THE BROTHERS' BOYS

THE FIRST 75 YEARS OF SAINT ALOYSIUS FOOTBALL 1912-1986

This is undoubtedly the toughest assignment ever given a Brothers' school eleven, and very few fans grant the Flashes the ghost of a chance to win. The Aloysius gridsters, however, have a habit of biting off more than they can chew and then proceeding to chew it."

<u>The Sunday Post Herald</u>
Vicksburg, MS
September 1, 1940

NOTE ABOUT THIS BOOK

With any project of this size, there will be errors. Knowing that you will misspell someone's name, not give credit to the right person at some point, leave off a player name in the roster, or worse is a terrific letdown. But, any mistakes or omissions were purely unintentional.

Great lengths were attempted to get it right. Early in reporting, a player was identified just by his last name. Team rosters were almost non-existent, and sometimes a player was noted as a substitute during a game who was never mentioned before. With the loss of so much valuable info in the Saint Aloysius fire, the only feasible way of getting it right was by looking at graduating class names, records of honor rolls reported in the paper at the same time, etc.

Unfortunately in that time period, not all students graduated. Once a great job opportunity arose, many would simply leave school and start their careers and their families. In the earliest years, some players would simply appear and seemingly disappear just as quickly.

As late as the 1970s, complete rosters were not always reported. Past year books were helpful, but even those may omit a player if one missed the picture or joined late. In the early years, the team would be reported with a certain number of players, but most of the younger ones would never see newspaper ink. Combined with inaccurate reporting and spelling of names, it is nearly impossible to do justice to those nearing 100 years before us. Perhaps that is one of the worst things about this effort.

Relative to statistics, they were very much a hit-and-miss commodity … even in later years. An opposing team paper may report stats that varied greatly. Added to that, the statistics reported were often impossible (2 fumbles lost, but a total of zero fumbles for the game). I have attempted to match game details with stats and give all benefit of the doubt to the Vicksburg reporters. Some coaches were very much against the reporting of individual accomplishments; rather putting the team before the person. In rare occasions, the paper would actually report play-by-play with yardages. Much of the info herein had to be taken by breaking down the report to provide the statistics. That section is simply for entertainment.

Finally, it seems certain that we have missed entire years of Flash football. Hints about a season from sentences here and there indicate that Saint Al was engaged in contests with other squads for potentially 13 years with no reporting. With no early yearbook records, and with so very few newspaper accounts, it could be that our brothers from those years will remain solely in the memories of those long gone. What follows is all that could be found as of now. Those that come after are encouraged add to our history.

DEDICATION

My deepest thanks go to my wife (Lee), my daughter (Haley) and my son (Ty). When dad was always unavailable, I was telling you the truth that I was working on a book! Don't hold it against me if you think I did a bad job and I won't hold it against you if you don't read it!

To the Flashes who gave their left high school halls to die on foreign soil, this is for you.

It's also dedicated to the memory of so many Vicksburg sports writers since just after the turn of the century who took interest in our program and the time to save our history. One person in particular should be highlighted. It seems that Billy Ray was Sports Editor at The Vicksburg Evening Post for more years than I can rightfully say. His *Press Box Views* gave us so much of the valuable information that brought our program to life before kickoffs and after the final whistles. To your memory, sir. I'm indebted.

To Clinton Bagley, the "elder statesman" of the Mississippi Department of Archives and History. And to everyone else who assisted me. Thanks for the friendship along with way. It was a pleasure.

To my teammates in David Atkins and Patrick Gordon. This book is also for you. I wish only that you were here to criticize me for not mentioning your names more often. You are not forgotten.

To Joe Baladi for the contant encouragement. Also to Tom Balzli, David Biggar, Ronnie McDaniel, Michael Mahoney, Corey Pinkson, Marvin Geter, James Peck, Lee Speyerer and Bill Garmon for providing funding to make this possible!

To the ex-Flashes who gave their time and resources to round out the team pictures, provide information, share memories, give a quote, uncover old game films, and encourage me. Thank you. Tom Balzli, Tommy Lee, Warren Doiron, Joe Durst, Louis Logue, Ray Terry, Jimmy Terry, Eddie Ray, Andrew Romano, Karl Nicholas, George Evans, Michael Mahoney, and so many others really made me feel like part of their band of brothers.

To the linemen of every single year. They are the one group of players who fight the hardest and who get the least credit, even in my rudimentary attempt on saving our history. On behalf of every person who is highlighted for scoring in the following chapters, it is because of you.

To The Vicksburg Post writers and your predecessors. Thank you for saving our history.

And finally, to everyone who has ever put on purple and gold, and to those that follow. We will always be brothers. Share your history with those that follow and your love to those who came before.

INTRODUCTION

This book didn't start as a plan to write the history of our football program. Rather, it was simply a small project to reclaim fading memories and details of the 1983 and 1984 seasons. Vicksburg will always be my "home town", but with a father in the military, you don't always stay in once place. By the grace of God, I was fortunate to finish at Saint Al after attending for only two years: 1984 and 1985.

I was no star athlete by anyone's standards, least of all mine. But I was proud to have been a part of two years of Flash football that left an indelible mark on me. During that time, it was common to hear people mention names of relatively-recent heroes that had worn the purple and gold in the past. But not having been a part of the first ten years, they meant very little. The storied history of our program that was sometimes mentioned was also of little relevance with no context. Shamefully, I had no idea who Joe Balzli or Tony Virgadamo were, nor how their lives impacted Flash football.

"Flash" forward to the 30th reunion of the Class of 1985. The leadership of the school was generous in opening the facilities for us one Saturday morning to go back in time; to go into our old classrooms and cafeteria, and also see the progress and improvements being made. Coach B.J. Smithhart was also kind enough to open the new football facility and allow those of us who played to relive a few memories on the field.

It's common for anyone who has played any sort of competitive sport to remember things in ways that may not have actually happened. Some details are still clear, like a play here or there that will never leave your mind. Locker room meetings at halftime that never see newspaper ink, practices designed for us to read one-another and act quickly, or a quick talk in the huddle about strategy exist only in our memories.

During our tour, I noticed that the school had wisely decided to save hundreds of aging VHS tapes of games stretching back decades. My first thought was to get them onto DVDs not only to save them from decay, but to allow once-eighteen-year-old kids the chance to watch their younger-selves in competition. Yes, it would be sometimes cringe-worthy, but it would also be guaranteed to bring a smile. And that is what we did, with over 200 games being made available for our future selves to see.

Since only one game surfaced during my time in pads, I decided to go to the Mississippi Department of Archives and History and pull anything ever written about that time in the vast collection of microfilm and archival material. What followed was an 8,000 word "story" from each season, complete with quotes, statistics, and anything that would give a bit of color to the narrative. However, once complete, I found myself wondering what happened the year before. So, I did the same for the 1983 season.

What you see now is the end. One year led to another, and another, and finally to the first 75 years of our storied program. As it unfolded, it became a project much like that of the DVDs. The goal was the same: to preserve the memories for not only those still around, but also for those that follow. And in the process, I learned something well more valuable than dates and statistics.

What I learned was something I hadn't realized, though it should have been obvious. Regardless of my talents, any accolades or honors, or bragging rights about my team's place in history, it was about a brotherhood. The kids of 1925, though different in approach and conditions, went through the same thing as the 1984 squad and every other ex-Flash football player. We gave our best, fought against one-another, depended on one-another, supported one-another, loved one-another. And all while representing the Flashes of Saint Aloysius; much of it on the same patch of dirt tucked away off Grove Street.

This could be seen as a historical account of a football team, or it may be viewed as the story of a fraternity of brothers. I choose to see it as a love story because the affection I now have for teenagers now aging or no longer with us is as deep as if we did it together. Because in some way, we did.

Perhaps names like O.E. James, Van Stewart, Clint Schlottman, Charles Guiney, Joe Durst, Warren Doiron, and more will take their rightful place when the history of our program is discussed. And perhaps when someone walks in Balzli Field, they won't just see the letters on the building, but envision a man who shaped this into what it stands for today and why so many fought to have it put there.

To everyone who played before me, with me, and after me, this is for you. My sincerest hope is that you take your rightful spot in purple and gold history all while remembering your brothers who gave you what is rightfully yours.

1912-1929

SAINT ALOYSIUS COLLEGE FOOTBALL: 1914

Very few details are found about the "birth" of Saint Aloysius football. Unfortunately, early accounts by newspapers were sparse as the new sport was gaining popularity. Perhaps the best source of early information would be found in now-yellowed, almost non-existent yearbooks from Saint Aloysius College and the teams they faced. But an unfortunate Saint Aloysius fire destroyed the most complete collection of archival history available and only a single yearbook exists in the Vicksburg Public Library from that time. So what is left to tell the story of those who laid the foundation?

While it has been reported that Saint Al was playing as early as 1911, nothing can be found relative to a team. The school opened classes on September 5th of that year, but no mention was made of any sports team in writings found to date. Vicksburg High School had fielded their first team in 1910, with results noted as *"the best they have done yet was to break even with their opponents in games won and lost"*. In their 1911 season schedule, there was no mention of a Flash opponent, so we can therefore confidently assume that the first Saint Al team was probably 1912.

1912 (1-1)

Much ado was made regarding the September 9th opening of Saint Aloysius College. Brother Lambert headed the local Brothers' school, and on October 12th, the paper recounted the very first recorded Saint Al game. The Vicksburg yearbook that year tells the story with a strange ending.

GAME 1:   SAINT AL (0-0) vs VICKSBURG (UNREPORTED)
                 FINAL: ST AL 6 VICKSBURG 0
                 October 23, 1912

The contest that was to be the first in a series of games took place at a location known as "Beck's Bottom", later mentioned as a another game site for the new sport. The paper noted that *"both schools were well represented on the sidelines, amongst them being several young ladies from the High School"*. Saint Al outweighed *"High School"* and it was noted that their *"light line could not stop the plunges made by the hefty Full Back of St. Aloysius team"*.

Saint Al focused on the run, while their opponents *"succeeded in putting through several perfect forward passes for long gain"*. The Flashes only score was in the 2nd quarter on a 15 yard Norbert Heron touchdown run up the middle. Palermo's kick was no-good. Vicksburg came close to scoring in the 3rd, but an incomplete pass finished their drive.

The Vicksburg yearbook went into more detail, saying: *"Upon our return home (from a game against Jackson High School), we were challenged by S.A.C, our local rivals, to play them on the next Wednesday. Both teams practiced hard for the next week, and when the day arrived the teams were about evenly matched. The first quarter passed with no scoring on either side, both teams showing their ability to its best advantage. In the second quarter, S.A.C. worked their 185-pound fullback through our line for a touchdown, but failed to kick their goal.*

S.A.C. failed to hold us down in the third quarter. After many good advances of the back field, especially those of Captain (Irvine) Scudder and Quarterback (Lester) Tinkelpaugh, eluded the opponent by calling an unexpected forward pass that was caught by Fullback (Henry) Allien who crossed the line for a touchdown. At the time it was considered that the pass was incomplete and again we were thought to have been defeated. A few days later the referee of this game was present at another game in a foreign city, and strangely the same incident occurred. Upon his return home he acknowledged his error and we were given our due credit. The score was '6 plus to 6' because we were not permitted to kick for our goal.

In the last quarter, much hard playing was done on both sides, but the efforts of both teams were futile."

GAME 2:   SAINT AL (1-0) vs VICKSBURG (UNREPORTED)
                 FINAL: ST AL 0 VICKSBURG 7
                 November 13, 1912

For their second game, it would be the Flash second-team against the High School first-team. Only a few players overlapped from the first contest for Saint Al and the paper said of them *"The college boys were outweighed, but played a plucky game from start to finish"*. For fairness, Brother

Williams (SAC) would be referee while L. Tinklepaugh (Vicksburg) would be Umpire. Timekeepers would be representatives from each school.

The paper's only notation of activity was that Bazinsky had the touchdown while captain Allien kicked the PAT. Vicksburg's Marshall sustained a broken collar bone and was forced *"to retire"*.

There was apparently at least one more game between the two teams, and was recorded in the VHS yearbook. *"In the second half the captain of S.A.C., not liking our methods of attack, refused to play after this half and was willing to take his defeat as it stood. The score was 13-0."* The paper failed to mention that game.

1913 (0-2)

Football practices under 1908 Ole Miss football star and Aloysius Coach Ike Knox began September 15th. It was to be called *"... the beginning of one of the most interesting years in S.A.C. football circles"*. The school reported that *"those who are trying to make the first or varsity team were at the college campus trying to get into shape and to limber up"*.

Normally, the following account of a practice would mean little: *"While the Varsity team was practicing the other day, the captain ordered the players to begin tackling and Mr. Cameron Fletcher tried to tackle the dummy, but only succeeded in ploughing up about two feet of dirt"*. Mr. J.C. Fletcher was my neighbor as a young man and I can still remember times talking with him about his years in school. So, this effort has come "full circle" as it turns out that I actually knew someone that helped start this storied tradition.

While individuals were open to practice, tryouts for the team would come after the 27th. Knox noted that *"with a little more practice, the varsity football squad will be able to tackle any school team in its class or weight. The scrub also has a lot of good material to draw from."* The 14 man squad would be led by Captain Don Wilson, left tackle for the Flashes.

The school was also now attempting to branch out and play squads outside of Warren County. *"The Lake Providence High School eleven will come first to tackle the SAC. Second team of Mississippi College at Clinton wants a game on October 4th but it is thought that they are too heavy for the local team. The team will average about 135 pounds."* If those games were played, they were not recorded in the paper.

GAME 1:   SAINT AL (0-0) vs VICKSBURG (UNREPORTED)
                           FINAL: ST AL 0 VICKSBURG 6
                           October 7, 1914

According to the 1914 Vicksburg yearbook (detailing the 1913 football game against SAC), *"Both teams were equally matched in weight and a hard-fought contest resulted. Owing to the inclement weather, both teams played under great difficulties. Our team kept the ball in the opponents' territory for the greater part of the game, but frequent fumbles prevented us from scoring.*

At no stage of the game was our goal in danger, but when on VHS's 20-yard line our team fumbled and one of the VHS backs, securing the ball, made a spectacular run of 80 yards for a touchdown. This, however, did not dispirit our team and they worked with redoubled vigor. When time was called, our Warriors found themselves on the verge of scoring, being on VHS's 10 yard line. The final score was 6-0 in favor of VHS.

After the first defeat we challenged VHS several times, but were unable to get a return game to decide the superiority. We, therefore, claimed the championship of Vicksburg".

From indications on October 18th, there had already been two games by the Junior Team against Vicksburg and it seemed that *"they are trying to 'show up' the Senior team as they have played VHS two games and walked from the field victors both times, while the Seniors have played only one and lost to the VHS squad by a small margin."*. That number would grow to three victories before the season ended according to the SAC yearbook. Unofficially, it would be a 3-1 season if one considers games such as those noted above.

GAME 2:   SAINT AL (0-1) @ DELHI, LA (UNREPORTED)
            FINAL: ST AL 0 DELHI 20
            October 26, 1914

The 1914 team played once more, on Thanksgiving Day, at Central High School in Delhi, LA. The yearbook from S.A.C. says *"We were defeated by the score of 20 to 0. In this game we were playing entirely out of our class, as our opponents outweighed us 30 pounds to the man and the score under these conditions was a great credit to S.A.C."*

1914

Saint Aloysius College opened its doors on September 8th. By the 19th, the football team had *"practiced every afternoon of the week and seem determined not to let the colors of the school trail in the dust."* Brother Sylvester's team, *"who seems to pass muster in the act of football"*, apparently was joined by an Alumni team led by Joseph Palermo and Hilton Hazel. Since Palermo graduated in 1913 and Hazel the following year, it appears that this team was an attempt to add opponents.

Looking to increase that schedule past just Vicksburg, SAC and the Alumni Team, *"A number of challenges have been sent out for games, but as yet, no reply has been received from any of them"*. In stark contrast to the previous season, and those that followed for some years, no records are found as to what happened by either of the teams.

1915

Only two notations have been found relating to the 1915 season for Saint Aloysius College football. First, The Golden Quill (SAC's school publication running every two months) featured a picture of Robert O'Connor, a player from that team. It had been reprinted from their publication of the day called The Hill Billy and pointed out his *"football togs (shoes)"*. Second, a short mention on October 7th, tucked away in the middle of the paper and drawing very little attention, noted an upcoming contest at Beck's Bottom.

GAME 1:   SAINT AL (UNK) vs LAKE VILLAGE, AR (UNK)
            FINAL: UNRECORDED
            October 9, 1915

"On Saturday afternoon at 3:00 the Vicksburg football fans will have the unique opportunity of witnessing the initial interstate football game of the season between St. Aloysius College and Lake Village, Arkansas. The game will be played at Beck's Bottom and a large crowd is expected to be present. A small admission of 10 cents for children and 20 cents for adults will be charged to defray the expenses entailed. Tickets may be had at Jones Smoke House. Come out and cheer the home boys to a victory. If you cannot come out, buy a ticket and help the boys along." Neither Vicksburg paper recorded the outcome, nor announced any future (or potentially prior) contests or results.

1916-1922

There is no mention of Flash football found between 1916 and 1922. It would be somewhat understandable for the 1917-1918 period as America was fighting in Europe during World War I and the outbreak of influenza was taking a devastating toll on the United States. On October 5th, 1920, The Vicksburg Evening Post ran a write-up called *"Saint Aloysius College Notes"*. It highlighted activities at the school, including athletics. While detailing their basketball progress, the only vague notation to other sports included the following:

"The athletic programs for this season are of the brightest, and if enthusiasm and good will count for anything, the boys of S.A.C. are sure to gain recognition." No other account was found.

1923

One write-up mentioning Saint Al's 1923 football team was found in an on-line discussion of that season's Tallulah, LA team. It was noted that the Louisiana boys had *"hired"* players from Clemson. And in one game against the Flashes, it was said that *"The hired team had trouble scheduling games. In one practice scrimmage with Vicksburg (S.A.C.), several of their players were broken up and hurt"*.

1924

The next official report of Saint Al football was found with the 1924 season. The call went out on September 8th for any young man who wanted to try out for the team. Roughly 20 boys were expected to report and each had to name a desired position. Brother Thomas would handle the coaching duties and would also serve as Athletic Director. Practices would begin on the 11th with John Tierney elected captain of the squad.

Only three players had playing experience and a schedule had not been announced as of the 17th. Letters were sent to other schools letting them know of the size of the Flashes (125-130 pound average) and asking for opponents in the same range.

PRACTICE: SAINT AL (0-0) vs "TIGERS" (N/A)
                 FINAL: UNREPORTED
                 September 20, 1924

A warm-up contest, open to the public and officiated by Athletic Director Professor Oliphant, was scheduled at 2:30pm with a team known only as "The Tigers". This team most-likely consisted of a local group of youths who competed in a recreational league environment. The paper for the following day is missing, so no details of the event are found.

No detailed record of other games after the announcement of the pre-season scrimmage was found in the paper. We do know that they played Vicksburg High School and lost during the season as an article on November 12th, 1927 called the result the 4th consecutive defeat for the Flashes. Later years point out that some members of this squad, called *"veterans"*, came back for scrimmages.

1925 (2-2-1)

Practices started somewhere around the second week of August and the team was in *"good condition"*. School opened on September 8th with 265 boys enrolled for all grades and President Brother Martinian said that *"prospects are bright for St. Aloysius College having a most successful year"*. Mike Morrissey, a former college gridiron star, would coach the squad and Brother Thomas would be the Athletic Director.

GAME 1:   SAINT AL (0-0) @ HAZLEHURST (UNREPORTED)
                 FINAL: ST AL 0 HAZLEHURST 6
                 September 30, 1925

The Flashes left at 9:30am on game day for Hazlehurst. It would be a tight contest with only one score between them as a result of a Hazlehurst interception at their 30 to end the 3rd. One play into the 4th, Slay pushed it in from the Flash 1. The final would end 6-0 after Hazlehurst reserves got a chance to play. In a display of sportsmanship and in spite of the loss, the *"S.A.C. boys … were loud in their praise for the splendid reception given them by the Hazlehurst boys"*.

GAME 2:   SAINT AL (0-1) @ DELHI, LA (UNREPORTED)
                 FINAL: ST AL 2 DELHI 0
                 October 10, 1925

Wearing new uniforms, Saint Al thought they had scored a go-ahead touchdown in the 4th on a pass from Joseph Brunini to W.H. Miller. However, *"the umpire ruled otherwise"* and had called the

Flashes off-sides. But in the closing minutes of play, Clarence Mackey blocked a Delhi punt from their 5, leading to an Earl Cronin tackle of Barfield in the endzone for the safety. Brunini was praised for his offense and his defense; especially in light of his interception return of 40 yards. *"As a whole the 'Purple Flashes' … looked like some great college team in action"*.

GAME 3:   SAINT AL (1-1) vs PORT GIBSON (UNREPORTED)
                FINAL: ST AL 6 PORT GIBSON 0
                October 16, 1925

Conditions were awful for the game before a small crowd. Playing the last part of the contest in *"semi-darkness"*, the paper put it as *"Playing in a sea of mud, surrounded by dark clouds…"* As a result, there was only one score. That was fortunately for the Flashes. In the 1st on Port Gibson's second possession, they fumbled to Vincent Canizaro. Immediately afterwards, Ernest Sheffield pulled a fake pass and took it 25 yards for the touchdown. Cronin's PAT missed, but the Flashes had all they needed.

Port Gibson got to the Flash 20 at one point but fumbled back to the home team. The Flashes *"displayed a well-balanced team and one which should make a good showing this season"*.

GAME 4:   SAINT AL (2-1) @ EAST CARROLL (UNREPORTED)
                FINAL: ST AL 0 EAST CARROLL 0
                October 23, 1925

The final practice for the contest was on Thursday the 22nd and the team was in good shape. The boys from Lake Providence, Louisiana had *"a strong team and have won the majority of games played this season"*.

The only real highlight of the game came late in the 4th with East Carroll having 1st down at the Flash 3. Three runs failed and then the incomplete pass gave the ball back to Saint Al to seal the tie. Afterwards, the Flashes *"were pleased over the splendid reception given them by the High school boys and the people of Lake Providence. They report having a most enjoyable day"*.

GAME 5:   SAINT AL (2-1-1) vs VICKSBURG (UNREPORTED)
                FINAL: ST AL 0 VICKSBURG 19
                November 11, 1925

Vicksburg practiced during the week against the *"Minnesota Shift"*, a formation supposedly the base of the Flash offense. After enough practice, Coach Oliphant declared that they would beat Saint Al 14-0. Before the game, students and players of both schools paraded together to The Fairgrounds for the contest. Former coach Ike Knox would be referee and future coach Ted Rogers would be head linesmen.

Vicksburg came close to scoring twice in the 1st but after driving to the Flash 28, the *"drop kick"* FG was no good. Later, they got to the Flash 1 but the purple defense held them on 4 downs. In the 2nd, a mixture of runs and passes got Vicksburg close enough for Nat Haynes to snare a 6 yard touchdown pass. Wells tacked on the PAT to make it 7-0 at halftime.

Turnovers would doom the Flashes in the 2nd half. The first was a fumble by Brunini as he attempted to pass. VHS picked it up at the 15 and took it in for a touchdown but the PAT failed. Later in the 3rd, Miller found Brunini for 25 at the VHS 45. But on the next play, *"the Old Gold and Purple"* fumbled it back to Vicksburg. Vicksburg's Schaffer scored their final touchdown on a 25 yard interception return.

The paper noted that the *"game was a good clean game and the two teams fought a good fight and everyone was well-pleased…"* They praised the play of many, but called E.W. Brown *"easily the star for S.A.C. His work was spectacular."*

1926 (2-4)

Practices under the watchful eye of new Head Coach Ted Rogers and Brother Thomas began September 7th and predictions of a strong team were reported as early as the 4th. The description of *"small but light"* would be a hallmark description of the Flashes for years to come. The school had 280 young men and was led by Brother Bonaventure, Thomas, Bernardine, Gabriel, Phillip, Benet and Benjamin.

GAME 1:   SAINT AL (0-0) @ EAST CARROLL (UNREPORTED)
                              FINAL: ST AL 0 LAKE PROVIDENCE 13
                              October 1, 1926

On Friday morning, Rogers, Brother Thomas and the team ferried across the Mississippi to Lake Providence to battle a *"proud and haughty"* team already with one game under their belt. The paper called Saint Al *"worthy of the emblems they bear, yet they do not claim any laurels beforehand They merely promise bringing home the bacon and … the scalp of Lake Providence … on their wampum pole…"* The article was flowery and noted our returning veterans and 155 pound weight as an advantage.

Though the poetry of the departure was well-written, little is noted about the loss. The *"Purple Flashes … played a steady game and their line held well turning back charge after charge. The backfield also showed up well."* East Carroll's two touchdowns were both pass plays, and the added PAT was enough to take away a number of first downs recorded by the *"practically new team (Flashes)"* in the contest.

GAME 2:   SAINT AL (0-1) vs TALLULAH (UNREPORTED)
                              FINAL: ST AL 39 TALLULAH 0
                              October 7, 1926

The Flashes again crossed the Mississippi for a game in which Saint Al *"baffled their opponents from across the river"*. At least four Tallulah boys suffered injuries, though none *"were of a serious nature and were fully recovered when … closed"*. Saint Al scored twice in the 1st and once in the 2nd to make it 19-0 at halftime. They added to the shutout with a touchdown in the 3rd and another two in the 4th. More details are unknown, but the Flashes had lived up to the billing from the write-up of September 30th.

GAME X: SAINT AL (1-1) vs NATCHEZ (UNREPORTED)
                              FINAL: NOT PLAYED
                              October 15, 1926

One of the reportedly best teams Natchez ever had was coming to Vicksburg. They had at least one victory in hand over East Carroll (Lake Providence). So, the paper said *"If dope counts for anything, the Natchez high squad will take the field as favorites over the local Collegians."* On game day, the paper reported that Natchez had cancelled the game.

It was supposedly due to *"some of the players on the Natchez eleven who had not been keeping up their studies as they should, and being unable to play without these students … called off the game"*. Apparently forfeits were not counted until 1928, as the Flashes would discover in Rolling Fork.

GAME 3:   SAINT AL (1-1) vs CHAMBERLAIN HUNT ACADEMY (UNREPORTED)
                              FINAL: ST AL 13 CHAMBERLAIN HUNT 0
                              October 22, 1926

Saint Al overcame a scoreless first half to gain their second victory of the year. In the 3rd, the Flashes put up two touchdowns and added a PAT to make it 13-0. The first was a Jack Eckoff interception of a CHA pass returned 75 yards for a score followed by a Clarence Mackey PAT. After runs by Ernest Sheffield, Vincent Canizaro and Jack Roberts, Canizaro took the final Flash touchdown in from the 25. CHA unsuccessfully tried to score in the 4th but Roberts picked off another Cadet pass.

GAME 4:   SAINT AL (2-1) @ MISSISSIPPI DEAF INSTITUTE (UNREPORTED)
                              FINAL: ST AL 6 MDI 10
                              October 29, 1926

The paper praised MDI by saying *"This team, composed of boys totally deaf, is a very good, very strong one and the local boys are going into the field at Jackson with a feeling of being already* beaten for the odds that are against them are overwhelming". Both Mackey (eye) and Canizaro (shoulder) would not play but were expected back soon. One of the many ways to illustrate the changing of the times is to note that despite the respect of the opponent, the MDI team was called "The Deaf and Dumb Boys".

MDI was first on the board in the 2nd with a touchdown and a PAT. Saint Al came right back on the opening kickoff of the 3rd when Roberts took one back 95 yards for the score to make it 7-6. MDI finished the scoring with a FG in the same quarter with the ball placed at the 12. The Flashes were primed to respond with seconds remaining at their opponent's 10, but the final whistle blew. The paper noted that "The Deaf and Dumb boys gave their signals by means of using their fingers." The loss was no surprise, but the score was. The paper had MDI as a predictive favorite by a 28-0 score.

GAME 5:   SAINT AL (2-2) @ ROLLING FORK (UNDEFEATED)
             FINAL: ST AL 0 ROLLING FORK 33
             November 5, 1926

The "Purple Flashes" was meeting "the leading squad of the Delta and a team which so far this season has not been beaten." Their analysis was right because "St. Aloysius college was handed their worst drubbing of the season when the Rolling Fork Tigers ran rough shod over (them) … by a score of 33-0" outplaying them "in every department of the game… Many members of the team have had their heads instead of their chins shaved. Mackey came to school the other morning with a pillow over his eye. It was later found out that his face had come into too close contact with the earth during a scrimmage practice, which was held in the yard after school".

Rolling Fork "dropped kick" a FG on their first possession from the Flash 10. They added a touchdown in the same quarter, as well as two more in the 2nd and a touchdown and FG in the 3rd. The Flashes had too many fumbles to be successful and the only highlight play was a T.A. Jamison interception for 15 yards. Other details weren't recorded.

GAME 6:   SAINT AL (2-3) vs VICKSBURG (4-2)
             FINAL: ST AL 0 VICKSBURG 48
             November 11, 1926

The paper predicted a two-touchdown victory for Vicksburg in the Armistice Day game due to size and experience. Their worst loss of the season was a 30-13 deficit to Central High in Jackson, but the Flashes had been trounced 33-0 by Rolling Fork.

On Vicksburg's first drive, Moorehad pushed in from the 2. The PAT missed but the Flashes were off-sides and somehow the point counted. Saint Al pushed back behind runs from Sheffield, James Fitzgerald and Roberts, but Roberts fumbled at the VHS 25. The 2nd saw big runs by VHS and a drive was capped by Thaxton from the 3. In a replay of the first touchdown, the PAT was missed, but Saint Al was again off-sides to make it 14-0. The third touchdown of the quarter came from the Flash 3 by Fowler to make it 21-0.

In the 3rd, another Roberts fumble at the Flash 3 allowed Matthews to score and convert to make it 28-0. The quarter ended on a Matthews interception at the VHS 40. Early in the 4th, Roberts went up the middle for a 48 yard touchdown and PAT that "brought High school rooters to their feet". Saint Al got as far as the VHS 9 on the next drive but was intercepted by Boyce. They immediately converted on the drive with a pass from Fowler to Roberts from the 9. The dagger came on the last set of plays when Boyce picked off another pass at the VHS 40. He was also the recipient of the ensuing 38 yard touchdown pass that sealed the game after Hunt's PAT.

The Flashes were also (apparently) scheduled for two more game in 1926. They were slated to play Port Gibson on November 19th and Delhi, LA on November 26th. Delhi was "considered the college's hardest rival" due to their record as of October 28th. However, no report of games played nor cancellations appear in the paper.

1927 (5-1-1)

Coach Ted Rogers' "Purple and Old Gold" team was reportedly "only a shell of last years' big team in size only". Captained by future head coach Jack Roberts, it featured a backfield averaging close to 115 pounds and a 140 pound line. In the first game, the Flashes would *"According to Hoyle"* ordinarily be expected to pass. But the paper said that *"There will be no forward passing nor trick formation; merely straight football is the plan of offense being arranged for."*

GAME 1:   SAINT AL (0-0) vs FAYETTE (0-2 AS REPORTED LOCALLY)
                         FINAL: ST AL 43 FAYETTE 0
                         October 7, 1927

Substitutions were anticipated by the coaches to *"give their men practical tests under fire"*. One player expected to perform was *"the plucky little capital"* in Roberts. *"This year he is fast reaching the point where the title of 'triple threat man' will be tacked over his place"*. O.E. James was expected to *"reach the top ranks also as he is sturdy on offense and a hugman catapult on defense. This small fellow will stop many line plays before the season has come and gone"*.

It was later discovered that Fayette's Mark Brown had broken his collar bone the week of the 12th and wouldn't play. Roberts scored the first two touchdowns for the Flashes in the 1st; the first a carry for 10 yards and the second another run to put Saint Al up 12-0 at halftime. Nick Lavecchia had the third effort early in the 3rd on a run and, after a Fayette punt in the same quarter, Will Davis did his part in the scoring. He also scored again in the 3rd from the 20 as the whistle blew to start the 4th.

Perhaps the most eventful quarter, Lavecchia hit Roberts for 20 but was picked off afterwards by Swarner. Forcing a punt after holding, the Flashes started their drive. Lavecchia hit Caston James for 30 and then found him again for the touchdown. Before the quarter ended, O.E. James blocked a Fayette punt. The next play was a Roberts pass to Caston James from the 35 for the final touchdown.

The Fayette Chronicle said that their team *"played better than they have in any previous game this season. The Vicksburg boys, however, which averaged 170 pounds, was superior to our light lads and won the engagement 37-0."* Their paper may have missed a score.

GAME 2:   SAINT AL (1-0) @ EAST CARROLL (1-0)
                         FINAL: ST AL 13 ECHS 6
                         October 14, 1927

The Flashes caught the 8:30am ferry across the river for Louisiana on game day along with Athletic Director Brother Thomas. T.A. Jamison, one of 1926's *"stellar performers"* had missed the first game, but was in the group for the second.

The beginning was not good for the Flashes against the boys from Lake Providence. Fumbles in the 1st quarter led to an ECHS touchdown. Afterwards, it was *"bitterly contested"*. With only 6:00 left in the 4th, Jamison scored and Davis kicked the PAT. Lavecchia later tacked on the last Flash points on a next possession run.

GAME 3:   SAINT AL (2-0) vs ANGUILLA (UNREPORTED)
                         FINAL: ST AL 33 ANGUILLA 7
                         October 20, 1927

The Flashes would play on Thursday at the request of the *"fast team"* from Anguilla to allow them to see the LSU-Mississippi State (A&M) game on Friday in Jackson. The State Fair was also in town and was another enticement for moving it up. Anguilla was said to be a *"low-charging and hard-plugging"* team that was *"well-coached"*. Though no details were reported, Vincent Canizaro would reportedly miss the remainder of the season whether by injury or otherwise. In comparison, future game recaps mention Canizaro action.

Anguilla's first drive resulted in a Davis interception, but the Flashes fumbled it right back. The visitors recovered and later ran in a touchdown from the 40. Saint Al came back with a Roberts score from the 20 and added the PAT. Saint Al later punted to Anguilla, they fumbled and Jamison recovered. It resulted in another touchdown and Davis tacked on the PAT. Roberts hit Jamison later for a 40- yard score and the Flashes converted the PAT. Roberts scored at least one more before the end of the game and the Flashes had a run-away victory.

GAME 4:   SAINT AL (3-0) vs CHAMBERLAIN HUNT ACADEMY (UNREPORTED)
            FINAL: ST AL 6 CHAMBERLAIN HUNT 6
            October 28, 1927

Other than their full year-to-date record, Chamberlain Hunt was much-written about before the game. Called "*a scrapping bunch of clean players*", they outweighed Saint Al by 15 pounds. They were "*primed to the brimful*" of talent, including Brehm and the captain R. Hayes. The only defeat this season was to VHS as a practice game, though the other game results weren't noted.

The contest looked like it would end in a 0-0 tie as the 4th was underway. But CHA got on the board on a touchdown run though the PAT was unsuccessful. With 7:00 left, Lavecchia found Jamison for 25 yards. Canizaro, now playing again, picked up good yardage and then on 4th down, Lavecchia found Jamison in the endzone from the 30. The kick for the PAT would have won the game, but it was no good. Saint Al's William Davis intercepted a pass at the end of the game, but a Lavecchia pass to Jamison would not convert.

The Port Gibson Reveille said that the game was "*one of the best played for a long time. The local boys (CHA) were at the disadvantage of playing on a strange field and in the enemy's hometown, but they acquitted themselves splendidly.*"

GAME 5:   SAINT AL (3-0-1) vs VICKSBURG (UNREPORTED)
            FINAL: ST AL 0 VICKSBURG 35
            November 11, 1927

The Vicksburg-SAC game would now have a new "*beautiful loving cup*" trophy sponsored by the Y's Men Club for the "*city championship*". Details were to be announced as of the October 3rd report. Additionally, the two teams would be guests of Manager John Q. Lambert after the game to see Tom Mix in The Last Trail at the Alamo Theater.

Though the score ended up 33-0, the paper said that would "*lead one to believe the game was one-sided. It was far from that. It was a stubbornly fought contest from beginning to end…*" Over 1,200 fans were on hand to see a game that had seemingly as many Flashes hurt as healthy. But the contest was so rugged that it resulted with big injuries on both sides. VHS's Blades broke a finger and Clark "*was knocked out for a few minutes*". Saint Al's Jamison broke his collar bone.

Vicksburg's Cunningham took advantage of a bad punt attempt for a 1st quarter safety and Blades added a touchdown near the end of the 2nd to make halftime 9-0. Teller added a score in the 3rd on a run but the PAT was unsuccessful. Vicksburg did most of their damage in the 4th. The first was on a Lavecchia fumble at the Flash 3 that resulted in an Abraham touchdown and Clark PAT two plays later. Abraham then picked off a pass for a 65 yard touchdown return. The final was the result of another pickoff, this one by Monger. He added the touchdown afterwards and Jabour converted.

Two days after the game, both teams came together again at the Y Men's Club at 6:30pm for the trophy presentation. It was presented by chairman of activities William F. Laughlin with speeches from both captains. VHS was led by Charleston Brent and Saint Al by Roberts.

GAME 6:   SAINT AL (3-1-1) vs JEFFERSON MILITARY COLLEGE (6-2)
            FINAL: ST AL 33 JMC 0
            November 18, 1927

Injuries from the Armistice Game with VHS sidelined several Flashes, including Joe Arenz, Canizaro, O.E. James and Jamison. Even the coach would miss the contest, with Walton Shannon taking his place. But, "*the local college lads are going to carry out their schedule and promise to make it interesting for the JMC boys…*" Arriving at noon, Lieul Wilser's team was treated to a tour of the YMCA.

More was written about the arrival of JMC's team to Vicksburg than about the surprising victory by the Flashes, especially by such a large margin. All that is known is that the Flashes scored in the 1st and Davis scored three PAT's. Either way, it was a big victory for the purple and gold.

GAME 7:   SAINT AL (4-1-1) vs PORT GIBSON (UNREPORTED)
                   FINAL: ST AL 25 PORT GIBSON 37
                   November 25, 1927

Port Gibson outweighed the Flashes and had a QB (Oberhauser) that was *"the prettiest passer that has ever appeared here, and his plays were uncannily accurate"*. The Port Gibson Reveille said that the visitor *"launched an aerial attack on S.A.C. … that would have dazzled an aviation brigade …"*

Port Gibson scored at least three times in the 1st, and *"dumfounded the Flashes"* so much that T.A. Jamison was brought into the contest with a still-broken collar bone. Behind the play of Jamison, Roberts and Lavecchia, the 3rd quarter score would be cut to 24-13 with at least one Roberts score. Roberts added another touchdown in the 4th on a 99 yard run that was described as *"the prettiest play seen here in years"*. Before the final whistle, Jamison and Davis added scores for the Flashes while Bennett and Atwood added for Port Gibson.

The Reveille said that the Flashes *"fought with the 'never-say-die' spirit and they played hard and square"*. Our paper summed up the 4-2-1 year by saying *"S.A.C. has enjoyed an unusually successful gridiron season, losing only two games of the dozen played"*. Author's note: Noting dates of the games, and discounting the possibility that they were referring to practice scrimmages, there was no "dozen" played. They probably intended to say "half dozen". It continued: *"Throughout the season they have played hard, clean football and deserve the credit they have received"*. If other games were played, they weren't reported.

1928 (4-2-2)

Not much is presented as to the team health or practices under first-year coach Walton Shannon. Specific game info is noted when available.

GAME X: SAINT AL (0-0) vs JACKSON HIGH SCHOOL (UNREPORTED)
                   FINAL: NOT PLAYED
                   September 28, 1928

Originally, the Flashes had the first tilt scheduled against Jackson High School. Word came on the 20th that they couldn't honor the commitment because rules allowed them only to play Vicksburg in that time period. Vicksburg businessmen were doing a *"good will tour"* of the Mississippi Delta the next Friday and Coach Shannon was trying to schedule an area team to be able to capitalize on the timing.

GAME 1:   SAINT AL (0-0) @ ROLLING FORK (UNREPORTED)
                   FINAL: ST AL 0 ROLLING FORK 1
                   September 27, 1928

The game was originally set for Friday, but a circus was in Rolling Fork and they asked to have the date moved back. Coach Shannon agreed since it still coincided with the aforementioned *"good will tour"*. Athletic Director Brother Thomas accompanied the 18 member team *"by motor"* to watch.

It wasn't the best start to the season, with the Flashes ironically forfeiting the *"good will"* game 1-0. Scoreless in the 1st half, both teams put up points in the 2nd. Rolling Fork scored and converted their PAT on a kick. The Flashes answered with a score and attempted a pass for the extra point. Though incomplete, Coach Shannon argued interference to no avail. With the score 7-6 and on the first play of the 4th, the Flashes drove to the Rolling Fork 10. An off-sides penalty was called on both teams, but after conference, the penalty was assessed only to S.A.C. This ignited a fight that spread not only to the players, but also to the fans.

After police intervention, the game was forfeited by Saint Al. The only good news was that before leaving, *"all differences were amicably settled"*. The Flashes had passed four times and were successful on two of them (Norman Wright to either O.E. or Caston James).

GAME 2:   SAINT AL (0-1) vs FLORA (0-0)
                   FINAL: ST AL 41 FLORA 0
                   October 5, 1928

Two Flashes would find themselves injured before kickoff. Joe DiRago was out at least two weeks and Jack Hummell for a week with undisclosed injuries. Even so, the team worked *"daily, and are preparing for a hard battle against the fast aggregation from Flora"*.

The Flashes dominated the game from the start with the visitor *"...unable to get beyond the middle of the field. The only times they were in possession of the ball was when the 'Purple Flashes' would kick off"*. Flora had three men in the game who had never played before. S.A.C. scored in the 1st quarter though details are unknown. At halftime, the Flashed led 21-0. We do know that Wright and Caston James were successful on pass plays, and T.A. Jamison was credited by noting *"This Jamison lad showed he can still snare them out of the air"*.

GAME 3:   SAINT AL (1-1) @ TALLULAH, LA (1-1)
                   FINAL: ST AL 7 TALLULAH 0
                   October 11, 1928

Originally scheduled for Friday, the game was moved back a day to allow Tallulah boys to attend a local pageant. Practices were *"strenuous"* for the Flashes because *"From reports, the elevens are well-matched this year and another closely contested game is expected..."* A crowd of 700 saw teams evenly matched in weight battle for four quarters.

A first half fumble by Caston James caused no damage. Later, starting at their 35 after a loss of 5, James hit Jamison for a 35-yard touchdown. Wright went through the middle for the PAT and final points. Saint Al could have scored twice more on Wright passes to a wide-open Jamison, but each time the ball was dropped.

The best review of the game came from Mr. Maurice Geisenberg, who said about a 3rd quarter event, *"When S.A.C. got into the huddle for the next play, 12 players were in a circle for the signals. Upon looking around, a player with a maroon jersey found out that he was with the S.A.C. team."*

GAME 4:   SAINT AL (2-1) vs JEFFERSON MILITARY COLLEGE (UNREPORTED)
                   FINAL: ST AL 21 JMC 7
                   October 19, 1928

No record for JMC was reported, but the insinuation was that they fielded a good team. *" (JMC) has a fast squad and judging from their record so far this season, will make it interesting for the local Collegians."* Fortunately for the Flashes, Will Davis was back after recovering from a foot injury and Caston James's neck had healed after the Tallulah game.

Much of the recap is missing, but Caston James scored first for the Flashes. The second was the result of a fumble recovery by James and a later run by Wilkerson to the JMC 3. The Flashes scored and Donovan converted. The Flashes made it 21-0 in the 2nd with just minutes left to play before half when T.A. Jamison caught the touchdown pass. JMC scored in the 4th on plays by Betheme and Washburn.

GAME 5:   SAINT AL (3-1) vs CRYSTAL SPRINGS (3-0-1)
                   FINAL: ST AL 13 CRYSTAL SPRINGS 13
                   October 25, 1928

The paper reported Crystal Springs as outweighing the Flashes and *"rated as having one of the leading high school elevens in this section of the state"*. That didn't stop the Flashes from jumping ahead in the 1st. A Wright punt to Crystal Springs was fumbled and recovered by T.A. Jamison at their 10. Wright found Jamison for the touchdown and William Davis gained the PAT. Running plays by Louis Hossley, Caston James, Wright and P. Donovan got the ball near the goal in the same quarter and Hossley did the honors for the touchdown. The PAT was unsuccessful.

Crystal Springs recovered a Flash fumble in the 3rd and converted it when Scott found Thurman. Johnson converted the PAT to make it 13-7. In the 4th with only 5:00 left in the game, the Flashes punted and pinned the opponent deep. But Thurman and Scott runs were accompanied by a

Porter pass to Jones at the 50. Porter then hit L. Scott for the long and agonizing touchdown. The failed PAT kept it 13-13.

GAME 6:   SAINT AL (3-1-1) @ DELHI, LA (UNREPORTED)
                        FINAL: ST AL 6 DELHI 6
                        November 2, 1928

Both Jamison brothers would miss the contest, perhaps by issues related to school in the form of grades. It wasn't welcome news since Delhi outweighed the Flashes by a reported 20 pounds. But "*Despite the odds, the 'Purple Flashes' are going into the struggle … with a determination to win*". Eighteen Flashes left for Delhi at noon, including DiRago who had been out with a knee injury.

The halftime was scoreless, with mostly punts by both after no "*worthwhile gains*". The exception was in the 1st when Delhi recovered a Saint Al fumble and got as far as the Flash 3 before losing the ball on downs. The Wildcats scored in the 3rd but couldn't convert the PAT. The Flashes tied the contest in the 4th with 4:00 left. Starting at their 15, they drove to the Wildcat 10. On a run for the endzone, Caston James fumbled but it was recovered by Saint Al's Davis for the touchdown. The PAT attempt by Davis was not good after slipping down "*due to the condition of the field. Had Davis remained on his feet he would have easily gone over the Wildcat's line as he had an open field before him*".

GAME 7:   SAINT AL (3-1-2) vs VICKSBURG (UNREPORTED)
                        FINAL: ST AL 0 VICKSBURG 6
                        November 12, 1928

This game almost never happened. On October 29th, the paper reported that "**SAINT ALOYSIUS, VICKSBURG HIGH SEVER RELATIONS**". Details are unknown, but it was reportedly a Saint Al cancellation. A conference the next day reported the "*matter settled*", though details aren't legible from reports. The Jamison brothers were still out, others "*suffering from minor injuries*", and Vicksburg was "*favored to win over the local collegians...*"

Vicksburg was the only team to score in a contest of penalties and great defense. After a 40 yard Wright punt in the 2nd, Vicksburg utilized the running of Jabour, Teller and Mounger to push the ball downfield. It was Howard who went over for the touchdown. Haskew's PAT was no good.

GAME X: SAINT AL (3-2-2) @ LAKE PROVIDENCE, LA (UNREPORTED)
                        FINAL: NOT PLAYED
                        November 23, 1928

Position changes were undertaken in anticipation of the trip to Lake Providence. The Jamison boys "*had rejoined the team*" and numerous players would see new spots. This was due, in part, to injuries to Charles Wilkerson (finger) and James (wrist). The Tallulah team was very good. They had lost to Ferriday, LA 12-0, and the only team to beat Ferriday was the LSU freshman squad.

On the 22nd, Coach Shannon received word that the game would have to be called off. First, numerous players would be unable to play as a result of the previous game against Bastrop. Second, the head coach would be in Baton Rouge for a school meeting. Shannon agreed and the Flashes team attended the Vicksburg-Philadelphia contest in town instead.

GAME X: SAINT AL vs SAINT AL ALUMNI
                        FINAL: ST AL 12 ALUMNI 0
                        November 25, 1928

A free game for the public was played on Sunday afternoon. Past "*star players*" put their skills up against the current team. Alumni playing included Jack Roberts, George Downey, Earl Fife, "Country" Brown, Robert Bankston, Fred Evans, John Ryan, Earl Jacquith, Ferguson Ryan, Nick Lavecchia, Vincent Canizaro, Bill Campbell, Earle Reynolds, Reginald Hossley, Wyatt James, Ernest "Fatty" Sheffield and C.H. "Moon" Melsheimer. The paper said the veterans were "*in fine condition and will give Coach Shannon's boys a good fight when the two squads meet*".

The crowd of 300 saw the youngsters score first in the 2nd. Joe Arenz blocked a punt and took it back 15 yards to the 5. Davis capitalized afterwards for the score. Their next touchdown came on a Wright pass to T.A. Jamison for 45 yards. Amazingly, the Flashes had no injuries going into their last contest of the season in just four days.

GAME 8:   SAINT AL (3-2-2) vs CHAMBERLAIN HUNT ACADEMY (UNREPORTED)
                          FINAL: ST AL 7 CHAMBERLAIN HUNT 0
                          November 29, 1928

The final game would be "Alumni and Dads Day" and feature a double-header. Younger players, called *"stars of tomorrow"*, would play after the CHA contest. Two teams made of grammar school kids would be known as the Sparks and the Flames. The Flames would end up victorious with Boolos garnering praise from the paper.

The Flashes would also end up victorious, though it didn't appear to be heading that way. The only score came in the 4th after a Burch punt to Saint Al. Davis plunged in from the Cadet 5 for the touchdown, added to the combination of Wright to T.A. Jamison for the conversion. The game was purely a defensive struggle with only 1 fumble being lost in the contest; that by CHA. Penalties also added to the lack of scoring.

The paper was quick to credit Shannon with a fine job in his first year as head man of the Flashes.

1929 (2-4-1)

Jack Roberts, the former Flash from the "Old Gold", would head the team in 1929. With a few returning veteran players, it was thought that he had enough experience to make this S.A.C. team *"one of the best teams in the history of the school"*. The team was captained by O.E. James.

GAME 1:   SAINT AL (0-0) vs OAK GROVE (1-0)
                          FINAL: ST AL 13 OAK GROVE 7
                          October 3, 1929

Articles by the paper on the game are nearly unreadable. Oak Grove was led by a former LSU star in Swanson whose team had been decimated by graduation in 1928, losing 17 players. Even so, Oak Grove was first on the board after a fumble at the Flash 40. A run for 25 and runs by Lee and Cotton took it to the Flash 6 before Torrance, a reported 17 year-old weighing 250 pounds, was able to move in for the touchdown. The PAT made it 7-0. Saint Al answered in the 2nd after an Oak Grove fumble was brought back to the OG 10. Charles Wilkerson got 6 and Norman Wright got the remainder to make it 7-6 at half.

The 3rd was scoreless, but the Flashes put the opener away in the 4th when T.A. Jamison scored. The PAT was good. Roberts brought the substitutes in at the end to finalize the game and the start of a 1-0 season.

GAME 2:   SAINT AL (1-0) @ TALLULAH, LA (2-0)
                          FINAL: ST AL 2 TALLULAH 2
                          October 11, 1929

The Flashes worked hard during game week in preparation for the trip to Louisiana. Caston James had been injured in the Oak Grove contest and, though out of the *"infirmary"*, would miss the road opener. A large crowd of Vicksburg fans made the trip to see the game and enjoy the Tri-Parish Fair.

Saint Al scored at the beginning of the 2nd when Joe Arenz knotted a Tallulah safety to make it 2-0 at halftime. A 40 yard pass play early in the 3rd by the Flashes was called back due to a time-out allegedly called by Tallulah. In the 4th, Tallulah tied the game when a punt return was marred by the player being tackled in the endzone.

The paper noted that *"The Purple Flashes were lacking in their usual 'pep' and smooth signal plays ... This change can be attributed to the tiresome journey, Fair excitement and the playing conditions of the field. Playing true to form, S.A.C would have defeated the Tallulah Tigers by three touchdowns."*

GAME 3:   SAINT AL (1-0-1) vs CHAMBERLAIN HUNT ACADEMY (3-0)
                       FINAL: ST AL 0 CHAMBERLAIN HUNT 6
                       October 18, 1929

More injuries were in store as both Captain O.E. James and QB Wilkerson would be forced to sit. Robert Geary would take the QB spot for the game. Caston James would return to play a portion of the contest.

After a scoreless first half, the game was won in the 3rd by Chamberlain Hunt. Behind runs and passes that involved Jolly, Brown, Landry and Murphy, Brown plowed in for the touchdown. The Flashes moved as far as the Cadet 18 in the 4th but could get no further. They also had an incomplete pass from Wright to Jamison ruled in favor of CHA. Afterwards, the Cadets ran the clock for the victory.

GAME x: SAINT AL (1-1-1) vs JEFFERSON MILITARY ACADEMY (UNREPORTED)
                       FINAL: UNREPORTED
                       October 25, 1929

O.E. James and Caston James would be back to give strength back to the Flashes against their visitors from the Natchez area, but John Grant would be injured and watching. Unfortunately, the paper did not report on the game or the results in the Saturday paper from October 26th or afterwards. Reports from The Vicksburg Evening Post in much later years would credit the 1929 team with a record that included only 7 games. So, it would seem that this contest did not take place. However, the write up for the next game noted that there were three injured players beforehand. So, either they were injured in practice or the game was simply ignored.

GAME 4:   SAINT AL (1-1-1) vs MAGEE (5-1)
                       FINAL: ST AL 0 MAGEE 6
                       October 30, 1929

Wilkerson (ankle), John Grant (knee) and Abraham (leg) were out for the game. Wilkerson and Grant were on crutches and Abraham was confined to his bed. It didn't help that the opponent was what the paper called "one of the best teams in Mississippi" that was "well balanced from end-to-end". There was hope that the rain falling in Vicksburg on game day would be the equalizer.

The paper reported that "The gridiron battle was waged in a field ankle-deep in mud." Not only had it rained before the game, it rained during the game. Perhaps the mud did equalize against the bigger and more experienced squad because the Flashes held their own until there was only :40 left remaining. A Wright punt was blocked by Magee at the 50. After a number of runs and passes, Cole swam over for the last-second winning touchdown. The PAT was understandably unsuccessful and the Flashes had lost a heart-breaker to a formidable foe.

GAME 5:   SAINT AL (1-2-1) vs VICKSBURG (UNREPORTED)
                       FINAL: ST AL 0 VICKSBURG 12
                       November 11, 1929

Before the game, the two teams were guests at the cozy Alamo Theater to see a movie appropriately named The Forward Pass. But on Monday, Saint Al would play yet another game in the rain and mud; this one for much more than just a victory. The city championship was at stake against a "balanced machine (Vicksburg) working in perfect unison".

A Caston James fumble at the Flash 20 in the 1st set up Vicksburg's first score when Howard pushed the ball over the goal to give them a halftime lead of 6-0. In the 3rd, the Flashes were pinned at their 5 and quick-kicked to the Flash 25. On a drive that saw more than one fumble, Brent got 8, Monger gained the first down, and then Jabour took it in for the touchdown. Again the PAT was unsuccessful.

The contest was a symphony of turnovers and penalties in the horrid conditions. But Vicksburg had retained control of the trophy and bragging rights for 1929.

GAME 6:   SAINT AL (1-3-1) @ EAST CARROL (2-4-1 ENDED)
       FINAL: ST AL 6 LAKE PROVIDENCE 0
       November 15, 1929

  Coach Roberts promised that the trip to Lake Providence, LA would see *"the boys ... play a clean, well fought game"*. His promise was kept as there were no penalties in the game. Eighteen Flashes made the trip to Louisiana.
  Rain fell during the contest but the field was in good shape for once since October 25th. The only touchdown came with 5 minutes left when F.X. McNamara took the ball 50 yards for the touchdown. Though the write-up is largely unreadable, the line work of T.A. Jamison, Francis Bliss, Milton Sadol and Arenz cleared the way for the victory. The yearbook from ECPHS has a section on *"The 1929 Gridiron Season"*. Unfortunately, they don't note the Saint Al game having been played.

GAME 7:   SAINT AL (2-3-1) vs FLORA (UNREPORTED)
       FINAL: ST AL 7 FLORA 14
       November 27, 1929

  There had been much written about an upcoming football battle between alumni. It would be the 2nd "Alumni Game" that featured "stars" of previous years. The game was set by November 20th, but it was announced on November 23rd that Coach Roberts had cancelled the contest due to the upcoming season finale against Flora, the bad weather and the holidays.
  Neither team lighted the scoreboard in a 1st. Near the end, Flora punted but Wright fumbled and it was retained by the visitor at the Flash 42. In the 2nd, a double pass from Cox to Hawkins for 6 and a Cox run for 9 put them at the Flash 5 and Cox took it in 3 plays later. He also converted the PAT. The quarter also saw a Wright pass picked off by Cox, but he was tackled by O.E. James before he could score and halftime would see a Flora lead of 7-0.
  The 3rd started with another Flora interception by Jackson but did not result in a score. On their next possession, runs by Nelson and James set up a 35 yard touchdown strike from Wright to Jamison. Wright converted the PAT to tie the game. Though they had threatened to score on the ensuing drive, Flora was unable to do so. But, on the next Flash drive, Bardin intercepted Wright and returned it 50 yards for the touchdown. Cox converted the PAT as the whistle ended the 3rd. That would provide the final points of the game and a 2-4-1 record for the 1929 Flashes.

1930-1939

SAINT ALOYSIUS 1939 TEAM (10-0)

1930 (4-3)

Walton Shannon's team worked hard through September to get into *"first class condition"*. Fundamental work and 60-minute scrimmages pitting regulars against reserves produced a team *"promise of giving its opponents a battle from the opening play till the final whistle"*. The paper noted no star player, but a team of *"green timber"*; a comparison to *"how 'green branches' refuse to bend, yield and burn to their opponents"*. Charles Wilkerson would serve as team captain while Frank Kelly would be alternate captain.

GAME 1:   SAINT AL (0-0) @ TALLULAH, LA (UNDEFEATED)
         FINAL: ST AL 7 TALLULAH 6
         October 3, 1930

The Flashes made the trip across the river to play a team that had *"practically its entire squad back from last year"*. The previous 2-2 game would provide a measuring stick for Saint Al and a win would change the perception of the team of *"green timber"* to one that *"has a better team than last year"*.

Saint Al was *"outweighed and handicapped by a grassy field"* but did bring *"a large delegation of rooters"*. Early in the 3rd, Robert Geary found Milton Seidel for a 25 yard reception. After 3 straight runs of 6 yards each, Ira Ellis plunged in for the touchdown. He also scored the PAT after a fake kick to make it 7-0. Tallulah, behind the work of Harris and Davis, provided a touchdown later, though specifics weren't reported. The paper noted that even though graduation had hit Saint Al hard, *"...their showing at Tallulah gave every indication that the Flashes are going to give all of their opponents a real battle"*.

GAME 2:   SAINT AL (1-0) vs MAGEE (2-0)
         FINAL: ST AL 0 MAGEE 18
         October 10, 1930

The Flashes were anxious to play well in front of their first home crowd and defeat a Middle Mississippi Conference foe that had beaten them in the waning minutes 6-0 in 1929. Practices to correct weak areas of play were in place on game week. Though Bill Jaquith (pulled muscle) and Marion DiRago (ankle) would miss the game, the paper predicted it to be *"one of the liveliest football battles of the season"* between the *"two well-matched teams"*.

Thames scored the first Magee touchdown in the 1st and added another in the 2nd behind a balanced Magee attack of running and passing by himself, Jones and Meyers. The PAT was again no-good. An interception by Magee late in the half almost gave them another score, but the halftime whistle sounded beforehand. The final touchdown came in the 3rd, this time on a run by Jones.

GAME 3:   SAINT AL (1-1) vs SAINT MATTHEWS (UNREPORTED)
         FINAL: ST AL ? SAINT MATTHEWS ?
         October 18, 1930

There was hope for a *"large crowd out as (Saint Al) is under considerable expense in bringing the St. Matthews team here"*. The starters would be the same *"well-developed"* players and the game promised *"to give the local collegians a tough battle"*. Unfortunately, there is no record of the game to be found. By reviewing the season record reported on November 24, 1930 by The Vicksburg Evening Post, we know that they won the contest. But the details and score remain unknown.

GAME 4:   SAINT AL (2-1) @ DELHI, LA (UNREPORTED)
         FINAL: ST AL 6 DELHI 0
         October 24, 1930

According to reports, at least 5 regular players were on the injured list and unlikely to play at Delhi. Team Captain Wilkerson was one and three of the others included Seidel, Francis Bliss and Ellis.

The Flashes had at least 4 miscues in the 1st half, throwing 3 interceptions and giving up the ball on a fumble, while Delhi had only an interception and a fumble. The 2nd half would see the same results until the 4th. After a Nelson punt to the home team, Delhi fumbled to Saint Al. Geary ran for 2, threw a 25 yard strike to Charles Garraton and then ran it in himself from the 10 for the touchdown. Nelson intercepted a ball near the end of the game to help run out the clock.

GAME 5:   SAINT AL (3-1) @ LAKE PROVIDENCE, LA (UNREPORTED)
                FINAL: ST AL 0 LAKE PROVIDENCE 25
                October 31, 1930

The injured list grew to 6 players, with Geary now watching due to an injured knee. With so many Flashes on the sidelines, Jack Swink was able to have a stellar day. He scored four touchdowns and "*dropped kicked*" once for the PAT. Numerous player changes by the Flashes that allowed each member to play couldn't stop the home team. Said the paper, "*Despite this, though, the Flashes played great football. They have no alibis to offer.*"

GAME 6:   SAINT AL (3-2) vs VICKSBURG (UNREPORTED)
                FINAL: ST AL 0 VICKSBURG 13
                November 11, 1930

It was time for the annual Allien Armistice Day game against the Greenies. The Flashes hadn't experienced success thus far against Vicksburg, but the paper indicated that this could be "*one of the closest contested game(s) yet played between the elevens*" with "*a good game promised...*" The Flashes were healthy again and "*in tip top shape*" with everybody returning. They had been working hard and changing position players to ready for the bigger opponent.

In one of the most detailed games written in any year, the contest really came down to a few plays on a field entirely of mud. In the 1st quarter, Beasley took the ball from his own 42 and darted for the touchdown. D. Fleming ran through the line for the PAT and it was 7-0. In the 2nd and after numerous slips and fumbles, Nelson punted to Hovious at the VHS 25. Beasley promptly gained 65 yards on a run, Hovious got 5, Fleming managed 1, and then Hovious went around the right for the 4 yard touchdown. Fleming's PAT failed and halftime was 13-0.

The remainder of the muddy game was simply a back-and-forth affair with the scoring having already been completed.

GAME X: SAINT AL vs JEFFERSON MILITARY COLLEGE and MADISON AGR. HIGH
                FINAL: UNPLAYED
                Set For November 21, 1930 and November 25, 1930

Originally, Saint Al was to host Jefferson Military College on Thanksgiving Day. But before the game could arrive, the college had "*disbanded for the season*". An attempt by the Flashes to schedule another opponent had apparently been successful. On November 19th, the paper reported that Madison Agricultural High School would play in Vicksburg on November 21st. The game fell through, though no details were given. The Flashes would have to gain another opponent to challenge their 3-3 record.

GAME 7:   SAINT AL (3-3) vs HAZLEHURST (6-4)
                FINAL: ST AL 19 HAZLEHURST 7
                November 26, 1930

The Indians took the spot for the last contest of the year. They had a strong team, had played more games and made it known they were coming to win. But the Flashes were healthy and "*not one complains of injuries of any kind*". Originally scheduled for Thanksgiving Day, it was moved to allow both fans to see other major games. "*Nothing outside of winning ... would please the team and student body of S.A.C. more than to be able to say that the ... game was a sellout and that standing room was at a premium.*"

An Indian fumble to start the 1st was recovered by the Flashes at the their 20. Bliss and Nelson gained a few yards before Wilkerson went in from 17 out. In the same quarter, a Flash punt to Hazlehurst was fumbled and recovered by Saint Al. Wilkerson drove the Flashes into the endzone on a run but Nelson's PAT missed. In the 2nd, Hazlehurst's Wade scored and added the PAT. Halftime saw the Flashes up 12-7.

The 3rd was scoreless and ended with an Indian punt that had Saint Al sitting at the Indian 26. To start the 4th, runs by Geary, Wilkerson and Nelson took it to the 1 and then Bliss got it in. Nelson converted the PAT and the Flashes had a winning 4-3 season. Injuries had cost the Flashes one game in all likelihood, but they had won 2 out of 3 on the road. The Hazlehurst Courier noted afterwards that "The team was led the first five games by Shirley Aldridge, snappy quarterback. The last of the season it was led by Burrell Young, better known as 'Rambling'. Our line was not up to par at the first of the season, but a little later, under the coaching of Coach Therrell, there were seven fighting Indians".

1931 (1-7)

As in previous years, newspaper coverage for pre-season outlooks was uncommon. The first writings about Flash football would take place just before the initial contest. Saint Aloysius College would be led by Gorman Schaffer and captained by guard William (Bill) Jacquith.

GAME 1:   SAINT AL (0-0) vs CLINTON (1-0)
               FINAL: ST AL 0 CLINTON 19
               October 1, 1931

On Wednesday, the coach took the team to the Fairgrounds for a few hours to allow then to get "acquainted as to surroundings and in perfecting plays". The game lineup depended on which "various players show up" in these practices. The paper said that Clinton was "reported to have one of the fastest teams in the history of that school. The visitors will have the edge on the local lads in the weight ... about 10 pounds per man. SAC expects to overcome this extra weight by speed." Schaffer reported his team "in fine shape" and "performed in fine style" in practices. That would change as their team captain would miss due to illness.

After kickoff and an exchange of punts in the 1st, Clinton scored on a drive from the 50 when Hitt got in from the 3. Musselwhite's PAT made it 7-0. Early in the 2nd, the Flashes fumbled and Clinton converted it immediately. Hitt found Meyer for 30 to the Flash 15. Hitt took it in for a touchdown after 3 runs but Musselwhite missed the PAT and it was 13-0 at halftime.

Saint Al's best chance came in the 3rd. A Flash punt was fumbled and Gerald Melsheimer recovered it at the Indian 5. Three runs and a pass were unsuccessful. Clinton closed the game in the 4th when Hitt found Musselwhite for a 25 yard touchdown. The paper gave credit to Clinton by calling them "a well-developed team", but said of the Flashes, "The local collegians showed enough stuff yesterday to indicate that the material is there and, under the direction of Coach Schaffer, the Flashes give every promise of coming through in fine style."

GAME 2:   SAINT AL (0-1) @ HAZLEHURST (4-0)
               FINAL: ST AL 7 HAZLEHURST 69
               October 8, 1931

The team left at noon for Hazlehurst "fit and ready". Many players were first-timers against Clinton and the paper said "now that the effects of the opening struggle has wore off, the boys are expected to put up a splendid exhibition this afternoon." They couldn't have been more wrong.

The undefeated Hazlehurst team had already played 4 games. The lack of ink devoted to the Flashes couldn't possibly detail each score, but Saint Al did put up their 7 points in the 1st on a pass from Robert Gabe to Melsheimer for a 30 yard touchdown. Charles Garraton ran for the PAT. Said the paper, "The SAC boys were outplayed in every department of the game ... and were also outweighed. Hazlehurst ... tore off yard after yard while the Indians line held like a stone wall. The SAC Flashes executed several plays, but the opposition was too much for them."

The Hazlehurst Courier said that "Ainsworth, Aldridge and Young showed up well in the backfield. Cowan, star halfback, scored 5 touchdowns; Ainsworth, three; Captain Young, one; and Aldridge one". Their paper reported the final as 67-7.

GAME 3:   SAINT AL (0-2) vs SIMPSON COUNTY (UNREPORTED)
                 FINAL: ST AL 0 SIMPSON COUNTY 13
                 October 16, 1931

Due to the size of the Aggies that *"easily outweighed"* the Flashes, Schaffer had worked that week on the passing game. Jaquith was back from his sickness and Saint Al was expected *"to do an about-face ... and hang up a win. With Jaquith at guard, the Flashes are expected to take on new life and flash their way across the Simpson goal line"*.

Much of the first half of the game is not available or incomplete. Simpson County scored first behind Williamson runs but the PAT was *"wild"*. Their second touchdown came in the 2nd quarter on a Robinson pass to Strait. Robinson then passed to Neal for the extra point.   The writing style of the reporters made it somewhat difficult to really get a feel for the game, but this much is clear: The game was almost literally a contest of fumbles, lost yardage and penalties.

GAME 4:   SAINT AL (0-3) vs SAINT MATTHEWS, LA (4-0)
                 FINAL: ST AL 7 SAINT MATTHEWS 13
                 October 23, 1931

The Flashes had beaten Saint Matthews the previous year. The visitor was *"reported to have a stronger and much better team in every department this year and a hard fought struggle is being anticipated"*. Though they lost the previous week, the paper said that *"the squad made a most impressive showing and, with the polishing up on the rough spots ... in the daily drill this week, the SAC boys are confident of ... a win over their 'friendly enemies' from across the Mississippi river"*. The Monroe boys on whom the Flashes were *"confident they will hang up their initial win of the year at the expense of the boys from our neighboring state"* were bringing a *"big delegation"* (50 fans) that promised *"to make themselves known at City Park..."*

Saint Matthews scored in the 1st after blocking a Flash punt at the Flash 20. They drove to the 4 and then Gebhardt took it in. McHenry converted the PAT on a run. Saint Al tied the game early in the 4th, when starting at the 50, William Booth crossed the goal. Jauquith converted the PAT to make it 7-7. Within the last 2:00 at the 50, Gabe punted to the SM 10. But an off-sides call pushed the Flashes back. On the ensuing attempt, Gabe's punt was blocked by Cicero and recovered at the Flash 35. A couple of plays later, McHenry went in from the right and scored. The PAT was no good.

GAME 5:   SAINT AL (0-4) vs SAINT MATTHEWS, LA (UNREPORTED)
                 FINAL: ST AL 0 SAINT MATTHEWS 14
                 November 2, 1931

A return tilt with the Louisiana team had Saint Al hopeful. The previous game was close and the Flashes were bigger than the Irish. The 1st half was scoreless at Forsyth Park, but the Irish opened up after the opening 2nd half kickoff put them at the 40. The Flashes immediately gave the home team 25 yards on 3 penalties. McEnery, the Irish QB, capitalized for the touchdown and the PAT. In the 4th, they scored from midfield after holding Saint Al on downs.

Runs by Ballard and Gebhardt gained 20 and the Flashes lost another 10 for *"profanity, a failing for which St. Aloysius paid dearly..."* McEnery ran for 3, Gebhardt gained 5, McEnery got 19, and then the QB scored after 3 runs. Turk hit Gebhardt for the PAT to make it 14-0.

GAME 6:   SAINT AL (0-5) vs VICKSBURG (UNREPORTED)
                 FINAL: ST AL 0 VICKSBURG 40
                 November 11, 1931

The Allein Post American Legion Armistice Day contest for the City Championship had been won by Vicksburg a number of years in a row. VHS's star quarterback Beazley would miss due to *"a severe charley-horse which he received in practice last week"*. Both teams worked to fine-tune their play and the paper predicted that *"a large crowd will be out to witness the game"*.

VHS scored their 1st touchdown in the 2nd when Hovious passed to Metz and *"the little quarterback raced down the field and over for the touchdown"*. Hovious converted the PAT. Their second score came in the 3rd behind a Hovious run and the PAT was successful when he found Brownstein. It was 14-0. In the 4th, Hovious hit Brownstein for a touchdown and Hovious converted.

An ensuing Flash fumble recovered by Red Strickland gave VHS the ball at the Flash 5. Strickland scored from there to make it 27-0. After giving the ball back, VHS strung together runs by Strickland, Metz, and Hovious to get to the Flash 10. Strickland scored from the 4 and Hovious made it 33-0. The final score came in the last minute. An K.P. Broussard pass was picked off by Biedenharn with a return to the Flash 7. Strickland went in from there and Brownstein converted as the whistle sounded.

GAME 7:   SAINT AL (0-6) vs MADISON COUNTY; CAMDEN, MS (UNREPORTED)
                FINAL: ST AL 6 MADISON COUNTY 25
                November 20, 1931

Somewhere along the way, Coach Gormon Schaffer was replaced by Fred Setaro, though no reports were found as to the rationale. The upcoming opponent was described as *"a fast and furious gridiron squad which has won the majority of its games this year"* and *"ranked as one of the leading teams in the regional district (and) has among its achievements for the season a victory over Canton."* With the *"kinks ironed out" from the past week"*, the paper said *"the game promises to be a hard fought affair and it is expected to attract a large crowd"*.

Rain and a muddy field was expected to overcome the bigger opponents. *"...it will not be so much weight, but the ability to plow through mud."* The prediction was accurate and the Flashes played in *"chilly and bleak"* conditions on *"a field that was virtually a sea of mud"*. Only a few fans came to watch.

The Aggies scored first in the 1st after starting at midfield. Drives pushed them close enough for Melton to push through for the touchdown. The Flashes responded in the 2nd behind *"stellar little halfback"* Booth to the 2. Garraton went in to tie it 6-6 going into halftime. In the 3rd, the Aggies faked a punt at the Flash 40 and Melton took it all the way for the go-ahead touchdown. They scored again early in the 4th when, again starting from midfield, Tatum hit Melton for the final 15 yards. The Flashes fumbled in the 4th and Madison's Scroggins made them pay with the final touchdown. Goolsy converted the PAT.

GAME 8:   SAINT AL (0-7) vs SATARTIA (UNREPORTED)
                FINAL: ST AL 19 SATARTIA 0
                November 25, 1931

Satartia brought a *"powerful"* team coached by a former MSU (A&M) and Vicksburg Greenie star player Miller Matthews. In this (his first) year, he had inherited an inexperienced team. But *"under his tutelage, the boys have learned fast and the squad is now rated as one of the best in this section of the state."* The Flashes were outweighed but expected to counter with *"fleetness of foot and an aerial attack"*.

The paper noted that the Flashes had suffered so many losses due to one reason: depth. *"Had the team had the reserve players to shoot in when the veterans became tired, there is no doubt they would have won several of the games which were lost."*

The Flashes were the only team to score in the 1st half. After a poor punt put them at the Satartia 40, the Flashes began running. Booth, Garraton and Broussard pitched in before Booth scored for a 6-0 lead. In the 3rd, more runs by Gabe, Garraton, Broussard and Ellis pushed it to the 5. Ellis converted for the 12-0 touchdown. Ellis' PAT was stopped at the line. Broussard ran the last touchdown on a fake pass and Jaquith converted the PAT for the final 19-0 tally.

1932 (1-6)

A meeting was held in September at Mississippi College to organize an organization known as The State Association of Coaches and Officials. In addition to a framework of regulation, it also served to clarify the rules and provide an interpretive body. Brother Thomas and Coach Jack Roberts attended on behalf of the Flashes. Roberts would be back to helm the team after his departure at the conclusion of the 1929 season.

The actual coaching of the Flashes was vague to start 1932. In a September 29th article, it was noted that Brother Thomas was the coach and Roberts was the assistant. As the year progressed, Roberts was called the coach and George Guider the assistant. In either case, the paper reported that they had *"whipped into shape a light, yet scrappy, team"*. Donald Price would serve as team captain.

GAME 1:   SAINT AL (0-0) @ TALLULAH, LA (1-0)
               FINAL: ST AL 0 TALLULAH 69
               September 30, 1932

Hopes were high for the first game of the season. Though outweighed 160 to 144 and playing a team already with a victory over Eudora High (LA) 52-0, it was expected that "*a large number of Vicksburgers will accompany the Flashes on the trip*". Also attending would be Clinton's MC football team and students. Those high hopes for a good opening were dashed soundly.

The paper writes only the following about the game: "*The Tallulah, LA high school football team administered a crushing defeat to the St. Aloysius College eleven of Vicksburg in Tallulah yesterday afternoon. The score was 69-0. The Tallulah squad outplayed their opponents in every department of the game.*"

GAME 2:   SAINT AL (0-1) vs SIMPSON COUNTY (1-2)
               FINAL: ST AL 0 SIMPSON COUNTY 13
               October 7, 1932: CITY PARK

After such a brutal beating to start the season, the paper reported that "*the Flashes have been working overtime, getting the rough edges off the squad*". Roberts put the boys through "*a long and strenuous work out (Thursday) afternoon which held forth long after the sun had disappeared*". The results were pleasing and "*The Flashes are expected to present a much better clicking machine this afternoon than on the first time out last week.*"

The Aggies had a good team and three contests under their belt for this Middle Mississippi Regional Conference game. Simpson County gained their first points as the half ended. After a Watson Sudduth punt and a few runs, Robinson hit Strait from the Flash 40 for a touchdown and 6-0 lead. The last points came midway through the 3rd when Walters streaked 40 yards for the touchdown. Williamson was able to convert the PAT this time. The Flashes got close as the game ended, having the ball near the Aggie goal as time expired.

GAME 3:   SAINT AL (0-2) vs MAGEE (4-0)
               FINAL: ST AL 0 MAGEE 20
               October 14, 1932

The paper noted that even though they suffered a loss, the Flashes had an "*impressive showing*" the previous week. They would be healthy for a Magee team that averaged 175 pounds and underwent strenuous workouts during the week. They included adding new "*deceptive*" plays and position changes. Wilmer Ford and Raphael Franco would now be in the backfield with Vito Canizaro.

Saint Al would shine in the 1st half but neither team could get on the scoreboard. In the 2nd half, after the Flash kickoff, Kees found Winstead for a 55 yard touchdown. The PAT pass was no-good. On their next drive, Winstead hit Kees for a 75 yard touchdown pass. Winstead converted the PAT and it was 13-0. Midway through the 4th, Suddith was picked off by Brister. On his second carry, Brister crossed the goal. Burnham converted the PAT.

Though disappointing in the loss, this was the best the team had looked so far. They had actually gotten close to the Magee goal twice, but the bigger undefeated team held. The performances by Ford, Donald Price, Canizaro and Sudduth were called "*stellar*".

GAME 4:   SAINT AL (0-3) @ LAKE PROVIDENCE, LA (UNREPORTED)
               FINAL: ST AL 0 LAKE PROVIDENCE 13
               October 21, 1932

Nothing was written before kickoff, but Lake Providence got on the board in the 1st when a Flash passing penalty put the ball at the 5. Both the touchdown and extra point came on rushes. In the 2nd, another penalty on the Flashes and a completed pass put Lake Providence near the goal. The home team ran in the touchdown but the PAT was no-good. As with the Simpson County game, the Flashes were at the opponent's goal when time expired.

The paper was complimentary of the Flashes, saying "*The splendid condition of the SAC team has enabled it to go through with its punishing schedule; the hardest schedule ever assigned to a S.A.C.*

team. The boys deserve praise for their heroic stand against all odds and they certainly deserve a better attendance at the games if for no other reason than local sportsmanship".

GAME 5:   SAINT AL (0-4) vs JEFFERSON MILITARY COLLEGE (UNREPORTED)
                 FINAL: ST AL 7 JMC 0
                 October 28, 1932

When originally scheduled, JMC was a high school. By game time, they were now a *"junior college"*. The Flashes used that as incentive and the paper said *"...the S.A.C. team promises to give a surprise to their friends and well-wishers by scoring their first points of the season and sending JMC home with the distinction of losing the first game to S.A.C."*
        The section of the paper that dealt with the opening of the game is illegible, but we know that Canizaro scored the season's first points in the closing minutes of the 4th quarter. James Andrews ran for the PAT and the Flashes had their first victory of 1932.

GAME 6:   SAINT AL (1-4) vs UTICA (UNREPORTED BUT WITH 2 TIES)
                 FINAL: ST AL 0 UTICA 7
                 November 4, 1932

The paper believed the Flashes *"in better shape now than at any time this season"*. Canizaro, fresh from his touchdown, would start at halfback. Utica, under Coach J.J. Turner, had tied Hazlehurst and Clinton and also had a few upsets. Their record as a whole, though, was unreported.
        The sole score of the game came in the 1st quarter when T. Jenkins plowed through the line and broke a long run for the touchdown. Davis added the PAT to make it 7-0. The Flashes had only 2 first downs in the contest but did get inside the Utica 20 on one drive.

GAME 7:   SAINT AL (1-5) vs VICKSBURG/CARR CENTRAL (UNREPORTED)
                 FINAL: ST AL 0 CARR CENTRAL 56
                 November 11, 1932

The opponent was not only undefeated against Saint Al, but the Flashes had never scored on them. The night before the game, a heavy rain soaked Vicksburg, but the field was determined to be in good shape for the Armistice Day contest. Both teams were healthy and both predicted to give the 1,400 fans a good show on a cold day.
        There is no recap of every touchdown Carr Central would pin on Saint Al. The first one was a Wilkinson run from the 20 in the 1st, but the barrage of scoring must have been relentless. At least two Sudduth punts were hampered by Parker, and Miner did the job for the Greenies in both punting and passing. In the end, the 1932 season was very similar to the one previously. It was obvious that the Flashes had work to do in order to gain consistent victories.

1933 (2-3-3)

Another season and another coaching change was in store. Jack Roberts would not head the Purple and Gold this year. Instead, Athletic Director Brother Harold and assistant coach George "Hank" Guider would lead the team. In September, the coaches put the boys through drills and scrimmages that lasted up to an hour. The paper noted that *"The squad looks mighty good. The boys are clicking well together. They displayed good fighting spirit in their work"*. There would be no permanent captain this year; but instead a game-by-game selection.

GAME 1:   SAINT AL (0-0) @ UTICA (0-2)
                 FINAL: ST AL 6 UTICA 18
                 October 6, 1933

The Flashes left at noon for the drive to Utica and were sporting new equipment courtesy of the S.A.C. Alumni Association. They would be playing a team with two games under their belt, albeit with losses to Canton and Madison AHS.

Little is written about this contest except that after a scoreless 1st, both teams hit the endzone in the 2nd. Utica got theirs on "*a series of line plays*" and the Flashes' Robert Donovan returned a kickoff 60 yards for their score. Utica also scored in the 3rd and 4th quarters though details are unknown.

GAME 2:   SAINT AL (0-1) @ SATARTIA (UNREPORTED)
                      FINAL: ST AL 14 SATARTIA 0
                      October 12, 1933

The game was moved from Friday to Thursday to allow Satartia students to attend the State Fair in Jackson. The Flashes would be without guard Joseph Bonelli (nose), guard Phillip Jones (shoulder), Raphael Franco, Robert Donovan and James Andrews due to injuries. Julius Melsheimer was elected Captain for the contest that had "*About 25 autos containing Vicksburgers (make) the trip … to witness the game*".

The Flashes scored in the closing minutes of the 2nd when Melsheimer picked off a Satartia pass and took it 85 yards for the opening touchdown. Charles Guiney went right for the successful PAT to end the half with the Flashes up 7-0. Guiney came close to taking the 2nd half kickoff back for another score but got only 55 yards before being tackled.

Melsheimer continued his attack in the 3rd when Guiney found him for a 40 yard passing score. Thomas McDaniel provided the PAT. Melsheimer also added another interception on his day as team captain, that coming in the 2nd quarter. Brother Harold praised the team and "*especially the linesmen. During the entire game they were continually stopping the Satartia backs at the line of scrimmage or throwing them back for losses. On the offense, they opened up holes wide enough for the usual bread wagon to go through.*"

The paper recorded a story on October 29th, 1995 about this contest. The game had gone longer than expected and it was turning dark. So, spectators were quick to move their cars near the sidelines and turn on their lights.

GAME 3:   SAINT AL (1-1) vs JETT (0-2)
                      FINAL: ST AL 26 JETT 6
                      October 18, 1933

Some players would be back for the game, but Guiney had hurt a knee and was limited. The paper said that the Flashes were "*slight favorites due mainly to their showing against Satartia and an advantage in weight…*" Practices were still strenuous to avoid over-confidence against a Jett team coached by former "*grid star*" Miller Matthews. Matthews had moved on from Satartia as their coach in 1931. Bonelli served as team captain.

The Flashes went ahead in the 1st after a Jett fumble. Guiney gained 35 to the Jett 1 and Donovan converted. The PAT was fumbled and it was 6-0. Saint Al put up two more touchdowns in the 2nd. A Guiney punt was recovered in Jett territory by Saint Al. Melsheimer gained 5 and Donovan did the rest. The second score was a result of a Bonelli blocked punt on Jett's Reaves that gave the Flashes the ball at the Jett 20. Guiney scored and Melsheimer added the PAT to make the halftime a 19-0 Flash lead.

Both teams got on the board in the 4th. Jett's C. Davidson found Hammond on a pass but the PAT failed. Saint Al responded when 20 yards of Guiney runs and 10 yards by Donovan put the ball at the Jett 1. Guiney did the honors and Melsheimer added the PAT.

GAME 4:   SAINT AL (2-1) @ SAINT MATTHEWS, LA (3-0)
                      FINAL: ST AL 6 SAINT MATTHEWS 6
                      October 29, 1933

From what can be read, Saint Matthews was in terrible shape as it related to injuries sustained in their previous game. Saint Al would also face injuries with at least Phillip Janes and Joseph Bonelli missing. New faces replaced to and play in front of "*a fair sized crowd*" including "*a big delegation of Vicksburg fans…*"

The Flashes could gain no ground on the weakened Irish team. Saint Al runs were opposed by Irish passes and the first three quarters were scoreless. In the 4th, Saint Matthews took possession after a Flash punt put them at the 50. Gerhardt then took the ball from there for an Irish touchdown.

Saint Al was able to respond afterwards when 3 runs by Melsheimer got them from the Irish 45 to the 10. Three plays later, Donovan took it in for the touchdown. The winning PAT was just inches short by Melsheimer as the whistle blew. In the contest, Saint Matthews had 7 first downs versus the Flashes' 1.

GAME 5:   SAINT AL (2-1-1) @ MENDARD, LA (UNREPORTED)
                 FINAL: ST AL 6 MENARD 6
                 November 1, 1933

        The Flashes had only 2 days before hitting the road back to Louisiana. Both days consisted of practice but the paper said "*The squad is in fine condition for the game. The boys are looking forward with much pleasure to the trip and expect a tough battle but are confident of victory*". The first Flash team to play under "*electric lights*" was reported "*in excellent condition and their fighting spirit was up to the n'th degree*".
        Only portions of the game recap are available. Saint Al scored in the 2rd after a Menard fumble put them at the 12. Franco scored for the Flashes but the PAT was unsuccessful. Menard answered in the quarter on a Nash run for a score, but their PAT was also unsuccessful. The Eagles had the ball at the one-foot line before fumbling just before halftime. The remainder of the game would be played mostly in Flash territory but Saint Al did drive deep before the game ended.

GAME 6:   SAINT AL (2-1-2) vs VICKSBURG/CARR CENTRAL (3-?)
                 FINAL: UNREPORTED
                 November 11, 1933

        The Armistice Day contest for the city championship had come. Saint Al's record thus far had been not worth mentioning. Year after year, the Flashes had been held scoreless against their cross-town rivals. Since 1925, Vicksburg had outscored Saint Al by a score of 229-0. The paper reported this year's Flashes as having "*about an even chance of winning the football game ...*" This was probably due to injuries on Vicksburg's Long and Mallory that would keep them sidelined.
        The paper for this pivotal game is missing from historical records found thus far. However, the game did end in the Flashes 3rd tie of the season.

GAME 7:   SAINT AL (2-1-3) @ JEFFERSON MIL. COLLEGE (UNREPORTED)
                 FINAL: ST AL 7 JMC 13
                 NOVEMBER 17, 1933

        The paper decided to forego details of the game in favor of the incident that happened afterwards. On the return trip from the Natchez area after the loss, 11 Flashes "*narrowly escaped death ... when the lights on a car in which they were riding went out and the machine was wrecked ... on the road between Washington and Fayette*". The injuries were light compared to what could have happened. Joe Boolos had an ankle injury, Martin Frohn had cuts on his face/ear/arm, and others had slight injuries.
        They boys returned to Natchez to spend the night and recover. Brother Harold was still there, stayed with them and reported back to S.A.C president Brother Gerald.

GAME 8:   SAINT AL (2-2-3) vs SIMPSON COUNTY (UNREPORTED)
                 FINAL: ST AL 0 SIMPSON COUNTY 20
                 November 24, 1933

        The Flashes would finish the season against a team that out-weighed them as much as 12-15 pounds and had only one loss. The paper was complimentary of the work done and called it "*one of the most eventful seasons the Flashes have enjoyed in sometime*" with "*Much credit ... to Brother Harold ... and to George Guider ...*" Guider had been the assistant for a portion of the season before Brother Albertus took his spot for whatever unreported reason. Two Flashes (Boolos and Bonelli) were still unavailable as a result of the incident following the JMC game.
        In the 2nd, the boys from Mendenhall received a punt at their 40 and brought it back to the Flash 23. A Williamson run to the 10 set up his touchdown a few plays later from the 3. He also added the PAT. In the 3rd, Robinson took a run to the Flash 13. Williamson then hit Moody for a touchdown

pass. The kick was blocked. In the 4th, defensive guard Lumaden grabbed a pass at the Aggie 30 and went the distance. Williamson finished the scoring with the PAT.

The paper wrapped the season by saying *"The Flashes have played well this year and when one considers the squad was practically green when practice began, their record for the year is all the more impressive"*.

1934 (6-2)

Brother Harold was back as head coach and was assisted by Brother Albertus, who took over for Hank Guider near the end of 1933. With the exception of 4 lettermen, the team would experience new faces in positions. Practices and scrimmages were heavy and the paper said that *"Plenty of pep has been manifested all over the lot and the squad is keyed up to a fine pitch for the opening encounter with Satartia under the lights..."*

GAME 1:   SAINT AL (0-0) vs SATARTIA (UNREPORTED)
                    FINAL: ST AL 41 SATARTIA 0
                    October 5, 1934

A scouting report on Satartia said that they were *"playing an unorthodox type of football which is very deceptive to the opposition. Among other things, they are apt to pass deep in their own territory or to run on the fourth down when there is as much as three yards to go for first down"*. Meanwhile in Vicksburg, the blocking was *"much improved over that of last year along with speed which will play an important part in the fortunes of the team..."*

Saint Al scored early and often. Guiney took the opening kick back 45 yards to the Satartia 10 before running in afterwards. He opened the 2nd with another long run but it was Jerry Campbell who took it in. Lloyd Mulligan converted the PAT on a run. Later, Campbell, Guiney and James Andrews moved it to the 5 before Campbell scored.

Early in the 3rd, Guiney ran for a 45 yard touchdown and Andrews converted to make it 27-0. Before the quarter ended, they scored twice more. Both were long runs; one by Guiney and another by Campbell. PATs were converted and the reserves took the place of the starters and almost scored before the final whistle. Said the paper, *"All in all, it looks like Brothers Harold and Albertus have assembled a winner this season and the Flashes appear to be on the brink of an extremely successful year"*.

GAME 2:   SAINT AL (1-0) vs JETT (UNREPORTED)
                    FINAL: ST AL 28 JETT 0
                    October 12, 1934

Guiney suffered an injury during the Satartia game and was thought at the time to be out. A large crowd was expected based on advance ticket sales to see two local teams play, one of which being a very impressive-looking Saint Al team. Early in the 1st, Martin Frohn recovered a Jett fumble at their 10. Campbell converted on the second carry and Mulligan's PAT made it 7-0. In the 2nd, a Jett pass was picked off by Mulligan and returned 40 yards for another touchdown. Campbell plunged in for the 14-0 lead. Saint Al intercepted yet another Blues pass as the 1st half ended.

Campbell was good on defense, too. He picked off the 3rd Jett pass midway through the 3rd. In the same quarter, Andrews dove in from the 3 and Campbell made it 21-0. Jett started passing to make up the difference, but Guiney (who was playing) picked off the ball. Campbell then found Milton Seidel from 15 out and Guiney converted to make the 28th point. Reserves then took the field and sealed the victory.

GAME 3:   SAINT AL (2-0) @ UTICA (1-0-1)
                    FINAL: ST AL 0 UTICA 7
                    October 19, 1934

Utica was reported as *"having one of the best teams in this section of the state"*. It was bad timing to have Andrews (leg and broken little finger) and Mulligan (ankle) out for a few weeks to go along with Jerry Campbell's broken shoulder blade that would cause him to miss the rest of the year.

Before game time, W. Hogan's mother passed away and he would also miss the contest. Brother Harold was unimpressed with team blocking thus far. "If the squad doesn't show up any better this week than it did against Jett, we are due for a licking". He also noted that many starters could see the bench if they weren't able to perform. Victor Veasey was an exception as the former reserve came on and did an admirable job the previous week.

Before 150 spectators in weather resembling "mid-summer", Utica found the endzone in the 2nd for the games only score. At the Flash 12, they tried 3 times to convert and were also penalized for being off sides. But on 4th down, Ford hit F. Scott for the touchdown. Cudd dove through to make it the final 7-0. The Flashes would get inside the Utica 30 in the 4th but an interception killed the drive.

With injuries predominant for the Flashes, the paper said that "All in all, with most of the regulars on the bench as they were, and playing a heavier team, the Flashes gave as heroic an account of themselves as anyone would wish to see".

GAME 4:   SAINT AL (2-1) vs CHAMBERLAIN HUNT ACADEMY (0-2)
                 FINAL: ST AL 47 CHAMBERLAIN HUNT 0
                 October 25, 1934

Back at somewhat "full health", the Flashes prepped for a team that was "hard and strategically well-coached". Long practices to polish the backfield had Brother Harold busy. The Cadets were "a fast and scrappy gridiron squad..." and a "number of Port Gibson fans and the entire student body of the Academy will accompany the team to Vicksburg for the game". An estimated crowd of 1,000 fans were in attendance.

If Guiney ever had a better day with the football, it's not recorded. His first score came just 3:00 into the game and (either Lloyd or Ray) Woods converted the PAT. In the 2nd, he ran one for 45 yards and Woods again made the PAT. Woods got a touchdown in the 3rd and Andrews converted. The Flashes next possession saw them drive 70 yards with Andrews diving in. Bragg, taking the place of Woods, gained the extra point.

In the 4th, Jack Melsheimer picked off a Cadet pass at the Flash 20 and brought it to the Cadet 4. Guiney ran it in 2 plays later and Odom converted. Guiney added his last touchdown after receiving a punt and brought it 75 yards "standing up" for the touchdown. The Flashes completely dominated their Port Gibson opponents. Not only did they rule in 1st downs (12-0) but also picked off 3 Cadet passes.

GAME 5:   SAINT AL (3-1) vs LAKE PROVIDENCE (UNREPORTED)
                 FINAL: NOT REPORTED
                 November 3, 1934

The Flashes now faced a "highly rated" Lake Providence team described as "light but exceptionally deceptive..." All injured players would be ready except Lloyd Mulligan who was still nursing an ankle injury. The write-up of the game has not been found, but the November 5th paper noted that it was "the roughest gained victory of years... Several of the boys came out of the Lake Providence game with twisted ankles and other minor injuries..." Hosemann had performed well in his punting duties and "gave promise of plenty power and he will be used again in future games as a constant threat".

GAME 6:   SAINT AL (4-1) vs PORT GIBSON (UNREPORTED)
                 FINAL: ST AL 33 PORT GIBSON 0
                 November 7, 1934

While the Port Gibson record isn't noted, the Flashes were obviously expecting a victory. Playing a team 10-20 pounds lighter, the paper said that "From the comparative records of both teams, the Flashes should emerge the winner." Brother Harold anticipated playing a number of younger guys to get an idea of who could play the following year.

Saint Al scored in the 1st on a Woods dive from the 2 but the PAT was stopped at the line. Port Gibson had also stopped Saint Al's opening drive at the goal with a big defensive stand. Additionally, they had gotten to the Flash 10 before Jack Hude picked off a pass and brought it to the 3. The 3rd featured a drive that started with a Guiney kick return of 25 yards followed by an Andrews run of 22 for the touchdown. Guiney hit Andrews for the PAT to make it 13-0.

In the same quarter, Andrews ran it in from the Port Gibson 13 and Woods added the PAT. In the 4th, Saint Al increased the lead when Woods ran a punt back 40 yards to the opponent's 25. Andrews gained 14 and Lloyd Woods scored from there. Ray Woods converted to make it 27-0. The final touchdown came with 2:00 left when Lloyd Woods ran one in from "*scoring distance*". The PAT was fumbled by Andrews.

The paper was complimentary of the outmatched Port Gibson team, saying "*The score of the game is a poor indicator of the game fight the little Port Gibson team put up against overwhelming odds. All in all it was one of the most praiseworthy ones ever seen on a local field in some time.*"

GAME 7:   SAINT AL (5-1) @ NEWELLTON, LA (UNREPORTED)
           FINAL: ST AL 20 NEWELLTON 0
           November 13, 1934

No pre-game write-up was found but the contest was well documented. The Flashes scored early in the 2nd when runs by Guiney and Andrews put them at the Bear 12. Guiney then found Milton Seidel for the score and Andrews added the PAT. Sitting at the Newellton 45 in the 4th, a fake run set up an Andrews pass to a leaping Seidel to the 27 and then into the endzone.

Just afterwards on a punt, Lloyd Woods took what was called "*a beautiful run of one hundred yards*" to the endzone. But it was brought back to the 40 for stepping out of bounds. Guiney and Andrews again carried the ball deep into Bear territory. From the 1, Odom plunged in for the score and Andrews' pass to Guiney was good for the PAT.

GAME X: SAINT AL (6-1) vs JEFFERSON MILITARY COLLEGE (UNREPORTED)
           FINAL: NOT PLAYED
           November 21, 1934: HOMECOMING

This was to be Homecoming for the Flashes, complete with an "*after-party*" for the alumni and ex-football players. Unfortunately on the 20th, the coach of JMC called to say that the bridge between Natchez and Vicksburg had been washed out and that they would be unable to get to Vicksburg. The game and celebration were cancelled with hopes that another date could be found for the match. In the end, the game wasn't played.

GAME 8:   SAINT AL (6-1) vs VICKSBURG/CARR (1-?-2)
           FINAL: ST AL 0 VICKSBURG 33
           November 29, 1934

It was time for what the paper called "*...perhaps the greatest athletic event in Vicksburg sporting history each year...*" The teams would be playing not only for bragging rights and the Y's Men Trophy, but Alex Habeeb had offered a silver football trophy for the victorious team. It was placed in his store window for all to see. Guiney would be the star for the Flashes, with his exploits now eliciting crowds yells of "*Watch Guiney Go*"! Brother Harold proclaimed his team "*...as fit as a fiddle.*" Bon fires and a takeover of the downtown streets on Wednesday night had anticipation through the roof and a crowd of over 3,000 was expected.

Vicksburg scored late in the 1st when Sam took the ball from midfield to the Flash 10. Runs by Mallory and Parker got Parker close enough to get into the endzone. Troxell pushed through for the PAT. The Flashes saw the 3rd start with heavy rainfall and a host of injuries. Seidel was out with a knee injury and as many as 5 others were hampered.

Early in the quarter, Parker hit Sam with a pass to the Flash 26. Montgomery added 16 on a run, Sam scored on his 2nd run and added the PAT. Afterwards, the Flashes fumbled on the Greenie 20. Sam gained a few yards and then Ellis took it the rest of the way. The PAT by Hunt was no good. Vicksburg kept pouring it on when Franklin LaHatte took a Guiney punt 45 yards to paydirt in the 4th. Troxell's PAT attempt was good. Their last touchdown came from the Flash 15 on a McDonald run.

On December 5th, the football banquet was held at the school to honor the team and departing seniors. Though the last game was disappointing, the year was a rounding success by any measure.

1935 (2-4)

Brother Harold's football team of now-called Saint Aloysius High School would be "... *rather small and light, but the team is said to possess plenty of speed and fighting spirit*". The team averaged 145 pounds for the starters and would drop significantly when reserves were called. But, at least 12 players on the squad had been there the past year and would provide a nucleus for the success of 1935.

GAME 1:   SAINT AL (0-0) @ SATARTIA (UNREPORTED)
             FINAL: ST AL 27 SATARTIA 0
             October 4, 1935

A bus that wouldn't work meant the entire Flash team, accompanied by their fans, would make the trip to Satartia in cars. The game was moved from Friday to Thursday due to the Louisiana Delta Fair. Like most teams of 1935, Satartia outweighed the Flashes and the visitor would "*rely on speed and deception to take the gridiron battle*".

Saint Al came close to scoring on the kickoff. They moved the ball to the Satartia 2 before Ralph Bendinelli fumbled back to the home team. But after an exchange of punts, Martin Frohn found one of the Veazey players for a 35-yard touchdown. In the 2nd, Albert Melsheimer recovered a Flash fumble by Ray Woods for the score. Halftime ended with Saint Al up 14-0.

The Flashes had a near-miss in the 3rd with the ball inches from the Flash goal. A Saint Al punt put Satartia back enough for the defense to hold. On the Flashes next possession, the Woods brothers and Frohn put it close enough for Frohn to score. In the 4th, Frohn found Veazey again for another touchdown and the two converted the PAT afterwards in the same fashion.

GAME 2:   SAINT AL (1-0) vs EDWARDS (UNREPORTED)
             FINAL: ST AL 48 EDWARDS 0
             October 9, 1935

Practice week keyed on blocking and tackling; two areas the Brothers thought lacking. Edwards was described as a "*scrappy team*" that was to "*make the Flashes watch their step every moment of the game*". Ray Woods would be hampered by a nasty cut over his eye.

In the 1st, and after a Woods punt reception and runs by Bendinelli and Frohn, Frohn hit Veazey for a touchdown that was "*received perfectly*". In the 2nd, Frohn ran successfully twice after a Veazey 30 yard punt return and then hit Woods for the score. The PAT was good for the second time. Frohn scored again in the quarter on a run after he completed a pass to Melsheimer. Bendinelli pushed the PAT across.

The Flashes' score in the 3rd came after Bendinelli recovered a Carlsley fumble and ran for 30 yards. Woods and Frohn put the Flashes close and Albert Bragg lugged it in for the touchdown. Woods converted the PAT. As if Frohn hadn't done enough thus far, he blocked an Edwards punt that set up the next score. Runs by Bragg and Bendinelli got near the 25 and then "*the most spectacular play of the game followed...*" Bendinelli lateralled to Frohn who hit Veazey for the touchdown.

Another score in the 4th was the result of a long Melsheimer run for a "*near touchdown*". Bendinelli pushed it in but no PAT was attempted. The final one was from Bragg after a big Frohn run and Woods reception to the 5.

GAME 3:   SAINT AL (2-0) vs UTICA (2-1)
             FINAL: ST AL 0 UTICA 12
             October 17, 1935

Utica had a "*slashing offense*" that would be hard to stop. But the passing attack of the Flashes was expected to counter the team that "*promises to give the S.A.C. boys a real scrap*".

On their first possession, after a series of runs, Beasley hit Barlow for a 15 yard touchdown. On the ensuing drive, Frohn was picked off by Barlow, but the Raiders returned the favor when Bendinelli picked off a Utica pass. After a big gain by Frohn, he then fumbled for lost yardage and the Flashes were forced to punt as the half ended. The 3rd started with good Flash defense. Kelly Garvey picked off a Utica pass but it was knocked out of his hands by Frohn and given back to the Raiders at the

Flash 40. On the second play afterwards, Beasley hit Barlow again for a 30 yard touchdown. The PAT was unsuccessful but the game would end up 12-0 in favor of Utica.

GAME 4:   SAINT AL (2-1) vs CLINTON (1-2)
                          FINAL: ST AL 7 CLINTON 18
                          October 24, 1935

The Flashes were in fine condition physically, but the Brothers had put them through hard practices after their defeat the previous week. Practices *"have begun early and continued until late"*, said the paper. Clinton had been shut out by a combined score of 85-0 in their first two games (including Vicksburg), but were much heavier than Saint Al. The Flashes worked heavily on the passing game to combat the size deficiency. As incentive to work hard, Brother Harold had told the boys that only those who performed for this game would make the trip to Louisiana the next week.

The game started as a slugfest with each team gaining yards but turning the ball back on fumbles. Though the box score was reported as a 1st quarter score, it was actually just before halftime that Clinton's Landrum pushed it in from the 5 for the 6-0 lead. Clinton started the 3rd with heaving passing that got them deep into Flash territory, but they fumbled before they could cross the goal.

The Flashes responded with Woods runs that got them to the goal, but with it *"just around the corner"* he fumbled it back to the Arrows. Their drive was capped when Middleton found Landrum from the 2 to make it 12-0. On the ensuing drive, Middleton came through again; this time intercepting a Flash pass for a touchdown and an 18-0 lead. Egger intercepted a Frohn pass in the 4th, but to no avail. Saint Al scored with only moments to play when Bendinelli picked off a Clinton pass and returned it 60 yards to avoid the shutout. Bragg converted for the PAT.

GAME 5:   SAINT AL (2-2) @ MENARD, LA (5-0)
                          FINAL: ST AL 6 MENARD 18
                          November 1, 1935

The Menard team from Alexandria was under the direction of Athletic Director Brother Brendan, *"a former member of St. Aloysius faculty"*. Not only had he promised the boys *"a wonderful time"*, he had also lined up a dance in their honor afterwards. The Flashes, in *"perfect condition after a strenuous workout..."* would have their work cut out to defeat a team outweighing them by 10 pounds.

We don't know how the dance worked out (Menard did stay the night and attend), but we do know that the Eagles were up 18-0 in the final seconds when Saint Al's Frohn hit Ray Woods for their only touchdown. Menard had blocked a punt in the 1st quarter and returned it 35 yards for the touchdown. In the 2nd, Nash picked off a Flash pass and brought it back to the Flash 26 to give the Eagles an eventual touchdown. They added their final touchdown in the 4th.

The Brothers were very proud of the Flashes and the paper said they *"were more than pleased with the fight and spirit shown by the Saints as they battled down the furious attack of the mighty Menard Eagles. Standing toe-to-toe, they gave ground grudgingly and although lacking the substitution power, nevertheless they completely outplayed their heavier rivals during the entire second half. ... Never during this season did the Flashes tackle as hard, drive as impetuously and block as wholeheartedly as they did under the lights last Friday ..."*

GAME 6:   SAINT AL (2-3) vs NEWELLTON, LA (3-1-1)
                          FINAL: ST AL 14 NEWELLTON 25
                          November 8, 1935

The Newellton team, *"said to possess a team with plenty of power and speed and are going to attempt to win this game in order to even the score of last year..."* scored in the 1st after a Flash fumble put them at the Saint Al 42. On his third run, T. Pierce went in from the 27. On the ensuing drive, Saint Al fumbled again and gave the ball back at their 41. Carries by Pierce, Smith and Fiser set up another Pierce touchdown. Again the PAT failed but it was 12-0. Saint Al responded in the 2nd behind runs by the Woods brothers when Frohn crossed the goal. He hit Bendinelli for the PAT and a halftime deficit of 12-7.

The Bears upped their lead in the 3rd when Pierce gained 9 yards to the Flash 1 and then dove in on the next play. He also converted the PAT to make it 19-7. Newellton almost scored immediately afterwards, but the Flash defense held at their 2. A quick punt to give them relief put the

Bears at the Flash 40. Pierce eventually carried the ball over again from the Flash 15 for their last points. Saint Al scored in the 4th on a Bendinelli touchdown and he also added the PAT.

Saint Al was scheduled to play up to three more games. Those included Vicksburg/Carr (November 15th), Jett (November 22nd) and at Chamberlain Hunt (November 28th). No record of these contests exists nor a reasoning for why the season ended after the Newellton game. The annual game against Vicksburg was a city favorite for Armistice Day, though Saint Al had never won. If any of these games were played, they were simply not reported.

1936 (2-4-1)

Brother Remigius was now the head coach and serve under Athletic Director Brother Clement. He had been the coach of the younger kids and would see them through to their varsity seasons. Brother Benet would be an assistant alongside a new face in Joe Balzli. Balzli, the future legend at Saint Al, was also *"handling the cafeteria in a swell way. He runs an A-1 cafeteria and holds down a job as assistant football coach."* Benet and Clement came to Vicksburg from Saint Stanislaus but Remigius had been at the school for 2 years. Brent Katzenmeyer and Sam Mesheimer were elected co-captains.

The first practice was held August 31st and would be from 9-11am until September 21st. During this time period, two players were spotlighted by the paper. Sam Melsheimer was *"as hard as nails. Wouldn't surprise me if he ate spinach between meals"*. Robert Hosemann was *"...a lad who knows all the answers of 'get your man'. We've seen him block two men at a time and do a darn good job of it, too."* The coaches were also putting in new rules. Said Benet, who *"slammed a fist into a palm"*, *"There'll be absolutely no smoking on this team!"* The Flashes were taking it seriously. Newcomer John Branciere was instructed to *"draw a mark on some wall and throw at it with a football"*. Any player who missed a practice had to make a *"special practice"*.

For historical records, it should be noted that the first recorded athletic booster group (S.A.H.S. Athletic Association) was formed on September 30th. At a meeting at the school, Mayor J.C. Hamilton and other school dignitaries were in attendance. Mr. C. Leonard Katzenmeyer was the first president and Mr. William J. Foley was Secretary-Treasurer.

GAME 1:   SAINT AL (0-0) @ EDWARDS (UNREPORTED)
                FINAL: ST AL 19 EDWARDS 0
                October 9, 1936

Prior to the season, the Flashes were to play Satartia on October 2nd. However, on September 25th, Saint Al was notified that the game was cancelled and a new opponent would have to be re-scheduled. A heavy rain took away practice on Wednesday, so they went over things in a school room instead. Practice injuries to Blaine Russell and Kelly Garvey had healed by Friday and the team left at 1:30pm for Edwards.

Very little was written about the victory except that there were a *"large number of (Flash) supporters"* and that Ralph Bendenilli scored all three touchdowns. Kelly Garvey ran for one PAT in the win. The Flashes played a lot of reserve players in order to bolster a young team. *"The Saint Aloysius eleven is made up mostly of inexperienced material. The team is light but played well yesterday and gave evidence that with the rough spots ironed out, it will be a fast-stepping aggregation."*

GAME 2:   SAINT AL (1-0) vs CLINTON (1-0-1)
                FINAL: ST AL 0 CLINTON 19
                October 16, 1936

Hopes were high for the Flashes against the 160 pound Clinton team. They, too, had played Edwards in their first game and won 13-6. *"A holding, fighting, determined line and an expert, swift and mechanical backfield will represent Aloysius..."* featuring a team with*"...a fighting zeal that helps much on the road to glory"*. Bendinelli was described as *"ready to rip up the line of Clinton"* with his *"rubber cleats digging into the turf and flashing legs working like well-oiled piston rods...."*

Again, almost no details emerge as to the game in front of a *"large crowd"*. The Arrows put points up in the 1st, 3rd and 4th and converted on one of the touchdowns. O.B. Lambert was praised for his defense as a *"linesman who can't be beat. Throughout the entire game, Lambert drove through the enemy line and cut down runner in the backfield"*.

GAME 3:   SAINT AL (1-1) @ NEWELLTON, LA (2-0)
                         FINAL: ST AL 0 NEWELLTON 20
                         October 23, 1936

After the loss, positions were adjusted and Sam Melshieimer moved from the line to the backfield. His size and experience made the paper say that *"When Sam hits the line, the fans will all sit up and take notice and know that the Blue and Gold is gaining"*. Lambert was also praised and the week saw the Flashes get 25 new helmets to sport for a Newellton team described as *"heavy and crackerjack"*.

Saint Al drove as far as the Bear 10 in the 1st, but by the end of the quarter both teams would be without points. In the 2nd, Newellton concentrated on the run and scored. They continued scoring in the 3rd early on a pass for a touchdown and a PAT. Though not reported, the Bears also scored again in the 3rd to close out the contest. Bendenilli, Garvey, Stewart, and Katzenmyer were *"star performers"*.

GAME 4:   SAINT AL (1-2) @ UTICA (UNREPORTED)
                         FINAL: ST AL 7 UTICA 7
                         October 30, 1936

Plans had been discussed for a Flash battle against a Houston, TX team the following Friday in New Orleans, but no details were worked as of the week. Meanwhile, the Flashes were favored over a slightly smaller Utica team and left campus at noon.

The Flashes were first on the board in the 2nd. Bendinelli intercepted a Utica pass with under a minute to go in the half and brought it back deep into Utica territory. This set up a Garvey pass to him for the touchdown and the PAT was good. In a heartbreaking moment with only a minute to go in the game, Utica scored with their second string QB's pass to Beasley to make it 7-6. A *"fake play"* gave Utica a run into the endzone to make the final score 7-7. The game was called *"a thriller ... from start to finish"*.

GAME 5:   SAINT AL (1-2-1) vs JEFFERSON MILITARY COLLEGE (3-2)
                         FINAL: ST AL 19 JMC 0
                         November 13, 1936

The circus came to town on November 5th and there would be no practice due to the players aiming *"to go 'circusing' and see all of the eight wonders of the world they've been missing all of their lives"*. The same day, Brother Clement received a letter from Saint Al's future opponent from Gilbert, LA that let them know they were playing a team averaging 165 pounds, something the paper called *"not to be sneezed at"*. The *"powerful eleven"* from Natchez would be a good opponent and Saint Al would be without Garvey due to a foot injury. The Flashes would wear gold jerseys trimmed in blue for the first time.

Bendinelli scored on the opening kickoff drive behind runs from him, Sam Melsheimer, and A.J. Cronin. He almost scored again in the 2nd after a run almost the length of the field. But it was called back for clipping and eventually given back to JMC on downs. He wasn't done, however, picking off a Jefferson pass in the quarter and later scoring. The Flashes fumbled on their first possession of the 3rd, but JMC could not take advantage of the turnover. Saint Al immediately used the running game to push the ball close enough for Cronin to score.

The paper reported that all three PATs were no good, but one was obviously successful. In spite of the absence of Garvey, the paper said that *"... changes were made in the lineup and it worked like Chandu's magic tricks. The Blue and Gold line held like a barrier of stone, and blocking tackling shown by the entire team was something to be marveled at"*.

GAME 6:   SAINT AL (2-2-1) vs GILBERT, LA (4-2-1)
           FINAL: ST AL 6 GILBERT 7
           November 19, 1936

Gilbert was reported as having a *"crack eleven"*. *"There'll be a struggle ... (until) the final whistle blows. But ... they can and will win tomorrow night"*. Practices were hard and the Flashes were expected to throw a lot. Garvey was still out and star player Bendinelli was a game-time decision due to a recent rib injury. It was said of him that he was *"a real thrill finisher. Occasionally Ralph gets loose for a spectacular run and spectators stand up on their seats, throw hats in the hair and cheer as the human speedbolt tears over the white stripes"*.

A large crowd came to see the contest, including *"about two dozen fans from Gilbert..."* The 1st half had only one touchdown, coming near the end of the 2nd quarter. After a Tiger punt, the Flashes sustained a drive of runs and passes that resulted in a Sam Melsheimer score. The crucial PAT was no good. Gilbert responded in the 3rd by taking a Flash punt at midfield back for their touchdown. With the PAT successful, the Tigers had defeated the home team.

Van Stewart *"worked like an eight day clock and the ball carrying men who came his way failed to make gain"* while Robert Bonelli *"...snagged several passes for fifteen to twenty yard gains and showed good blocking and tackling ability"*. Blaine Russell and Brent Katzenmeyer also garnered praise.

GAME 7:   SAINT AL (2-3-1) vs CHAMBERLAIN HUNT ACADEMY (UNREPORTED)
           FINAL: ST AL 0 CHAMBERLAIN HUNT 12
           November 24, 1936

The final game of the season would be against *"a powerful and heavy..."* team from Port Gibson. The *"Flashes will have to use every cell in the old hatrack to defeat the enemy gridders. This writer (Sam Ewing) predicts a 19-12 win for Aloysius"*.

Turnovers and special team mistakes spelled disaster for the final game of 1936. The Cadets scored in the 1st after blocking a Bendinelli punt at the Flash 20. Simrall carried for the score on the next play. In the 3rd, Bendinelli punted to a waiting Reynolds at the Flash 40 who *"gave a splendid exhibition of broken-field sprinting"* for the touchdown. Saint Al also threw 3 interceptions in the contest.

This game would mark the last Flash game with the Brothers of the school in charge of football except for fill-in time between 1942-1945 due to the war. The assistant coach who did such a splendid job in the cafeteria would soon change the face of the program for future generations.

The football team was given a banquet led by William Ivory at the Coral Room (Hotel Vicksburg) at season's end. Each player received tiny, golden football for their faithful service and practice.

1937 (5-3)

Joe Balzli's first year as head man had an interesting start. All city and county schools were closed on September 10th due to an outbreak of polio. It would be September 20th before classes resumed. He still held practices both morning and afternoon in the interim and told the Saint Aloysius Athletic Association on September 14th that *"indications were for a good season"*; this in spite of an entirely new backfield. Only Gordon Nelson had seen some reserve action in 1936.

A historical note of interest is that the very first Saint Al football player pictured in a newspaper would be on September 28th in the form of junior Van "Butch" Stewart.

GAME 1:   SAINT AL (0-0) vs CLINTON (0-0)
           FINAL: ST AL 13 CLINTON 21
           October 1, 1937

Clinton had beaten the Flashes the previous year but *"this fall ... the Flashes are out to bring in the Arrows scalps"*. A.J. Cronin would quarterback a team Balzli called *"still a question"*. Said Balzli, *"We may lose, but will look good losing"*. To build anticipation, a large rally and bonfire was kicked off by Vicksburg Mayor Hamilton and Brother Ignatius on the evening of September 30th.

Behind a *"drizzling rain ... practically throughout the game"*, the Flashes held the bigger visitors throughout the first half. In the 2nd, Cronin grabbed a lateral and took it 30 yards to the endzone. The PAT was good. The 3rd, however, showed that lack of reserves would wear down the starters. The Arrows scored early in the quarter and added the PAT to tie the game. The Flashes responded before it was over when Billy Hatchette ran one in for the score. The PAT failed.

On the second play of the 4th, with the Flash line tired from a continuous running assault, Clinton passed for the tying touchdown and added the PAT. With minutes left, the Arrows scored once more and, with the PAT, iced the game at 21-13. The paper credited, among others, the play of Cronin. Balzli was not as complimentary. *"I was not at all pleased by the way A.J. Cronin played against the Arrows ... as I believe him capable of giving a much better performance than he did Friday."*

GAME 2:   SAINT AL (0-1) vs NEWELLTON, LA (0-1)
                 FINAL: ST AL 0 NEWELLTON 73
                 October 8, 1937

A Louisiana team outweighing Saint Al by 30 pounds per player came to Vicksburg on game day. The paper was *"...expecting some really stiff opposition from the boys across Ole Man River"*. The Flashes were without Katzenmeyer (collarbone), Cronin (leg), Miller Evans (hand) and O.B. Lambert (ankle). Position changes were underway to compensate. *"There'll be plenty of surprises in the starting lineup"*, Balzli said on game week.

There is no detail for each touchdown scored; nor is there a need. The paper summed it up by saying *"The visitors outplayed and outclassed their opponents in every department of the game."* HB Gerald White scored six touchdowns and a PAT alone. Others who crossed the Flash goal included Vines, Smith, McCarthy and Thomason. It was 29-0 at half and the Bears tacked on 44 more points in the 2nd half. This would stand as the worst defeat in history by a Saint Aloysius football team.

GAME 3:   SAINT AL (0-2) vs JEFFERSON MILITARY COLLEGE (NOT REPORTED)
                 FINAL: ST AL 33 JMC 6
                 October 14, 1937

Balzli's luck on injuries wasn't improving. For the JMC game, he now had Lambert, Ed Williams and Vincent Battalio definitely out as a result of the previous week's game. Nevertheless, the Flashes got on the board in the 1st with a 70 yard drive that was capped by Robert Hosemann to make it 6-0. Saint Al struck on defense twice in the 2nd. First, Hosemann picked off a JMC pass and took it back 70 yards for the touchdown. Cronin matched the feat in the same quarter with another interception return. Hosemann lit up the board in the 3rd with a 25 yard touchdown run and the 4th saw both teams reach the goal.

JMC's Brame accounted for the first touchdown for the Cadets and Van Stewart added the last one for Saint Al. PATs were added at intervals by Stewart (2) and Gordon Nelson (1).

GAME 4:   SAINT AL (1-2) vs FLORA (UNREPORTED)
                 FINAL: ST AL 26 FLORA 0
                 October 21, 1937

Some players would be back, including most of Balzli's starting line. One Katzenmeyer was definitely out with a broken collarbone and could miss the season. Flora's squad was a mystery and Balzli was *"preparing for the worst and expecting almost anything in the way of good football"*.

The Flashes scored in the 1st after the other Katzenmeyer picked off a Flora pass and returned it 30 yards before being tackled. Behind runs of Hosemann and Cronin, Hosemann took it in for the score. Stewart kicked the PAT. Hosemann scored again in the 2nd on a run and Hatchette added the PAT on a pass to put the Flashes up 14-0 at halftime. In the 3rd, Hosemann added another touchdown. His final score was in the 4th on yet another plunge across the goal. Balzli brought in the reserves afterwards to play in a game beset by rain after the half.

Said the paper, *"St. Aloysius outweighed and outplayed their opponents in every department of the game. The local squad should have run up a larger score, but fumbles and penalties prevented this."*

GAME 5:   SAINT AL (2-2) vs CHAMBERLAIN HUNT ACADEMY (UNREPORTED)
                          FINAL: ST AL 12 CHAMBERLAIN HUNT 0
                          October 28, 1937

Balzli would now enjoy the return of most of his players and *"have his strongest team on the field"* for the game. Lloyd Woods would also return to the Flash team after a year's layoff. As for the game, no scoring details were provided aside from the fact that Hosemann and Cronin scored one touchdown each. CHA only got close once; that in the 4th when Carriere had broken a 30-yard run. Hogan was able to stop him to preserve the shutout.

GAME 6:   SAINT AL (3-2) vs MENARD, LA (UNREPORTED)
                          FINAL: ST AL 26 MENARD 6
                          November 7, 1937: HOMECOMING

The coach would have a chance to watch Alexandria, Louisiana's Menard High play beforehand. He reported the team a few pounds heavier, would be *"hard to handle"*, and expected *"his men to be hard-pressed for a good showing"*. Therefore, the team worked *"with unprecedented vigor and determination to pluck the feathers of the proud Eagles"* to prepare for the team Balzli called his second toughest foe behind Newellton.

On the Sunday before the game, the Athletic Association sponsored a parade in honor of Homecoming. A reported 1,400 fans attended and heard a *"speaking apparatus and microphone"* manned by Charles Colmery and Souphie Habeeb from WQBC. This could have been the first broadcast featuring the Flashes.

Menard pushed out early in the 1st on a DeStenio touchdown. The Flashes responded with four touchdowns over the next three quarters. The first was by Hosemann; the second on a Cronin pass to Woods, Woods crossed again later, and the final one was a Floyd Bragg touchdown on a blocked punt. Hosemann added 2 PATs. The performance highlighted a number of activities throughout the game, including the Flash band, the American Legion Troop 5 Drum and Bugle Corps, the cheerleaders from both teams, and a speech from Brother Ignatius to the assembled crowd.

GAME 7:   SAINT AL (4-2) @ YAZOO CITY (UNDEFEATED)
                          FINAL: ST AL 12 YAZOO CITY 39
                          November 12, 1937

Yazoo City had an unknown team to the Flashes, but Saint Al was *"going prepared to give a good account of themselves."* Practices had been hampered by rain during the week, but they had done some preparations and left at 3:00pm on the new bus for Yazoo County with supporters in tow.

The only notations about the contest were that Hosemann ran for the first touchdown and Woods caught a Cronin pass for the second. Both PATs were unsuccessful. From the write-ups, the Indians had not given up a touchdown in 1937 and Saint Al *"achieved the distinction"* of crossing the goal twice.

GAME 8:   SAINT AL (4-3) vs UTICA (UNREPORTED)
                          FINAL: ST AL 13 UTICA 0
                          November 19, 1937

The Flashes were reported to be in *"pink condition"* for the last game of 1937 against a *"much heavier"* Maroons team. Utica had owned Saint Al in their 5 contests and Balzli prepared by *"running his charges through stiff workouts all week..."* The coach also had a nice going-away present for his seniors. For "Senior Day", all of them would start in the contest for the *"Hill City fans"*.

A *"bitter cold"* game for the seniors would be a good one. In the 1st, the team drove the field and Hosemann capitalized from the 5 when he *"crashed the line ... for the home lad's first touchdown"*. Woods ran in the PAT. Halfway through the 2nd, Utica punted to Saint Al to start the next drive and it was finished by an Ed Williams' score from the 6. The PAT was unsuccessful.

Hosemann almost added to the final but dropped an interception for a sure touchdown. Utica got only as far as the Flash 25; that being in the 3rd. The *"razzle dazzle"* Saint Al offense of laterals, passes and runs *"proved baffling to the visitors"*. Reserves finished the game for the appreciative Homecoming crowd.

1938 (9-0)

Coach Balzi began practices for *"the Aloysius parade of pigskinners"* mid-August. By the first day of school on September 6th, his roster hovered around 30 players with 16 being experienced returners. The starters averaged around 160 pounds while the younger guys, under the tutelage of Brother Lloyd, averaged around 135 pounds.

The week of their first game, Balzli put the boys through 7-day practices. A scrimmage against *"alumni stars"* was scheduled for the 15th in order to get the squad accustomed to playing at night. In spite of thin depth and early injuries to Billy Hatchettee, Charles Bell and John Cesare, the paper still called them *"the best pigskin pack Aloysius has presented in many a moon"*. On game day, the paper led with **"One Of Strongest Squads of School History Presented"**.

GAME 1:   SAINT AL (0-0) vs GLEN ALLEN (UNREPORTED)
                     FINAL: ST AL 57 GLEN ALLEN 0
                     September 23, 1938

Saint Aloysius would live up to predictions in their first outing against a *"lighter and badly bewildered Delta aggregation"*. They scored twice in the first quarter. The first was on an A.J. Cronin run and the second 12 plays later was a Joe Booth run. Ed Williams converted the PATs. Things got worse for Glen Allen afterwards, though individual scoring was not noted. The Flashes put up 18 in the 2nd, 6 in the 3rd and finished the game by adding another 19 points in the 4th.

George Katzenmeyer, later termed *"the Flash with the legs of lightning"*, ended up scoring 4 touchdowns on 5 carries. But reserves were seeing a lot of action and proving that they could play.

GAME 2:   SAINT AL (1-0) @ BELZONI (UNREPORTED)
                     FINAL: ST AL 7 BELZONI 6
                     October 6, 1938

Balzli went back to scrimmages against former players to keep his players fresh during an off-week. They would be playing a Belzoni team described as boasting *"one of the finest grid teams it has ever had"*. Balzli called the game an *"acid test"* and worked the guys hard to prepare. A large number of Vicksburg fans would accompany the squad to the Delta.

The contest would be rugged. Belzoni intercepted a Booth pass in Flash territory but the defense held them to a punt. Toward the end of the quarter, Saint Al had moved the ball to the Warrior 1 twice, but each time was pushed back for penalties. Belzoni put the first points up in the 3rd with a Turner touchdown run and 6-0 lead. At the end of the same quarter, Saint Al answered when A.J. Cronin picked off a Warrior pass and brought it back for a touchdown. Booth converted the eventual game-winning PAT and Saint Al was now 2-0.

GAME 3:   SAINT AL (2-0) vs MENARD, LA (0-1-1)
                     FINAL: ST AL 7 MENARD 0
                     October 16, 1938: HOMECOMING

The team from Alexandria had revenge on their mind from the previous year, but had lost all but 3 players from that squad. On the other sideline, Saint Al had sustained a number of injuries in the form of *"bruises and sprains"*. It would not be until game time that Balzli knew who would, and wouldn't, be able to play.

Homecoming was a big event for the Flashes. A *"uniformed pep squad of 74 members"* from Saint Al and Saint Francis were adorned in purple jackets and white pants. They joined the *"Peppers"* cheer squad to put on a show for the game. The Elks band and the Flashes band under the direction of Tacitus Bucci were also performers at the contest. A *"large crowd was on hand"* in weather *"more suitable for baseball than football"*. Brother Jerome, former faculty of Saint Al and now principal of Menard, would attend along with the Menard coach Brother Patrick. He was also an alumnus of the Saint Al faculty. The visitors came to Vicksburg the evening before, stayed in a local hotel and were treated with *"special affairs"* before leaving after the game.

The Flashes kicked off Homecoming in the 1st with a drive from their 35. A triple lateral (Joe Canizaro to Hatchette to Booth to Vincent Battalio) gained 30. Booth capped the work with a 2 yard touchdown and Blaine Russell provided the PAT for the only points of the game. The Eagles did threaten by getting to the Flash 2 before fumbling. They also scored when Phillips went in from 28, but it was called back for being out of bounds. Finally, Menard was at the Flash 4 after a fumble but gave the ball back immediately afterwards due to their own.

GAME 4:   SAINT AL (3-0) vs CLINTON (2-0-1)
                                FINAL: ST AL 19 CLINTON 6
                                October 20, 1938

Vicksburg was hosting "Neighbor Day" for the game. That meant that anyone (with a pre-approved badge) living outside of Vicksburg got into the game for free. The Flashes were healthy and "out after their fourth scalp..." versus a team deemed "evenly matched".

Clinton opened in the 1st after a Flash fumble at their own 16. McPherson capitalized on a run but the PAT failed. Saint Al responded in the 2nd on a Booth run. As with Clinton, the PAT failed. The 3rd was scoreless and "looked like a certain tie game as neither side seemed able to push over a marker". But the Flashes exploded in the 4th. At the 6:00 mark, Cronin hit Hatchette from the 33 for a Flash score. With 2:00 on the clock, they sealed the victory on a Cronin plunge from the 3. The paper said that Clinton was "bewildered by the spurt of power (and) at a total loss as to their method of battle. They wallowed helplessly into the inspired Aloysius defenses and caved before the thrust of offensive power".

GAME 5:   SAINT AL (4-0) vs SAINT JOHN, LA (2-3)
                                FINAL: ST AL 32 SAINT JOHN 0
                                October 30, 1938

The Shreveport boys were an "aggregation ... highly recommended and from all reports ... anything but up a set-up for the victor". Balzli was "drilling his charges diligently this week to prepare them for what promises to be a true gridiron thriller here on the Sabbath". Their 2-3 record didn't reflect the higher level of competition they had been playing and the squad was reported as "somewhat light but fast" with a weight "in proportion to the weight of the Purple Flashes". Balzli called them "the strongest foe of the season".

To prepare, "the Grid Magician" dismissed the scrimmages for the week. Katzenmeyer was back for the first time since the Glen Allen game. The opponent, made up of 25 players, arrived late Saturday. The game would feature national baton champion Steve Borne, the Saint Al band in new uniforms and a "surprise feature ... 'Snow White and the Seven Dwarfs".

Saint Al scored in the 1st on a drive from the Flash 27. Three plays in, Booth scored from the 8. Russell's kick was unsuccessful. The Fliers fumbled at the close of the quarter on their 29. Numerous runs set up another Booth touchdown and Battalio added the PAT to make it 13-0. The Flashes put up another in the 2nd on a "bullet-like" pass from Williams to Hatchette. Russell was good this time to make the halftime lead 20-0.

The Flashes continued the onslaught in the 3rd when Cronin found Hatchette for a 50 yard strike. Russell's PAT was unsuccessful. Katzenmeyer picked off a pass in the same quarter and returned it 45 yard to the Flier 13. Booth then hit Battalio for the touchdown from there but Battalio's PAT missed. Said the paper, "The Flashes outplayed the Fliers in all departments of the game. ... The passing attack of the local boys bewildered the boys from Shreveport."

GAME 6:   SAINT AL (5-0) vs HOLLANDALE (UNREPORTED)
                                FINAL: ST AL 58 HOLLANDALE 0
                                November 4, 1938

Practices were light and Monday was an off-day for the now fully healthy team. The Hollandale team had defeated a common opponent (Belzoni) by one more touchdown than the Flashes, so expectations were for a tough contest. While no individual plays were mentioned, we know that touchdowns were scored by Booth (3), Battalio (2); Williams (2), and Katzenmeyer (3). PATs were from a Battalio run, a Cronin pass to Charles Finane, a Finane kick, and a Cronin pass to Williams. The paper perhaps under-stated the result. "The boys from the Mississippi Delta fought gamely but the powerhouse of the local lads was just too much for them"

GAME 7:   SAINT AL (6-0) @ CHAMBERLAIN HUNT ACADEMY (UNREPORTED)
               FINAL: ST AL 25 CHA 0
               November 11, 1938

The Academy outweighed the Flashes by 10 pounds and had *"one of their best teams in years"*. Balzli still paced the team in *"vigorous workouts"* in order to avoid overlooking the Cadets. The coach said that *"his team's many tricks, speed and precision will rival the weight and power which the CHA squad will present on the gridiron"*. A large crowd of supporters, "Peppers" and more left Vicksburg on game day a bit after noon.

Booth was the touchdown leader of the day with one from the Cadet 18 in the 1st and one in the 2nd. That one was set up by a Cronin pass to Hatchette for 30 yards. Russell made the second PAT and halftime stood with the Flashes up 13-0. Williams scored for the Flashes in the 3rd and Cronin scored in the 4th behind runs from himself, Katzenmeyer and Cronin.

GAME 8:   SAINT AL (7-0) vs NATCHEZ CATHEDRAL (2-5)
               FINAL: ST AL 44 NATCHEZ CATHEDRAL 0
               November 20, 1938

The first-year Natchez squad was though *"a supposedly weaker team than Saint Aloysius"* but Balzli still spent the time honing the finer aspects of the fundamentals. A few thousand were expected for the last game and baton-twirler Steve Borne would be back to entertain the crowd, as would acts of tumbling and the Saint Al band and "The Peppers". Balzli again let the seniors play together during the game, with all of the younger players on the field at the same time later to prepare for the 1939 season. *"These that play today will have to step into the shoes which the graduating Flashes leave vacant"*.

The first of many Flash touchdowns was from Williams in the 1st behind running from Cronin, Booth and himself. Booth scored the second one in the same quarter and reserves starting seeing action. Williams hit Lloyd Ray for the last touchdown of the 1st and Russell hit Harry Hude for another touchdown to start the 2nd. Eli McKinney picked off a P. Burns pass in that quarter and returned it 42 yards for another score. Finane made it 31-0.

Natchez avoided the shutout in the 3rd when Canizaro picked off a pass and returned it 60 yards for a touchdown, but it was called back for off-sides. Cronin scored to start the 4th and Williams added the PAT. Cronin added another on a drive from the Flash 49. To make matters worse, Katzenmeyer picked off another Natchez pass for a 75 yard score, but that was likewise called back for clipping.

The Greenies lost most of their weapons when the two captains (Jimmy Jones and Bobby Perrault) were injured. *"It fell to Harold Hicks and little R.L. Lanchart to bear the brunt of the CHS offensive with Jesse Jones and Kilpatrick outstanding in the line for the losers"*. Natchez brought more than 150 supporters to the contest led by former Vicksburg resident and Athletic Director Father Joseph Brunini.

GAME 9:   SAINT AL (8-0) vs TALLULAH (UNREPORTED)
               FINAL: ST AL 13 TALLULAH 0
               December ?, 1938

It had been noted that the Flashes finished the 1938 year with a game against Tallulah in "The Goodfellow Benefit Bowl". Until recently, no record could be found regarding the event. However, a recent finding of the December, 1938 version of <u>The Golden Quill</u> (Saint Al's school newsletter of the day) aptly recorded the event.

"Continuing the spirited playing that had carried them through eight scheduled games undefeated and untied, the Aloysius Flashes smashed through the really powerful Tallulah Trojans to gain a hard-earned 13-0 victory... Recovery of a Tallulah fumble on the Trojan 44 by the Flashes midway in the second quarter eventually led to the first Aloysius touchdown. From the 44, the Flashes marched steadily to the three-yard stripe where a gallant stand by the Trojans staved off a score. The Trojans kicked out of danger, but the Flashes came right back to drive 23 yards for a touchdown.

A quick-kick on third down by the Flashes in the middle of the fourth quarter led to the second marker. Rolling to the goal line, the ball was scooped by a Trojan back who fumbled the oval and Aloysius recovered. In one play, the Flashes pushed across the touchdown and then scored the extra point through the line.

The Louisiana boys played a splendid game but the inspired playing of Aloysians with an undefeated record to maintain and a topnotch Class A team to vanquish was more than they could handle. So, undefeated and untied, the 1938 Flashes rest in victory over teams ranking among the best that this section can offer."

The season was perhaps the most successful one ever for the purple and gold. They outscored their opponents 249-12 and gave up one of those touchdowns on a fumble near their goal on the road. The only thing that kept them from claiming the Class A Championship was "too few games with teams in this region". And Balzli did live up to his final game promise. At one point, all Flashes on the field consisted of seniors.

"Joe Balzli had a big influence on my life and I will never forget it. To this very day, I feel honored and blessed to had the Brothers of the Sacred Heart and Joe educate me in the classroom and on the playing field. He was like a father figure to me and stressed fundamentals that I have used my entire life; such as the importance of teamwork, respect for people, and the love of God. Joe would never expect you to do something he wouldn't do himself. He will always in my mind be a part of my extended family for what he did for me".

Charles Finane; October, 1995

1939 (10-0)

Coach Balzi's team described as in "excellent shape" was practicing on "limbering up drills, getting the 'feel' of the ball ... and hard tackling" along with light scrimmages in preparation for their opener. Balzli had anticipated 22 players with eleven of them returning as lettermen. The paper said that "the places left vacant by graduation would be capably filled by these lads, who have all the qualifications for first class "gridsters". By August 20th, the roster was up to 25 and the schedule was called "the toughest ... in the history of the school".

Anticipation for a great season was evident. Said the paper, "Hunting should be very good for the Purple Flashes this season, sports authorities in the section assert... From the looks of the team, the Flashes this year should make Aloysius grid history. Though adequate reserve forces is lacking, authorities believe that the aggregation will repel severe offensive force".

GAME 1:   SAINT AL (0-0) vs SAINT MARY'S, LA (UNREPORTED)
           FINAL: ST AL 30 SAINT MARY'S 0
           October 1, 1939

Balzli's first opponent from Natchitoches boasted "of a fine grid record and is rated as one of the classist teams in northern Louisiana". The paper predicted "... a real contest of smart football and spirited sportsmanship. St. Mary's comes here sporting a very good record" and "has the determination to beat Aloysius". Not only did they have the determination, they had the size. The line of Coach Charles Loomis averaged 165 and had a 223 pound tackle. The backs averaged 160 and were much bigger than the Flashes.

The visitor arrived on September 30th and stayed at the Carroll Hotel. Game day would honor Mayor J.C. Hamilton, Aldermen J.J. Williamson and Alderman Julius Buchanan; all of whom would be in attendance to "officially witness the replay as the game will be dedicated to them and played in their honor." Harry Piazza and Dan Mahoney would be missing for the game as they were in Chicago with the American Legion.

There was more written about activities surrounding the game, including "The Beer Barrel Polka" and the heat of the surroundings, than the actual contest action. Harry Hude picked off a pair of Buccaneer passes for touchdowns to set the tone for 1939. Joe Booth did very well, too, with at least one touchdown. The only criticisms of the Flashes "lay in the lack of timing of plays but this will be ironed out in time ..."

GAME 2:   SAINT AL (1-0) @ TALLULAH, LA (1-0)
               FINAL: ST AL 13 TALLULAH 6
               October 5, 1939

Tallulah was holding *"Vicksburg Day"* at the Louisiana Delta Fair and the 8:15pm game was a big part of the festivities. Up to 750 Vicksburg citizens took part of the special Bridge rates of *"$1 for automobiles regardless of the number of passengers therein"* to see the Flashes against *"The Blue and Gold Trojans..."* with their *"well-developed passing attack and their offense ... aided by a very deceptive running game"*. When asked about the contest, the only quotes by Balzli or the team were *"Tallulah will know that they have been in a ball game"*.

As with the game versus Saint Mary's, much was written about the Fair. The only words about the contest were that the Flashes trailed 6-0 at halftime due to an Emmett Lancaster touchdown, but scored twice in the 3rd. Both scores were by Booth and he added one PAT from a *"center plunge"*. Said the paper, *"The Vicksburg squad had no easy time in defeating the hard-fighting Tallulah aggregate"*.

GAME 3:   SAINT AL (2-0) vs CHAMBERLAIN HUNT ACADEMY (UNREPORTED)
               FINAL: ST AL 7 CHA 0
               October 13, 1939

Practice week for the Flashes worked to get most *"of the stiffness out of the squad which has been resting since Thursday's thriller at Tallulah"* and *"polishing off some of the rough sports discovered in the first night games of the year"*. Major E.S. McCallum's CHA team was reported *"somewhat the same squad as last year with a little added speed."* They were later noted as *"one of the heaviest teams in recent years"* and outweighed the awaiting Flashes.

On Wednesday, the paper reported that it *"had been necessary due to injuries ... to completely revamp (the) lineup ..."* Billy Hatchettee, Piazza, George Katzenmeyer and *"possibly one or two others"* would be sidelined, but Balzli was still planning on putting *"the fastest backfield of the current season"* on the field. Hude and Robert King would play alongside now-returned Battalio in the backfield. Van Stewart would return to the line to handle the bigger visitors.

The only score of the contest would come toward the end of the 1st. Following a Cadet fumble at the CHA 15, Saint Al ran twice for 7 yards and then Booth ran it in for the touchdown. Hude hit Mahoney afterwards for the PAT. CHA came close to tying in the 2nd after a Flash fumble at their 24. A Littrell pass to Pearson reached the Flash 8 and a QB keeper put CHA inches away but the Flash defense held. In the 3rd, Hude found Mahoney for 32 yards at the Cadet 26 but Cadet captain Smith picked off a Flash pass to end the threat.

The paper reported that there were numerous fumbles that killed drives on both sides. In front a large crowd, it was noted that *"The CHA boys displayed one of the best balanced and fighting teams from that school seen here in some time. The game was a bitterly contested grid battle with both teams playing a fine brand of ball all the way."*

GAME 4:   SAINT AL (3-0) vs BRANDON (3-0-1)
               FINAL: ST AL 14 BRANDON 7
               October 19, 1939

The Class A state championship runner-up from 1938 was touted with a stronger team than the previous year. The good news for Saint Al was that Dr. A.J. Messina, team physician, pronounced *"the Purple and Gold 'cripples' will be in condition to take their respective places in the Catholic lineup"*. The Flashes worked long and hard in practices to prepare for *"one of, if not the, hardest game on the 1939 program"*.

A crowd of 1,500 barely had time to find a seat before Brandon put up points. After the kickoff was returned to their 31 by Billy Agard, HB Cotton Hardy found Rufus Campbell for 30 yards and team captain Campbell did the rest. Freeman Webb's PAT made it 7-0. Saint Al responded in the 2nd after Miller Evans blocked a Bulldog punt at their 33. A triple reverse netted Katzenmeyer 20 yards to the Brandon 13. Booth took the fifth run in for a touchdown and then added the PAT to tie the game.

The Flashes blocked another Bulldog punt at the Brandon 46 at the close of the 3rd, and capitalized in the 4th after Booth, Hude and Katzenmeyer moved the ball to the 3. Booth did the honors and again made the PAT. The paper labeled it *"one of the best games ever played on Johnson Field…"* It also marked Saint Al's 14th straight victory.

GAME 5:   SAINT AL (4-0) vs CLINTON (2-2-1)
                           FINAL: ST AL 27 CLINTON 0
                           November 3, 1939: HOMECOMING

The great news was that almost all of their players would finally be together for the same game, including an injured Hatchettee. Saint Al also had an open date the week before to get healthy and prepared. The Flashes hosted a Homecoming *"Pep Parade"* on game day that saw cars motor through the business and residential districts prior to the 8pm kickoff.

A big crowd sat in cold weather for a scoreless 1st quarter. In the 2nd, the Arrows used a triple pass to get the ball to the Flash 18. But then Arrow QB Boggan threw an unwise pass that was picked off by Battalio. He raced the full 82 yards for the Saint Al touchdown and Booth made it 7-0. Before the quarter was over, the running tandem of Hude, Katzenmeyer and Evans pushed the ball from the Flash 43 to the Arrow 10. From there, Katzenmeyer ran it in and Hude capped it.

In the 3rd, the Flashes padded their lead on a blocked Boggan punt by Evans at the Arrow 12. Hude gained 9 and was rewarded with the touchdown carry. Stewart's PAT kick made it 21-0. The final touchdown was in the 4th on an Evans run. Clinton did come close to avoiding the shutout by reaching the Flash 5 but could not get past the stingy Saint Al defense.

GAME 6:   SAINT AL (5-0) vs HAZLEHURST (6-1-1)
                           FINAL: ST AL 19 HAZLEHURST 0
                           November 10, 1939

Scouts had been watching Hazlehurst and reported them as a *"…well-balanced, smart-coached eleven … that is equally good in the air as well as in their ground driving attack".* The Flashes were healthy, described by the paper eloquently. *"The Aloysius Hospital' is empty at the present time and all 'cripples' are out for practice … with their best squad".* That would change by the 10th. Reserve back William Stewart had broken his collar bone and would miss most of the remainder of the season. Even though the paper thought the visitor a *"two or more touchdowns"* favorite, the Flashes *"feel confident that they can turn the trick".*

The red-clad Hazlehurst team battled the Flashes to a scoreless first quarter in driving rain. The Flashes actually scored on a Katzenmeyer run, but it was called back for roughing. They got to the Indian 19 in the same quarter but could not convert. In the 2nd, Katzenmeyer brought a Hazlehurst punt back to the Indian 32. Saint Al almost lost the drive on a Hude fumble but he recovered at the 8. Afterwards a 4 yard run by Katzenmeyer set up a 4 yard touchdown by Booth. The PAT by Katzenmeyer failed.

Saint Al added another touchdown in the same quarter when Hude took a punt to the Indian 11 and then scored on the next play. The rain hindered the PAT and halftime was a 12-0 Flash lead. The 3rd was scoreless though Saint Al got to the Indian 19 before turning the ball over on downs. Katzenmeyer added one more touchdown in the 4th and it was capped by Hude. One football observer said *"The punting of Battalio and the centering of Piazza won the game for Aloysius. Give these two men to Hazlehurst and the score will be reversed."*

GAME 7:   SAINT AL (6-0) vs NEWELLTON, LA (1 LOSS)
                           FINAL: ST AL 20 NEWELLTON 0
                           November 17, 1939

In 1937, the Newellton team beat Saint Al 73-0 behind a 27 pound weight advantage. Ten of the Flash starters were on the sidelines during that contest and this was their first game to get revenge. They were so serious about beating Newellton that *"Let loose against the reserves, the regulars went at it so seriously that it was necessary to call of the scrimmage to save the second-stringers for possible service".*

In the 2nd, with time closing, Evans fell on a Newellton fumble at their 29. On the third play, Booth lateraled to Battalio who, in turn, lateraled to Hude. Hude then found Evans for a 23 yard touchdown. Hude capped the play with the PAT. With 1:00 left in the 3rd, Katzenmeyer fielded a Roby punt and took it back 52 yards for the touchdown. Hude again converted. The Flashes sealed the victory late in the 4th after a Hatchettee punt block. On the same play that counted their first touchdown, Battalio lateraled to Booth who lateraled to Hude. He hit Evans in the endzone for the last score. A pass from King to Evans for the PAT was no good.

GAME 8:   SAINT AL (7-0) vs YAZOO CITY (3-3)
                   FINAL: ST AL 33 YAZOO CITY 6
                   November 24, 1939

With a 190 pound average player, Yazoo City greatly outweighed the Flashes. And like Saint Al, they were also in the running for the Class A championship. The team practiced hard against the Notre Dame offense used by their opponent and it was reported that "blocking is ferocious, both in the line and down field". Said Balzli, "Aloysius will be satisfied to beat Yazoo City be it by only one point". The Flashes dedicated this last home game of the season to Louis Cashman and his staff at The Vicksburg Evening Post and The Vicksburg Morning Herald "in appreciation of their cooperation not only in the season about to close but in former years..."

Saint Al scored quickly when Yazoo City fumbled the kickoff to the Flashes at their 18. Katzenmeyer gained 5, Booth gained 9, Booth ran for 2 and Katzenmeyer pushed it in. Hude added the PAT for a 7-0 lead. In the 2nd, the Flashes started from the Yazoo City 25. Katzenmeyer, Hude and Booth took turns moving the ball deep before Hude hit Hatchettee for the 15 yard score. Hude converted again to make the halftime score 14-0. The Oilmen would score in the 2nd with a Wilburn pass to Hamliton from the 20. Hogan blocked the PAT.

The scoreless 3rd saw only two Flash highlights. The first was a Katzenmeyer interception return of 32 yards and the other was a Flash advance to the Yazoo City 6. Neither would produce points. The 4th, however, was a scoring barrage by Saint Al. The first touchdown came on a 32 yard Hude pass to Evans. Hude picked off a pass on the ensuing drive and returned it 43 yards for the touchdown but Stewart couldn't convert. The final score was set up by a Hude pass to Evans for 40 yards. Evans followed that up with a 22 yard touchdown run and Hogan conversion to make it 33-6.

Worth noting is that Katzenmeyer, already with a number of pickoffs on the year including some that were brought back, did it again. He picked off one for 35 yard touchdown but it was brought back on a penalty. In contrast to other reports, The Yazoo City Herald reported the loss as the Indians' seventh loss of the 1939 season.

GAME 9:   SAINT AL (8-0) @ MENARD, LA (4-4-1)
                   FINAL: ST AL 20 MENARD 0
                   December 3, 1939

On Monday, the Middle Mississippi Board selected Magee as the Flashes' opponent for the Class A championship. Both were undefeated and untied. Vicksburg, in order to get the game played locally, guaranteed the expenses of the game, opponents and district percentage of gate profit. But there was work to be done beforehand. The Flashes had one more game to play to keep their undefeated regular season and 19-game win streak going. They left on December 2nd for Alexandria in special busses alongside a large delegation of fans. They would stay the night and return Sunday to prepare for the conference tilt against Magee.

Saint Al was the aggressor in the 1st, driving deep into Menard territory only to lose the ball on a fumble. In the 2nd, the defense set up the first Flash touchdown when William Stewart picked off a Menard pass at the Flash 38. The first play thereafter was a Hude to Mahoney pass for 39 yards followed by a triple lateral (Battalio, Booth, Hude) that gained 13 to the Eagle 10. It took Booth two runs before he crossed the goal, and he added the PAT for a 7-0 halftime lead.

Menard kicked to Saint Al to start the 3rd and Evan returned the ball to the Flash 45. Runs by Battalio, Booth, Hude and Katzenmeyer put it at the 10. On 4th down, Hude blasted in from the 1 and Booth made it 14-0. The final touchdown came in the 4th after a Hude interception at the Menard 38. Steve Mattingly gained 18 and Hude eventually tacked on the score. The PAT was no good.

Though celebrating the win, it came at a cost. Billy Hatchettee suffered a "spinal injury" and would stay in Alexandria's Baptist Hospital until December 7th. Louis Theobald, owner of Guion-Theobald, had their ambulance pick him up and bring him back to Vicksburg.

GAME 10:   SAINT AL (9-0) vs MAGEE (8-0)
                FINAL: ST AL 13 MAGEE 7
                December 8, 1939

The Flashes were in for their toughest fight of the year against the undefeated Magee "Burrheads". They had trounced Class B Champion Madison 39-6, outscored their opponents 179-26 on the season, and averaged between 170-185 pounds up front. By comparison, Saint Al had outscored their opponents 183-19. Hatchettee would be the only Flash missing, though a cold epidemic had hit during practice week. By game time, the symptoms were gone and the team pronounced "*in the pink of condition*". While keeping the motto "*Win the game for Hatchettee*", the game was dedicated to The Vicksburg Chamber of Commerce for their role in securing the home-field advantage. Hatchettee, in a body cast, would watch the contest from an ambulance parked on the sideline.

Things started roughly for the Flashes. On the opening kick, Hughes lateraled to Kenneth Robinson and he took it 75 yards for the touchdown. Hughes' added the PAT. Saint Al responded before the quarter ended after a bad snap caused a fumble at the Magee 5. Miller Evans fell on the ball and, two plays later, Booth plunged in. Hude converted the PAT to tie the game 7-7. There would be no more scoring until the 4th quarter. Evans blocked a Magee punt at their 20, Van Stewart picked it up and crossed the goal for the winning touchdown.

The paper said that "*The Vicksburg Evening Post's sports department extends congratulations to Joe Balzli … and to the Flashes for their victorious season and string of twenty consecutive wins*". Back-to-back undefeated and untied seasons and a string of 20 consecutive wins would not be matched again by a Saint Al team for the remainder of the century.

1940-1949

SAINT ALOYSIUS 1947 TEAM (8-1)

1940 (5-3)

Coach Balzi returned five lettermen in Hogan, Battalio, Hude, King and Billy Stewart. Others had seen playing time and new faces were counted that had promise but were "*rather weak*" in experience. Practices started around the second week of August with the exception of Battalio. He had spent several weeks in National Guard camp and came back the first week of September. Two-a-days began the last week of August with scrimmages against former players.

The schedule would not be kind to the Flashes. Others teams weren't excited about playing Saint Al, so they had to step up and scheduled the tougher available teams. With a host of fine football players lost to graduation, Balzli would have his hands full to "*win its share of games*". "Big Tom" Hogan, who had played every minute of every game for the past three years as tackle would be team captain and call plays.

GAME 1:   SAINT AL (0-0) @ BATON ROUGE, LA (0-0)
                        FINAL: ST AL 0 BATON ROUGE 26
                        September 20, 1940

This game was called "*undoubtedly the toughest assignment ever given a Brothers' school eleven and very few fans grant the Flashes the ghost of a chance to win. The Aloysius gridsters, however, have a habit of biting off more than they can chew and then proceeding to chew it.*" With practices described as "*heavy*" in their "*dog-fighting style of play*", the Coach suspended much of the physical activities to keep what little reserves they had from being hurt.

The Flashes offered their fans a chance to take a special train to Louisiana from the Cherry Street Station at a round-trip cost of $3.25. It would leave at 3pm and return at 2am. The Saint Aloysius Mothers' Club would "*operate a luncheon car*" for patrons. The Flashes were donning new uniforms and "*every piece of protection that can be put on a football player*". The boys left at 7:30am Friday "*in the pink of condition*".

The drizzle on the Baton Rouge field was indicative of the start of the Flash season. The Louisiana boys scored in the opening quarter on an Ivy Thompson run from 15. He scored again in the 2nd on a 14 yard run. In the 4th, Pourciau got in from the 27 and Thompson got his third touchdown on a pass from Pourciau. Pourciau also had two PATs. The Flashes seemed to have gotten close only once; that being in the 4th quarter when a triple-lateral got them to the 22.

The paper reported that a number of Bob King's passes were dropped to make the contest even tougher on the visitors. That was echoed by the Baton Rouge paper who said "*If King had not fumbled so much, and if the receivers had held a few more of his passes, the story might have been different*". Balzli's win streak was over, but one had to admire the guts to step up to such heavier competition on the road. Great things were now expected from purple and gold football teams.

GAME 2:   SAINT AL (0-1) @ YAZOO CITY (0-1)
                        FINAL: ST AL 13 YAZOO CITY 7
                        September 27, 1940

The boys had a practice-free day on Monday to heal from the Baton Rouge tilt. Thirteen Flashes had played in the game and 9 had gone the entire contest. Yazoo City was bigger, but so was almost every team Saint Al would face this year. But after playing a team reportedly outweighing them by 20 pounds, these were minor obstacles. Baton Rouge had two players over 6'0" on the line, with one weighing 212 and the other 235.

Battalio was still the only one somewhat injured. He had been doubtful for the previous week, but came on to play and was expected against Yazoo City. The plan of attack was to "*take the air route to gain a victory...*" Balzli was quoted as saying "*The air will be just full of passes*". The team left for Yazoo City at 1pm in good spirits and The Yazoo City Herald announced that "*tonight's contest will be a severe test, as the visitors, while losing their veteran center Captain Van Stewart, have found needed replacements in the last year's reserve crop.*"

In a game before 800 fans at Crump Athletic Field described as "*... a thriller and one of the best seen here in a long time*", the Flashes hit the scoreboard right away. Saint Al kicked to W.N. Permenter's red-clad Yazoo City squad but it was fumbled by Frank Smith and recovered by the Flashes. Bill Stewart gained 7 to the Yazoo City 18 and then King went in for the touchdown to make it 6-0. In spite of the fact that the Flashes were at the Indian 8 as the halftime whistle sounded, that one score would hold until the 3rd quarter.

There, James Fagan found Carl Henry Johnson for 20 yards to the Flash 5. Tom Rainer moved it to the 1 and then Frank Smith pushed through for the touchdown. Rainer converted the PAT after a Flash penalty for a 7-6 advantage. But in the 4th, Saint Al pulled out the win on a 67 yard drive climaxed by a Hude score and a King PAT. It started with by runs by King, Battalio and Hude, as well as a 10 yard pass to Mahoney to the 10. The Indians tried to snatch the last-minute victory, but the injured Battalio picked off a pass to seal it.

GAME 3:   SAINT AL (1-1) vs TALLULAH, LA (UNREPORTED)
                       FINAL: ST AL 7 TALLULAH 13
                       October 3, 1940

The Flashes were back at home for the first time since December 8th but would be playing "*Louisiana Rules*", also used by the pros, for the contest. They permitted "*... passing anywhere behind the line of scrimmage*". There were no practice scrimmages due to injury risk. Being healthy, the Flashes planned to "*shoot the works*" in front of the home folks.

Saint Al got the scoring going in the closing minutes of the 1st after Battalio returned a Trojan punt to the 26. Hude broke off a 49 yard scamper but was tackled by Cagnolatti at the Trojan 25. Battalio, King and Hude pushed the ball to the 8, and Battalio scored from there. Hude hit Evans for the PAT to make it 7-0. Tallulah came right back on a Gilbert interception at the Flash 17. The visitor was rewarded with a catch (interference) at the Flash 8 after a Cagnolatti toss to Gilbert was dropped. Two plays later, Cagnolatti hit Gilbert for a 7 yard score. The PAT was no good. In the 3rd, a costly penalty on the Flashes gave the Trojans new life and they capitalized. Starting at their 42, they used three runners to get to the Flash 34, Leoty hit Cagnolatti for 15, Leoty ran for 12 and the Cagnolatti punched it in on the second run. The PAT was good and the scoring was done. The Flashes had lost their first home game since October 8th, 1937.

GAME 4:   SAINT AL (1-2) vs CHAMBERLAIN HUNT ACADEMY (UNREPORTED)
                       FINAL: ST AL 38 CHA 0
                       October 11, 1940

The boys were working harder than ever to erase the bad taste from a home defeat. Chamberlaint Hunt was described as a "*strong eleven*" and the injuries to Hude (ankle) and Evans (boils) were concerns. Since Saint Al would be the only home football game this week, a large crowd was expected and the Flashes didn't plan on letting them down.

Running "*rough shod*" over the visitor, Saint Al put up their first points in the 1st on a lateral from Stewart to King and his pass to Mahoney from the Cadet 37. King hit Hawkins and it was 7-0. Midway through the 2nd, King ran one in from the Flash 34 and scored again on the ensuing drive from his HB position. Halftime had the Flashes in command 19-0. Battalio scored the next touchdown in the 3rd on a run and he put up two more in the 4th for good measure. The first was a 1 yard plunge and the second was a 25 yard interception return. The best way to recover from a bitter defeat was to transfer the taste to the next opponent.

GAME 5:   SAINT AL (2-2) vs INDIANOLA (3-?)
                       FINAL: ST AL 0 INDIANOLA 20
                       October 18, 1940: HOMECOMING

Indianola was predicted on September 1st as "*likely the most powerful opponent on the 1940 schedule.*" In 1939, they "*went undefeated in its regular season, piling up four hundred some odd points against their opponents' twenty five*". They also won the Lions Bowl game against Pascagoula 33-12. The squad was so good that Balzi had "*continually affirmed that Indianola's is the best team the Flashes have every attempted to play, not even Baton Rouge excepted*". Said the paper, "*The visitors will be favored to win, but with that old fighting spirit kindled, the Flashes are confident they can spring a surprise stunt*". With Hude and Evans back from injuries, hopes were high that they could in spite of a Battalio knee problem that could be exaggerated during the contest.

The Alumni Association, led by Mr. Charles Wilkerson, recruited as many alumni as possible *"to demonstrate their loyalty for the old alma mater"* to attend. To make the experience even better, a huge parade through downtown Vicksburg had been arranged.

Indianola's first touchdown of three on the night was in the 2nd. After a 30 yard run by Majure, and numerous other runs afterwards, Majure took it 39 yards for the score. The PAT by Wilson made it 7-0, and behind solid defense, that score held until halftime. The Flashes threatened twice in the quarter but came up empty. They could get no further than the Indian 28 on the first opportunity, and after a fumble recovery on the Indian 23, they again stalled.

Indianola's second touchdown drive started in the 3rd with a 40 yard run by Dickerson to the Flash 22. Majure scored from the 9 on the fourth play afterwards. The Flashes blocked an Indian punt at their 38 but then threw an interception. Majure hit Bellipani for 52 yards to the Flash 10 and then Pinkerton for the touchdown. The last PAT was unsuccessful after the defense stopped a QB sneak attempt. The Flashes' last series consisted of runs that put the ball as far as the Indian 35 but could not get further.

Balzli was *"satisfied with the game his charges played..."* being able to *"keep up the ferocious charging..."* of the opponent in light of the old injuries that had been reopened in the game.

GAME 6: SAINT AL (2-3) vs CLINTON (5-0)
FINAL: ST AL 13 CLINTON 12
October 24, 1940

The district championship was still in reach having beaten the other conference opponent in Yazoo City. But after losing 27-0 to the Flashes in 1939, the 165 pound Arrows would be out to avoid to any repeats. And injuries were mounting, with both King and Evans having *"face injuries"*. King's was described as a *"severe nose injury"*.

The taller and heavier Clinton team started the 1st with a drive to the Flash 20, but a fumble to Hude gave the ball back to Saint Al. Both teams managed to get all of their points in the 2nd. Clinton reached first after a Stewart pass was picked off by Price at the Arrow 44. A pass from F. Langston to Lilly gained 20 and then James Langston took it in from the 36. An off-sides call on Clinton negated the PAT. On the first play after the kickoff from the Flash 33, King found Mahoney for a 67 yard touchdown pass. Hude gave the Flashes the lead on the PAT run. An exchange of punts (on first down in some cases) followed and Clinton sat at the Flash 48. Clyburn hit Lilly for 25 yards, Saint Al had a 5 yard penalty, and Lomax took in in from there. Though the PAT pass was incomplete, the lead was now 12-7 in favor of Clinton.

Saint Al averted disaster afterwards. At their 34, King was picked off by Boggan for a touchdown. But Clinton was called off-sides and the play was brought back. The drive ended with a King pass to Evans for a 40 yard touchdown and the 13-12 lead. Saint Al got to the Arrow 3 in the 3rd but could not convert. The teams exchanged interceptions afterwards, with Piazza getting one for the Flashes.

Clinton got to the Flash 2 in the 4th, but fumbled. They also got to the Flash 1 but could not penetrate. Amazingly, they finished the game at the Flash 4, unable to get further. The game play was described as *"brilliant, and at times it bordered on the spectacular. It was one of those grid battles that one sees in the movies"*.

GAME X: SAINT AL (3-3) vs BRANDON (UNREPORTED)
FINAL: NOT PLAYED
October 31, 1940

The Flashes had the weekend off to prepare for heavy practices on game week. Brandon had scouted the Flashes on the 24th to prepare for the conference tilt, but Balzli was pleased with where his team stood on the 30th and those injured were expected to be in full health. However, Mother Nature had other ideas.

A *"downpour of rain"* hit Johnson Field the night before the game that was bad enough to *"make play practically impossible"*. Brother Ignatius, principal of Saint Al, said that *"unless the ... Brandon game had a bearing in the district play-off later in the season, it would not be played"*. Brandon ended up losing to Yazoo City in their next contest and the folks from Brandon thought the game unnecessary.

GAME X: SAINT AL (3-3) vs MADISON (UNREPORTED)
                              FINAL: NOT PLAYED
                              November 7, 1940

In initial reports, the Flashes were to play Madison on the 7th. The game was apparently called off much earlier in the season since an article on October 29th noted that the Flashes had another off-week after the Brandon game.

GAME 7:   SAINT AL (3-3) vs MAGEE (UNREPORTED)
                              FINAL: ST AL 7 MAGEE 0
                              November 22, 1940

A repeat of the Championship Game from 1939 was in store. Balzli put the Flashes through *"Their hardest practice week of the season"* in anticipation. The coach loved what he saw and *"was elated over the appearance of the team and felt confident enough to predict that his charges would take Magee and roll on to a second Class A championship"*. Magee's roster included Robertson, the man who scored on the initial play with a big reverse for their lone touchdown.

After initial hitting, *"Very little heavy work (and) timing of plays and perfecting the types of defense will be stressed"*. For the contest, the team elected to wear their gold jerseys, significant because those not only had been worn during the two-year steak, but also because they were worn during the last Magee game; a win. *"Fans ... will see some real straight football with a sprinkling here and there of razzle dazzle"*.

A muddy field made *"Passes ... conspicuously dangerous ... and a treacherous footing and were used rarely except in emergencies"*. But it was a pass that allowed the Flashes to play for the conference championship the next week. On the first play of the 2nd, Bob King hit Edwin Evans for a 48 yard touchdown strike and King converted the PAT. Saint Al reached the Magee 1 at least once and got close two other times. When the game ended, the Flashes were at the Burrhead 10. The crowd was *"small"* and the both teams *"came out looking as though they had been through the traditional 'hog wallow"*.

GAME 8:   SAINT AL (4-3) vs FOREST (?-2)
                              FINAL: ST AL 39 FOREST 0
                              November 28, 1940

Though not undefeated, the Flashes were playing for another Mississippi Class A title. It would be played in Vicksburg thanks to the city picking up expenses on faith of a good turnout and loss of very little money. A very good opponent awaited in weather predicted as *"clear and cold"*. Forest's two losses had come to Big Eight Champ Meridian and higher-ranked Newton, a team playing in the Lions Bowl later.

Said the paper, *"The eleven-cylinder St. Aloysius powerhouse made Johnson Field look like a two-way track... The offense and defense of Aloysius was planned around barriers that resembled a string of seven concrete posts standing in formation across the field. Behind these bulwarks, the four horsemen who made up the Flashes' backfield could run and pass to their heart's desire. These boys in the Aloysius line ripped the Forest team to pieces with such force that the Flashes' backfield needed only to charge through. They could have driven a parade through some of the same holes."*

The Flashes' first score came on Battalio run from the 4 and a King PAT. A 2nd quarter fumble by Saint Al gave Forest their only sniff of the goal in the game. After 4 downs from the Flash 14, the ball was turned back to the home team. Afterwards, King found Hude for a 65 yard touchdown. Before half, a Stewart QB sneak from the 10 got to the one-foot line and Stewart followed with a score. Mahoney converted and it was 20-0 at intermission. Though scoreless in the 3rd, the Flashes scored on the first play of the 4th when King found Evans for an 80 yard touchdown. Theobald added to the lead afterwards from the 6 and Hude picked off a Forest pass for a 30 yard touchdown to end the contest.

"Joe Balzli's philosophies and principles assisted in molding the character of hundreds of athletes, band member and students. He gave us a a competitive and winning attitude which lasted throughout his tenure. He was an excellent teacher of techniques and emphasized physical conditioning and mental toughness. He established sound ball control game plans, developed attack-style defense and a productive set of backs and receivers. He always demanded a maximum effort.

My impression, as one of his players, is that he would have made a fine college coach. His 25-year record should have merited consideration for nomination to the Mississippi High School Coaches Hall of Fame."

Harry Hude; October 1995

1941 (1-6)

The defending Class A champion coach was *"...forced to lie awake at nights in an attempt to devise ways and means of replacing last year's starts lost by graduation"*. He would have 7 lettermen with which to work and the paper said *"A fighting team is hard to beat, and from all indications Balzli's men will be a scrappy squad. Playing against stiff competition, the Flashes may possibly not win all their games, but they will definitely be very logical contenders for the conference championship"*.

The first few weeks of practice were devoted to conditioning and fundamentals of the "T-Formation". The keys to this machine would be held by team Captain Dan Mahoney, Richard Hawkins, and "Little Butch" (William) Stewart. Their competition would be stiff, with the paper promising a *"grueling grind for the team handicapped by a shortage of varsity caliber material"*.

GAME 1:   SAINT AL (0-0) @ YAZOO CITY (0-1)
                      FINAL: ST AL 13 YAZOO CITY 14
                      September 26, 1941

The Indians had just lot to a powerful Indianola team 26-15 the week before, but it was known that they were a capable squad. Revenge for the previous year's defeat was also going to be on the minds of the home kids as they prepped for the Division tilt in front of 2,500 fans. Balzli took 18 of his squad on the afternoon of game day to the Delta town.

Rugged action early in the 1st resulted in Shelby Flowers having to leave the game with a knee injury. The first score of the game came from Yazoo City in the 2nd. Mastering a 62 yard drive, Tom Rainer finished it with a touchdown run and extra point. Early in the 3rd, a fumbled kickoff forced Saint Al to start at the Flash 19. Mahoney ran 4 times, the last being from the 13 for the touchdown. Saint Al would take the lead in the same quarter on a 77 yard march highlighted by a King run of 60 yards to the Indian 23. Five plays later, King went through from the 12 for the go-ahead touchdown. Mahoney smashed through for the extra point.

Before the quarter ended, Yazoo City would put together a 69 yard effort for the tie and lead. Rainer again was the victor, racing 39 yards for the score. He added the crucial extra point kick for the eventual win. *"Saint Aloysius displayed a fine passing attack, but the line defense was ragged"* said the paper.

GAME 2:   SAINT AL (0-1) @ FOREST (0-1)
                      FINAL: ST AL 19 FOREST 20
                      October 3, 1941

Balzli put his charges through a tough practice to fix needed areas of the game. The injury to Flowers would further weaken his forward wall and scrimmages were focused on finding the answer. *"The weaknesses that brought defeat to his purple and gold clad gridsters were given a good going-over..."* This was another division game and *"...they are determined to go all-out in an effort to break into the win column..."*

The Flashes got on the board in the rainy 1st after Robert King broke off a 52 yard run to the Forest 10. In two plays, Mahoney went off left tackle for the touchdown. The missed PAT, as the previous week, would come back to haunt them. Early in the 2nd, a Bearcat runner skirted Saint Al defenders for a 58 yard touchdown run. The PAT was good to make it 7-6. Later in the quarter, Forest added another behind a 34 yard run to make it 13-6.

The Flashes added two touchdowns in the 3rd stanza. King took the kick back 32 yards for the first one and Mahoney added the PAT. The second one was annexed by David Theobald from 32 away but again the extra point went for naught. Late in the 4th, Forest sealed the win on a 48 yard drive that included addition of the extra point. Saint Al tried in vain to pull out the win, sitting at the Forest 10 as the final whistle blew.

GAME 3:   SAINT AL (0-2) @ NATCHEZ CATHEDRAL (2-1)
               FINAL: ST AL 20 NATCHEZ CATHEDRAL 0
               October 10, 1941

Before the season began, Cathedral boasted of "*one of the best teams in the history of the school. They have been pointing to this engagement for the past several months, saying that revenge is sweet and that they intend to taste it for the defeats suffered by them in the days of 'Butch' Stewart, A.J. Cronin, Tom Hogan, etal*". That history had started in 1938. Meanwhile in Vicksburg, the Flashes had played good ball, punting only once thus far, but fell by one point in both contests. Flowers was due to return against Cathedral, but Claude Ferguson had injured his shoulder in practice and was out indefinitely.

Straight runs on the opening Flash drive resulted in a 72 yard march for a touchdown. Theobald did most of the carrying but it was Stewart who dove in for the score. That touchdown would be the only points through halftime. In the 3rd, starting from the Flash 28, King once again showed his skills with a "*slashing ground attack*" that set up the next touchdown. Theobald would take it in from the 14 and Stewart's pass to Theobald gained the extra point.

The final tally by Saint Al came in the 4th with much of it through the air. An 84 yard drive was realized when Stewart passed to King from the 8, followed by a Stewart pass to Theobald for the PAT. A large crowd from Vicksburg was on hand to watch "*The Aloysius line (play) invincible ball and (come) through in the pinches*".

GAME 4:   SAINT AL (1-2) vs INDIANOLA (5-0)
               FINAL: ST AL 14 INDIANOLA 34
               October 17, 1941

Balzli called Indianola's squad "*better than Baton Rouge*" the previous year. That squad had eventually gone all the way to the Delta Bowl against Tupelo. Their main player was "Fruit" Majure and the paper said that he was "*The stubborn type and can only be halted by rocking, convincing tackling*". Indianola, by virtue of a convincing win over Yazoo City, was deemed "*... ten points better than Aloysius, but the Catholic eleven has taken great strides forward since the meeting with Yazoo City*".

On the kickoff, Indianola fumbled and Saint Al grabbed it at the Indian 36. They managed to get to the 2 before being penalized. Four efforts afterwards weren't successful. Indianola managed to get going in the 2nd on a 56 yard drive mastered by the running of Majure and Dickerson. Majure was able to break through for a 43 yard touchdown and Thompson added the point. Jake Bellipani fell on a Flash fumble thereafter and Dickerson bested Majure's feat with a run of 45 yards for the touchdown. Thompson's kick made halftime a 14-0 affair.

Saint Al opened the 3rd with another fumble that was recovered by Indianola at the Flash 29. Dickerson broke around the left six plays later for the 15 yard score. The Flashes responded with a 65 yard scoring drive immediately afterwards. A 27 yard pass from King to Richard Hawkins highlighted the drive that saw Theobald score from the 4. Stewart's pass to Flowers made it 20-7. But in the same quarter, Saint Al fumbled again and Thompson recovered at the Indian 44. The next play was a Majure run and pass to Pierce for a 45-yard touchdown strike. The kick put Saint Al down 27-7.

A mixture of Flash passes and runs started the 4th and got the ball to the 11 before Stewart found King for the touchdown. Now at 27-14, Indianola put the dagger in the Flash hearts. Majure gained 21 to the Flash 35 and then Dickerson did the rest. Thompson's PAT finished the game.

GAME 5:   SAINT AL (1-3) @ NEWTON (UNREPORTED)
               FINAL: ST AL 13 NEWTON 39
               October 24, 1941

Newton had finished 1940 by beating Columbus in the Lions Bowl. Nothing else was noted during game week about the opponent, but they turned out to be a very good team. The Flashes started by fumbling the kickoff at the Flash 5. Newton immediately converted. They then blocked a punt at the Flash 10 and later walked in. In the 2nd, they scored twice more to make it 27-0 at halftime.

The 3rd saw both teams hit the endzone. King picked off a Newton pass for an 85 yard return to the Newton 6. Theobald shot over tackle for the touchdown. Newton would respond with a touchdown of their own in the quarter and add another in the 4th. King, Theobald and Flowers drove the ball downfield as the game ended with King getting the score. *"Despite the score, the game was a well-played contest with the Flashes scrapping every inch of the way with no let up."*

GAME X: SAINT AL (1-4) vs MORTON (UNREPORTED)
                       FINAL: NOT PLAYED
                       October 31, 1941

It was back to division play with the third Class A opponent of the year. *"Coach Balzli delivered a rousing harangue to his gridmen yesterday afternoon, and the practice that followed showed that he had infused into his protégés a super-dose of that fighting spirit for which Balzli-coached teams have been noted"*. Despite reserve depth, light weight and inexperience, the coach though they *"must accept all handicaps"* and win their last three home games. To give them an advantage, he had installed a set of new plays for the contest and practiced them daily.

A downpour of rain hit Vicksburg Thursday night and early on game day. The field would be a muddy stage for a desperate Flash team. With that in the minds of the coaches, the game was postponed until November 11th for an Armistice Day event. That plan would eventually fall through due to conflicts on either one or both sides and would not be played.

GAME 6:   SAINT AL (1-4) vs HAZLEHURST (UNDEFEATED)
                       FINAL: ST AL 0 HAZLEHURST 19
                       November 7, 1941: HOMECOMING

The Flashes would enjoy some time off to heal and practice, but would be facing a *"Hazlehurst powerhouse"* for Homecoming. The paper though that due to comparative scores, *"... the Indians are some twenty points better than the Flashes. Joe Balzli's boys will be considerably outweighed, but ... the Flashes will be in there fighting them all the way"*. One of the Homecoming activities would include a full quarter of football played by *"old timers"*. The Alumni team would be led by Charles Wilkerson and the Exchange Club team would be helmed by Pat Kelly. *"What though bones may crack and muscles be sore, this is Homecoming Day and it must be 'all out' for the old Alma Mater"*.

Hazlehurst started the 2nd by mixing passes with runs, driving to the Flash one-foot line before Smith barged in from there. As the half closed, Julian Yates put up more Indian points when he broke off a 37 yarder. Again the PAT missed, but halftime would sit at 12-0 and stay that way until the 4th. Saint Al had managed to furiously drive to the Indian 4 in the 3rd, but the visitor's defense held and got the ball back on downs. In the 4th, Hazlehurst would get to the Flash 2 and G. Ford would go in from there for the score. The Flashes attempted to avoid the shutout afterwards but got only to the 19 before time expired.

The paper noted that Hazlehurst had a couple of opportunities in the game for touchdowns, but the passes to wide-open receivers were missed by inches. As for the "Old Timers" game, the Exchange Club beat the Alumni 6-2 on a "Red" Strickland touchdown. *"The play of the two teams gave the crowd plenty of entertainment"*.

GAME 7:   SAINT AL (1-5) vs MAGEE (UNREPORTED)
                       FINAL: ST AL 6 MAGEE 12
                       November 14, 1941

The last game of the season was also a division contest with the Flashes having beaten the Burrheads in their only two games played. But this time, Magee would be called *"... one of the strongest teams in the Middle Mississippi Conference"*. Bob King was doubtful after the last game and Balzli was again switching personnel. For the record, the paper called this game "Homecoming" though it was actually the prior week.

Yet again, the Flashes would taste defeat in another game that was up-for-grabs late. This in spite of the paper's quote that *"The Magee team outplayed their opponents practically all the way, but the Flashes put up a game fight"*. In the 2nd, the Flashes were driving and stood at the Magee 37. A Stewart pass was picked off by Earl Holmes and returned 85 yards for the first touchdown but his PAT effort was unsuccessful. Saint Al would have another picked off, this time by Bell, and they got as far as the Flash 6 as the half neared expiration.

Midway through the 4th the Flashes got a gift in the form of a bad punt that put them at the Magee 10. Flowers scored four plays later but their PAT failed and the game was now tied 6-6. Magee would put together a couple of long runs afterwards that set up a Brooks run of 32 yards for the winning touchdown. Magee's Carr had actually picked off another Flash pass in the 1st but the Burrheads could get no closer than the Flash 9. Saint Al also dodged bullets in the 2nd (a Brooks run of 36 for a score was called back for holding) and twice in the 4th (getting to the Flash 5 and Flash 10) before the defense held.

Balzli would see his last game as head of the Flashes until 1945, entering the USMC early the next year. But, in lieu of noting his upcoming Marine Corps stint, the paper said, "*The game was the last that the Flashes will play under the direction of Coach Joe Balzli, who is leaving soon to enter another field of endeavor*".

A new trophy would be awarded for the first time in 1941. Initiated and sponsored by Mr. Walter W. Cunningham, Superintendent of the Illinois Central Railroad, it would be awarded to the Saint Aloysius football player proving to be the most outstanding in the classroom and on the gridiron. Dan Mahoney would be the inaugural winner of The Cunningham Trophy.

1942 (6-2)

With the introduction of the United States into World War II at the close of 1941, reporting changed considerably for the next three years when it came to high school sports. Many citizens, including students AND Joe Balzli, were now serving their country. Balzli enrolled in February with stations that took him from Guadalcanal to Palau. Rationing was underway and the affordability to travel to away games simply to report on the high school football results was rare.

Since Saint Aloysius would play 12 of the next 14 games on the road, results and statistics until 1944 are largely unavailable if not covered more thoroughly in the paper of the home team.

The school opened for classes on September 7th, but the football team would still remain a mystery. There was no mention of the players, preparations, coaches, or such until the day before the Yazoo City game. It was only slightly mentioned much later that the team was coached by Brothers John and Roderick. The paper thought the team was "... *not as heavy as it had been in previous years. The line's average weight is 150 pounds. The backfield, which is exceptionally light, averages 130 pounds in weight. However, what the team lacks in weight, it hopes to compensate for in spirit and deception*".

The squad would by captained by Vincent Cassino and have 9 experienced players returning. In fact, the squad would number only 17 in total according to records found, but two would be potentially missing for the first game: John Kolb (shoulder) and Willie Walker (eye).

GAME 1:   SAINT AL (0-0) @ YAZOO CITY (0-1)
                        FINAL: ST AL 6 YAZOO CITY 0
                        September 25, 1942

All schools were facing the fact that the War had started taking its toll on enrollment and, therefore, players. Still, Yazoo City was a much more formidable opponent against the small and light Flashes. Yazoo City threatened to break the scoreless game in the 3rd after recovering a Flash fumble at the 35. The Flashes held and forced a turnover on downs. Saint Al's William Henegan hit Cassino with a pass that put them at the Indian 40, but the Flashes promptly threw an interception to kill the drive.

Holding Yazoo City once more, the Flashes put up the only points of the game. Runs by Cassino and Charles Kette got the ball to the 12 before Kette plunged in from the 3. Cassino's PAT attempt failed. The Indians threatened in the last minutes but the defense once again held.

GAME 2:   SAINT AL (1-0) @ TALLULAH, LA (0-1-1)
                        FINAL: ST AL 13 TALLULAH 0
                        October 2, 1942

The Flashes headed to Louisiana to meet "*one of the best high school teams in Louisiana*". A large crowd of supporters were following to see a first half of exchange of punts and an intercepted pass, though by whom we don't know. Starting at midfield and behind rushes of Cassino, Evans, David Theobald, and Kette, the Flashes got the ball to the goal but could not cross. Holding Tallulah on the next possession, Kette "...*faded back and heaved a pretty 35 yard pass to Cassino...*" for the game's first score. Earl Evans' try for the PAT failed to keep the game 6-0.

Both teams fought desperately for yards in the 3rd, but Saint Al finally got control at the end of the quarter. The 60 yard drive was highlighted by a Kette pass to Cassino for 13 to the Tallulah 2. "*One the next play, little David Theobald went over tackle into pay dirt for the six points*". Kette would convert and end scoring with yet another win while holding opponents scoreless.

GAME 3:   SAINT AL (2-0) @ JEFFERSON MILITARY COLLEGE (UNREPORTED)
               FINAL: ST AL 40 JMC 6
               October 9, 1942

Irving Cotton would be injured in the previous game and a newcomer would take his place in Joseph Derivaux. Despite this, the Flashes would score at will. Theobald got the first and Kette added the PAT. A JMC fumble on the ensuing kick was recovered by Paul Bellan at the Jefferson 20 but the Flashes could not convert. Theobald took a later punt and raced to the JMC 10. Kette scored and Earl Evans added the extra point.

Kette quickly picked off a pass and Saint Al converted early in the 2nd with an Evans run and a Kette PAT. John Weimar recovered another fumble at the Cadet 35 and Kette made it count a few plays later. The Cadets only score came afterwards when Breaux picked off a Flash pass for a 75 yard score. Saint Al would not be deterred, with Willie Walker picking off a pass for a touchdown. Kette added the PAT and followed Walker by picking off a pass for a touchdown afterwards. Backup players took the field in the 4th and kept JMC from scoring from the Flash 5.

GAME 4:   SAINT AL (3-0) @ LAKE PROVIDENCE, LA (UNREPORTED)
               FINAL: ST AL 0 LAKE PROVIDENCE 13
               October 23, 1942

Though outweighed, the Flashes actually held an advantage over Lake Providence by comparisons of teams played. Saint Al beat Tallulah 13-0 while Lake Providence lost to them 33-0. Cotton was back but Earl Evans (knee) would be replaced by Bill Henegan. Practices during the off-week were intense to keep their record intact. "*All along in their current campaign, the Flashes have played a wide open brand of football and their skill and deception in ball-handling have often had the opposition in doubts as to the whereabouts of the pigskin*".

The only mention about the contest noted that Henegan and Cassino were out at some point due to injuries. Shawbuckles, now back, scored both touchdowns and added the sole PAT. The paper said that "*Lack of reserves hurt ... in the opening minutes of the contest (due to injuries). The visitors fought back hard and stood off several Providence goal line thrusts. The final whistle saw the Flashes playing the same type of ball for which they have always been known.*"

GAME 5:   SAINT AL (3-1) @ NATCHEZ (7-0)
               FINAL: ST AL 0 NATCHEZ 19
               October 30, 1942

The Brothers made position changes after their first loss. "Wee Willie Walker", voted unanimously as the best blocker, would see a new spot as would others. The center of the line was called "... *a second Guadalcanal for any opponent. This 'new' Flash team, combined with numerous plays, no less flashy, will thoroughly convince the Natchez eleven that the Purple and Gold clad boys from the Hill City are a hard-fighting team, unsurpassed in that well known art of 'carrying that pigskin*".

The game was played on a muddy field. The quarters in which Natchez scored their three touchdowns are unknown. Sonny Jenkins broke free on a long run for the first one, and Hall hit Curly Blankenstein for new next two. The paper reported that "*The Flashes displayed plenty of fight and played a fine game*".

GAME 6:   SAINT AL (3-2) @ CHAMBERLAIN HUNT ACADEMY (UNREPORTED)
                 FINAL: ST AL 34 CHA 6
                 November 6, 1942

Both teams had lost to Natchez and the paper though them to be well-matched. A *"hard-fought gridiron battle"* was promised and some fans were expected to make the trip to Port Gibson with the boys.

Midway through the 1st, Bellan, Walter Reynolds and John Kolb played a hand in the block of a CHA punt. Reynolds would take the ball on the next play for a 50 yard touchdown run and Kette would get the extra point. Late in the 2nd, they mastered a 70-yard drive behind the running of Theobald, Kette and Cassino. From the 3, Theobald crashed in for the score and Kette kicked the PAT. In the 3rd, Cassino capped a Flash drive with a touchdown run and Theobald converted.

Theobald would continue his fine day by taking the ball 30 yards to the Cadet 5 and, on the first play of the 4th, punch it in. Kette redeemed his missed PAT with his own touchdown in the frame. As the game was ending, CHA took to the air and completed a few nice passes that got them to the Flash 2. The Cadets would get in from there but miss the PAT. The paper announced afterwards that this marked the final game of the season. However, two more games were played with one the very next weekend. So, it is assumed that these contests were late additions.

GAME 7:   SAINT AL (4-2) @ PORT GIBSON (UNREPORTED)
                 FINAL: ST AL 13 PORT GIBSON 7
                 November 14, 1942

A return trip was underway to Port Gibson, this time taking on *"high-school"* instead of the Academy. Bellan had injured his knee in the CHA game and would not play. The contest found both teams tied at 7 at halftime, though exact scorers are unknown. Since the paper said *"Lugging the pigskin in the victory march were Derivaux, Evans, Kette and Theobald...",* it must be assumed that it was run by one of these Flashes. It would get to the final minutes of the game before Saint Al would retain the ball at the Flash 35 and start the victory march, ending with a pass from Kette to Theobald for the win.

GAME 8:   SAINT AL (5-2) vs MAGEE (UNREPORTED)
                 FINAL: ST AL 14 MAGEE 6
                 November 26, 1942: HOMECOMING

The only home appearance for the Flashes this season would be on Thanksgiving against Magee. They were *"... rated as having one of the best teams in this section of the State and promise to give the Vicksburgers a hard fight from start to finish. The Flashes are out to chalk up a win over the Magee team, but are firmly convinced it will be rather a tough task."* Saint Al had an off-week to prepare, with light workouts followed by *"stiff practice sessions"* on game week. Bellan would still be out but Earl Evans had healed and would return to the QB spot.

Saint Al started quickly, sustaining a 75 yard drive after Holmes' kickoff. Theobald would do the honors for the touchdown and then add the PAT. There would be no more scoring until the last frame. In the 4th, Magee picked up a loose Flash ball at the Saint Al 32. Six plays later, Holmes would find Everett from the 19 for the touchdown. Holmes' attempt at the extra point was blocked *"... by a half dozen or more Flashes"*. During this drive, Magee had a scare when Hilton Stewart was carried from the field on a stretcher with an apparent back injury.

The Flashes would respond on the ensuing kickoff. Starting at their 35, Theobald gained 25, Kette ran for 13, and Evans got 5 more. Kette *"on a spinner"* would crack the Burrhead goal from the 4 and *"... Evans on a run around end crossed the coveted line standing up"*. The Flashes recorded a 6-2 season, which is admirable since they had a new coaching staff and played all but one game on the road.

John Kolb would be awarded the second-annual Cunningham Trophy.

1943 (4-2)

The day before the first game, head man Brother Philip said *"...that the team is in fine condition and that he is looking forward to a successful season"*. It would be a very light six-game schedule. Most of the other schools in Mississippi had also seen their ranks drop due to recruitment and the War effort, so the season would simply be the best that any high school could offer.

Saint Al had *"...practically a completely new team ... with many of the former members now in the armed forces or their country"*. Those ranks included Irvin Cotton, Vincent Cassino, Willie Walker, David Theobald and Walter Reynolds. Joe Derivaux and Joe Marsicano would be the two "veterans" on the squad. The Flashes would play all but one game on the road this year.

GAME 1:   SAINT AL (0-0) @ CHAMBERLAIN HUNT ACADEMY (0-1)
                FINAL: ST AL 35 CHA 0
                October 8, 1943

The annual rivalry *"aroused"* many fans and a large number would follow the Flashes to Port Gibson. Saint Al was described after the game as having *"... a small but light squad, but the team clicks well and has plenty of speed"*. After a number of runs early in the 1st, Joe Derivaux found Jimmy Bres for the touchdown. John Barber's kick was good. Derivaux added the second touchdown and Barber made it 14-0.

In the 2nd, Bres caught a 27 yard touchdown and Preston Ammon added the PAT. After picking off a Cadet pass, Derivaux and Barber tacked on another with Derivaux going over for the score. Barber's PAT run was good. In the 3rd, Donnie Derivaux came in and took a long run for the final touchdown. Ammon added the PAT.

GAME 2:   SAINT AL (1-0) @ PORT GIBSON (UNREPORTED)
                FINAL: ST AL 20 PORT GIBSON 0
                October 15, 1943

Saint Al, rejoicing from the opening win, was wary of their next opponent. Therefore, significant practices were held in preparation. *"The Flashes realize they are playing opposite a determined opponent who will outweigh them slightly. With this in mind, and with the sound of last week's victory march ringing in their ears, the Aloysius squad will take the field intent upon adding another scalp to their belt"*.

The game was called *"closely contested"*. The Flashes had taken the ball to the 5 in the 1st but Port Gibson had repelled them on four downs. Later in the 2nd, a Port Gibson flag put the Flashes in position for Barber to run to their 6. From there, Ammon took it around end for the touchdown *"standing up"*. Bres' PAT run failed but halftime saw the Flashes up 6-0.

Bres started the 3rd with a long pass to Ammon for the 1st down at the Port Gibson 8. Bres rushed for 6 but the next run was fumbled by Barber. In the 4th, Harry Evans recovered a fumbled punt attempt at their 1. Bres smashed though for the touchdown and added the PAT kick for a 13-0 lead. In the last minute of the game, Barber picked off a pass at the Port Gibson 20 and took it to the 4. Derivaux bulled in and Bres tacked on the kick. The whistle blew right afterwards.

GAME 3:   SAINT AL (2-0) @ LAKE PROVIDENCE, LA (UNREPORTED)
                FINAL: ST AL 26 LAKE PROVIDENCE 7
                October 22, 1943

Though Saint Al sat 2-0, the paper was wary of the lion's den in which Saint Al was marching. *"Aloysius has shown plenty of scrap and fight in the pair of contests, but the Vicksburg team is light and it will be the first time a big charging back (Shauberger) has attempted to come though the line. ...but the Aloysius boys feel confident they can (stop him)"*. The boys made the trip over that morning and returned the same day.

"Behind a light but spirited and fast-charging line, the Flash backs roamed far and wide; usually in enemy territory". Saint Al held the Panthers after kickoff and took over on their 45. Derivaux ran to the 15 and the Ammon took the reverse in for the touchdown. Ammon would score again in the 2nd from the Panther 5 on the same play. Shauberger *"...carrying the ball 3 out of every 4 times"*

eventually got in on his plunge from the 2. Before the halftime whistle, Shauberger got off a 70-yard punt, but Ammon (on a reverse) "... *went on a dazzling 94 yard run to 'Touchdown Town'*". Bres' PAT kick made it 19-7.

The Flashes were at the Panther 12 when the 3rd ended but were held on downs. They forced a punt but Bres was immediately intercepted. The Panthers fumbled at the Flash 2 recovered by J.B. Logue and, on the next play, Bres hit Ammon for a 98 yard touchdown for the final points.

GAME 4:   SAINT AL (3-0) @ TALLULAH, LA (UNREPORTED)
                      FINAL: ST AL 0 TALLULAH 26
                      November 5, 1943

Tallulah was "*training hard*" to get revenge. Their record was unknown, but they had outscored opponents 160-46. Approximately 75 Vicksburg fans made the trip to see Tallulah hold the Flashes on the initial possession but give up a fumble by Wilkins afterwards. Saint Al was forced a punt that eventually started Tallulah at their 19. A combination of runs, along with two great passes from Gilbert to Grace got them to the Flash 24. From there, Gilbert hit his captain Grace for the touchdown. Gilbert's PAT made it 7-0.

Starting from the Flash 10, Derivaux gained 11 and then 10, but Ammon suffered a broken leg on the drive and was carried to Mercy Hospital. Barber replaced him after delay and then Bres found Logue for 31 yards to the Tallulah 42. Wilkins picked off the following pass and returned it 60 yards for a touchdown. Gilbert made it 14-0. The next Saint Al punt was blocked to give Tallulah the ball at the Flash 31. Three plays later, Gilbert hit Grace for the 5 yard score and, though the PAT failed, it was 20-0 at halftime. Tallulah received the 3rd quarter kick and Gilbert would eventually hit Jim Ellis for a 41 yard touchdown to make it 26-0.

GAME 5:   SAINT AL (3-1) @ YAZOO CITY (AT LEAST ONE LOSS)
                      FINAL: ST AL 7 YAZOO CITY 12
                      November 12, 1943

Ammon's broken leg would finish his Flash career. "*Ammon was rated as one of the fastest men on the Flashes squad and, of course, this speed will be missed*". The practices had otherwise been good during the week and Saint Al was "*... out to re-enter the win column*".

It was called "*... one of the best football games seen here this season...*" but the Flashes still chalked up another loss. The Indians scored the only touchdown of the half on a "*...beautifully executed forward pass...*" The second was the result of a "*...drive down the field...*" The Flashes added their points in the 4th when Derivaux went in and Bres kicked the PAT. "*St. Aloysius threatened the Yazoo City goal line time and again, but were never able to muster up the necessary combination for a score*".

GAME 6:   SAINT AL (3-2) vs PORT GIBSON (UNREPORTED)
                      FINAL: ST AL 18 PORT GIBSON 0
                      November 19, 1943

Ammon was definitely gone, Rudolph Kolb had an ankle injury, and Derivaux was out after a practice injury. But, the Flashes were going against a team they out-weighed, had beaten before and who's record the paper called "*not impressive*". Since the band could not play for halftime, the "*future greats*" of Saint Al would play for the crowd. The "Fleas" played the "Flies" and most of the names would become the Flashes' future.

Saint Al started off with a 46 yard drive that was capped by a Barber touchdown. As the 2nd ended at the Port Gibson 16, Barber went in again on a reverse only to be called back for a penalty for clipping. Not to be held, Derivaux gained 9 on the first run and then hit the goal on the second run. In the 3rd, Bres took a Cohn punt at the Flash 43 and promptly took it all the way back for the score.

Joe Derivaux was named the winner of the Cunningham Trophy for 1943.

"*The Evans family has so much respect for Joe Balzli. He was a leader, coach, confidant, gentleman and above all a Christian. He taught us much on and off the field and court that has been beneficial in life. We all loved him*".

Earl Evans; October, 1995

1944 (5-4)

Eighteen players reported for Brothers Alvin and Philip's first practice on August 23rd. They would be assisted by Billy Quinn and play under direction of new Saint Al principal Brother William. Others joined the squad who were out of town and unable to begin drills. Four lettermen would be suiting up while others had game experience.

Scheduling continued in earnest as of the 27th with 7 definite games and as many as three pending. The Flashes had only one home game and the push for more was in full-swing. By September 24th, the team had 9 games on paper. Meanwhile, practices were underway and the paper said that "… *the boys show plenty of fighting spirit and speed, and these are two elements which go into the making of a winning combination*".

The squad had later grown to 22 and "…*some are out for their first venture in football*". There were 9 Flashes lost to graduation and others to the armed services. Benny Hogan and Dick Bolton, both experienced players, were now serving in the war effort. If that wasn't bad enough, Donald Reddoch, Billy Baugh, and Tony Virdadamo were injured during pre-season practices.

GAME 1:   SAINT AL (0-0) @ PORT GIBSON (0-0)
                                    FINAL: ST AL 19 PORT GIBSON 0
                                    September 29, 1944

Coach Goodwin's Port Gibson team was unknown except that they outweighed the Flashes and "… *it is said to be small but full of fight*". The inexperienced Flashes had a major setback on the 27th when one of the largest boys on the team (Frank Muirhead) fell on campus and broke his arm. Tommy Morrissey took his spot. The team left at 2:30 on game day along with supporters to see how the "*fighting spirit*" would carry them for the year.

After holding on the kickoff, the Flashes took over in Port Gibson territory. Foley, James Bres and J.B. Logue marched the ball downfield on runs and the Bres hit Logue for the touchdown. Bres converted the kick for the PAT. Late in the 2nd, Donnie Derivaux returned a punt 46 yards to the Port Gibson 14. Derivaux crashed through on the next play and Bres found Logue for the PAT. Saint Al drove 45 yards in the 3rd for another touchdown in three plays when Bres hit Logue again and ended scoring.

GAME 2:   SAINT AL (1-0) @ FOREST (1-1)
                                    FINAL: ST AL 12 FOREST 0
                                    October 6, 1944

The Flashes came out of the first game fairly healthy. The closest thing to an injury was to backup center Dan Hogan who was kicked in the knee during a play. He would miss a day or two but be back for limited service. Bobby Theobald was praised for his play at the blocking back position and "*performed like a veteran*". Forest was described as about equal in weight and in returning lettermen (3), so the paper said "… *it is likely the breaks of the game will be the deciding factor*".

The prognosticators were right as to an evenly matched game. The first three quarters of the contest were scoreless, though Saint Al did drive to the one-foot line before losing on downs. They also managed to get to the 10 in the 3rd unsuccessfully. Only in the 4th did Saint Al manage to get their two touchdowns. Both would come from Robert Foley with the first being a 44 yard reception for the score. Bres set up the second one with a run of 40 yards that put the ball at the Forest 3. Foley went in from there for the final 12-0 score.

"*On both Foley's and Bres' long runs, Bobby Theobald did some fine down the field blocking, which greatly aided his fellow team members in their sprints.*"

GAME 3:   SAINT AL (2-0) vs CULKIN (2-0)
                                    FINAL: ST AL 12 CULKIN 0
                                    October 13, 1945

Culkin had the weight advantage over Saint Al with "… *two large boys at the tackle positions and (speedy youngster) Sam Swett in the backfield…*" This was the first meeting of the teams in football, though they had a "*keen*" basketball rivalry. Culkin had suspended football due to the War, but decided to bring back *"this truly American sport"* in 1944. With great weather in store, this promised to be a big seller for fans of Vicksburg football.

After a scoreless 1st, the Flashes went to the air and got on the board late in the 2nd. Bres hit Derivaux for 5 and then Theobald to the Blues 44. Bres found Derivaux for 21 more and then Foley hit Bres at the 17. Finally, Foley found Bres from the 15 for the touchdown. In the 4th, a mix of great Culkin defense, Flash penalties, and short yardage runs had kept the ball at the Blues 26. Bres-to-Foley-to-Theobald gained 13 and then Derivaux added one more in rushing to put the ball at the 12. From there, Foley hit Derivaux but the Bres pass to George Roesch failed.

GAME 4:   SAINT AL (3-0) vs CHAMBERLAIN HUNT ACADEMY (UNREPORTED)
           FINAL: ST AL 25 CHA 0
           October 20, 1944

The Flashes had made such a stir in the community with the unexpected 3-0 start that citizens requested the game be moved from Port Gibson to Johnson Field. Unbelievably, the Cadets approved. The CHA squad *"... boasts of a speedy, shifty backfield quartet which operates behind a powerful and fast line"*. The Flashes endured the toughest practice sessions to date to polish up *"several departments of the game in which they did not look too impressive last week"*. Coach G.E. Floyd's CHA team had revenge on their mind from the opening season loss of 1943 saying *"We are not coming to Vicksburg to be beaten"*.

Bres opened with a 15 yard kick return to the Flash 25. After a 15 yard penalty, Bres ran for 18 and Theobald gained 6 to put the ball near midfield. Derivaux and Foley got to the Cadet 37 and then Bres broke away from there. Saint Al almost added to it immediately on a drive to the Cadet 11, but fumbled away the opportunity to Bergeron. Midway through the 2nd, a Flash interception of Schultz put the ball at the Cadet 48. Bres banged through for 37 and was followed with runs by Derivaux before Robert Foley crashed through from the 3.

Just before the intermission whistle, Saint Al held CHA to take over on the Flash 39. Two short runs by Derivaux and Foley were followed by a Bres touchdown from 59 away. The Flashes went into the locker room up 19-0. Numerous long runs were nullified by penalties in the 3rd, but Foley was still able to find Bres from the 50 for their final touchdown. Bres' kick hit the crossbar but scoring was done.

"Practically the entire Flashes squad got to see action, and among the reserves who did well were Jerry Derivaux and Jack Geary. Bres, in the stellar role, was ably assisted by Robert Foley, Theobald and Donnie Derivaux".

GAME 5:   SAINT AL (4-0) vs PORT GIBSON (UNREPORTED)
           FINAL: ST AL 20 PORT GIBSON 0
           October 27, 1944: HOMECOMING

The Flashes prepared to once-again play Port Gibson. It would be the last home game for Saint Al, with the next four games on the road. *"The hard knocks and lusty cheers heard on the St. Aloysius campus during the past few days mean only one thing: the Flashes are hard at work in preparation for their homecoming game."* The Flashes dedicated the game to *"... former wearers of the Purple and Gold now serving with Uncle Sam's armed forces. In view of this, all service men in uniform will be admitted to the game free of charge."*

Late in the 1st, a Theobald punt catch put them at the Port Gibson 43. Bres runs and passes set up his pass to Robert Foley for the touchdown. In the 2nd, after failing on their drive at the visitor 11, the Flashes were able to block Harrell Billingslea's punt and Logue recovered at the 1. Theobald ran an immediate QB sneak for the second touchdown. Bres converted to make it 13-0 at halftime. The Flashes did score once more, though nullified. Port Gibson marched the ball to the Flash 27, fumbled, and Roesch picked it up for a 73 yard run for the score. The officials ruled the ball was simply turned over on downs.

The 3rd was scoreless though Saint Al had driven to the visitor 12 before turning over on downs. A highlight of the drive was a 30 yard connection between Bres and Logue. In the 4th, the Flashes put up the last points of the game. A punt to Port Gibson was fumbled and recovered by Roesch at the PG 30. A reverse from the 14 allowed Theobald take it in for the score. Bres' end-run for the PAT was good.

GAME 6:   SAINT AL (5-0) @ YAZOO CITY (UNREPORTED)
           FINAL: ST AL 0 YAZOO CITY 25
           November 3, 1944

Yazoo City was called "...*possibly one of the toughest opponents the Flashes will face this season*". It would be a Middle Mississippi Conference game and the Indians were keen on ruining the undefeated and unscored-upon Flash season. Saint Al left for Yazoo City with Bres doubtful due to a charley horse. Tony Virgadamo was announced as his halfback replacement on the 3rd.

Saint Al would have some fight in them, even with second-stringers in key positions. Four times in the 1st half the Indians attempted to cross the goal. But the Flash defense held strong and both teams went to the locker room scoreless. Yazoo City opened the 3rd with another drive, this time to the Flash 10. But once again the defense pushed them back. They would do it again on the next Indian drive that got to the Flash 3. Saint Al was simply playing a "*bend but don't break*" game and immediately punting to get themselves out of danger.

Finally, in the 3rd, Glisson, "*the outstanding back on the Indian team*", broke off a 38 yard touchdown run. It was called "*the most spectacular play of the game*". The score would stand at 6-0 until the 4th. Saint Al began a march that was killed when Glisson picked off a Bres pass at the Flash 46. It took 5 plays against a tiring Saint Al defense before the Indians put up the next points and the PAT.

Yazoo City added insult to injury when Bres was picked off again, this time by Crawford, for a 46 yard touchdown return. Though the PAT failed, it was 19-0. Robert Foley was injured on the ensuing play and had to leave the game. The Indians scored on the next drive on runs starting at the Flash 41.

GAME 7:   SAINT AL (5-1) @ ANGUILLA (?-1)
           FINAL: ST AL 6 ANGUILLA 27
           November 10, 1944

Anguilla's eleven was "...*rated as being one of the best in the lower Mississippi Delta and they promise to make the going plenty tough for the Flashes*". The going was already rough, as injuries were killing the team. Bres had still not recovered, Charles Koestler was in bed with a cold and throat infection, Foley had a sprained ankle, and Morrissey had been out all week with sickness. By game day, Frank Ditto was also noted as expecting to watch from the sidelines. Reserves would see much of the playing time in Anguilla.

Saint Al would be no match with such an injury-riddled squad. Bres, still recovering, fumbled on the first drive near the Flash 37. Two plays later, Moore took it in for the touchdown. The Flashes stopped an Anguilla drive to their 32 by forcing a fumble, but couldn't capitalize. On the third play at the Flash 31, Danny Hogan broke his hand. Runs by Moore and Stevens pushed the ball close enough for Stevens to get in for the score. Holloway hit Noble for the PAT. Derivaux would fumble on the ensuing drive but the Flash defense held to keep halftime only a 13-0 score.

Stevens opened the 3rd with a touchdown after a sustained Anguilla drive. He also added the PAT to make it 20-0. After an exchange of possessions, runs by Foley and Derivaux pushed the ball to the Anguilla 43. Foley then found Tommy Thomas for a 35 yard touchdown pass. Stevens got in once more for Anguilla on a run and, with the PAT, secured the 27-6 victory.

GAME 8:   SAINT AL (5-2) @ TALLULAH, LA (UNREPORTED)
           FINAL: ST AL 0 TALLULAH 21
           November 17, 1944

Practices were tough as the coaches shuffled the lineup to get a more effective combination. Even more new players would see time but the paper still called it a potential "*nip and tuck affair*". Tallulah's first score came from a Wilkins run from the 4 set up by his pass to Fortner the play earlier. Wilkins dove in for the extra point. In the 2nd, Wilkins hit Van Zelfden for the second touchdown, and late in the 4th, Wilkins ran for a 40 yard touchdown scamper after not being able to find an open receiver. The Trojans ended the game by blocking a Flash punt for a safety.

GAME 9:   SAINT AL (5-3) @ ALEXANDRIA (MENARD HIGH), LA (2-4)
                   FINAL: ST AL 6 MENDARD 20
                   November 26, 1944

In spite of Thanksgiving holidays, the boys still went through strenuous practices for the tough Alexandria team. Bres was limited with a bad knee and Charlie Foley had a dislocated knuckle. The team left on Sunday morning and returned late that night. Menard was reported as having played some of the *"high-ranking teams in Louisiana and has won the majority of its games. The squad is reported to be in excellent condition and promises to make things interesting from start to finish"*.

The only article found on the contest was brief. Menard opened with an 82 yard kickoff return by Matthews *"through the entire Vicksburg team"* for a touchdown. Wilks was able to nearly copy his feat with a 73 yard run for the second score. Both teams added points in the 4th. Saint Al's came on a 9 yard carry by Derivaux but the last for Menard was not reported. The paper said, *"As a whole, the Alexandria boys were much heavier than Vicksburg, and this advantage was underscored by the seasoned type of men in their lineup."* Bres played only 2 minutes with his bad knee and a host of others were injured during the game.

In the 1944 yearbook for Menard, it was noted that the victory was 45-6 in lieu of the reported 20-6.

As a whole, the year was a successful one. The team started with only 3 returning lettermen and prospects for a winning season were questionable. A 5-0 start was remarkable, but injuries and lack of depth would eventually take their toll against bigger competition. James Bres was the winner of the Cunningham Trophy for the season.

1945 (4-5)

Brothers Regis and Alvin put out the call for interested players with practices beginning on August 20th. Twenty-two potential players came forward and as many as six more were a possibility the following week. Saint Al would have 7 lettermen back. *"(The Brothers) are directing the workouts and the boys are putting out their best efforts to clinch a place on the team."* With such a light squad, it was a devastating blow when many veterans found themselves injured before the first game arrived.

J.B. Logue sustained a leg injury, Tony Virgadamo had injured his foot, Donald Reddoch was suffering from a back injury, Jack Geary sprained his arm, and Griffin Chatham was dealing with malaria. The Brothers still ran strenuous practices through Wednesday with only light drills on Thursday. In between the first call for practice and the first game, World War II would formally come to a close. Though Japan had surrendered on August 15th, the formal agreement would be signed on the USS Missouri on September 2nd.

GAME 1:   SAINT AL (0-0) @ YAZOO CITY (0-1)
                   FINAL: ST AL 0 YAZOO CITY 25
                   September 21, 1945

Yazoo City had beaten the Flashes two-straight years and their strong squad was reported to be *"hard to beat"*. They lost their opener to Greenwood 23-6 but had been *"well-balanced"*. Alongside a *"large delegation of local supporters"*, the Flashes left on Friday afternoon to *"prove their mettle"*.

Jimmy Glisson was the main clog for the Indians, scoring touchdown in each quarter. His first was from the 10, the second from the 1, the third from the 37 and the final one from 41 yards away. Glisson hit Comola for the PAT after his first touchdown. *"At intervals, the Flashes took the air route but were successful in completing only one. Straight football was the play. The game was hard fought and was clean with very few penalties being called on either team."*

GAME 2:   SAINT AL (0-1) @ NEVILLE HIGH, LA (1-0)
                   FINAL: ST AL 0 NEVILLE HIGH 33
                   September 28, 1945

Practices focused on blocking and tackling, an apparent weakness the previous week. With the exception of Baylot, the team was reported to be finally healthy. But they would face *"one of the toughest teams on the Flashes' schedule ... reported to have a strong, heavy team again this year."* They must have been since they opened their season with a 53-0 trouncing of Minden, LA.

Neville's opening kick went only 15 yards, but it hit Frank Ditto's knee and was recovered by the Tigers. Six plays later, alternating Brown and Dawkins, Neville hit the endzone for a touchdown. In spite of a Donald Derivaux kick return of 37 yards, the Flashes were forced to punt. A bad snap gave the Tigers the ball at the Flash 20 and Smallwood capped their drive from the 2. Hugh Smith's PAT kick made it 13-0. Exchanging punts afterwards, Neville scored from the Flash 20 when Dawkins ran it in on the second play. Luffey ended the half with the PAT to make it 20-0.

Thomas fumbled at the Flash 20 early in the 3rd and Neville capitalized. It took three plays before Brown had his touchdown. The Tigers scored their last in the same quarter via the air. The fourth pass from Brown was good for a 19 yard touchdown. The Flashes battled *"valiantly"* against a Monroe squad with *"... superior odds and a definite (advantage) in weight... At the end of the game and behind 33 points, they were playing as hard as at the opening whistle."*

GAME 3:   SAINT AL (0-2) vs FOREST (1-0)
            FINAL: ST AL 2 FOREST 13
            October 5, 1945

Coach Marcus Garrett's squad had revenge on their mind, having lost last year to Saint Al 12-0. Forest had *"... an entirely experienced team carried over from last year, and they boast of a powerful fullback in Richard Spence."* The Bulldogs had 21 returning lettermen but weight was about the same as Saint Al. The Flashes would not know that four star players from Forest would be inured and out.

Since many Flashes were beat-up after the Neville game, Monday's practice was light with attention stressed on passing offense and defense. Heavier practices would follow. Kickoff would be on a muddy Johnson Field made worse by continuing rain. With poor conditions, fumbles were high but scoring was low.

Forest took advantage of one of those fumbles early when Guy Henderson recovered on the Flash 30. It took three plays before Weems crossed the goal from the 5. David Lee hit W.N. Jones for the PAT and a 7-0 lead that would stand until the 3rd. The Flashes had gotten only as far as the Forest 20 in the interim. Starting on their 8, the Flashes fumbled again to Forest and gave them possession near the goal. Kelly scored on a double-reverse from the 3 on the third running play but the PAT was unsuccessful.

Saint Al put together a march in the 4th that got to the Bearcat 3 before stalling. Forest's Lee attempted to punt out of danger, but Derivaux would cause a safety for Saint Al's only score. *"While there was no spectacular playing, the game was hard fought and well-played. (Saint Al) displayed a fast, though light, well-balanced clicking squad. Time and again Aloysius players reeled off substantial gains, but seemed to lack the necessary punch to continue a downfield march."*

GAME 4:   SAINT AL (0-3) @ CHAMBERLAIN HUNT ACADEMY (0-3)
            FINAL: ST AL 26 CHA 6
            October 11, 1945

The game took place on Thursday in lieu of Friday at the request of CHA. The Flashes would reportedly see limited action from starters Donald Reddoch, Charlie Baylot, Donald Derivaux and Bill Harrison due to injuries. Nevertheless, the Flashes promised to bring home *"one of many"* victories in what the paper called *"...one of the best grid tussles of the year..."* A big delegation of Saint Al and SFXA students, as well as parents and friends, made the trip to Port Gibson.

Taking the opening kickoff, the Flashes marched downfield to the Cadet 2 before Earl Matherne punched it in. He added the PAT on a pass to John Pinkston for the 7-0 lead. Matherne would score again just before halftime on Flash runs that steadily moved the ball toward the Chamberlain Hunt goal. On one, Tommy Thomas was able to gain 24 on a reverse. Tony Virgadamo and others had runs called back by penalties that the paper called *"...highly questionable..."* Another questionable call was the spot on a PAT that was ruled no-good.

Matherne continued his great play in the 3rd by picking off a Cadet pass and returning it to the Flash 47. Charlie Foley found J.B. Logue for 38 yards and Virgadamo pushed it to the Cadet 12 on an ensuing run. The Flashes then pulled out the triple-pass (Foley-to-Matherne-to-Virgadamo) for the touchdown and a 19-0 lead. Chamberlain Hunt responded when Cadet captain Hopper took the kick on his 20 and ran it 80 yards for the score.

Thomas added another interception in the 4th at the Cadet 38. Virgadamo's reverse gained 23, Foley spun for 5, and Thomas drove in for the touchdown. Thomas' drop-kick for the PAT brought delight to the crowd since *"... that is rarely seen in the modern game"*. In the end, it was Ray Bankston and Billy Harrison who didn't play due to injury. Donnie Derivaux saw only a couple of snaps.

GAME 5: SAINT AL (1-3) vs CULKIN (2-0)
FINAL: ST AL 18 CULKIN 6
October 19, 1945

Rivaly week was here with the paper saying that *"... fans can expect the best that football has to offer"*. Culkin was undefeated and looking for payback after the loss in 1944. W.C. Sullivan's team was thought evenly matched with Saint Al, and both had their share of injured players.

Saint Al scored in the 2nd after recovering a fumble at the Culkin 14. Matherne gained 7, Derivaux gained 5 and Virgadamo capped it with a 2-yard touchdown. None of the Flash PATs were successful in the contest. Their second score came late in the 3rd after taking over at the Culkin 26. Matherne gained 4 and Virgadamo took it to the 15, but penalties and mistakes forced Saint Al back to the 30. That's when Foley spotted Virgadamo in the endzone for the touchdown and a 12-0 lead.

The Flashes final touchdown came in the 4th. Eventually starting at the Flash 45 due to penalties, Thomas lugged the ball to the Culkin 32 and then Derivaux took a reverse from Thomas the rest of the way for the touchdown. Culkin answered when Shelby Price broke off a 47 yard run to the Flash 5 and then finished it from there on the next play. Virgadamo was able to stop Price on the big run, but was injured and had to leave the game. Saint Al had deeply penetrated the Blues side of the field on two other occasions in the 4th, but drives to the 2 and the 6 were repulsed.

GAME 6: SAINT AL (2-3) @ JEFFERSON MILITARY COLLEGE (UNREPORTED)
FINAL: ST AL 19 JMC 6
October 26, 1945

The Flashes were to present a *"rather weak squad against the Cadets"* due to continued injuries. Matherne, Bankston and Virgadamo were expected to watch from the sidelines and that had the Brothers scrambling to *"... make shifts in the team"*. With question marks as to the team strength, the squad left for Washington, MS at noon on game day with *"some 35 Vicksburgers"* in tow.

One article on the game is missing and the other is mostly illegible. The first half was a *"see saw affair"* but Saint Al would put up three scores in second half of play. Thomas scored the first on a run and John Pinkston would cross the goal for the second. The last was by J.B. Logue that was set up by a 52 yard pass from Foley to Pinkston. Thomas converted the only PAT.

GAME 7: SAINT AL (3-3) @ TALLULAH, LA (UNREPORTED)
FINAL: ST AL 0 TALLULAH 13
November 2, 1945

Tallulah was healthy after a win against Ferriday that kept them *"... still in the running for Class B honors"*. The same couldn't be said for Saint Al. Many were still questionable and others deemed "out" for the contest as the team bus crossed the Mississippi River.

The home team would put up the only two touchdowns of the game. Their first came in the 2nd after blocking Anderson's punt at midfield. Jones gained 32 and then Holly passed to Anderson for the 19 yard score. Holly successfully kicked the PAT. In the 3rd, Tallulah gained the ball at the Flash 37. Jones scampered for 15, Tallulah connected on a 20 yard pass, and then Ogden dove over from the 2 to make it 13-0.

Saint Al threatened twice in the game. Early in the 1st, a Trojan fumble was recovered by Saint Al at the Tallulah 41. Successive drives got the ball to the 1 where Thomas dove over for the score. One official noted it a touchdown while the other waved it off. On their second attempt from the 1, the Flashes fumbled and the opportunity was gone. In the 4th, they marched to the 20 but were held on downs. Though they tasted defeat, the injured Flashes *"... turned in one of their best games of the season... Both teams played hard, clean football and the result was an interesting game from start to finish"*.

GAME 8:   SAINT AL (3-4) vs PORT GIBSON (4-2)
               FINAL: ST AL 13 PORT GIBSON 0
               November 9, 1945

Coach G.S. Goodwin's Port Gibson team boasted "... *one of their fastest and strongest squads in recent years and are determined to get revenge over the Flashes for defeats suffered in the 1944 and 1943 seasons.*" With Matherne back, rigid and strenuous practices were underway on Tuesday and Wednesday. But by Wednesday, John Pinkston had sprained his ankle and would be watching the game alongside Virgadamo and Bankston.

The Flashes were this time on the right side of a 13-0 scoreboard. Donnie Derivaux blocked three punts on the night, and the first one led to a Flash touchdown. Starting at the Port Gibson 33, Logue and Virgadamo blazed through the line with runs that put the ball at the visitor 5. Logue cross the goal and Virgadamo hit Bob Williams for the PAT. Saint Al would get to the 2 in the 2nd but lose on downs. Port Gibson quick-punted and Virgadamo hauled it in at the 50. Foley found Anderson for 32 yards and then saw Matherne for the touchdown. Two tries at the PAT failed. Saint Al would have other trips to the visitor goal rebuffed. They got to the Blue Wave 5 in the 2nd and their 8 in the 4th.

It was noted by <u>The Port Gibson Reveille</u> afterwards that the Blue Waves were missing three first-string players in Gerald Montgomery, Everett Hammett and W.W. Gordon. "*In spite of the drawback, our boys held the score comparatively well*".

GAME 9:   SAINT AL (4-4) vs ANGUILLA (7-0-1)
               FINAL: ST AL 0 ANGUILLA 56
               November 16, 1945: HOMECOMING

Anguilla wasn't the best team to schedule for Homecoming. The paper said "*Anguilla has the best record of any school team in entire Mississippi. They have won 231 points to the opposition's 43. They boast of the best backfield man in the state in Jimmy Moore*". As for the home team, they said "... *the fighting Flashes ... are out to win this game no matter what the price may be*". Festivities were underway, including a parade from the corner of Cherry and Crawford that would extend to Clay and Monroe. All students, including the SFXA girls, would be in attendance along with many decorated cars and bicycles.

The paper said of Moore (who scored 7 times), "*In Moore, the Anguilla team presented one of the best backs seen here this season. The lad can certainly run, and time and again he got off for long jaunts.*" Anguilla's 10-pound-heavier team took it to the Flashes, with Saint Al getting no closer than the Anguilla 21 late in the 4th. A recap of each score would be tedious, but the Anguilla squad seemingly walked in each time they had possession.

They scored once in the 1st, twice in the 2nd, three times in the 3rd, and added two more in the 4th. Moore's stats would have been historical. He scored touchdowns on runs of 4, 77, 6, 43, 20, 41 and 7, giving him 198 yards of rushing just on touchdowns. Adding his other runs for yardage must have made the total staggering. But as for the Flashes, the injury-riddled season was over at 4-5. And 1946 was awaiting the return of "The Father of Saint Aloysius Football" to bring the team back to glory.

GAME X: SAINT ALOYSIUS VICTORY BOWL
               FINAL: "CRIMSON TIDE" vs "BLUE WAVE"
               November 16, 1945

In cooperation with the Victory Loan Drive, the school put on a Victory Bowl to raise Bond sales. Admission would be a .25c Victory Stamp for kids and a .50c Victory Stamp for adults. Bonds were also sold at the game. The teams would be "*from the Saint Aloysius League*"; both made up of Flashes. One was named the Crimson Tide and the other the Blue Wave. While serving a good cause, it also gave some up-and-coming players a chance to get an early start on the 1946 season.

Donnie Derivaux would be awarded the 5th annual Cunningham Trophy.

1946 (7-1)

Joe Balzli was back. His four-year stint in the Marine Corps was over and he took his rightful spot as head man of the Flashes when practices began on August 15. With so many entering the service as he had during that period, the coach faced the task of *"building a team virtually from the ground"*.

The first few weeks were light, with intensity picking up afterwards. He was installing the speedy T-Formation in lieu of the Single-Wing run previously. By kickoff, he had a healthy team not counting Rip Baker (broken leg) and Neil Watson (knee). He originally hoped to field two teams, but that had *"faded though the failure of several men to live up to expectations. The Aloysius mentor believes he has eighteen men he can use without weakening the team very much"*.

The Flashes had new uniforms consisting of two-way purple stretch-knit pants, purple lightweight jerseys with gold numerals, and purple helmets. Balzli was also ensuring his team had *"every item of protection known to the game and every item the best that money can buy"*. Bob Foley would be the captain and Jerry Derivaux would eventually be Alternate Captain.

GAME 1:   SAINT AL (0-0) vs NATCHEZ CATHEDRAL (0-0)
                      FINAL: ST AL 18 NATCHEZ CATHEDRAL 0
                      September 19, 1946

Coach Carson Green's team was led by Louis Sandel, a returning USMC vet with *"triple-threat ability"*. He was also the leading punter. Billy Byrne would also be a danger with his deception. The *"forward wall"* was noted as light, but *"their speed is expected to give the heavier Aloysius line considerable trouble"*.

Giving *"every indication of being a fast and snappy aggregation with a little more practice"*, the Flashes got off to a great start in front of 1,200 spectators. Midway through the 1st after a Sandel punt, four runs were mixed with a 26 yard Jerry Derivaux pass to Charlie Foley. Bob Foley finished the drive with a 2 yard run. Just before halftime, Natchez fumbled to Logue at their 31. The Flashes got to the six-inch line but Virgadamo would turn the ball over to leave it at 6-0.

Nearing the close of the 3rd, Sandel heaved a pass that was picked off by Charlie Foley and returned 47 yards for the touchdown. Now 12-0 early in the 4th, Robert Foley would find the outstretched arms of Logue for the third and final touchdown. All three PATs would miss. Balzli was pleased with the performances but thought the key to get *"his T to really boiling is … just a little more timing in the backfield and to give halfbacks and safetyman more attention on pass defense"*.

GAME 2:   SAINT AL (1-0) vs NEWELLTON, LA (0-0)
                      FINAL: ST AL 54 NEWELLTON 0
                      September 27, 1946

The Flashes worked even over the weekend to prep for Newellton. The paper said they were *"noted for consistently having a strong and powerful team and this year will probably be no exception"*. To simulate game conditions, intense practices under the lights were held and pass defense was highly stressed. Grif Chatham had sustained a shoulder injury against Natchez and would join Watson on the sidelines for the year.

The worst loss of Saint Al history, a 73-0 massacre in 1937, would be revenged in this rubber game between the two squads. Foley quickly went through center for the 1st touchdown. In the 2nd, using the same formula of solid running by many backs, they moved to the Bear 18 and then Foley found Anderson for the touchdown. Foley made it 14-0. The Flashes scored immediately afterwards with Foley going in for his second to make halftime 20-0.

Derivaux started the 3rd with a touchdown run and Virgadamo followed him in the same quarter from the 13 on a reverse. Both had touchdowns previously called back for penalties. In the 4th, Frank Ditto picked up a loose Newellton ball at the Bear 47 setting up the next score. Virgadamo again twisted his way through the crowd before sprinting for the 33 yard touchdown. Knowing they needed quick scores, Tatum launched a pass but it was picked off by Foley for a 64 yard pick-six. Thomas picked off the next Tatum throw and returned it 33 yards to the Bear 13. Foley then found Virgadamo for the touchdown. Thomas added the extra point on a run.

GAME 3:   SAINT AL (2-0) vs CHAMBERLAIN HUNT ACADEMY (2-1)
               FINAL: ST AL 13 CHA 0
               October 10, 1946

The game was originally scheduled for Friday, but the visitors requested a change to Thursday due to a conflicting program. With a 12-day rest period, Balzli agreed. G.S. Goodwin's team outweighed the Flashes by 5 pounds and had just beaten a powerful Edwards team 20-7. But the extra practice time, combined with the shutouts his defense had been throwing, had everyone confident.

Moyers picked off a Foley pass at their 24 after the kickoff but couldn't advance. On a wet field, Derivaux fumbled on the second play afterwards to Prophet, but redeemed himself with an interception as the 1st ended. Runs by him, Thomas and Virgadamo got to the Flash 49. Foley and the Flash rushing machine got them to the 3 and Derivaux then hit Virgadamo for the touchdown pass. Foley made it 7-0. Foley was next with a pickoff but Saint Al couldn't do anything due to penalties. Chamberlain Hunt would pick off a Flash pass at the Cadet 1 to end the half.

The 2nd was a continuation of penalties and fumbling. After getting to the Cadet 11, they fumbled to Kettle only to get a loose ball back on the next play by Koestler at the 11. The Flashes had 30 yards in penalties on that drive and Foley managed a 17 yard touchdown run, only to have it called back on another penalty. Eventually losing the ball on downs, Chamberlain Hunt again fumbled. They recovered and punted twice, the last because of a Flash penalty.

Derivaux fumbled on the next drive but the defense held. From the 48, Thomas cashed after runs to the 8 for a touchdown. Foley's kick hit the crossbar and scoring was finished. A win was a win, and the shutout streak continued. But penalties and fumbles was cause for concern.

GAME 4:   SAINT AL (3-0) vs JEFFERSON MILITARY COLLEGE (UNREPORTED)
               FINAL: ST AL 39 JMC 0
               October 24, 1946

Practice during another off-week looked good. Scrimmages were so intense that linemen *"still smarting from the poor showing against CHA … had to be slowed down in order not to ruin the pony backfield men on whom they were knocking"*. Injured players like McCormack could possibly be back and Balzli was polishing 12 new plays he couldn't use last week due to field conditions. Of JMC, it was known only that they were very heavy in all areas. Originally scheduled for Friday, the game was moved to allow the boys a chance to see the circus in their town.

Saint Al raced out with runs by Foley, Virdadamo, Thomas and Derivaux to the 1. Thomas then crashed through to make it 6-0. There would be no more scoring in the half and Jefferson got only as deep as the Flash 18. Saint Al almost had a touchdown on a pass from Derivaux to Foley, but it was incomplete. Gordon Bailey started the 3rd with a fumble recovery in Jefferson territory. Thomas would convert but Foley's kick was blocked to keep it 13-0. The next touchdown of the quarter was a pass from Derivaux to Foley set up by huge runs by Thomas and Logue.

The Flashes added 3 touchdowns in the last frame. The biggest was an 87 yard run by Charlie Foley followed by a Derivaux pass to Carl Wallace for the PAT. Foley then grabbed a loose Cadet ball at the Jefferson 21. Virgadamo and Robert Foley took it to the 14 and then Thomas scored from there. They recovered another fumble at the Cadet 42 after and Robert Foley took it all the way on the next play. As the game ended, the heavens opened and the crowd raced for their autos.

In four games, Saint Al had put up 124 points versus 0. That wasn't bad for a coach who was rebuilding his program against good competition. The paper noted that with the Flashes holding only a slim lead at half, *"Whatever Balzli said during halftime certainly put some fight in the Flashes because they showed the best fight they had since the first game of the season"*.

GAME 5:   SAINT AL (4-0) @ TALLULAH, LA (UNREPORTED)
               FINAL: ST AL 7 TALLULAH 26
               November 1, 1946

Saturday and Sunday were practice days in Vicksburg to prepare for the Notre Dame Box. The Tallulah team had multi All-State players and Balzli told the team *"… that this is the hump they must get over to have a great season"*. The Trojans were highly rated and reported as of the best high school squads in Louisiana. It wouldn't help that before game time, McCormack (illness) and Robert Foley (back) would be sidelined.

The game was summed up by The Vicksburg Herald as, *"Heavily outweighed by their opponents, the Flashes were magnificent in defeat as they played the finest game of their season against the Trojans. The wear and tear of the hotly contested battle told on the lighter Flashes and four of their number (Derivaux, Virgadamo, Charlie Foley and Reddoch) were injured..."* The Trojans quickly scored with an 80 yard drive capped by Wilkins from the 2. Saint Al attempted to hit stride in the 2nd but a Jones interception of a Derivaux pass to Robert Foley gave them the ball at the Trojan 33. The defense would hold, but Tallulah regained the ball afterwards and allowed Jones to run 65 yards to paydirt. Saint Al attempted to answer but had another pass intercepted.

Derivaux went out two plays into the 3rd *"as the result of a head-on collision"*. Tallulah took the Flash punt and Wilkins ripped off a 45 yard run for a score three plays later. His PAT made it 20-0. The defense would hold Tallulah after a Flash fumble at the 27 but the next Trojan drive would be 40 yards with Jones going in from the 3 to make it 26-0. Worse, Virgadamo was hurt on the play and was carried off the field.

Saint Al's only score came in the 4th when Thomas took a Wilkins punt back 65 yards for their score. Charlie Foley hit his brother Robert for the PAT. *"The Flashes left Legion Field with the plaudits of the crowd for a well-played game. There were no standouts to cope with the power of the fine Tallulah team"*.

GAME 6:   SAINT AL (4-1) @ PORT GIBSON (2-3)
                      FINAL: ST AL 13 PORT GIBSON 0
                      November 8, 1946

Practices were lighter due to the Flashes' health. Virgadamo and Reddoch would not travel to Port Gibson due to their injuries. Jack Stamm would move into Reddoch's position while Gene Henegan would take the spot of Virgadamo in the backfield. It was to be seen whether the beat-up Vicksburg team could get back into their old form.

Saint Al would provide the only points of the game in the 1st half. On their first drive, the Flashes took 5 plays before Thomas bowled over for the touchdown. It was called back due to Glen Anderson failing to report, but on the next play, Derivaux found J.B. Logue for a wide-open touchdown. Foley made it 7-0. In the 2nd period, Derivaux pulled a QB sneak from the 1 to get the next. The Flashes had two fumbles in the 2nd half to kill scoring drives and others stopped due to penalties. *"The blocking and tackling of the Flashes showed improvement over their previous games and they played a bang-up game even though held to a smaller score than was expected"*. Another 12 day off-period awaited the Flashes, but this one would be useful.

GAME 7:   SAINT AL (5-1) vs CULKIN (8-0)
                      FINAL: ST AL 14 CULKIN 0
                      November 22, 1946

The Flashes held off of heavy practices for 5 days to mend. Thomas and Virgadamo were potentially coming back after healing, but John McCormack, Hogan and Reddoch would be gone for the year. Anderson had the flu and was questionable. Culkin had injuries as well, but did have a *"slight edge"* over Saint Al based on common opponents. They were no pushover having outscored their opponents 304-20.

There would be only two scores in the contest and both for the Flashes. The first came after Culkin's kick to Saint Al. Foley and Williams runs, along with a penalty, put the ball at the Culkin 26. Robert Foley got a first down, but Culkin eventually held Saint Al to a 4th and 10. Here, Foley gained a 1st at the Blues 15 and then two plays later went in from the 13. His PAT kick made it 7-0. The Flashes would get to the half-yard line in the 2nd, but Culkin would stop the drive.

In the 4th, Saint Al held Culkin at their 28 and took over. Foley fumbled the first play, lost 5 yards but recovered, and would eventually take a 4th down run 22 yards to the endzone. His PAT kick *"looked wide"*, but officials ruled it good. The game would end a few minutes later. Balzli *"... was enthusiastic over the way his charges played... To those that know the Aloysius mentor, this in itself is a something most unusual"*.

GAME 8:   SAINT AL (6-1) vs NEVILLE HIGH, LA (UNREPORTED)
            FINAL: ST AL 25 NEVILLE HIGH 0
            November 28, 1946: HOMECOMING

The original opponent for Thanksgiving was Anguilla. But during the season, the Anguilla coaches told Balzli that they were hard-hit by graduation and wanted to cancel. Balzli went to Anguilla to watch them play and came back in agreement, saying that *"an Aloysius-Anguilla contest this year would be no contest at all and certainly not a Thanksgiving and Homecoming feature"*. So, an offer was extended to North Louisiana Class AA Neville High School in Monroe, the team who beat Saint Al 33-0 the previous year, and they accepted within 2 hours. *"... Balzli and his protégées know that they are in for a terrific tussle (but) they welcome a shot at so formidable an opponent. Win, lose or tie, local fans are in for a football treat on Thanksgiving Day"*.

After the Culkin game, Saint Al *"... was as fresh as they went into it, and with not a bruise nor a scratch (they) are in the pink of condition..."* On Monday, they *"... ran through short snappy signal drills with little contact work ..."* This was because *"practically the entire first eleven were a bit weary after touring to New Orleans to see the Notre Dame-Tulane game..."* Both Thomas and Virgadamo were back and in *"top shape"*. The paper said that *"With its full complement of backs now on call, Coach Balzli can balance his aggregation out at a strength never used this season. It has always been the policy of Coach Balzli to start all the seniors off in their last game and will do so against Neville"*.

Tuesday rain stopped practices and held the boys to just a light practice on Wednesday. Balzli still felt them ready. *"The Flashes are anxious to demonstrate to their following that although they are in a Class B according to enrollment that they can step out and play in the Class A"*. Though they had lost to Neville last year 33-0, *"This time, stated Balzli, Neville will know that they have been in a football game"*. The Homecoming parade *"traversed the business section of the business section of the city"* including, among others, the SFXA Pep Squad, the Homecoming court, Flash sponsors and band, the police,and decorated autos and bicycles.

Saint Al took the opening kick to the Neville 4 behind Virgadamo, Thomas and Foley. Foley would get the touchdown from there to make it 6-0. In the 2nd, Derivaux found Anderson from the 40 for a touchdown pass and a 12-0 lead. There would be no more scoring until the 4th, with both teams fumbling to one-another in the 3rd. Neville got further than anyone other than Tallulah when they hit the Flash 3 ½ yard line only to see Fisher fumble back to Charlie Foley.

On the first play of the 4th, Robert Foley got to the Neville 34 before being brought down. He would amend afterwards for the touchdown. The Flashes would also march 80 yards before the game was over. Thomas runs pushed the ball down to the one-foot line and he was rewarded with the scoring plunge. The game was described as *"cleanly fought all the way and (of) the few penalties inflicted, none were for rough tactics"*.

When considering one of the greatest teams of Saint Al history, some could point to this one. A record of 7-1 wouldn't indicate such a term, but considering that they never gave up a score against great competition excluding one game, while playing the "best" in Tallulah, it does merit consideration. Gordon Bailey was the winner of the Cunningham Trophy.

1947 (8-1)

If Balzli had ever been happy with the initial showings of a team, it was this year. The *"Aloysius pigskin professor"* stated that *"... both line and backfield has the chance to be the finest the local Catholic school has ever fielded"*. Even with heavy losses from graduation, ineligibility and injury, he loved his chances. He even confidently started the season's practices with scrimmages but kept them to once-a-days through the 31st due to heat.

Griff Chatham hadn't practiced due to the brace on his shoulder, and both Danny Hogan and Tony Virgadamo had knee issues. *"At times Coach Balzli has seemed to be in doubt as to the possibilities of his football machine. The Catholic coach seems to be in the position of a mechanic who has built, tested and checked out an efficient and powerful machine with confidence that it is ready to roll only to find that it seems to falter at certain points along the test run"*.

He stressed speed as only one back out of eight weighed over 150 pounds. The Vicksburg Herald said, *"Fielding one of the lighted teams to represent the Grove Street school in years, Balzli will depend upon the scoring punch of his jack-rabbit backfield to equalize the weight register"*. The team would have new solid purple uniforms uniforms trimmed in gold for the season. On the 18th, Tony Virgadamo was elected team captain and Jerry Derivaux was named alternate captain.

Balzli had told the paper that he thought the team *"capable of scoring at least five TDs a game with the system they are using and the speed they possess. Some other teams might outscore us, but we should be able to cross their goal line at least several times"*.

GAME 1:   SAINT AL (0-0) vs LAKE PROVIDENCE, LA (UNREPORTED)
                         FINAL: ST AL 20 LAKE PROVIDENCE 14
                         September 20, 1947

Lake Providence was heavier, so Balzli worked on new offensive attacks to keep them off-balance. Originally, the game was scheduled for Thursday but moved due to weather. Saint Al jumped out early in the 1st after recovering a Panther fumble at the Flash 48. Two long runs by Jerry Derivaux and Tommy Thomas set up a Thomas 11 yard touchdown run. Lake Providence threatened on the next drive by getting to the Flash 2, but the defense held. The Panthers scored in the 2nd when Trieschman hit Clement from 13 away and Deal converted to make it 7-6.

A Virgadamo fumble on the ensuing drive recovered by Fred Phillips at the Flash 40 was held to a punt. Derivaux received and raced 86 yards for the score. Wallace converted to make halftime a 13-7 Flash lead. Derivaux got in again in the 2nd half and, with a Carl Wallace PAT, made it 20-7. Derivaux got his third of the night in the 4th on an 83 yard run. Lake Providence scored late in the quarter when Trieschmann again hit Clement for 50 yards and Deal converted.

GAME 2:   SAINT AL (1-0) @ NEWELLTON, LA (1-0)
                         FINAL: ST AL 47 NEWELLTON 0
                         September 26, 1947

The Vicksburg Evening Post praised the team for their efforts. Almost every starter was named with the only point of criticism being *"Though the purple and gold gridders had a few early season weaknesses, which can be expected of any team at the initial contest, they pleased both the crowd and their mentor by their playing"*. Balzli's team had now shaken their colds and sniffles, had Chatham back, and was expected *"to field an eleven equally as strong as the team that opposed Lake Providence"*. They left at 3:30 for Newellton for the 8pm game.

The Flashes kicked off the scoring with a Tommy Thomas 2 yard run after a 59 yard haul by Jerry Derivaux. Wallace made it 7-0. Holding the Bears on the next possession, Derivaux again put up long yardage with a 50 yard run for the next score. Before the 1st ended, Thomas had run another in for a touchdown. In the 2nd, Dick Palermo padded the lead and Wallace converted again. In the 3rd, Tony Virgadamo got in from the 22 after a long drive. Saint Al nearly scored again in the frame following an 80-yard interception return by Will Jabour to the Newellton 3. However, the Flashes fumbled away the opportunity. On the next play, the *"entire Aloysius forward wall went crashing through and dumped the Bear back behind his goal for a safety..."* Thomas would score next from roughly 17 yards out.

Jabour hit Wallace in the 4th on a long pass and the paper reported afterwards that Thomas had a couple of more totaling 63 yards. Frank Ditto, Jack Geary, Chatham and Jack Stamm *"turned in bang-up performances and made their presence felt along the first line of defense"*. Wallace had also done a nice job on the extra points and kickoffs.

GAME 3:   SAINT AL (2-0) vs BILOXI NOTRE DAME (UNREPORTED)
                         FINAL: ST AL 12 BILOXI NOTRE DAME 6
                         October 11, 1947

This game was predicted to be a *"strenuous test"* due to Biloxi's weight. Rough scrimmages were held throughout the week and it was expected that *"The Aloysius forward wall"* would have the outcome rest *"upon their shoulders"*. The Commercial Appeal's E.E. Litkenhous rated the game as a *"near toss-up with the teams being almost on a par from their performances to date"*. The Vicksburg Herald thought Saint Al *"a few percentage points above the invaders from the coast..."* An interesting description of QB Pat McCormack said that he *"has proven himself a deft magician bewildering the opponents by playing the 'old shell game' with the pigskin and his trio of pigskin toters"*. Notre Dame arrived in Vicksburg on game day and would return the following day.

Biloxi's opening play of the 2nd was a Kuluz pass to Pickard for 75 yards and a touchdown. The PAT by Gutierrez failed to keep it 6-0. Starting on the Flash 35 after the kick, Virgadamo ran for 44 to the Notre Dame 21. Thomas took the next handoff to paydirt to tie it 6-6 where it stayed though the half. Biloxi threatened in the 2nd after a Flash fumble but could get no further than the Flash 16.

Gutierrez picked off a Pat McCormack pass at the Notre Dame 42 in the 3rd and got as far as the Flash 7 but the defense stiffened to retake the ball on downs. McCormack then fumbled on the Flash 5, but again the defensive wall held to get the ball back. In the 4th, the Flashes put together a 60 yard drive capped by a Virgadamo plunge to seal the win.

GAME 4:   SAINT AL (3-0) vs FOREST (3-0-1)
                           FINAL: ST AL 41 FOREST 6
                           October 17, 1947

Balzli now faced a Class A (Middle Mississippi) team for the first time in 6 years, getting his chance "*at grabbing a brass ring on the district pigskin merry-go-round this Friday night...*" The red and blue visitors had "*served notice that they are ready and able to do battle...*" Said the paper, "*Aloysius gives no warning from any special department but rather makes it known that if anyone plans on halting them, they will find it necessary to stop 'them all' – eleven, that is.*" The team was healthy and ready for conference play.

Virgadamo wasted no time putting the Flashes up by running in a 61-yard touchdown on the Flashes 2nd play. A fumble by Wallace at the Forest 27 stopped the next drive. In the 2nd, Virgadamo capped a 52 yard drive with another score; this one from the 17. Jabour found Derivaux from the 24 on the next drive for a score and, despite a 79-yard Forest push to the Flash 6, ended 1st half scoring with a 20-0 Saint Al lead.

The 3rd started with a McCormack pick at the Flash 25. Runs got to the 13 and then McCormack hit Stamm for the touchdown. McCormack and Stamm again connected from the 34. Derivaux put up the last Flash points in the 4th with a 17 yard run. With less than 1:00 to go, Richard Spence avoided the shutout with a run from the 4. The PAT attempt at the whistle was unsuccessful.

GAME 5:   SAINT AL (4-0) @ CRYSTAL SPRINGS (?-2)
                           FINAL: ST AL 6 CRYSTAL SPRINGS 7
                           October 24, 1947

Class A (Choctaw League) conference foe Crystal Springs featured a 240-pound center that had "*built up a hard-hitting reputation*". Saint Al would not only be on the road, but without the services of Thomas (ankle). McCormack (illness), Ditto (foot) and Donnie Tuminello (foot) weren't in great shape but expected to see action. "*The pony backfield of Coach Balzli has shrunk into a Shetland pony foursome with the average weight of the backs registering 133 pounds. Again the Aloysius mentor is depending upon his forward wall to show these pony backs some wide open, unobstructed, green pastures in which to gallop*".

Saint Al scored first on the second drive after the opening kickoff. Baylot carried for 23 yards to the Trojan 25 and, two plays later, Derivaux took it in off-tackle for the touchdown. Crystal Springs answered in the 3rd with their touchdown. A Rogers run of 33 put the ball at the Flash 26 and a pass moved it to the 5. The Flash defense held on 4th down, but a penalty gave new life. Ingram, the 240-pound center, came in for one play and pushed in from the 1. Frizzell kicked the winning PAT.

The Flashes had a chance to win. Earlier in the 2nd, they had driven "*to within the shadow of the Crystal Springs goal*". Baylot fumbled as he crossed the goal and it was picked up by the home team and brought out to the 4. The paper said, "*Cheered to the closing minutes by a large delegation of Vicksburg supporters who made the trip ... the Aloysius club was outdone in nothing but shifting winds of fortunate, and a 240- pound center.*"

GAME 6:   SAINT AL (4-1) vs MENDENHALL (3-3)
                           FINAL: ST AL 12 MENDENHALL 0
                           October 31, 1947

The last game was more costly than just a number in the loss column. Left End Carl Wallace broke his collar bone and was now expected lost for the season. Thomas was still two or three weeks before full-time service. Meanwhile, the Flashes were undergoing long-and-hard practices to prepare for the heaviest team thus far. Class A Mendenhall averaged 160 pounds and the paper called the Flashes underdogs.

Conditions at kickoff were abysmal. The contest was played in a sea of mud and a heavy downpour hit the players in the first half and drove most of the spectators to cover. Fumbles were frequent and conditions limited any effective plays or scoring until the 4th. As the 3rd was ending, Saint Al sat at the Mendenhall 37 after recovering a fumble. When the 4th started, they were at the 6. Thomas and Virgadamo pushed it to the 4 and then Thomas took it in for the touchdown. The duo also combined for the last touchdown: a 64 yard drive that resulted in Thomas going 26 yards for the score. Neither PAT was successful due to conditions.

"The Flashes simply took the oval behind eye-opening, bone-rattling blocking to reach the prized territory. So long as their pony backs were able to hold on to the slimy pigskin, the seven workhorses along the purple and gold line cleared passages through the heavy Mendenhall eleven. In the shifting sea of mud and rain, two objects appeared securely anchored. These solid abutments were the Aloysius men down the middle: Griff Chatham and Jack Logue".

GAME 7:   SAINT AL (5-1) vs CULKIN (1-LOSS)
                 FINAL: ST AL 7 CULKIN 0
                 November 14, 1947: HOMECOMING

The Flashes had a week-off, but Balzi was still busy. In addition to preparations for Culkin, he was also at the A Club meeting on the 6th where new president H.E. Mackey was elected. He *"congratulated those present on organizing the club and outlines some of the services the members could render, not only to the team but the school as well"*. The club was high praise for the progress of the team thus far. He was also at another meeting on the 13th where the LSU-Tulane game was being shown.

Virgadamo, McCormack and Thomas were slightly banged up but were ready to go against their Warren County rivals. Culkin also had injuries, with Bishop out for the season with a severe hand injury. Both teams were even in weight and lacking in quality reserves. *"Both for the Flashes and the Blues, this isn't just another ball game. Both consider this tussle as THE ball game"*. That ball game would be moved up one day due to the *"heavy down pour of rain throughout the morning"*.

In a battle of wills before a record crowd on a muddy field, there would be no score for the first three quarters. Culkin managed to get to the Flash 2 but the defense held. Culkin blocked the ensuing punt, but Saint Al would recover. They drove to the Culkin 24 before Derivaux fumbled to Culkin's Downey. The Blues got another Flash fumble in the 3rd but immediately returned the gift in the same manner. Saint Al pushed that possession to the 18 but lost the ball on downs.

Midway through the 4th, Culkin turned the ball over on downs at the Flash 24. After runs to the Flash 42, Thomas *"got loose over his left guard and galloped 58 yards for the only score of the game"*. Derivaux added the PAT.

GAME X: SAINT AL (6-1) vs FLORENCE (UNREPORTED)
                 FINAL: NOT PLAYED
                 November 19, 1947

Florence was originally scheduled to play Saint Al, but the game was never registered.

GAME 8:   SAINT AL (6-1) @ MENARD HIGH, LA (UNREPORTED)
                 FINAL: ST AL 18 MENARD 16
                 November 27, 1947

During the Culkin game, it was announced by Lions Club President H.C. Decell that Saint Al had been selected to play in the Lions Bowl. Potential opponents were discussed but there could be no consensus as the season wasn't over and other bowls were vying for teams. This game would be labeled the C.Y.O. Bowl. As for the upcoming opponent, Menard boasted *"one its best elevens in a decade and Coach Balzli is prepared to field the most versatile combination possible...."* The only injury from the last game was a wrist sprain by McCormack that kept him out of the Culkin second half. He would be ready to go.

Saint Al struck quickly when, after a Menard fumble, Derivaux grabbed it and ran 36 yards for the score. Menard answered immediately when Deville ran in a touchdown followed by a Kelso plunge for the PAT. In the 2nd, Derivaux scored again; this time from the 17 to make halftime 12-7. Thomas took the first run of the 4th in from 7 away for the touchdown. Menard added points after with a safety and a Deville run. Kelso's PAT finished scoring.

GAME 9:   SAINT AL (7-1) vs TYLERTOWN (5-5)
                 FINAL: ST AL 26 TYLERTOWN 0
                 December 4, 1947: LIONS BOWL

The 4th Annual Lions Bowl would be held at Johnson Field with two *"well-matched"* teams though Tylertown held a slight weight advantage. The visitors had requested 500 tickets by the 29th, so a large crowd was anticipated. Saint Al had won the C.Y.O. trophy for the Catholic Diocese of Alexandria, LA and Natchez, MS and the trophy was to be displayed in a downtown window. The Delta Blue Devils left Tylertown on the 3rd to stay overnight. They had a week off due to scheduling and The Tylertown Times thought that *"the Devils will turn in their top performance of this season"* after some injured players were ready to return.

According to their paper (the Vicksburg accounts were unavailable), the scoreless first half was highlighted by a Tylertown interception by Marion at the Flash 46. But *"A transformed St. Aloysius team took the field in the opening of the third"*. The first score was from Virgadamo at the 3 set up by a Thomas 42 yard run to the Tylertown 10. Tylertown's Scott fumbled afterwards on his 37 and Derivaux and Thomas runs pushed it to the 2. Thomas would go in from there to make it 14-0 after the PAT.

After holding the Devils the Flashes started at their 20. Thomas broke off a 76 yard run to the Tylertown 4 before being tackled by Oliver Scott. Three plays later, Virgadamo went in to make it 20-0. Derivaux picked off a following Devil pass and returned it to the Tylertown 20. Virgadamo put in his second touchdown two plays later.

By virtue of the win, the Flashes were co-champions (along with Morton) of the Middle Mississippi Class A Conference Championship. Balzli called them *"... the fastest and cleverest team he has ever coached."* The A Club would promise the boys a trip to the Delta Bowl on January 1st for the Ole Miss-TCU game in Memphis.

For his efforts in the classroom and on the field, Tommy Thomas received the Cunningham Trophy for 1947.

1948 (3-5)

Incredibly little was written about the opening of the season except that 9 of the starting 11 from *"Balzli's dream team of 1947"* were gone. Final preparations for their kickoff game were reported on September 22nd, with Balzli saying that *"his squad was in tip-top shape and ready for the Lake Providence Panthers"*. Graduation had changed the team to a *"light though fast aggregation"* though the line was actually heavier than 1947.

The backfield, nickname the *"Little Three"*, would average 117 pounds. It consisted of Bobby Baylot (127), Dick Palermo (103) and Bobby Koestler (123). When relieved, it would be by the *"Big Three"* of Jack Logue, Pat McCormack and Buddy Wood. The co-captains would be Jack Stamm and Pat McCormack. *"These two lettermen of last year are 'twin brothers' of precision and timing perfection"*.

GAME 1:   SAINT AL (0-0) vs LAKE PROVIDENCE, LA (1-0)
                 FINAL: ST AL 0 LAKE PROVIDENCE 32
                 September 24, 1948

A large crowd on hand included many from Louisiana. Lake Providence held the Flashes on the kickoff and mastered a 70 yard drive that culminated in a Denny touchdown dive from inside the 1. Saint Al responded with a 25 yard Stamm reception from McCormack and a Palermo run for 25. Now at the 23, McCormack's intended pass to Palermo was picked off by Clement who raced 77 yards for another touchdown.

The visitors almost scored to start the second, but a Hopkins fumble at the Flash 1 was recovered by Evans. Being held, Pat McCormack punted to the Flash 35. Clements and Phillips gained 24, Trieschmann got to the 3 and Phillips took broke off the right for the touchdown. The remainder of the quarter saw a tradeoff of interceptions: Denny for Lake Providence and Logue for the Flashes. Halftime would be 18-0.

Logue got another gift in the 3rd when a Trieschmann pass to Brown was fumbled. Saint Al was forced to punt to set up the next Panther touchdown. Trading passes and runs, the Panthers worked to the Flash 5 before Clements ran in. Trieschmann's PAT pass to Clement was good. McCormack opened the 4th with a blocked punt that put them at the Flash 33. They could get no closer than the 7 before losing on downs. Their next possession resulted in the last score of the contest. At the Flash 41, Trieschmann spotted Clement for the touchdown pass and then Phillips for the PAT.

GAME 2: SAINT AL (0-1) vs TALLULAH, LA (3-0)
FINAL: ST AL 7 TALLULAH 37
October 8, 1948

The Flashes worked under the lights on the 4th on all phases of the game. "*I expect a lot more out of the line for the Tallulah game than it showed in the Lake Providence game. For six of the seven linemen, it was their first starting assignment, Jack Stamm being the only really seasoned man on the line. But with a full game under their belts, much more is expected of them*". Tallulah ran from the Notre Dame box and had a fine leftie-do-everything player in Jackie White. So, Balzli dressed his left-handed manager (John Horton) for practice to simulate the Tallulah offense while "*erasing many prominent errors*" committed last week.

Tallulah got going in the 1st and didn't look back. Running by White and Martin Verhagen was unstoppable. Verhagen scored from the 3 twice in the 1st behind runs from White, Ervin and Bernard Cox. In the 2nd, a Wood fumble of a Verhagen punt gave Tallulah the ball at the Flash 45. Clark Christian registered the score from the 6. White's only PAT of the game followed and halftime sat 19-0.

The Flashes started the 3rd with a McCormack pass intercepted. Tallulah would score on a Sonny Clark pass to Ira Hugh Erwin from the 15. Saint Al took the kick and drove to the Tallulah 7 courtesy of Wood and Milton Emfinger runs coupled with a Jabour pass to Stamm for 45 yards. McCormack found Stamm from the 5 and then kicked the PAT to make it 25-7. In the closing seconds of the 3rd, a Flash fumble put Tallulah at the 18. Clark would find White from the 3 for the touchdown. Tallulah chalked up their last points in the 4th. After taking a Saint Al punt on the Flash 45, White did "*some fine broken field running*", raced the rest of the way for the touchdown.

GAME 3: SAINT AL (0-2) @ FOREST (1-0)
FINAL: ST AL 7 FOREST 13
October 15, 1948

Balzli worked the team hard and shifted men around trying "*several new formations which seek to be clicking*". The paper said "*Forest, always boasting of a fast well-clicking squad, is reported to have one of its best teams in history this year. They promise to make things most interesting for the Aloysius boys tonight.*" A large group of Flash fans accompanied the team to support.

McCormack started off with a pass to Stamm for 25 yards that set up the Stamm touchdown run "*standing up*". Wallace, who had been suffering from a broken collar bone, converted the PAT for an early 7-0 lead. In the 2nd, Forest responded when captain Harry Massey found Richard Spence for the touchdown. Massey's kick made it 7-7. Forest added to the lead in the 3rd with a 79 yard drive that resulted in a Bobby Henderson touchdown.

The heartbreaker for the Flashes came as the game ended. Starting at the Forest 32 after holding them for downs, Bobby Koestler broke off a long run to the Forest 22. McCormack then hit Jabour at the Forest 6. Two plays later, Saint Al was at the Forest 2 but time expired. The paper said, "*Father Time stepped in a denied the St. Aloysius High School Flashes the opportunity of breaking into the win column...*"

GAME 4: SAINT AL (0-3) vs CRYSTAL SPRINGS (4-1)
FINAL: ST AL 0 CRYTSTAL SPRINGS 41
October 22, 1948

With mostly varsity returners playing, Choctaw Conference opponent Crystal Springs was considered "*... one of the best teams in this section...*" They had just lost to highly-rated Brookhaven but only 12-2. If there was good news for Saint Al, it was that Dr. A.J. Messina pronounced Carl Wallace and

Frank Muirhead available for the last 3 games. Wallace was now being used solely for kicking. *"Coach Balzli plans to continue using his two sets of backs with McCormack directing both the feather merchants and the bit-heavier three"*.

The first half was described as *"a beautifully played contest"*. In the 1st, the Flashes got to the visitor's 15 before a Wood fumble. Midway through the 2nd, Crystal Springs was at their 32 when Charlie Sojourner broke a long run to the Flash 37. Seven plays later, he punched through for the 1 yard touchdown. Rogers ran for the PAT and a 7-0 halftime lead. McCormack would not see the second half as a knee injury would put him on the sidelines.

Things got out of hand from there. Crystal Springs capped a 68 yard drive on a Sonny Rogers touchdown followed by a Garland Harris interception at the Flash 9 that resulted in a Smith touchdown pass to Harris. In the closing minutes of the 3rd, Batton finished a 38 yard drive from the 9. Sojourner's PAT run made it 27-0. Jabour was picked off in the 4th by Robert Smith at the Flash 45 and was rewarded with the 1 yard touchdown run later. Rogers ran in for the PAT. Their final score came on another nab by Smith of a Jabour pass. Carroll Henley converted from the 8 and hit Bush for the PAT.

GAME 5:   SAINT AL (0-4) @ MENDENHALL (5-1)
                 FINAL: ST AL 7 MENDENHALL 26
                 October 29, 1948

The game against *"... a fast, well-balanced eleven..."* in Mendenhall would be tough. *"Mendenhall is rated to defeat the Flashes by two or three touchdowns. However, the Flashes are entering the contest with the determination of upsetting the dope."* Part of the reason for low expectations was that McCormack and Jabour (knee) would be sitting out alongside Muirhead, Wallace and Ford. By kickoff, both Palermo and Koestler were bedridden for two days with colds. Said Balzli, *"This squad is in the worst crippled condition of any Aloysius team since I took over in 1936"*.

As against Crystal Springs, Saint Al started the 1st half strong. They drove to the Tiger 12 in the 1st before losing on downs. Mendenhall's first score was in the 2nd. Lester Magee received a bad snap and, under pressure from the Flash defense, heaved a 48 yard pass to Fred Morris for a touchdown. Durr Cockrell's PAT made halftime 7-0. The 3rd would begin to show the weakness in depth of the visitors.

Mendenhall's Billy Slay added two touchdowns in the 3rd frame. The first was a 48 yard run that *"... with the blocking of his teammates, made Slay's beautiful run look comparatively easy"*. The second was a slash off right tackle from the 11. Saint Al got their only touchdown against the reserves as the 3rd ended. At the 50, Wood found Stamm at the 1 and then Stamm got the call on a pass the next play. Wallace converted the PAT. Slay added his 3rd touchdown of the game in the last quarter to seal the win.

GAME 6:   SAINT AL (0-5) @ BILOXI NOTRE DAME (3-4)
                 FINAL: ST AL 14 BILOXI NOTRE DAME 6
                 November 12, 1948

Though Muirhead was still out, the Flashes were *"in tip-top share, in fact they are in the best condition they have been this season"*. In Biloxi, Coach Louis Presti's squad was dealing with rain in preparation for the Flashes. That was significant since the defending Class B champs were a passing team and could not work on that part of their offense. The Flashes left Thursday at noon for an overnight stay at The White House Hotel in Biloxi. They would leave on Saturday for Baton Rouge to see the Mississippi State-LSU contest.

A crowd reported to be near 4,000 was on hand to see the Flashes *"in the role of conqueror"* by gaining their first win of the season. After holding the home team to an opening drive punt, Saint Al responded with a workman-like effort by Wood that resulted in his touchdown. Wallace converted for a 7-0 lead. Saint Al added another when Jabour *"got loose and raced sixty yards"* for a score, but it was nullified for motion. The Flashes would have the same thing happen again and eventually lose the ball on a fumble. The halftime whistle sounded as the Flashes were knocking on the Biloxi door just feet from the goal.

Saint Al got to the Biloxi 20 twice in the 3rd with no results, but scored in the 4th when Wood again crashed the goal. Wallace converted his second PAT. Biloxi's Larry Toups took the ensuing kick at the Biloxi 10 and returned it 71 yards to the Flash 19. Stamm saved the touchdown run, but Toups would score from the 4 after a Flash penalty. Afterwards, Stamm would be called "... *the best that's been on the Biloxi field all year*".

GAME 7:   SAINT AL (1-5) vs FLORENCE (UNREPORTED)
               FINAL: ST AL 51 FLORENCE 7
               November 19, 1948

Florence had gotten off to a bad start but improved as the year went along. They were heavier than Saint Al on the line, but with the expected return of Muirhead, that would even out somewhat. The paper said that "*Frustrated fans will not recognize the team as being the same Flashes who performed in the early part of the season, so greatly are they improved.*" Though dealing with a horrendous year, Balzli now felt that "... *the defensive play of this squad even surpasses that of his 'dream team' of last year and their offensive play is not trailing far behind*".

The week was dreadful relative to practice. Balzli called off Tuesday and Thursday drills due to inclement weather, wanting to avoid at all costs the threat of someone catching the flu. But the Wednesday practice saw "*the rejuvenated Flashes look like their 'season-ago brothers' and a fan who saw them ... remarked ... that it will take a better-than-average team to out-score the Aloysius squad*".

Saint Al would score at-will against Florence, with every member seeing valuable playing time. The first score was on the second play of the game when Wood scored from the 6 after a Wallace return of 69 yards. Florence fumbled at their 31 and Al Ford recovered. Koestler took it in from there. Palermo got the 3rd touchdown as the next quarter started, racing in from 19. Next, McCormack hit Stamm for a 49 yard strike and then he hit Jabour for the PAT. Florence got their only score afterwards when Bill Frazier took a Muirhead kick back 65 yards. Harry Ferguson converted the PAT.

Saint Al responded with a Logue run on a reverse for 34 yards and the touchdown. Baylot tallied the next touchdown on an 11 yard scamper and halftime would be a staggering 39-7. Baylot picked off a Ferguson pass at the Florence 25 to start the 3rd and Palermo "*wiggled his way through the center of the line*" for his score. Saint Al added another 3rd quarter touchdown when O'Neill hit Emfinger from the 19. Sanders' PAT run failed. There would be no more scoring, even though O'Neill would pick off a Frazier pass at the Florence 18.

GAME 8:   SAINT AL (2-5) vs MENARD HIGH, LA (?-4)
               FINAL: ST AL 48 MENARD 0
               November 25, 1948: HOMECOMING

The final game of the season would be on Thanksgiving against "*a powerful bird*" from Alexandria. The Flashes squeaked by the Eagles last year 18-16 and Menard was "*reported to have every bit as powerful a team this season as last*". The team was healthy, having watched the majority of the game from the sidelines against Florence while their "*little brothers*" saw playing time. "*The Flashes are more in shape and ready for this game than any other game of the season. Every boy, from the most valuable player to the lowest scrub is in the peak of condition and raving to go*". Menard arrived on Wednesday and stayed at The Hotel Vicksburg.

Saint Al seemed to be in the endzone whenever they wished. The first touchdown was a run by Jabour from the one-foot line set up by numerous Flash runs. Menard's James Chatman fumbled on their first drive at the Eagle 17. Runs by Logue, Jabour and Koestler allowed McCormack to find Wallace for the touchdown and the 13-0 lead. Menard turned it over again on the kick when White fumbled at the Eagle 40. McCormack made them pay by finding Wallace from the 11.

The 2nd started with numerous exchanges of punts before Saint Al finally set up shop at the Menard 46. Two plays later, Jabour hit Wallace for the touchdown from the 18. Saint Al added one more on the final play of the half after a Chatman fumble at their 21 was recovered by Stamm. A Palermo run and an Eagle penalty put the ball at the 6 where McCormack found Jabour for the touchdown and a 33-0 halftime lead. The Flashes started the 3rd with a safety on Menard when Stamm blitzed in for the sack on Lazarone.

The ensuing kick was returned 47 yards by Jabour to the Menard 26. McCormack hit the center of the line for an 18 yard touchdown three plays later and Wallace padded the lead to 42-0. The 4th started with the Flashes at midfield. Koestler would get the 10 yard running touchdown and McCormack would find Emfinger for the extra point. Saint Al scored another touchdown on an O'Neill strike to Jabour from the 11, but it was called back.

The season would go into the book at 3-5, but one has to wonder what it would have held if the Flashes were afforded the strength they had since November 12th. Jack Stamm won the coveted Cunningham Trophy for the season.

1949 (4-5)

Balzli set the first practice for August 15th. Brother Mark, the principal of Saint Aloysius (New Orleans) for several years, would take over from Brother Gerard. Practices would be once-a-day at 4pm until the weather cooled. Seventeen experienced players, including 10 lettermen, returned to make up the tentative 35 member group. Balzli was high on the prospects in spite of only 4 home games.

To prepare, the coach had the new team face the Alumni from 1947 and 1948 on September 6th. The elders won by a score of 7-6 in front of "*a large crowd of interested spectators*". The season looked promising with Will Jabour and Carl Wallace selected as co-captains by their teammates.

GAME 1:   SAINT AL (0-0) @ NEWELLTON, LA (0-0)
                          FINAL: ST AL 21 NEWELLTON 0
                          September 16, 1949

Balzli wasn't impressed with the running of the "T" formation thus far and was "*... leary as to whether his squad (was) ready*" for their first game. He thought it would take well-more time to get it running smoothly and hoped the defense would be able to provide the necessary help. Newellton promised Saint Al that the Bears would not be the "*Cubs*" they saw in 1948. The paper described them as "*an excellent ball club ... much improved one the '47 team that the Flashes easily took*". Roughly 200 Flash fans made the trip to Louisiana.

The Flashes still got off to a good start for the season on Newellton's field. Though the Flashes made tremendous strides in yardage in the 1st, but it would be the 2nd quarter before Dick Palermo went for 54 yards and the initial touchdown. Carl Wallace's PAT made it 7-0. Will Jabour stopped the ensuing Bear drive and put an exclamation point on it with a 50 yard interception return for a touchdown "*standing up*". It was 14-0 at halftime.

In the 4th, with Newellton at their own 13, Tatum was picked off by Clint Schlottman who returned it 25 yards for the final score "*with no opponent near him*". Balzli sent in every reserve afterwards but they would not let Newellton past the Flash 27. Saint Al had limited their offense to the run except for 2 passes. Schlottman and Baylot exited afterwards with apparent leg injuries, and time would tell if they were OK for the next game.

GAME 2:   SAINT AL (1-0) @ LAKE PROVIDENCE, LA (UNREPORTED)
                          FINAL: ST AL 13 LAKE PROVIDENCE 25
                          September 23, 1949

When asked about his prospects for Game 2 with Schlottman out, Balzli said "*When a coach says that one of his boys will not play, it is taken as an alibi. So let me just say that the ones who will play are in top shape*". Lake Providence pounded the Flashes in 1948 by a 32-0 score, but their main clog (Lloyd Clements) was their only graduating lettermen. "*A large delegation of Aloysius supporters...*" crossed the river with the team in early afternoon.

On the opening kick, Buddy Wood and Carl Wallace attempted a reverse but it was fumbled at the Flash 21. John Hopkins made it count 4 plays later with the touchdown. Lake Providence added another in the 1st when Treischmann found Hopkins from the 16 for the second score. The PAT pass to Fortenberry was good. The 2nd saw Wood leave the game with a hip injury and Baylot re-aggravate his knee and also leave. Even so, the first play would see Jabour hit Carl Wallace for a 55 yard touchdown. Wallace placed the PAT to close the halftime lead to 13-7. Starting the 3rd and after holding Lake Providence, Dick Palermo fumbled the punt and gave the Panthers the ball at the Flash 32. Hopkins capitalized with a 20 yard touchdown run.

The Flashes fumbled again on their next drive but held the Panthers without a first down. Palermo, on receiving the punt, signaled for a fair catch but was tackled with no penalty. The drive was still successful when Jabour crashed in from the 1. The Flashes chance to pull out a victory was squashed when Hopkins pulled off a 58 yard touchdown run.

GAME 3:   SAINT AL (1-1) vs FLORA (2-0)
FINAL: ST AL 18 FLORA 0
September 30, 1949

After two trips to Louisiana, it was time to come home. Flora was a major team in the Middle Mississippi District Conference and went to the State Class B football final in 1948. And most of the team was back and prepared to *"give the Flashes a hard tussle"*. Milton Emfinger, Wood and Baylot would miss the game but Schlottman would be back. Wood was still in the *"infirmary"* and would miss several weeks. Balzli felt that Flora would *"be one of his strongest opponents of the year"* and was working the guys hard in preparation. He took it light toward the end of the week to save more from injuries. Saint Al would have 4 sophomores starting out of the 19 sophomores on the squad. Not all names were released for the team roster.

Flora's Matrick picked off a Flash pass to start the 1st, but they wouldn't be able to use it. On the ensuing drive, and after a number of Flash runs, George Ellis burst through for the 6-yard touchdown. Flora came close to tying or leading at the half closed. Jabour's pass to Wallace was picked off by Price at the Flora 20. They would drive to the Flash 1, but could not get in to keep halftime 6-0.

In the 3rd, Saint Al punched in again when Palermo ran in from 23 away. It was set up by a Schlottman reception of 39 yards from Jabour. They held Flora on downs afterwards at the Lion 47 and closed the 3rd on the 17. On the first play of the 4th, Palermo would make it count on a 17 yard touchdown run. They were 2-1 but would now go back to Louisiana two more times and then to Crystal Springs before coming home.

GAME 4:   SAINT AL (2-1) @ TALLULAH, LA (3-0)
FINAL: ST AL 7 TALLULAH 30
October 7, 1949

Balzli had more obstacles than powerful Tallulah. First, the weather was horrible and prevented all but one day of practice. Second, Wood would now be out for the season; Palmero and Baylot were still injured and not playing; and Emfinger would leave the squad probably due to injury. *"Coach Balzli sees little hope for a win over the Trojans, but says that they will have to earn victory."* He had little reason to expect it. The reigning State Class B Louisiana champions had 10 straight victories and 16 out of 17.

There were 3,500 fans on hand for the contest to see the "**Mighty Trojans Of Tallulah Trample Aloysius Flashes**". Tallulah put up two touchdowns in the 1st, the first after a blocked Jabour punt was recovered by Bob Laird. Jackie White ran it in and Lamar Loe converted. Later, the Flashes fumbled to the Trojans and Wallace Hargin found Marlin Christian for a 9 yard touchdown pass. Martin Verhagen's kick also counted.

The 3rd touchdown came in the following quarter after starting on the Flash 45. Jackie White moved it to the 18 from which Verhagen reversed for the score. Loe made it 21-0. As time expired on the Flash 5, Jabour would be tackled for a safety to make it 23-0 at intermission. Another Flash punt was blocked in the 3rd at the Flash 35 and recovered by Loe. Bill Christian plunged through the middle from there and Loe made it 30-0.

With Tallulah reserves playing, the Flashes pushed the ball to the Trojan 2 behind runs by Will Sanders and Ellis. Bob O'Neill snuck over for their only score of the evening. A bad snap to O'Neill prevented the kick, but Wallace picked it up and ran in for the extra point. Balzli's rare praise for one person did single out the work of George Evans, whom he thought *"... not ready for action against a team like Tallulah, but only did George play guard on defense, he also carried the ball 3 times out of 4"*.

GAME 5:   SAINT AL (2-2) @ FERRIDAY, LA (3-1)
FINAL: ST AL 13 FERRIDAY 0
October 14, 1949

Ferriday was a Class A school *"even larger than that of Tallulah"* and *"... one of the top-ranking high school teams in Louisiana and ... is slated to win"*. Palermo would return, but Baylot would not. Al Ford was thought lost, but was cleared on the 13th to play. Wood left the hospital on the 12th and was out for the year. Due to the punt blocks against Tallulah, Balzli took special time to work on this aspect of his game. The team left at 2pm on game day for Ferriday.

Off-and-on rain during the game would make conditions tough. The Flashes would hold after kicking off to Ferriday and take control at their 28. Numerous runs got to the Ferriday 11 before Palermo rushed in from there for the touchdown. Wallace's second try after penalty was good for a 7-0 lead. Saint Al almost scored again after a Schlottman reception of 23 yards put the ball at the Ferriday 4. But an Ellis fumble at the 1 gave the ball back. Halftime would end 7-0.

Palermo opened the 3rd when he crashed in from the Ferriday 1 to finish a 90 yard drive. Jabour picked off a Loomis pass on the next drive and the Flashes got to the Ferriday 10 before a "*slippery ball was fumbled*" at the Ferriday 15. Wallace would recover a Ferriday fumble afterwards to stop their only deep drive.

GAME 6:   SAINT AL (3-2) @ CRYSTAL SPRINGS (5-1)
                FINAL: ST AL 7 CRYSTAL SPRINGS 14
                October 21, 1949

The Flashes simulated Crystal Springs formations during a week of intensive practices. Reserves were utilized heavily since Crystal Springs would have the decided advantage in depth. Baylot was still not expected to play and the paper said "*The Aloysius go into the game once again slated to lose according to pre-game ratings. However, Balzli is hoping for another upset.*" Thursday practice was almost impossible since many squad members were in Natchez with the band celebrating Bishop R.O Gerow's "*jubilee*". Balzli was noted as considering his opponent "*...equal to if not better than Tallulah...*" A large contingent of Flash fans left with the team early in the afternoon for Crystal Springs.

The 1st and much of the 2nd was a back-and-forth affair. Midway through the 2nd, a Flash fumble allowed Gerald Bush to hit C. Lingle for a 42 yard touchdown pass to give the Tigers the early lead. Lingle's PAT made it 7-0. Just before the half ended, Jabour picked off a Bush pass at the Flash 1 and kept the deficit to 7 points. Saint Al fumbled in the 3rd but the defense held. On the first play of the 4th, Bush found a wide-open Kenneth Bailey for a 24 yard strike. Lingle made it 14-0.

After being held on the ensuing possession, the Flashes punted but Crystal Springs fumbled to Wallace at the Flash 42. The next play was a Jabour pass to an "*unmolested*" Wallace for the 58 yard score. Saint Al would be as deep as the Tiger 17 when the game ended. The paper praised the play of Schlottman, Wallace, Billy Bufkin, and Palermo. Balzli was also proud of his defensive line play and "*thought his team played its best game*".

GAME 7:   SAINT AL (3-3) vs MENDENHALL (6th GAME)
                FINAL: ST AL 21 MENDENHALL 6
                October 28, 1949

Balzli devoted three days to offensive practices and scrimmages and came though pretty well with the exception of a Sonny Schaff ankle injury. The Flashes would "*take the field ... and literally live up to their name in their uniform dress. New football pants of purple nylon with two-way stretch old gold backs, white jerseys with purple stripes and numerals and purple headgear will be worn*".

A crisp and clear night was in store at City Park for a game described as "*one of the best seen on the local field this year, and despite the score, the two teams gave a great exhibition of football*". Saint Al fumbled the kickoff at their 38 but would hold the Tigers for only 1 yard and take over on downs. Short runs set up a Jabour pass to Wallace for 23 yards at the Tiger 39. More runs to the 7 allowed Palermo the touchdown from there. Wallace made it a 7-0 ball game. In the half, the Flashes drove to the 11 and Palermo recovered a Morris fumble at the Mendenhall 35 for naught.

On their second possession in the 3rd, Morris threw an interception to Jabour at the Tiger 32. The Flashes got to the 1 but fumbled to Bailey at the Tiger 7. Saint Al held and then blocked the punt to put them at the Mendenhall 9. Will Sanders ran for 8 and then Palermo cashed in from there. Wallace's kick increased the lead to 14-0. Midway through the 4th, Ford sacked Morris at the Tiger 8 to set up a Bufkin punt block and touchdown. Mendenhall put up their points on the next drive, starting with a 74 yard kick return by Jim May to the Flash 11. Morris hit Benton for 9 and then ran it in two plays later. Allison's attempt for the PAT failed.

GAME 8:   SAINT AL (4-3) vs ROLLING FORK (UNREPORTED)
            FINAL: ST AL 20 ROLLING FORK 27
            November 4, 1949

The pattern thus far had been to lose the week after a win. *"Coach Balzli is fearful that the pattern will again prevail and his charges be defeated again."* The team had lengthy practices with the exception of Evans, Palermo and Sanders. Each had missed due to illnesses. The sophomore squad was looking very good and gave Balzli hope if only his team would not be looking forward to Homecoming.

The Bearcats struck quickly when Saint Al fumbled on the opening drive. Ernest Mangrum recovered at the Flash 20 and, on the 3rd play, John Fenton went in from the 11. Mangrum added the PAT. The Flashes responded immediately with a Jabour touchdown pass to Wallace from the 24. Wallace added the tying PAT. Rolling Fork wasted no time in regaining the lead. Runs by Mangrum, Fenton and Cassanova got the ball to the Flash 15 and then Fenton hit Norris for the score and C. Bodie for the PAT. It looked like the game would be a slugfest, because Jabour took the Maranto kickoff and raced 85 yards for the touchdown. Wallace ended the 1st with the game at 14-14.

Rolling Fork opened the 2nd with a fumble recovered by Evans on the Bearcat 41. One play later, the Flashes returned the favor with Maranto recovering. The Flashes held but fumbled again on their next drive at the Rolling Fork 44. Unbelievably, the Flashes held again but fumbled for the third straight time; this one at the Flash 40. Turnovers would continue in large numbers. Fenton threw a pick to Jabour, Jabour threw an interception to Cassanova, Mangum fumbled to the Flashes, and Jabour was picked off by Reed as the half ended.

The Bearcats increased the lead in the 3rd on a Fenton run up the middle for the 20 yard touchdown. Both teams would finish the game with touchdowns though reports with details are missing. Rolling Fork did get to the 1 as the game ended, but the defense held numerous attempts to score. Afterwards, the boys would note that Ernest Mangrum was the finest back they had faced all year and was admirable in his sportsmanship. The same went for John Fenton.

In spite of the loss, the boys were treated to a trip courtesy of the Saint Aloysius A Club. They left on Saturday for New Orleans to see the Navy-Tulane game and returned on Sunday.

GAME 9:   SAINT AL (4-4) vs CATHOLIC HIGH, TN (2-?)
            FINAL: ST AL 6 CATHOLIC HIGH 32
            November 11, 1949: HOMECOMING

Homecoming festivities were being finalized for the season's last game. Balzli met with the A Club and *"athletic authorities"* on the 5th to give *"a report on the team's trip to New Orleans..."* He felt his squad to be in shape and planned for hard drills for the week. Catholic High was in the Memphis Prep League and, though known as *"Little Catholic High"*, were nearly equal to Central High of Memphis on the field the previous week. Said Balzli, *"We will take them as we have the rest of the tough nine-game schedule."* The Tennessee team flew in to Jackson on game day and returned the same night.

Holding on the first drive, the Flashes took the ball to their 41 but fumbled to Malley. Runs to the 17 finally resulted in a Malley pass to Valley for the 17 yard score. Wallace blocked the PAT to keep it at 6-0. Midway through the 2nd, Valley picked off a Jabour pass at the Flash 42 to set up shop. Bailey would take advantage with a pass from the 23 to Valley for the touchdown. Bailey hit Valley again for the PAT and a 13-0 halftime lead.

After taking the 3rd quarter kick to the 4 on numerous runs and passes, Palermo squeezed through for Saint Al's only touchdown. Catholic followed that with a touchdown of their own. It took 6 tries from the 1, helped by a penalty, before Edwards would get though. Bailey's PAT was blocked by Evans. On the 3rd play of the 4th, Burke burst in from the 2 for a score, but Saint Al again blocked Bailey's kick; this time by Wallace. Catholic added two more touchdowns in the final frame. One followed a Jabour interception by Owens at the Flash 7. Two plays were run before Jensen went in. He also drop-kicked the PAT.

Said the paper, *"The Flashes fought hard all the way, but their best was not sufficient to compete with the hefty lads from Memphis"*. Homecoming festivities ended on the 13th with Balzli giving a review of the season and stating that *"he expected to have a very good team next year, as his sophomores had come along very well and should be ready for next year."* The group also wished to have future games played at Saint Aloysius Athletic Field, but it would take improvements to become reality.

A final game against Clinton for November 18th was originally scheduled but cancelled somewhere along the way. Al Ford would be the recipient of the final Cunningham Trophy; to be named the Virgadamo Trophy the following season.

1950-1959

SAINT ALOYSIUS 1955 TEAM (8-0)

SAINT ALOYSIUS 1958 TEAM (8-0)

1950 (6-3)

Balzli addressed the A Club on August 27th where support was reported high. Classes started on the 5th and the season started 10 days later at City Park against Newellton. Intensive drills had been ongoing for the past three weeks. Balzli was a *"devotee of the T-system"* but was now putting in the Single-Wing for 1950 since his team was *"heavy .. this year"* and *"was best adapted to the single wing"*. The paper thought *"The grid machine presented by Balzli on that night will be reminiscent of the Balzli-coached teams of the late thirties"*.

A scrimmage against alumni on September 10th was described as *"very helpful in several ways"*. They worked out each afternoon starting at 3pm and had their last hard work out before the first game. Thin in reserves, they still had the *"spirit"* undaunted by the rain that fell after 5 weeks of practice in the heat. Balzli thought them *"just about the best he has ever had during his years at St. Aloysius High"*. Buddy Wood would co-captain the team.

On the other side of the river, Newellton was going through its own changes. Two or three players on a team described as *"small in number"* and *"especially lean this year due to graduations"* had decided not to play.

GAME 1:   SAINT AL (0-0) vs NEWELLTON, LA (0-0)
                     FINAL: ST AL 35 NEWELLTON 6
                     September 15, 1950

Saint Al hosted *"Eight adult polio patients from Lutheran Hospital"* in the north side of the field across from the stands to join *"One of the largest crowds to ever witness a St. Aloysius game..."* Saint Al scored midway through the 1st after starting at the Newellton 47. Sonny Schaff gained 10 and Bob O'Neill hit Jack Davidson to the 1. Buddy Wood carried in from there and Clint Schlottman made it 7-0. Before the quarter ended, a Schlottman punt was fumbled by Newellton at their 28 and recovered by "Bubber" Evans. Runs by Schaff, Baylot, O'Neill, and Wood put the ball at the Newellton 3 before Shaff crashed in for the touchdown. Schlottman's kick made it 14-0.

As the 2nd closed, Saint Al held Newellton on downs at the Flash 43. On 2nd down, Wood took a pitch and went 57 yards for the score. Schlottman made his 3rd PAT for a 21-0 halftime lead. The 3rd saw the Flashes start from their 15 and drive for a score behind a John Durst run from the 4. Schlottman made it 28-0. Newellton's only tally came in the 4th when Douel dove in from the 2. The Woods PAT was blocked by Evans. The final score came when another Schlottman punt was fumbled and recovered by the Flashes at the Newellton 7. Durst gained 4 and then Fred Groome plunged in. O'Neill hit Mike Riddle for the PAT and the final points.

GAME 2:   SAINT AL (1-0) vs DELHI, LA (1-0)
                     FINAL: ST AL 0 DELHI 25
                     September 22, 1950

Though Balzli was pleased with the win, *"when he refers to the game with Delhi, he reaches for the crying towel. It is no secret that the Aloysius coach is doubtful that his boys can cope with the fine eleven from Richland parish"*. The Delhi boys had lost only 3 games in two years, and Balzli was putting his second-stringers through strenuous 45-minute scrimmages to build depth. In fact, long and hard scrimmages were norm that week. Durst would start after his performance against Newellton. *"The Flashes are showing excellent spirit and refuse to concede that the Louisiana boys will be victorious."*

Saint Al stopped the visitors just as the whistle sounded at the Flash 5 to keep halftime 0-0. But starting the 3rd, a fumble put the Bears at the Flash 23. Hopkins ran to the 1-foot line a few plays later and then Best scored. As the 3rd drew to a close, Brunley scored to cap a 33 yard drive. Andrews made it 13-0 with the PAT. The Bears took over at the Flash 40 midway through the 4th. Snider came in for Andrews and then hit Best for a 15 yard touchdown pass. The Flashes threw an interception afterwards that set up the last touchdown. On 4th down, Andrews found Hall at the Flash 7. Andrews would go in from the 2 but could not hit his receiver for the PAT.

GAME 3:   SAINT AL (1-1) @ FLORA (UNREPORTED)
                   FINAL: ST AL 32 FLORA 0
                   October 8, 1950

The paper said "*The Aloysius coach is preparing just as hard for the Flora game … as for any other… The Flashes should be returned the victors in that contest, but this will be the only light game remaining on the schedule…*" Focusing on his 2nd string, he put the boys though tough practices on the 26th with intensity tapering off before game-time. Baylot and Evans had colds and Quirk had a sprained ankle, but all were expected to compete. The team left that in the afternoon "*accompanied by many students and supporters*".

The Flashes took out frustrations on the Hinds County boys by scoring three times in the opening frame. After holding Flora on the kick, the Flashes took 5 plays before Durst went through for the score. After holding the Lions again, O'Neill hit Schlottman for a 75 yard strike. The quarter closed with two runs by Buddy Wood for a touchdown. The PAT made it 19-0.

O'Neill started the 2nd with an untouched 55 yard punt return for a score. Every reserve player took the field in the game; many as early as the 2nd. Up 26-0, the Flashes put up their last touchdown in the 3rd. O'Neill returned a punt 40 yards to the Lion 35, Durst and Wood got it to the 10, and Wood bulldozed in from there. The reserves continued to hold for the remainder, stopping the only deep Flora drive at the Flash 5.

GAME 4:   SAINT AL (2-1) vs SAINT JOHNS, LA (0-3)
                   FINAL: ST AL 18 SAINT JOHNS 7
                   October 8, 1950

Saint Johns, with an enrollment three times that of Saint Al, was "*definitely favored, but the Flashes are not conceding anything to the Shreveport boys…*" The visitor's line averaged 174 pounds, they regularly scheduled the top Louisiana teams as opponents, and were "*reported to have a smooth operating machine*". Balzli put his group though heavy scrimmages during the week and the paper noted that "*A vastly improved Flash team could well upset the dope over the favored Shreveport boys.*" Saint Johns arrived in Vicksburg on the 7th and stayed overnight at The Hotel Vicksburg.

Saint Johns scored first in the 2nd after a Flash fumble gave them the ball at the 50. Only a few plays in, Jerry Lynch found Joe Pistorious for a 45 yard touchdown strike. Gottee's kick made it a 7-0 Flyer lead. On the ensuing kick, Wood used his blockers to get the 75 yards and the touchdown. In the closing minutes, Saint Al pinned the Flyers on their 20. Saint Johns' Gottee fumbled on the first play and Bob Marlett recovered at the Flyer 12. Durst, on several runs, crossed the goal for the lead. The PAT was wide, but halftime was in favor of Saint Al 12-7.

Midway through the 3rd, Gottee fumbled again at the Flyer 38 and it was recovered by Billy Bufkin. O'Neill hit Schlottman for 32. Consecutive runs by Wood eventually paid off with a dive from the 1. The "*battered and bruised but highly elated*" Flashes would hold the Shreveport team for the remainder of the game and provide the upset for local fans.

GAME 5:   SAINT AL (3-1) vs FERRIDAY, LA (3-1)
                   FINAL: ST AL 0 FERRIDAY 6
                   October 13, 1950

The previous game had been brutal on the Flashes. Horace "Bubber" Long had a leg injury that would keep him out for 2 weeks, Evans had a sprained ankle, and O'Neil had a head blow so serious that "*he suffered a temporary complete loss of memory*". Practices were therefore lighter this week in spite of the fact that Ferriday had scouted the Flashes last game.

The first half was a "*see-saw*" struggle. The Flashes recovered a Ferriday fumble in the 1st, but couldn't convert. In return, Ferriday drove to the Flash 19 but was held. The second saw the Flashes get as far as the Ferriday 19 before O'Neill was intercepted by Cuthbertson. The Flashes held, and even blocked the ensuing punt, but again could not make it count.

The game was decided in the 3rd. Starting at the 20, a series of runs put Ferriday at their 36. Cuthbertson broke through the Flash center and raced 64 yards for the touchdown but Durst blocked the Massey attempt for the PAT. Ferriday came close to scoring again in the 4th but lost on downs at the Flash 21. Saint Al would get no further than the Bulldog 39 the remainder of the game.

GAME 6:   SAINT AL (3-2) vs CRYSTAL SPRINGS (4-2)
                        FINAL: ST AL 12 CRYSTAL SPRINGS 13
                        October 19, 1950

With injuries and lack of hard scrimmages, the Ferriday loss wasn't a complete surprise to Balzli. He still had banged-up players this week, now including Jack Canizaro, but began scrimmages after a light Monday workout. The coach considered *"the Crystal Springs Tigers as the finest team to appear against Aloysius on the home field this year"* and was *"staying awake at nights trying to figure ways and means of stopping the Tigers and getting the Flash offense rolling."* They enjoyed a nice winning record against the Flashes over the last few years. Prospects weren't helped by injuries to Evans, Long and Canizaro that would probably limit their use. Rain had fallen throughout the 18th, but the field was expected to drain well and be in better shape than the health of the Flashes.

Crystal Springs hit the board on their initial drive. Starting at their 43, Phillips capped it on a plunge from the 2. Purvis' PAT was good. Baylot closed the quarter with a 15 yard return of a Sojourner punt that gave the Flashes the ball at their 25. Wood ignited the crowd by starting the 2nd with a 65 yard touchdown pass to Schlottman. The Schlottman PAT was blocked. Before the 2nd ended, Crystal Springs put together a 52 yard drive highlighted by a 30 yard pass completion from Sojourner to Purvis at the Flash 10. Bush took it on a reverse from there for the touchdown and a 13-6 halftime lead.

Saint Al got their answering touchdown midway through the 3rd. Starting at the Flash 44, and behind numerous runs and passes, Baylot took it 25 yards for the score. The Flashes had two attempts for the PAT after a penalty, but could get neither. That would be the difference in the contest. While Bufkin had picked off a Tiger pass afterwards, Baylot also fumbled away another drive that could have change the outcome. Highlighting difference in reporting in the time before information was widely available, Vicksburg had the Tigers as 1-1-1 but their paper reported them as 4-2.

GAME 7:   SAINT AL (3-3) @ MENDENHALL (4-2)
                        FINAL: ST AL 33 MENDENHALL 7
                        October 27, 1950

The Saint Aloysius A Club sponsored a trip to New Orleans for the boys on the previous Saturday to see the Tulane-Ole Miss game. They stayed at the Bienville Hotel and came back on Sunday. Upon return, they faced at least three scrimmages to prepare for a team *"considered by Coach Joe Balzli much stronger than last year. Their 13-13 tie with Clinton indicates their strength."* Mendenhall had scouted Saint Al twice this year and was comparable to Crystal Springs in play.

Mendenhall was praised for playing *"the game for keeps, but they have been coached to play a good, clean game and the series ... with the Tigers has been noted for sportsmanship. The Flashes are not overconfident about the contest, but believe they will get back on the winning side after two straight defeats"*. All injured players were expected back and *"Physically, the Flashes are at about their best since the season's opener, while mentally, the boys seem to be up"*.

Saint Al dominated the entire 1st half. Mendenhall fumbled their first possession on their 10 and Canizaro recovered. On the 4th play, O'Neill found Schlottman for a 3 yard touchdown. Schlottman converted to make it 7-0. Taking over on the Tiger 25 after a bad snap, Wood wasted no time in scoring the next one standing up. The 2nd saw O'Neil recover another Tiger fumble at their 39. The drive had 3 first downs before Wood burst in from the 2. Schlottman's kick made it 20-0 at halftime.

Mendenhall's Peacock scored from the 2 early in the 3rd, but Saint Al would respond. It took 8 plays before O'Neill hit Baylot from the Mendenhall 23 for the touchdown. Schlottman made the PAT and subsequently picked off a pass in the same quarter. The final score would be set up by a 69 yard run by Wood to the Tiger 21. O'Neill finished the drive with a 6 yard touchdown pass to Schlottman. Mike Riddle's attempted conversion catch was not good.

GAME X: SAINT AL (4-3) @ ROLLING FORK (5-2)
                        FINAL: NOT PLAYED
                        November 3, 1950

The game was to be Rolling Fork's homecoming tilt and *"rated the best game of the week in Class BB circles in Mississippi"*. The Flashes worked hard during the week since they knew the toughness of the Bearcats. While readying themselves to leave Friday afternoon, all eyes were on the sky. It had rained heavily the past night and this day wasn't much better. The game would be cancelled as the Rolling Fork "field was in no condition to play". The two teams proposed alternate dates but neither worked with the other. "It seems unlikely the contest will be played at all". It was not.

GAME 8:   SAINT AL (4-3) @ CATHOLIC HIGH, TN (UNREPORTED)
                FINAL: ST AL 18 CATHOLIC HIGH 0
                November 12, 1950

        Since the Rolling Fork game was cancelled, Balzli gave the boys Monday off. When they started on Tuesday, he put them through heavy pass defensive drills considering what had happened in their last contest. He was expecting a pass-heavy attack and was counting on a secondary that had been playing well thus far.
        Some players were suffering small colds on Friday, so Balzli had chalkboard sessions instead of scrimmages. On Saturday morning after 8am Mass, they left for Memphis and worked out at Hodges Field in the afternoon. They stayed at the Catholic Club of Memphis that evening and awoke with cold conditions to greet them. Fifty Flash fans followed and would return with them on Monday. "The Flashes will be against Class AA opposition next Sunday, but they are capable of pulling an upset. They have had two weeks rest since their last game and are in top condition."
        Both teams turned the ball over on fumbles in the 1st, but neither was able to capitalize. The 2nd started the same as both teams turned the ball over on fumbles. Saint Al took advantage of one when Wood hit Schlottman for a 79 yard touchdown pass. After another Saint Al fumble, the Terriers then did what Balzli expected by taking to the air. Saint Al was up to the task with O'Neill picking it off to keep the half a 6-0 lead.
        O'Neill kept up the barrage by picking off another Ryan pass to start the 3rd at the Terrier 24. Baylot and Wood pushed to the 9 and then Wood found Schlottman for an 8 yard touchdown. In the 4th, Ryan was intercepted for the 3rd time by Wood but the drive wouldn't last. On the punt, however, Catholic fumbled and Davidson recovered at the Terrier 1. O'Neill quickly took it in on a QB sneak for the final score and the win. The Durst try for the PAT was costly. He was hurt on the play and taken to Saint Joseph's Hospital, but the evaluation was positive.
        As a sidenote, on that Wednesday, the S.A.C. principal of what was thought to be the first Flash football team passed away. Brother Lambert served from 1911-1913 and had died in Saint Louis. His funeral would be attended by Brother Mark.

GAME 9:   SAINT AL (5-3) @ CLINTON (2-6-1)
                FINAL: ST AL 40 CLINTON 13
                November 17, 1950

        Durst wasn't the only one banged up. Bob Marlett was hit in the mouth hard enough to have "several teeth … loosened, but the fine guard will be ready against Clinton." The Flashes had only three days to prepare for Clinton after their Monday return, and Balzli would focus that time on the defense since he was pleased with the offensive production in Memphis. "As this is the last game of the year for Aloysius, they will use every play at their disposal to close the season with a victory."
        In his final game as a Flash, "It was Baylot night over Clinton… Bobby Baylot was the brightest star on the field. The diminutive left half wound up his school playing days in the proverbial blaze of glory scoring four touchdowns and sparking his teammates to victory". He started by returning the opening kick 86 yards to the Arrow 6. Two plays later, he broke tough for the touchdown. The Arrows fumbled on ensuing drive at the Flash 4 to keep the score 6-0.
        Baylott started the 2nd by running 75 yards for a touchdown. Schlottman made it 13-0. Clinton immediately responded when Byrd crossed the goal from the inside the 10. That play was set up by his pass to Tann for 44 yards. Byrd fumbled as he went into the endzone, but the officials determined he had crossed the goal beforehand. The Flashes came right back after O'Neill returned the kick 44 yards to the Arrow 41. From the 23, O'Neill found Baylot and, with Schlottman's PAT, made it 20-6 at halftime.
        The 3rd found the Arrows going for 4th down but failing at their 36. O'Neill hit Baylot for 26 yards and then Canizaro did the rest from there. Schlottman made it 27-6. Bufkin stalled another Clinton drive midway through the 3rd with a pickoff but the home team held. They did fumble on the next possession, however, with Saint Al getting the ball at the Arrow 15. Baylot scored again; this time from the 12 to make it 33-6. The Arrows' best drive came immediately afterwards, going 70 yards in 9 plays with Byrd diving in from the 4. His PAT made it 33-13.

The bench cleared to start the 4th for Saint Al and forced Byrd into a fumble at the Arrow 38 that was recovered by Marlett. O'Neill would find Schlottman for the last touchdown from the 12 and a 40-13 win. Both teams had accumulated exactly 312 yards of offense, but *"It was by far the best game played by Aloysius this year"*. One touchdown and one PAT would keep the Flashes from an 8-1 season.

Bobby Baylot won the inaugural Virgadamo Trophy for 1950 and later said about the year:

"Many of us, not only athletes, but everyone who came in contact with Coach Balzli shared a special friendship. I can remember when I was in the eighth grade. We would play a tag game at recess in which everyone tagged would help hold you to be tagged by whoever was 'it'. I was pretty fast and would hardly ever get caught. Joe would watch us at recess. One day he invited me to play on the varsity football squad. This was a great time of my life; a time when I learned from the best.

I remember in my freshman year playing Crystal Springs. Early in the first quarter, Tommy Thomas sprained his ankle. Well, you know who was Tommy's sub? Oh yes; all 120 pounds of me. Well I did pretty well except for a fumble late in the game. It was on their one-yard line. Instead of a win, we lost. Boy did I feel bad. The next day, Coach Balzli taught me how to learn from my mistakes. After a talk with Joe that day, I felt a little better about myself. I learned how to hold on to the ball and can't remember fumbling after that.

I can remember a touchdown, a pat on the back by Joe, winning game, winning the Virgadamo Trophy. These things made me feel great. But what I remember most of all about Joe Balzli was his dedication, his show of character, his confidence, and how he helped us grow as young Christian men.

Joe had confidence in me and taught me many things that made my life a little better. There are many things I remember about those years, but I can't share them now for it would take a book to do so. God bless my friend Joe Balzli."

Bobby Baylot; October 1995

1951 (4-3-1)

Joe Balzli put his charges through *"... lengthy workouts each evening on the Aloysius athletic field"* as reported on September 7th. The paper thought that, though losing several key pieces due to graduation, the team was rounding into shape and promised *"... to give a good account of itself as the season progresses"*. John Durst, providing *"... the greatest punch in the Flash backfield"*, and Bob O'Neill, *"A tall boy ... very cool under pressure and regarded as a brainy QB..."*, served as team captains.

GAME 1:   SAINT AL (0-0) @ DELHI, LA (1-0)
            FINAL: ST AL 6 DELHI 38
            September 21, 1951

Delhi had won 14 of the last 15 games, had won the District B crown, and were in the finals of the Louisiana State Playoffs. It would be even tougher on the Flashes relative to injuries. Clint Schlottman would be used sparingly due to a pulled muscle but Mike Riddle would be out due to an infected foot. John Campbell already had a broken wrist and Henry Bauni had a severe cut on his eye. Balzli bemoaned the fact that he couldn't get a game scheduled before this one. In his mind, this would be the toughest of the year.

Following a Charlie Wyly run to the Flash 16, Delhi's first touchdown came on a Milford Andrews pass to Norman Derouen. The Bears recovered an O'Neill fumble at the Flash 20 and Andrews hit Derouen again from there. Andrews' PAT made it 14-0 at the end of the 1st. In the 2nd, an O'Neill pass to Mike Riddle was picked off by Derouen on the Flash 34. They got to the Flash 1 before losing on downs. Wyly scored on the next possession from the Flash 5. After putting together a decent drive, O'Neill was picked off again by Patterson at the Delhi 25 who took it to the Flash 34. Andrews found Hartley from the 16 to cap the drive and make halftime 26-0. Delhi got in twice in the 3rd when Andrews snuck in from the 2 and later when Derouen took an O'Neil punt for 85 yards.

After a bad snap on a 4th quarter punt, the Flashes took control of the ball at the Delhi 1. John Durst burst in for the touchdown but Schlottman's PAT was missed. While praising the effort against a clearly better squad, the paper said *"... the Flashes never had the necessary stamina ... and also were found wanting in means to stop (the passing and running of Delhi)"*. However, *"There were no alibis offered for the Delhi loss. Players and coach were unanimous in their praise of the Bears for the fine team they put on the field. They were also highly complementary of their opponents in the matter of clean playing and good sportsmanship. The Flashes to a man stated this was one of the cleanest games they ever played."*

GAME 2:　　　　　　SAINT AL (0-1) vs HOLLANDALE (UNREPORTED)
　　　　　　　　　　FINAL: ST AL 44 HOLLANDALE 6
　　　　　　　　　　September 28, 1951

Balzli was undaunted by the Delhi loss, noting satisfaction of the play of the backfield. Practices concentrating on line play were held starting the 24th in preparation for a Hollandale team that had *"not been playing for several years"*. Rain hampered his practices on both Monday and Tuesday, and Balzli was unhappy about practice attitudes. So, instead of one scrimmage, the coach would have two. The good news was that the team was healthy when kickoff came.

Early in the 1st, Sonny Schaff rushed for 20 to the Hollandale 40. The drive got to the 15 on runs by John Durst and Schaff, and to the 2 on a pass from O'Neill to Schlottman. Schaff went in from there for a 6-0 lead. At the end of the quarter, John Durst recovered a fumble at the Flash 40. On the opening play of the 2nd, Durst got in from the 3 for the touchdown and Schlottman added the PAT.

The Flashes scored three more times in the quarter. The first was a Riddle run from the 8. The second followed a Bill Carrigan punt block that Jack Davidson brought back to the 7. Joe Durst plunged in from the 1 to cap the drive. The third followed an interception by John Durst at the Flash 48 when O'Neill ran for 43 on a QB sneak. Halftime gave the Flashes a 32-0 lead. Hollandale's lone touchdown came in the 3rd against the Flash second and third-string when Cope ran in from 21. Saint Al responded immediately with a Mickey Koestler kick return of 81 yards for the touchdown. To open the 4th, Carrigan blocked another punt at the Hollandale 17 and then ran it in.

GAME 3:　　　　　　SAINT AL (1-1) @ NATCHEZ CATHEDRAL (2-0)
　　　　　　　　　　FINAL: ST AL 20 NATCHEZ CATHEDRAL 0
　　　　　　　　　　October 7, 1951

Cathedral was undefeated despite the loss of several injured players. They would return against the Flashes and Balzli held *"long and strenuous workouts to prepare"*. The Flashes had a few players who were sitting out hard practices due to injuries. They included Riddle (shoulder), Davidson (arm), and Carrigan (finger). Natchez had respect for Saint Al, with their paper saying *"... it's just possible that Coach Joe Balzli's St. Aloysius squad might be better all-around than (Chamberlain Hunt's) eleven, which was terrific in spots. St. Aloysius plays several very strong teams each football season, some of which are in a higher class, giving them the benefit of experience gained under very tough circumstances."*

The Flashes' promising first drive was dashed by a fumble at the Cathedral 18. The defense held and forced a terrible punt that gave Saint Al the ball at the Natchez 14. John Durst gained 4 and Riddle gained the other 10 for the touchdown. Their next drive ended poorly when O'Neill's pass was picked off by Ferguson. Durst was next into the endzone for Saint Al from the 2 and Schlottman made it 13-0. There would be one more touchdown before halftime; a 45 yard run by Schaff, but it was called back for offsides.

In the 3rd, the Flashes threatened when Koestler ran for 50 to the Cathedral 19. But the offense sputtered and Natchez took over at their 6. The Flashes got the last score of the contest following a Cathedral fumble recovered by Walter Smith at the CHS 35. Schaff would take it in from 29 out and, with Schlottman's kick, seal the game.

GAME 4:　　　　　　SAINT AL (2-1) vs BYRAM (3-1)
　　　　　　　　　　FINAL: ST AL 13 BYRAM 7
　　　　　　　　　　October 12, 1951

Byram was considered a strong contender for the Class BB championship. They had been runner-up in District 6 in 1950. The Flashes were fairly healthy, however, and were now battle-tested. In spite of Schlottman (shoulder) being questionable for the game, the paper called it *"evenly matched"*.

The game would be a slugfest, with both teams scoring in the 1st. Saint Al's came on a 68 yard run by O'Neill and a Schlottman PAT. Byram would put theirs up on a Durwood Martin pass to

Dexter Scruggs from the 18. Their PAT was also good. The next two quarters would be a back-and-forth affair. *"The Aloysius line played a whale of a game stopping the heavy Byram backs on the ground. It was only when the Bulldogs took to the air that they could penetrate the Aloysius defense."*

Early in the 4th, the Flashes put together a drive that allowed John Durst to punch through for the game winning touchdown. *"The tilt last night was an exceedingly rough one. Byram received a number of penalties for unnecessary roughness"*. Among the *"number of injuries"* was O'Neill. Though taken from the field, he did manage to return before the game was over.

GAME 5:   SAINT AL (3-1) @ YAZOO CITY (3-2)
                      FINAL: ST AL 7 YAZOO CITY 33
                      October 19, 1951

Yazoo City fielded a tough and heavy team featuring 14 returning lettermen and a stable of strong running backs in Bubba Barrier, Billy Coleman, Bobby Rhodes and Robert Pugh. The Flashes had recovered from the Byram scrap and were prepared to keep their unexpected winning streak going. Balzli and the team were reported to have scouted the Indians two weeks previously against Cleveland.

The Indians scored immediately after blocking a Saint Al punt at the Flash 46. Runs and passes put the ball at the 12 before Coleman hit Rhodes for the touchdown. The PAT was blocked by Carrigan. In the same frame, Barrier ran in from 12 to finish a 75 yard drive. They added to that in the 2nd when Coleman took a Schlottman punt back 48 yards for a score. Guthrie's PAT made halftime 20-0.

Saint Al opened the 3rd by fumbling to Yazoo City at the Flash 40. After driving to the 12, Nowlin raced for the touchdown. Saint Al put up their only points in the frame when Durst dove in from the 4. The drive was set up by O'Neill passes to Riddle and Carrigan. O'Neill converted the extra point. The Indians would score once more in the 4th when Barrier broke though the secondary.

GAME 6:   SAINT AL (3-2) vs MENDENHALL (4-2)
                      FINAL: ST AL 19 MENDENHALL 12
                      October 26, 1951: HOMECOMING

Homecoming week would find Schlottman injured in a scrimmage and out for the game. Durst and Schaff were also banged up, meaning that *"… injuries might lessen the Flashes chance against the Tigers"*. Mendenhall was traditionally tough and their split-T formation was *"hard to handle at times"*. Homecoming festivities were in swing with a big pep rally held on the 25th. Durst, O'Neill and Balzli gave speeches and a replay of the 1951 Kentucky-Oklahoma Sugar Bowl game was shown.

The Flashes had won three of the four games played against the Tigers, but the relationship between the schools had always been *"particularly cordial"*. Mendenhall had a new coach in A.J. Mangum and had lost two close games to good teams. Clinton had beaten them 12-0 and Magee (considered the number one team in District 6) had squeaked by 6-0. The Tigers, unbeknownst to Saint Al, had numerous men on the *"crippled"* list.

The Flashes went straight to work with O'Neill completions to Koestler and Riddle that got the ball to the 4. John Durst then burst through for the touchdown. Midway through the 2nd, O'Neill hit Carrigan for a 76 yard strike and a 12-0 lead. After the play, Carrigan would leave the game due to sickness and not return. Just before half, O'Neill threw another touchdown pass; this time to Leo Seymour from the 23. His PAT made the halftime lead 19-0 and would end Flash scoring.

Mendenhall attempted a comeback with two 4th quarter touchdowns. Gerald Morgan scored from the 3 on a QB sneak to cap a 40 yard drive. Morgan hit Arthur Weathersby for a 40 yarder to the Flash 12 to set up their last. A Magee run took the ball to the 3 and then Dan Peacock went in from there. Mendenhall missed on both PAT attempts.

GAME 7:   SAINT AL (4-2) vs CLINTON (UNREPORTED)
                      FINAL: ST AL 7 CLINTON 26
                      November 3, 1951

The only injury other than Carrigan was to John Groome. A lacerated lip took him out of the Mendenhall game, but he was expected to return along with Schlottman for the last home game of 1951. Clinton was acknowledged as the favorite, having beaten Byram and Mendenhall by larger scores, but the paper said *"…Aloysius will have a psychological factor which may upset pre-game calculations"*. Balzli actually took it somewhat easy during practices with little scrimmaging and workouts without pads to tune their timing. He also focused on *"... keeping the boys up mentally..."*

Clinton scored in every quarter with their first score via a Turcotte run from the Flash 25. Gilmore made it 7-0. The 2nd featured a series of turnovers. The Flashes fumbled 2 but recovered one; O'Neill threw 2 interceptions; and the Arrows fumbled one. In the end, Turcotte ran 66 yards to the 1 foot line before Gilmore took it over for the next touchdown. Halftime had Flashes down 13-0.

Turnovers continued in the 3rd with another O'Neill pick and a George Ellis fumble recovery. The Flashes took advantage of theirs with Mickey Koestler plowing through from the 12 to score the lone touchdown. Schlottman converted for a 13-7 deficit. Clinton responded with passes to Turcotte and Gilmore to move the ball to the Flash 15. Wright would score a few plays later from the 3. Hammond's kick was good. The 4th saw the 4th interception of O'Neill, this time by Wright, to give Clinton the ball at the Flash 23. Kelly then found Livingston a few plays later from the 13 for the final score of the contest.

GAME 8:	SAINT AL (4-3) @ SAINT JOHNS, LA (UNREPORTED)
	FINAL: ST AL 6 SAINT JOHNS 6
	November 11, 1951

The Flashes, along with roughly 60 fans, traveled to Shreveport on Saturday night to face a Louisiana Class A team equal to a Mississippi Class AA. Practices were extensive but not overly-rough in order to stay healthy. The boys stayed overnight both Saturday and Sunday awaiting a team with *"weight and experience"* on their side. Even with the loss of JoJo Pistorius, the Flyers were still two touchdown favorites.

The field had seen action the night before and was drenched from heavy rains. As such, the slippery field made the going tough for both squads. Saint Johns took advantage of a rushed Wood punt that gave them the ball at the Flash 26. LeBlanc went in from the 5 but Sardino's PAT missed to keep halftime a 6-0 affair. With 2:20 left in the game, Carrigan became the hero by blocking a Fulcoe punt at the Flyer 25. O'Neill found John Durst for 13 yards and a first down, Durst gained another 11, and Schaff and O'Neill each gained 1. John Durst then cracked the center to tie the game. The crucial PAT by Schlottman was blocked. Schlottman would pick off a late Beuven pass attempt to seal the tie. It would be *"... the first time in Coach Balzli's coaching career one of his teams played a tie game"*.

Clint Schlottman would win the Virgadamo Trophy for the year. He later commented:

"It was my privilege, both as a teenager (when he was my coach and role model) and as an adult (when he was my friend) to know Joe Balzli as a true Christian gentleman. His stern manner, raucous voice, and the ever-present cigar concealed a kind and gentle inner self. Joe demanded hard work and clean sportsmanship as prerequisite for victory. He required rededication to excellence after defeat. Except for my father, Joe Balzli was the most influential person in my life."

Clint Schlottman; October, 1995

1952 (5-1-1)

The Flashes started practices August 18th without 10 of 11 starters and 13 of 14 leading players. The coach noted that he had *"one of the smallest and the most inexperienced squads he has had in his seventeen years at Aloysius"* but despite the fact, ... the boys are all willing and anxious and are taking their football seriously." The paper called the upcoming season "... *an off year for the Flashes, with Balzli faced with the task of rebuilding his grid machine. ... Though they may not win a game, none of the gridiron contests scheduled for this year will be walk-aways for the opponents"*.

By September 10th, the coach though the squad to be *"rounding into shape"*. They were healthy thus far, *"but how long we will be free of injuries is not known"*. Returning player William Carrigan would serve as team captain.

GAME 1:   SAINT AL (0-0) @ TCHULA (0-0)
               FINAL: ST AL 13 TCHULA 13
               September 12, 1952

The boys and the fans left on Friday afternoon. Balzli said "*Though Tchula may beat us, it will give the boys on my team a real test which will afford me an opportunity to see what they can do under fire*". In the game, Tchula took an early lead when Lacey Chapman ran for a 31 yard touchdown. Saint Al responded as the 1st ended when John Wood ran one in at close range. Early in the 2nd, Fred Groome returned a Tchula punt to the Panther 20. Wood found Warren Doiron for 8 and then Wood crashed through for the 12 yard touchdown and extra point. Halftime would have the Flashes up 13-6.

The home team tied the contest as the 4th was coming to a close. A Wood punt was blocked at the Flash 35 and Tchula capitalized. Runs by Chapman, Spivey and Gordon put the ball at the 7 and Gordon went in from there and added the valuable extra point. The paper noted that the game was hard fought and that "*Fumbles were plentiful on the part of both elevens. However, Aloysius fumbles proved more costly than their opponents'. Aloysius had several opportunities to score, but on each of these occasions, the drive was halted. The Flashes stopped two scoring attempts of the Tchula squad.*"

GAME X: SAINT AL (0-0-1) vs ROLLING FORK (0-0)
               FINAL: NOT PLAYED
               September 19, 1952

On Sunday the 14th, it was announced that the contest would not be played. A "*polio situation*" plagued Rolling Fork and surrounding area and medical authorities advised Bearcat head coach Kelly Horn to cancel the game. Rolling Fork had actually told Balzli a couple of days before, but the head man endeavored to schedule another opponent before announcing plans. No open date would match for either team at a later date, so Saint Al would enjoy an open week.

GAME 2:   SAINT AL (0-0-1) vs SAINT MATTHEWS, LA (0-1)
               FINAL: ST AL 19 SAINT MATTHEWS 0
               September 28, 1952

The Monroe team was reported by Coach Jay Broussard as light and inexperienced, but enjoyed a weight advantage. They had just lost to Wisner (LA) the previous week 10-7 but came to Vicksburg with a large delegation to see the contest at City Park. Between practices, Balzli attended the Aloysius A Club meeting on the 24th. As the game neared, he would be missing three players to injuries in Sam Tuccio, John Marsicano and Harry Sutton.

On a "*rather dusty field before a large crowd*", the Flashes went to work. On the opening play of the 2nd, Wood secured a QB sneak for a touchdown. His pass to John Hartley for the extra point failed. Midway through the 3rd, Saint Matthews fumbled to the Flashes. Warren Doiron and Wood got the ball to the 50. Fred Groome, Leo Seymour and Joe Durst moved the ball to the 14. The final two plays were from Wood with a 13 yard run and a QB sneak. A second PAT pass to Seymour failed.

In the 4th, a Riddle punt block set up the last score. After runs and penalties, Groome took a Balfour Wallace pitch for the touchdown. Woods pass to Riddle completed scoring at 19-0. Saint Matthews gained their only 1st down of the game afterwards against reserves but an ensuing fumble was recovered by Bob Alvarado to seal the win.

GAME 3:   SAINT AL (1-0-1) vs NATCHEZ CATHEDRAL (3-0)
               FINAL: ST AL 0 NATCHEZ CATHEDRAL 27
               October 5, 1952

Upon hearing The Natchez Democrat proclaim Saint Al a touchdown favorite, Balzli disagreed. "*True we won by a 20-0 score (in 1951), but we have lost 10 of our starting 11, and 13 of our first 14 men. Natchez has suffered the loss of only 2 men from its entire squad and certainly these comparative losses do not substantiate this prediction. Further, their backfield outweighs our backfield by 29 pounds per man and as much, if not more, in the line.*" Our paper said "*It is a general consensus of unbiased opinion that Natchez is at least a three touchdown favorite this year...*" Balzli put that number as high as six.

With odds already against them per Balzli's evaluation and the injuries to Carrigan (head), Wood (ankle) and Groome (toe), the Flashes were put even further behind by injuries to Joe Durst (broken collar bone) and Doiron (lacerated left hand requiring 3 stitches). Durst would stay overnight in the "Infirmary". Natchez also had concerns with fullback Charles Ferguson injured in an auto accident that Friday. He would play, and in the first minute, he broke loose for a 70 yard touchdown run. In the final minute of the 2nd, they scored again when Gerald Pitchford blocked a Flash punt on the 30 and took it in for a touchdown. Halftime was a 13-0 lead.

Early in the 3rd, the Saint Al fumbled to Cathedral at the Flash 31. Runs by Pat McDonough, Eddie Davis, Charles Burke and Ferguson took the ball to the 3 before Burke crossed the goal. Davis' kick made it 20-0. The Greenies put the last touchdown in the 4th from Pitchford. Davis made the PAT and sealed the 27-0 shutout. Said Balzli afterward, *"They had too many horses and we had too few ponies"*. Both Burke and Ferguson would have over 1,000 rushing yards on the season.

GAME 4:   SAINT AL (1-1-1) vs WASHINGTON (0-3)
                    FINAL: ST AL 25 WASHINGTON 6
                    October 10, 1952

Durst was now gone for the season, Doiron was doubtful (but would play), and other injuries were costly. Balzli had to *"revamp his entire squad"* and started practice on Sunday. Against Washington's spread formation, Saint Al was called *"on paper ... several touchdowns better than Washington, but with the injury situation as it is the teams should be pretty evenly matched and the prospects all point up the fact that Friday's game will be a thriller"*. L.M. Rogers of the (Jackson) Clarion-Ledger put the Flashes as 2 point favorites.

Saint Al's first drive of the 1st was behind runs from Doiron, Hartley and Wood. Doiron would get the touchdown from the 15. Carrigan picked off a Washington pass on the ensuing drive followed by big runs by Doiron and Hartley. From the 19, Hartley found Wood for a touchdown and then Wood added the PAT a sneak. In the same quarter, Doiron scored again; this time from the 43 to make halftime 19-0.

On the final play of the 3rd, Carrigan picked off another Pirate pass to set up a Wood touchdown from the 10 in the 4th. Washington's only score came after a 20 yard Frank Roberts run and 20 yards of Flash penalties. On 4th and 4, Roberts went in for the touchdown.

GAME 5:   SAINT AL (2-1-1) vs SALLIS (UNREPORTED)
                    FINAL: ST AL 25 SALLIS 0
                    October 24, 1952

Sallis had been conference champions on several occasions and were heavier. However, they were also in a rebuilding season and injury-plagued in their second string. The paper praised the *"know how"* of the defensive line play and gave *"hats off"* to Campbell, McTaggart, Franco, Hennessey, Scott, Madison, Seymour and Riddle. *"Spirit wins ball games and the once-beaten Flashes are out to add another win ... at the expense of Sallis"*. Brother Cecil's junior teams would open the evening, with Purple versus Gold. The Gold would win with a Hebert pass reception from McCormick to make it 6-0.

As for their big brothers, Saint Al put up three touchdowns in the 1st before stalling in the 2nd and 3rd. The opening drive saw Doiron gain 15 yards on two runs before taking the next one for a 42 yard touchdown. It was brought back on a motion penalty, but Wood passed to Carrigan on the next play for the score. Doiron hit again from the Sallis 43 immediately afterwards to make it 12-0. Before the quarter ended, Crowder fumbled to Hartley. Passes from Wood to Marsicano and Carrigan gained 23. A penalty hurt the Flashes but didn't stop Marsicano from converting on the following run. Wood made it 19-0.

Seymour's pickoff of Sallis was the only highlight of the 2nd, while the 3rd saw a Sallis fumble and a Wood pass intercepted. In the 4th, Hartley reeled off a 55 punt return that was returned 15 yards *"for slipping"*. On the following play, Doiron went the distance but was again called back; this time for off-sides. Not to be stopped, the Flashes mixed runs by Doiron and a pass to Carrigan to and Riddle. During the drive, yet another penalty stopped the march when Wood's pass to Riddle gained 15 but was called back. Wood eventually crashed in for the score from the 2. John Banchetti stopped a late Sallis drive by recovering a fumble on the Flash 39 one play before the game ended.

GAME 6:   SAINT AL (3-1-1) vs GREENVILLE SAINT JOSEPH (UNREPORTED)
               FINAL: ST AL 27 GREENVILLE SAINT JOSEPH 13
               November 2, 1952

It was becoming evident that Balzli's efforts to secure an eighth game were going to be unsuccessful. In the interim, he prepared for a team about which the only things known were that they had depth and a 180 pound fullback named Glen Powers. It was also reported to be the first football year for Greenville Saint Joe. Balzli was hard at work on practice week with concentration on *"various defensive maneuvers designed to confuse even the best-clicking offensive combinations."*

Reserves saw a lot of playing time in the contest as Balzli's boys jumped out early and often. The second-stringers took the field in the 2nd with regulars in only long enough to stay in condition for the Saint Joe game. Carrigan gave the Flashes the first score on an interception return for a 35 yard touchdown just minutes into the game. Wood made it 7-0. After holding the Irish to a punt, runs by Marsicano, Wood, and Carrigan moved the ball from the Greenville 38 to the Flash 7. Wood then took it in for the touchdown and Wood made it 14-0.

The third touchdown drive of the quarter started at the Irish 43. Doiron ran for 20 and then passed to Riddle at the Greenville 8. Wood took two runs before getting in and then made the PAT. The Irish responded when Azar returned a Flash punt 68 yards for the touchdown. Power made the PAT kick and it was 21-7 at halftime. In the 3rd, Riddle returned an Azar punt to the Flash 43. Then, Doiron found him for a 57 yard touchdown to make it 27-7. The last score came from Greenville in the 4th. Azar gained 30 to the Flash 15 and then took it the distance two plays later.

GAME 7:   SAINT AL (4-1-1) vs JACKSON SAINT JOSEPH (5-1)
               FINAL: ST AL 31 JACKSON SAINT JOSEPH 14
               November 9, 1952: HOMECOMING

Homecoming week featured a number of festivities. On the 6th, the A Club sponsored a pep rally at the Saint Al auditorium. The Homecoming Queen (Rita Faye Riddle), faculty, coaches, players, SFXA cheerleaders and the Saint Al band all participated. The Strauss-Stallings trophy was shown and Balzli was recognized for this being his 100th game as the Flashes head man.

Practices were spent on perfecting their game, but Balzli was aware that they couldn't survive another injury. *"The Jackson Rebels will afford the Flashes just about the strongest opposition (they have) encountered this year. While the Rebels are doped to win, the Flashes are a fighting outfit and are never licked until that final whistle"*. The Clarion Ledger had Saint Joe as three touchdown favorites.

The opening kick by Tucker Latham was returned by Wood to the Rebel 20 and then Doiron blasted through for the touchdown. Wood's run for the PAT made it 7-0. A few minutes later, Larry Hennessey blocked a David punt and the Flashes took over at the JSJ 8. Wood gained his second touchdown from there for a 13-0 lead. Before the quarter ended, Doiron returned a punt to the Rebel 45. His runs, along with those of Wood, Marsicano, Hartley and Carrigan, got the ball to the Jackson 3. Wood scored again from there.

Saint Joe capitalized on a nice punt and a penalty in the 2nd when they tackled Doiron for a safety. Right afterwards, Latham found Simon at the Flash 1 and then Amis plunged through for the touchdown to make halftime 19-8. Both teams would score in the 3rd. A mix of runs and passes by Saint Joe got the ball to the Flash 4 before Dupuy carried for the touchdown. Saint Al did likewise behind runs from Marsicano, Wood and Doiron to the Rebel 7. On 4th down, Wood got in and gave Saint Al a bit of breathing room headed to the 4th.

After holding the Rebels on downs at the Flash 37, Saint Al scored immediately when Carrigan snared a Doiron pass for a 63 yard touchdown run and season-ending victory. The paper said that *"The line play of the Flashes was just about the best of the season. Time and again they thwarted attempts by the Rebels to get through. The Flashes certainly concluded the year's schedule in a blaze of glory"*. After the game, the Rebel captain presented the Strauss-Stallings Trophy to Flash captain William Carrigan.

The team was rewarded by the A Club for their success by sponsoring a trip for everyone to see The Tulane-Vanderbilt football game in New Orleans on the 15th. The boys would stay overnight at the Jung Hotel and come back late Sunday. At the December banquet, Balzli was presented with a pen and pencil set, a chair, and glass cover for his desk and a hat. William Carrigan was presented with the Virgadamo Trophy.

"Our 1952 team was in a rebuilding mode, having lost 10 starters from the previous year. We had 5 seniors and a large class of us juniors. Our first game ended in a tie. Coach Balzli didn't like what he saw and junked the T-Formation we were running. The next time we hit the field, we were in the Princeton Single Wing. Throughout his coaching career, Joe was one of the most innovative coaches in the south; particularly on offense. He ran this offense with profound success until he retired. But we got it started in 1952!"

Joe Durst; August 5, 2016

1953 (6-2)

The 1953 edition of Flash football featured 13 returning lettermen for Balzli's 18th season. Sportswriter Billy Ray thought that the coach *"should field one of the best teams, according to size of players that he has ever turned out. All told, the Flashes line will average approximately 155 pounds with the backfield 5 pounds lighter, which is a fair high school average but doesn't compare with the powerful St. Aloysius teams of the past"*. Balzli said, *"I've coached bigger teams before but think this will be the best 'little' ball club I've ever coached. Their hustle and determination during these first few days of practice have been something to make any coach smile."*

Night practices started on the 18th with two-a-days beginning the following week. By September 1st, Balzli had the boys emphasizing defense and passing. On the 9th, Balzli attended the Saint Aloysius "A Club" to discuss the season and to *"tell about the team's prospects as he has analyzed up to this time"*. The starting lineup was announced on the 10th.

GAME 1:   SAINT AL (0-0) vs TCHULA (0-0)
                      FINAL: ST AL 26 TCHULA 0
                      September 11, 1953

The Flashes were originally scheduled to play *"a strong Tchula"* team there on Thursday, but a scheduling conflict moved the game to Friday and to Vicksburg. Starting Fullback John Wood would be doubtful due to a twisted knee but otherwise the team was healthy and would try to erase the tie from the last game against the Delta squad.

Saint Al scored on their first possession, managing a 56 yard drive capped by Warren Doiron from the 5. In the 2nd, John Hartley found Mike Riddle for a long *"beautifully-executed"* touchdown. James Peacock took the ball in for the extra point. Midway through the 3rd, Doiron broke away for a 30-yard touchdown on a fake handoff. Balzli sent in the reserves for valuable experience in the 4th and they managed to force a Tchula fumble at the 15. Peacock and Ted Helgason pushed to the 3 before Peacock scored his first touchdown of the year. He also added the PAT.

GAME 2:   SAINT AL (1-0) vs ROLLING FORK (0-0)
                      FINAL: ST AL 0 ROLLING FORK 12
                      September 25, 1953

Balzli attempted earlier in the year to get the open date for the 18th filled, but to no avail. The team would be guests on the 15th of the Council 896 Knights of Columbus for a chili dinner in honor of their inaugural victory. Rolling Fork, having lost only 3 starters from the previous year, would be playing their first game of the year. While the visitor was an unknown to the Flashes, their coaches had scouted Saint Al on the 11th against Tchula. *"We do not know what offense or defense we are going to meet against Rolling Fork on Friday night. An advantage Aloysius will have is the fact that they have engaged in a gridiron battle"*.

On doctor's orders, Wood would not suit up. The 175-pounder was described as the *"main cog on the makeup of the Flashes eleven. He called the signals, did the passing, punting and kicked off"*. News worsened before kickoff when Tom McTaggart, starting guard, had an emergency appendectomy. Additionally, Peacock missed 5 days of school due to sickness. Playing a team outweighing them by 20 pounds, losses to the bigger players was huge. Nevertheless, the paper picked Saint Al 19-12.

The Flashes held their own in the contest, keeping the Bearcats from penetrating the entire first half. They stopped one drive on their 30 and forced a fumble on another at their 13 that was recovered by Howard Madison. In the 2nd, the Flashes scored when Warren Doiron plunged up the middle from the 30, but it was called back for being off-sides. Rolling Fork's first score came midway through the 3rd when Bob Smith hit Billy Carr for a 60-yard touchdown. Their final points came in the 4th after a John Hartley fumble at the Flash 38. Smith found Carr again from there. Both PATs were stopped by the Flashes.

GAME 3:   SAINT AL (1-1) @ NATCHEZ CATHEDRAL (3-1)
                      FINAL: ST AL 20 NATCHEZ CATHEDRAL 33
                      October 2, 1953

The game originally was set for Sunday, but it was moved to Friday due to the Greenies using Natchez High's field. Balzli visited with the Vicksburg Kiwanis Club during the week to discuss the team, their offense and player health updates. Wood and McTaggart would still be missing. Down in Natchez, coach Don Alonzo was running the Greenies "*long and hard*" after a loss to Waterproof, LA.

Despite a crowd of 1,200 deemed "*disappointing*", The Natchez Democrat called the contest "*a slow, very poorly officiated football game*". Little was noted about the contest by either Vicksburg paper. Doiron put the Flashes up early in the 1st with a 41 yard touchdown run and pass to Joe Durst for the PAT. Natchez responded when Eddie Davis picked off a Flash pass at the Greenie 10. Andrew Eidt passed to Eddie Davis for a touchdown 75 yards later but the PAT was blocked. Doiron again put the Flashes ahead on a run from the 1 and a pass to Mike Riddle for the PAT. The 1st quarter ended 14-6.

Natchez mastered a 56 yard drive on their next possession capped by an Eidt pass to Pat McDonough from the 19. Stopping the Flashes at the Cathedral 39, the home team went ahead on the next drive. Runs by Pete Frank and James Broussard got the ball to the 34 and Frank ran in from there. Eidt's kick made it 19-14. Saint Al turned a blocked kick into a first down on the ensuing drive at the Flash 45. Doiron pushed in on a 20-yard run and the Flashes were back on top 20-19.

As time was expiring, Frank caught a Davis pass for 46 yard score. Eidt made halftime a 26-20 Cathedral lead. As noted by the Natchez paper, "*... the Flashes ran completely out of condition in the last half and could do very little*". Frank ran for a 16 yard tally in the 3rd, added by an Eidt kick. Saint Al had controlled the stats in rushing and penalties, but little else.

GAME 4:   SAINT AL (1-2) vs WASHINGTON (0-4)
                      FINAL: ST AL 33 WASHINGTON 7
                      October 9, 1953

The paper had done "*the math*" by comparing common opponents and deemed Saint Al "*just about one touchdown favorites. But in a close game like this, one touchdown doesn't mean much. The tables can be reversed in a moment's notice.*" The new Farrell Stadium was almost ready and dedication ceremonies would come the next week. It seated "*comfortably around 1,200 fans*" and also had "*... press box facilities ... a flag pole, continental fence ... and a new dressing room for the visiting teams*". Wood would return for the game, though Balzli said "*Although (he) may not start, he will probably see some action if we need him*". Strenuous preparations were underway for Washington's passing attack and game night would have some 1,000 fans in attendance.

Saint Al used "*practically every player on the ... roster...*" and "*perhaps could have run up a larger score had they wished.*" On the first possession, a 21 yard touchdown pass from Hartley to Riddle was called back for off-sides. They still finished the drive with a Peacock run from the 5 and a Wood PAT kick. Wood would see action only in punting and kicking. On their next possession, three Flash runs provided the next score. Sam Tuccio and Doiron both gained 22 and Hartley finished it from the 20. Wood's kick was true. The last touchdown of the half came after Riddle blocked a Billy Sebille punt to give the Flashes the ball at the Washington 10. Doiron ran for the score on the next play to make it 19-0.

Saint Al scored on their first possession of the 3rd behind a 60 yard drive highlighted by a Doiron touchdown pass to Riddle from 11 yards away. Doiron picked off a 4th quarter Sebille pass and ran it back for a 50 yard touchdown to cap the scoring for the Flashes. Ray Terry later picked off another pass and returned it roughly 68 yards to the 1. Terry later recounted that the FG attempt was only because everyone thought the Flashes had scored. Washington's only tally was on the last play when Sebille hit Charles Wallace from 25 yards followed by a Sebille PAT.

GAME 5:   SAINT AL (2-2) vs UTICA (UNDEFEATED)
                 FINAL: ST AL 24 UTICA 7
                 October 22, 1953

        Courtesy of the Knights of Columbus, the Flashes would now have a new stadium. It was named in honor of James B. "Jim" Farrell, a former member of the organization who had passed away several years before. George Downey, Grand Knight, would make the presentation to Principal Brother Mark. Monsignor D.J. O'Beirne and Leonard Katzenmeyer would also participate in the ceremonies.

        Utica had not lost a game since 1951 and was on a sixteen-game win streak. Balzli had not been happy with practices during the week, but Saint Al was up to the test. An opening possession drive of 66 yards was finished when Doiron took it in from the 10. Utica came back in the 2nd when Morris Curry hit Billy Templeton for a 29 yard strike on 4th down. The PAT by Neal made it 7-6. But after kicking to the Flashes, it was Doiron again on a long touchdown run to finish a 70 yard drive. Halftime had the Flashes up 12-7.

        On their first possession of the 3rd, the Flashes drove 78 yards for a score. Wood, now playing, set it up on runs of 20 and 5 and Doiron took it in from the 2. Unfortunately, Wood would re-injure the same knee on the play and be taken off the field by teammates. He would be lost for the season. The Flashes intercepted a pass in the 4th leading to the final touchdown. It would come when Doiron powered in from the 4. In all, Doiron had four touchdowns and the paper said *"That is something to be proud of, no matter how you look at it"*.

GAME 6:   SAINT AL (3-2) vs SAINT MATTHEWS, LA (UNREPORTED)
                 FINAL: ST AL 35 SAINT MATTHEWS 13
                 October 30, 1953: HOMECOMING

        Having *"... practically the same team they had last year when the Flashes won 19-0"*, the Monroe team was one Balzli was practicing to beat for Homecoming. The defense was stressed that week against the *"highly patented Monroe eleven"*. A parade was held on the 30th through the downtown area before *"nearly 1,000 near freezing fans"* filled the stadium. Doiron would again please them by putting on a stellar performance.

        Saint Al scored on their opening possession with a 62 yard drive in 9 plays finalized when Peacock got in from the 5. Tuccio slammed in for the PAT. They got to the Monroe 3 before fumbling thereafter, but Saint Matthews' next play resulted in a safety. In the 2nd, Doiron found Riddle for a touchdown pass and added the PAT for a 16-0 lead. Doiron finished the half from the 2 to cap a 41 yard march. Monroe answered in the 3rd when Jungina scored from the 8 but Fruge missed the PAT. Saint Al came right back on the visitors when Doiron yet again hit the goal; this one from 28 yards. Saint Matthews scored for the final time in the 4th when Brown capped a 61 yard drive from the 6 and Fruge added the PAT. The Flashes sealed the game when Doiron passed to Hartley from the 27 for a touchdown.

GAME 7:   SAINT AL (4-2) @ JACKSON SAINT JOSEPH (4-1)
                 FINAL: ST AL 18 JACKSON SAINT JOSEPH 13
                 November 6, 1953

        The second battle for the Straus-Stallings Trophy would be in Jackson against a reported strong team. It would be homecoming for Jackson Saint Joe but Saint Al would be focused on retaining the trophy and finishing the year strong before a *"large crowd of chilled spectators at Pearl Stadium..."*

        Early in the 1st, Doiron ran for 63 yards and a score followed in the 2nd by a Hartley run from 18. In the 3rd, passes led the way to the next tally. Doiron hit Durst and Johnny Marsicano found Riddle that put the ball at the 9. Peacock ran it in from there. The Rebels fought furiously in the 4th, gaining two scores. The first was set up by a Hall to Amos pass that allowed Hall to get in. Minutes later, Hall found Courtney for a 3 yard touchdown and Amos converted the PAT. The final whistle blew with Saint Joe at the Flash 30. The paper reported their headline as **"Losers Give Coach Balzli Jitters In Last Quarter As (They) Score Two Touchdowns"**.

GAME 8:   SAINT AL (5-2) vs PUCKETT (6-2)
               FINAL: ST AL 39 PUCKETT 7
               November 13, 1953

Saint Al would be rewarded, win or lose, on the day after the season-finishing contest with a trip to New Orleans to see the Tulane vs Vanderbilt football game. A stay overnight in the Jung Hotel, along with the game expenses, would be sponsored by the Saint Aloysius A Club.

The Friday game was called *"... an evenly matched contest"* against *"...one of their (Puckett's) strongest teams in years"* according to comparisons of common teams played. Saint Al would have an injury-laden team with Tuccio, Campbell, Riddle, Alvarado, and Durst all hobbled. It was noted that *"The Flashes are expected to meet one of their toughest opponents of the season in Puckett"*. Unfilled open dates were still possible, but would not come to fruition. Said Billy Ray, *"The Flashes are crippled, yes, but we're sticking with Coach Balzli, who's done such a remarkable job this year, especially with injuries piling up, every week. St. Aloysius 26, Puckett 13"*.

The *"Blaze of glory..."* to mark the last game of the year saw *"... every St. Aloysius player that was able to get in the game..."* Puckett started well by driving to the Flash 35 but Joe Durst picked off a Puckett pass at the 20 for the stop. After holding, and on the next possession, Peacock took the punt back 66 yards to the Puckett 6. The Flashes got the 1 foot line before giving the ball back. Their next drive, though, would prove fruitful. Starting at the Puckett 47, Doiron blazed through the middle for 40 yards, hit Durst for a 3 yard touchdown, and passed to Hartley for the PAT.

In the 2nd, Howard Madison gave the Flashes a bigger lead when he picked off a Puckett pass and took it back 75 yards for the score. Doiron's pass to Riddle for the PAT was good to make halftime 14-0. Balzli's intermission speech must have been impressive because the Flashes scored on each possession of the 2nd half. Peacock ran for a 4 yard score, Doiron hit Riddle for a 12 yard strike, Hartley returned a punt 55 yards for a touchdown, and Marsicano capped a 41 yard drive with a plunge from the 4. Puckett's lone score came against reserves late in the 4th when Purvis ran a 30 yard touchdown and Rhodes converted the PAT. The Flashes carried Balzli off of the field in a victory celebration.

After the game, Brother Mark told Billy Ray that the team declined to take advantage of any post-season activity as *"... Aloysius had played eight games this season and it was their policy not to play anymore, regardless."* That statement conflicted with the earlier reports of that week that unfilled spots for off-weeks were under discussion. Eight games were the norm and the Flashes did well after starting 1-2 considering injuries that took its toll on the squad. But rebounding to beat Utica and finish strong were commendable.

Season statistical recaps were published on November 22nd. Doiron had 731 yards of rushing, followed by Hartley (537) and Peacock (403). In all, Saint Al rushed for 1,852 yards, passed for 342 and had 29 touchdowns. The Virgadamo Trophy was presented to Joe Durst.

"We were ready to roll in 1953. We had the largest squad ever assembled at Aloysius up to that time, and 16 of our 19 classmates participated in football. Raymond Ray found time from his business to assist Joe daily in coaching the defense. We lost two close ballgames; one to Rolling Fork (two key players determined the outcome) and one to Natchez Cathedral (home-cooking at its very best). We had a great offensive game and were the better team. We had a great win over Utica; our best game of the year.

Three stalwart players were out for the year in John Dorsey Wood, Freddy Groome (injury) and Johnny Ellis (out of town). With them we would have really been something."

Joe Durst; August 5, 2016

1954 (5-3)

The Flashes were in a *"rebuilding stage from last year's graduation"* but *"would wield an aggressive aggregation who will give a good account of themselves"*. Said Balzli, *"They want to play football and, if they do that, I'll be proud of them. We may not win every game we play, but if the boys do their part the way they're coached, and not lay down on the job, we'll make all the teams on our schedule know they've been in a game."* September 9th would find them finishing up *"intensive training"*. Additionally, the newly-constructed concession stand would now be in service for the capacity crowds.

Balzli, alongside Brother Cecil and new principal Brother Anselm, attended the first meeting of the 1954 Saint Aloysius A Club on the 1st to discuss the prospects for the year. The head man *"said the boys were inexperienced in the fine arts of the gridiron, but they were learning the techniques rapidly..."* There were reportedly 30 less boys trying out than 1954. Only 6 lettermen returned and, of those, only three (Peacock, Tuccio and Banchetti) were considered starters. *"... so it's not much of a question that the Purple Flashes have a tough road out for them. However, Coach Balzli reports that the Flashes are about the scrappiest bunch of boys he's ever coached and he's expecting them to make a commendable showing in every game; win, lose or draw"*. Each of the three would serve as alternating team captains.

GAME 1:   SAINT AL (0-0) vs PUCKETT (0-0)
                        FINAL: ST AL 7 PUCKETT 6
                        September 10, 1954

Despite an easy time against Puckett in 1953, the paper called it closer this season in favor of the Flashes 20-6. They noted that it could be *"even closer"*, and they were right. A large crowd got their money's worth on a hard-pressed Flash victory. The only highlight of the first half was a Balfour Wallace run of 26 yards at the whistle that didn't make it across the goal. As the 3rd closed, Jimmy Peacock gained 32 yards and then opened the 4th with a 3 yard touchdown. Wallace hit Eddie Lucchesi for the PAT to make it 7-0. Puckett almost tied it midway through the 4th when Kelly Cook blocked a Flash punt at their 28 and ran it back. His PAT was unsuccessful and the Flashes secured the first win of the season.

GAME 2:   SAINT AL (1-0) vs CARY (1-0)
                        FINAL: ST AL 19 CARY 13
                        September 17, 1954

The Panthers returned 12 lettermen and *"their 1953 eleven almost intact"*. They had just beaten a tough Cleveland team 13-7 and the paper said that Balzli had his work cut out for him *"and we're afraid the road is going to be too tough to cut"*. Hence, they predicted a Flash loss of 26-13. Fortunately, Frank Logue had provided a great scouting report.

The Flashes played *"before home folks and one of the largest crowds to ever see a football game at Farrell Stadium"*. And though the stats were in Cary's favor, the score was not. Lucchesi blasted through the Panther kicking team to block a punt that gave them the ball at the Panther 7 to close the 1st. Peacock took advantage and scored on the next play. Wallace hit Lucchesi for the PAT and a 7-0 lead. With *"cheers still ringing throughout the stadium"*, Cary immediately tied the game on a Jack Beard 37-yard touchdown run. He then hit his brother Jerry for the PAT to make it 7-7 at halftime.

Billy Ray noted a particular play late in the 2nd when Ray Terry took out two potential tacklers on a Peacock pass. Leaving his line position, Terry scrambled back to free Peacock and took out two Cary victims that freed him for a long run. *"That block thrown by Ray Terry, 147 pound quarterback that sent two Panthers sprawling, will be talked about for a long time"*. The Flashes got a break on the 2nd half kickoff when Cary fumbled at their 35 and Norbert Johnson recovered. Wallace gained 26, Peacock gained 4 and then Wallace scored. The Panthers then fumbled to Jesse Jones at the Cary 34. They got to the Panther 3 before Wallace went over right tackle for the score. James Hossley's pass to Andrew Romano for the extra point was incomplete.

Cary tried to come back early in the 4th when John Wessinger ran for a 24 yard score but Beard's PAT was unsuccessful. On the last play of the game, a 22-yard Jack Beard pass to Jerry Beard pass appeared destined for a touchdown, but he was caught from behind on his way *"into the clear"*.

GAME 3:   SAINT AL (2-0) @ ROLLING FORK (1-0)
                        FINAL: ST AL 6 ROLLING FORK 14
                        September 24, 1954

Romano, after having been *"shaken up"* in the Cary game, was expected to be out against a team *"reported a notch better than Cary"*. Rolling Fork was *"reported with many more reserves than the Flashes. If (they) can keep going at the pace they set last week against Cary, they'll let Rolling Fork know they've been in a ball game. IF (and that's an 'if' in capital letters) the Flashes could get by Rolling Fork, then Joe Balzli's Flashes ... could have a remarkable year... By playing on their own field tonight* gives (them) the edge, but don't be too surprised if the Flashes fool you again. They're capable. Rolling Fork 20 Saint Aloysius 12".

A first half of tough football changed when Sam Tuccio suffered a leg injury at the close of the 2nd. Saint Al managed an interception in the quarter, but could not penetrate. In the 3rd, Delaney put up Rolling Fork's first score on a 35 yard run followed by a Billy Carr pass to Barnard Danzig for the PAT and a 7-0 lead. They increased the lead when Carr hit Delaney for 23 and then Geno Stokes afterwards for the score. Stokes also caught the PAT from Carr to make it 14-0.

With 5:00 left, Rolling Fork scored on a Delaney run for 62 yards, but it was called back. Saint Al got on the board when Peacock ran in from the 5. The PAT was unsuccessful and the Flashes had lost their first game of 1954. The Deer Creek Pilot said of the contest, "All in all, it was a good game with both teams displaying fine sportsmanship and both playing a hard, clean-fought football game".

GAME 4:   SAINT AL (2-1) vs NATCHEZ CATHEDRAL (3-0)
                FINAL: ST AL 0 NATCHEZ CATHEDRAL 27
                October 3, 1954

A Sunday contest awaited the Flashes against Catholic rival Natchez Cathedral. They had 9 first-teamers back against only John Banchetti in the same Flash position. The paper called Saint Al "scrappy by outclassed", probably due to the fact that the Greenies outweighed the Flashes "... 29 pounds in the line and 16 pounds in the backfield". The Natchez Democrat said that their three consecutive wins were by "lop-sided scores which could have been even bigger..." Tuccio would be out after the Rolling Fork game, and Romano and Joe Crevitt were injured.

The Greenies almost scored immediately by driving to the Flash 26 before Ray Terry picked off a Greenie pass at the Flash 1. They had to punt and Natchez drove for the 24 yard score behind a Pat McDonough run from the 7. Sammy Eidt kicked the extra point for a 7-0 lead. Saint Al drove to the Cathedral 35 on the next possession but a fake punt gave the ball back to the Greenies. Two possessions later, the Wave scored on a 65 yard punt return by Eddie Davis only to be called back for clipping. On the ensuing play, McDonough rambled 82 yards for the make-up touchdown. Eidt's kick was off.

The next Natchez score came in the 3rd on their first possession. Eerily like the previous play, Davis took a punt return 80 yards for the score. Eidt made it 20-0. Saint Al got their deepest penetration of the game in the 4th to the Wave 9, but lost the ball on downs. The Greenies capitalized when Gay Necaise caught a pass at the 11 and then Pete Frank took it in for the score. Eidt finished the game with the PAT.

GAME 5:   SAINT AL (2-2) vs SAINT MATTHEWS, LA (UNREPORTED)
                FINAL: ST AL 27 SAINT MATTHEWS 6
                October 17, 1954: HOMECOMING

Balzli was playing a strong Monroe team but his squad was healthy. He had "been cooking up a little 'special' for Sunday" according to Billy Ray. "The Flashes want to win this one badly, especially since it their homecoming, and we think they will. St Aloysius 20, Monroe 7". A near capacity crowd in "cool sunshiny weather" would be on-hand.

The homecoming crowd wasn't happy in the 1st as the Flashes had driven deep into Monroe territory twice without points. Fumbles by Wallace at the SM 3 and 4 cost Saint Al two early touchdowns. The next drive was to the Monroe 25, but that was stopped as well. Finally, in the 2nd, and at the Monroe 34, James Hossley got things going with a run to the 30. Two Peacock runs got to the 3, Wallace got to the 1 and then Peacock took it in. Sam Tuccio split the uprights to make it 7-0.

In the same quarter, Peacock picked off a pass at the Flash 47. Wallace found Lucchesi for a 30 yard scoring pass and Tuccio added another PAT. Monroe fumbled to start the 2nd half and Saint Al took over at the Saint Matthew 34. Wallace went to the 12 and Hossley took it in from there. Tuccio made it 21-0. Monroe fumbled on the very next possession at their 38 and Saint Al took advantage with a Wallace pass to Lucchesi for a 20 yard score. Saint Matthew would get on the board in the 3rd though details highlight specifically a "circus catch" to Bruscale to make it possible.

GAME 6: SAINT AL (3-2) vs UTICA (UNREPORTED)
FINAL: ST AL 27 UTICA 0
October 22, 1954

Romano was back in the lineup against a *"young, inexperienced squad"* in Utica. They had *"shown improvement in each game played this year and has averaged close to two touchdowns per game"*.

In a seeming replay of the Monroe game, Saint Al committed two early turnovers that should have been scores. The first was a Peacock pick by Utica after the Flashes had gained 50 yards. The second saw Saint Al at the Utica 3 before fumbling. Utica returned the favor at their 25 on a fumble and Saint Al took advantage. After driving to the 1, Peacock went in for the score. Utica fumbled again on the next possession and Saint Al recovered. Wallace scored but the play was called back for motion and Utica would eventually get the ball back.

In the 2nd, plays by Peacock and Wallace got the ball to the Utica 17 and Wallace converted from there. Tuccio's kick made it 13-0 going into halftime. The Flashes scored again in the 3rd when Peacock hit Romano for 38, Wallace ran for 10, and Banchetti took it in from the 3. Tuccio's kick was good. On the next possession, Banchetti picked off a Utica pass and returned it 31 yards for the touchdown. Tuccio finished the scoring at 27-0 with the PAT. Balzli sent in the reserves in the 4th.

GAME 7: SAINT AL (4-2) @ EUDORA, ARK (WINLESS)
FINAL: ST AL 13 EUDORA 18
October 29, 1954

A large crowd of Flash fans followed the team across the river to Victory Stadium in Eudora to see the game against a *"heavier"* opponent. Some Flashes were on the doubtful list due to injury, but Balzli thought spirits to be good in preparation.

Saint Al jumped out early recovering a Badger fumble at their 40. Wallace made it pay from the 3 and Tuccio made it 7-0. In the same quarter, Peacock ran one in from 18 but Tuccio's PAT was blocked to keep it 13-0. In the 2nd, Eudora hit the board on a pass from Wright to Nichols to make it 13-6. In the 3rd, Wright found Criswell but the PAT was again not good. *"In the 4th period, the Badgers completely outplayed the Flashes"*. Nichols ran one in from 30 and sealed the upset win 18-13.

GAME 8: SAINT AL (4-3) vs JACKSON SAINT JOE (0-5-1?)
FINAL: ST AL 27 JACKSON SAINT JOE 6
November 7, 1954

Saint Al had held the Strauss-Stallings trophy since the 1952 inception, but the paper predicted a closer contest this year. *"Sticking with the hometowners in a closie. Tuccio's foot probably the difference. 14-13 or 21-18"*. Saint Al worked very hard to ensure they retained the precious trophy and bragging rights over their Catholic rival. *"... they'll be going all out trying to make their finale a crowd-pleaser for hometown backers"*.

The first possessions were turnovers with the Rebels fumbling at their 48 and the Flashes fumbling two plays later. Then, Philip Simpson fumbled to Wallace at the 40 and then Saint Al was picked off by Wayne Hall. The Flashes marched as far as the Rebel 11 after a punt, but Peacock fumbled back to Saint Joe. Fittingly, a Rebel fumble afterwards was picked up by Tuccio at their 1 and taken back for the touchdown. His PAT made it 7-0. Saint Joe's only points came early in the 2nd on a Hall run from the 6. In the 2nd, a 30-yard Wallace to Jackie Wood pass was tipped by Con Maloney but caught at the Rebel 6. As time was expiring, Ray Terry bulldozed in and Tuccio converted the 2-pointer. Halftime would see the Flashes up 14-6.

In the 3rd, the Flashes immediately scored on a 73 yard drive capped by a Wallace 8 yard run. In the 4th, Wallace found Lucchesi for a 92 yard touchdown pass. Lucchesi *"reached high in the air to grab the pigskin at the 46 and the 'lanky end outraced three defenders to the goal"*. Saint Joe tried to rally but a Hebler interception at game's end sealed the Flash victory, the Strauss-Stallings Trophy and a 5-3 season.

John Banchetti was the recipient of the Virgadamo Trophy for 1954.

"1954 was a rebuilding year for St. Aloysius after the large graduation class of the year before. It set the stage, however, for an undefeated season in 1955. The Flashes played the Single Wing with an unbalanced line (Princeton-style). As was the norm at that time, SAHS played an 8-game schedule. The 1954 season started with Puckett and we were favored but won only 7-6. With that in mind, Billy Ray said that we would have no chance against powerhouse Cary the following week. We fooled everyone by winning a hard-fought game; the only one Cary lost all year.

Three of our players went on to play college ball. Tuccio went to Southern Miss, Nicholas went to Ole Miss and Lucchesi attended Princeton."

Joe Setaro; July 31, 2016

"Saint Aloysius played a very important role in my life. It taught me great discipline, teamwork and leadership. Joe Balzli was a wonderful person and my friend. He loved Saint Aloysius, football and Notre Dame. When I first met him, he was determined that I would play football on the first team and I did for two years. We did well this year, winning five out of eight games against some very good teams which considerably outweighed us. We were light, but good and tough."

Andy Romano; August 6, 2016

1955 (8-0)

The Flashes returned 8 lettermen from a 5-3 rebuilding season. Balzli put more development into the passing game to compliment the Single Wing running attack. They appeared to be a little faster than 1954 so prospects were high. "On paper, we have a mighty good club, but we won't definitely know until we see them in action. The team has been looking very good in practice and especially the scrimmages. The fans can look forward to a grudge game (with Cary) and we are out to win this one. We have a great chance to repeat a victory." Ray Terry and Teddy Marshall would serve as team co-captains.

GAME 1:   SAINT AL (0-0) vs CARY (0-0)
                 FINAL: ST AL 13 CARY 7
                 September 15, 1955

The Flashes started the season with miscues. Twice in the 1st, they lost opportunities. The first was a fumble at the Cary 4 and the second was an erased Hebler touchdown of 75 yards due to clipping. Just before halftime, the Flashes got as far as the Cary 6 but could not get in. In the 3rd, the Flashes finally hit paydirt when Perry Hale capped a 53 yard drive from the 6. The PAT made it 7-0.
In the 4th, Saint Al would get their winning touchdown after holding Cary on downs at their 40. Hebler found Paul Loyacono from there. Cary got its lone score in the period after a Tim Vollor fumble at the Flash 38. Three plays later, Bozo Shields ran in from the 26. Jimmy Jenkins added the PAT on a run from the 7, but there would not be enough time for the Panthers to come back. Playing "grades" after film review showed Jessie Jones as the outstanding player, followed by Leo Koestler and Ray Terry.

GAME 2:   SAINT AL (1-0) vs ROLLING FORK (UNREPORTED)
                 FINAL: ST AL 26 ROLLING FORK 0
                 September 23, 1955

When asked about prospects for the upcoming game, Balzli said, "To win this Friday against Rolling Fork, we will have to play better ball than we did last week… We looked horrible in the game. We have a good ball club but it didn't show. The big question is for the Flashes to prove themselves against good competition." Rolling Fork had a nice win streak against the Flashes and had just shut out Glen Allen 27-0.
Over 2,000 fans watched the Flashes jump on the Bearcats from the opening kick when John Hebler took the ball 85 yards for a score. Perry Hale's PAT made it 7-0. With both teams fighting in midfield for the remainder of the quarter, Norbert Johnson was able to partially block a Rolling Fork punt to give Saint Al the ball at the Flash 45. When the quarter ended, the Flashes were at the Bearcat

27. A Jerry Cronin reception from Hebler and two Terry runs got the ball to the 4 before Terry bulldozed in for the touchdown. Hebler's pass to Teddy Marshall was good for the PAT and a 14-0 lead.

Early in the 3rd, the Flashes drove from their 33 to the Bearcat 32 before Hebler found Loyacono at the 3. Hale went in two plays later only to have it called back for clipping. Hebler hit Loyacono immediately afterwards for the score to make it 20-0. Attempting to come back, Rolling Fork began passing. But Cronin snatched a pass and took it back 39 yards for the final touchdown.

GAME 3:   SAINT AL (2-0) vs WESSON/COPIAH LINCOLN (1-1)
                   FINAL: ST AL 33 WESSON 12
                   September 30, 1955

Wesson had 9 returning lettermen, had a *"hot passing attack"* and were *"reported to have a couple of men hitting the 200 pound mark"*. Hale sustained a shoulder injury against Rolling Fork, but Balzli noted that he *"… would probably see some action, though"*. Terry, Jones and Koestler were also banged up but expected to play.

An *"average but noisy crowd"* was on hand to watch *"John Hebler, a tremendous ramrod (do) everything one man could possibly do in a football game…"* The Flashes scored in the 1st on a Terry run from the 1. On Wesson's first possession, they fumbled to Jesse Jones at the Co-Lin 28. Hebler ran for 14 and then hit Wood for the touchdown. Hale's PAT made it 13-0. In the 2nd, Wesson's Glyn Beasley dove in from the 1 after running and passing plays by QB Robert Newsome. Randall Smith's PAT run was not good.

The next Flash score came in the same quarter after Loyacono gained 30-plus yards on a reverse. Marshall caught a Hebler pass for the touchdown from the 5 for a 20-6 lead. Loyacono did the same on the next drive and gained 48 yards to the Wesson 2. Hebler ran in the touchdown to make it 26-6 at halftime. He also added another touchdown in the 3rd on a 59 yard run and hit Cronin for the PAT. With reserves in, Newsome scored from the 1 to finish the game.

The paper reported that *"Perry Hale was injured during a second period play and removed to a hospital. First reports indicated that he received a broken collar bone"*.

GAME 4:   SAINT AL (3-0) @ NATCHEZ CATHEDRAL (4-1)
                   FINAL: ST AL 51 NATCHEZ CATHEDRAL 7
                   October 13, 1955

The first road game would be against their Catholic rival with three straight wins. They had five members over 200 pounds and ran the Split-T formation. Their only loss came to 30 consecutive game-winning Ferriday, LA and the paper said *"Losing to this club is like losing to Notre Dame; one feels proud to have played on the same field with the club"*. Balzli told the reporters that *"The Flashes do not play good ball when they are away from home. Cathedral will be our toughest game this season. However, I think we have a wonderful chance of winning; that is if we have a good night, we definitely have the boys who are capable of outplaying Cathedral."* Perry Hale's injury was confirmed and he would miss the remainder of the season.

The Flashes put up their highest point total of the year against the team expected to be the toughest competition. The first two touchdowns were courtesy of Cathedral fumbles. On their opening play, the Greenies fumbled at their 36 and Hebler ran it in from the 11 two plays later. The second was on the ensuing drive at their 15 and Hebler again ran in on the very next play. The 1st quarter saw Saint Al with a 12-0 lead.

Saint Al put up three touchdowns in the 2nd. Hebler hit Lucchesi from 35, Loyacono ran from 50 out, and Hebler found Loyacono from the 14 to make halftime a 31-0 affair. Terry scored in the 3rd on a run from the 5, Cronin romped the same distance in the 4th for a touchdown and a Vollor pass to Wood marked the final Flash touchdown. The Greenie's only score was in the 4th on a Mike McDonough run of 15 yards. Sammy Eidt added the PAT.

GAME 5:   SAINT AL (4-0) @ UTICA (UNREPORTED)
                   FINAL: ST AL 34 UTICA 6
                   October 22, 1955

The Vicksburg Herald's Pete Finlayson described the effort by the Flashes as *"Only in score did the Flashes resemble the well-trained and alert team which has tolled to 5 straight victories without an unblemished mark, otherwise a worthy opponent would have belabored this force unmercifully. Never before has dullness and non-spirit forsaken the ... Flashes as pitifully as it did last night in Utica ...Penalties, excessive injuries and incomplete passes prolonged and marred the game."*

Hebler put the Flashes up in the 1st with a touchdown run from the 17 and the PAT. Aided by one of two fair-catch penalties on Utica and a fake punt by Terry, Saint Al scored again on a 36 yard pass from Hebler to Loyacono and a Hebler PAT. Terry increased the lead in the quarter on a run from the 6 and Hebler's PAT pass to Cronin made it 21-0. Utica's lone points came before halftime on a Morrison dive from the 1. The final two touchdowns came in the 3rd. Hebler capped a 55 yard drive with a run from the 30 and Terry added the PAT. It was Terry who added the last touchdown from the 12.

GAME 6:   SAINT AL (5-0) vs DAVIDSON HIGH, LA (WINLESS)
                          FINAL: ST AL 40 DAVIDSON 7
                          October 28, 1955: HOMECOMING

With Carr Central not playing this week, the largest crowd ever was predicted to fill the Farrell Field stands. Davidson, a team from Saint Joseph, Louisiana, was only in its 3rd year of football and their odds for victory were slim. *"Coach Joe Balzli can probably name the score to suit the Flashes as his boys are assumed capable of winning over a light regarded opponent by any number of points".* The only negative would be the soggy playing conditions resulting from a big rain earlier in the day.

Finlayson's description of Hebler's performance was notable. *"John 'Cooter' Hebler's playing has been as habit-forming as smoking tobacco as for the fourth straight week, 'Mr. Dasher's' superb contributions paced the Flashes to victory by chalking up tallies twice and having a hand passing in another."*

Saint Al scored quickly in the 1st after Lucchesi returned the kick to the Flash 37, Hebler ran for 42 and Loyacono took it in from the 10. Teddy Marshall's PAT made it 7-0. Davidson promptly fumbled at the Flash 43 allowing Hebler to find Marshall for 12 before the Flashes ran for a 45 yard score. Marshall's PAT ended the 1st at 14-0. The 2nd started with the Flashes at their 36. Runs by Hebler, Terry and Vollor moved to the 15 before Hebler found Cronin for the touchdown. Falling behind quickly, the Warriors tried the air but Vollor picked off an errant pass. A Wood run on a reverse got the ball to the 1 and Habert converted from there.

Saint Al continued the assault in the 3rd with another pickoff, this time by Loyacono at the Warrior 44. Hebler finished it off with a touchdown run that *"thrilled the crowd"* and made it 33-0. Davidson came close to scoring by getting to the Flash 8 before a third interception was recorded; this time by Marshall. It would be costly as Vollor hit Wood for a 75 yard touchdown pass. With reserves on the field, Davidson avoided the shutout when Hoover went in from the 5 midway through the 4th.

GAME 7:   SAINT AL (6-0) @ JACKSON SAINT JOE (7-0)
                          FINAL: ST AL 27 JACKSON SAINT JOE 0
                          November 4, 1955

The undefeated Rebels had not beaten Saint Al since they started their rivalry in 1952, but returned 7 starters for the season. The contest would be held at Pearl High School and a big crowd was expected to see who would take home the Strauss-Stallings Trophy.

Saint Al set the tone on the third play of the game when Terry went up the middle for a 47 yard touchdown run. Marshall's PAT made it 7-0. Both teams fought until just before halftime when a Flash drive enabled Terry to plunge in from the 1. Hebler's pass to Loyacono was good and gave Saint Al a 14-0 lead at intermission. The 3rd would prove fatal for the Rebels. They fumbled at their 25, Hebler gained 15 and Terry finished it off from the 10. Marshall converted for a 21-0 lead and Terry added another score on a 30 yard run afterwards. Saint Joe came close to avoiding the goose-egg but fumbled at the Flash 3 in the 4th to seal the game.

GAME 8:   SAINT AL (7-0) vs PUCKETT (UNREPORTED)
                          FINAL: ST AL 47 PUCKETT 0
                          November 10, 1955

The final game was originally scheduled for Friday but Balzli moved it up a day to allow fans to attend the tilt between Carr Central and Greenwood. A win over Puckett would give Balzli his first perfect season since 1939, but the paper said *"An upset is like a tornado. There is no previous warning as what to expect, but even a possibility of an upset is given little light in this approaching game…"*. Considering that Saint Al barely got by Puckett in 1954 by a score of 7-6, and with the Wolves returning 8 of 11 starters, Balzli warned his team about overconfidence and stressed having the *"proper mental attitude"*.

The Vicksburg Post Herald said, *"…the 47-0 score could have been 147 as the Flashes found their opponent less than a drop in a bucket"*. Scoring was relentless. Hebler hit Loyacono for a 26 yard touchdown and followed it up with a touchdown pass to Marshall from the 16 after a Puckett fumble. The Wolves' Phillip Warren promptly threw an interception to Jesse Jones at the Puckett 33 resulting three plays later in a 25-yard Loyacono reverse for a touchdown. Puckett was able to stop a Flash drive to the goal, but immediately stepped out of the endzone for a safety afterwards to make it 21-0.

Balzli put in the reserves early which allowed Puckett to get to the Flash 1. He sent the first team back out and they held them on 4 attempts. The 21-0 lead would hold through halftime. Three plays into the 3rd, Terry picked off a Warren pass and took it back 33 yards for a touchdown. On their next possession, Hebler ran it 52 yards to make it 33-0. Before the quarter ended, Loyacono would grab another Puckett turnover at the Flash 38 and then took it 63 yards three plays later. Cronin added the last touchdown of the undefeated season from the 5 after a nice run by Terry of 32. Marshall's PAT gave the experienced coach a season to remember.

In calculation of points for academic and football criteria, Ray Terry was awarded by the coaches as MVP. The fast-learning and much-liked William Gargaro was the sixth recipient of the Virgadamo Trophy.

"The 1955 season was the highlight of my youth. It was formative of my character and developed traits of leadership which carried over into my long career as a civil rights lawyer, law professor and executive. One of my proudest moments was when my teammates voted Teddy Marshall and me team captains.

For the first time since 1939, we enjoyed an undefeated and untied record. We prevailed against a Rolling Fork team who had beaten us 3 years in a row and one we had never beaten. Similarly, arch rival Natchez Cathedral had beaten us the last three times we played them; two of which were humiliating. Saint Joe (Jackson) always played us tough and was undefeated when we beat them 27-0 on their field (which involved all kinds of unsuccessful efforts on their part to "psych us out"). If I had one "do-over", it would have been to personally thank Norbert Johnson, Jesse Jones and Jackie Mackie for the 8-foot holes they opened for me, and the entire line for escorting me through the "wedges". I'm confident that John, Jerry, and Paul were equally as appreciative.

We were blessed to have not one, but two, great tailbacks in John Hebler and Perry Hale, an outstanding QB in Jerry Cronin (who always set up the left end so I could "bring him down") and wingback in Paul Kelly Loyocano. Our offensive line opened holes you could drive a tank through and, on defense, we were impregnable. The scores of our games, aside from Cary, bore that out.

But most of all we were honored to have great coaches led by the incomparable Joe Balzli, Raymond Ray and Brother Cecil, as well as an incredible scout in Frank Logue. Joe spent the most time with us and provided us with a model of integrity, grit and striving for excellence. He taught us to play by the rules, be magnanimous in victory and accepting in defeat. Not bad for a small all-boys Catholic school in the 1950s."

Ray Terry; July 18, 2016

1956 (6-2)

Balzli opened drills on August 15th with 8 returning lettermen and was asked right afterwards about the prospects of another undefeated season. *"Joe wouldn't go out on the limb and predict how he would finish, just said he hoped his team would be as colorful to watch as last year's team"*. Much of that team had graduated, but promising new faces were joining returning lettermen. One young sophomore was Eddie Habert, a 150 pound back who caught the coach's eye while playing for Brother Cecil's "pee-wees". With him in the lineup, Balzli added the deceptive "T-Formation" to go along with his powerful Single Wing.

As the season neared opening day, Balzli reported *"satisfactory progress"* with one exception. Jimmy Monsour, a blocking back who was deemed instrumental to the squad's success, received a simple fracture to his left arm during August 20th scrimmages and would be lost for at least six weeks. Balzli spoke with The Vicksburg Touchdown Club on September 4th using a chalkboard to show patrons how his offense worked and who would be expected to start. His prediction for the season would be *"... if his first team stayed intact, the Flashes would be hard to beat, but an injury here and there and anything could happen"*. Balzli followed that up the next night with a similar presentation to the Vicksburg Lions Club either just before or after he spoke with the Aloysius "A" Club.

GAME 1:   SAINT AL (0-0) vs WESSON/COPIAH-LINCOLN (0-0)
                     FINAL: ST AL 34 WESSON 13
                     September 7, 1956

The Flashes were up against *"the (9) lettermen-laden Copiah-Lincoln High School of Wesson"* who were expected to be *"throwing a lot of weight at the Flashes with ... lettermen whose combined weight averages 177 pounds"* and *"...gunning for a 'spoilers' role in the St Aloysius encounter"*. Karl Nicholas would be team captain while Eddie Lucchesi and Jesse Jones would co-captain. Billy Ray called it 26-13 for the Flashes in his usual close predictions.

      A crowd of 1,900 were rewarded with an opening Flash scoring drive. On the 5th play, Paul Loyacono ran a reverse *"like a scared rabbit"* from the 35 for the touchdown and Joe Hossley made it 7-0. The duo repeated the performance minutes later with Loyacono going 76 yards *"and the stands went wild"*. With Wesson at the Flash 30, George Evans picked off Nickey Purvis but it was short-lived as the Flashes returned the favor. Wesson would get to the Flash 6 before the half ended.

      Starting the 3rd, Tim Vollor hit Lucchesi with passes of 20 and 24 yards to pad the lead to 20-0. Paul Chatham added the next touchdown on an *"untouched"* run of 47 and Hossley converted. Chatham added the same minutes later, but a penalty called it back. Habert added the last Flash points from the 4 to cap a 37 yard drive. With Balzli *"cleaning the bench"*, Wesson managed to score twice. The first was a Robert Hales 26 yarder to Robert Newsome, and the second was with almost no time left when Hales got in from the 6.

GAME 2:   SAINT AL (1-0) vs CARY (0-1)
                     FINAL: ST AL 33 CARY 6
                     September 14, 1956

A healthy Flash squad was cause for a two-touchdown prediction by Billy Ray. But due to Cary's toughness and the close game from the previous year, Balzli took no chances and ran his kids though *"high-geared workouts"*.

      Receiving the kickoff before the largest crowd of the season, the Flashes went 63 yards in 11 plays capped by a Chatham to Don Riddle pass from the 11. Runs by Habert, Vollor and Chatham set up the play and Hossley made it 7-0. In the same frame, Saint Al went 55 yards in 4 plays with Loyacono getting in from the 11. The last score of the half came in the 2nd when Loyacono ran in from 23 away to make it 20-0.

      Tim Vollor started the 3rd by faking a handoff to Loyacono at the Flash 47 and taking it all the way. Cary fumbled at their 33 and Habert converted two plays later from the 31. Reserves took the field and gave Cary their only touchdown. In the 4th after a fumble put the Panthers at the Flash 36, Rudy Holcomb dashed in from the 21 after runs by him and Buddie Summerall.

GAME 3:   SAINT AL (2-0) @ ROLLING FORK (1-0)
                     FINAL: ST AL 33 ROLLING FORK 0
                     September 21, 1956

Balzli planned to use a *"forked stick"* to repel the Bearcats. Rolling Fork was reported as *"loaded"* with 13 returning starters *"... and this game could turn out to be one of the toughest on the Aloysius schedule"*.

      The Flashes put up two scores in the earliest minutes of the game. Four plays after the kickoff, and starting at the Flash 40, Loyacono gained 27, Habert gained 38 and then pushed in for the final 3 yards. Hossley made it 7-0. Shortly thereafter at the Flash 12, Loyacono went 88 yards on a touchdown run and a 14-0 lead. Loyacono ran one in from 52 in the 2nd but it was called back for clipping. They made up for it when, starting on their 40, Habert gained 39 and Paul Chatham ripped off 18 for the touchdown. At half, it was 20-0.

Habert continued the assault in the 3rd with a 72 yard run and Hossley added the PAT. Before the quarter was over, Loyacono hit Vollor for a 55 yard strike. The Bearcats almost scored just before the game ended on a Mallie Price run of 45 yard to the Flash 5. The defense stood and ended the drive23 yards backwards. Balzli was *"well pleased with the Flashes performance"*, praising both the offense and defensive units.

GAME 4:   SAINT AL (3-0) @ LAKE PROVIDENCE (UNREPORTED)
                             FINAL: ST AL 45 LAKE PROVIDENCE 0
                             September 28, 1956

Lucchesi and Mike Morrissey would return and the paper said that *"unless something unexpectedly happens to the Flashes' first team before game time, Joe Balzli should be able to name his score"*. Ray predicted a 40-12 win while The Vicksburg Herald writer John Hallbach called it 34-7.

The Flashes scored 32 points in the 1st half alone while having two other 55 yard Loyacono runs called back due to penalties. Chatham scored first on a run from the 10. The next drive saw a Panther interception by Douglas Patrick only to give the ball back to Jackie Mackey on a fumble the very next play. Habert scored from the 3 to start the 2nd and Koestler added the point. A Vollor fumble recovery later opened the door for a Habert 10 yard touchdown. A few plays after, Lucchesi blocked a Panther punt at their 40. Loyacono capped it six plays later from the 8 on a reverse. Koestler made it 32-0 at halftime.

The reserves held the second half position in large part. Hossley drove in from the 1 in the 3rd and George Ettinger picked off a Panther pass for a 70 yard touchdown return. Said Hallbach, *"Coach Balzli admitted he was looking for keener competition from Rolling Fork, but speculated that St. Aloysius' two lightning fast touchdowns in the first minutes of play dampened the Bearcats spirit"*.

GAME 5:   SAINT AL (4-0) vs SAINT MATTHEWS, LA (0-2)
                             FINAL: ST AL 34 SAINT MATTHEWS 13
                             October 5, 1956

Balzli told the Vicksburg Touchdown Club on the 1st that *"he was real proud of his Flashes for their performances thus far, but that the real tough games were just about ready to start"*. The paper said that *"The Flashes are reported ... in fine shape and from all indication should annex their 5th win of the season and their 14th in a row"* and called it 47-7 in favor of Saint Al.

The coach's pre-game speech was *"It looks like rain, so you better hit 'em hard in the first period because you never know what will happen in a ball game when it starts raining."* Saint Al did just that; putting up two touchdowns within three minutes. On the second play of the game, Habert hit Loyacono for a 60 yard touchdown. Next, Loyacono *"streaked through the center of the St. Matthews defensive barrier like a bachelor expecting a shot-gun wedding"* for a 69 yard touchdown.

On their 3rd drive, Lucchesi finished a 63 yard march with a touchdown run of 31 yards. The Flashes fumbled the rain-soaked ball at their 34 afterwards, allowing J.G. Zagona a pitch to Julian Fontere for a 60 yard score. Loyacono came right back with a 40 yard touchdown run, but it was called back for clipping. Now at the 25, Chatham went in and Koestler's PAT made it 27-6.

The reserves played the entire 3rd and all but 3 minutes of the 4th. In the frame, Zagone capped a 70 yard march from the 1 and converted the PAT. The three minutes devoted to the starters in the 4th was more than enough time. Habert would run in from the 13 after a 37 yard run by Chatham and two 10 yard catches by Lucchesi. Said Balzli afterwards, *"Man, did I foul up these local sports prognosticators who are always picking my ... boys to win by 40 and 50 points when I let the reserves play nearly all the last half"*.

GAME 6:   SAINT AL (5-0) vs NATCHEZ CATHEDRAL (3-2)
                             FINAL: ST AL 32 NATCHEZ CATHEDRAL 0
                             October 11, 1956: HOMECOMING

The Thursday night contest was scheduled as not conflict with the Carr Central-Yazoo City game on Friday. Natchez's offense ran the Split-T and had Martell and Verucchi on the line totaling 405 pounds. *"They are said to be as good as any in the state"*. The Greenies, however, had lost key starting HB in Mike McDonough with a separated shoulder and Guard David Guercio the week before but counted 11 returning lettermen to their credit. After consideration, Billy Ray called it for the Flashes 27-13.

Early in the 1st, Nicholas blocked an Arthur Eidt punt and recovered it at the Cathedral 10. Vollor converted from the 2 three plays later and Koestler kicked the PAT. Before the quarter ended, Loyacono ran one 63 yards for a score and returned a punt 65 yards for another. The return was a reverse handoff by Vollor that surprised the visitors. There would be no more scoring until the 4th. After a Vollor pass to Jesse Jones of 25 yards, combined with Greenie penalties, Habert punched in from the 1. The last score would be a Vollor touchdown pass to Loyacono of 46 yards. The paper noted that *"the fourth quarter elapsed with Natchez Cathedral and St. Aloysius nearing a fist-slinging feud in a midfield battle"*.

GAME 7:   SAINT AL (6-0) vs DURANT (8-0)
               FINAL: ST AL 7 DURANT 20
               October 26, 1956

The *"Kings of the Big Black Conference"*, had outscored their opponents 227-31 and had won 39 of 40. *"Everything could break loose in this one, or it could turn out to be a knock down-drag out affair. Only time will tell."* Both teams had been scouting one-another for a while. The Flashes had rugged workouts after a week off. Balzli yelled at his squad at the close of the Wednesday practice, *"The pressure's going to on Friday night! You boys haven't been in a tight spot this year, but I think you can go in there and beat the Durant team if you have the determination to do it."* Halbach said that pre-game predictors had Saint Al as 6 point underdogs. *"It is the first time in two years that St. Aloysius hasn't been forecast a favorite"*.

Said Balzli, *"The Durant ball club works on pin-point precision. They have a fast, tricky offensive unit and (the coach) has been grooming them to perfection... Pressure hasn't been on the ...squad any time this year. The Flashes haven't had to reach a performance peak in a single game of the current campaign. They'll have to do it tonight, and if they have the proper determination, the Durant Tigers will go back to their northern lair a loser"*.

The *"largest expected crowd ever to attend a football game at Farrell Stadium"* would mean extra bleachers and preparations. Said Billy Ray, *"... it's our personal belief that the bigger Aloysius line will prove too much and Durant will leave the Hill City with their second loss in the past four years while Joe Balzli's Flashes will rise to new heights ... St. Aloysius 26 Durant 7"*.

Durant scored on their first three possessions; twice in the 1st and once in the 2nd. Starting at the Flash 40, Dale McBride rushed for 30 on a fake handoff. On 4th down, Jimmy Ferguson gained the 4 yards for the touchdown. Jimmy Kealhofer's kick made it 7-0. On their next drive, Durant knocked off the entire 30 yards on a run. Saint Al would come right back and get as far as the Tiger 5 but could not cross the line in 4 plays. The Tigers dagger would come in the 2nd when McBride faked a handoff to Wallace Reid and scampered 72 yards to the Flash 5. Reid got in from the one-foot line three plays later and the Flashes found themselves down 20-0 at halftime.

The Flashes got their only score in the 3rd. After a Durant fumble was recovered by Nicholas at the Tiger 20, Habert hit Loyacono to the 5 and then took the ball in himself afterwards. The Koestler kick made it a final 20-7. *"The Durant game is past history. We were beaten by a good ball club that played heads-up ball and hustled every minute. I'm not ashamed of the way our boys played the game, either. They were aggressive, played their hearts out and really came back in the second half."*, Balzli said afterwards.

GAME 8:   SAINT AL (6-1) vs JACKSON SAINT JOE (6-0)
               FINAL: ST AL 7 JACKSON SAINT JOE 14
               November 2, 1956

Balzli appeared before the Vicksburg Touchdown Club for the third time on the 30th. This time he showed game film and *"pointed out costly mistakes"* of at least 15 assignment errors, 7 fumbles and 2 costly 15 yard penalties. *"We hope to correct these errors and be ready to go full blast against another powerful club this week"*. The undefeated Rebels had lost only 1 game in the last two seasons, and that was to Balzli's Flashes. The coach was hoping *"to have costly kinks ironed out but (warning) that the Rebels will be nearly as tough as the Tigers and any kind of let down would mean their second straight defeat"*. In spite of the flashy passing game of Con Maloney and Jim Conway, the paper picked Saint Al 27-14 *"to end their season in a streak of rebounding glory..."*

Saint Al charged out of the gate by holding Saint Joe on downs and getting as far as the Rebel 4 before a Chatham fumble was given back to the Rebels. Holding again in the 2nd, the Flashes started at the Rebel 45. After a short pass to the 40, Loyacono found Riddle for the remaining yards. A Koestler run made it 7-0. Five seconds before half, Childress picked off Maloney to preserve the halftime lead.

A Flash punt to start the 3rd was downed by Nicholas short of the goal, but *"a pudgy official waddling some 30 yards back up field (ruled) the pigskin bounced into the endzone and the Rebels were granted possession on their own 20..."* The defense but turned the ball over on downs after reaching the Rebel 8. After another Saint Joe punt, the Flashes would throw an interception to Tom Cambre at the Rebel 32.

The Rebels got on the board in the 4th when Johnny Anoulih went 31 yards into paydirt and Lewis Drane ran in the PAT. The Flashes took the onside kick at the Rebel 48. A Habert touchdown run was nullified for *"backfield in motion"* and Logue fumbled shortly thereafter at the Rebel 38. The Rebels would score again on a fake punt when Anouilh ran for 33 to the Flash 29. On 4th down, he then took it in from the 22 for the game-winning touchdown. Maloney bullied through for the PAT.

John Halbach was brutal in his description of the ability of the referees; one in particular. *"A bush league referee from central Mississippi, who should have been home reading the rule book, shaked away two second half scoring marches of the Flashes in the 3rd and 4th quarters. Once, the short, squatty fellow ... tossed down the red handkerchief after St Aloysius slammed to the Rebels 4 yard stripe. He inflicted a backfield-in-motion penalty on a play that the Flashes single wing formation sent a 'man in* motion'*."*

Balzli put the blame only on Saint Al. *"We beat ourselves again, just like last week. We beat ourselves. Why, we were inside their 14 yard line and didn't score. We were in their 20 twice and with the same result. You can't lose these chances and win ball games. Heck, we seem to be getting worse instead of better. But it's all in the game. The game is over and so is the season. We played as well as were able to. I just hope we can do better next season."*

Karl Nicholas and Eddie Lucchesi would share the Virgadamo Trophy for 1956.

"In the grand scheme of things, the Durant game is barely a ripple. It certainly doesn't compete with such memories as my wedding day, Viet Nam, finishing my dissertation, or the births of my three children. Nevertheless, it has haunted me for sixty years. Some of it is a blur, other moments are sickeningly clear – like the first touchdown, when we knew we were in for a challenge we'd not faced before that season. I've dreamed about that game, and there's one recurring scene that I've conjured up, one that never occurred, but should have. We held those guys scoreless during the second half; we just couldn't pick up the two touchdowns we needed to tie or go ahead. And I know what we could have done – how we could have won that game and, riding on a wave of adrenaline, go on to finish the season unbeaten.

My dream tells me that it could have happened in the third quarter. By then, even I could see that our staple plays – the wide sweeps that had gained us mega-yardage consistently in the first six games – had been successfully scouted and neutralized. But something else was clear. They could not stop our fullback dive up the middle. Every time we ran Buck 38 or the Wedge, with Morrissey and me shoulder-to-shoulder leading the way for Eddie Habert, we gained a sure three or four yards. Eddie called the plays for us, but he was a sophomore and reluctant to call his number too often, deferring to Paul Kelly and Tim to run those sweeps and get creamed.

In my dream I remember that I was the team captain, and I called a timeout. I told Habert, 'Look, kid, run up the middle until they stop you. We won't let you down.' And in the dream we win. Then I wake up. And my heart is a little heavy all day long."

Karl Nicholas; July 20, 2016

1957 (7-0-1)

Balzli started two-a-days on August 19th. He had a rebuilding job in the backfield with only Eddie Habert returning with experience. Ten lettermen were back, however, so the paper said that Joe would *"have to do a little line robbing in order to have a balanced diet"*. He did, and noted that *"We'll probably do a lot more shifting around too before the curtain lifter September 13 against Cary"*.

GAME 1:   SAINT AL (0-0) vs CARY (0-0)
                              FINAL: ST AL 14 CARY 6
                              September 13, 1957

Little was known about Cary except that they had 8 returning starters. Billy Ray said that they were *"expected to field their best team since 1955"* and thought Balzli to be *"worried about tonight's contest"*. He still picked the purple and gold to win 20-12.

In the 1st, the Flashes had driven to the Panther 27 but a Lindigrin fumble killed the momentum. Cary got within the shadow of the goal afterwards but also fumbled at the Flash 6. Saint Al got to the Panther 2 but halftime remained 0-0. Saint Al scored in the 3rd when Billy Howell found Paul Hosemann with a huge 57 yard touchdown pass. Eddie Habert ran the PAT to make it 7-0.

Cary answered when Rudy Holcomb ran 60 yards on a Tom Martin lateral but his PAT failed. The play should have been a 4th down sack of Martin, but a pitch to Holcomb as he was falling gave them the points. The last points came on a bad punt by Cary's Jimmie Jenkins that gave the Flashes the ball at the Panther 25. Habert capitalized from the 1 and the PAT was good.

GAME 2:   SAINT AL (1-0) vs ROLLING FORK (1-0)
                              FINAL: ST AL 0 ROLLING FORK 0
                              September 21, 1957

On the 17th, the Vicksburg Touchdown Club showed film of the Saint Al-Cary game. The upcoming contest against Rolling Fork *"had the markings of a real humdinger"* and matters were not helped when Hosemann broke a bone in his arm that afternoon *"while prepping around in the school yard during recess"*. He was to miss at least 6 weeks and Leo Koestler was also now suffering from an ankle injury. Rolling Fork claimed *"one of their strongest teams in years and are reported with most of last year's star performers back in uniform"*. The game was originally scheduled for the 19th, but both teams postponed the contest due to inclement weather. The ever-accurate Billy Ray called for a tie at 13-13.

The overflow crowd waited for the big play that would propel their Flashes to another victory. It would not come. In fact, Rolling Fork had a chance to win the game late in the 4th. Taking a Logue punt at their 30, they worked to the Flash 13 before Mallie Price fumbled to the Flashes. They had done the same on one drive to the Flash 16 in the 2nd and got to the Flash 27 later before the defense held. Saint Al would get no closer than the Bearcat 20.

Saint Al had thrown 2 picks in the contest while Rolling Fork only 1. That one was by Evans at the Bearcat 49 but he fumbled it back at the 27. The paper said *"The game was a real 'ground' contest'"*. Statistics favored Rolling Fork in the 1st and Saint Al in the 2nd.

GAME 3:   SAINT AL (1-0-1) vs LAKE PROVIDENCE (2-1)
                              FINAL: ST AL 21 LAKE PROVIDENCE 0
                              September 27, 1957

A flu outbreak took its toll on Vicksburg this week and Culkin was hit hard enough to cancel their homecoming game against Rolling Fork. The Flashes were luckily healthy, but Balzli warned that *"Lake Providence will be just as tough, if not tougher, than Rolling Fork"*.

The Flashes' first drive was for 61 yards before fumbling. Joe Lindigrin had hit Don Riddle for 44 in the march to no avail. They did score on their second possession after 10 plays that started at their 43. Runs by Lindigrin, Habert, and Evans got to the 19 before Evans went in from there. Habert made it 7-0. Adding to it afterwards from the 50, Riddle raced for 26 to highlight a drive capped by Habert runs of 4 and 1. He also added the PAT and it was 14-0 at halftime despite a late Mike Hosemann fumble recovery.

The final Flash points came in the 3rd. Runs by numerous players starting at the Flash 49 put the ball at the goal for Habert to crash in and convert the PAT. Lake Providence would get no further than the Flash 20 before the whistle blew. Credit was given to Habert and the other *"Fancy Dan"* runners in Lindigrin and Evans. Others receiving praise were Hosemann and *"the whole line of the Flashes"* for holding Lake Providence to 80 yards of rushing and only 1 *"tally in three games"*.

GAME 4:   SAINT AL (2-0-1) vs GREENVILLE SAINT JOE (1-2)
               FINAL: ST AL 39 GREENVILLE SAINT JOE 6
               October 4, 1957

The coach shifted his team around to provide more scoring potential, but realized that they had scored more points in the last game than in the first two combined. *"We'll go along with that lineup pretty much tomorrow night"*, he had said on Thursday. Saint Joe had two of *"the finest tackles in the state"* in Paul Fava and Harvey Keiler and the team had been practicing hard to stop Balzli's offensive formations. Habert would miss the game due to injury. The Irish would also have a missing key in Center J.R. Low.

Two minutes in, Evans ran for a 54 yard touchdown. He scored the second touchdown of the quarter from the 10 aided by two Riddle runs of 13, a Lindigrin run of 7, and two Monsour plays. Lindigrin hit the goal in the 2nd with a 1 yard dive. The drive's biggest play was a Lindigrin run of 29. It was 20-0 after Evan's PAT.

After an Irish fumble eventually gave the ball to Saint Al at the Flash 33, Lindigrin ran 65 yards to the 10 and Riddle scored from there. Holding Greenville on their downs, the punt went to Billy Howell. He *"criss-crossed"* to Evans who ran it in from 60 and yet another Flash score to make it 32-0 at halftime. The 2nd half started with a Mackey pick on 4th down at the Flash 44. Eight plays later, Lindigrin scored from the 10 and Koestler made it 39-0. Third stringers played thereafter with the last play of the game being a Fred Bordleon to Raymond Olremari touchdown pass. Evans would move into 2nd place in Warren County scoring with 31 points behind Culkin's Tommy Akin (43).

GAME 5:   SAINT AL (3-0-1) vs NICHOLAS BLACKWELL, TN (3-2)
               FINAL: ST AL 25 NICHOLAS BLACKWELL 7
               October 18, 1957

The scouting report on the Bartlett, TN boys said *"they were loaded"*. With 190 pound-plus line and some *"rip-snorting backs"*, Saint Al was in for a fight. Nicholas Blackwell ran *"the Tight T and belly series to perfection, similar the Ole Miss offense"*. The paper called it the "Game of the Year" against the AAA school with Saint Al a *"one to two touchdown underdog against the higher classed Tennessee invaders"*.

The 100-person crowd, *"disappointingly small"* for such a big game, saw the Flashes start quick. The Panthers' punt on 4th down was blocked by Logue and recovered by Mike Hosemann at the Bartlett 28. Evans plowed through for the last 11 to make it 6-0. Nicholas Blackwell responded midway through the 2nd on a 72 yard drive in 8 plays. Mixing passing and running, Farley found Balote from the 10. Brown's PAT gave them a 7-6 advantage going to halftime.

The opening drive of the 2nd half was a Flash march from their 47 in 7 plays. Behind Evans, Riddle and Meyer, it would be Evans taking it untouched for the last 11 yards and the touchdown. Three plays later, Habert picked off Farley at the Panther 35 and took it to the 14. After a few penalties, Lindigrin connected with Hosemann for a 22 yard score and an 18-7 lead. The game was sealed in the 4th when Hosemann recovered a fumble on the Panther 41. Two plays later, *"Evans made like a little sputnik around right end..."* for the remaining 20 yards. Koestler finished the game with the extra point.

Billy Ray was quick to say *"Coach Joe Balzli ... owes us a big, fat cigar. We, not his coaching, caused his Flashes to upset powerful Nicholas Blackwell ... Friday night. We picked the Tennessee squad to trample the Flashes. That got (them) so mad nothing could have stopped them...".* The coach had a lot of praise for his squad, saying *"he had never seen a bunch of boys rebound from a half-time deficit to win so decisively... They had to scrap or the score would have been just the other way around."*

GAME 6:   SAINT AL (4-0-1) @ ANGUILLA (1-2-1)
               FINAL: ST AL 32 ANGUILLA 13
               October 24, 1957

Balzli warned against a *"letdown"* against Anguilla. Their opponent also ran the Single Wing and had a *"beefy, well-conditioned squad who will be going all out for an upset..."*

Saint Al scored immediately on a 97 yard drive capped by a Habert run of 49. Koestler made it 7-0. Their next possession was a 65 yard drive in 7 plays again capped by Habert; this time from the 35. The third score came early in the 2nd after a Panther fumble at their 17. Evans runs of 14 and 11 resulted in the touchdown and a 19-0 lead.

Anguilla cut the lead before halftime after a Flash fumble at the 31. Hal Lyn Green did the honors from the 1 and then passed to Frank Baykin for the PAT. In the 3rd, a Habert run of 53 yards was good for the score and a 25-7 lead. The Flashes could actually have had two more touchdowns in the frame. One was a 62 yard punt return by Evans that was called back for a penalty. The second was a 61 yard run by Riddle who, thinking he crossed the goal, spiked the ball at the 1. Anguilla smartly grabbed the fumble.

The Flashes got another touchdown in the 3rd when Riddle redeemed himself with a 53 yard run. Koestler's PAT made it 32-7 and the "scrubs" took over. Against that unit in the 4th, Anguilla recovered a fumble at the Flash 31 and capped it when Green found Chester McDaniel from the 11. Said the paper, "Coach Balzli mercifully played every boy suited out in an effort to hold down the slaughter".

GAME 7:   SAINT AL (5-0-1) @ JACKSON SAINT JOE (UNREPORTED)
                 FINAL: ST AL 34 JACKSON SAINT JOE 0
                 November 1, 1957

Saint Al was attempting to regain the Strauss-Stallings Trophy taken away by Saint Joe the previous year. With no injuries reported for the week, the paper said "The Flashes appear too strong in our books, and after what Culkin did to Saint Joe last week (33-0), the Rebs spirits won't be quite as high. Saint Aloysius 22 Saint Joseph 6".

On the second play of the game, Tommy Gordon fell on a Rebel fumble. Habert gained 8, Riddle got 11 and then Habert blasted in for the touchdown. The Flashes took the next possession to the Jackson 11 but penalties stopped the drive. Midway through the 2nd, Habert returned a punt 51 yards to the Rebel 23. Evans gained 14 on 3 carries and Habert reached the 15 before a penalty pushed them back to the Rebel 21. Eventually Lindigrin hit Mike Hosemann for a 14 yard strike and Habert added the PAT for a halftime lead of 13-0.

Evans added another touchdown from the 3 late in the 3rd, and the Flashes added two more in the 4th. The first was after runs by Riddle, Habert and Evans put the ball at the 6. Habert took it in from there and, after a penalty, Lindigrin hit Hosemann for an 18 yard PAT. The second was an Evans run from the 1 that capped numerous team rushes. Habert added the last points of the game on the PAT. In the end, Saint Al had limited the Rebels to 2 first downs and only 62 net yards (all rushing). The Flashes had 16 first downs and 333 total yards, and had regained the Strauss-Stallings Trophy.

GAME 8:   SAINT AL (6-0-1) vs WESSON/COPIAH-LINCOLN (UNREPORTED)
                 FINAL: ST AL 48 WESSON 0
                 November 15, 1957: HOMECOMING

The Flashes sat idle over the past two weeks and had to deal with rain on game week. Howell and Hosemann were sick while Saint Al prepared for a team returning 10 of their 12 key players. "Wesson is reported with one of their best elevens in years … and to make matters worse on locals, they've had their eyes set on the Flashes all year". Yet, the paper also noted that "George Evans … has been to the Flashes what Sputnik and Mutnik have been to the Russians: Can see but can do nothing about it. St. Al 20, Wesson 7".

Saint Al scored on their first four possessions. Evans and Habert accounted for most of the rushing in the first drive that was finalized when Evans hit Riddle in the endzone from 15 yards away. Riddle returned the next punt 29 yards to the Flash 44. Ten plays later and at the start of the 2nd, Evans dragged a man into the endzone from the 8. Evans ran in the PAT for a 13-0 lead. The next possession saw Howell pick off a Wesson pass back to their 43. Six plays later, Habert outran Wesson 31 yards to the goal. Evans made it 20-0. The Flash defense held the last Wesson drive as far as the Saint Al 12 before halftime.

The opening kick of the 3rd was taken by Evans 43 yards to the Wesson 10. Habert's two runs resulted in a touchdown and Koestler made it 27-0. The ensuing kick kept Wesson at their 3 and then Jackie Mackey sacked R. Spell for a safety. Saint Al scored three more times before the game was over. Hosemann from the 2 with a Koestler PAT; Hosemann for 56; and a Lindigrin pass to Hosemann from the 20.

Balzli's team would earn not just their 7th win and another undefeated season for the Flashes, but they would rightfully take their place in history among the school's best.

Mike Morrissey and Paul Hosemann would share the Virgadamo Award for the season.

"As I look back on the last game we played, we were all jubilant in the field house after a winning season, but then things turned quiet as we all knew that was our last time together on the field. Joe Balzli had molded us into a family of loyal brothers. When we meet today, it's like we just played that last game last night remembering every play. We can laugh and poke fun at one-another and talk for hours."

Louis Logue; August 6, 2016

1958 (8-0)

Could Joe Balzli continue expectations from an undefeated year? He had some experienced players back but said of his line *"they are too few in number and too light to let me rest easy at night"*. Jackie Mackey and Harold Logue were the only line returners, though Ivan Cunningham and Gordon Sutton had played. The backfield was solid with Eddie Habert and George Evans running the Single Wing so hopes were high. Said Balzli, *"my deepest concern at present is fielding a representative first unit that will make us look good early in the game at least"*.

Workouts began the 15th and *"they really got down to business…"* Practices were positive, but for the schedule he said *"We should be able to hold our own in our league, but we're playing too few teams in our league"*. The paper was high on Balzli and his record. *"But if we know Joe, he'll field a team that will make all Vicksburg proud, no matter who he is playing. He always does"*.

Before the season stated, returning letterman Gordon Sutton would have knee surgery and be sidelined for the year.

GAME 1: SAINT AL (0-0) vs LEXINGTON (0-0)
FINAL: ST AL 19 LEXINGTON 13
September 4, 1958

The Flashes were in *"fair shape"* against a team returning 8 starters and the predictive Mid State Conference champions. The line was *"still causing him to have sleepless nights"* But, he added *"We're just about as ready as we can get. We've shown a lot of pep and spirit in practice, but I'm afraid it's going to take a lot more than that to have a winning season"*. Lexington outweighed Saint Al on the line 176-157 and the paper hesitatingly picked the visitor 19-12 because *"We don't know if Balzli has had time to get his Flashes fired up to meet this tough test or not…"*

With score being kept by the first *"electronic scoreboard"* and in front of the *"second largest crowd to ever attend a football game at Farrell Stadium according to Joe Balzli…"* the home town fans would witness the coach's 100th win as head man. Saint Al marched 54 yards on their first possession for the score. A mix of Lindigrin passing to Monsour and running by Evans and Habert put the Flashes at the Hornet 3 before Evans crossed the goal. They nearly added to that in the 2nd while at the Lexington 1-foot line, but fumbles and lost yardage stopped the drive.

Saint Al took over in the quarter at the Hornet 25 and two passes later (one to Monsour to the 10 and the final to Louis Logue) the Flashes padded their lead. Lexington responded early in the 3rd from the Flash 39 behind runs from Donny Holder and Doyle Hale. Holder took it in from the 5 and he converted to make it 12-7. The Flashes immediately responded on a 64 yard drive. Lindigrin hit Logue for 23 and Evans for 15. Lindigrin then found Evans from the 20. The paper said *"It was like taking candy from a child"*. Evans hit Monsour for the PAT. With :07 left, the Hornets notched their last touchdown after a Flash fumble at the 4. Hale hit Donny Autry for the score but Holder's PAT missed.

GAME 2: SAINT AL (1-0) @ MENDENHALL (3-0)
FINAL: ST AL 12 MENDENHALL 7
September 26, 1958

A game was originally scheduled against Rolling Fork for September 19th, but rain forced a cancellation that would be move the game to November 7th. So, the Flashes next opponent would be the defending Little Dixie Champions. Balzli said that *"We found our weaknesses during the first game and for nearly two weeks have worked hard to correct them. Nine fumbles are too many for any team in one game and we have worked very hard with our backs on this weakness. We definitely have improved* our team with a lot of hard work. Last week we did quite a bit of scrimmaging and I think it will pay off".

Facing a 0-2 team in Rolling Fork quickly changed to being one that would take "an unexpected upset" for a win. The boys had been idle for over three weeks. "Experience is what we needed the most and we were really hurt when our game ... was postponed... However, we are in good physical shape for the unbeaten Little Dixie champions and we may make it an interesting contest." Only Ivan Cunningham would be ailing due to "a sore arm as a result of a recent vaccination shot".

The Flashes put up the first points in the 2nd when Lindigrin nailed Evans for a 52 yard touchdown. In the 3rd, a 60 yard Flash march was highlighted by a Lindigrin pass to Evans of 31 yards. Evans capped it with a 2 yard dive. Mendenhall threatened twice, getting to the Flash 10 and the Flash 7. But in each instance the defense stood tall. Their only score came in the 4th when Wesley Sullivan ran for 22 and Truett Powell scored from the 1 to finish a 65 yard drive.

In typical fashion, Balzli would not call out an individual for accomplishments, instead calling the team victory "terrific". John Downey, playing his first game on defense, suffered a cut requiring six stitches. Perhaps the players were inspired by bus driver W.C. Orr, who said "he didn't drive losing teams and if they didn't want to walk back to Vicksburg, they would have to win."

GAME 3:   SAINT AL (2-0) @ GREENVILLE SAINT JOSEPH (1-2)
                       FINAL: ST AL 32 GREENVILLE ST JOE 0
                       October 3, 1958

Joe was wary of over-confidence after two "upsets" but playing a Catholic rival was always reason to be ready. "We are in good shape and if we play the type of ball as in the first two games, we shouldn't have too much trouble" but added "over-confidence and not being able to get his boys 'up' for this game loomed as a big problem. ... they can be mighty tough if we don't play our best. After all, for the past two years it's been the underdog that came out on top. These underdog teams are the ones that can really hurt you if you are not careful because you know the boys are more than apt going to 'put out' when they play a tough team." Ray's prediction for a Flashes win of 33-6 was nearly perfect.

Evans, suffering from an injured foot, would see only one play before sitting. The Flashes scored three times in the 1st. Habert had the first two on runs of 2 and 51, and Lindigrin ran the next in from the 2 and hit Logue for the PAT. Before the quarter's end, Lindigrin plunged in from the 2 and found Logue for another PAT. Saint Al continued the barrage in the 2nd when Lindigrin again found Logue from the 15. Mackey then picked off an Irish pass at their 44 and returned it for the final tally.

GAME 4:   SAINT AL (3-0) @ NICHOLAS-BLACKWELL, TN (UNREPORTED)
                       FINAL: ST AL 33 NICHOLAS BLACKWELL 13
                       October 17, 1958

Balzli visited the Vicksburg Touchdown Club on the 6th to discuss the Flashes' Single Wing offense. President Buster Rawdon announced it to "be one of the top programs of the year". As for Nicholas-Blackwell, little was known except that the AA team had lost one game to Corinth of the Big Eight Conference 19-7. Saint Al had another off-week and had played only 3 games in a month and a half which caused the coach to worry about "staleness". They left at 7:30am on game day for the 200 mile trip with a stop in Clarksdale for lunch. Ray picked the Flashes 20-13 for a number of reasons, not the least of which was "every time we pick him (Balzli) to lose, he makes us eat our own words and we must admit they don't taste very good".

The Flashes opened on their 34 after a 14 yard Lindigrin kickoff return. After Habert gained 6, Evans went up the middle for 62 yards and a touchdown. Logue was good on the PAT. Their next possession started at the Flash 45 after a Gordon 20 yard punt return. After hitting Evans for 17, Lindigrin took the reverse to the Panther 12. A penalty put them at the 1 and then Lindigrin went over on 4th down. Logue was again good to make it 14-0.

Saint Al got to the Panther 15 in the 2nd before a pass was picked off by Reece Davis. The defense gave them the ball back at the NB 39 where Evans eventually got in from the 8. Logue ended the 1st half scoring at 21-0. The effects of the long travel showed in the 2nd half when Larry Thomas found Curtis Gabbard on an 8 yard Panther score. In the 4th, the Flashes padded the lead when Gordon fell on a loose Thomas punt attempt at their 30. Evans and Habert rushed the ball to the 1 and Lindigrin scored from there.

Nicholas Blackwell added one more against the second unit with a Thomas 32 yard touchdown pass to Billy Pleasants and PAT pass to Davis. Saint Al iced the contest with less than 1:00 left when Lindigrin threw to Evans for a 28 yard score. The paper labeled the Flashes *"... as one of, if not THE top independent team in the state barring none"*.

GAME 5:   SAINT AL (4-0) vs ANGUILLA (UNREPORTED)
                        FINAL: ST AL 33 ANGUILLA 14
                        October 24, 1958: HOMECOMING

Ray's homecoming week pick was 26-6 in favor of Saint Al. Almost nothing was written about the opponent during the entire week, but the game article was lengthy.

Two fumbles by Saint Al and two very long quick-punts by Hal Green of Anguilla kept the first quarter scoreless. In the 2nd, and starting at the Anguilla 43, Habert went 6 plays to paydirt after runs by him and Lindigrin. Logue made it 7-0. The ensuing Anguilla punt gave the ball to the Flashes at the 30 and started a drive of frustration. Lindigrin found Logue for a 66 yard strike but it was called back for a motion penalty. Habert runs and receptions, along with an Evans run to the 24, allowed Gordon to race around end for the touchdown. That, too, would be called back for clipping. Lindigrin would eventually hit Logue at the 5 and then Habert went up the middle for the touchdown to make it 13-0.

On their first possession of the 3rd, Gordon passed to Evans for a 44 yard score and Logue made it 20-0. Evans next punt return was for 49 yards, but Anguilla picked off a Flash pass. They gave it right back when Habert returned the favor for a 22 yard pick-six. Habert did the honors on the next drive by running in a touchdown from 62 yards away and Logue added the last Flash points.

Balzli *"once again demonstrated his fine sportsmanship by playing his substitutes throughout most of the last half of the game, even putting in the substitutes' substitutes or what might be called the St. Aloysius Rinky-dinks"*. It was then that Anguilla scored their two touchdowns. A Flash fumble and a Sam Garrett pickoff allowed Anguilla to start at the Flash 29 and then Green ran in from the 10 for the score and (later) the PAT. He also put up a 53 yard run for a touchdown and a PAT as time expired.

GAME 6:   SAINT AL (5-0) vs JACKSON SAINT JOSEPH (UNREPORTED)
                        FINAL: ST AL 39 JACKSON ST JOE 0
                        October 31, 1958

The Flashes started the week ranked 22nd in the Top 25 Poll. Bragging rights against a Catholic rival and the Strauss-Stallings Trophy were at stake. The paper noted that Balzli had *"his share of (unreported) injuries"* but though Saint Al too much to handle saying *"... we expect St. Joe is going to need more than 14 points in the last quarter to win this one. St. Al 33 St Joe 4"*.

On the kickoff, Lindigrin took the ball 29 yards to the Saint Al 44. Evans went for 13 before Habert took it the rest of the 43 yards for the touchdown. Evans rushed for the PAT and the rout was underway. Habert added another long touchdown of 44 yards on the next drive courtesy of his 13 yard run and Evans' 17 yard push. Evans' run made it 14-0. He put up his third touchdown on the next possession from 19 away after a combined effort from himself, Evans, and Lindigrin. Their last score of the half came from Evans from the 4 after a highlight pass from Lindigrin to Evans for 35 yards. Halftime would be a Flash lead of 26-0.

Saint Al put up two more in the 3rd with a Lindigrin pass to Evans from 36 and a Monsour run from 9. After that, the *"rinky-dinks"* came in and continued the shutout. Notwithstanding the phenomenal rushing game he had, the paper called Habert *"a real terror on defense"*. Logue, Mackey and others were called *"the rock-ribbed Saint Aloysius line"*.

GAME 7:   SAINT AL (6-0) @ ROLLING FORK (UNREPORTED)
                        FINAL: ST AL 27 ROLLING FORK 0
                        November 7, 1958

The game cancelled on September 19th was here. *"No one was hampered with an injury in last week's game"* according to the coach. The Flashes were now 17th in the state. Calling Rolling Fork *"vastly improved"* and noting that they were the team to tie Saint Al the previous year, the paper still predicted a 27-12 Flash victory. *"... the Colonels are a much better team this time and could give Joe Balzli's blazing Flashes gobs of trouble. They'll be going all out to knock the props out from under the highly-touted Flashes"*.

In usual fashion, Saint Al scored on their opening possession. Evans gained 20, Lindigrin gained the same to the RF 10 and Evans took it in from the 7 on 4th down. Logue made it 7-0. That score would hold until the 3rd when they used 6 plays to go 69 yards for the touchdown. Habert gained 56 of the yards and added the points on a 28 yard run. Logue made it 14-0. In the same quarter, they went 63 yards in 8 plays highlighted by a Lindigrin pass to Evans for 39 yards. Evans pushed in from the 1 and Logue made it 21-0.

The last Flash points came in the 4th when Evans went up the middle for 60 yards. "*Coach Joe Balzli then called on the 'Japanese Bandits', his second unit, and they managed to contain the Colonels without a score*". Rolling Fork had only 73 yards of total offense (10 on one pass) and only 3 first downs compared to 381 net yards for Saint Al.

GAME 8:   SAINT AL (7-0) vs KILMICHAEL (?-2)
                             FINAL: ST AL 59 KILMICHAEL 25
                             November 13, 1958

The contest for this week was supposed to feature a North Carrollton opponent. But Kilmichael, "*considered the Mid-State Conference's Cinderella team, was substituted … because it was felt Kilmichael could furnish stronger opposition to the undefeated, untied Flashes and … provide loyal fans with a real opponent for the season's climax*". North Carrollton was "*crippled and small and didn't care to engage in grid battle …*" Kilmichael, on the other hand, had lost only 2 games (each by 1 point) and was considered "*one of the strongest small teams in North Central Mississippi*".

Balzli commented that "*… the bad thing about it, we haven't been able to scout them. Therefore, we don't know what to expect from them*". Said Billy Ray, "*So, Joe and his Flashes face quite a tough foe, it seems; one that's not used to being pushed around very much. It'll be quite a challenge to the Flashes to see if they can crack this tough defense and possibly score more points in this one game than has been scored against the Hornets all season*".

The paper said "*Touchdowns came a dime a dozen here … as Joe Balzli's St. Aloysius Flashes climaxed their 1958 football season by running roughshod over helpless Kilmichael. It was an offensive crowd-pleaser that left fans gasping for air. However, had Balzli not shown mercy, the visitors would not have scored near that many points*". Saint Al scored first on a Lindigrin 36 yard pass to Evans. Afterwards, Habert ran one in from 62, Evans picked off Kilmichael pass and lateraled to Gordon; and a Kilmichael fumble at their 39 set up the last of the half. Nine plays later with :15 before halftime, Lindigrin found Logue for a 44 yard touchdown to make it 32-0.

Kilmichael put up points against "*the Japanese Bandits*" in the 2nd half on a Farris Jenkins keeper from the 7, two by LaDell Harrington of 50 and 71 yards, and a Jenkins 7 yard strike to Bobby Howell. The "*Flashes offensive punchers re-entered the game and bombardment right back whenever Kilmichael would 'sock their little brothers'*". In the 2nd half, Habert ran one for 62, Logue caught one for 46, Monsour caught one from 13 and Gordon tallied the last from 14.

The Flashes had completed another perfect season under Balzli. A section in the paper congratulated him on his accomplishment. "*Two losses a season isn't considered too bad, but when a team goes four seasons and suffers only two defeats, well, that is something. If ever a coach deserves a pat on the back, brother Joe does.*" The Virgadamo Trophy for 1958 went to Eddie Habert and George Evans.

"*The 1958 season crowned four years of varsity football with a total of two losses. We could not have been prouder. We wanted to please our beloved coach, Joe. He was like a second father to us. To win our first two games in which we were decided underdogs and a bit unknown was terrific. To beat Mendenhall, defending Little Dixie Champions, was the highlight of four years. I'll never forget warming up on their home field and them running around us to warm up with more on their team than we had in high school. But Joe had us prepared and we hung on. A feeling all the great guys on that team will never forget.*"

George Evans; August 8, 2016

1959 (4-4)

Joe Balzli's Flashes reported on August 10th with only 1 two-way starter in Jimmy "Monk" Monsour. As a whole, only 4 total returning lettermen were suited up (Bobby Gordon, Jerome Johnson and John Downey) but the remainder were *"...a galaxy of eager sophomores and juniors"* For the first two-weeks, starting August 17th, they held two-a-day practices but tapered off to daily workouts.

Billy Ray prepared fans that had seen the Flashes go 29-2-1 since 1956 with a stark reality by saying *"... the season could turn out to be a little longer than St. Aloysius fans have been accustomed to in the past. The main reason is that the Flashes ARE NOT loaded this time..."* They would play 7 of their 8 games against Class A opponents. *"Balzli won't take defeat beforehand, nor will he have a defeatist attitude before the game is played. One thing certain though, if there's any tricks up Balzli's sleeve, he'll more than likely have to pull them out this season."*

From behind his massive cigar, the coach said *"We won't be humiliated. And I'd like to pay tribute to these boys. We have the greatest potential of any squad we've had in recent years. I don't mean by that that we'll win every game; just look forward to seeing us in the future."*

As the first game approached, Balzli said *"We're about as ready as we can possibly get under prevailing circumstances"*. He noted that it was hard to pick a starting eleven because the *"entire squad has been showing spirit, determination and that ever so important 'want to win' attitude. We may not go undefeated as in the last two seasons, but we're getting to be in there all the way and other teams had better not go to sleep on us"*.

GAME 1:   SAINT AL (0-0) vs LEXINGTON (0-0)
                     FINAL: ST AL 0 LEXINGTON 7
                     September 4, 1959

Saint Al started the rebuilding year against the defending Mid-State Conference champions. Like Mendenhall, the only loss they had the previous year was to the Flashes. The paper said that the team with 9 returning lettermen would be *"hot and mad and (would) go all out in an attempt to knock-off the ... Flashes in their own back yard"*.

The opening kickoff saw Lexington fumble at their 25 and recovered by Dan Hossley. The offense had only two plays before fumbling the ball back when a bad snap by Hossley was recovered by Lexington at the Hornet 40. They put together runs by Tommy Holder (18) and two by Eddie Harrison (11 and 16) to set up a Harrison 16 yard scoring sprint. Holder split the uprights for the PAT.

Saint Al came right back by driving to the Hornet 28 but Gordon was picked off by Pat Barrett. They got no deeper than the Lexington 22 in the game due to the numerous fumbles that stopped every drive. In fact, they actually rushed for 73 yards, but fumbles cost them 64 for a net of 9 yards. It would be the first Flash loss since the end of the 1956 season. Losing by 7 points combined with 12 Flash fumbles to such a big opponent must have been heart-breaking.

GAME 2:   SAINT AL (0-1) @ CLINTON (2-0)
                     FINAL: ST AL 13 CLINTON 36
                     September 18, 1959

During the off-week, Balzli put the Flashes through *"rugged drills during the past two weeks trying to correct some of the weak spots"*. Billy Riddle and Bobby Gordon were injured, with Gordon termed *"out indefinitely"*. The coach switched numerous players around to new spots and introduced new faces into the lineup. Clinton had two Little Dixie wins along with 200 pound FB Jimmy Dukes.

The re-vamped Flashes surprised the hosts in the 1st by taking a 13-7 lead. On the first drive, Dukes fumbled to Saint Al at the Arrow 39. David Nohra gained 15 on one of the twelve plays before Mike Franco crossed the goal from the 3. Clinton answered immediately on their second play when John Quissenberry hit Jack Walker for a 41 yard touchdown. Dukes converted for the 7-6 lead.

Saint Al's next possession started at the Flash 31 after a "Monk" Monsour return. Franco found John Downey for 17 and Nohra hit Larry Falgout for 34 to put the ball at the Clinton 17. On his second run, Franco was able to score and add the PAT. That would be the last Saint Al points but Clinton would begin a scoring barrage. In the 2nd, Quissenberry hit Jerry Rankin for an 18 yard score and then Jack Watkins for the 14-13 PAT. The Flashes fumbled at the Arrow 34, resulting in a 12 play drive with Dukes going in from the 1. He also converted the extra point for a 21-13 halftime lead.

In the 3rd, a David Bacon punt pinned the Flashes deep and eventually resulted in a safety on Nohra. Later, Dukes ran for 41 yards with one shoe for the next touchdown. Quisenberry found George McMullan for the PAT. Dukes capped the scoring in the 4th from the 6. The paper noted that the Arrows actually had a few more touchdowns that were called back due to (125 yards of) penalties.

GAME 3:   SAINT AL (0-2) vs MENDENHALL (0-0)
                 FINAL: ST AL 6 MENDENHALL 32
                 September 25, 1959

Though Saint Al sprung the 12-7 upset in 1958, only 3 of the 14 boys who played in that game were back. Mendenhall, described as *"what will probably be its toughest foe of the season…"* was defending Little Dixie champs. Called *"undefeated"*, The Simpson County News probably incorrectly showed St Al as their first opponent since the victory was the 10th straight. The paper called it *"a genuine challenge for (Balzli's) Flashes"* and said *"St. Aloysius seems destined for another defeat…"* Riddle and Gordon were still out.

The contest started with Nohra taking the kickoff from the Flash 15 to the Tiger 18. But a Franco fumble shortly thereafter, recovered by Dudley Nichols at the Flash 10, resulted in an 8 yard touchdown pass from James Sullivan to Tommy Lucas. Later in the quarter, the orange-clad Sullivan found Lucas for 36 yards to the Flash 24. Sullivan gained 24 yards on 2 runs and then capped it himself from the 16.

Mendenhall's next score was in the 2nd via a Stephen Pittman run of 51. Don Whitman hit Lucas for 11, Sullivan got 6 and then Whitman found Lucas for the 9 yard touchdown. Sullivan's PAT made it 19-0. Before intermission, Douglas Grubbs picked off Franco and returned it 23 yards for the score. Each team would put up points in the 4th. The Tigers' Robert Kline picked off another pass but Mendenhall fumbled it back seconds later at the Tiger 36. Seven plays later Greg Doiron scored from the 1. It took no time before Mendenhall responded. On their first play after Cecil Puckett's return to the Tiger 46, Sullivan hit Dudley Nichols for a 53 yard score. Sullivan's PAT finished the 32-6 game. As the last seconds elapsed, Nohra took a reverse at the Flash 36 all the way to the Tiger 13 before being tackled. They would get as far as the Mendenhall 4.

GAME 4:   SAINT AL (0-3) vs GREENVILLE SAINT JOE (2-1)
                 FINAL: ST AL 13 GREENVILLE SAINT JOE 6
                 October 2, 1959

Balzli confirmed on Thursday that Bobby Gordon and Frank Gugert were lost for the season due to their injuries, but Billy Riddle would be back in the lineup. The team worked hard on pass defense and offense that week and reported *"a good week of practice"*.

The Flashes finally cracked the win column this night in Vicksburg, but not without a slippery start. Starting at the Flash 29, a fine play by Franco was brought back 15 yards for penalty. Nohra gained 11 and then Franco burst for 48 before fumbling back to the Irish. After a defensive stand forced a punt, Nohra returned for 21 and then broke off a 79 yard touchdown run. The 2nd saw more Flash fumbles and an ejection of "Monk" Monsour.

Saint Al's last touchdown came in the 3rd. Doiron ran for 32, Franco got 8, a penalty pushed them back to the Irish 32, and then Franco hit Norha with a pass to the Irish 2. Franco pushed over for the touchdown and then hit Downey for the PAT. Greenville's response came late when Richard Mascagni engineered a 72 yard drive ending with his run from the 5.

GAME 5:   SAINT AL (1-3) @ WASHINGTON (5-0)
                 FINAL: ST AL 13 WASHINGTON 36
                 October 9, 1959

The Class A Pirates had won 12 straight and the paper predicted a 26-13 loss, calling it *"just a little too much"* for Saint Al. Said Balzli, *"If we can cut down on mistakes tonight, we may not win but we'll strictly let the Pirates know they've been in a battle"*. A crowd of 2,500 fans were on hand for the Homecoming game.

Washington took advantage of their first possession after a Flash punt. Joe Ditzler ran in from the 30 and Dick Dollar converted the PAT. On the Flashes' ensuing drive, Nohra ran 41 to the Pirate 21. Two plays later he got to the 9 before going in from there on 4th down to finish the 64 yard drive. Franco hit him for the tying PAT. Washington answered two plays afterwards for 60 yards when Ditzler ran for 41 followed by a James Boyett score. Dollar gained the PAT.

Washington opened the 2nd with a Milton Smith punt return of 70 yards cushioned with a Dollar PAT. On the kickoff, the Flashes fumbled on the 19 and Vernon Myers recovered. After a Dollar run to the Flash 9, Boyette scored again. Dollar made it 28-7 at halftime. The 3rd had both teams knocking on their opponent's door. Saint Al got to the 18 and the 5 while Washington got to the 3 and 1-foot line. Defenses held each time.

But in the 4th, a punt snap at the Flash 1 went over the punter's head and the Pirates chalked up a safety. Saint Al's on-side kick was recovered by Washington on the 31. Runs by Acy Arnold, Smith and Boyett put the ball near the goal. Smith took the pitchout and scored. The Flashes' last score came with :40 remaining when Franco hit Falgout from the 21.

GAME 6:   SAINT AL (1-4) @ PEARL (UNREPORTED)
                             FINAL: ST AL 20 PEARL 12
                             October 23, 1959

An off-week was what the Flashes needed after a brutal start to the rebuilding season. There was still a chance for a .500 season and Pearl was a good way to start. The paper predicted a 19-6 victory.

Pearl got off to a good start by blocking a Monsour punt at the Flash 15. Danny Neely then hit George Puckett at the 5 and Bobby Stribling went in from there. Saint Al responded quickly when Falgout picked off a Pirate pass at their 37. Three plays later from the 31, Franco hit Monsour from the 27 for the touchdown. Franco added the PAT to re-take the lead. Moments later, Charles Amborn blocked a Pirate punt at their 32. Franco again found Monsour from the 8 five plays later. As the half was ending, Pearl put together a 72 yard drive capitalized by a Larry Jones touchdown from the 12.

The last score came in the 3rd after a 29 yard punt return by Monsour put the Flashes in business at the Pirate 18. Runs by Doiron (3) and Franco (14) pushed the ball to the 1 and Monsour did the rest. The 4th was played in the rain, causing both teams to slog through the plays. The Flashes' only fumble came in this quarter, but it was recovered by the purple and gold. With his performance, Monsour moved to 2nd in Saint Al scoring with 18. Franco held the lead with 21.

GAME 7:   SAINT AL (2-4) vs JACKSON SAINT JOSEPH (3-5)
                             FINAL: ST AL 28 JACKSON ST JOE 6
                             October 30, 1959: HOMECOMING

The plan to finish .500 was still on track and the Flashes would "*be shooting the homecoming works for victory number three*". Another Little Dixie foe waited in rival Saint Joe, but the team had worked hard on defense and was "*in good physical shape for the Friday game*". Saint Joe had just upset highly favored Culkin 7-6. For Homecoming, a joint parade between SFXA and Saint Al would be staged through downtown streets.

Saint Al started quickly when runs by Nohra, Doiron and Franco produced big gains and Doiron capped the 61 yard drive from the 13. The Rebels stormed back to the Flash 8 but fumbled to Saint Al. In the 2nd, however, they closed the gap to 7-6 when Randy Kuriger danced in from the 8. Saint Al almost scored again, getting as far as the JSJ 1 before time expired.

The Flashes did their damage in a rainy 2nd half. They took the opening kick 80 yards with Monsour closing the final 16 for a touchdown. Later in the 3rd, Jimmy Buell crossed the line from the 23 on a drive that started at the Rebel 44. Saint Al's final score would be from Doiron's 9 yard run to cap a 46 yard drive. Said the paper, "*Joe Balzli's young Flashes, dominated by freshmen and sophomores this year, are beginning to jell and the outlook for the next two years is promising indeed. The Flashes are improving in every game and perhaps played their finest game of the season … with a 28-6 rout of rival St Joseph of Jackson*".

GAME 8:   SAINT AL (3-4) vs ROLLING FORK (NOT REPORTED)
                             FINAL: ST AL 26 ROLLING FORK 7
                             November 5, 1959

A chance to break even would come without the services of Nohra. He was now out with the chicken pox and Jimmy Buell would take his place alongside a healthy Flash squad. The Flashes scored first in the 2nd after Doiron returned a Colonel punt 10 yards to their 27. Franco gained 8 and three consecutive Doiron runs got into the endzone. Franco converted the PAT. Doiron also added more in the quarter on a touchdown from the 9 that capped a 60 yard endeavor. Franco's pass to Monsour for the PAT gave Saint Al a 14-0 halftime lead.

In the 3rd, Monsour picked off a Colonel pass and returned it 54 yards for the next touchdown. Both teams hit the scoreboard in the 4th. Runs from Larry Jenkins, Ray Garcia and Phil Thomas brought the ball to the 16 where Thomas was able to maneuver through the Flash defense for the score. Jimmy Hastcock hit Thomas for the PAT to make it 20-7. Franco was able to score once more for the Flashes before the end of the contest from the 5.

Doiron had 198 yards on 20 carries which the paper called *"Not bad for a freshman"*. More importantly, the Flashes had beaten the odds against higher-quality opponents to close 1959 at .500 and set the stage for a promising future.

Bobby Gordon and Jim "Monk" Monsour would share the Virgadamo Trophy for the year.

1960-1969

SAINT ALOYSIUS 1963 TEAM (5-2-1)

1960 (3-5)

Balzli was celebrating his 25th year as head man. As a present from past players, he received the gift of a new Rambler station wagon. Another gift was the returning 13 lettermen from the previous year; though most were juniors and sophomores. Injuries were limited to reserves in Paul Brown (broken ankle) and Freddie Angelo (broken foot).

The Flashes had an eight-game schedule led by senior captains Danny Setaro, John Downey and Larry Angelo. Their lead game was the team picked as winner of the Little Dixie Conference. The paper predicted a *"bang-up game and possibly the Flashes' toughest opponent on their schedule."* And while saying that the Flashes *"could be off to one of their better and most thrilling seasons"*, they also predicted a loss to open the year. Clinton outweighed the Flashes. Therefore, it was predicted that *"... when it comes to the explosive charging of* (RB Jimmy) *Dukes, the Flashes fall a little short."*

GAME 1:   SAINT AL (0-0) vs CLINTON (0-0)
                 FINAL: ST AL 6 CLINTON 21
                 September 16, 1960

A standing room only crowd came to see if the Flashes could defeat a highly regarded team that had been victorious 36-13 the year before. Both teams returned the majority of their players, but Saint Al was still younger. The 210 pound back Dukes would be the man to stop.

Saint Al scored first on a 65 yard drive with only 3:00 left in the half. Greg Doiron ran 36 yards up the middle to the Clinton 20, and then Jimmy Buell hit tailback Mike Franco for a one-handed and deflected touchdown catch. The Flashes were up 6-0 at halftime. Clinton came right back in the 2nd half. The Arrows drove after the kickoff, with Dukes going for 35 to set up his own score. Doiron and David Nohra stopped him, but Dukes eventually got in from the 3 and scored the extra point. In the same quarter starting at their own 33, Robert Williams hit David Bacon for 30 yards to the Flash 21. Ken Johnson moved it to the 13 and then Dukes ran twice more for the touchdown from the 11. Johnson added the extra point to make it 14-6.

Scoring was finished in the 4th when Williams hit Bacon for 60 yards to the Flash 30. Dukes pushed in the final 14 yards for the score and Bill Thornton added the extra point. The Flashes were optimistic on the drive after Williams had hit Bill Moore for a 79 yard touchdown only to have it called back for a penalty. The paper noted that *"Balzli's Flashes gave a good account of themselves, especially during the first half, but found Clinton a more experienced and heavier outfit."*

GAME 2:   SAINT AL (0-1) vs CHAMBERLAIN HUNT ACADEMY (0-1)
                 FINAL: ST AL 19 CHA 7
                 September 22, 1960: HOMECOMING

The Flashes scored on their first two possessions and on their last. On the opening kickoff, the Flashes moved 75 yards with Franco later finding paydirt and Riddle adding the PAT. In the 2nd, Franco went in from 5 to cap a 70-yard march. They almost scored again from the CHA 7, but the halftime whistle blew before they got any further. The Wildcats managed a 68-yard drive for their score. Riley Nelson ran for 35 followed by Randy Sims' run of 28 for the touchdown. Billy Alexander's PAT made it 13-7 at half.

Chamberlain Hunt had an opportunity to take the lead at the end of the game. Jimmy Boyd picked off a pass and brought it back to the Flash 27. The paper in Port Gibson said it was the Flash 20. They got to the 3 when Boyd hit Ellis, and on their final attempt, pitched to Nelson. The Flash defense stood tall and stopped him inches from the goal. Taking advantage of the momentum, Franco ran 59 yards to the Wildcat 23, Doiron gained 16 yards in 2 attempts and Franco took it to the 1. In a drive of 100 yards, Doiron went over for the touchdown.

GAME 3:   SAINT AL (1-1) @ GREENVILLE SAINT JOSEPH (3-0-1)
                 FINAL: ST AL 12 GREENVILLE ST JOE 33
                 October 1, 1960

The game was moved to Thursday to avoid conflict with Greenville High School's homecoming game with Corinth. Coach Dom Bevalaqua's Irish was, according to reports, *"sporting one of their best elevens in many a moon"* and had outscored their opponents 60-7. Balzi reported the team healthy and in good condition, but said *"We'll have to play our best game of the season or we're in for a licking."*

The Flashes started well when a Pat Downey punt block put the Flashes at the Irish 5. Franco went in from the 1 but missed Downey for the conversion. In the same quarter, the Irish fumbled a kickoff and Saint Al had it on the Saint Joe 33. Franco got to the 21 and then the 15 before Doiron took it in to make it 12-0. Saint Joe took the game over afterwards. Starting at their 10, Jimmy McCoy ran to the Flash 35, Billy Swain and Richard Mascagni got it to the 20, the tandem of Johnny Ventura, McCoy and Mascagni pushed it to the 9. McCoy went in to make it 12-6. They later scored when the Flashes fumbled and Benny Strazi returned it 55 yards for a touchdown. Before halftime, Jimmy McCoy picked off a Flash pass for a 60 yard touchdown. At half, it was now 18-12.

In the 3rd, Mascagni found McCoy and Swain to get to the Flash 20. Mascagni then found McCoy for a 9 yard score to make it 24-12. In the 4th they scored immediately when Al Fava hit Dade McCoy from the 7. The final score was a safety when Saint Al ran from their own 2 but were pushed back.

In the end, Balzli summed up his team by saying *"… they aren't quite as good as we thought they were. Speed is lacking but we're hoping to improve as the season goes along. St. Joe also had a fine team; the finest team they've had in some time … and they just seemed to want it a little more than we did."* He also noted that the Flashes *"hit the hardest they've had all season, they just had misfortune with breaks and that St. Joe took full advantage."*

GAME 4:   SAINT AL (1-2) vs WASHINGTON (4-1)
                 FINAL: ST AL 21 WASHINGTON 26
                 October 7, 1960

Balzli had his team working to *"weed out mistakes and improve on their offense."* They also focused on defense to stop an expected *"high power offense".* Washington also had a big line. Roger Idom (263), Pat Harrigill (235) and Marion Felternberger (195) were mentioned as obstacles to overcome.

Saint Al had two close 1st quarter drives. One got to the Washington 17 before losing the ball. But it was the Pirates who scored first after a fake 4th down punt. The snap went to halfback Joe Ditzler who went 61 yards to the Flash 2. Charles Freemen finished it for the score and quarterback Acy Arnold converted the PAT to make it 7-0. The Flashes came right back on a 55 yard drive capped by a Doiron score from the 28. Franco's PAT tied it 7-7. But the half ended when the Pirates drove 77 yards, aided by two James Boyette catches. The last one was from the 22 and a touchdown. At half, it was 13-7. On the opening kickoff of the 2nd half, Saint Al moved 52 yards to the endzone with Doiron running the last 13 for the score. He also converted the extra point to give the home team a 14-13 lead.

In the 4th, Washington had moved from their 19 to the Flash 30. Saint Al had appeared to stop the Pirate march on a 3rd-and-7 Arnold pass. Ditzler and Doiron both went for the ball. Doiron knocked it to the ground but a flag was thrown for interference. The ball was now at the Flash 15. Arnold would hit Eugene Ham from the 13 to give them a lead of 19-14. Washington added to the lead when John Bhonn hit James Lofton for 16, Boyette for 22, and Ditzler for a 10-yard touchdown. Bhonn found Lofton for the extra point to make it 26-14. The Flashes scored on the last play of the game; a 58 yard drive with Jimmy Buell hitting Downey from the 12. Franco found Nohra for the PAT.

The Vicksburg Evening Post said that *"the hometown fans went away shaking their heads and moaning, 'we were robbed' and rightfully so because it was a disputed pass interference play that set up the Pirates third touchdown early in the fourth quarter."* Later, they commented on the effort of the Vicksburg boys. *"Although the Flashes lost their third game of the season, they showed much more hustle and determination than at any time this year…"*

GAME 5:   SAINT AL (1-3) vs HAZLEHURST (5-1)
                 FINAL: ST AL 28 HAZLEHURST 21
                 October 14, 1960

The Little Dixie Conference Hazlehurst team was described as *"one of their all-time great teams"* and *"well-rounded"* with *"an explosive offense spearheaded by 190-pound fullback Powell. Their line is built around Guard Wallace and Tackle Bolan, both 190-pounders and Center Mangold, a 185-pounder."* Balzli noted of his squad, *"We have shown a lot of improvement from our opening game. I just hope we have improved enough to give Hazlehurst a good game."* In preparation, he worked them overtime to improve both sides of the ball. The paper had said that with their *"well balanced attached ... it will take 100 per cent effort on the part of all St. Al players to make the game interesting."*

Before a *"large, cheering crowd"*, Hazlehurst scored first to make it 7-0 on the shoulders of Hunter Kergosien from the 16. But St Al responded with 1:00 left in the half via a 58 yard drive that had Doiron plunge in for a 3-yard touchdown. Franco hit Billy Buell for the PAT to make it 7-7. In the 3rd, Saint Al sent Franco up the middle from the 3 for a score, followed by a Franco-to-Falgout pass for the EP. With two minutes gone in the 4th, Doiron went in from the 2 after a 61-yard drive. Hazlehurst responded with a Kergosien score from the 2.

Franco then struck again with an 80-yard run for the endzone. Buell found Falgout again for the conversion. Kergosien had one more score in him on a pass from Don Raggio from the 29, but it was too late. The paper called it *"the best they've looked all season ... in a big upset, and even played their subs in the last quarter while doing so."* Said Balzli *"We jelled in the ... game. I was real proud the way our boys bounced back. If we keep playing like that, we'll win another game or two this season."* Doiron's efforts put him 2nd place in Warren County in scoring with 45; 3 behind Fred Windham of Jett.

GAME 6:   SAINT AL (2-3) vs PEARL (0-6)
                 FINAL: ST AL 14 PEARL 21
                 October 20, 1960

Balzli wasn't overlooking winless Pearl. He thought that they had the best looking team in their league with key players in Bill Clay (170) and center George Benton (235). *"They have too good of a team not to win one pretty soon, and if we're not careful, it's liable to be us they beat. They're plenty big and tough and we're not in the best shape of the season, either. We had quite a few players 'shook up' last week against Hazlehurst and one or two of them may see very little action, if any."*

One of those players who were "shook up" was starting tackle Billy Buell. He had injured his arm and would be replaced by the 183-pound Billy Riddle. By game time, he was joined on the sidelines by tackle Amborn and end Falgout. As with Game 2, the date was changed to avoid conflict as The Sisters of Mercy were having their 100th anniversary celebration.

On their first possession, Pearl drove 83 yards behind rushes of Bobby Stribling (36 yards) and Danny Jones (23 yards). Stribling went in from the 3 for the touchdown and then Clay found Jones for the PAT. It was 7-0. The Flashes almost answered with a 50 yard pass Buell to Setaro, but they got no farther than the Pirate 30 before giving the ball back.

Nearing halftime, the Pirates marched 59 yards ending in a Danny Neely touchdown run from the 14. Stribling once again converted the PAT to make it 14-0. This time the Flashes were able to respond. In six plays, Saint Al went 60 yards. Buell ran for 28 and 20 to set up a Franco score from the 3. Franco then hit Buell for the PAT and trimmed the Pearl lead to 14-7 at intermission.

The Pirates copied their first possession of the game to start the 3rd. Going 54 yards in 6 plays, Stribling finished the drive from the 9. Tommy Curtis converted and it was 21-7. Saint Al responded with a 55 yard drive behind runs from Nohra (15) and Buell (17). Franco hit Pat Downey for a touchdown from the 19 and then converted the PAT to make it 21-14.

Pearl had blown a 19 point lead to Forest Hill the week before and Saint Al almost made them repeat the performance. Late in the game, the Flashes put together a long drive to the Pearl 25 behind Buell runs of 11 and 26. Franco moved it to the 15 and then found Buell on a completion to the 6. Doiron moved it to the 5, but the Pirate defense stiffened. Two passes were incomplete and the runs gained nothing. It was *"like running into a stone wall"*, noted the paper.

GAME 7:   SAINT AL (2-4) @ JACKSON SAINT JOSEPH (2-4-2)
                 FINAL: ST AL 21 JACKSON ST JOE 0
                 October 28, 1960

"We think we can win." That was what Balzli was feeling on game week in spite of the continuous and growing injury list. Amborn had a separated shoulder and would miss the remainder of the season. Four others were questionable (Nohra, Setaro, Falgout and Mickey Mahoney). Two days before the game, Balzli couldn't even determine who would be in the lineup.

Jackson Saint Joe had an impressive team with an unimpressive record. Culkin had barely beaten them the week before and they had tied Greenville Saint Joe as opposed to the Flashes 33-12 loss. They had a powerful running attack that could *"really rip to threads the opponent's line"*. The

Flashes were an underdog. What Saint Al didn't know was that Ronnie Surguine and Pat Nataro were out for the season, and Jerry Dietrick was out with a pulled muscle.

The Flashes were beset by penalties in the first half, but put up a great defensive stand that kept the Rebels out of the endzone at the Saint Al 4. In the second half, they were a different team. Doiron ran for 40 yards on one drive that allowed Franco to get in from close range and add the extra point to make it 7-0. In the same quarter, Franco punched it in again from the 3. A penalty on the PAT pushed them back to the 17, but Jimmy Buell hit Falgout for the conversion to make it 14-0. The Rebels aided the Flashes when they fumbled the ensuing kickoff. Doiron ran it in from the 20 and Franco hit Buell for the extra point. Though the reserves that came into the game managed to get to the JSJ 25, the whistle blew and scoring was complete.

Balzli was pleased with the efforts, saying they played possibly their best game of the season. He praised Mahoney, Downey, Angelo, Doiron and Franco in particular.

GAME 8:   SAINT AL (3-4) @ ROLLING FORK (6-2)
               FINAL: ST AL 0 ROLLING FORK 26
               November 4, 1960

The boys were playing a strong Delta Valley Conference team and aiming to break even for the 1960 campaign. Balzli called the Colonels *"as strong, if not the best, of any club his team has faced this season."* He even said that their defense was better than Clinton's. Balzli knew there were bumps and bruises and slight sickness with Riddle and Mahoney, but thought only Amborn would be missing the game. However, Doiron would be injured early and would also watch from the sidelines.

Rolling Fork set the tone early with a 60-yard scoring drive that was capped by a Charles Strong touchdown pass to Ralph Miller. They scored again in the same manner when Strong hit Tim Robertson for 51 yards. Jack Jenkins converted the extra point and it was 13-0. Still in the first half, the Colonels marched 85 yards with Eddie Touchberry ripping off a run of 70 yards for the third score.

The final points were added by Rolling Fork in the 4th when Jack Jenkins ran in from the 11 to cap a 47 yard drive. Touchberry converted and the scoring was done. The best drive of the game for the Flashes was afterwards. They had driven all the way to the opponent's 4 thanks to a 36 yard Downey reception but surrendered the ball after a penalty.

The boys from Vicksburg came into the season with a bit of hope. Though expected to be *"one of their better and most thrilling seasons"*, they ended with a record of 3-5; the first losing season since 1948.

John Downey was recipient of the Virgadamo Trophy.

1961 (5-3-1)

The much-beloved Joe Balzli had given 25 years of his coaching life to the purple and gold, and now the Andy Bourgeois Era was here. A football and baseball standout at LSU, he brought with him Loyola graduate Mike Conlin. There were also new team leaders with Billy Riddle and Mickey Mahoney as permanent captains, and a new Wing T formation patterned after Bourgeois' LSU Tigers.

They opened against the formidable Clinton Arrows, a team that overpowered them the previous year 21-6. Big running back Jimmy Dukes was back, and to make matters worse, Mahoney and David Nohra would not play due to injury. Mahoney had a back injury from weight lifting in the summer and Nohra suffered a broken hand during scrimmages. John Cronin had a shoulder injury and was doubtful as well. Much more about the Flashes pre-season isn't readily available, but it was time for the new coach to put his stamp on the Saint Al program.

GAME 1:   SAINT AL (0-0) @ CLINTON (1-0)
               FINAL: ST AL 7 CLINTON 28
               September 15, 1961

In the 2nd, the Flashes gave Clinton the ball at their 10 on a fumble. Dukes made them pay three plays later by way of a touchdown and Benny Moore gave the Arrows a 7-0 lead. On the next possession, Mike Franco hit Jimmy Buell for 14 yards before the Vicksburg boys fumbled again; this time at their own 27. Quickly, Richard Stacy (or Buddy Rankin) caught a touchdown and Bill Thornton provided the PAT. It was 14-0. Clinton added to their lead in the 3rd when Dukes scored from the 5 and

Thornton converted the extra point. On the ensuing kickoff, Herman Guimbellot returned the ball before fumbling at the Flash 40. Bill Moore would score and Frank Keenum got the PAT to makeit 28-0.

A quick response was waiting when, on the kickoff, Mike Franco went 72 yards for the touchdown. Billy Riddle converted to make it 28-7 and end the scoring in the game. It was obvious that the miscues were the difference in the game. Many of the stats were surprisingly close. Clinton had one more first down (6-5), one more completed pass (4-3), 18 more rushing yards (133-118) and more penalty yards (50-20).

GAME 2:   SAINT AL (0-1) vs FOREST (0-3)
                        FINAL: ST AL 0 FOREST 0
                        September 22, 1961

Hopes were high that playing a winless Forest team after keeping it close against Clinton would bring a victory. In the contest, Forest had driven to the Flash 19 in the 1st but got no further. In the 2nd, the Flashes got as far as the Forest 10. The next half did feature an interception by Franco to give hope to the home team, but the Flashes had to punt and give the ball to Forest at their 15. Roy Woody also had a pick and returned it to the Forest 16, but a penalty moved them back to the 31. The closest scoring opportunity came here, when Saint Al got within inches but could not convert. One last chance within the last minute saw the Flashes get to the Bearcat 32, but again could not get in.

Mahoney returned to play offensive and defensive tackle. Buell, Guimbellot, Billy Buell and Greg Doiron powered the rushing attack, while Jimmy Terry was noted for his defensive efforts.

GAME 3:   SAINT AL (0-1-1) v GREENVILLE SAINT JOSEPH (3-0)
                        FINAL: ST AL 32 GREENVILLE ST JOE 0
                        September 30, 1961

Mahoney had returned the week before and now Nohra would re-join after getting doctor's approval. But sitting undefeated and outscoring the opponents 54-6 thus far, the Irish were big favorites this night. The paper said (afterwards) that they hadn't been *"given a ghost of a chance against the Fighting Irish who beat them 33-12 last year in Greenville and had already won three games this season against no defeats."* Greenville never got past the Flash 40.

The Flashes started off early when Mahoney blitzed through the Irish line, grabbed the ball from QB Billy McCoy, and raced 20 yards for the touchdown. In the 2nd, Franco finished a 54 yard drive in 13 plays by scoring from the 3. The Flashes held the Irish on their next possession, but were starting from the Flash 10 after a Greenville punt. Runs by Nohra, Doiron, Guimbellot (with a 24 yard run) and Larry Falgout had them at the Irish 48. After seven plays, Franco hit Falgout at the 18 and he ran it the rest of the way to paydirt. Riddle made the 19-0 halftime PAT.

Early in the 3rd, Wilsey Kelly recovered an Irish fumble at their 30. After five plays, Nohra finished it from the 10 and Riddle was good again. The paper says that *"St Al cheers rocked the stadium."* In the 4th, Nohra ran for 14 yards to the 7. Doiron eventually took it in from the 1 and the 32-0 score was solidified. Billy Ray said afterwards, *"Don't believe we've ever seen two happier coaches than we did Saturday night right after St. Aloysius had just put the finishing touches to a 32-0 rout of favored GSJ here at Farrell Stadium. We're speaking of course of Andy Bourgeois and Mike Conlin, the young St. Al mentors who had just sacked their first victory as high school coaches."*

After noting that Andy was happier here than when Billy Cannon raced to beat Ole Miss, he said *"But the Flashes never looked better. They kicked the odds in the left field bleachers, looked the Fighting Irishmen squarely in the face, applied the knockdown punch early and never let the Greenville visitors get off the floor. That was quite a game to win and could give the Flashes that much needed confidence to produce a winning season after all. At any rate, here's a big pat on the back to Andy and Mike and all the Flashes for a job well done ... and the Irish weren't even scouted. It couldn't have been finer, even if every play had been rehearsed for months."*

GAME 4:   SAINT AL (1-1-1) @ HAZLEHURST (3-2)
                        FINAL: ST AL 26 HAZLEHURST 6
                        October 12, 1961

Franco had an emergency appendectomy on game week and would miss the Hazlehurst tilt. Sophomore Roy Woody, who had seen only four offensive plays in 1961, would replace him at QB. The

Flashes would be playing their third Little Dixie opponent and were winless in the first two (Clinton and Forest). Hazlehurst was the number one team in the league and playing their homecoming game.

After holding the Indians four-and-out on their initial possession, Nohra took the punt to the Indian 39. Two plays later, *"Gallopin"* Herman Guimbellot went the distance for the touchdown. Riddle was good and it was 7-0. On the next Hazlehurst possession, they fumbled with a Flash recovery at the 37. Jimmy Buell took the next handoff and ran 63 yards for the score. Riddle was good again to make it 14-0 going into halftime.

In the 4th, Falgout punted to the home team and pinned them at their 6. The defense held and Saint Al had the ball at the Indian 22. Nohra took them to the 10 on two runs, Woody got to the 7, and Guimbellot to the 4. Jimmy Buell then hit Nohra for the touchdown to make it 20-0. Hazlehurst answered with a Marlin Granger touchdown from the 4 but the PAT was fumbled and recovered by the Flashes.

Saint Al started the next drive at the Flash 35. Buell went to the Indian 40, Nohra to the 24, and Guimbelllot to the 3 before he took it in from there to make it 26-6. And with that score, Guimbellot tied his teammates of Nohra, Franco and Buell for the team lead in Total Points with 12.

Everyone played well. Center Freddy Angelo went the entire game minus one play. Of Woody, Bourgeois said *"He looked swell … he stepped up like a champ. He got in there and played hard. We only brought him out a few times on defense to catch his breath. It's a nice feeling to know we have two good boys in that position now. We knew Woody was a good ball handler, but it takes game experience to prove it."*

GAME 5:   SAINT AL (2-1-1) @ PEARL (UNREPORTED)
            FINAL: ST AL 0 PEARL 7
            October 20, 1961

Of the little written during game week, we know home-standing Pearl was *"highly favored"*. The Flashes almost scored in the 1st but missed a FG from the 6. The defense stood up on the next drive and stopped Pearl just before time expired at the Flash 4. At half, it was a scoreless affair. In the 3rd, the Flashes marched to the Pirate 5, but a 15-yard penalty killed the opportunity. In the 4th, Pearl got the only touchdown of the game on a Bill Clay run from the two and his PAT. The play was set up by a 38 yard pass from Danny Neely to Tom Hedgepeth. The Flashes were back down in scoring position at the 7 when time expired. In all, the Flashes were inside the Pearl 10 three times but got no points.

Speaking at the Touchdown Club, Balzli said that he was well pleased with the performance of the Flashes and was looking forward to another tough game here against rival Jackson St. Joseph.

GAME 6:   SAINT AL (2-2-1) vs JACKSON SAINT JOSEPH (4-1)
            FINAL: ST AL 14 JACKSON SAINT JOE 0
            October 27, 1961

A meeting was held on the 24th alongside Jett & Culkin at the Elks Club to discuss the possibility of playing in the Leo Puckett benefit game. There were complications due to uncertainty of the Magnolia Conference winner's obligation, but The Touchdown Club wanted Saint Al to play the loser in such an instance. Bourgeois and Principal Brother Foster were in favor. Meetings took place later to discuss the matter further. Of more importance was the Jackson St Joe Rebels. They had lost only once; a 7-6 upset to Port Gibson. The Rebels had three named playmakers in Marty McCubbins, Billy Yoeste and Jerry Dietrich. Doiron was out with a swollen gland and Riddle would miss due to a nose infection. The paper says that a large crowd on a *"real cool night"* came out to see a *"real rock 'em, sock 'em football contest."*

The Flashes threatened early by moving the ball to the 13 in 2 plays. But penalties snuffed out the opportunity and the Rebels took over on the Flash 18. On their possession, Yoste hit Johnny Lange at the Flash 42 for a long yard gain, but they were eventually forced to punt to the Saint Al 11. The Flashes gave the ball back on the next drive when Franco threw an interception at the Rebel 24. The next two plays were give-and-take. Mahoney found a Yoste fumble at the Rebel 15, but Franco threw another pick two plays later at the Rebel 14. Saint Joe almost scored behind Yoste and McCubbins, getting as far as the 2 before being tackled before reaching the endzone. The entire drive was beset with Flash penalties that almost cost them a Rebel touchdown.

In the 3rd, Falgout got off a 55 yard punt and pinned Saint Joe at their 11. Jerry Woods then picked off a McCubbins pass at the Reb 40. Nohra got to the 26 after 2 runs, Woody moved it to the 15,

Franco advanced to the 8, and Guimbellot fell just short at the 1. From there, Woody scored to make it 7-0. On the next Rebel possession, they fumbled and Jimmy Terry fell on the ball at the 30. Franco, Woody and Guimbellot rushes powered them 17 yards before Franco was sacked back at the 30. A Franco pass to Nohra to start the 4th was good for the touchdown. Saint Joe came back and got to the Flash 6 before, on 4th and 1, Yoste fumbled to Jimmy Terry to kill the drive.

The Flashes would punt and give the Rebels another chance. Franco, though, picked off another Yoste pass and returned it 27 yards to the Rebel 47. The drive went nowhere and Falgout punted again. Time ran out, however, and the Flashes were winners.

GAME 7:   SAINT AL (3-2-1) vs ROLLING FORK (6-1)
                FINAL: ST AL 7 ROLLING FORK 27
                November 3, 1961: HOMECOMING

The week started with Saint Al officially named by The Touchdown Club to play in the benefit "bowl" for Leo Puckett. President Charles McBride noted, *"...this time we think we have really come up with one of the best post-season attractions the club has ever offered and it should be a real crowd pleaser, as well as benefit the two competing schools, and most of all, Leo Puckett for which the game is being staged."*

The Flashes still had two games to go and the Delta Valley Conference Colonels were coming for Homecoming. They had lost only one game, were two-touchdown favorites and outweighed the line 185-173. Said Bourgeois, *"We've met several real strong teams this season, but Rolling Fork will probably be the strongest we've ran up against all year."* Doiron was originally doubtful for the second straight week but was now playing.

The Colonels went to work early, scoring one touchdown on a 55 yard pass and Jerry Hill run from the 15. Two others (a punt return TD by Charles Strong of 69 yards and a 39 yard Strong TD run) were fortunately called back. In the 3rd, the Flashes got on the board when Jimmy Buell took the kickoff back 92 yards for the score. Riddle's PAT made it 13-7. Shortly afterwards, Buell picked off a Colonel pass and the Flashes drove to the 25 before Franco was intercepted in the endzone by C.J. Perkins.

The fourth, however, saw two more Colonel touchdowns. A snap to the punting Falgout sailed over his head and put the ball deep in Flash territory. Billy Adams scored the touchdown thereafter. Adams scored again from close range and added all three PATs.

GAME 8:   SAINT AL (3-3-1) vs ROSEDALE (UNREPORTED EXCEPT 3-0-1)
                FINAL: ST AL 32 ROSEDALE 6
                November 10, 1961

Friday's game was moved to Saturday so as not to *"conflict with the big Jett-Culkin Magnolia Conference showdown battle carded for City Park on Friday night."* The paper noted that *"Imagine Andy will want a chance to scout both teams too ... ".* Rosedale was reported to have *"one of its finest teams in years"* and had two All-Conference players returning as seniors. The Flashes would be missing only defensive halfback Jerry Woods.

On Rosedale's first possession, they drove 89 yards for a 3 yard Vicky Couey touchdown to make it 6-0. The Flashes came back in the 2nd when Jimmy Terry recovered his third fumble in 3 games at their 14. Woody, Buell and Doiron drove it to the 2 before Woody got in from the 1. The game would go into halftime tied. The 3rd started with another fumble recovery for the Flashes, this time by Freddie Angelo at the Rosedale 19. Franco pushed it in from the 7 four plays later and Riddle made it 13-6. Another fumble was recovered by Guimbellot at the Flash 38. Franco threw three passes: Buell for 12, Falgout for 10 and Paul Brown for 11. From there, Doiron scampered the 29 yards for the score. Riddle tacked on the PAT.

Unbelievably, Rosedale fumbled yet again. This time, Falgout got the ball at the Flash 40. It took two plays before Buell hit Guimbellot for a 50 yard gain to the 10. Franco took it the remainder on the next play. Nohra ended the contest with :10 left when he picked off James Alford and took it back to the Rosedale 37. With :02 left, Franco found Buell for the touchdown. One Rosedale player, receiver J.M Tweedle, was injured during the game and had to be taken off via stretcher.

GAME 9:   SAINT AL (4-3-1) vs JETT (8-0)
                      FINAL: ST AL 25 JETT 0
                      November 10, 1961: VICKSBURG MEMORIAL STADIUM

Abysmal weather forced Saint Al to work in the mud to prep for Magnolia Conference Champion Jett. They had allowed only 32 points all year, were undefeated, fielded the county's leading scorer in Red Kleinman, and boasted *"their best team in school history."*　Bourgeois told the Touchdown Club, *"We're certainly not taking Jett easy and we're going to go all out to win."* Jett head man Othel Mendrop scouted the Rosedale game in order to prepare. *"I dread these Flashes; their record is not as good as ours, but I know they can knock because I've seen them play. They'll really be after us Friday night and we'll have to go all out and make very few mistakes if we're to keep our fine unblemished record intact."* Though the game was certainly for pride, it would also benefit Leo Puckett.

Puckett played for Jett in 1953 and was described as a *"jet-like runner"*. In a game against Satartia that year, he had broken free on a long run but was tackled and *"crashed into the hard ground on Redwood High's field. He didn't get up."* Puckett broke his neck and suffered major spinal damage. The injuries were life-threatening, but he pulled through only find himself paralyzed from the waist down. The fifth-annual affair, marred once on its inaugural by the December 5th Vicksburg tornado, assisted in the large medical bills incurred. The cold and blustery day featured many entertainers for both pre-game and halftime. The Warren County and Saint Al bands, the Hinds band and "Hi-Steppers", the "Southern Belles" and the "Hoffmanettes" would put on shows for the 3,000-plus crowd.

On the Flashes' second possession, runs by Buell and Doiron were added to a 10 yard Franco pass to Doiron. The 73 yard drive was culminated when Doiron went in from the 1. Down 6-0, Jett came close to answering in the 2nd. QB Percy Boell's passing to Jimmy Smith and the running of Kleinman, Eddie Taylor and Bob Hollingsworth moved the Bulldogs 62 yards to the Flash 12. Boell barely missed Hollingsworth in the endzone and then overthrew the 4th down pass to give the ball back to Saint Al.

In the 3rd, Jett moved the kickoff to the Flash 46 but fumbled. Subsequent runs by Buell (14), Doiron (6), Guimbellot (12 and 6) and Franco got the ball to the Bulldog 15. From there, Buell passed on the run and hit Falgout for the touchdown. Riddle capped it to make it 13-0. The Flashes blocked a Jett punt four plays later to retain the ball at the 4. After a penalty pushed them back to the 9, Franco hit Terry for the score.

Jett would fumble again at their 32 but the defense held the Flashes to a punt. With 3:04 remaining, Buell capped a 67 yard drive with a 29 yard touchdown run and the game was over. The Vicksburg Evening Post said it best: *"the real winner was Leo Puckett"*.

David Nohra was recipient of the Virgadamo Trophy.

"The 1961 season was a new beginning for the Flashes in several ways: new coaches and new offensive and defensive schemes (Wing-T and Six-Two, respectfully). Players had been taught the Single-Wing and Five-Four from the grammar school years to varsity years. The new coaches made a positive impression on the players, proving to be above average motivators and earning the respect of their players. The coaches' basic philosophy was that the Flashes would always be in better condition than their opponents. With that and fewer mistakes, winning would follow. Coach Bourgeois informed the seniors that their conduct and effort would set the example for the team.

The first game was a learning experience for the team and coaches. We fumbled three times, two inside Clinton's own 30 yard line, giving them short scoring opportunities. Basically, those three scores were the difference in the final score. Additionally, Clinton had only 18 more yards on offense. In the remaining eight games, we outscored our opponents 136-46. Our offense in all nine games averaged over 211 yards per game. Passing yards were not available for two games. Notwithstanding, the first touchdown from scrimmage was scored in the third game by defensive tackle Mickey Mahoney (co-captain playing in his first game of the season) when he took the ball away from the quarterback and ran untouched twenty yards."

Jim Terry; July 28, 2016

1962 (7-2-1)

The Vicksburg Evening Post said that the head man at Saint Al had been *"eating and sleeping football"* since the Jett victory the previous season. His attention to detail included outfitting the team in professional travel dress. The ensemble was dark blue jackets trimmed in gold with a SA logo of his design, gray pants and gray, red and black ties. His captains were Paul Brown and Greg Doiron and fall practices had gone, in his opinion, particularly well. Roy Woody now led the team at QB after having done a nice job in second place the previous year. There were a few position changes, but solid players were manning their spots. Only Freddie Angelo would miss the first game with injury. Depth, however, was a question mark.

Bourgeois knew little about his first highly-ranked Little Dixie opponent. *"We're expecting a tough game. I just hope we'll be ready to meet this early challenge."* The paper had predicted a Flash win by a score of 19-6. Not much else was written except that the Flashes had a great turnout for their *"Meet The Flashes"* night and spirits were high among fans and students for the first Catholic Conference championship.

GAME 1:   SAINT AL (0-0) vs BRANDON (0-0)
                 FINAL: ST AL 27 BRANDON 7
                 September 6, 1962

The paper said *"The game was played before one of the largest crowds ever to witness a football game at Farrell Stadium. Every seat was gone and fans lined the sidelines, and a thriller they did see."* Saint Al was first on the board after a punt gave them the ball at the 42. Jerry Woods ran for 18 and bullied in eight plays later from the 5. Brandon came right back after starting at the Flash 43. On eleven plays, QB Stark King went in from the 2 to tie it. His PAT made it 7-6 lead. The Flashes, after just having missed a 32 yard FG by Falgout, came back just before halftime. Woods brought a King punt 66 yards to the Bulldog 24 and Doiron cashed it in from the 2. Saint Al was up 12-7.

Midthrough the 3rd, a punt snap went over King's head. It landed in the endzone and he was tackled by the Flashes for a safety. Later in the 3rd, the Bulldogs fumbled at their 22 and it was recovered by Tommy Lee. In the 4th, after penalties, Woody found Freddie Jones at the 5 for 32 yards. It took two sneaks before Woody reached the endzone. Brandon's Stark King had to pass to make up the gap in score. That's when Doiron intercepted King at the Flash 35 and returned it to the Bulldog 44. Woody hit Jones for a second time; this one for a 27 yard touchdown. Falgout's PAT made it 27-7. Joe Maggio sealed the win with another King interception at the Saint Al 5 that was returned to their 42.

GAME 2:   SAINT AL (1-0) vs CLINTON (0-0)
                 FINAL: ST AL 7 CLINTON 0
                 September 14, 1962

With the overflow from the previous week, the school put in new seats to accommodate the expected crowd. Said Principal Brother Foster, *"We're doing everything possible to try and see that fans have seats tomorrow night."* They were coming to see Saint Al play Clinton, a Little Dixie team who had beaten them the last four years. Bourgeois said, *"They have a big line and some fast backs and we'll have to play even better than we did last week to have an even chance."* The good news was that RB Jimmie Dukes was out, replaced by his brother Donnie.

Roy Burkett, head man at Clinton, had watched Saint Al beat Brandon the week before and *"thought they looked much stronger this year than last when Clinton won easily"*. He also knew that two of their starters in Frank McCollum (wisdom tooth) and Claude Gholson (head injury) were limited for the game.

For the first three quarters, the overflow crowd saw a slugfest. The paper says that behind the running of the younger Dukes, the Arrows got no more than 30 yards on a drive. Saint Al did little better with 40 yards. The half ended with the Flashes at the Arrow 20. The 3rd saw Clinton running once again, but this time Dukes fumbled to the Flashes. The Arrows held and got the ball back only to throw an interception to Jerry Woods. After a Flash penalty, they punted once more. Ironically, Clinton ended up fumbling again, only to be recovered by Wilsey Kelly. Again they held strong and forced a Flash punt.

In the 4th, Clinton punted to Franco. He took it from the Flash 40 to the Arrow 5. A few plays later, Woody burst through for the winning touchdown. The game finished with Saint Al at their 7 and ready to punt when time expired. Arrow turnovers didn't help their cause, but it was Franco's big return and the solid Flash defense that won the day. Said the paper, *"Andy Bourgeois' ... Flashes did it again Friday night, and a commendable showing they did make. It's been a long time since St. Al has* whipped two Little Dixie Conference teams in a row, but they've done it their first two games this season." Roy Burkett called it *"first game mistakes"*.

GAME 3:   SAINT AL (2-0) vs BILOXI NOTRE DAME (2-1)
                 FINAL: ST AL 20 BILOXI NOTRE DAME 13
                 September 28, 1962

The Flashes had a week off to prepare for a big Biloxi Notre Dame team. By all accounts, this would be the coast boys testing the Flash defensive secondary with their passing game. The paper noted that *"They know what Notre Dame's going to do. It's up to them to do something about it. ... A St. Al win and Andy's boys could go all the way."* Passes from Sam Boney to Bobby McGinn resulted in touchdowns in every game this year, but that wasn't the only obstacle. They outweighed Saint Al on the line 192-166 and had just played a Big Eight school (Hattiesburg) though losing 26-14.

Saint Al got to the BND 13 in the 1st before relinquishing possession. The Rebels also had great movement via Boney passes to McGinn and Billy Wilkes. In the 2nd, the Flashes were knocking on the door again at the Rebel 2. A fumble in the endzone was recovered by Eddie Hardin for the Flash touchdown. Larry Falgout made it 7-0. Still in the 2nd, Boney was picked off by Woody and he brought it back to the Rebel 27. Woody then hit Freddie Jones from the 25 for the score to make it 13-0. Notre Dame hit the scoreboard afterwards when Boney found McGinn for a touchdown and the half ended with the Flashes up 13-6.

In the 4th, Woody found Franco for a 41 yard touchdown to make it 20-6. Notre Dame's final points came on a Boney 6-yard run and a Larry Hart PAT. Their on-side kick afterwards was recovered by the Flashes to seal the game. Defensive standouts included Woody and Falgout with 9 tackles each. Tommy Lee had 7. The Flashes were now leaders in the northern half of the Catholic Conference. It remained to be seen if they would play a probable Saint Stanislaus or a BND team for the crown.

GAME 4:   SAINT AL (3-0) vs GREENVILLE ST JOSEPH (3-0-1)
                 FINAL: ST AL 0 GREENVILLE ST JOE 0
                 October 6, 1962

Two undefeated teams would be playing one-another, and Saint Al had beaten the Irish the previous year 32-0. Irish coach Dom Bevalaque said that he was *"about as ready as possible"*. The Flashes had *"several injuries"* though names weren't noted in print. That, and a possible letdown, had Bourgeois worried. *"However, we'll be there. Just how good we'll do, I have no idea"*.

The Irish got as far as they would all night on their first drive to the Flash 15. The Greenville team dominated the first half with 9 first downs versus the Flashes' 2. Like the Irish's first kickoff drive, the Flashes took the second half kick to the opponent 14 for their deepest drive of the night. That came on a Franco return to the Greenville 48, a Woody pass to Franco to the 33, and a screen to Doiron to the 23. Between Woody and Doiron, they drove to the Irish 14. But a 4th down sack back at the 21 stalled a promising drive. The Irish got as far as the Flash 29 before the game ended in a tie.

The telling part of this game for the undefeated Flashes was the penalties. They had racked up 95 yards in the game on flags with many of them coming at inopportune times.

GAME 5:   SAINT AL (3-0-1) @ JACKSON ST JOSEPH (3-1-1)
                 FINAL: ST AL 20 JACKSON ST JOE 0
                 October 6, 1962

Saint Al beat Greenville Saint Joe 30-0 while the Rebels had tied them 20-20 the week before. Starters Freddie Angelo and Jerry Woods weren't playing; perhaps the same two missing from the previous game against the Irish. The Rebels had only 4 starters back, but none were the tandem of Yoste/McCubbins/Dietrich from the previous year.

The Flashes took the kickoff at their 39. Runs got them to the 2 after 8 plays. Woody went in from there and Falgout added the PAT to give a quick 7-0 lead. Their next possession took only two plays. Starting at their 44, Doiron ran for 4 and then Woody found Freddie Jones for the touchdown. The Rebels drove all the way to the Flash 1 courtesy of two receptions by Bill Perron. They ended up losing possession before the half expired.

They also tried to close it in the 3rd, but Buell recovered a Jimmy Bittner fumble at the Flash 23. Franco ran for 14, Woody passed to Steve Foster for 12, and Woody ran it to the eight to set up the score. After eleven total plays, Doiron took in in from there to cap a 77 yard drive. Falgout made it 20-0. Before the game ended, Jones picked off a Rebel pass and returned it 36 yards to the Rebel 26. They eventually got to the 10 before time expired.

Woody sat tied for 3rd in Warren County scoring with 19 points. The leader was Wayne Roberts from Cooper with 25. Freddie Jones was tied for next place with Cooper's Harvill Weller at 18.

GAME 6:   SAINT AL (4-0-1) vs HAZLEHURST (3-2)
                         FINAL: ST AL 6 HAZLEHUST 7
                         October 19, 1962: HOMECOMING

The heavier (182-165) Indians were coming to a crowded Farrell Field to repay the Flashes for the 28-6 beating in 1961. It appeared that Jones and Woods would be back. Bourgeois said, "*This will probably be as tough an opponent as we've played all year and it'll take 100 percent effort on the part of every player if we're to win.*" The paper agreed by giving Andy's boys "*a slim chance over Hazlehurst, but only because they are playing at home.*" Hazlehurst was described as having "*an aggressive outfit that doesn't mind hitting no matter how large the opposition.*"

In the 2nd, the Flashes scored first with 3:00 to play. Woody found Franco for 23 yards to the 2, and Doiron took it in. The Indians came back passing, but Woody picked one off at the Flash 42. They moved it all the way to the Indian 8 as the halftime clock expired. The 3rd saw Saint Al get no closer than the Hazlehurst 7. In the 4th, the Indians started inside their own 20. After drives that got them to the Flash 12, QB Alex Bass kept it for the score. Afterwards, he rolled out and found Ronnie Woods for the extra point to make it 7-6 . On the stat sheet, the game was close with the exception of the passing yards by Saint Al (139-12).

GAME 7:   SAINT AL (4-1-1) @ ROLLING FORK (7-0)
                         FINAL: ST AL 7 ROLLING FORK 13
                         November 2, 1962

There was no "*coach speak*" on this game. The paper said the Flashes were hitting the road to "*battle a powerful monster*" and a "*steam roller*". They called it the "*toughest opponent in many years*" or "*the toughest team St. Aloysius has played in the last two years…*" It wasn't hard to see why. Rolling Fork had outscored their opponents 270-19 this season. But Bourgeois was optimistic. "*We should be in good shape for the contest. We have lost center Bill Lauderdale, but Freddie Angelo is ready to go again after being sidelined most of the season.*

Rolling Fork's depth was fantastic, prompting the coach to say "*they have the finest high school team for the size school* (he had) *ever seen.*" In his eyes, their second team was almost equal to their first. "*The odds are against us, but we're not going up there to be added another four-touchdown victim. We're going up there to win if at all possible.*" The paper gave good odds to the Flashes, predicting a 20-7 loss.

The Colonels scored in the 1st when Charles Strong found Danny Martin from 38 yards. The PAT missed and it was 6-0. But in the 2nd and after a punt put the Flashes at the 45, Steve Foster took it 31 yards on a pitch to the 5. One yard gains by Doiron and Woody, and a penalty against Rolling Fork, set the ball at the 1. Foster did the rest for the score and Falgout put them ahead 7-6. Saint Al barely missed scoring at the end of the 2nd when Woody hit Franco for 60 yards down to the 10. But the Flashes held the halftime lead 7-6.

The kickoff by Rolling Fork to start the 3rd was fumbled by Saint Al at the 32. Billy Adams took it in from the 1 and then added the extra point to finish the scoring. The Colonels threatened to score before the end, but Jerry Woods intercepted a pass. The Flash drive afterwards went nowhere, but they did very well against a powerhouse Rolling Fork team expected to dominate the contest.

Doiron led the team with 7 tackles, followed by Brown (6) and Kelley and Foster (5).

GAME 8:   SAINT AL (4-2-1) @ ROSEDALE (UNREPORTED)
                         FINAL: ST AL 68 ROSEDALE 14
                         November 9, 1962

The paper said, "*Saint Aloysius, who gave unbeaten Rolling Fork such a tremendous battle last week before being nosed out 13-7, will be in good shape for their Delta journey and barring a tremendous letdown, should re-hit the win column*" and predicted a win of 33-6. There was not much ink devoted to what the paper deemed: **"Saint Aloysius In Rampage Wallop Rosedale 68-14"**. They called it *"perhaps* (their biggest point production) *in the history of the school"*. And only four Flashes did the scoring: Franco, Woods, Foster and Falgout. And that was before Bourgeois brought the reserves in for duty.

Franco had a 90-yard kick return, touchdowns on runs of 2 and 32, and a Woody pass from the 35. Woods had scores on runs of 80, 41 and 38. Foster had a 50-yarder and two 10-yard runs. Rosedale had a 45-yard pass from Davis to Pace and a Billy Adams 4-yard run. At halftime it was 34-7. One pass was attempted, and it was a Woody to Franco touchdown. The accomplishments of many Flashes were lost in this contest for historical record.

GAME 9:   SAINT AL (5-2-1) vs CULKIN (3-4-1)
                           FINAL: ST AL 40 CULKIN 7
                           November 16, 1962: CITY PARK

With local teams battling for the first time in more than 10 years, the paper was leaning both ways. Billy Ray said *"St Al is reported in good physical shape with only center Bill Lauderdale sidelined. Culkin is still crippled although several of their injured are expected to be back for part time action. The Cats had an off week last go round to try and get ready and you can bet that Coach Bill Tate will shoot the works and hold back nothing. The Cats could make it interesting for a while, but the Flashes will wear them down and will probably be able to move at ease near the end. One thing for sure. It'll be Culkin's toughest test of the year and it's just possible they could rise to the occasion and surprise, especially if the Flashes are feasting on too much overconfidence. Should be a game well worth attending and quite a few fireworks should pop. Make it St Al 33, Culkin 13."*

The Flashes were *"impressive"* but said that Culkin *"with an off week last week to get ready promises keen competition, especially if they can catch the Flashes a little over-confident."* Culkin QB Jamie Jones was expected to throw a lot since he had 6 TDs already in 1962. An aerial assault was anticipated on both sidelines.

A big crowd sat through driving rain to watch the contest. The Flashes drove in the 1st to the Wildcat 15 but fumbled to give it back. Saint Al held after two Culkin first downs and Woods returned a Lloyd punt 31 yards to the Culkin 44. Woods ran it in on the next play and Falgout made it 7-0. Five seconds later, Pete Hearn fumbled at the 21 and Foster recovered the ball. Woods gained 10 and then Doiron scored from there. With Falgout good again, it was 14-0.

Culkin answered in the 2nd on a 72 yard drive that was capped by a Gene Gray catch to make it 14-7. But on the ensuing kickoff, Franco took it all the way only to be ruled out at the Wildcat 32. Nine plays later, Woody went in from the 3 and, with a blocked Falgout PAT, it was 20-7. The next drive saw a Jamie Jones fumble recovered by Angelo at the Culkin 47. Woody hit Franco three plays later for the 44 yard touchdown for a halftime lead of 26-7. Midway through the 3rd, Franco went in from the 30 to cap a 55 yard drive. Falgout quickly made it 33-7. The final points came at 9:28 when Foster went in from the 30. Falgout made the final score 40-7.

GAME 10:   SAINT AL (6-2-1) vs SAINT STANISLAUS (UNREPORTED)
                           FINAL: ST AL 47 SAINT STANISLAUS 0
                           November 23, 1962

The very first Mississippi Catholic Conference title was on the line. The paper said that it would be a *"climax to a most successful season and Coaches Andy Bourgeois and Mike Conlin would like nothing better than to end it with the newly formed loop's first title and trophy"*. The Rock-A-Chaws were well-heavier than the Flashes (187-167) on the line and ran a Single Wing offense that the Flashes faced previously from Biloxi.

Both teams had beaten Biloxi Notre Dame (Saint Stanislaus 20-7 and Saint Al 20-13). The opponent played bigger schools in the Big 3 and Louisiana AA and AAA schools, so it was hard to find a common denominator outside of Biloxi. When picking a winner, the paper said, *"It looks like a real hum-dinger, but we'll take the Flashes something like 14-7"*. They added later, *"The Flashes aren't big, but they're well-conditioned and operate as a well-oiled machine.* The game featured the Saint Al band, the "Hoffmanettes", Saint Stanislaus bands, and the "Rock-A-Cheers". But the Flashes were without Paul Brown who was hospitalized with a throat infection.

Jerry Woods picked off a SSHS pass on their first possession. Four plays and a penalty later Doiron went in from the 16 to cap a 41 yard drive. It was now 6-0. After holding their opponent to a punt, the ball was at the Flash 29 after a "*quick-kick*". The next play saw Doiron go from the Flash 38 to the SS 39. Woods went for 25 and Doiron took it in four plays later for the score. Falgout made it 13-0.

In the 2nd, Franco hauled in an interception for 75 yards and the score. In the same quarter, Woody got it in from the 6 on a 27-yard drive to make the halftime score a lopsided 27-0. The Flashes continued the assault in the 3rd with a Franco kickoff return of 78 yards for the touchdown. In the 4th, Foster ended a 56 yard drive by scoring from the 4. The Flashes were standing at the 9 after Franco caught passes of 22 and 29 yards, but the final whistle blew.

They had posted a 7-2-1 record and lost one of those (Rolling Fork) to a heavy favorite on the road by 6 after leading. The Flashes were invited to play against that team in the Delta Bowl, but turned down the invitation. Said Bourgeois, "*It was a hard decision to make. I would dearly love to get another crack at them. The reason we turned the invitation down was because our basketball season starts next week and we have had absolutely no practice as yet, and too, Brother Foster is scheduled to take eight boys (all key football players) down to the coast for a Catholic convention next Friday ... it would be useless to try and play a football game without them, especially against such an opponent as Rolling Fork.*"

Greg Doiron was recipient of the Virgadamo Trophy.

"*Our class was the second for Coach Andy Bourgeois. Many of us had gone to Saint Aloysius together since the first grade. We had a number of returning lettermen, so we knew we could be successful. The schedule was tough as we played many schools that were much larger than ours. That was the norm then. Two games were very memorable. The first was beating Clinton and the second was beating Saint Stanislaus for the first Catholic school championship.*
One thing, though. Coach Bourgeois was tough. But it paid off."

Greg Doiron; August 3, 2016

1963 (5-2-1)

Saint Al faced a rebuilding year after a 7-2-1 season. They had lost Doiron, Foster, Franco, Hardin, Kelly, Brown, Jones, Angelo, and Falgout. Additionally, Jerry Woods had transferred to Redwood. It would be a smaller team in numbers (30) than in previous years. Of the starting 11, only 5 had experience and many had never played a down before. Warren Guider and Roy Woody were elected team captains.

Bourgeois told the Lions Club that "*If our juniors and sophomores can play ball like seniors, we will have a good ball club. We lack depth and experience, but we will be in shape to play at top speed. They are hustling.*" The paper echoed it. "*You don't play for Bourgeois unless you give it everything.*"

GAME 1:   SAINT AL (0-0) @ BRANDON (0-0)
                   FINAL: ST AL 20 BRANDON 20
                   September 5, 1963

Saint Al had beaten a younger Brandon team 27-7 in 1962. Now the Flashes were youngsters, making Brandon a two or three touchdown favorite. It started as many anticipated. Though they opened by fumbling at the Flash 40 (recovered by Tommy Lee), Brandon held the Flashes to a punt. The snap eluded Ray and put the ball at the Flash 7. Seven plays later, QB Sonny Shamburger went in for the score.

In the 2nd, the Flashes fumbled at the 30 and it took Brandon 11 plays before Henry Moody went in for the touchdown to make it 12-0. With 3:00 left in the half, the Flashes went on a tear. On the first score, Woody hit Eddie Ray at the 18. Six plays later, Bill Lauderdale crashed through from the 4 and Charles Antoine made it 12-7. Brandon ran three times behind Jimmy Hardy but had to punt with: 50 left. That's when Woody, receiving the ball at the Flash 40, took it all the way for the touchdown. Antoine added to it to for a 14-12 game. After the kickoff, Shamburger threw an interception to Lauderdale who returned it from the 33 to the 9. Woody, behind a Lauderdale block, ran it in from there. The Flashes had scored 20 points in three minutes to lead at half 20-12.

Brandon, in their red and white, came out by driving from their 9 to the Flash 2. The Flash defense held but on the ensuing Flash punt, Butch Lawrence blocked it and the ball rolled out of the endzone for a safety to make it 20-14. In the same quarter, Brandon fumbled and Tom Balzli was there to recover at the 39. The offense came within *"a smiff"* of the 1st down on a Woody run, but turned it over to Brandon on downs.

The Bulldog game-tying drive consisted of many Hardy runs, but Shamburger eventually got the score from the 2. The PAT would decide the victor. Hardy took the handoff but the Flashes held strong to force the *"upset"* tie.   Pat Ring led in tackles with 11, followed by Ray (9), Joe Maggio and Tommy Buell (7), and Lee and Guider (6). Bourgeois was *"well pleased at this young club's initial performance and the way they bounced back from apparent defeat to almost pull it out."* The paper called his squad *"one of the 'fightingest' ever assembled at the Vicksburg school."*

GAME 2:   SAINT AL (0-0-1) @ CULKIN (1-0)
                 FINAL: ST AL 23 CULKIN 0
                 September 13, 1963

After a "severe cold", Wood returned Wednesday but would *"probably not* (be) *at top speed"*. Ernie Albritton's Wildcats had beaten Redwood 13-7, but Bourgeois thought they may have been *"holding back ... and would come prepared to throw the book at (Saint Al)... I just hope we're ready."* When asked about it, Albritton laughingly said *"I certainly don't plan to hold anything back tomorrow night. We're hoping to make it a real interesting game."* The paper predicted *"a cat-mouse contest"* since both teams were so young. Three thousand fans came out on Friday the 13th.

In the 2nd, Woody returned a Culkin punt 36 yards to the Wildcat 19. Four plays later, Lauderdale got the touchdown from the 4 and Antoine made it 7-0. Later, Culkin QB Jamie Jones was sacked in the endzone by Marvin Quin and Dave Bridgers for the safety. The Flashes scored again in the half when Woody found Lauderdale for a 27 yard touchdown pass. The previous play had seen Woody run for a 12 yard score, but it was called back on a penalty. Antoine upped the halftime lead to 16-0. The Flashes actually had a chance to add to the onslaught but time expired while driving at the Culkin 1.

In the 3rd, Balzli blocked a Wildcat punt at the 26. Woody capped the drive on a 1 yard plunge and Antoine made the PAT to end the scoring. It could have been worse as a 70 yard Woody run for a touchdown was called back for clipping. Culkin tried to avoid the shutout late in the 4th at the Flash 36, but couldn't move. The game put Woody into a three-way tie in the Warren County Scoring Leaders. His 18 points were matched by teammate Lauderdale and Jerry Woods from Cooper.

GAME 3:   SAINT AL (1-0-1) vs OAK GROVE, LA (2-0)
                 FINAL: ST AL 0 OAK GROVE 20
                 September 19, 1963

Bourgeois said the undefeated and unscored-upon opponent *"could be the toughest team on his schedule. They are quick and aggressive and concentrate on moving the ball."* The paper predicted a loss, saying *"Oak Grove is a slim choice here, but we believe if they win, it will be because of manpower. We do not believe they will outscrap the Flashes. Make it 13-7 in a real belly-buster."* Harry Piazza missed due to illness and center Quin was nursing a bruised knee from the previous week.

A full house was there to watch the contest. Oak Grove scored in the 1st after starting from their 46 when David Kennedy went all the way for the touchdown run and Mitchell Broadway made it 7-0 on the PAT. The Flashes were able to recover an Oak Grove on-side kick at the Tiger 48 and put together their longest drive. The big play was Woody's pass to Eddie Ray at the 23. The 2nd had just begun with the Flashes at the 15. Woody went for 9 and seemingly a 1st down. But not only was the play called back for illegal procedure, Woody would be carried off with a knee injury.

Backup 124-lb Billy McCain came in to replace him, but fumbled on 4th and 1 at the 13. Oak Grove used the ground game of Mike Gammill and Broadway to get to the 44. The paper describes what happened after as *"the most dazzling, confusing might be a better word, magician-like play of the night..."* Similar to the "fumble-rooski", QB Jim Boyles faked a run but laid the ball on the ground. While the Flashes were chasing the *"ball carriers"*, guard Benny Murphy picked it up and went 56 yards for the score. It was 13-0 at halftime.

In the 4th, Ray was punting for the Flashes at their 35. The punt was partially deflected and Oak Grove came up with it at the 33. Eight plays later, Gammill went in from the 6 to give the Flashes their first loss of the young season. Saint Al would have an off week off to prepare for rival Greenville .

GAME 4:   SAINT AL (1-1-1) vs GREENVILLE ST JOSEPH (4-0)
                 FINAL: ST AL 12 GREENVILLE ST JOE 6
                 October 5, 1963

Said Bourgeois, "*The off week last week did us much good. And, it couldn't have come at any better time. We've improved in many positions and I'm hoping we'll be able to make tonight's game interesting.*" Not much more was written other than Woody would still be out. It was time to play against a team unbeaten entering the Saint Al game for the fourth straight year since 1960.

The first three quarters were scoreless. The only highlight was a Tommy Lee fumble recovery on the Irish 36 that resulted in no points due to a Buell fumble. But the end of the 3rd and entire 4th quarter was worth admission. The Flashes took a punt at their 25 and moved 13 plays to the Irish 4, mostly due to runs from Maggio (13) and Lauderdale (11). They battled to the Irish 2 and, on fourth down, they elected to kick the FG with Antoine. He missed, but the Irish were off-sides. So, Saint Al went for the touchdown and got it when McCain scored from the 1 to finalize a 65 yard drive with a 6-0 lead.

Greenville came right back via a David Wallace kick return to the Flash 44. Mike O'Brien found Wallace on a pass to the 7. Three plays later, Joseph Bennett took it in from the 1 to tie it 6-6. The ensuing kickoff was to Maggio. He received at his 38 and brought it all the way back for a touchdown. Antoine was low, but with 7:17 left the final score was 12-6.

The Irish responded by driving into Flash territory. Penalties were traded, but O'Brien hit Wallace again at the Flash 15. However, a penalty put them back at the 32. Two running plays and a David Cobianchi run got them to the Flash 12. O'Brien ran to the 6, but then Ray sacked O'Brien back at the 14. His next pass was picked off by Maggio at the 3 and brought back to the 29. Three plays later, the final whistle sounded.

GAME 5:   SAINT AL (2-1-1) vs JACKSON SAINT JOE (1-?)
                 FINAL: ST AL 14 JACKSON ST JOE 7
                 October 11, 1963: HOMECOMING

The Vicksburg Evening Post called the Irish game a "*magnificent performance*" by the Flashes. As for Saint Joe, they said "*they're in good position to victimize another St. Joseph team, but only if they play like they did last week. ...They'll be out to tame the Flashes for sure and it'll take an all-out effort on the Flashes part. But it's homecoming and spirits should be high. We'll take the Flashes 13-7.*" The Rebels had players that could add "*misery*", but Bourgeois told Billy Ray that the team was in good shape injury-wise. Saint Joe would miss starter Harry Yoste (wrist) and the paper said that the injury would "*no doubt hurt Saint Joe*". They did have Mike Frascogna in the lineup who had just been named "Player of the Week" by the Jackson Touchdown Club for his performance against Rosedale.

"*One of the most exciting games of the year for the home team*" was in front of a "*standing-room only crowd*" and "*in perfect weather.*" The 1st was rocky when Lauderdale fumbled a punt at the 33 and recovered by David McDonald for the Rebels. The defense held and forced a punt to Lauderdale who, this time, took it to the Flash 20. Buell had runs of 14 and 17 and a couple of plays into the 2nd, Buell went in from the 3. The 80 play drive was capped by Antoine to make 7-0.

In the same quarter, both teams threw interceptions, but Saint Joe converted one. From their 36, they reached the endzone behind a 17 yard pass from Bobby Head to Frascogna . Bill Perron's PAT made it 7-7. The 3rd almost saw another Flash touchdown after a bad punt put Saint Al at the Rebel 41. The Flashes managed to get to the ½ yard line but could not convert. In the 4th, Saint Al sealed the win. Starting at their 40, they marched to the Saint Joe 38. Ray then found Joe Maggio for the touchdown pass and Antoine made it 14-7. The Rebels tried furiously to tie it with 3:30 to go. They got as far as the Flash 4, but the offense could not get in despite pass completions of 18, 12, and 14 yards.

GAME 6:   SAINT AL (3-1-1) @ HAZLEHURST (UNREPORTED)
                 FINAL: ST AL 21 HAZLEHURST 19
                 October 19, 1963

Woody was still out with injury and the Flashes were looking to repay their homecoming defeat from 1962 at Hazlehurst's homecoming. In the 1st, Hazlehurst's Harold Kergosen had his pass deflected by a Flash lineman but it ended up in the QB's hands and he gained 7 yards. The Indians eventually pushed it in behind a Pat Amos run from the 1 for a 6-0 lead. The Flashes responded in the

2nd when Maggio caught an 11 yard touchdown pass. Antoine made it 7-6. Maggio was also a presence on defense, intercepting a pass at the Flash goal. They would eventually have to punt and it would be 7-6 Flashes at half.

The 3rd was a trade of touchdowns. The Indians' Amos scored again from the 1 and carried it in himself for the PAT to make it 13-7. The Flashes responded on the kick when Maggio went 75 yards for the touchdown. Antoine was good to make it 14-13. Like the 3rd, the final quarter was a trading of touchdowns. Roy Harris scored from the 1 early. For Saint Al, Lauderdale did the honors by scoring from the 16. Though backed up by a penalty, Antoine was good and the Flashes had spoiled homecoming in Hazlehurst.

Instead of Maggio, it was Buell who won both of Bourgeois' offensive and defensive honors. He had 10 tackles and a 6 yard rushing average. Ring had 9 tackles, Piazza and Balzli had 7, and Maggio picked up 6. But there was no mistaking Maggio's efforts. He had a 75 yard kick return, ran for 64.5 yards and had three interceptions.

GAME 7:   SAINT AL (4-1-1) @ ROLLING FORK (?-1)
            FINAL: ST AL 0 ROLLING FORK 7
            November 2, 1963

Woody was back, if just for limited action, after being out since September 19th. Though the Delta Valley Conference Colonels had dropped only 1 game this year, the Flashes had lost only 13-7 to them last year and were ready to play. The Flashes had moved to the Colonels' 12 but given up a fumble and an interception before the half to keep it scoreless. In the 3rd, they opened up with an on-side kick and took possession at the Rolling Fork 43 after a fumble. Saint Al could not take advantage of the play and gave it back to Rolling Fork.

At 4:10, the Colonels scored the game's only points. A John Taylor run to the 45 was complimented by Jerry Bishop runs to the 25. Bishop eventually scored from the 4 at the :22 mark and Bobby Burns made it 7-0. The Flashes came very close to answering with a drive to the Colonel 48, but it was not to be. Saint Al intercepted a pass in the very end to stop another Rolling Fork attempt. Ring led the Flashes in tackles with 10; his 5th game with double-digits. Guider and Ray had 5 each. Ring also had an interception, while fumbles were recovered by Eddie Canizaro, Piazza, Guider and Buell.

GAME 8:   SAINT AL (4-2-1) vs LAKE PROVIDENCE, LA (8-0)
            FINAL: ST AL 20 LAKE PROVIDENCE 12
            November 8, 1963

The big Louisiana team, coached by former Ole Miss Rebel Pete Mangum, outweighed the Flashes by as much as 12 pounds and was senior-laden with 8 players. Saint Al had only Guider and Woody as seniors. The paper noted that the prospects for a victory "appear slim since the Flashes will be playing minus two starters." Ring had dislocated his shoulder at practice and Canizaro had developed the flu. But Bourgeois noted that "sprits have been high all week", probably due to Woody's full-time return. A standing-room only crowd would be on hand to watch.

Saint Al was first on the board after a Panther fumble was recovered by Dave Bridgers at their 49. A penalty put the Flashes at the 34 and then Woody found Ray for 31 yards. Three plays later, Buell went in from the 1 to make it 6-0. Saint Al appeared to have a chance to widen the lead when Lee fell on a Lake Providence fumble at the Panther 43, but the drive couldn't be sustained. The visitors came back in the 2nd on an 8 play drive of 61 yards. A punt return of 33 yards by Panther David Clarkson was brought back to the 34 for clipping. But QB Billy Bayles found Johnny Overby for 26 yards to the Flash 11 and then hit Kenneth Frith on the 11-yard score. Clarkson was true to make it 7-6 at halftime.

In the 3rd, the Panthers' Harry Murrah took the opening kick from his 17 to the Flash 41. It took 5 plays before Overby, described by Billy Ray as "running like a deer and was as slippery as an eel", took a reverse for 23 yards and paydirt. Clarkson made it 14-6. When Saint Al could gain no ground, Lake Providence took three plays to go 62 yards and score. It was set up by a 43 yard run by Overby to the Flash 19 that was stopped by Maggio. Don Washam gained 4 and then Clarkson took it in.

The Flashes answered the three-touchdown barrage with one of their own. The ensuing kickoff run and a penalty spot them at Flash 35. Woody found Ray for 11 and 4 yards and Delbert Hosemann for 9. After 10 plays, Woody found Ray from the 32 for the touchdown. The defense was led by Buell with 6 tackles. Lee, Guider and Maggio had 5. Both Bridgers and Canizaro, playing with the flu, gained a fumble recovery. But with Ring already lost with the shoulder injury, he was now joined by

Woody and Balzli (knees). Reserves in Mike Fontenot, Fisher Calloway, Frank Vollor and Bobby Lucchesi would also be unable to go. The worst news would come 14 days later.

GAME 9:   SAINT AL (5-2-1) vs BILOXI NOTRE DAME (6-0)
                              FINAL: CANCELLED
                              BILOXI, MS: Originally Set For November 22, 1963

This game being played in Biloxi would decide the Catholic Conference Champion. Notre Dame had advanced by destroying Saint Stanislaus 44-7. They were led by an impressive eighth grader in Jesse Truax, a 6'2" and 190-pounder who was also brother of LSU's Billy Truax.

The team left at 10am on game day and were scheduled to stay that evening at the Tradewinds Hotel. Saturday morning was to be a deep sea fishing trip courtesy of Reese Oil Company. The team was on the way to Biloxi when, at 1:25pm CST, the tragic news broke that President John F. Kennedy had been assassinated in Dallas. It was an event that shook not only the sports world, but indeed the entire world. All games were immediately cancelled or postponed with decisions to be made later. The official announcement came from Brother Mark later. The game would not be rescheduled. In only its second year, the Catholic Conference would have no champion.

Roy Woody was recipient of the Virgadamo Trophy.

"The 1963 season started with only two seniors who were returning. We were young, but scrappy, and determined to follow the tradition established in the 1962 season. Our first game at Brandon was stifling hot but we were able to end the game in a tie. Several players lost a tremendous amount of weight in the game, but spirits were high around the school. Culkin was next and we handled them fairly easily. We knew a lot of their players and were determined that we wouldn't succumb to them. We didn't.

We were a cocky bunch heading into the next game with undefeated Oak Grove. We had a great game plan and came our executing it. However, Roy Woody was injured on a QB keeper around left end. Freshman QB Billy McCain was inserted and played well, but he was restricted on what plays he could run. We couldn't overcome this problem and were defeated. But we left the field with our heads held high.

We had a week to heal and prepare for the Fighting Irish of Greenville. They were at tough opponent with an undefeated record, but we handled them in a brutal game with sheer determination. Billy played a steady game and our offensive line paved the way for our victory and prepare for the rest of the season. Saint Joe of Jackson was our next opponent. We knew quite a few of their players and it was a tough, nip-and-tuck game. We were plagued by fumbles and several promising drives were stopped by turnovers. Most were caused by hard hitting.

We wanted to repay Hazlehurst on their Homecoming and it was a good game. The right side of our line opened numerous holes by increasing the distance between right guard and right tackle. Coach wanted to know what we were doing and we told him we were moving out and their tackle was playing on the outside shoulder of our tackle. He told us that if they continue to do that, we should move on our as far as they would go. The victory, along with a week off, set us up for the next game against Rolling Fork.

It hadn't rained in a couple of months but Coach had us bring our rain cleats. It started pouring when we pulled into Rolling Fork and the field was already soaked at kickoff. The game went down to the very end and was a disappointing defeat. We hosted an undefeated Lake Providence team next made up of a tough bunch of country boys. We have them a heck of a game but could not pull out a win in the end due to injuries and sickness.

We prepared for the next game against Biloxi Notre Dame for the CAC championship. We had a raucous pep rally and then loaded for the long trip to the coast. Woody was in the back with the scrubs and he came to the front with news that President Kennedy had been assassinated in Dallas a few moments before. We pulled over around Magee, piled out onto the shoulder of the road and said prayers. Everyone was upset. We finally got to Biloxi and had a pre-game meal before going to the hotel. The game would be cancelled and our season ended on a sour note."

Warren Guider; July 22, 2016

1964 (3-5)

Andy Bourgeois entered his 4th year with a new assistant in former Ole Miss player Jerry Worsham. Foret had resigned to return home to New Orleans. Bourgeois was also contemplating other changes. In January, he had written a letter of application to the Little Dixie Conference. The new consolidated Warren County schools had done the same. Saint Al was members of the Mississippi Catholic Conference with only two other schools (Saint Stanislaus and Biloxi Notre Dame) and had trouble scheduling other opponents due to the success of the Flashes. Logistics also proved troublesome.

Andy was optimistic but cautious on the season outlook. According to The Vicksburg Evening Post, he was *"looking with anticipation of having his best team since he's been head coach here."* They were in good shape, no injuries, and sporting 13 seniors. Team captains included Tommy Lee and Joe Maggio. However, the coach was quick to tell the Lions Club, *"We could have the finest team since I've been at St Aloysius and still have my worst record yet. You win with seniors, and we have 13 this year. So, we expect to win our share."*

GAME 1:   SAINT AL (0-0) vs BRANDON (0-0)
                         FINAL: ST AL 7 BRANDON 13
                         September 4, 1964

Like Saint Al, Brandon returned many key players from the previous season. Running a pro-style offense, a good game was anticipated since both teams played to a 20-20 tie in 1963. Bourgeois said *"...we expect a tough one. Their quarterback is potential SEC material."* It was time to see what his offense (dubbed *"the Purple and Golds"*) and his defense (called *"Apaches"* and *"Commanches"*) would look like before *"perhaps the largest* (crowd) *to ever see a St. Aloysius game here."*

In the 1st, QB Sonny Shamburger picked off a Kelly pass and brought it back 66 yards for the touchdown. Bill Lauderdale blocked his PAT and it was 6-0. In the 2nd, Brandon was driving before Steve Stubblefield fumbled at the Flash 14. Saint Al took over but had to punt 3 plays later. Shamburger, who had just intercepted Saint Al, was now intercepted by Lauderdale. And the result was the same. Lauderdale took it 71 yards to paydirt and Antoine gave the Flashes a 7-6 lead. The Flashes actually scored again just before the closing of the half when Maggio hit Ray from the 19 for the touchdown. But a flag for movement was thrown, costing them a larger halftime lead.

The ensuing kickoff to Brandon was full of action. Runs by Shamburger, Stubblefield and Freddie Farmer, a pass to JoJo Payne and a 4th-and-18 conversion via a Farmer reception put the ball at the 1. After 70 yards in 15 plays, Shamburger took it in for the score. He was also good for the PAT to make it 13-7. In the 4th, the Flashes threatened when Maggio took the kickoff back to the Flash 35. Following a McCain run of 27, Ray then took the ball to the Bulldog 19 but fumbled and gave possession back to Brandon. The Flash defense held and forced a Bulldog punt. It went only 12 yards and Maggio returned it to the Brandon 34. It was here that the game was won by the Brandon defense midway through the 4th.

Lauderdale gained 5 to the 29 and Maggio got through for 7 and the 1st down. A Brandon facemask penalty put the ball at the 12, Lauderdale went for 9, and Kelly got it to the 4. Maggio ran the next three and gave the Flashes a 1st down at the 1. Three sneak plays were handed to McCain, but he got no closer than just inches away. On 4th, Maggio's pass was overthrown to Mike Kelly and the game was heartbreakingly sealed. The last prayer by the Flashes came on a Maggio punt return to the Brandon 47. But with :50 left, Saint Al could not convert a 1st down. Eddie Ray hit Buell at the 31 on a 4th down pass, but needed the 29 to continue.

Pointing out at least 15 mistakes after watching film, Bourgeois graded only three players as "pass". They were Billy McCain, Lee and Mike Kelly. The paper said *"A loss like this is hard to get over, but with the fine personnel the Flashes have, we're sure they won't let it get them down. The season is just beginning and there's plenty more football, and thrills, ahead."*

GAME 2:   SAINT AL (0-1) vs CULKIN (1-0)
                         FINAL: ST AL 6 CULKIN 7
                         September 12, 1964

Great feelings over being injury-free last week were gone. Starting QB McCain injured his hand against Brandon and would be out. But Culkin suffered the same fate as QB Jamie Jones had broken his foot and would be out a month. Saint Al would rely on Al Brown and Bernard Calloway, while Culkin would depend on Cecil Simmons and Donald Frith. As such, the paper said that Culkin would "promise an all-out effort in an attempt to gain revenge for losses to the Flashes the past two seasons, and they have the material which could make it interesting."

Culkin coach Ernie Albritton said, "...we're certainly not going to roll over and play dead. We know St. Aloysius has a fine team and they should have won against Brandon last week ... They'll probably be real mad tonight, but we hope to be ready, too. ... I think we'll be ready to give the Flashes a real good game." Bourgeois said "I expect this to be the closest of our series and unless we do play better ball than we did last week, we're going to be in for our second loss." Kickoff was moved up 30 minutes because of the Miss America pageant being show on television. That was important because Vicksburg's Judy Simono was Miss Mississippi.

The scoreless first half belonged to the Wildcats. In the 2nd, Maggio fumbled to give Curtis Brewer the ball at the Flash 24. Culkin drove to the Flash 7 behind a Preston Riley run, but multiple penalties pushed them back to the 34 forcing a punt. On the next Culkin drive, George Zorn picked off Frith at the Flash 10. A fumble by new QB Brown gave the ball right back to the Wildcats at the Flash 15. With :10 left in the half, Frith found Jeff Burton for the touchdown and Brewer gained the PAT. At intermission, it was Culkin up 7-0.

In the 3rd, Brown found Ray from the 21 but a penalty put them at the 24. A few plays later, Preston Riley intercepted Brown to end the quarter. In the 4th, the Flashes would make it interesting. Punting from their 20 on 3rd and 12, Ray faked and hit Zorn who went to the Culkin 45. Maggio, Brown and Lauderdale pushed it to the 25. After an incomplete pass, Ray got the 1st down on a run to the 18. Lauderdale took it to the 11 and Brown found Ray for the score. Antoine hit the upright on the PAT and it was 7-6.

The Flashes had one more chance to win in the final 3:00. Lauderdale ran for 26 to the Flash 41 and three Maggio runs got them to the Culkin 34. Between incomplete passes and a sack back to the 41, the drive and the game were over. There was talk that Saint Al didn't show much of their playbook due to Oak Grove scouts in the stands. Said Billy Ray, "We certainly want to give Culkin every bit its due and the way they popped they deserved to win. They just seemed more fired up and wanted the game a little bit more. We believe St. Aloysius should have won, but Culkin was the best team on the scoreboard."

GAME 3:   SAINT AL (0-2) @ OAK GROVE, LA (2-0)
                 FINAL: ST AL 10 OAK GROVE 13
                 September 24, 1964

Undefeated Oak Grove returned 7 offensive and 9 defensive starters from a team that beat the Flashes 20-0 in 1963. They were picked to finish high in Louisiana Class A football. But Bourgeois was upbeat after a week off, saying "They've got a real fine ball club, but I believe we're going to get after them." Frank Cassino was out with a broken finger but McCain was coming back to play defense.

After holding the Tigers to a first possession punt, Saint Al marched to the Oak Grove 15 behind Maggio's running. But a flag for holding pushed them back and forced a punt. Oak Grove had gambled on 4th downs as far as their own 21, and one of them resulted in a Bridgers interception to the Tiger 42. An errant punt snap recovered by Eddie Ray put the Flashes at the Tiger 14 to set up the first score. Kicking from the 13, Antoine "split the uprights" to make it 3-0 at half.

In the 3rd, Eddie Ray recovered a Jim Boyles fumble at the Flash 10. Two Tiger penalties and a 29 yard Ray pass to Zorn got to the Tiger 42. Another penalty put Saint Al at the 27 and then Tommy Ray ran to the 13. Ray and Maggio got it to the 9 and then with only :45 to go, Eddie Ray converted a 4th down with a 9 yard touchdown run. Antoine made it 10-0.

On the ensuing drive, Maggio picked off a Tiger pass and brought it to their 15. Tommy Ray started the 4th by getting to the 13 before disaster struck. Maggio took Brown's pitchout and then passed, only to be intercepted by David Butler at the 10. Butler went 90 yards for the touchdown. Mickey Broadway's PAT, made it 10-7. Saint Al couldn't drive afterwards but Eddie Ray punted to their endzone and hopes were high that they could still win. A booted Tiger fumble and a 31 yard pass from Boyles to Mike Pollard put them at the Flash 15. Six plays later, Boyles went in from the 1 to cap the 80 yard drive. Oak Grove attempted the onside kick, but Buell grabbed it and brought it back to the Tiger 46. The Flashes got as far as the 34, but with 1:30 left, could get no further. The Tigers simply ran the clock out for the win.

Bourgeois was pleased, saying *"we played our best game of the season and should have won."* Eddie Ray had 6 tackles and an assist, Lee had 6 tackles, Bridgers had 5 tackles and 2 assists, and Buell had 5. Balzli, with an injury, would probably miss the St Joe contest.

GAME 4: SAINT AL (0-3) @ GREENVILLE SAINT JOSEPH (3-0)
FINAL: ST AL 3 GREENVILLE ST JOE 7
October 2, 1964

The Flashes went to play a Greenville team going for their third straight Little 8 Championship. Bourgeois' told Billy Ray, *"We've been plagued by bad weather this week, but our spirit is still high and one of these days I believe we'll win one, and I hope tonight's the night."* Irish coach Dom Bevelaque had scouted the Flashes and, in spite of the 0-3 start, called them *"a real good team"*.

In the 1st, Eddie Ray recovered the fumbled opening kickoff. Carries by Ray and Maggio got the 1st down, but the Irish held and took over at their 4. Runs by Mike O'Brien were not enough to advance and the Irish resorted to a Charles Sherman punt. The Flashes fumbled it and gave the ball back to Greenville at their own 45. The Irish drove to the Flash 2 but then fumbled back to Saint Al.

The 2nd was highlighted by Tommy Ray runs, but the Flashes had to punt. On the ensuing drive, O'Brien unleashed a 40-yarder to David Wallace for a touchdown. Fortunately for Saint Al, a flag on the play erased the score. The Greenville team almost capitalized later on that drive but the ball went back to the Flashes at their 25. Saint Al went to the run with Zorn, Maggio, Brown and Tommy Ray combining for 4 first-downs to the 4. A penalty put the ball back to the 15 and Antoine hit the FG as time expired to make it 3-0 at half.

In the 4th, the Flashes made their costly error by fumbling on the 10. Joseph Bennett fell on the ball for the Irish and Wallace capped it off a few plays later from the 8. Wallace also made the PAT and it was 7-3. The Flashes came very close to winning afterwards. On a drive to the Irish 4 with under 2:00 left, Maggio fumbled and it was recovered by Greenville. They ran the clock for the victory.

GAME 5: SAINT AL (0-4) @ JACKSON SAINT JOSEPH (1-4)
FINAL: ST AL 20 JACKSON ST JOE 0
October 9, 1964

Bourgeois was feeling good in spite of being 0-4. *"Despite our four losses, spirit is still good and we feel like the ball is going to bounce in our direction one of these nights. St Joseph is a dangerous club and with an off week … they should be in top shape. And it's their homecoming, too, so we're looking for nothing but trouble. We just hope we're ready and will play as we're capable."*

The cold weather contributed to two early fumbles: the Rebels on their first possession and the Flashes on the very next play. The Flashes did end up scoring on their second possession when Maggio went in from 36 yards. McCain made the PAT to make it 7-0. But it was all fumbles afterwards until the halftime whistle blew. Saint Joe got to the Flash 29 but fumbled; the Flashes fumbled 4 plays later; Saint Joe 5 plays later; 4 plays later by the Flashes; and 8 plays later by the Rebels.

Saint Al started the 2nd with a 15 yard drive for 70 yards. Brown's pass to Eddie Ray got 25 and was highlighted two plays later by a Maggio run from the 1 for the touchdown to make it 13-0. After a Saint Joe punt to the 20, the Flashes added to the lead in 10 plays. Maggio and Tommy Ray ran for 16; Brown hit Eddie Ray for 19; and then Ray went over from the 7. McCain made it 20-0. The defense held the final Rebel drive to the Flash 6 to get the victory.

GAME 6: SAINT AL (1-4) vs HAZLEHURST (2-3)
FINAL: ST AL 12 HAZLEHURST 0
October 15, 1964: HOMECOMING

The Friday game was moved to Thursday to accommodate patrons of the State Fair in Jackson. Antoine and Lauderdale would be out with knee injuries, but the coach was still in high spirits. *"…We haven't had a bad week of practice yet. It's just that we've lost four real close games that could have gone either way. Maybe the second half of the season will balance and be in our favor. We'll have to be at our best tonight to win. We know the Indians are hungry and they'll be after our scalps. But we're hungry, too."*

In the 2nd, Saint Al scored from the 31 with Maggio running all the way. McCain made it 7-0. Bridgers recovered a Hazlehurst fumble at the Indian 39 on the kickoff but the Flashes ended up punting from the 28. Hazlehurst responded with a Harold Kergosien pass to Fred McDonnel for 9; Robert Hattison's run for 13 and Derrel Granger's 22 yard pass completion that put them at the Flash 22. But Bridgers recovered his second fumble to end the drive and the half.

In the 3rd, Kergosien picked up a Flash ball at the Flash 28, but fumbled it two plays later and was recovered by Kelly. Nearing the end of the quarter, Zorn took a Hazlehurst punt from his 33 to the Indian 44. Zorn ran twice for 5, McCain went for 35, Maggio found Eddie Ray for 14, and Zorn got 2. A delay penalty put the Flashes back the 19 before Kelly ran it in for the last touchdown and the win. The Copiah County Courier called the Flash defense "one of the best that Hazlehurst has been up against this year". Bourgeois graded the offensive line at 80% and the backs at 60%. He reported grades for each player in the paper on October 27th, but Tommy Buell at 83% was highest. On defense, Zorn took a 90% grade with McCain at 85%.

GAME 7:   SAINT AL (2-4) vs ROLLING FORK (6-1)
                 FINAL: ST AL 0 ROLLING FORK 20
                 October 31, 1964

Said Bourgeois "We'll have to be at our season's peak Friday night. This is one game that will make or break our season." This game wouldn't be a conference game since Rolling Fork didn't have the required number of Delta Valley Conference opponents. The defending champs had lost the opener against Greenville but not since. Lauderdale would be out but the coach said that, "spirit and determination were at a fever pitch." The paper said that the expected standing-room only crowd could "look for leather to pop".

A 1st quarter drive that started with a Kelly fumble recovery at the Colonel 24 was the closest the Flashes would get to scoring. After runs by Brown, Maggio and Zorn, Antoine missed a 34 yard FG. In the 2nd, the Colonels went 52 yards in 8 plays that saw John Schimmel, Harry Cauthern, Gary Bond and Terry Bradshaw get yardage. Bond then found Russell Atchley for the 4 yard touchdown.

Rolling Fork scored again in the 3rd when Bond found Danny Martin for a 71 yard touchdown to make it 13-0. The Flashed attempted to respond but got only to the 38 before having to punt. The Colonels started at their 25 and finished the scoring after 10 plays when Bond found Atchley from the 19. Martin finished with the kick to make it 20-0. The Colonels almost scored before the end after a Bradshaw interception was returned to the Flash 29. While still at the Flash 7, time expired. After the game, Colonels coach Charles Peets told The Deer Creek Pilot that "the Flashes hit harder than any team (they) had played. It was anything but an easy victory, and that's why it was so sweet."

GAME 8:   SAINT AL (2-5) vs MAGEE (5-1)
                 FINAL: ST AL 10 MAGEE 0
                 November 6, 1964

Bourgeois had predicted a potential 5-loss season when speaking to a local civic club before the season. He had been right. And now it was time to play the defending Little Dixie Conference Champions from Magee. Though both teams had defeated Hazlehurst (Magee 14-6 and Saint Al 12-0), the paper thought the Magee was deeper in reserves and predicted a Magee victory of 13-7.

Saint Al's first possession took them to the Magee 35 before Eddie Ray fumbled to Wyck Neely. The Trojans responded by driving to the Flash 40 but couldn't complete a 4th down pass. In the 2nd, Neely fumbled a Flash punt that was recovered by Maggio. Ray then found Zorn for a touchdown on the next play but a flag for motion erased it and had the Flashes back to the 11. Ray responded with a run to the 1 and then plunged in for the touchdown.

The 3rd started with a Lamar Carter fumble on the kickoff at the Trojan 44 that was recovered by Balzli. However, Neely picked off a Ray pass at the 15 afterwards to give it back. In the 4th, Ray drove the Flashes 89 yards to the 3 by hitting Zorn for 13 and 22, and then Maggio for 12. Combined with Ray rushes for 44 yards on 6 carries, Antoine made the 19 yard FG. Magee almost scored on their next possession by moving the ball to the Flash 1 behind plays by McAlpin, Neely and David Tedford. But the 4th down pass was overthrown and "the St. Aloysius stands rocked." The Flashes would finish Bourgeois' last year and the 1964 season with a record of 3-5.

Joe Maggio was recipient of the Virgadamo Trophy.

"The 1964 season can be characterized by the values that Andy Bourgeois taught us: having pride in ourselves, fighting through adversity and never giving up. Playing with this "Band of Brothers" was totally awesome because we certainly lived up to those values both on and off the field. We valued ourselves and cared and supported one-another while fighting through insurmountable odds. We had each other's' backs no matter what the circumstances.

Expectations for the season were extremely high, but mainly because of early injuries to key players, the results might not have turned out as anticipated. The "never-say-die" attitude kept us fighting and scraping the entire season. The highlight of the year was defeating the Little Dixie Conference champion Magee Trojans. This was a perfect way to conclude our senior season and the winning era of Coach Bourgeois."

Tommy Lee; July 21, 2016

1965 (7-2)

Saint Al had lost 13 of 19 lettermen to graduation and, equally as important, their head coach. Bourgeois returned to his home in New Orleans to take over the AAA program in Cor Jesu and was replaced by Elmo Broussard. Broussard was nominated for *"Coach of the Year"* at Holy Savior Central High in Lockport, LA the previous year. Assistant Jerry Worsham stayed at Saint Al to assist the new man.

Whereas Bourgeois was using the "Wing T", Broussard introduced the new "Split Slot T" to the Flashes. The weeks leading up the first game were spent adjusting and determining which guys would hold which positions. Eddie Ray was the obvious choice for QB and was, along with Tom Balzli, elected team captain. The Flashes also had added a transfer from Jackson St Joseph in George Booth. Broussard was pleased with the addition, saying, *"Booth was a very pleasant surprise and he should help us tremendously."*

The Flashes added two night practices in preparation for a *"little known"* team *"... reported with one of the toughest lines in the Little Dixie..."* Broussard prepped his passing game, saying *"We'll definitely throw a great deal tomorrow night. I have been impressed by the way our passing game has been clicking in practice this week and I just hope we can continue to click. If we can hit on a few early, that will make our running-game function better."*

GAME 1:　　　　SAINT AL (0-0) @ BRANDON (0-0)
　　　　　　　　FINAL: ST AL 19 BRANDON 13
　　　　　　　　September 3, 1965

The paper had Saint Al as one-point favorites (14-13) based on an unknown Brandon team. *"Just a hunch, since we know absolutely nothing about Brandon, we're picking the Flashes to make* (Broussard's) *debut ... a successful one."* There were *"packed stands"* to see what the paper called "**BIG EDDIE SPARKS ST. AL'S TRIUMPH**".

In the 1st, Ray found Al Brown from the 3 to cap a 58 yard drive and Bridgers added the 7-0 PAT. The Bulldogs answered in the 2nd when Freddie Farmer ran in from the 8 and then tied it 7-7. In the 3rd, Farmer scored again but his PAT was blocked by John Hardin and Pat Hogan. In the same quarter, the Flashes responded after traded punts when Booth *"bullied his way through the Brandon line"* for the touchdown. In the 4th, Ray broke through the line for 61 yards and the winning score.

Brandon's Farmer had 2 touchdowns, a PAT, and averaged 41.4 yards punting. In spite of three TD passes dropped in the endzone from Ray, Broussard said, *"Of course we made mistakes, but we also learned a lot, too. And we really looked better that I thought we would. I was really proud of our defense. They really came through for us. It made me feel mighty happy, not only for myself, but for the kids. They've been working awfully hard and I was proud of everyone, especially ... when we got behind and instead of folding up they seemed to try harder."*

GAME 2:　　　　SAINT AL (1-0) vs CHAMBERLAIN HUNT ACADEMY (UNREPORTED)
　　　　　　　　FINAL: ST AL 27 CHA 0
　　　　　　　　September 11, 1965

This was the first year of play for CHA. As for Saint Al, Danny Cappaert had injured his knee and was doubtful. Practice week wasn't impressive, but the coach said that *"maybe we'll come around before game time."* Game day was moved back a day due to Hurricane Betsy and then up an hour (according to Brother Mark) in order for fans to get home and watch the Miss America Pageant.

In the 1st, Eddie Ray recovered a Wildcat fumble and went 46 yards for the score. They almost scored again but couldn't convert from the Wildcat 5. In the 2nd, they threatened again from the 10 but could not get in. In the 3rd, it was Tommy Ray who picked off a CHA pass and took it 25 yards for the touchdown. CHA was later at the Flash 5 but Eddie Ray picked it off at the goal and went 100 yards for the touchdown. And in the 4th, fullback Robert Sadler took it in from the 10 to score. Bridgers was good on all PAT attempts beforehand, but Eddie Ray missed the final one.

Broussard was pleased with the running game but disappointed in just 50 passing yards. Ray had 9 carries for 85 yards and two touchdowns and had taken the Warren County lead in total points with 18. Second place was Mike Lips (Cooper) with 7.

GAME 3:   SAINT AL (2-0) @ WARREN CENTRAL (1-2)
           FINAL: ST AL 14 WARREN CENTRAL 12
           September 24, 1965

Warren Central was "new" as Jett, Redwood and Culkin were merged into one school. At the Vicksburg Touchdown Club, both coaches were complimentary of the other. Noting the tandem of Eddie and Tommy Ray, WC head man Ernie Albritton said to laughter, *"If we can hold down their passing and stop their running game, I believe we'll have a chance".* Broussard complimented the Vikings much-bigger line and said *"we're gonna get after them and hope we can come out on top".*

Over 1,000 fans were *"frostbitten"* when the game began. On the Flashes' first series, they went 55 yards in 9 plays for the score. Ray was 4-4 in passing and found Bridgers for the first touchdown from the 8. Bridgers made it 7-0. Warren Central responded 9 plays later when Donnie Frith found Cecil Simmons for a 44 yard touchdown. Sid Beauman missed the PAT to keep it 7-6. The Flashes dominated the 2nd on the ground, getting as close at the 27, but remained scoreless.

In the 3rd, Eddie Ray had a punt go only 1 yard and then threw a hurried pass that was intercepted by the Vikings' Bill West. West went 35 yards for the score but Beauman missed and it was 12-7. In the 4th, the Flashes stopped a Beauman run to regain the ball at the 38. Ray gained 22 on a run and then a Viking penalty moved it 8 more yards. The Flashes tried four plays from the 8, but could get no farther than the 1 and gave it back to Warren Central.

With 4:11 left, Eddie Ray dropped the ball and then picked it up to go 21 yards for the touchdown. Bridgers made it a 14-12 victory. Warren Central was attempting a drive, but Billy McCain picked off Frith to ice the game. Ray moved up to 24 total points in Warren County for a clear lead. Teammate Bridgers was tied for 2nd with 12 points.

GAME 4:   SAINT AL (3-0) vs GREENVILLE SAINT JOSEPH (4-0)
           FINAL: ST AL 14 GREENVILLE ST JOE 7
           October 1, 1965: CITY PARK

The Irish had outscored opponents 109-13, were undefeated, had lost only 1 game in 2 years and were going for their 4th straight Little 8 title. The paper 's prediction was *"The odds say St. Joe, but the Fighting Irish haven't run up against anything like Eddie Ray and company. A 20-14 upset, Flashes."* Said Broussard, *"We'll really be put to the test tonight. I just hope we can make the game interesting."*

The Flashes held the Irish after the kick and took over on their 30 after an offsides penalty. Ray moved the team to the Irish 22, but after a 10 yard loss on a run, an official ejected him for what the paper called *"using his elbow a bit too freely".* Without their star player, the Flashes still came through. In the 2nd, they started at their 47 and drove to the Irish 40. Tommy Ray ended up punting, but a holding penalty gave the Flashes the ball at the Irish 26.

They gained new life at the 11 when Greenville was called for pass interference on a 4th down attempt. Brown rushed 3 times to the 4 and then Ray pushed it in for the touchdown. Bridgers connected to make it 7-0 as the halftime clock was expiring. The Irish tried a long pass but it was intercepted by McCain at the Flash 47 who returned it to the 19.

Their first possession of the 3rd found the Irish at their 38. Andy Schmitt hit Gregory Cassio for 22 yards, kept it for 14 and then Richard Shapley ran it to the 3. Cassio took it in from there and then Charles Sherman hit Tommy Fava for the extra point to tie it 7-7. Balzli recovered a fumble at the 38 in the period, but the Flashes had to punt. Ray put it at the 1. Greenville got to the 15 before a Sherman punt to Ray. He collected it at the Flash 49 and took it to the Irish 21. Ray then went 16 and followed it with a touchdown from. Bridgers made it 14-7. The game ended on a McCain interception while guarding receiver Mickey Marante.

Broussard complimented Danny Cappaert and Mike Woody on Ray's last touchdown for their blocking. Said Billy Ray, "*The St. Aloysius Flashes grew up in a hurry last night. They became men, real men as they convinced a standing room only crowd here at Farrell Stadium that they were not a one man team after all.*" Little brother Tommy closed the scoring leader gap to put the Rays 1st (24) and 2nd (18) in points. Bridgers was in 3rd with 14.

GAME 5:   SAINT AL (4-0) vs JACKSON SAINT JOSEPH (2-3)
            FINAL: ST AL 27 JACKSON ST JOE 0
            October 8, 1965: HOMECOMING

Saint Joe had "*a light but fast team … (that would be) going all out to upset the Flashes' apple cart*". On the 3rd play of the 2nd, Eddie Ray went 69 yards for the touchdown and Bridgers made it 7-0. Eddie later threw a screen to Tommy for a 46 yard score. It was 14-0 at half. In the 3rd, the Flashes went 38 yards in 8 plays with Eddie Ray getting in from the 8. After holding the Rebels to a punt, Ray collected it and went the 31 yards for the final score. Ashley Mahoney hit the PAT for the final score of 27-0. In the 4th, second and third team Flashes were in and held the visitor scoreless.

The paper reported that the "**RAY BOTHERS TAKE COMMAND**" in scoring. Eddie had 42 points and Tommy had 24. The next total was 12 shared by 4 players from the county.

GAME 6:   SAINT AL (5-0) @ HAZLEHURST (3-2)
            FINAL: ST AL 20 HAZLEHURST 6
            October 15, 1965

The Flashes were facing a 3-2 Little Dixie foe and the paper said "*This will be perhaps the Flashes toughest opponent thus far … But if St. Al wants to continue their honeymoon, they'll have to play one of their best games. Hazlehurst has a big team and they're even bigger on defense, the line averaging around 195. With the Ray boys in the lineup, and the others going all out, we'll go along with the Flashes for one more time at least. Make it 21-13.*"

Flashes fans were chanting "*Let's get number six*". On the kick, the Flashes went 53 yards on 8 plays before Eddie Ray dove in from the 3. Bridgers made it 7-0. After forcing a Hazlehurst punt, they went 75 yards in 9 plays and Ray went in from the 1. With a minute left in the 1st, Bridgers made it 14-0. Ray had completed 3 passes in those drives: McCain (22), Tommy Ray (25) and Bridgers (37).

The Indians scored in the 4th after Saint Al held a goal-line drive only to give it right back on a fumble. Fred McDonnell then hit Ray Bridges from the 9. The Flashes put their final drive in order midway through the 4th. Eddie Ray moved them 67 yards in 12 plays and then scored from the 2.

GAME 7:   SAINT AL (6-0) vs ROLLING FORK (7-0)
            FINAL: ST AL 20 ROLLING FORK 14
            October 29, 1965

Rolling Fork had outscored opponents 177-10 this season. The Flashes hadn't won against the Colonels in 6 years, and the paper said "*They're not expected to tonight either, but you can't convince … Broussard, his players and loyal St. Al supporters of this fact*". Said Broussard, "*We're in about as fine shape as any coach could ask and our spirits seem to be the highest they've been all season. If we get beat tonight, we'll just have to say a better team beat us.*"

The standing room only crowd saw the Flashes hold the Colonels opening drive to a punt. But Tommy Ray fumbled it and gave them the ball at the 15. After getting to the 3, Terry Smithhart dove in for an apparent lead, but it was called back for clipping. Jimmy Wade's pass to David Blanchard could not convert 4th down and the Flashes had held. After holding a Colonel 4th down attempt at their 33 in the 2nd, it looked as if the Flashes would give the ball back on a punt. But a flag was thrown for holding. Starting at the 21, Tommy and Eddie pushed the ball to the 1 where Tommy scored. Bridgers capped the 11 play drive to make it 7-0. The Colonels answered on 9 plays from their 36. Smithhart gained 51 and Harvey Spurgeon went in with 1:50 left in the half to tie it.

The Flashes took the opening kickoff and drove 72 yards in 14 plays to regain the lead. Eddie gained 29 on a fake 4th down punt and added 35 more on 8 carries including the 1 yard touchdown. Rolling Fork answered on a 55 yard drive in 5 plays when QB Joel Richardson hit Blanchard from the 26.

Phil Griffin converted for a 14-12 lead. In the 4th, Eddie found McCain on two passes, hit Bridgers for 9 yards and spotted McCain again for 16. Tommy gained 8 and then Eddie took it the remaining 19 yards for the winning score. Bridgers was good to make it 20-14. Fans were on their feet as the Colonels took the ensuing kick back to the Rolling Fork 36 to set up shop.

The running of Smithhart, Richardson, Wade and Spurgeon moved them all the way to the Flash 1. With 3:00 to play, and on 3rd down, Wade fumbled and it was picked up by Danny Cappeart at the 2. The *"Saint Al fans, now sensing a mighty upset, went into near hysterics."* Billy Ray noted that *"Minutes later, Coach Broussard was given probably the best ride he has ever had off the field on the shoulders of some thrill-happy youngsters."*

The headline was **"FLASHES SAID THEY WOULD AND THEY DID, 20 TO 14"**. *"The Saint Aloysius Flashes kicked the dope bucket into the left field bleachers here … last night"* and *"This was one of the finest high school games we have ever seen and we doubt if any person who witnessed the contest will disagree, not even Rolling Fork fans"*. The Flashes reached number 13 in the UPI Top 25 football teams in Mississippi. Their upcoming opponent, Magee, was 8th.

GAME 8: SAINT AL (7-0) @ MAGEE (7-0)
FINAL: ST AL 0 MAGEE 13
November 5, 1965

Magee had outscored opponents 230-6 and entered the game with memories from the previous year's 10-0 shutout. The paper noted that *"The defending Little Dixie chaps will be ready. We believe the Flashes will go all out, too. They realize what's riding on the outcome and it's not altogether just an undefeated, untied season."* Said Broussard, *"We're just going to do the best we can and if the boys will give … 100 percent effort, like they have done all season, that's all we can ask".*

It had been many seasons since the Flashes ended undefeated. Saint Al fans were at the school for the rainy 3:30 departure to Magee with what was called *"a plane load of noise-makers, pom-poms and special t-shirts"*. Additionally, the *"Friends and Supporters of Saint Aloysius High School Flashes"* published a full-page ad in the paper on game day as motivation.

The Flash fumbles in what Phil Maclin called a *"backyard mud puddle"* started immediately. Eddie Ray lost the handle on the first drive and recovered for a 13-yard loss. Starting on the 10 on their next drive, Ray gained 24 but the run was brought back for a penalty. Ray then fumbled twice, and the second one was recovered by the Trojans at the Flash 4. Four plays later, Bubba Carter went in from the 2 for the touchdown and Royce Foster made it 7-0.

The Trojans started the 2nd at the Flash 38. Six plays later, Foster plunged in from the 2 to make halftime 6-0. The Flashes got as far as the Trojan 30 after but Ray was intercepted. More penalties in the 3rd killed a Flash drive with catches by Brown of 16 and 6. When Magee got the ball back at their 26, Foster fumbled. Saint Al immediately gave it back with a Ray fumble. Magee fumbled their punt on the ensuing drive, the Flashes fumbled it back on the next play, and the Trojans fumbled it back to Saint Al on the next play! In the end, Magee got to the Flash 3 before time expired.

The paper summarized the game *"played on a field standing several inches deep in water in many places"* by calling it a heartbreaker and saying that Saint Al had nothing ashamed of. Said Broussard, *"I am truly proud of the entire squad for their fine spirit, hustle and determination this season. It has been one of my finest hours."* Eddie Ray still doubled the next person in the Warren County Scoring Leaders (73). Tommy was next with 30.

On November 9th, Brother Mark announced acceptance of a bid to play in the Mississippi Bowl on Thanksgiving Day. Broussard was *"tickled to death at the bowl invitation"* and *"thought his players were strictly deserving of a post-season bowl game and would give a good account of themselves win, lose or draw."* The team had been invited to the Red Carpet Bowl, but McComb's higher classification was not attractive.

GAME 9: SAINT AL (7-1) vs FOREST HILL (8-2)
FINAL: ST AL 6 FOREST HILL 7
November 25, 1965: CLINTON, MS

The Flashes had a week off before prepping for their fourth post-season appearance; the previous ones all coming under Joe Balzli (1938, 1947, 1947, 1961). Broussard had watched his opponent beat Clinton the previous week 26-7 and commented that *"It certainly will be a great challenge for our boys. I saw (them) beat Clinton Friday night and they have a quick, alert and smartly coached ball club. I don't see how they've lost a game."*

The Rebels lost 6-0 to Rolling Fork in the 1964 Red Carpet Bowl but were returning most of their players. They outscored their opponents 215-55 and the common foes for both were nearly identical in scoring margins. The paper tagged Forest Hill as slight favorites. Said Broussard, *"We're in fine shape. I know Forest Hill has a fine team with speed to burn, but I believe we'll be ready to give them a real good battle. Practice has been real good this week and team spirit is still high. We're sure going to try and win, just for our loyal fans if for no other reason. They've really been great and have meant so much to us this season.*

A Robinson Field crowd of 4,000 saw the Flashes score first. On a Ray punt to the Rebels, Travis Eldridge called for a fair catch but fumbled to Billy Goodman at the 10. Ray ran for 8 and finished the drive from there to make it 6-0. Previous to that, the Flashes were driving but were intercepted by Jimmy Stewart who brought it back to the Flash 38. The defense held and got the ball back after a fake punt went wrong for the Rebels.

At the close of the 3rd, Ray thrilled the crowd with a 63 yard run from the Flash 15 to the Rebel 22. Charles Nicholson saved what would have been a sure touchdown. After getting to the 12, Harry Edwards picked off a Ray pass at the 8 and took it back to the 17. Two running plays got them to the 40 but the Rebels fumbled and it was recovered by Cappaert. The Flashes managed to get to the 16 before Ray was hit during a pass and it was intercepted by Stewart.

Eldridge took the first play for 25 yards on a run followed by a Chuck Allgood run for 9. A Flash penalty was added to put the ball at the Saint Al 40. The Rebels got to the 16 on two Stewart receptions, Allgood got to the 5 on two runs, and then Joe Rutledge went in from there. Steve Sparks drove home the PAT to end the scoring. A final attempt by the Flashes got to the Rebel 37 before time expired.

Eddie Ray won the 1965 Tom McAn Grid Trophy, the award given by The Vicksburg Evening Post for the player most valuable to his team during the season. The trophy was actually the playing shoe of the recipient, bronzed and mounted. All Warren County Awards went to David Bridgers (End); Tom Balzli (Guard); and the Ray brothers (Backs). Honorable Mentions went to Al Brown (End), George Booth (Back) and Jim Schultz (Center). Balzli won the Virgadamo Trophy.

The season is best summed up by Broussard's comments to the Vicksburg Civitan Club on October 27th. *"We may not have the best 11 football players in the state, but I think we do have the best 50 boys. No one can beat them in the department of desire. I am as proud of them as any boys I ever had. We realize that somewhere along the line we will probably meet a better team. That's true of life. Somewhere you will find a man that is better than you and you won't be able to do anything about it. But you must give your best anyway. You have to make certain sacrifices to win; on the football field or in life. And this is the lesson that we hope football teaches our kids."*

"My recollection of the 1965 season is bittersweet. It was my senior year at Saint Al and we entered the season with unbridled enthusiasm, led by our new Coach Elmo Broussard. Our confidence grew with each successive win and the dream continued. The high point was beating undefeated Rolling Fork with a 4th quarter goal line stand. That put us a 7-0 with just undefeated Magee in our way. But we lost 13-0 in terrible rain and mud. It hurt. It really hurt.

But we licked our wounds and went on to the Mississippi Bowl on Thanksgiving Day to play Forest Hill. Our old coach Andy Bourgeois came to cheer us on. It was 85 degrees at kickoff. We lost that one 7-6 and thus the final two games were disappointments, but the season remains a great memory for me. The entire Saint Al family had been so supportive during the season. We were proud of our effort and proud to represent our beloved Saint Aloysius."

Tom Balzli; August 9, 2016

"Beating Rolling Fork could be called the greatest victory in Saint Al history. They were not only intimidating in size, but also in their records and number of players. Playing as a team, we overcame unbelievable odds.

But the best memory I will take will be playing alongside my teammates. While I may have gotten more publicity, it was always about us. Everybody had the "team" attitude put into us early by Coach Bourgeois. We made one-another better. They certainly made me better. And for that, I love them all."

Eddie Ray; August 9, 2016

1966 (3-5-1)

Anyone expecting a 7-2 repeat season would be in for a surprise. Gone were big Eddie Ray, Tom Balzli, and others to graduation. Additionally, the Flashes lost three more players (David Bridgers, Jett Evans and Billy Goodman) as a result of moves. That left 13 lettermen on the squad. Said Broussard, "*We just haven't got that 'zip' we had last year, but I'm hoping it will come around this week. ...we'll just have to take things as they come and hope for the best.*"

He found a replacement at QB in converted end Mike Booth, who was named team captain alongside Billy McCain and Jim Schultz. The Flashes averaged well in size on the line (181) and in backs (170). The first game would be against Little Dixie foe Brandon, ranked 3rd in the division. The paper's prediction was in favor of Broussard's boys by a score of either 20-13 or 14-13.

GAME 1:   SAINT AL (0-0) vs BRANDON (0-0)
                               FINAL: ST AL 25 BRANDON 7
                               September 2, 1966

A standing room only crowd came to Farrell Stadium to watch Broussard's second season commence. On the Flashes second possession, Booth went 54 yards for the touchdown to make it 6-0. The Bulldogs tried to answer but fumbled on the Flash 32 and it was recovered by Danny Davis. However, Booth fumbled back to Brandon on the next possession and it was recovered by Cecil Wells at the Flash 30. Five plays later, Jimmy May went in from the 4 to tie the game. Carl Swilley added the PAT to make it 7-6.

The Flashes started at their 44 after Ray's kickoff return. Booth got 11 and then hit Frank Price to put the ball at the Brandon 29. Ray then converted from there to make it 12-7. The Flashes almost scored again when Booth hit Price in the endzone, but the ball was dropped. In the 4th, the Bulldogs had gotten deep into Flash territory after starting at their own 20. Tommy Ray then picked off a Troy Mashburn pass and returned it 83 yards for the touchdown. McCain made it 19-7. Only 1:10 later, it was Bobby Ray who picked off a Brandon pass and took it 25 yards for the last Flash touchdown.

GAME 2:   SAINT AL (1-0) vs OAK GROVE, LA (0-0)
                               FINAL: ST AL 7 OAK GROVE 13
                               September 8, 1966

The father of Charles Hagan, Mr. Claude Hagan, passed away this week and the team attended services on game morning. As for the opponent, Oak Grove had officially played no games, but did impress in their victory the previous week over Eudora (AR) in a Jamboree. Broussard attended the game and compared them to Rolling Fork, saying "*They are big, fast and they hit hard.*"

The Flashes were now hampered with injuries. Mike McNamara was out, Danny Cappaert was doubtful and Claude had missed the week for obvious reasons. As for the game, Broussard said "*We've got to play a much better brand of ball against Oak Grove or we won't be around for the second half. And our injuries to key players certainly won't help us an. Our bench has really got to come through.*" Billy Ray added "*...every game* (against Oak Grove in the past) *has always been a rip-snorter and tonight's contest is not expected to be an exception.*"

The "*overflow crowd*" at Farrell Stadium saw the Flashes score first. After a couple of punts, Saint Al drove 54 yards in 9 plays behind Ray runs of 7 and 9, McCain's 13 yard catch, and a 5 yard run by Booth. Booth found Ray on a 20-yard screen for the touchdown. McCain's PAT made it 7-0. Mark Evans intercepted an Oak Grove pass at the 10 to stop the ensuing Tiger drive though they answered in the 2nd when David Butler threw a pitchout pass to Mike Pollard good for a 54 yard touchdown. Harvey Hempill converted to make it 7-7 going into halftime.

In the 4th, Butler took a pitch from Donald Ray Hurley 34 yards for the touchdown. The Flashes tried to come back for the go-ahead score when Booth found Bernie Callaway for 10 and Ray for 15. Booth and Ray pushed the ball to the 9 behind rushes and a penalty. But the next play found Booth fumbling, picked up by Hemphill, and returned all the way for an apparent touchdown. The refs said that he had stepped out of bounds at the 16, however. After running clock, and 3 errant Flash passes, the clock ran out for an Oak Grove victory.

GAME 3:	SAINT AL (1-1) @ GREENVILLE SAINT JOSEPH (2-0)
	FINAL: ST AL 7 GREENVILLE ST JOE 7
	September 17, 1966

Broussard attempted to change the game to Thursday to avoid the MSU-Georgia game in Jackson but was turned down by school officials. Greenville had beaten local teams in Shaw and Lambert by a combined 90-12 without injured key players. For Saint Al, McCain was injured and would play defense only for the contest.

The Irish scored on their kickoff, capping an 80 yard drive when Andy Schmitt found Gerald Keigley from the 30. The Flashes responded with a McCain pickoff at the Saint Al 40 and brought it back to the 27. Booth and Ray took it to the 4 and then Ray went in for the score. Ashley Mahoney's PAT tied it 7-7. The remainder of the game saw Saint Joe get only to the Flash 22 and Saint Al only to their 37. Broussard was not happy with offensive production, but he praised his defense. *"We intercepted four passes to run our pass interception total to 10 in our first three games."*

GAME 4:	SAINT AL (1-1-1) @ WARREN CENTRAL (0-3)
	FINAL: ST AL 39 WARREN CENTRAL 0
	September 23, 1966

The Flashes entered the local rivalry with a load of injuries. Sadler and Evans were definitely out, Callaway had a *"gash in the head requiring eight stitches"* and 5 others were hampered. Warren Central was fairly healthy and getting ready with a *"Burn The Flashes"* bonfire. Said coach Donald Oakes, *"... spirit has been booming this week and I believe our boys are going to go all out for this one."* Broussard said *"We know we've got our work cut out. We're not looking at Warren Central's records their first three games. This is a new game, a big one for the Vikings and I know they'll be throwing the book at us. I'm really scared."*

The paper called the Vikings underdogs, but said *"don't look for a wop-sided score and with the good place kicking of Ernest Myers, we would be surprised to see the Vikings dot the scoreboard with a field goal. ... make it Saint Al 26, Warren Central 10."*

On the Flashes' kickoff drive, Booth found McCain for a 26 yard touchdown with only 4 minutes gone to make it 6-0. They almost scored again at the Viking 8, but a Jimmy Salmon fumble was recovered by Mike Beauman. Continuing the pressure, Tommy Ray picked off Steve Carlisle at the Viking 34, but later fumbled at the Viking 9 to be recovered by George Brent. To make matters worse, a 50 yard touchdown pass from Booth to McCain in the 1st was called back. It would be part of the 125 total penalty yards assessed on the purple and gold that night.

The Flashes finally put up another touchdown in the 2nd when a punt snap got by Warren Central and gave Saint Al the ball at the Viking 30 with 1:16 remaining. Three plays later, Booth found McCain from the 10. Mahoney made it 13-0 at halftime. In the 3rd, Ray took it from the 3 to cap a 38 yard drive of 6 plays. Booth added another later with a 3 yard touchdown. In the 4th, Ray scored from the 7 and backup QB Joe Gerache ran one in from the 12.

GAME 5:	SAINT AL (2-1-1) @ JACKSON SAINT JOSEPH (2-2)
	FINAL: ST AL 6 JACKSON ST JOE 7
	October 7, 1966

Injuries were still a factor as Danny Davis and Sadler were out and others again were questionable. Broussard would have to start 4 seniors, 6 juniors and sophomore. The Flashes had managed to move from their 20 to the Rebel 21 on their first drive before Mike Ray fumbled to Saint Joe's Mike Davis. The Rebels got to the Flash 5 in the 2nd after a 35 yard connection from Thomas to Jimmy Carroll and a pass interference penalty. But St Joe was turned back by the Flashes. On the first play thereafter, Ray fumbled to Davis at the Flash 11. Again the defense rose and prevented a score at the 7. Ray took the next play 73 yards to the Rebel 20 as time expired in the half.

The Flashes got on the board when Ray ran for 49 yards and the touchdown in the 3rd. After both teams exchanged punts, Booth found McCain on a 55 yard bomb that was brought back for a penalty. The Rebels' Leonard Thomas later found Jimmy Carroll from the 42 for a game-tying touchdown. Bobby Anger added the PAT to make it 7-6. Saint Al's response got to the Rebel 29 before Booth coughed up the football. No other drive was successful and St Joe had upset the visiting Flashes.

Broussard told the paper afterwards that it was probably his team's worse performance since he's been head coach. *"We just made too many mistakes. Penalties and fumbles killed us."*

GAME 6:   SAINT AL (2-2-1) vs HAZLEHURST (4-2)
                 FINAL: ST AL 6 HAZLEHURST 13
                 October 13, 1966: HOMECOMING

Broussard held a *"rugged"* Sunday practice to *"iron out a few kinks"*. The paper said, *"Homecomings are supposed to be happy occasions and the home team is expected to win to please old grads. But the St. Aloysius Flashes really have their work cut out this week when they host powerful Hazlehurst…"* Mahoney would miss with a fractured foot for the game moved to Thursday to avoid coinciding with the State Fair. By game day, Broussard was a bit more upbeat, saying *"I think we have improved some, but just how much I'd be afraid to say. However, I think we're going to get after some Indians tonight."*
    The Flashes were able to avoid disaster in the 1st half by holding the Indians on two long drives. The first got to the Flash 13 but was stopped by a fumble. The second got to the Flash 8, but the defense held Hazlehurst four-and-out. After an Indian punt to the Flash 47, Booth found an open Salmon behind the safety at the 25 for the 53 yard touchdown. Richard George's PAT was good, but after a penalty, the second attempt was short.
    Hazlehurst started at their 32 after the kick. The first play was only a 2 yard gain from Ray Bridges to Billy Wyatt, but a penalty for *"piling on"* added 15 more to the 49. Behind runs by Robert Higdon and Eldon Pitts, Hazlehurst got to the Flash 15. Wyatt then passed to Charles Callaway for the touchdown. Bridges PAT made it 7-6. The Flashes got a break in the 4th when Ray was thrown to the ground on a punt. With the ball now at the Indian 40, Ray fumbled and it was recovered by Poagie Wyatt. Saint Al held Hazlehurst to a punt, but an off-sides penalty allowed the drive to continue. Billy Wyatt broke a run of 33 to the 1 and Pitts dove in from there. Trying to recover, Booth hit Ray for a 13 yard pass to the 50 and then Ray broke a 41 yard run to the 9. Ray got as far as the 7, but two passes fell incomplete and the last one was picked off by Billy Goodman. Hazlehurst got to the Flash 15 before time expired.

GAME 7:   SAINT AL (2-3-1) @ ROLLING FORK (8-0)
                 FINAL: ST AL 0 ROLLING FORK 47
                 October 28, 1966

Broussard knew well the Delta Valley Conference this week. *"… we're not conceding defeat by any means. We hope to make the game plenty interesting, but I know we'll have to play our best game of the season in order to do this. This will definitely be the toughest opponent we'll meet all year. They're much tougher than they were last year, having scored 305 points while holding seven opponents to only 27. We know they're going to score on us. Our only hope is to match them blow-for-blow and point-for-point and hope for the best. That's what we're going to try to do."*
    They were facing a team Broussard later complimented by saying *"We consider it an honor to be on the same field with them"* and without the services of McCain for the remainder of 1966. To make it worse, three others (White, Mahoney, and Leo) may not see action either. *"I just hope we can make the game interesting."*
    The game was best evidenced in the 1st when Ray went to punt, had the snap go over his head, and forced a quick kick. Two plays later, Terry Smithhart scored after runs of 30 and 20. Willard Miller made it 7-0. Ray took the kickoff on a fumble and returned it to the Colonel 35 but got no further than the 12. The home team answered with a 43 yard Jimmy Wade pass to Donnie Baggett for the touchdown. Miller was no good and it was 13-0.
    The Colonels continued scoring at will in the 2nd. Harvey Spurgeon scored from the 8, Smithhart ran one in, and Baggett caught one from 41 yards out to make it 34-0 at half. In the 3rd, Wade found Baggett for 39 yards and Smithhart capped it from the 5. Rolling Fork's last was with 1:00 left when Wade found Smithhart for 55 yards. Dennie Frisbee's PAT made it 47-0. It was one of the worst defeats that Saint Al had in recent memory; a testament to the team from Rolling Fork.

GAME 8:   SAINT AL (2-4-1) vs MAGEE (7-0)
                              FINAL: ST AL 0 MAGEE 19
                              November 4, 1966

Because of the 13 injuries, and though the Flashes were the last team to beat Magee (1964), the paper predicted another Flash loss (20-13) in their last home game. An opening kick to Magee was fumbled at their 40 and recovered by Saint Al. But three plays later, Booth was picked off by Don Beatty and returned to the 49. Later, the Flashes got to the Trojan 34, but Booth was picked off again. This time Wyck Neely took from the 15 to the 32.

The Trojans first touchdown came in the 2nd. Chuck Akers, Royce Foster, Neely, Jim McAlpin and Ronnie Garner pushed it to the 4. Akers then converted on 3rd down. He was hit at the goal and fumbled, but ruled as having crossed the line for the score. Foster made it 7-0. The Flashes tried to respond when Ray ran for 19 and then hit Frank Price for 41. But the halftime whistle sounded while still at the Trojan 19.

In the 3rd, Magee capped a 78 yard drive in 6 plays when Akers scored his second touchdown from the 31. After the ensuing kick, Booth fumbled on a pass and it was taken back by Bob Everett 25 yards for another score. The Flashes attempted to get on the board after a recovered fumble by John Evans at the 22 and a pass interference call on Gil Israel at the Trojan 11. Booth and Ray put it inches from the goal, but on 4th down, Booth fumbled and it was recovered by Magee at the 3 to end the game. Magee's streak of victories continued.

In spite of the lopsided score, Broussard complimented Martin White, Ray, Jimmy Salmon and Booth. "I thought White and Booth probably turned in their best defensive games of the season."

GAME 9:   SAINT AL (2-5-1) vs CHAMBERLAIN HUNT ACADEMY (0-8)
                              FINAL: ST AL 42 CHAMBERLAIN HUNT 0
                              November 11, 1966

Broussard noted in advance that he was hoping to play as many reserves as he could against the winless Wildcats. The paper predicted a 33-6 victory. On their first possession, the Flashes needed only 4 plays to score. Ray and Booth took it to the 50; Salmon ran one for 45; and Ray finished it for the touchdown. Later in the quarter, Robert Sadler took one in from the 10 for another touchdown. In the 2nd, runs by Gerache, Sadler and Ray got them to the 2 before Ray capped it. The Cadets got only to their 35 before turning it back to Saint Al. Booth then hit Ray for the 32 yard touchdown. Ashley Mahoney found a Chamberlain Hunt fumble on their next possession and behind runs from Salmon and Ray, Ray took it in from the 5. Ray almost scored again before half, but the whistle sounded with the Flashes at the Cadet 10.

The 2nd half was played by the reserves. Marion Conerly rush for 52 yards and then Mark Evans hit Lester Koe for another score. Richard George made the PAT. The Flashes scored again when Eddie Solomon, playing LB, intercepted a Cadet pass at the CHA 30 and returned it to the 13. Saint Al converted it into a touchdown. The only threat from the Cadets came in the 4th when they got to the Flash 9 but were unable to score. The Port Gibson paper noted that the Cadets were "outclassed from the beginning".

The season was over at 3-5-1; just eight points from points from being 7-3. Billy McCain was recipient of the Virgadamo Trophy.

1967 (4-2-3)

Broussard entered his third year at the helm of Saint Al with Charles Hagan and Tommy Ray co-captaining the squad. Very little was reported on pre-season activities. The paper noted that the first Flash opponent (Brandon Bulldogs) was rebuilding and had a new coach. So, barring "overconfidence and first game butterflies", they had picked the Flashes 26-7.

GAME 1:   SAINT AL (0-0) vs BRANDON (0-0)
             FINAL: ST AL 13 BRANDON 6
             September 8, 1967

On the first Brandon drive, Ray picked off a pass to eventually allow Wade Evans to score from the 5. Frank Price converted the PAT to make it 7-0. In the 3rd, the Flashes received and were driving only to have a pass picked off and returned to the Flash 16. Before they could score, the Bulldogs fumbled to give the ball back to the purple and gold. The Flashes were able to make it count when Charles Ring ran for 36 yards to set up an Evans 40 yard touchdown pass to Price.

In the 4th, Troy Mashburn found Larry Herring for a 12 yard Brandon touchdown but they missed the PAT. The Flashes started with a win, though the paper noted that there were too many penalties that cost them scoring opportunities.

GAME 2:   SAINT AL (1-0) vs CLINTON (0-0)
             FINAL: ST AL 0 CLINTON 13
             September 15, 1967

With a number of returning lettermen, the Arrows were picked as North Little Dixie favorites and had scouted the game versus Brandon. The paper said that *"… this one should be a dilly and a toss-up could be in the making. However, while the Arrows are reported loaded with lettermen returning at every position, the Flashes do have two advantages if you call them that. They have a game under their belt while the Arrows do not, and they'll be playing at home. But look for a big crowd of Arrow boosters here, too. Make it Clinton 20 Flashes 14, but hoping it's the other way around."*

Wayne Muse hit Mike Sellari from 68 yards out for an opening possession touchdown. Muse's PAT made it 7-0. Jimmy Salmon returned the ensuing kickoff to the Flash 42, but Evans eventually picked off a pass at the Arrow 31. The Flashes turned it over again at the close of the 1st on a fumble at the Arrow 29. The 2nd started with a Ray punt to the Arrow 25. On the first play, Clinton got all the way to the Flash 25. Muse hit Philip Booth several plays later for the touchdown, but the PAT was fumbled to make the final 13-0. The Flashes had a chance to answer set up by a Salmon punt return into Arrow territory. But after getting to the Clinton 25, David Brunson intercepted Evans at the 4 to end the half.

The 2nd half included a fumble and two more interceptions of Evans; one at the Flash 45 and the other at the Arrow 13. Two fumbles and four interceptions stalled chances to beat the heavy favorites at home; but the defense did a remarkable job holding them scoreless in the 2nd half.

GAME 3:   SAINT AL (1-1) @ WARREN CENTRAL (0-1)
             FINAL: ST AL 0 WARREN CENTRAL 0
             September 28, 1967

Billy Ray summed up the game by saying *"This is the big one as far as the two teams are concerned. A county-city rivalry at its best that should pack the fans into Viking Stadium tonight. Both will go all out and both teams are reported in good shape. … The Flashes are favored, but in a game of this kind, anything can happen. As Viking coach Dewey Partridge said 'the team that gets the breaks and can capitalize on them will probably be the winner'. Because Saint Al has more experienced veterans, we like the Flashes … Make it 13-3."*

Nearly 3,000 fans were on hand for the contest. In the 1st, Warren Central drove from their 42 to the Flash 31. Facing 4th down, the FG attempt by Richard Rogers was low and went to Frank Price at the Flash 5. The Flashes were eventually forced to punt from their 32. Ray got off only a 6 yard effort but a roughing call kept the drive alive. It didn't last long as the Flashes had to punt again from the Viking 34.

In the 3rd, the Flashes were punting from their 31. The snap was high to Ray who, at his 2, got off a desperation punt to the 50 to avoid disaster. In the 4th, the Vikings threatened when Robin Stroud barely missed a first down at the Flash 17. It gave the ball back to Saint Al, starting at the 6 due to a penalty. Ray found Larry Rocconi at the 26, had yards added on a personal foul, but the Flashes were unable to move and punted.

With the clock winding down, the Flashes found themselves at their 29. Salmon ran twice for 18, Price ran for 4 and Ray got the first down at the Viking 46. Ray hit Bernie Callaway for a 1st at the 31, ran for 4 and then pitched to Price. He got as far as the 20 but fumbled to Bill Allgood to give the Vikings the ball at their 18. The Vikings tried to take advantage with under 2:00 left, but got no further than the Flash 26.

GAME 4:   SAINT AL (1-1-1) vs CHAMBERLAIN HUNT ACADEMY (2-0-1)
            FINAL: ST AL 52 CHA 0
            October 5, 1967

The Wildcats sported a team *"much improved over last years' squad ... out to upset the Flashes."* They had not been scored on but the paper said *"The Flashes could be pushed but we look for them to get win number 2 in a hard fought contest 20-6."* In the 1st, they scored on a 67 yard drive in 12 plays. Ray capped it with a plunge from the 1. Their third touchdown came in the 2nd, when Price ran one in from the 27. Three plays later, Wade Evans found Price for a 32 yard score. In the 3rd, Ray went in from the 19. Other scores included a run by Ray of 55, Salmon from 5, and Ricky Antoine from 4 and an Evans touchdown to Bernie Callaway from the 34. Price had 3 PATS and Charles Ring had another.

The reserves played heavily for the Flashes, and were at the 1 when time expired. The Wildcats actually scored in the 2nd frame; a 19 yard pass from Tim Laughlin to Ralph Van Fossen. But it was called back on a penalty.

GAME 5:   SAINT AL (2-1-1) vs JACKSON SAINT JOSEPH (4-0)
            FINAL: ST AL 21 JACKSON ST JOE 6
            October 13, 1967: HOMECOMING

On paper, Jackson Saint Joe was a bad choice for Homecoming. They were undefeated and had outscored opponents 170-13. Though the paper was picking the Flashes 14-13, Broussard wasn't so sure. *"We've scouted them and they have a real fine team. They are big and quick hitting. It's going to take our best effort if we are to make it close."*

The Flashes hit the scoreboard in the 1st after Evans received the Rebel punt and brought it to their 45. After getting to the 12, Ray scored on his third rush to make it 6-0. Price added the PAT. That would be all of the scoring for the first half, with the Flashes getting no closer than the Rebel 17. In the 2nd half, the Rebels fumbled the opening kick and it was recovered by Ray at the JSJ 43. After holding, the Rebels fumbled to Ray yet again. But they could get no further than the Rebel 11.

On the ensuing JSJ punt, Salmon brought the ball to the Flash 43. Numerous runs got them to the 34 and then Price went up the middle for the touchdown. Saint Al was able to get to the Rebel 1 later, but was held. On the ensuing Rebel drive, the Flashes were able to put up their final points. John Landry threw a quick pass, but it was bobbled into the waiting hands of Charles Hagan. The tackle then took it all the way for the final touchdown. Jackson Saint Joe got on the board afterwards on an 85 yard kick return but the two-point conversion failed.

GAME 6:   SAINT AL (3-1-1) vs HAZLEHURST (UNREPORTED)
            FINAL: ST AL 26 HAZLEHURST 7
            October 20, 1967

The paper predicted a slim Saint Al victory of 14-6 because of the 13-6 loss in 1966. Jerry Hosemann would miss the game and the Flashes had a host of injuries. Broussard was noted as saying *"... if we play as we are capable, I think we will make the game interesting."*

There is very little written about the game, but we know that the 1st was scoreless and closed with a Ray 40 yard run to the Indian 2. Ray got the next run and took it in as the 2nd quarter began. Frank Price's PAT made it 7-0. Evans had the next score before half when, after finding no open receiver, he tucked the ball and ran for a 35 yard toucdown.

Ray scored again in the 3rd with a 35 yard run to the Indian 20 followed by a touchdown run four plays later. The 3rd ended 19-0 in favor of the Flashes. Price converted the last touchdown in the 4th and Ronnie Muffaletto made it 26-7. Price actually had one other touchdown called back for motion. Hazlehurst got on the board on a Pogey Wyatt reception 42 yards out followed by a successful PAT. Ernie Albritton, writer for The Vicksburg Evening Post said that *"One of the main reasons for the fine defensive play of the Flashes was Bernie Callaway, who made tackles all over the playing field; not only in his halfback territory, but also in the enemy backfield on a couple of occasions."*

GAME 7:   SAINT AL (4-1-1) @ ROLLING FORK (3-3-1)
                 FINAL: ST AL 0 ROLLING FORK 0
                 November 3, 1967

Bad weather forced indoor practices. Equally as glum, the paper noted that one of the main reasons the Flashes wanted this final home game so badly was that *"there may not be a Saint Aloysius High School next year and fans, players and coaches are wanting this one badly."* The school's future was in flux and a *"capacity, standing room only crowd"*, quite possibly to see the last game at Farrell Stadium, was a possibility.

Hosemann was now declared lost for the season and was replaced with Frank Koe and Paul Banchetti. On the other side, the Delta Valley champs not only had injuries, but also suffered rumored disciplinary setbacks for some starters. Coach Cotton Robertson made nothing public and the Flashes would have to find out on game day. The paper predicted a 14-7 Flash victory.

It was a cold evening on a field pounded by rain during the week. The Flashes got as far as the Colonel 8 behind two Evans passes. One was to Ray for 26 and the other to Ring for 38, but penalties and sacks for losses ended the threat. Rolling Fork moved inside Saint Al territory 3 times in the game unsuccessfully. A fumble at the Flash 22 killed one of those drives. In all, the Flashes recovered 3 fumbles and Evans had 2 interceptions.

GAME 8:   SAINT AL (4-1-2) @ MAGEE (4-3)
                 FINAL: ST AL 6 MAGEE 14
                 November 10, 1967

Though both teams had improved over a season with three home losses, the paper called this one for Magee 7-6. Saint Al tried to put together a drive on the opening kick and got to the Magee 20 before being stopped. In the 2nd, after a Magee punt, Evans was swamped on a pass and fumbled back to the Trojans. They drove to the Flash 5 before Marion Conerly and Robert Foley sacked the QB on a 4th down play back to the Flash 22.

In the 3rd, after a couple of traded punts, the Flashes began a drive on their 25. Ray made this one count as, on a handoff from Evans, he tore through the line and raced 75 yards for the score. Ray said afterwards, *"I've been waiting for that all season. I wanted to get one long one!"* It was short-lived as Magee drove right back and scored on a pass from the 2. Mike Taylor's PAT made it 7-6.

The 4th found Magee inches from the Flashes goal, but a Colonel fumble was recovered by Salmon in the endzone for the touchback and the ball at the 20. The paper complimented Salmon by saying that he *"turned in a fine night of defensive football"*. The drive was not sustained and Magee's Chuck Acres was able to score from the 3 with just minutes left to seal the game. Ray commented on Acres by saying *"He's not that fast or hard to bring down, but he's got some moves. He's hard to catch."*

GAME 9:   SAINT AL (4-2-2) vs ITAWAMBA COUNTY (7-2)
                 FINAL: ST AL 14 ITAWAMBA COUNTY 14
                 November 24, 1967: JAYCEE BOWL; BATESVILLE, MS

On November 16th, the Flashes unanimously accepted the invitation to play the Tombigbee Conference Indians in the Mississippi Delta Jaycee Bowl. Said Broussard of chances against the team from Fulton, MS, *"We're mighty proud to have been invited to a post-season game, but this is strictly a business venture and not a good time trip. We'll have time to celebrate after the game, if we win."*

Broussard held *"stiff workouts each afternoon"* and had scouted the Indians. He found them to be *"a big, solid club that specializes on the aerial game. … This has me worried some since we have shown a weakness in pass defense. We have been working hard trying to make some adjustments this week"*. The team left early Friday morning and was guests of the Batesville Chamber of Commerce for lunch with their opponents. The evening would be spent at the Skyline Motel in preparation for the 8pm kickoff.

Hosemann had now returned and the paper had predicted a Flash victory, saying *"…we don't think the Indians have run against a line quite as strong as the Flashes and if they can rush the passer, this could be the defense they need. And if Tommy Ray and Frank Price are at their best, the Flashes should put some points on the scoreboard, too. Make it the Flashes … maybe something like 20-19."*

In front of 2,000 fans, it was Itawamba that scored first. Dan Holified found Tommy Roberts on a 40 yard pass to the Flash 25. The drive got eventually got to the Flash 6. On third down Holified hit Roberts again; this time for a touchdown pass from the 6. With a Wiygul PAT, it was 7-0. Before half, the Flashes answered twice. On the first, Evans found Ray on a screen pass of 60 yards. Price tied it at 7-7. With 1:05 left after giving the ball back to Saint Al at the Flash 23, Evans faked to Ray and pitched to Price. He went the entire 75 yards for the score. Price made it a 14-7 halftime lead.

In the 3rd, the Flashes got to the Indian 15 but fumbled. Itawamba got to the 10 and the 5 on two drives, but came up empty. In the 4th, a Flashes' punt put the Indians at the Flash 30. Jerry Senter took it in from the 6 and Wiygul tied it at 14. In the last 6 seconds, Price was called on for a 42 yard FG. The Flashes had gotten to the 20 behind an Evans pass to Marion Conerly, but a clock penalty moved it back 5 yards. Price's kick fell short by 5 yards and the game ended in a tie.

Broussard was complimentary of his defense and named them individually. Everyone carried home a miniature trophy, but Price won the big one for MVP for the contest. Bernie Callaway, who started the following year at the Air Force Academy, won the coveted Virgadamo Award.

1968 (3-5-1)

Broussard kicked off his final year as head man with only 5 seniors in his starting lineup. On top of that, injuries had already bothered the Flashes and one player, Andy Booth, was definitely watching from the sidelines. He was high on the backfield, saying that they may be better than 1967, but the other positions were lacking in depth. *"I just hope our lineman can stay in one piece. We can't afford to get any of them hurt."* Elmo would also be starting off 1968 against a bigger team that returned 9 lettermen from the previous year.

GAME 1:   SAINT AL (0-0) vs BRANDON (0-0)
                         FINAL: ST AL 20 BRANDON 13
                         September 6, 1968

The paper predicted a 13-12 St Al victory, perhaps being just a bit biased. But the Bulldogs were the ones that started strong. The Flashes' Paul Banchetti received the opening kick but, on third down, Saint Al fumbled to Brandon. After runs by Aldridge and Nash pushed the ball to the Flash 6, Aldridge went in for the touchdown. Herring made the PAT for a 7-0 lead. Brandon went up 13-0 in the same quarter when they scored a long touchdown but missed the point after.

In the 2nd, Marion Conerly scored and Ronnie Muffaletto made it 13-7 to end the half. The 3rd saw the Flashes strike quickly when Conerly took it 58 yards for a touchdown to make it 13-13. Saint Al's Jerry Hosemann iced the game in the 4th when he picked off a Brandon pass and took it 51 yards for the touchdown. Muffaletto's PAT connected. The Bulldogs had a valiant effort to tie it at the Flash 3 but could not convert.

GAME 2:   SAINT AL (1-0) @ CLINTON (0-0)
                         FINAL: ST AL 6 CLINTON 21
                         September 13, 1968

The Flashes traditionally had trouble with the Arrows squad. The paper reported that because they were idle the previous week, *"practically the entire team came over to see the Flashes play Brandon"*. Said Broussard, *"I just hope they make some opening game mistakes and that we can capitalize off them. We've been drilling hard all week on pass defense. One mistake and those long bombs can kill you."* Because the Flashes had *"one game under their belt"* and were picked 6th in North Little Dixie, the paper predicted a Flash victory of 13-7. Marion Conerly and Paul Banchetti would be game captains.

Clinton scored in the 1st on a Boyde Sullivan run of 38 yards that capped a 61 yard drive. Harold Wright hit Tommy Saul for the PAT to make it 7-0. The only other 1st half highlight was a Jimmy Salmon run of 31 yards that was well-short of the endzone. In the 3rd, Clinton padded the lead after 4 passes to Burkett, Sellari, Sullivan and McNeer set up a 5 yard touchdown run by George Dennis. David Bishop made it 14-0. The Flashes did get on the scoreboard in the quarter when Salmon took a Donnie Price pass of 53 yards *"dancing across the scoring stripe"*. Muffaletto's PAT was blocked and it was 7-6.

Clinton sealed the game with :25 left when Wright found Saul from the 20. Bishop's PAT made it 21-6. The paper noted that Wiley Piazza and Jerry Hoseman were lost to injury during the game, but Robert Baylot emerged as a *"fine young sophomore … especially in the running department"*.

GAME 3:   SAINT AL (1-1) vs GREENVILLE SAINT JOSEPH (1-1)
                    FINAL: ST AL 28 GREENVILLE ST JOE 15
                    September 20, 1968

After a year hiatus, Saint Joe was again playing the Flashes. The game, *"always a bitter struggle between these two Catholic schools"*, was expected to be close with the Flashes edging the Irish 20-13. Broussard said of the opponent, *"Our scouting reports reveal that St. Joseph has two fine running backs and a hot passing attack with four receivers usually going down for passes on every … play. They have a good size line, too, averaging about 175 pounds."*

Baylot returned the opening kick to the 42, drove to the 28, and then Donnie Price found Muffaletto for the score. Muffaletto's PAT made it 7-0 early. The Irish answered immediately on a 73 yard drive capped by Al Crawford's 1 yard dive. Greenville was able to score yet again when a snap went over the punter's head resulting in a safety. The call was incorrect as the punter had actually run out of the endzone, but the inadvertent whistle resulted in 2 points for the Irish.

Saint Al regained the lead in the 2nd behind the solid running of Salmon. It was Price, however, who got the touchdown from the 3 and it was 14-8. In the 3rd, Saint Joe scored on the opening drive. Ralph Thompson returned the kick to the Flash 25 and then Crawford found John Hinkle from the 13 for the score. Crawford, with Joe Dantone's hold, made it 15-14. The Flashes came right back with a Salmon carry to the 2 and then an eventual touchdown to make it 21-15.

After a Flash fumble at their 40 in the 4th, the Irish began their passing attack. Muffaletto, however, picked off their pass at the Flash 6. On the next play, Salmon dashed the 94 yards for the touchdown for a 28-15 lead. Wiley Piazza managed to pick off another pass late in the game at the Flash 1 to seal the win before the open week.

GAME 4:   SAINT AL (2-1) @ CHAMBERLAIN HUNT ACADEMY (1-3)
                    FINAL: ST AL 0 CHA 0
                    October 4, 1968

For the contest, Broussard said his team was in *"their worst shape of the season"*. At least 7 players, including Salmon, Baylot and Evans, were out. Additionally, Hosemann was questionable with a shoulder injury. *"We've been trying not to get anybody else hurt and our biggest job right now is to try and come up with a starting eleven."* Though saying that *"the stage could be set for an upset"*, the paper did pick Saint Al 20-12 because *"they should have enough reserve strength to get them by."*

The Flashes could have pulled out the victory. Late in the 1st, Saint Al picked up a Cadet fumble and managed to drive to their 10 before failing. The Cadets fumbled to Saint Al again in the half, but Price returned the ball to CHA via an interception. In the 2nd, the Flashes drove more than 79 yards to the Chamberlain Hunt one-foot line, but were unable to get over the stripe. In the end, the Flash defense was able to do an admirable job, but even with nice running by Marion Conerly, the offense couldn't get on the board.

GAME 5:   SAINT AL (2-1-1) @ JACKSON SAINT JOSEPH (4-0)
                    FINAL: ST AL 7 JACKSON ST JOE 26
                    October 11, 1968

Saint Joe was rumored to have *"their best team in years"*. And even though the Flashes were returning 6 players from injuries, they were the underdog against the undefeated Rebels at Homecoming. JSJ had outscored their opponents 147-6 and had an open date the previous week.

The 1st half was a back-and-forth affair. Each had fumbles and neither could gain significant ground. In the 2nd, the Flashes' Joe Gerache was tackled by Bob Hitchens at his own 9 on an attempted punt. On 4th and 1 at the goal line, John Landry finally worked his way in for the Rebel touchdown. Landry then Bob Hitchens for the PAT and it was 7-0 at halftime.

In the 3rd, and after a Saint Al punt put the ball at the Saint Joe 48, Donnie Knoblock took their first play 52 yards for the score. In the 4th, the Flashes fumbled at their 29 and the Rebels drove to the Flash 20. On 4th and 1, Roger Parkes broke through a hole on the right for the touchdown. Fred Knobloch made it 20-0 with the successful PAT. The Flashes tried to respond on the next kickoff with a drive to the Rebel 18. But Price threw an interception intended for Gerache to Donnie Knobloch to end the drive. Their first play afterwards was a Parkes 80 yard touchdown to put the game out of reach.

The Flashes managed to get on the board in the quarter when Evans threw a 16 yard touchdown pass to Preston Harris. Muffaletto added the PAT to make the final 26-7.

GAME 6:   SAINT AL (2-2-1) vs FRANKLIN COUNTY (5-0)
                        FINAL: ST AL 3 FRANKLIN COUNTY 10
                        October 18, 1968: HOMECOMING

Another unbeaten team awaited the Flashes this week for Homecoming. The paper predicted a loss of 20-7 due to continuous injuries and sickness. Salmon was out again since *"He's been out of school this week running a pretty high temperature"*. Four others were uncertain for the contest and had Broussard say about scheduling the boys from Meadville, *"This could have been one of my biggest boners ever. Franklin County has only about 24 players on its entire squad, but they're practically a senior outfit and will be the biggest we'll run up against this season."*

The 1st saw a Flash opening drive punt by Gerache to the Bulldog 38. On their first play, Mike Speyerer recovered a fumble at the Flash 38. They moved to the Bulldog 41 before fumbling themselves. In the 2nd, Franklin County was moving toward a score but fumbled at the Flash 40. Unable to move, the Flashes had to punt back to FCHS. On the ensuing drive, the Bulldogs Jimmy Causey found Ken McLemore all the way to the Flash 12. On 4th down, John Monroe converted the PAT with :40 left to make it 3-0 at half.

After Homecoming ceremonies, the Flashes held the Rebels and regained the ball. Marion Conerly runs got to the Franklin 24. Evans got them to the 13 and Muffaletto kicked the 4th down FG of 23 yards to tie the game. In the 4th, a bad Flash punt snap gave the Bulldogs the ball at near the 50. Runs by McLemore moved FCHS to the Flash 38, Causey ran to the 10, a flag put the ball at the 5, and McLemore got to the one-foot line. McLemore then took it in and, with the PAT, it was finalized at 10-3. Without key players, the Flashes had fought extremely hard against a much bigger Bulldog team for a victory that was only a "moral" one.

GAME 7:   SAINT AL (2-3-1) @ WARREN CENTRAL (3-4)
                        FINAL: ST AL 9 WARREN CENTRAL 2
                        October 25, 1968

A capacity crowd was expected for the Warren County rivalry. Warren Central was predicted with *"their best chance this time, and it will also be homecoming … which will be an added incentive"*. While their opponent was in good shape, Saint Al was still bothered by injuries. Salmon was out again and others were questionable. The paper said both teams had reliable FG kickers (Frank Johnson and Ronnie Muffaletto) and that *"in a rival game of these kind, records can be tossed out the window"*.

Ironically in the 2nd, the Vikings tried a Johnson 17 yard FG that was wide. The Flashes' Muffaletto also missed one; a 31 yarder with only :34 seconds left. It was set up by a Viking fumble at their 31 where Conerly had actually gotten to the 6 before the Flashes lost yardage.

After a 3rd quarter penalty, Frank Koe blocked a David McClurg punt and recovered at the Viking 8. Conerly could not get past the 3 on his carries and Muffaletto booted the FG for a 3-0 lead. On the ensuing Warren Central drive, Price picked off a 3rd down Bill Mendrop pass at the Viking 30 and took it back for the only touchdown of the game. Viking points came in the 4th when a high snap to punter Gerache forced him to be tackled for a safety. The Flashes came close to scoring at the close of the game. Paul Banchetti picked off a Mendrop pass and took it to the half-yard line. Price couldn't get in and the time expired.

GAME 8:   SAINT AL (3-3-1) @ ROLLING FORK (5-1)
                        FINAL: ST AL 0 ROLLING FORK 27
                        November 1, 1968

The Flashes had everyone, except Bill Steinriede out with an infected arm, back and ready to play. Conerly had a cracked rib from the Viking game but was predicted to play. Salmon would also be back, though he had to come in against Warren Central for a bit due to a Piazza ankle injury. *"We hope Salmon will be of more value to us tomorrow* night", said Broussard.

In the 1st, a Colonel pitch by QB Jim McNeely was deflected by Bubba Booth and recovered by Mike Speyerer who returned it to the RF 30. They missed the scoring opportunity by giving the ball back to the Colonels at the 30. This resulted in the first Rolling Fork touchdown behind the running of

Doss Shropshire to the 4 and then the eventual score. Jackie Fleeman added the PAT. In 3rd, a snap over punter Gerache's head put the ball at the 19. Tom Griffing ran for a 17 yard touchdown and Fleeman made it 14-0. The Colonel's held Saint Al to a Gerache punt and it was returned 65 yards for a touchdown by Randall Atchley. Reserves came in for Saint Al and saw Evans hit Price for 7 passes in the final quarter but for no points. Rolling Fork padded their lead when Griffin ran in from 25 yards.

GAME 9:　　　　　　SAINT AL (3-4-1) vs MAGEE (5-3)
　　　　　　　　　　FINAL:　ST AL 0 MAGEE 29
　　　　　　　　　　November 9, 1968

The paper was generous by saying that *"This one could be close. Magee hasn't been as powerful this season as in the past ... St Aloysius has had its ups and downs and they're still not in the best shape of the season. Make it Magee 14-3 and hope it's the other way around."*
　　　　A *"rain drenched field"* embodied the final game and the season. The Trojans garnered a safety in the 1st when yet another (for the season) punt snap went over Gerache's head. Later in the quarter, Tommy Meador pushed one in from the 5 to make it 8-0 before the PAT. In the 2nd half, Magee recovered a Saint Al fumble at the Flash 25 that resulted in a Lane Stewart touchdown from the 3. Barrett made the PAT and it was 15-0. Stewart scored twice more in the 4th. One was set up by an interception that allowed him a 35 yard run, and the second was another 35-yarder. The season was over for the Flashes and for Broussard, who would walk off the field as head man for the purple and gold for the last time.

　　　　Frank Koe won the Virgadamo Trophy.

　　　　"Elmo Broussard was a great motivator and as tough as nails. He stressed being prepared for the game, knowing your position, playing as a team and giving 100% while you were on the field. He developed character in his men and made a huge difference in my life."

　　　　　　　　　　　　　　　　　　　　　　　　　　　Ronnie Muffaletto; July 30, 2016

1969 (2-7)

As with the previous head coach, Saint Al lost another to the state of Louisiana when Elmo Broussard resigned and took a job back home at Central LaFource High School in Matthews, LA. In his place would be Don Alonzo, a 16 year veteran with experience at Natchez Cathedral and Vidalia, LA. The main drawback would be that the new coach could not be there in time for spring workouts and everyone would have to adjust quickly. As for the team, there were 13 returning lettermen that included Donnie Price, Bobby Baylot, Jimmy Salmon, Wade Evans.
　　　　Before the first game, at least 3 would be unavailable and no less than 3 others doubtful. The Flashes were now significantly underweight on the line and playing the pre-season North Little Dixie pick as champions. Said Alonzo, *"Nevertheless, we'll show up and hope for the best. This is the worst shape I've ever been in for an opener."* Not knowing that Magee also had significant injuries, the paper predicted an opening loss of 26-14.

GAME 1:　　　　　　SAINT AL (0-0) @ MAGEE (0-0)
　　　　　　　　　　FINAL:　ST AL 14 MAGEE 24
　　　　　　　　　　September 4, 1969

The Trojans took command early in the 1st. After a punt put them at midfield, they fumbled (and recovered) three times before Jonathan Styron kicked a 24 yard FG. On their next drive, they added a 97 yard touchdown run by Butch McKenzie to make it 10-0. On the kickoff, Salmon brought it to the Flash 28. Jerry Hosemann and Price runs got to the 26 before Price hit Ronnie Muffaletto to the 1. Johnny Alonzo came in at QB and gave to Hosemann for the touchdown. On the ensuing Magee drive, Jimmy Harris fumbled and Muffaletto recovered at the Trojan 43. Hosemann got 5 and then Price hit Salmon to the 11. Hosemann got to the 3 and then Salmon converted for the score. Price hit Muffaletto for the 2 points to make the halftime score 14-10 in favor of the Flashes.
　　　　On their second play after the kickoff, Magee put the ball in the endzone. Ronnie Herrington blasted up the middle for 48 yards and the score. Styron made it 17-14. The game was iced with :15 left when McKenzie went in from the 1.

GAME 2:   SAINT AL (0-1) vs CLINTON (0-0)
                 FINAL: ST AL 0 CLINTON 3
                 September 12, 1969

After an off-week, all players were ready to return except Andy Booth with a kidney infection. Another Little Dixie opponent awaited; one with 8 lettermen returning. In spite of this, the paper predicted a Flash victory of 20-14.

The Flashes threatened on their opening possession to the Arrow 32 but couldn't sustain the drive and punted. The Arrows came back as far as the Flash 28. In the 2nd, the Arrows got to the Flash 23 before pass interference put them at the Flash 9. The defense held on 4 downs to get the ball back. An exchange of punts again put the Flashes back to work at their own 1. On the next play, Hosemann went up the middle for 35. But in the closing seconds, and after Price hit Muffaletto at the Arrow 31, Wright picked off a Flash pass to finish the half.

The Arrows got all they needed in the 3rd after a drive got them close enough for Jim Blackwell to connect on a 27 yard FG. The 4th was a trade of punts as both teams tried to gain advantage to no avail. Said Alonzo, "... I'll have to say this about our boys: They showed much improvement from their opening 24-14 loss to Magee ... and we've had some spirited workouts this week".

GAME 3:   SAINT AL (0-2) @ GREENVILLE SAINT JOSEPH (1-1)
                 FINAL: ST AL 0 GREENVILLE ST JOE 6
                 September 19, 1969

Though Irish coach Dom Bevalaque had lost only 17 games in 10 years, the paper said that this game "rates about even. The Flashes haven't won a game yet. We're picking them to this time. Make it close though; Flashes 10 Saint Joseph 6. This one always produces the thrills and usually the underdog comes out on top. The Flashes rate the favorite by a smidgen, and that ain't much".

The Flashes first drive saw Price fumble at the Saint Joe 46 only to be recovered by the Irish's Buster Mascagni. They managed 47 yards before Salmon got a fumble at the 7. The quarter ended after a Salmon run to the Irish 35. In the 2nd, Price attempted a pass to Preston Harris but was picked off by Jim Crawford who took it to the Flash 22. The defense held but the Flashes could get no further than the Irish 37 before halftime.

On their first drive of the 3rd, the Irish used runs by Doe Signa and Ralph Thompson along with penalties on Saint Al to enable Thompson to score from the 1. Signa's PAT was no good and it was 6-0. The quarter ended on a Price pass to Muffaletto at the Irish 30 and a Muffaletto run to the 30. The 4th saw the Flashes get to the 9 but a Howard Fisher tackle caused an Alonzo fumble. Saint Al stopped a late Irish drive when Price picked off Signa on the 12. The drive got as far as the Irish 30 but ended on a Price interception by Thompson at the 1 with 2:13 remaining and the clock eventually ran out.

GAME 4:   SAINT AL (0-3) vs LAKE PROVIDENCE, LA (3-1)
                 FINAL: ST AL 30 LAKE PROVIDENCE 38
                 October 3, 1969

Lake Providence was led by three All-State players and was dominant enough to have punted only 4 times in the year. Additionally, Center Bob Franco had a sprained ankle and second stringer Phillip Vedros had a broken ankle. The paper said that "stopping the Panthers hot-passing attack will be a headache that could even cause Mr. Bayer some problems. Make it Lake Providence 27-14."

The Panthers hit the board first in the waning moments of the opening quarter when Joe Kennedy found Mike Wilson for the touchdown to cap a 12 play drive. Allain Gossein made it 7-0. Later in the 2nd, a Price pass was intercepted by Butch Sumrall at the Flash 35. The defense held and gave the ball back to Saint Al, where a Price pass to Muffaletto was lateralled to Piazza to the Flash 49. But the Flashes fumbled two plays later to give the ball back. With 8 plays, Kennedy found Wilson again for a 10 yard touchdown and a 12-0 lead.

The ensuing kickoff was on-sides and recovered by the Flashes. Price eventually found Piazza from the 4 for the touchdown and Muffaletto for the 2 point conversion to make it 12-8. Ten plays later, and after a Flash fumble, Kennedy found David Hopkins for a touchdown. Gossein made it

19-8. The Panthers scored again after a Price fumble was recovered by James Ellis at the Flash 23. In two plays, Kennedy took it in to make it 25-8.

A penalty on the Panther coach gave the kick to Saint Al at the Flash 39. After not converting, the Panthers took over but Kennedy fumbled to Wade Evans. Price then threw an interception intended for Salmon that was costly. The Panthers' Kennedy found Ray Meredith for 67 yards and the 31-8 lead. But on the ensuring kick, Piazza took the ball at the 11 and returned it 89 yards for the Flash score. Price added the 2 for a 31-16 tally

The Flashes were not giving up. The 4th opened with a Kennedy turnover at the Flash 25. Price took the team down in 4 plays and hit Muffaletto to make it 31-22. Next, Kennedy was picked off by Salmon who brought it back to the Panther 27. Hosemann took it in 9 plays later from the 1. Price threw to Piazza for the PAT and it was 31-30. Though it was a valiant comeback for the Flashes, Lake Providence sealed it when Kennedy found Wilson again to make it 38-30.

GAME 5:   SAINT AL (0-4) @ FRANKLIN COUNTY (3-1)
                    FINAL: ST AL 36 FRANKLIN COUNTY 12
                    October 17, 1969

Franklin County had only 13 points scored on them this year and had a skilled FG kicker who had made a 55 yarder the week previous. On a hunch, the paper predicted a 14-10 Flash upset. What they called the "Crystal Ball" was clear that week in spite of it being Homecoming for the Bulldogs.

In the 1st, Hosemann picked off a Bulldog pass at the Bulldog 49. Price found Muffaletto from the 16 to cap the drive, and a Price to Salmon pass made it 8-0. They scored again in the 2nd when, starting on their 27, Price found Salmon to the Bulldog 6. Piazza took it in and it was 14-0. Franklin County answered on the kickoff by driving from the 18 for the James Cotton touchdown. It was now 14-6. The half ended with a Bulldog attempted FG at the Flash 6 that wasn't good.

The 2nd half kickoff was taken by Baylot and returned 90 yards for the touchdown and Salmon converted to make it 22-6. Franklin County got deep into Flash territory later but Piazza picked off Cotton in the endzone. In the 4th, the Flashes received a Bulldog punt and started at their own 24. Salmon took the ball to the Bulldog 15 on the first play and then, three plays later, took it in for the touchdown. Price found Muffaletto for the 2 and it was 30-6.

The Bulldogs recovered a Flash fumble at the Saint Al 35 and converted on a Cotton pass to Elton Lewis from the 21 to make it 30-12. But with :48 left, the Flashes recovered the on-sides kick at the Bulldog 40 and Salmon finished it with a 21 yard touchdown.

GAME 6:   SAINT AL (1-4) vs JACKSON SAINT JOSEPH (5-0)
                    FINAL: ST AL 12 JACKSON ST JOE 34
                    October 24, 1969: HOMECOMING

With the progress the team had made, coach Alonzo said that *"I wish this football season was just now beginning. We're in good shape and I hope we'll be in the right frame of mind. If we are, I believe those attending will see a heck of a football game."* The Rebels were undefeated in their last 16 regular season games, having on a 6-6 tie with Hazlehurst to blemish the mark. The paper said that *"It should be a rip-snorter and it will take the Flashes best game of the year. We think the fans will see it. Make it Saint Al 22-20; another finger-biter"*.

As a sidenote, there had been a hunting accident during the week involving two students. For this reason, and considering it was Homecoming, the game was originally scheduled for earlier but moved to October 24th.

The Rebels scored first after a drive of 67 yards in six plays when Bernie Trebotich took it in from the 13 for the touchdown. Saint Al answered in the 2nd when Price hit Salmon for a 53 yarder but it was brought back for a penalty. The Flashes had two touchdowns brought back due to penalties that may have made a difference. Saint Joe got another touchdown from Andrew Mattiace at the 3 after a 33 yard drive on 7 plays. Mattiace kept for the 2 and it was 14-0. Later in the 2nd, Roger Parkes got in from the Flash 31 and, after the kick, it was 21-0.

The Flashes fumbled in the 2nd half at their 31. Seven plays later, Mattiace found Tom Lange from the 9 and it was 28-0. A Mattiace interception by the Flashes to close the 3rd went nowhere, but in the 4th, Hosemann returned a Rebel punt to their 44. After 6 plays that got them to the 9, Piazza took it in. The 2 point conversion wasn't good and it was now 28-6. The last two scores came from a John

Puddister interception return from the 9 and a Saint Al drive of 68 yards capped by a Price pitch to Baylot from the 1.

GAME 7:   SAINT AL (1-5) vs ROLLING FORK (7-0)
                          FINAL: ST AL 8 ROLLING FORK 28
                          October 30, 1969

An undefeated Rolling Fork averaged 193 pounds on the line. Said Alonzo, *"Maybe Rolling Fork will be overconfident this week and maybe if they are and we can put forth our best effort of the season, we might be able to make the game a little interesting."* The paper's prediction was a 27-14 Rolling Fork victory at Farrell Field.

Four plays after the kick, the Colonels drove 75 yards and scored when Tom Griffing went in from the 4 to make it 7-0. Saint Al fumbled to Rolling Fork at the Colonel 42 and, nine plays later, Jim McNeely kept it for a QB touchdown from the 2 to make it 13-0. The Flashes answered in the 2nd when Salmon picked off McNeely at the Colonel 45. It took 12 plays before Hosemann went in from the 2. Price hit Salmon for the 2 and it was 14-8.

In the opening seconds of the 4th, a 22 play drive was capped by a Doss Shropshire touchdown from the 4 and it was now 21-8. The quarter was wrapped up when Shropshire scored again from the 4 after 3 plays from the Flash 46.

GAME 8:   SAINT AL (1-6) @ BRANDON (2-6)
                          FINAL: ST AL 19 BRANDON 32
                          November 7, 1969

Against a 2-6 Brandon team, this game was predicted by the paper as *"just about … a toss up"*. Afterwards they would say *"The Dogs had their day here last night, the real kind, and those of the Brandon kind…"* They referred not only the score, but also the fact that three dogs got onto the field in the 2nd half before being "escorted" off to *"roaring approval"*.

Brandon got to the Flash 5 at the close of the 1st behind QB Chris Benton. From there, David Morrow went in for the touchdown to cap an 83 yard drive and give them a 6-0 lead. The Flashes answered immediately in 7 plays though a previous touchdown had been called back. Salmon took a Johnny Alonzo handoff from the 3 and pushed it in. Not to be outdone, Brandon took the kickoff and scored behind a run and a 71 yard pass play. Delaney Ware caught the scoring pass to make it 12-6.

In the 3rd, Price's punt gave the Bulldogs the ball at their 25. It took 8 plays before Benton scored again on a QB keeper from the 2 to make it 18-6. After an ensuing Flash punt put the ball at the Brandon 20, a second play pass to Charles Reeves went 78 yards for the touchdown. The 2 point play made it 26-6 to end the 3rd. In the 4th, Preston Harris intercepted Benton at the Flash 46. Here, Price pitched to Muffaletto, who passed to Baylot, who ran 42 yards for the touchdown. Booth picked off another Brandon pass a few plays later, and five plays afterwards, Price hit Salmon from the 4. The PAT made it 26-19. Brandon finished the game with a 4th and goal touchdown run from the 1 foot line by Jerry Palmer.

GAME 9:   SAINT AL (1-7) @ WARREN CENTRAL (3-5-1)
                          FINAL: ST AL 33 WARREN CENTRAL 19
                          November 14, 1969

The Flashes had only one win going into the game. The Warren Central team had a better record, their QB Frank Ford was the second highest scorer in Warren County (56 points), and they were playing at home. But, the Vikings had never beaten the Flashes. A capacity crowd would be there to support both teams for what the paper predicted to be a Flash victory 21-20.

The Flashes were first to score when Baylot took a Bill Mendrop punt at the 33 all the way for a touchdown. The PAT was a fake that failed to keep it 6-0. The half almost ended at the same score, but Mendrop picked up a fumble at the Flash 4. After runs and penalties, Ford hit David Chaney with :33 left. Ford's PAT put the Vikings up 7-6 at half. Two plays after the 3rd quarter kick, Mike Ard found a Flash fumble at the 37. They got to the Flash 6 in 9 plays only to see Harry Weissinger fumble at the 1. Piazza gained 12 on the next play that resulted in only 6 due to a penalty, but then Baylot went the 94 yards for the touchdown and it was 13-7.

Warren Central responded with a 73 yard drive in 9 plays. Ford found Chaney for 34, Wayne Smith for 32 and then the 8 yard cap to Smith. The Flashes answered in the same quarter in 5 plays of 63 yards. Piazza got 28 for the big play to the Viking 35 and Alonzo hit Mufaletto for a 33 yard strike. Though the PAT was no good, it was now 19-13. In the 4th, the Flashes scored again after a Mendrop punt went to Baylot at the 38 and he went the distance for the touchdown. Price found Harris for the 2 pointer to make it 27-13. To make matters worse for Warren Central, Salmon took his next touch 64 yards for a touchdown and a 33-13 lead.

The Vikings put the final points up at the 3:34 mark when Ford went in from the goal on 4th down to finish a 58 yard drive. The PAT failed and the "**FLASHES JINX OVER VIKES**" continued.

This would be the first and last season for Coach Don Alonzo. He left Saint Aloysius after his first campaign with the Flashes and accepted the head coaching role at Greensburg (LA) High School. The Virgadamo Trophy would go to Carl Franco.

1970-1979

1977 St. Aloysius Football team from left to right: Chris Cox, Donnie Head, Tommy Alonzo, Les Bumgarner (head coach), Denis Hogan, Gerald Maxey, Carl Smith. 2nd row, Mike Ray, Randy Johnson, Carlos Lee, Pete Tarnabine, Bobby Nelson, Tony Patton, Danny Fordice, Matt Halford. 3rd row, Philip Hogan, Jay Barnett, Donnie Gordon, Tim Smith, Billy Coomes, John Kellum, Joe Battalio, David Tuccio, Tim DeRossett. 4th row, Pat Koestler, Tony Franco, John Laboda, Perry Cox, Sam Brown, George McConnell, Mike Yarbrough, Steve Butler, Bob Steinriede, Ben Hardy. 5th row, Coach Bob Hitchins, Mike McCain, Barney Koestler (head manager), Leo Koestler, John Ennis, Coach Salmon.

SAINT ALOYSIUS 1977 TEAM (11-1)

1970 (7-4)

Taking the place of departed Don Alonzo was Glen Rhoads, a three-year letterman at Mississippi State and past assistant under Elmo Broussard in 1968. He served at Picayune High before the opportunity arose to return to Saint Al. *"I realize we've got a tough road ahead. Especially by my coming in late and missing spring practice, but the players have come along real well the short time we've been out and I've been well pleased with their spirit and determination to be a winner. But this opener in two weeks … it could be the toughest on our schedule. I just hope we'll be ready. I know they will be"*.

GAME 1:   SAINT AL (0-0) @ WARREN CENTRAL (0-0)
                        FINAL: ST AL 0 WARREN CENTRAL 14
                        September 4, 1970

The Flashes had the advantage in returning lettermen, but the Vikings had several transfers in their starting lineup. WC coach Dewey Partridge said *"While we are big and fairly strong, we don't have the speed and quickness so important real good football must have. We also lack experience"*. Rhoads responded by saying *"We'll have to have a lot of luck tomorrow night. They are so big I'm afraid they will just power over us."* The paper thought the Vikings may be best, saying *"The Vikings have been tagged a one touchdown choice to break the Flashes' monotony…"*

An estimated 4,500 people continued to fill Viking Stadium through halftime and was called *"the largest ever to see a sporting event here."* The Flashes special teams gave a foreshadowing of what fans would see early in the 1st. A low snap to punter Mike Foley resulted in the Vikings starting at the Flash 17. The defense held and disaster was avoided when a Donald Oakes FG attempt from the 9 was no good. Another low punt snap went to Donnie Price, allowing Mike Flowers to block it. David Chaney picked up the loose ball and took it in for the touchdown. Oakes was good to make it 7-0. Saint Al responded by driving to the Viking 24 on two passes to Jimmy Baylot and one to Donnie Piazza, but time expired before they could capitalize.

The Vikings controlled the 3rd by allowing the Flashes only 3 plays and a punt. In the quarter, Mike Flanagan got in from the 6 for a WC touchdown but it was called back for off-sides. Oakes tried his 2nd FG from the 20 unsuccessfully. In the 4th, Warren Central duplicated their first touchdown almost exactly. Price was punting from the Flash 34. Another low snap forced another Flowers block, and Chaney again took it in for a touchdown. Oakes made it 14-0. Saint Al attempted a response when Baylot took a reverse to the Viking 17 with the touchdown-saving tackle by Dean Hearn. But after a short gain and a couple of penalties, the drive was over and the Vikings had ended the streak.

Hughes Jewelers presented trophies afterwards to Bob Franco for his offensive performance, and to Bubba Booth for defensive. Harry Weissinger and David Chaney were Viking recipients.

GAME 2:   SAINT AL (0-1) @ CLINTON (1-0)
                        FINAL: ST AL 19 CLINTON 14
                        September 11, 1970: MISS COLLEGE

Rhoads noted that, *"We've worked hard this week trying to correct what we did wrong last week"*. Saying of Clinton, *"We just hope we can make it interesting for them"*. The Arrows had just shut out Jackson Saint Joe 27-0 and appeared strong. The paper thought it an Arrow advantage 20-12. Originally scheduled as a home contest, the game was moved to Mississippi College due to an anticipated crowd of over 5,000 fans.

The 1st was scoreless, but only because a Bobby Baylot 75 yard punt return was called back for a penalty. Clinton put up points in the 2nd on an 80 yard drive behind running from Jim Waters capped by a Terry Harrison run from the 7. Jim Blackwell made it 7-0 at halftime. The Flashes responded midway through the 3rd when Baylot took one 68 yards for the score. In the 4th, Bill Sellari fumbled the Arrow ball at their 15. David Hosemann snatched it up and took it in for the touchdown. It was now 12-7. Saint Al held on the next drive but Baylot fumbled the ball back to the Arrows' Ken Richardson at the Flash 35. The Arrows converted two plays later on a Harrison pass to Phil Frazier for a lead of 14-12.

Baylot took the ensuing kick back to the Clinton 44. Price hit Hosemann to the 24 and Jimmy Baylot plunged to the 4. Two Arrow penalties put the ball at the goal and then Baylot took it in for the game-winner. Said Rhoads, *"They've been coming along real well and I'm proud of all of them"*.

GAME 3:   SAINT AL (1-1) vs GREENVILLE SAINT JOSEPH (1-0)
            FINAL: ST AL 22 GREENVILLE ST JOE 20
            September 18, 1970

The Irish returned 15 seniors but Saint Al was healthy and spurred by a great victory. The paper was cautious, saying "...*this is a rival feud and anything can happen. Hopefully Saint Al 20-13*". Meanwhile, the <u>Delta Democrat-Times</u> quoted Bevalaqua afterwards as "*We're short on depth. We don't have but 14 men that we're playing and we have to maneuver them around like chess pieces.*"

The Flashes scored in the 1st after a turnover on downs by the Irish at their 8. Ricky Antoine capped the drive from the 1 and Vedros made it 7-0. Greenville came right back when Doe Signa took the kickoff 72 yards for the answer. The 2nd started with a punt snap over Nickie Crawford's head resulting in a Flash safety and a 9-6 lead. Before the quarter was out, Ralph Thompson picked off Price to give the visitor the ball. Crawford hit Barry Brady for the touchdown to finish an 89 drive. The Irish converted the 2 to make it 14-9 at half.

In the 3rd, a Flash interception on their 40 resulted in a 7 play drive that saw Price hit Joe Williams from the 10. It was now 15-14. Saint Al padded the lead when Bobby Baylot went in from the 27. Vedros was good and it was 22-14. But Greenville would respond right away. Crawford found Thompson for an 11 yard score though the 2 point conversion to tie the game was unsuccessful. The fans stormed the field and Saint Al had a winning record again for the first time since October 11, 1968.

GAME 4:   SAINT AL (2-1) vs CHAMBERLAIN HUNT ACADEMY (1-1)
            FINAL: ST AL 19 CHAMBERLAIN HUNT 0
            September 25, 1970

Rhoads wasn't entirely happy with their performance. "*We've been working this week trying to overcome costly mistakes and I hope we have made progress*". The paper, in a nod to Parent Appreciation Night at Saint Al, picked the Flashes 33-6 "*with reserves able to get some game experience*".

The rain falling on Farrell Field made the 1st a sloppy one with nobody scoring. At the close the quarter, the Wildcats punted to Bobby Baylot who brought it back to the CHA 44. After 6 plays, and: 05 into the 2nd, Baylot took it in from the 10 and Vedros made it 7-0. Later in the half, Baylot ran to the Wildcat 2. From here, Antoine pushed in another Flash touchdown and it was 13-0.

The last score of the game came in the 3rd when David Hosemann picked up a CHA fumble and took it 42 yards for a touchdown. The now-muddy field made the PAT impossible and hampered any further scores. The Flashes did, however, get to the 1 foot line later before fumbling. The <u>Port Gibson Reveille</u> noted that two scores came as a result of two "*wet ball fumbles*" and that "*Offensive blocking broke down again and again, never allowing the backs much running room nor QB Cameron Dean a chance to mount an effective passing attack*".

GAME 5:   SAINT AL (3-1) @ MANGHAM, LA (UNREPORTED)
            FINAL: ST AL 21 MANGHAM 12
            October 2, 1970

The head man warned his players not to be overconfident about the Louisiana opponent. "*Mangham runs from an unbalanced line and they can hurt you. We will strictly have our work cut out.*" At some point during the week, the team received a setback in the form of a season-ending broken leg for Jimmy Baylot. Even so, the paper picked the Flashes 26-6.

On their first series, the Dragons drove to the Flash 2 behind a Mike McConnell pass to Joel Williams. McConnell scored from there but a missed PAT left it 6-0. On the ensuing kick, the Flashes were able to answer when Price hit Alonzo for 28 yards and the touchdown. Vedros put the Flashes up 7-6. The Dragons came right back to start the 2nd with another McConnell to Williams pass to the 2 and another McConnell touchdown plunge. The Flashes came very close to responding in the final seconds of the quarter. Hosemann recovered his third fumble of the game at the Mangham 20 and Saint Al got to the 1 before time expired.

In the 3rd, the Flashes got as far as the Dragon 11 behind Bobby Baylot runs before fumbled back to Mangham. After holding them, Williams dropped the punt and Mangham had the ball at their 37. Unbelievably, the defense held and the next punt was also fumbled back to Mangham; this time at their 25. Once again the defense held and the 3rd quarter came to a scoreless end.

The 4th was time for reversal. This time, Mangham fumbled at their 20 and it was recovered by Alonzo. Starting at the Flash 35, the drive was capped with a Piazza plunge from the 4 to make it 13-12. The game was put on ice when David Hosemann went in from the 3 half way through the 4th. Price found Piazza for the 2 points resulting in a 21-12 victory.

GAME 6:   SAINT AL (4-1) @ JACKSON SAINT JOSEPH (4-1)
                     FINAL: ST AL 28 JACKSON SAINT JOE 24
                     October 9, 1970

This was touted as *"one of the state's most rival feuds"*. Both teams were 4-1 but after seeing film, Rhoads said *"They'll outweigh us a good bit. We'll just have to try and out-scrap them. It'll take a superior effort"*. The Rebels had been quoted as saying they wouldn't lose another game this year. The Flashes used that as motivation and had newspaper clippings displayed in the locker room all week.

Perhaps the most thrilling victory of the year unfolded this night in Vicksburg. It was all Saint Al in the 1st half despite 3 interceptions from each QB. On the first drive, the Flashes started at their 25 and got 17 yards. That's when Baylot took a pitch for 58 yards and the touchdown. Vedros made it 7-0. In the 2nd, as time wound down to 2:19, Rebel QB Pat Maloney threw a pick to Hosemann at the 10. He made it count with a touchdown and Vedros added the point. On their next possession, a Rebel fumble was picked up by Bob Franco at the Rebel 37. Baylot scored again, this time from the 31. Vedros made the halftime score a lop-sided 21-0 in favor of Saint Al.

Nearing the end of the 3rd, the Rebels drove 79 yards and put up their first points on a Rob Parkes touchdown from the 4. Parkes found Miquel Mora for the 2 points and it was 21-8. Midway through the 4th, Fred Cunningham took one in from the 1. Parkes hit Kurt Schweigert for 2 points and it was now 21-16. The following kickoff was on-sides and recovered by Vedros at the 50. Hosemann made them pay from the 7 and Vedros made it 28-16 with just 2:25 left.

On the ensuing kickoff, Ken Kestenbaum took the ball to the Flash 42. Parkes found Mora from the 25 and, with a Cunningham 2 point conversion, the game was 28-24. To make tensions high, the Flashes fumbled at the 45 with just 1:20 remaining. The Rebels got to the Flash 6 with only :06 to play, but that's when Gus Williams broke through the line and sacked Parkes to dash the hopes of the home crowd.

GAME 7:   SAINT AL (5-1) @ VIDALIA, LA (5-1)
                     FINAL: ST AL 6 VIDALIA 30
                     October 16, 1970

With Franco (knee) and Piazza (shoulder) doubtful for the game against a reportedly *"loaded"* AA school, Rhoads said *"We'll have our work cut out just like we have in our other games."* The paper said that *"Vidalia looks a little too tough in this one, especially with Franco and Piazza (two real workhorses) injured. Vidalia 20-17. An upset here and the Flashes could go the rest of the way"*.

The Flashes received the ball and drove to the Viking 33 but fumbled it away. On the ensuing drive, Vidalia went 67 yards for a Kerry Craft 7 yard touchdown run. Bill Moseley made it 7-0. In the 2nd, Price was picked off by Bobby Eubanks at the Viking 30. Again the Vikings converted with Craft scoring from the 1. It was now 13-0 going into halftime.

On their opening play of the 3rd, Gene Brasher went 62 yards for another Viking touchdown. Tommy Barr added 2 for a 21-0 lead. The Vidalia defense came through again when Obie Jones sacked Price in the endzone for a safety. The Flash on-sides kick was recovered by Vidalia at the Flash 26 and they made the Flashes pay when Brasher scored from the 4. Moseley made it 30-0. The Flashes only points came on the ensuing drive. Baylot took the kick at the 10 and moved it to the Vidalia 40. Price found Tony Kolb at the 19 and then Alonzo with the touchdown. Price was sacked on the 2 pointer and the game was over.

GAME 8:   SAINT AL (5-2) @ OAK GROVE, LA (4-2)
                        FINAL: ST AL 16 OAK GROVE 6
                        October 23, 1970

Rhoads said of Oak Grove, "*They are big and we'll be outweighed again. We made quite a few bad plays last week, but (Vidalia's) blocking was the best we've run up against. I doubt if we could have beaten then had we played a perfect game. We'll have to depend on hustle, desire and cut down on mistakes if we're to beat (Oak Grove) on their own field*". Franco was doubtful with a knee injury but the paper said "*...keep your fingers crossed*" for a 21-19 Flash victory.

Ernie Albritton called the environment "*A rain-soaked field on a dismal night... sometimes coming in wind-blown torrents...*" The Flashes took the opening kick and drove to the Oak Grove 20 before being intercepted. The Tigers returned the favor on their ensuing drive by fumbling at the Flash 45 with Bubba Booth recovering. Behind runs of Baylot and Antoine, Price took it in from the 2 and Hosemann added 2 more. It was 8-0.

Before the quarter was over, Booth blocked a Tiger punt and Vedros recovered at the Oak Grove 35. Three plays later, Baylot went 23 yards behind Tommy Beasley and Wally DeRossette for the touchdown. Baylot also added the 2 to make the halftime score 16-0. Oak Grove responded to begin the 3rd from their 27 behind running from Mark Barnett and a 35 yard pass from Vic Dalrymple to Raymond Harris. On 4th and 1 from the 1 foot line, Dalrymple pushed it in to make it 16-6. The remainder of the game was simply a muddy affair of no mention.

GAME 9:   SAINT AL (6-2) vs NATCHEZ CATHEDRAL (2-4)
                        FINAL: ST AL 34 NATCHEZ CATHEDRAL 6
                        October 30, 1970: HOMECOMING

This week saw Baylot (hip) and Hosemann (ankle), along with others, out due to injuries. Said Rhoads about Cathedral, "*They have a lot of reverses, bootlegs and passes and if you don't stay wide-awake they can hurt you quickly.*" Said the paper, "*While the Flashes may not be in the best of shape, it's Homecoming and they'll put it out for the ol' grads somehow or another. Make it Saint Al 26-6*".

The Flashes had an opportunity after a bad Cathedral punt in the 1st. Starting at the Natchez 37, Piazza got 16 and Baylot 2 before they were forced to punt. In the 2nd, the Flashes started at their 32 and drove to the Greenie 34. On 4th and 2, Price found Alonzo for the touchdown. Vedros missed but it was 6-0. On their next possession, Saint Al went 72 yards in 10 plays. Antoine gained 16 to the Cathedral 8 and then Price hit Baylot from there. Piazza converted the 2 after a penalty and it was 16-0. The Flashes added points on their first possession of the 3rd on a 60 yard drive of 7 plays finalized by a Price run from the 14. Vedros made it 21-0. Natchez drove 75 yards in 7 plays with Wilson taking it in from the 19 to keep it 21-6.

Cathedral put their only points up in the 3rd by going 75 yards in 7 plays that resulted in a Cutis Wilson draw from the 19. Richard Spence would not get in for the 2 points. Both teams picked off passes (Cathedral's Steve Guido and Saint Al's Joe Williams), but Saint Al scored again to start the 4th with a Price touchdown from the 3. They scored again in 58 yards on 11 plays when Price snuck in from the 1. Vedros made it 34-6 to give the Flashes a 7-2 record.

GAME 10:   SAINT AL (7-2) vs BRANDON (1-7)
                        FINAL: ST AL 6 BRANDON 7
                        November 6, 1970

Though the Bulldogs record was not stellar, Rhoads was still worried. "*They are real big and have a fine defense. I've been looking for them to explode on somebody all season and now if they do; it looks like it could be against us. Unless we are ready, we could be in for real trouble*". Expecting all injured players to play, the paper predicted a victory of 20-7 saying "*We don't believe the Flashes will let their loyal followers down*" in from an anticipated overflow crowd.

The Flashes, with bowl representatives on-hand, scored first. Starting at their 19, they moved 8 plays including a 23 yard pass to Theobald before Antoine ran one in from the 4. The crucial PAT was not good. The only other score of the game was with 1:10 left in the 1st half. At the Flash 44, Brandon's Sam Waggoner handed the ball to Charles Reeves who went the distance. Larry McLeod added the PAT that would seal a devastating Flash loss 7-6. The headline read "**FLASHES' BOWL HOPES MAY HAVE GONE DOWN THE DRAIN**".

GAME 11:   SAINT AL (7-3) vs CRYSTAL SPRINGS (6-3-1)
                     FINAL: ST AL 0 CRYSTAL SPRINGS 40
                     November 21, 1970: CRYSTAL BOWL; CRYSTAL SPRINGS, MS

The Flashes were now invited to play Crystal Springs in the Crystal Bowl. "*We are delighted over the invitation. Our boys played real hard this season and we consider this bowl invitation as a big and deserving bonus which they earned.*" The game was never close.

The Tigers put up their first points in the 2nd on a blocked punt by Hugh Allen Knight at the Flash 4. Johnny Stewart took it in from the 1 but Mike Barlow's PAT was wide. Price fumbled two plays after the kickoff and Bill Thomas recovered at the Flash 31. Barlow scored from the 8 and then Stewart found Kent Newman to make it 14-0 at half.

On their first play of the 2nd half, Crystal Springs pulled the "hideout" pass from Barlow to Stewart from 52 yards out. Knight converted the 2 pointer. Then on their next possession starting at their 33, the Tigers went 10 plays that included catches by Mike Berry of 34 and 4 yards. The last was a touchdown. Knight converted the 2-points. It wasn't over, as the Tigers picked off a Flash pass to start the 4th and capped it with a Barlow run from the 10.

Crystal Springs scored twice more in the last quarter. Kent Newman hit Berry from the 42 and Knight picked off Price for a 47 yard touchdown return with :26 left. It was a bitter ending for what had become such a nice season.

Bobby Baylot was recipient of the Virgadamo Trophy.

1971 (8-3)

With much consolidation in Mississippi schools, a new classification came out from MHSAA. Saint Al was now a "B" school since enrollment of 200 missed by one student making the Flashes a "BB" school. They were back in the CAC and would play 10 games. Rhoads returned with assistant Joe Curtis, as did 9 lettermen. The pre-season coaches' poll had the Flashes tied for 3rd in the district with Pelahatchie.

Before the first game kicked, injuries and dropouts had given the coach "*some 20 working varsity candidates*". Depth would be an issue. "*This could really hurt us in the second half. Will just depend mostly on how our opponents are fixed with reserves.*"

GAME 1:   SAINT AL (0-0) vs RAYMOND (0-0)
                    FINAL: ST AL 19 RAYMOND 13
                    September 3, 1971

Raymond was supposed to be returning a good squad, including much of their backfield. Before kickoff, Rhoads' depleted depth took a hit when Gus Williams would have to miss a couple of weeks with a sprained ankle. Even so, the paper called it for the Flashes 27-13 in their first Colonial Athletic Conference tilt. The Flashes scored in the 2nd when a Ranger fumble at their 34 set up a Jimmy Baylot touchdown run from the 25. A short time later, Donnie Piazza got in on a 55 yard scamper to make it 12-0. Raymond answered in the quarter on a big 68 yard touchdown run by J. Reeves. The PAT afterwards closed the gap to 12-7.

The Flashes had 2 touchdowns called back in the 2nd half, but got on the board when David Hosemann broke off a run of 85 yards. Vedros made it 19-7. Raymond closed the gap in the 4th on a Steve Davis dive from the 3. The onside kick was recovered by Saint Al to end the game.

GAME 2:   SAINT AL (1-0) vs PUCKETT (0-1)
                    FINAL: ST AL 6 PUCKETT 0
                    September 10, 1971

The Raymond win had consequences. QB Reggie Head broke his collarbone in the game and would be out for at least six weeks. Harvey Landers would step into the role. Steve Cappaert had an emergency appendectomy on Sunday and couldn't play for three-to-five weeks. Rhoads' concerns about depth were getting worse, but the paper was *"tagging the Flashes to come out on top"* 13-7.

In the 2nd, the Flashes had gotten to the Wolves' 10 before fumbling to Puckett's Ray Williams. Later in the frame, Bobby Coomes fell on a Puckett fumble at their 15. But the Vedros FG was wide and halftime was met with a 0-0 score. Late in the 4th, the Flashes returned a punt to the Wolves' 41. Five plays later, Landers pitched to Hosemann for a 15 yard touchdown. The 6-0 score would hold for the second straight CAC victory.

GAME 3:   SAINT AL (2-0) @ UTICA (1-1)
                              FINAL: ST AL 31 UTICA 3
                              September 17, 1971

As if it couldn't get worse from the injury perspective, tackle Larry Anderson had hurt his knee and was now on crutches. *"We're really up a creek with our short reserve supply. We'll just have to move a lot of players around and hope they come through"*. Utica had 185 pound RB Clarence Flowers of whom Rhoads commented, *"He can blow you out of there on offense and is hard-rocked on defense. If we're not right, Utica will put it on us."*

Saint Al fumbled on their second play of the game at their 33 and it was recovered by Utica. The defense held the Gold Wave to a 30 yard FG by Bland Walker. Afterwards, the Flashes drove to the Utica 20 where Piazza found Mike Foley for a 20 yard touchdown. Vedros made it 7-0. In the 2nd, Piazza threw another HB pass. This one was from the Utica 37 to Jimmy Baylot who made a one-handed catch at the 1 while on his back. Piazza finished it from there. The snap for the PAT was bad and it was 13-3. Utica's next drive resulted in a fumble at their 29. It took 3 plays for Piazza to score from the 11. The Flashes scored their 3rd touchdown on a Baylot carry from the 39.

The 2nd half would consist of the reserves and they held their own. With 1:20 left in the game, Piazza (now playing QB) took it in from the 7 to make the final 31-3. The Wave came close to putting up points but ran out of time at the Flash 10. Piazza was now 2nd in Warren County scoring with 24 points; 6 behind Lummy Wright. He also shared Hughes Jewelers Player of the Week honors with Gus Williams. Said Rhoads, *"We are showing improvement and if we keep winning, we'll have to keep it up for our road ahead is going to be plenty tough."*

GAME 4:   SAINT AL (3-0) @ TERRY (0-3)
                              FINAL: ST AL 34 TERRY 6
                              September 24, 1971

Bill Loyacano, a transfer from Carr who had been forced to sit out due to transfer rules, would now join the team and step in at QB. He was tabbed as an outstanding college prospect by scouts and the Flashes could use more manpower. At 3-0, the Flashes were all alone at the top of the standings. Billy Ray perfectly predicted a resounding victory of 34-6.

Saint Al started strong with two touchdowns in the 1st and one in the 2nd. Loyacono took the first one for 59 yards with a Vedros PAT. Piazza returned the next punt 56 yards for another. The final 1st half score was set up by Loyacono on a 37 yard pass to Piazza to the 5 followed by a Piazza score and a Vedros PAT. It was 21-0 going into intermission.

The Flashes kept the quick scoring going in the 3rd when Gus Williams picked off a Terry pass and took it 30 yards for the touchdown. Vedros made it 28-0. Peter Andress added the final tally halfway through the 4th on a 30 yard run. The 2nd half consisted solely of reserves that included 9 freshmen. Even so, Terry managed to get only one score late in the 4th when Kenneth Granberry got in from the 2. The Hughes Jewelers Players of the Week included Paul Rocconi and David Gordon.

GAME 5:   SAINT AL (4-0) @ MADISON RIDGELAND (3-0)
                              FINAL: ST AL 17 MADISON RIDGELAND 0
                              October 1, 1971

Another game and another injury; this time with Fred Anklam suffering a sprained ankle. Madison Ridgeland and their 14 seniors were undefeated and defending their CAC championship. *"We've got our work cut out. We'll have to mix up our passing and running plays quite a bit if we're to move the ball. Our running game alone will not get it … through their big line. Our defense will also have to be alert for they have a good running and passing game that's hard to contain. The only* advantage we'll have is that we'll be playing at home." Said Billy Ray, "*This alone won't be enough. Make it Madison Ridgeland 20-13.*"

Madison threatened in the 1st when Columbus McDonald intercepted a Loyacono pass and brought it back to the Flash 21. But the defense came through and took over at the Flash 14 on downs. In the 2nd, the Braves moved to the Flash 20 on a 32 yard pass play from Steve Pope to Luther Simon. But again the swarming defense forced a punt. On the ensuing drive, Saint Al got the 1st down at the 30 on run plays. Loyacono found Joe Israel for 9 and Piazza got to the Flash 41. Loyacono then hit Hosemann at the 40, and behind blocking from Baylot, went the distance. Vedros gave the Flashes a 7-0 halftime lead on the PAT.

The 3rd was scoreless despite a fumble recovered by the Braves' Wilbert Daniel. They moved as far as the Flash 25 before penalties forced a punt. The 4th would belong to Saint Al. Madison's Pope, while attempting a pitchout, was hit and fumbled. Mike Foley was there and took the ball back to the Braves 12. Vedros kicked a 24 yard FG to make the score 10-0. Later, the Braves moved to the Flash 17, but a Pope pass was picked off by Piazza in the endzone. Long runs by Hosemann, Loyacono and Piazza got to the MR 9. Loyacono then found Piazza for the touchdown pass. Vedros ended the scoring at 17-0. Jack Leist finished the game with a fumble recovery for Saint Al.

GAME 6:   SAINT AL (5-0) @ BYRAM (1-3)
            FINAL: ST AL 20 BYRAM 7
            October 8, 1971

Said Rhoads, "*I hope we're not in for a letdown after last week's outstanding performance. We haven't been looking any too good in practice this week, but I guess that can be expected. I just hope we can pull ourselves together and get ready in time. We just don't have any reserves; one or two injuries can really hurt a club like ours. We only played 14 boys last week and that meant that most of them had to play every second. Another thing, Byram will be hungry to get after us with all to gain and nothing to lose and they have the personnel to do it.*"

Billy Ray still predicted a Flash victory of 21-14 while saying "*The Flashes won't be as high for this one as they were last week, but they are sitting in the driver's seat for the CAC title. One win in their next two games would give it to them.*"

Byram started by driving to the Flash 15 but fumbled to Hosemann. After a few traded punts, Saint Al started the 2nd at the Flash 28. Runs by Piazza, Loyacono and Baylot got them to the 3. Piazza finished it with a touchdown and Vedros made it 7-0. Byram responded with a 75 yard drive capped by Gary Cooper's run with :50 left. Sid Holcombe tied it going into halftime.

The Flashes fumbled on their opening possession and it was recovered by Arthur Sutton at the Byram 44. The defense forced a punt and the offense started at the Flash 20. They quickly got to the Bulldog 15 behind runs from Piazza and Hosemann and a 51 yard pass from Loyacono to Baylot. Leist, Vedros, Tommy Beasley and Kenneth Coomes opened a hole at the 4 for Piazza's scoring run. The kick was wide and the 3rd ended with a Flash lead of 13-7.

The 4th saw a lot of traded punts even though Byram's Jimbo Burton had recovered a Flash fumble at the Bulldog 28. With time running out, Byram went to the air. That's when Joe Israel picked off a pass and took it back to the Bulldog 45. After 2 runs, and as the horn sounded, Piazza broke off a 38 yard touchdown run for the win. The Flashes were now CAC Champions.

GAME 7:   SAINT AL (6-0) @ PELAHATCHIE (2-1-1)
            FINAL: ST AL 14 PELAHATCHIE 34
            October 15, 1971

The CAC champions still had 4 games left to play that would decide the fate of a bowl invitation. Said Rhoads of the Chiefs, "*They have a very impressive team. They have two fine running backs, an excellent quarterback and good receivers. They, in my opinion, even have a better running game than did Madison-Ridgeland. I just hope our success so far hasn't gone to our heads and we will play ball like champions are supposed to do. We'd better, or it could be a long trip home.*" Billy Ray smelled an upset, but said "*A shaky vote for the Flashes, but only if they play ball like champions should. Make it Saint Al 21-19 in another closie.*"

On their opening drive, Loyacono hit Foley from the 33 for the touchdown and Vedros made it 7-0. Pelahatchie immediately answered on a 64 yard drive with Charles Weakley hitting Frank Boyd for a 36 yard touchdown pass. The Chiefs scored again in the 2nd on a Boyd run of 61 yards. Not to be outdone, the Flashes had an interception by Hosemann that was brought 37 yards to the Chief 3. Piazza pushed it in from there and Vedros was good again for a halftime lead of 14-12 in spite of a 2nd quarter fumble, interception and 40 yards in penalties.

The 3rd was dominated by Pelahatchie. They drove 67 yards after the kickoff for a 4th down touchdown from the 1 by Lawrence McKee and added 2 points on a Weakley pass to Charles Gibson. After trading the ball, the Flashes touched a Chief punt at the Flash 28. Weakley found Glen Gray from the 10. Two more points came from Boyd and it was 28-14 to end the 3rd.

The Flashes fumbled to start the 4th. Pelahatchie's Gibson then ran a reverse to the Flash 3 allowing Weakley to go in from the 1. The PAT was missed but the final was 34-14. The good news was that Saint Al would have a week off to rest many injured Flashes and regroup to finish the last 3 games before bowl selections.

GAME 8: SAINT AL (6-1) @ NATCHEZ CATHEDRAL (5-1-1)
  FINAL: ST AL 29 NATCHEZ CATHEDRAL 21
  October 29, 1971

Saint Al used the off period to work on fundamentals. They would get Head and Anderson back but Paul Rocconi had stretched a knee ligament and would be out. It was Cathedral's homecoming and Rhoads said "They are big, quick and have a real fine quarterback. We've had our work cut out every week and this week is no exception." Said Billy Ray, "...we think they have already shown that they can win and we're sticking with them to bring back number seven. Flashes 26-13."

Ernie Albritton summed it all up pretty well. "The Greenies ran such plays as the flea-flicker, tackle eligible pass, double handoffs on quick kick-offs, quick kicks, a take-off on the old 'statue of liberty' play and the regular slot, double slot, flanker, wing, (and) I and T formations..." The Flashes scored first 5:00 into the 1st on a drive from their 25 when Baylot went in from the 3. Natchez responded when Bill Byrne found Curtis Wilson for 26 and Bart Brown for 24, and then Curtis Wilson for the touchdown from the 18. Wilson added the PAT for a 7-0 lead. They followed that with an onside kick recovered at the Flash 44. Byrne hit Paul Sanguinetti for the touchdown and Wilson added the PAT. Before ending the half, Cathedral scored again on a Steve Phillips run from the 19 to make it 21-6. Midway through the 3rd, Baylot picked off a pass at the Flash 30 and took it to the 42. Loyacono took them down the field and Piazza went in from the 3 to tighten the game. In the 4th, a 68 yard drive was capped by a 34 yard touchdown pass from Loyacono to Foley and the 2-pointer was caught by Baylot. Then, from their 22, Loyacono broke open for a run to the Greenie 3. The Wave defense held and forced a Vedros 22-yarder that put Saint Al ahead. Piazza sealed it with a Byrne to Pat Biglane interception return to the Natchez 12. Four plays later, he went in from the 1 to give the Flashes their 7th victory.

Billy Ray commented that "The ... Flashes are ... to be commended for their great comeback ... A lot of teams would have given up that far behind and that late in the game. But the Flashes did not. Somebody said Coach Glenn Rhoads was dripping wet when the game was over. Well, he had a right to be." Players of the Week from Hughes Jewelers included Piazza, Baylot and Hosemann. Also, a tight scoring battle in Warren County now went in favor of Piazza. Previously tied at 66, Piazza now led 78-72 over Warren Central's Wright.

GAME 9: SAINT AL (7-1) vs JACKSON SAINT JOSEPH (7-1)
  FINAL: ST AL 0 JACKSON ST JOE 21
  November 5, 1971: HOMECOMING

The Rebels had "one of their strongest teams in years ..." coming to Farrell Field. In their sole loss by 7 points, they had a number of injured players. All of them were projected to be back for the contest and caused the paper to call the Flashes the "Underdog".

Six turnovers by the Flashes on Homecoming would be the story of the night. Saint Al had only one significant drive; that in the 2nd that got only to the Rebel 33. And it was fumbled back to Saint Joe. The Flashes also fumbled in the 1st that gave the Rebels a score. On a pitchout, Robert Dow recovered the loose ball at the Flash 12. Fred Cunningham took it in from the 3 and Norman Katool converted the 2 to make it 8-0. That would be all of the scoring for the half.

Jackson's Billy Taylor pick off a 3rd quarter pass and brought it back to the Flash 7. But Guy Franco picked off a Rebel pass at the 7 to stop the threat. It was to no avail after a turnover on downs. In the 4th, Ken Kestenbaum finished a 36 yard drive by running 19 yards for the touchdown. Mark

Frascogna made it 15-0. After the ensuing kickoff, Tony Daniels picked off Loyacono at the Flash 37 and took it to the 11. Daniels took it in from the 2. The two-point conversion attempt by Rob Parkes was unsuccessful.

Said Rhoads, "*It's hard to beat anybody with that many unscheduled exchanges. We're trying to shake off that game and regroup.*"

GAME 10:   SAINT AL (7-2) @ GREENVILLE SAINT JOSEPH (2-6)
                        FINAL: ST AL 37 GREENVILLE ST JOE 0
                        November 12, 1971

Knowing that the Flashes had a post-season bowl in their sights and that there were no significant injuries from the game, the paper said the Flashes "*could want to bounce back from last week's homecoming blanking and climax their season with an impressive showing. ... Make it Flashes 34-21.*" Perhaps they knew that two-way players in Sam Mansour (ankle) and David Ventura (knee) would be out along with other Irish starters.

The Flashes scored on their first drive when Piazza got in from the 11. On their second drive from the Irish 37, Piazza took it all the way for the touchdown and a 12-0 lead. In the 2nd, the Flashes went from the Irish 48 to paydirt behind an 11-yard pass from Loyacono to Foley. Loyacono picked up his fumble to convert the 2 points. On their fourth possession, Vedros missed a 47 yard FG. And on their 5th drive, they moved it 40 yards behind a 33 yard Hosemann run and got the points when he ran in from the 2. Vedros made it 27-0 at halftime.

The 2nd half kickoff to the Flashes resulted in an 83 yard romp to the endzone by Hosemann. It was 34-0. It was time for freshman and sophomore reserves and they held the Irish out of the endzone the entire half. Vedros added to the final with a 37 yard FG in the 3rd. Saint Al would hold the Irish to 3 yards rushing and end the regular season 8-2.

GAME 11:   SAINT AL (8-2) vs WARREN CENTRAL (8-2)
                        FINAL: ST AL 0 WARREN CENTRAL 34
                        November 26, 1971: CITY PARK

On Saturday, it was released that 5 Flashes made the All-CAC team. They included Rocconi, Vedros and Piazza for Offense. Steve Cappaert and Hosemann made the list for Defense with Williams and Baylot getting Honorable Mentions. Additionally, Piazza had wrapped up the Warren County Scoring Leader award over Wright 90-84 and Reggie Head had won the Hughes Jewelers Player of the Week award.

On the 15th, the team met to decide what, if any, bowl they would choose. Two invitations were on the table: The Mississippi Bowl in Clinton versus Mendenhall, or the 10th annual Red Carpet Bowl at home versus Warren Central. "*We'll let the players vote to see if they want to go to a bowl, and if they do, then we'll vote again to see which one.*" The vote was unanimous to stay home and play Warren Central. Piazza and Wright would be playing against one-another. But Rocconi and Anderson would apparently miss because of lingering knee issues.

Warren Central, under new head coach Elbert Wright, had their first winning season ever. But as Billy Ray said, "*...you can throw past records out the window. It's a new game and more is at stake than just a regular season contest*". Rhoads was more concerned. "*I know we are outnumbered and outweighed as a whole, but we have pride, desire and quickness, and that's what I am counting on.*"

This game was all Warren Central from the start. They scored after the opening kickoff with a drive of 73 yards in 10 plays. Butch Newman went the last 26 yards for the touchdown. The Vikings punted on their next possession, but Loyacono fumbled at the Flash 16 and it was recovered by Keith Wright at the 10. Lummy Wright ran three times, the final from the 1 for a touchdown. Newman hit Ellis Tillotson after a fake PAT for the 2 points.

In the 2nd, Newman gained 44 to the Flash 11. Four plays later, David Bliss finished the 52 yard drive by plunging in from the 1. Bo Oakes made it 21-0. Unfortunately for the Flashes, Baylot fumbled a few seconds later at the Flash 32 and Tommy Antoine recovered for Warren Central. One play later, Wright ran for 32 and the touchdown. Oakes made it 28-0. Saint Al pushed as far as the Viking 32 before the halftime horn sounded.

The game's last score was in the 3rd when Wright moved the club 58 yards in 12 plays and kept it from the 3 to score. The Red Carpet Awards Banquet was held immediately after the game. Saint Al's Hosemann was voted Saint Aloysius Outstanding Back, Williams was Saint Aloysius

Outstanding Lineman and Piazza won the Sportsmanship Award. Viking winners included Robert Erves (lineman) and Wright (MVP, Outstanding Back). Though it was a disappointing finish, the paper said that the Flashes *"8-3 overall record, plus the CAC championship, certainly is nothing to be ashamed of."*

Paul Rocconi was recipient of the Virgadamo Trophy.

1972 (9-1)

Twelve lettermen returned along with a new assistant coach in Richard Gontz, previously coaching at Biloxi. The only questionable Flash for the defending CAC team was Larry Anderson. Coaches picked Saint Al as the pre-season favorite to repeat with 44 votes. Said Rhoads, *"We've been looking pretty good in practice but we still have a long way to go if we're to be a championship contender again. Our first two games are of utmost importance. I just hope we will do better Friday night than we have done in some of our practices or it could be a long season."*

GAME 1:   SAINT AL (0-0) @ RAYMOND (0-0)
                    FINAL: ST AL 22 RAYMOND 12
                    September 8, 1972

Raymond was predicted third in the CAC behind a new coach but had returning All-CAC QB Steve Davis and two backs in John Downing and Jay Reeves. Even so, the paper said that *"Flashes like to win and it's the first game for jittery Coach Phillip Hannon of Raymond. 26-13 Flashes."*

On a hot and humid night, a Raymond punt put the Flashes at the Ranger 47. On the second play, *"Hosemann started around right end, cut back to the middle of the field and weaved his way to the endzone..."* With the PAT it was 7-0. The Flashes almost scored again shortly after but fumbled at the Ranger 17. It was costly, as the first play of the 2nd was a Laurie Davis touchdown from the 6 and it was 7-6. On the ensuing kick, Hosemann took it from the 7 to the Ranger 25. Hosemann's 35 yard FG was good to make it 10-6. Raymond answered immediately when Downing took the kickoff 86 yards for the score. Raymond almost scored after a Flash fumble at their 14 was recovered by Hiram Gatewood. The halftime horn sounded before they could convert.

The 3rd was back-and-forth until Hosemann scored from the 12. Saint Al tried to capitalize on a Bobby Coomes pick of Davis at the Ranger 24 in the 4th but the FG missed. Again, they had a chance when Francis Williams got a fumble at the 23, but the FG missed yet again. But when the Rangers fumbled again on their 20, Bill Loyacono was there. With :15 left, Hosemann took the ball toward the endzone but fumbled at the 5. However, Loyacono recovered and took it in for the final score.

GAME 2:   SAINT AL (1-0) @ PUCKETT (0-1)
                    FINAL: ST AL 20 PUCKETT 6
                    September 15, 1972

Saint Al started as number 3 pre-season pick for the CAC and now sat number 2. Puckett had gone 8-2 in 1971 and played in the Red Carpet Bowl. But the week before, they had lost at home to Madison Ridgeland 16-13 while on the 6" line late. Of the week, Rhoads said *"We have been trying to polish our attack ... with emphasis on timing, blocking and fundamentals. Our overall team spirit is good and our goal is to win the CAC title again, but it's certainly not going to be easy as every team will be after us."* The paper's prediction was 14-13 Flashes.

Starting at the Flash 19, Loyacono found Harvey Landers for 40 yards to the Wolves 3. Hosemann took it in from there but missed the PAT. The Flashes fumbled at their 25 but got it back when Coomes picked off a pass at the 1 foot line. In spite of a 40 yard run by Loyacono, a Hosemann run for 22 and a fumble, the score would remain 6-0 at half.

Loyacono started the 2nd half by taking it in from the 29 and Hosemann made it 13-0. After a plethora of Flash reserves filled the field, Saint Al put up their final points on a drive that started at the Flash 42. Loyacono took it in from 8 and Hosemann made it 20-0. Puckett put their points up when James Crain found Steve Boone from the 20. The two-point conversion was picked off by Coomes, his second of the game.

Said Rhoads afterwards, *"We showed much improvement over our opening game in both offense and defense but we're still making mistakes that we shouldn't"*. Saint Al had both leader and co-leader in Warren County scoring in Hosemann (24) and Loyacono (18). After beating projected numbers 2 and 3 in the CAC, it would seem that the Flashes had everything under control. But Billy Ray noted that *"...pre-season polls don't always turn out the way they are supposed to. A lot of water can run under the bridge between the opening and closing of a football season. But the Flashes are off to a good start, and nobody can deny that."*

GAME 3:   SAINT AL (2-0) vs UTICA (1-1)
                      FINAL: ST AL 32 UTICA 0
                      September 22, 1972

Rhoads echoed Ray this week. *"Preseason ratings mean little. Every game is a hurdle for us and Utica will certainly be a tough one. We'll probably have to take to the air a lot. We certainly can't sit back and rest on our laurels."* Utica featured All CAC back Clarence Flowers but Saint Al was finally at home. Ray said *"... this is the first home appearance after two straight weeks on the road. The Flashes are going to get after some people this year. Make it Flashes 26-7"*.

A Harvey Landers opening kick return to the Utica 25 didn't produce results. But on exchanged punts afterwards, Saint Al recovered a fumble at the Wave 36. From there, Loyacono hit Foley from the 23 for the touchdown. The Flashes started the 2nd with a Peter Andress 17 yard touchdown added by a Pat McNamara PAT to put the Flashes up 13-0. Andress also picked off Bob Walker at the Utica 48 afterwards, and after 2 plays, Hosemann ran it in for a 42 yard score.

As the half was ending, another Utica mistake allowed Hosemann to score from 8 yards and McNamara made it 27-0. Reserves filled the 2nd half *"playing toe-to-toe"* with the Wave. With 7:30 left, Guy Franco plunged in from the 2 to finish the scoring.

GAME 4:   SAINT AL (3-0) vs TERRY (0-3)
                      FINAL: ST AL 43 TERRY 0
                      September 29, 1972

The county's leading scorer in Hosemann had a swollen knee from the Utica game and Rhodes said *"We probably won't play him unless it is absolutely necessary."* The paper said that Terry may be *"fired-up"* but *"hasn't done too much this season"* and predicted the Flashes 34-12.

Saint Al scored early and often in the rain. After the kick, it took 8 plays before Reggie Head went in from the 1. McNamara made it 7-0. Saint Al drove next to the Terry 10 before fumbling, but Andress got the ball back on an interception of Kenny Granberry. He brought it back 20 yards to the 10 but the Flashes would get no further than the 5. After forcing a punt, the snap went over the kicker's head for a safety and it was 9-0 in the 2nd. The Flashes received the ensuing Terry kick and, one play later, Loyacono found Coomes for the 48 yard connection. Granberry threw another pick, this time to Phillip Bucci, on the next possession. Three plays later, Landers went 42 yards for the touchdown. McNamara added to the lead and it was 23-0 at half.

Loyacono joined the interception party in the 3rd and returned it to the Terry 10. Running by Landers put McNamara in range for a 24 yard FG. Chuck Trahan took one in from 33 yards and, in the same quarter, Saint Al's Coomes picked off yet another Terry pass. Loyacono recovered a fumble at the Terry 7 and McNamara converted the FG to start the 4th quarter 36-0. Saint Al's last score came late in the 4th on a Kyle Lawler run from the 1 after the Flashes recovered a punt touched by the Yellow Jackets.

GAME 5:   SAINT AL (4-0) @ MADISON RIDGELAND (UNDEFEATED)
                      FINAL: ST AL 47 MADISON RIDGELAND 0
                      October 6, 1972

Against an undefeated CAC opponent, this could be "winner take all". The paper picked the healthy Flashes 24-13 since Hosemann was back and emphasized the importance of the kicking game for Saint Al. On the first Flash drive, Landers ran for 65 and a score. McNamara made it 7-0. On their next possession, Loyacono received the Braves punt and took it to the endzone from 63 yards away. Andress then picked off a McDonald pass at the Flash 46 and returned it to the MR 34. Hosemann gained 23 and Landers took it the remaining 11. Still in the 1st, Hosemann gained 68 and then 9 for another Flash touchdown to make it 27-0.

Midway through the 2nd, Loyacono returned a Braves punt for 50 yards to the 8. Hosemann did the honors and McNamara converted. Reserves were called upon for the 2nd half and they performed. Landers scored from the 6 in the 3rd and Ed Lawler hit Joe Tarnabine from the 20 in the 4th. The defense had held MR to no deeper than the Flash 29 the entire game.

GAME 6:   SAINT AL (5-0) vs BYRAM (UNREPORTED)
                         FINAL: ST AL 31 BYRAM 0
                         October 13, 1972

The 5-0 Flashes were getting better each week, could wrap up a repeat CAC title and were playing a conference foe that Billy Ray called *"certainly not the toughest foe on the Flashes' schedule".* Rhoads said *"Our players know that, too. And that's what I'm afraid of: a big let-down."* Ray predicted a 42-6 victory.

Byram came out strong after the kick and drove as far as the Flash 19 before turning the ball back to the Flashes on downs. Hosemann immediately ran for 41, Landers for 16 and then Hosemann capped it from there. McNamara made it 7-0. Loyacono picked off a Bobby Bruce pass and brought it back to the Flash 23 to end the 1st, but fumbled on the ensuing play. Marvin Hill recovered but the offense could not produce.

The Flashes had a Loyacono touchdown pass of 51 yards to Coomes called back, but they did score on the drive. Loyacono pushed it to the 8 and Hosemann got in for the touchdown. McNamara made it 14-0. On the kickoff, Pat Beard both caused a fumble and recovered it at the Bulldog 25. Hosemann scored his 3rd of the night from the 7 and McNamara padded the lead to 21-0. Before the half was done, Byram fumbled to Coomes at the 11. It took 3 plays before Loyacono hit Hosemann from the 8 and McNamara made it 28-0.

The final half was handled by reserves. They allowed McNamara to hit from 30 yards out to finish the scoring at 31-0. The Flashes were now CAC champions for the second-straight year.

GAME 7:   SAINT AL (6-0) vs PELAHATCHIE (UNREPORTED)
                         FINAL: ST AL 35 PELAHATCHIE 0
                         October 20, 1972

Saint Al entered the Pelahatchie game almost like last year. They were conference champs, 6-0 and had outscored their opponents by a good margin. But Pelahatchie had won. *"They have a team than can be awfully good when they want to be, and since we've already won the conference title, I'm afraid they'll be high as a kite again and will probably play their best game of the season against us, trying to duplicate what they did last year. We'll have to try and be ready."* Billy Ray still thought the Flashes would be too much. 38-18.

The Flashes started by driving to the 19 where Hosemann capped it with a score. "Toe" McNamara made it 7-0. After the Chief punt was returned to the Pelahatchie 45, Loyacono went up the middle for the score. "Toe" made it 14-0. The 2nd also saw a missed FG by the Flashes and a Larry Lock fumble recovery for the Chiefs. The defense rose up and held but it remained 14-0 until halftime.

Saint Al padded their lead in the 3rd with a Loyacono touchdown pass to Mike Foley from the 40. McNamara's PAT ended the 3rd 21-0. The Chiefs punted to Loyacono in the 4th and he returned it 58 yards for another touchdown and a 27-0 lead. Saint Al's last scoring drive started at the Pelahatchie 30. Hosemann quickly went in from there and Loyacono annexed the 2 points at game's end.

GAME 8:   SAINT AL (7-0) @ JACKSON SAINT JOSEPH (6-0)
                         FINAL: ST AL 21 JACKSON ST JOE 28
                         October 27, 1972

The Flashes had outscored their opponents this year 224-18 but now faced *"their stiffest challenge of the year. (They) are reported with an even stronger eleven (than the previous year)."* Said Rhoads, *"I know we won't have a letdown. This is our big game and I think we're up for the game. I know they are, too. We've got to play a near-perfect game, and even that may not be enough. They have a tremendous team, big in size and fast afoot."* Billy Ray picked Saint Joe 23-17 *"mainly because the Rebels will be playing at home".*

The tough Saint Joe squad drove on their opening possession 73 yards with Fred Cunningham scoring from the 3. Mark Frascogna's PAT was no-good. Hosemann returned the ensuing kick to the Flash 45. Runs by Loyacono, Head, Landers and Hosemann pushed the ball to the 3 and Loyacono capped it from there. McNamara gave Saint Al the lead on the PAT. The Rebels came right back when, starting at their 20, Rob Parkes hit Robert Dow at the 50 and he ran the remainder for a touchdown. Cunningham converted for 2 for a 14-7 lead.

In the 2nd, Loyacono hauled in a punt at the Flash 47 and took it all the way for the score and McNamara tied it. Another quick score came immediately afterwards when Dow pulled in the kick at the 10 and wound his way 90 yards for the touchdown. Frascogna made it 21-14. The Flashes managed to tie it up before halftime when Hosemann took a pitchout in from the 18 and McNamara converted.

The final score came in the 3rd. Foley had pinned the Rebels back at the JSJ 25, but after runs and passes, Cunningham dove in from the 9. Frascogna converted for the 28-21 final. The Flashes had a ball picked off by Dow in the endzone in a final attempt to even it up. Ernie Albritton said that *"The Flashes put on a tremendous team effort in the contest…"* and Rhoads *"called it one of the Flashes best performances in his three years as a head coach…"*

GAME 9:   SAINT AL (7-1) vs NATCHEZ CATHEDRAL (3-3)
                     FINAL: ST AL 44 NATCHEZ CATHEDRAL 0
                     November 3, 1972: HOMECOMING

"We've just got to shake off that loss last week and regroup. We've still got two big games left and they are very important to us", said Rhoads. Murray Whitaker (knee) and David Gordon (ankle) were doubtful against a team termed better than last year. Because it was Homecoming, the paper predicted a *"bounce back"* victory of 35-14.

The rain didn't stop Saint Al from dominating the game. Hosemann scored on the initial drive but the PAT snap was mishandled. After a Steve Cappaert fumble recovery at the Greenie 40, Hosemann started the 2nd by gaining 16 followed by a Head touchdown from there. McNamara made it 13-0. Hosemann scored twice more in the quarter. The first capped a 70 yard drive and the second on an 87 yard run. Halftime would be in favor of Saint Al 27-0.

With reserves taking over, the Flashes drove to the Natchez 5 before allowing McNamara a 23 yarder in the 3rd. In the 4th, runs by Franco and Beard moved the ball to the 8. Hosemann returned and ran twice, with the latter gaining the touchdown. The final score would be a Landers plunge from the 1 that capped a 49 yard drive. Natchez crossed the 50 yard line only once and only by a yard. They were driven back on the next play.

GAME 10:   SAINT AL (8-1) vs GREENVILLE SAINT JOSEPH (3-5)
                     FINAL: ST AL 33 GREENVILLE ST JOE 13
                     November 10, 1972

The final game was marked by penalties and turnovers for the Flashes. In all, there were 3 lost fumbles and 2 interceptions. But it wasn't enough to keep them from putting up their 9th win of the season. The 1st ended on a 34 yard pass from Loyacono to Coomes to the Irish 6. Hosemann took it in from there for a 6-0 lead. The Flashes fumbled their next possession at their 25 but the defense held. Starting at his 8 after the punt, Loyacono hit Hosemann for 36 and Foley for 15. Hosemann then took it 29 yards for the touchdown ending 1st half scoring with the Flashes up 12-0.

Saint Joe closed the gap to open the 3rd behind running by Paul Mauceli. Phil Mansour scored from the 6 and Steve Cascio converted to make it 12-7. The Flashes started next at their 35. Irish penalties aided the drive and Head finally capped it from the 15. McNamara made it 19-7. The Irish fumbled the ensuing kick and Cappaert recovered at their 22. Head and Hosemann got it to the 1 and Loyacono sprinted in. It was 26-7.

Greenville responded with a 75 yard drive that included a 45 yard completion from John Sherman to Mauceli at the Flash 10. Mauceli went in from the 1 later, but the 2 point attempt was stopped by Andress. In the 4th, Loyacono put up the last points when an attempted pass situation turned into a 59 yard touchdown run. Hosemann converted the PAT.

The Flashes decided not to accept either offered bowl invitation: one in Ellisville and the Lions Bowl in Kosciusko. Said Rhoads, *"We've accomplished a lot this season and our main objective was accomplished early, that to win our second CAC championship. We've worked awfully hard and the players, as well as the coaches, are a little tired right now. And, too, our basketball season is about to start and some football players and cheerleaders are members... Participating in a bowl game would mess up the start of our season, but I certainly appreciate those bowl folks thinking about us."*

When the All-CAC selections came out, the Flashes were well-represented. Rhoads was "Coach of the Year", and 8 Flashes earned spots. They included Hosemann (Most Valuable Back); Cappaert (Most Valuable Lineman); Bobby Coomes and Peter Andress (Linebackers); Reggie Head (End); David Gordon (Tackle) and Mike Foley (End) and Bill Loyacono (Back). Hosemann would also win the Virgadamo Trophy.

"Coach Rhodes had offensive linemen calling the blocking schemes at the line of scrimmage. It was pretty impressive to trust the O-line, but these were smart players well-practiced during the week. The CAC was new and we were used to playing bigger, more organized schools. We were good enough to basically break out with big first half leads and then just mop up in the second half. Our season, in my opinion, came down to one game: Saint Joseph of Jackson.

If Coach Raphael were alive today, he would tell you their 1972 team was one of the most talented he had the pleasure to coach. Several future D1 players were seniors. The game was a slugfest, with Saint Joe winning 28-21. We played our hearts out but just came up a little short. We went 9-1 and had a good football team. At season's end, the decision was made to not play in a bowl game. This as before high school playoffs and bows were few and far between. I think our mentality was that the Saint Joe game was like a bowl game to us.

Saint Joe would be pitted against Murrah in the capitol bowl in Jackson. Nobody gave them a chance. Some stated the game to be "ill thought out". Saint Joe beat Murrah and we felt some vindication for our only loss."

David Hosemann; August 7, 2016

1973 (9-1)

Despite losing 5 All-Conference players to graduation, Glenn Rhoads' Flashes were picked as favorites for the Capital Athletic Conference three-peat. Madison Ridgeland, the Flashes first opponent, was second while Raymond finished third. Rhoads had steadily increased his record with each passing year. In 1970, he was 7-3. In 1971, he was 8-2, and in 1972 he went 9-1. The goal this year, he told the Vicksburg Lions Club on September 12th, was to be undefeated.

GAME 1:   SAINT AL (0-0) @ RAYMOND (0-0)
                       FINAL: ST AL 33 RAYMOND 6
                       September 7, 1973

Before game time, Harvey Landers (thigh) and John Gerache (ankle) were injured and game-time decisions. *"We don't know right now if either will be able to play, but I'm hoping they will be ready for at least part-time action"*. Many were already playing both ways, and no depletion in depth was good. Team captains would be Larry Nichols and Bobby Coomes. Despite a prediction of *"opening game jitters"*, Billy Ray picked Saint Al 14-7.

In the 2nd, Raymond fumbled at the Ranger 34 and it was recovered by Lynn Jefferson. Bill Loyacono hit Guy Franco at the 11, and two plays later, Loyacono took it in from the 9 to make it 6-0. Saint Al added to that score on the ensuing kickoff when Raymond fumbled again. This time, Terry Alonzo grabbed it on the Ranger 32. Two plays afterwards, Loyacono hit Joe Tarnabine for the touchdown. Loyacono made it 13-0.

With just 3:58 remaining in the half, Loyacono brought the crowd to their feet with an 80 yard punt return for a touchdown. It was 20-0 at intermission. Loyacono found Bobby Coomes late in the 3rd and the QB made it 27-0 with the PAT. From there, the reserves came in. Joe Tarnabine found yet another Raymond fumble, this time at their 22. The Flashes got to the 1 foot line but the Rangers held. The Flashes managed another touchdown in the 4th from Chuck Trahan behind running by him, Dennis Southard and Ed Lawler. The 47 yard drive made it 33-0. Raymond managed to avoid the shutout on a 77 yard kickoff return by Robert Drone.

GAME 2:   SAINT AL (1-0) vs PUCKETT (0-1)
                        FINAL: ST AL 35 PUCKETT 6
                        September 14, 1973

Rhoads had scouted Puckett in their loss to Madison Ridgeland the previous week. *"Puckett has a big ball club and their split end is one of the finest I've seen since I've been here."*

Saint Al came out as barn-burners by scoring 21 points in the 1st. Loyacono aided the first one with a 40 yard punt return to the Wolves 14. In two plays, Franco crashed in for the score. Loyacono converted to make it 7-0. On their next drive, Puckett's Phillip Shotts threw an interception to Coomes who took it back 55 yards for the score. Loyacono again converted. After holding Puckett's next drive, the Flashes drove to the 4 where Loyacono cashed in and capped the PAT.

The visitor responded in the 2nd behind a Jimmy Miller run for 48 yards and a Shotts pass to Parker that got them to the Flash 1. Shotts then snuck over for the touchdown. They recovered a Saint Al fumble a bit later at the Flash 45 but ended up throwing another interception, this time to Franco, to kill the opportunity. After a third Saint Al interception by Loyacono at the Flash 4, they had time for one play. It would be a Loyacono fake pass and run for 96 yards and the touchdown with an expired clock. He converted the PAT and it was 28-6 at the half.

The Flashes were able to put up one more touchdown before the game ended. Trahan took a pitchout from Lawler 43 yards to paydirt. Loyacono made his 5th PAT to seal the game.

GAME 3:   SAINT AL (2-0) @ UTICA (2-0)
                        FINAL: ST AL 21 UTICA 0
                        September 14, 1973

This CAC tilt would be a major deciding factor for the future of both teams. Both were undefeated and a victory would put destiny in their own hands. Utica had outscored their opponents 33-0. Saint Al had given up 12 points but doubled the output of their opponent. *"Utica will probably be one of our toughest foes. They have most of their players back including a tree-year veteran QB and a 195-pound fullback. They are big defensively and very aggressive on offense"*. Billy Ray predicted a Flash win of 27-7.

At kickoff, Loyacono was on the sidelines as a result of a *"training rules violation"*. Ed Lawler took his place admirably. Utica threatened in the 1st with a drive to the Flash 30, but the defense held on a fourth down fake punt by Bob Walker. That would be the deepest drive of the night for the Wave. The Flashes finished the 1st when, starting at the Flash 39, Trahan peeled off a deep run to the Utica 7 and then finished it on the next play from there. Despite two attempts near the goal for Saint Al in the 3rd, that score would hold until the 4th.

To start the quarter, Utica's Don Curtis was tackled in the endzone by Nichols, Coomes and Franco for a safety. The Flashes would score twice more before the whistle. When Landers and Trahan got the ball to the Flash 29 on runs, Lawler was able to find Landers for a touchdown. Charles Mayfield blocked Landers' PAT. With 1:20 remaining, Coomes picked off Walker at the Wave 2 and stepped in for the last touchdown. Landers converted to finish the contest 21-0.

GAME 4:   SAINT AL (3-0) @ TERRY (0-3)
                        FINAL: ST AL 33 TERRY 0
                        September 28, 1973

Despite an off-week, Loyacono would still lead the CAC in scoring with 32 points. He was also tied with Utica's Shotts for touchdown passes with 3. This week should be a time to pad the lead with a healthy Flash team against a winless Terry team.

Saint Al started slow but managed to put up a touchdown in the 1st. On a 47 yard drive, Loyacono ran in from the 7 and added the PAT. The Flashes got as far as the Terry 11 and Terry 8 in the 1st half on other drives without success. But in the 3rd, Saint Al began marching. Trahan started the quarter with a 70 yard touchdown run. After a bad punt put the Flashes at the Terry 10, Patrick Beard added another touchdown from the 1. Loyacono made it 20-0.

In the 4th, Terry fumbled at their 15 and Loyacono was able to recover. Franco took it in from the 8. With just 1:10 remaining, Lawler found James Smith from the 24 for a score. Loyacono made the final 33-0 with his PAT. The Flashes could have made the score much worse had they been able to convert on the two drives in the 1st, or on the missed FGs from 27, 40 and 41.

GAME 5:   SAINT AL (4-0) vs MADISON RIDGELAND (2-2)
                                FINAL: ST AL 30 MADISON RIDGELAND 8
                                October 5, 1973: HOMECOMING

Said Rhoads of the healthy Flashes, *"Heck, we didn't hit hard enough to get hurt"*. Madison Ridgeland lost their first CAC game the previous week to Utica, a loss believed by Rhoads and the Utica coach from looking ahead to Saint Al. Rhodes praised his opponent and noted that their line was bigger, their defense was impressive and they had key players that could easily bring the first loss of the season. *"This is it; the game we've got to win. We'd better be at our best Friday night. I know they will be."*

Saint Al opened by driving to the Braves 4, but was moved back on a penalty. Loyacono was called upon and converted a 26 yard FG to make it 3-0. On their first drive of the 2nd starting from the Braves 46, Franco dove in from the 4 and Loyacono made it 10-0. On their ensuing drive, Loyacono hit Landers for a 41 yard strike. Loyacono added the PAT to make it 17-0 at halftime.

The 3rd started exactly like the 1st. The Flashes drove to the Braves 6, were moved back by penalties, and Loyacono converted a 26 yard FG. Madison Ridgeland put up their only points afterwards, driving to the Flash 2 before Jimmy Martin plunged in. Martin found Ralph Daughtry for the two-point conversion and the quarter ended 20-8.

The final two Flash scores came in the 4th. The first was highlighted by a Landers run of 21 followed by a 25 yard Loyacono pass to Terry Alonzo. Loyacono was able to convert his 3rd FG, this time from 25 away. Madison Ridgeland fumbled on their ensuing possession and Dennis Southard fell on it at the Braves 37. Franco gained 22, Loyacano finally scored from the 8 and then converted to give the Flashes a 30-8 victory and their 5th straight victory. Rhoads was complimentary this time of his team. *"Our offense moved well and I was real pleased with our defensive line play. But we must continue and not have a big letdown at this stage".*

GAME 6:   SAINT AL (5-0) vs BYRAM (2-2-1)
                                FINAL: ST AL 47 BYRAM 0
                                October 12, 1973

Everyone knew a victory would give the Flashes their 3rd straight CAC title. But Rhoads noted that Byram was *"real big across the line, averaging around 190 pounds and they have an offense … that can really move"*. Billy Ray predicted a score relatively close to the one in 1972 (31-0) and called it a 31-13 Flash win.

The 1st was an exchange of turnovers. The Flashes fumbled to Jessie McGee at the Flash 29 and then Loyacono picked off a Bobby Bruce pass at the Flash 5. Saint Al then fumbled once more to McGee at the Byram 42 to end the stanza. Afterwards, it was all Saint Aloysius. Loyacono found Coomes for 49 yards and then hit Neil Randall from the 18 for the touchdown. On the ensuing drive, Byram's Charles McLendon lost the handle at their 10 into the waiting arms of Francis Williams. His touchdown made it 12-0. Before the half was done, Franco picked off Byram at the Bulldog 24. Landers ran in from the 20 two plays later and it was 18-0 at half.

The 3rd was a nightmare for Byram. A fumble to Dennis Southard at their 20 resulted in a Loyacono touchdown from the 5. They fumbled again at their 17 and Franco made them pay from the 5. As the quarter ended, Loyacono picked off a Bruce pass at the Flash 30. Lawler hit Joe McCain from 32 yards and Lawler culminated the drive from the 1. Loyacono converted the two-pointer after a fumbled snap.

The contest fittingly ended on a Byram fumble to Joe Tarnabine at the Bulldog 25. Led by John Smith, the give to David Holloway from the 6 was good and Loyacono wrapped up the bludgeoning with the PAT. The Flashes had gotten their title and now eyed the perfect season.

GAME 7:   SAINT AL (6-0) @ PELAHATCHIE (0-6)
                                FINAL: ST AL 55 PELAHATCHIE 8
                                October 19, 1973

Loyacono was now firmly in the CAC scoring lead with 70 points; more than three times the amount the Flashes had given up on defense. With so many points scored against *"an injured, error prone Pelahatchie eleven"*, a simple recap will suffice. A Chief fumble at their 26 resulted in a Loyacono score from the 6. Franco scored next on a run from the 14, and Loyacono later finished off a Southard run for 24 by diving in from the 1. Another Chiefs fumble was recovered by Southard at the Chief 28. Loyacono ran it in from there one play later. Loyacono found Landers on the next drive for a 46 yard touchdown and the half ended with Saint Al up 33-0.

Reserve players took the field for the 2nd half. After the kickoff, Southard was able to score from the 1 and Loyacono added the PAT. Pelahatchie fumbled to Saint Al at their 11 and Robert Koestler plunged in from the 3 to end 3rd quarter scoring. In the 4th, Pelahatchie avoided the shutout on a Joe Keith McKay touchdown from the 1 and a Larry Latham PAT run. Fittingly, Pelahatchie fumbled just before the end of the game and Joe Tarnabine took the ball back for a 30 yard score. Loyacono hit Alonzo after a bad snap for the two-pointer.

GAME 8:   SAINT AL (7-0) vs JACKSON SAINT JOSEPH (3-4)
                FINAL: ST AL 19 JACKSON ST JOE 0
                October 26, 1973: SENIOR NIGHT

A Catholic rivalry such as this one meant that "you can throw the records out the window". Rhoads thought the JSJ defense would be the best one they would play in 1973. Billy Ray thought it would be a close one with a Flash victory 24-14 due to this and the fact that a powerful Clinton team only beat the Rebels 14-7.

First quarter defenses were strong on both sides. The Rebels held Saint Al deep and forced a 25 yard FG from Loyacono. The Flashes next score came in the 2nd on a 60 yard drive capped by a Franco run from the 8. Loyacono made it 10-0. Holding the Rebels on the Flash 22, Saint Al took over and pushed the ball to the Flash 47. Then, Loyacono "pulled off one of his patented sideline, sidestepping runs" for the 53 yard touchdown. Jackson blocked the PAT but halftime would be a 16-0 Flash advantage.

Saint Al came close to padding the lead in the 3rd on a 40 yard drive that got to the Rebel 2. But Loyacono fumbled and Saint Joe took over at their 17. The Rebels returned the favor after getting to the Flash 19 with a Curtis Barefield fumble that was recovered by Franco. In the 4th, a Rebel fumble at their 40 was returned to the 17 by Alonzo. The Flashes continued give-and-take a few more times afterwards when Loyacono was picked off by Paul Rossie. They pushed to the Flash 25 before Coomes intercepted a Rebel pass.

Saint Joe threw another interception on their ensuing drive. Mike Henderson threw an errant pass to Loyacono at the Rebel 42 and he returned it to the Rebel 15. With just :05 left, Loyacono split the goal from 26 for a FG behind Landers' hold.

GAME 9:   SAINT AL (8-0) @ NATCHEZ CATHEDRAL (7-1)
                FINAL: ST AL 0 NATCHEZ CATHEDRAL 6
                November 2, 1973

This game would be the key to the season and one paper said "could be a stumbling block". Said Rhoads, "It's going to take a tremendous effort on our part. They're explosive and they make big plays..." He called them the "best team the Flashes have faced and playing in Natchez certainly won't make things easier". A Flash win of 17-13 was predicted.

The paper summed up the loss by saying "The inability of Bill Loyacono's receivers to hang onto his passes, fumbles, a pass interception, penalties and the punting of Cathedral's Phillip Ladner were among the multitude of problems that the Flashes encountered". The defense, though, did very well with the exception of one play. Late in the first on 3rd and 4 at the Flash 49, 201-pound Jamie Arnold ran straight up the middle to the Flash 1 and then plunged in on the next play. The PAT was not good, but the scoring was done for the game.

In the 2nd, Loyacono hit Coomes at the 3 but a penalty negated the gain. A Loyacono FG attempt of 49 yards later was no good. Before the half ended and after getting to the Greenies 13, Brown picked off a Flash pass. Landers returned the favor by intercepting a Greenie pass at the 49 but Saint Al could not get closer than the 24. The 3rd saw another Flash fumble at the Greenie 44 but the defense held. Cathedral did likewise on a punt that was recovered by Koestler at the 49, but Natchez held the Flashes for no gains. Time and again, the Cathedral punter put Saint Al deep in their territory and forced long drives. Loyacono would finish 3 for 21 in passing with 1 interception.

The following week, Rhoads would say of his team "We're more mentally hurt ... than physically. I just hope we can regroup and play like we're capable. Our goal at the start of the season *was an undefeated season. That's now gone out the window. I just hope we can end on a winning note. A 9-1 season isn't all that bad".*

GAME 10:   SAINT AL (8-1) @ GREENVILLE SAINT JOE (UNREPORTED)
               FINAL: ST AL 27 GREENVILLE ST JOE 0
               November 9, 1973

A big line awaited the healthy, but morally down, Flashes. *"We should be at full strength, but must play much better or we'll go down in defeat again".* Ray predicted a 34-7 Flash win since they *"wanted their pride restored".*

Saint Al had a chance to score in the 1st on a blocked Ken Radigan punt but missed a 25 yard FG attempt. They missed another in the 2nd from the Irish 30. But two touchdowns would follow before halftime. The first was a 92 yard interception return by Coomes that Loyacono capped with the PAT. The next was the result of another blocked punt recovered by Southard at the Irish 15. Loyacono hit Landers at the 1 and then Loyacono carried it over afterwards and converted the PAT.

In the 3rd, Loyacono pulled off a 33 yard scoring run and PAT to pad the lead. The Flashes may have scored again save an interception by Ronnie Gross at the Flash 6. The Irish couldn't convert on that drive, nor on a later one courtesy of a Kenny Azar interception. The defense held at the Flash 13 to keep the shutout alive. The Flashes' Terry Alonzo did pick off an Irish pass in the 4th, but scored when Radigan's punt was fumbled in the endzone and recovered by Coomes. The Flashes would end up 9-1 but turn down bowl invitations this year as they had done in 1972.

The Flashes ended the season with a win and a loss. Coach Glenn Rhoads, *"after thinking it over prayerfully for three months",* ended his tenure as head man and took a job with Vicksburg Paint and Glass. *"I have really enjoyed my stay at St. Aloysius and people there have been mighty good to me. I have gotten more out of them than I have put into their program, and I will always be grateful to them for letting me be associated with so many fine boys".* He had three straight CAC championships and a combined record of 33-9 was topped only by the respect others had for him. Billy Ray said *"We think Saint Al was really lucky to hang on to a man of Rhoads' character and ability as long as they did. Men like him are in great demand."*

The All-CAC list came out on December 6th. Loyacono (41/95 for 753 pass yards) was named Most Outstanding Back and Coomes (11 for 204 receiving on offense) was Most Outstanding Lineman. The other Flashes with honors included Lynn Jefferson, Larry Nichols, Francis Williams, Murray Whitaker and Guy Franco (98 for 411 rushing). Honorable Mentions went out to Harvey Landers (45-255 rushing and 9 for 202 receiving), and Glenn Rhoads finished second in Coach Of The Year voting behind Utica's Terry Clark. Loyacono also won the Virgadamo Trophy.

"The 1973 football season was a great year. For us to lose to Natchez Cathedral is something that will never be forgotten. Always hard to win in Natchez."

Mike Jones; August 6, 2016

1974 (10-1)

Glenn Rhoads' departure opened the door for Tommy Autrey. The Jackson Wingfield assistant and ex-Forest Hill player inherited a team that lost many starters to graduation, but had 9 returning lettermen and chasing Saint Al's fourth straight CAC title. Coaches picked the Flashes to end 3rd behind Utica and Madison Ridgeland. *"It hurts my feelings that the CAC coaches picked us third. We've got a dedicated bunch of kids who aren't going to give up that title merely because of some coaches' opinions. You can't judge a football team's pride by the number of returning lettermen and starters it has. Pride's about 95% of the game in my opinion, and we are blessed with an abundance of it."*

Autrey had practiced hard and was installing the Multiple-I offense. Nearing kickoff, he thought that he *"… was more nervous than his players for (Raymond). I know Raymond is going to be laying for us as well as the other teams. That's the price you've got to pay when you have successful years like the Flashes have been enjoying".*

GAME 1:   SAINT AL (0-0) @ RAYMOND (0-0)
                    FINAL: ST AL 21 RAYMOND 8
                    September 6, 1974

Saint Al opened impressively, scoring in the 1st when Ed Lawler hit David Holloway for 58 yards and a 6-0 lead. Raymond coughed up the ball in the 2nd at their 7 and it was recovered by Murray Whitaker. Two plays later, Chuck Trahan blasted in from the 4 and Beasley's PAT made it 13-0. The Rangers responded with a 67 yard drive in 8 plays, with Richard Garrison finding Earl Lee White from the 14. Their two-point pass attempt to J.W. Freeman was unsuccessful.

The final score came in early in the 3rd after an exchange of fumbles. Saint Al gave up the ball at the Ranger 27 and then got it back 2 plays later at the Raymond 17. It took three plays before Dennis Southard muscled in from the 3. Trahan capped it with a 2 point conversion. The Flashes actually scored again on a 75 yard run by Holloway, but a personal foul brought the ball back. Greg Head's pick off a Garrison pass ended the game.

GAME 2:   SAINT AL (1-0) @ PUCKETT (0-1)
                    FINAL: ST AL 41 PUCKETT 6
                    September 13, 1974

Puckett was coming off of a 44-8 drumming by Madison Ridgeland and was beaten soundly by Saint Al in 1973. In spite of a good practice week, that didn't stop Autrey from seeing *"flies in the ointment"*. First was the size of Puckett. *"They are as big as we are and may be a little faster"*. Second was a hip-pointer injury to Trahan that had him listed as *"doubtful"*, though he would eventually play. Trahan would still be co-captain alongside Greg Head.

As an editor's note, The Vicksburg Evening Post sportswriter Billy Ray passed away the afternoon of this contest. He is noted in this book under Dedications due to his tireless efforts that preserved the history of Saint Aloysius sports. The Flashes would dedicate the game to him.

A *"soggy field"* didn't stop the Flashes from soundly thrashing the home team. The opening drive score came on a 10 play march (6 by Holloway) capped by Trahan from the 4. Beasley made it 7-0. The Flashes went on to score on their 2nd, 3rd, 4th, 5th and 6th possessions. Trahan again scored from the 2 and Beasley converted. James Smith picked off a Parker pass on the next play for a 32 yard touchdown and Bobby Nelson ran in the two points.

Southard opened the 3rd with a 2 yard dive and Beasley's PAT made it 35-0. Another James Lockett fumble into the hands of Robert Koestler set the Flashes up at the Wolves 8. Nelson went in from the 4 two plays later. With reserves on the field, Puckett avoided the shutout on a Lockett run from the 6. Parker's pass to Robert Burnham added the two points. The Flashes had two touchdowns called back for penalties. One was a Trahan 44 yard run and the other was a Lawler pass to Smith from the 34.

GAME 3:   SAINT AL (2-0) @ UTICA (2-0)
                    FINAL: ST AL 7 UTICA 0
                    September 20, 1974

Saint Al had their third straight road game; this time against CAC-favored co-champion Utica. Their wins had been against Byram (19-0) and Raymond (14-9). *"We can beat Utica if the team wants it bad enough. We played a fair game against Puckett. If we play a fair game against Utica, they'll blow us clear across the Pearl River"*. The team was healthy and Trahan had taken top spot in CAC scoring with 26.

In the heat and humidity, the battle between the two undefeated CAC opponents waged through three scoreless quarters. As the 3rd ended, Saint Al forced Utica to punt on 4th and 8 from the Utica 24. The Flashes started on the Wave 45 to begin the 4th and then marched 14 plays to put up the deciding score. Runs by Trahan, Lawler, Koestler, and James Smith moved the ball to the 1 before Trahan crashed through. Beasley converted to make it 7-0. A fumble by Utica was recovered by Saint Al to run out the clock.

Two times earlier, the Flashes had threatened. Once was a missed Murray Whitaker FG from the 22 that was blocked and the second ended on a fumble at the Utica 20.

GAME 4:   SAINT AL (3-0) vs TERRY (1-2)
                 FINAL: ST AL 40 TERRY 0
                 September 27, 1974

The Flashes were now a game ahead in the CAC standings. *"They have a good QB who can roll out well and throw well, and a good fullback, too. Terry will be better than Puckett."* The bad news was that Southard was nursing a swollen knee and Lawler was ill with pleurisy during game week.

Saint Al scored in all 4 quarters with the first from Trahan from the 5. The drive took only 3 plays and started from the Jacket 31. Beasley converted the PAT. Five plays later, the Flashes picked off a Terry pass at Terry's 48. Trahan went in from the 1 six plays later. In the 2nd, Trahan punched in his third from the 8 after a 52 yard drive. Beasley made halftime 20-0. The Flashes scored quickly in the 3rd. The first was a 57 yard drive capitalized by Holloway from the 26. The second resulted from a Terry fumble recovered by Steve Jefferson at the Jacket 23. Two plays later, Koestler went in from 10 out. The last Flash score came in the 4th. Starting at the Terry 46, Saint Al used 7 plays before Southard crashed in from the 1. Patrick Beard converted the 2 points to give them a 4-0 CAC record.

GAME 5:   SAINT AL (4-0) @ MADISON RIDGELAND (3-0)
                 FINAL: ST AL 0 MADISON RIDGELAND 7
                 October 4, 1974

"They're tough and extremely quick. They swarm all over you like a bunch of mosquitoes. They've got more offensive formations that we have plays. We've seen them in 13 different sets. It will all be decided Friday night on the chalk, not by some pre-season poll". That was Autrey's description of his opponent, a team described by Coach P.H. Walker as *"the best team he's had at Madison Ridgeland"*. The team was healthy with the exception of James Smith who was out with the flu. *"We'll do what we've been doing all year. They kids have worked hard this week, attitudes are real rippin' good and we're convinced we can win it"*. Captains would be Southard and Whitaker.

The one play that would be remembered would also be the only score of the game. With just 1:52 gone in the game, Robert Russell took a Flash punt back 67 yards for the game's only touchdown. Alvin Carter added the PAT. There were other opportunities in the game for both teams. Madison fell on a Flash fumble at the 15 but the defense held. Another fumble in the 3rd at the Flash 16 ended up at the Flash 5, but the FG by Carter was missed. Steve Jefferson found a Braves fumble at their 43 in the 4th but they couldn't get past the Braves 24.

Madison had only 1 first down and 0 yards in the 1st half of football. *"Our defensive effort was the best of the year. If we get the same effort the rest of the way, we are going to win five more ball games. I really don't see anybody on Madison-Ridgeland's schedule who can stop them. They would have to lose twice now under conference rules, since they beat us. He who gives all is a winner. We gave all we had to give, and as far as I'm concerned, we're will winners. We're the same ball club today that we were before last night's ball game. We had to have maximum effort and we got it. It was our best game of the year. We just couldn't get the ball into the endzone."*

GAME 6:   SAINT AL (4-1) vs BYRAM (3-2)
                 FINAL: ST AL 53 BYRAM 0
                 October 11, 1974

"There's a natural letdown after losing to Madison. But a club with character will come back, and we've got character", said Autrey. With 53 points being scored, a short recap of the contest should suffice.

With 9:25 on the clock, Trahan went in from the 12. He picked off the next pass for a 45 yard touchdown scamper. Holloway finished the quarter with a 10 yard touchdown and, combined with 2 Beasley PATs, it was 20-0. Cockrell started the 2nd with a pick-six of Kerry Robinson for 35 yards and the score and Southard finished a 60 yard drive from the 1 to make it 32-0 at halftime. Beard actually put up one more touchdown at the whistle, but it was called back due to penalty.

The Flashes put up three more before the game was over. Two plays and 35 yards saw Trahan cross from the 7. Southard converted for two points. Lawler picked off Robinson to put the ball at the Byram 30 and Trahan took it in from there on the next play. Finally, Nelson went in from 4 to finish a 49 yard drive and a 53 point victory. Each team had at least one other turnover; Byram with a fumble and Saint Al with an interception.

"We're probably a week too late hitting mid-season form. If we had the same execution against Madison-Ridgeland that we had against Byram, we'd be 6-0 right now. Our kids came back like I knew they would. We played good ball ... because we love the game and we love St. Al, and I don't know of two better reasons for playing."

GAME 7: SAINT AL (5-1) vs PELAHATCHIE (0-6)
FINAL: ST AL 47 PELAHATCHIE 0
October 18, 1974: HOMECOMING

Game week mentality against a winless foe was summed up by Autrey as *"Folks around here still remember the 33-12 upset by Pelahatchie three years ago and our kids are hungry"*.

Trahan took control of the first Saint Al drive, taking each of the 5 plays for 34 yards and a touchdown from the 3. Beasley added the PAT. Two plays later, Head recovered a Pelahatchie fumble at the Chief 32. Trahan scored again, this time from the 5 to seal an 8 play drive. Saint Al came up with the ball again a few minutes later at their 40. Lawler then hit Koestler to the Chief 7 and, after a penalty, Nelson went 13 for the score. Southard blocked a Pelahatchie punt at the Chief 2 and Trahan went in from the 3 two plays later. Beasley made halftime a 26-0 Flash lead.

Pelahatchie problems intensified in the 3rd after Southard picked off Mike Kelly and went 26 yards for the touchdown. Later, Lawler hit Koestler for a 36 yard touchdown pass and Beasley converted. In the 4th, Koestler ran in a reverse from the 13 and Beasley again converted to end the game at 47-0.

GAME 8: SAINT AL (6-1) @ JACKSON SAINT JOSEPH (5-2)
FINAL: ST AL 21 JACKSON ST JOE 0
October 25, 1974

The game was one predicted by some to be a Rebel win. It would be first of three straight Catholic school showdowns and with it in Jackson, the Flashes were expected to be in trouble. Thanks to 3 fumbles, 3 interceptions, 3 punt turnovers and keeping Jackson from Flash territory, they weren't.

Forcing a Rebel fumble late in the 2nd, Trahan went in from the 2 and Beasley added the PAT to make it 7-0. In the scoreless 3rd, Saint Al controlled the ball 21 out of 25 plays. The final two touchdowns by the Flashes would be in the 4th. A 47 yard drive in 8 plays resulted in a Southard touchdown from the 4. Shortly afterwards, and starting at the Flash 34, Nelson went in from the 1 after 11 plays. Lawler hit Trahan for the 2 points. Koestler sealed the win on a last second interception.

Autrey was ecstatic. *"(This is) the finest rippin' effort I've ever seen by a high school football team!"*

GAME 9: SAINT AL (7-1) vs NATCHEZ CATHEDRAL (3-5)
FINAL: ST AL 27 NATCHEZ CATHEDRAL 0
November 1, 1974

The Greenies had ruined the perfect season attempt in 1973 with a 6-0 upset. *"When two Catholic schools get together, you can throw the records out the window."* Trahan was hampered with an injured knee, Koestler had a bad ankle and shoulder, and Holloway was suffering from a hip-pointer.

The Flashes started early after a Greenie fumble by Glen Foley that was returned 38 yards for a touchdown by David Baylot. Two drives later, with Saint Al was starting at their 49, Trahan and Koestler drove the ball to the Greenie 5. Trahan then scored from there to start the 2nd. James Smith intercepted an Ed D'Antoni pass and brought it back to the Natchez 20 but the offense could not convert. Immediately after getting the ball back after a Greenie punt to the Flash 45, Trahan broke off the remaining 55 yards on a touchdown run. Beasley's kick was good for a 20-0 lead. Koestler was next with an interception returned to the Flash 39 but there would be no further movement before halftime.

The Flashes put up their last points in the 3rd after a punt kept them at the Flash 39. Trahan and Nelson moved the ball to the Greenie 1 and Trahan plunged over for the score. Beasley iced the game at 27-0. Two more Flash possessions resulted in an interception and a fumble but Natchez could not take advantage of the gifts.

"Physically, they were as tough a club as we've played this year. They hit us hard. We did a good job considering the fact that we didn't really get fired up for the game. We were flat in spots and

executed rather poorly at times, but our offensive line did a good job of picking up Natchez's stunts." Cathedral managed only 24 yards of rushing due to the stalwart defense.

GAME 10:   SAINT AL (8-1) vs GREENVILLE SAINT JOSEPH (UNREPORTED)
                 FINAL: ST AL 27 GREENVILLE ST JOE 0
                 November 8, 1974

The Irish would be the biggest opponent of the year *"featuring a defensive line the size of a pro team"*. Said Autrey, *"If David beat Goliath and the Indians beat Custer, then we can beat St. Joseph"*. That "Goliath" measured 290, 271, 257, and 235 up front. *"I believe our kids will be ready. It's the last home game for our seniors and we should be mentally right. For our seniors, it's been a fairly successful high school football career. I think they've got too much pride to end it on anything short of a winning effort"*. The Flashes had two starters suffering from a virus during game week. Southard and Holloway were tabbed "doubtful" as a result.

It took Saint Al until the 2nd before Holloway broke off a 58 yard run for a touchdown. With Beasley's PAT, it was 7-0. They had fumbled away one opportunity in the 1st and looked lifeless until Holloway's run. With :18 left in the half, Lawler hit Koestler for a 30 yard touchdown that followed a David Baylot fumble recovery. The 14-0 halftime lead came with a cost; that being a separated shoulder by Koestler that would finish his season.

Saint Al put up their last two regular season touchdowns in the 4th. Smith hit the endzone from the 8 to cap a 52 yard drive highlighted by a Trahan 13 yard run. Later, Joe McCain picked off Mike Campbell and went 51 yards for the final score. Said McCain, *"It feels great. I just got lucky. Coach said keep an outside rush on the QB and I was there"*. Afterwards, it was announced that the Flashes would accept the invitation to play in The Red Carpet Bowl. The opponent was to be determined.

GAME 11:   SAINT AL (9-1) vs TALLULAH, LA (6-3-1)
                 FINAL: ST AL 20 TALLULAH 0
                 November 29, 1974: RED CARPET BOWL

On November 15th, the paper announced the matchup against Tallulah, LA. It would be the second Flash appearance in the RCB; the last one being a 1971 loss to Warren Central. Billy Ray, the sports writer who died earlier in the season, was one of the founders and the game would be dedicated to his honor. A $500 scholarship to Mississippi State University (Billy's alma mater) was in store for one recipient.

Saint Al's opponent was also a small school that barely lost their conference title. They had outscored opponents 153-87 while the Flashes posted a 284-23 record. *"They are a well-coached, well-disciplined aggressive club. They are as sound fundamentally as any team we've seen this year"*. Both teams had been off since November 8th, and Autrey commented by saying, *"I believe they've got enough pride in themselves and St. Aloysius to meet the challenge. Practice has improved each day, and based on Thursday's workout, I'm convinced we're ready"*.

Both Autrey and Don Pennington were ex-Mississippi College graduates and teammates at Morton High School. Many Flashes made statements about the importance of this bowl game. Trahan may have been best in saying, *"Sometimes you wonder whether or not it's all worth the pain and hard work, especially those long, hot hours in the late summer. But when it comes to this, you realize that it is"*.

The Flash defense assisted in the first touchdown when Holloway caused Ronnie Jones to fumble a screen pass. Whitaker picked it up and took it 15 yards to the Trojan 33. Five Trahan runs took the ball to the 17 before he was able to convert three runs later. In the 2nd, Greg Head fell on a Marty Nolan fumble at their 32. Holloway went in from the 6 five plays later and then converted the two-pointer for a 14-0 lead. Their last points came in the 3rd on a 69 yard drive. Holloway again hit paydirt on a run from the 26. Though the PAT was unsuccessful, the game was not. Saint Al would win their final game and the Red Carpet Bowl.

Southard won the game's *"Most Outstanding Offensive Player"* while Lynn Jefferson received *"Most Outstanding Defensive Player"*.

When All CAC selections were announced, the Flashes were well-represented. Murray Whitaker received *"Most Outstanding Lineman"* and other first-teamers included Chuck Trahan, Lynn

Jefferson, David Baylot, and Dennis Southard. Honorable Mentions went to Mike Koestler, Greg Head, David Holloway, Patrick Beard, John Smith, Robert Koestler and James Smith. Chuck Trahan would take the CAC Scoring Leader award with 118 points. That was well above Madison Ridgeland's Jackson with 68. Murray Whitaker won the Virgadamo Trophy.

"The fellowship I experienced during my time as a player at Saint Al far exceeded any further experiences that I've had in my life. It was a special time; a special moment never forgotten."

Murray Whitaker, MD; August 8, 2016

1975 (9-0-2)

After just one year as Saint Aloysius football mentor, Tommy Autrey left a 10-1 team with a bowl win to turn around a Jim Hill High School program with 3 wins in the last two years. The Flashes put their program in the hands of Les Bumgarner, a varsity assistant coach from Warren Central. He retained Bob Hitchins as an assistant but added Tom Johnson to replace Richard Gontz.

With at least 9 key players lost to graduation, Bumgarner was expected to be in "rebuilding" mode. Madison Ridgeland, returning 12 lettermen from the CAC title year, was expected to repeat as champions. *"We've got a long way to go. We're actually a spring training behind everybody else. We're already young in the line with only one senior and two lettermen. We've got a good group of backs but we've got to work hard."*

That hard work opened on August 11th with two-a-days through the 22nd. Midway through, the coach was pleased with the progress. *"I believe we're a little ahead of schedule. They're picking up the new system real well. We're getting good leadership from our upperclassmen and attitudes are good. They have been through some hard practices this past week. These kids have a winning attitude and a lot of pride."*

GAME 1: SAINT AL (0-0) vs RAYMOND (0-0)
FINAL: ST AL 0 RAYMOND 0
September 5, 1975

Raymond was a perennially tenacious CAC opponent. *"We've got a lot of respect for them, but we've worked real hard and I think we're ready."* In the game, offense was non-existent with the deepest penetration no deeper than the Ranger 25. And that play was called back for illegal procedure. The game could easily have been chalked up in the Raymond win column. In the 4th, a Rangers 25 yard FG attempt by Richard Garrison was blocked by Dennis Southard. As the game closed, Ray Smith blocked a David Holloway punt that gave Raymond the ball at the Flash 30. They got as far as the Flash 10 behind a pass from Garrison to Gil Gillespie, but the defense under Bart Neal, Steve Jefferson, Kyle Flowers and Dennis Southard stopped the threat with no time remaining.

GAME 2: SAINT AL (0-0-1) vs PUCKETT (0-1)
FINAL: ST AL 21 PUCKETT 0
September 12, 1975

Bumgarner wasn't happy with the *"punchless offense"*. *"We've been working on blocking assignments and techniques of our offensive line especially and we see some improvement. We've corrected a lot of the mistakes we made last week. We're still looking for somebody to step forward and take over. We've got a lot of potential leaders sitting back and waiting for someone else, and we've got a lot of folks who are leading themselves but not the team."*

Holloway was ill during the week and his status was uncertain. Southard would also be less than 100% with a leg injury. That paled in comparison to what was to come. Approximately an hour and a half before kickoff, Bumgarner received the news that his mother had died in an automobile accident. Handing the reigns over to Hitchens, the coach left for Jackson to be with his family, but not before telling the assistant to *"not let the team get carried away with emotions"*.

The Flashes first score came in the 2nd behind a *"bone-jarring"* tackle by Ricky Cockrell on Frank Morehouse. The back fumbled into the waiting hands of James Smith who took it 20 yards for the touchdown. In the 3rd, John Smith ran one in from the 10 and in the 4th, the Flashes went to the air. Smith hit Cockrell twice for 14 and 20 yards with the last catch being a touchdown. Beasley added all three PATs.

Puckett threatened once in the 2nd half when Steve Miley found Cleve Brown for 49 yards at the Flash 8. Puckett ended up fumbling on 4th down to be recovered by Southard. In desperation, they began passing in the 4th, but Southard and Pinkston each picked off a Wolves pass. Said Hitchins, "*Puckett didn't think we could run on them because Madison-Ridgeland couldn't. But we improved 100% in our offensive line from last week*". The victory was dedicated to Coach Bumgarner.

GAME 3:   SAINT AL (1-0-1) vs UTICA (1-1)
                      FINAL: ST AL 6 UTICA 0
                      September 19, 1975: HOMECOMING

Bumgarner said of his team "*I think we're going to be alright. We grew up a lot last week … we've got to continue to improve. Overall it was a real fine effort. We still made a few mistakes, but we did a lot of things right.*" Coach Terry Clark's Gold Wave was a running team. "*Like us, they play a lot of boys both ways, so conditioning will probably play a key factor in the outcome. They've got a young secondary, so we're going to try to throw more on them*".

There would be only one score in the contest, that coming in the 1st. Utica punter Kenny Broome muffed the kick and the Flashes recovered in Wave territory. Southard gained 3, Smith hit Southard for 13, Southard gained 2, and Koestler gained 10 to the Wave 1. Smith picked up his fumbled snap and took it in for the score. The Flashes got back to the Wave 10 later but fumbled over to Utica's Arthur Durse. Another fumble in the 4th was left scoreless by the Flash defense. Ricky Cockrell also got an interception off of Henry Drayton.

"*You're always happy to win, but we fumbled away two other scoring chances and had seven bobbled snaps. We're making too many mistakes. We're missing too many blocks. While our line is blocking much better, we still aren't blocking as a unit. I couldn't ask for any more out of (the defense). They've put up five goal-line stands inside the 10 in three games*".

GAME 4:   SAINT AL (2-0-1) @ TERRY (1-1)
                      FINAL: ST AL 33 TERRY 0
                      September 26, 1975

As the clock was winding down in the 2nd, the Flashes picked off a Terry pass at their 42. Five run plays by Koestler, Southard and Holloway put the ball at the Terry 5. Southard capped it with :46 remaining and Beasley gave the Flashes the 7-0 halftime lead. The first possession of the 3rd had the Flashes starting at their 28. Smith pitched out to Gerald Maxey who then found Cockrell for a 72 yard touchdown to make it 13-0. An eight-play drive later in the quarter resulted in a Southard dive from the 1. The Flashes padded their lead when Maxey picked off Tommy Burleson and ended up at the Yellow Jacket 25. Southard took it the distance on the next play and the two-pointer from Smith to Southard made it 27-0. Cockrell ended the 3rd with the second Flash interception.

The final quarter had a mix of starters and reserves. Maxey, now at QB, handed off to Holloway and he slipped in from the 5 for the final points. Murray Pinkston had exited the game in the 2nd with a badly sprained ankle. The next week, he was on crutches. Said the coach about prospects against Madison Ridgeland, "*… if he plays, he won't be anywhere near 100 percent*".

GAME 5:   SAINT AL (3-0-1) vs MADISON RIDGELAND (4-0)
                      FINAL: ST AL 7 MADISON RIDGELAND 7
                      October 3, 1975

The winner would have the upper hand at the CAC title. Madison had 18 consecutive wins with the last being to Saint Al. The Flashes had last lost to Madison Ridgeland and boasted 9 straight wins with 10 shutouts (Raymond was a tie). Noted Bumgarner, "*They have a lot of quick backs and a good passing attack. They have overall team speed and are real aggressive. They react real well to the football and we feel like play action passes, traps and counters ought to go because they pursue so well.*"

In the 1st, a Southard punt was fumbled by James Smith in Braves territory. Five plays later, Southard bullied in from the 1 and Beasley's PAT made it 7-0. The Braves added their only score in the 2nd after a Flash fumble at the Saint Al 46. After 16 rushes, future USM star Sammy Winder took it in from the 1 and Bobby Malone added the PAT. In the 3rd, the Flashes attempted a 47 yard Southard FG, but it fell short.

The 4th was full of action but no points. Robert Russell picked off a Flash pass, Southard blocked a FG with :50 on the clock, and Smith picked off a Brave pass with no time left but could get no further than the Brave 39. *"I felt we played well enough to win. We outplayed them, but just weren't able to take advantage of a couple of scoring opportunities"*, said Bumgarner. Amazingly, both teams had 35 rush attempts and the Braves bested Saint Al only by 1 yard (105-104).

GAME 6:   SAINT AL (3-0-2) @ BYRAM (3-2)
                          FINAL: ST AL 47 BYRAM 0
                          October 10, 1975

Pent-up frustrations over their second tie of 1975 were taken out on Byram. The Flashes put up 395 rushing yards even with 135 yards of penalties against them. On their first possession, the Flashes went 86 yards in 14 plays with Southard scoring from the 1. Smith found Southard on a fake for the two points. James Smith scored from the Bulldog 8 to start the 2nd, Koestler added another from the 1 and Holloway added the fourth from the 3. Southard set up the score with a 21 yard run. At halftime, it was 27-0.

Saint Al started at the 25 to open the 2nd half. A few plays afterwards, from their own 29, Smith hit James Smith for 71 yards and the score. The next touchdown was a 59-yard run from Southard and Beasley made it 40-0. Maxey came in to lead the game late in the 3rd. Driving them 85 yards, he finished the scoring with a 15 yard keeper with 4:15 left. Beasley made it 47-0.

GAME 7:   SAINT AL (4-0-2) @ PELAHATCHIE (1-5)
                          FINAL: ST AL 41 PELAHATCHIE 12
                          October 17, 1975

The 1-5 home team stunned the Flashes by getting on the board first after a Holloway fumble at the Flash 26. After 5 running plays, Harold McGee faked a pitch and hit Earl Jordan for a 20 yard score. The Flashes responded 3 plays later when Cockrell dashed 50 yards for the score. Beasley put them up 7-6. On the next Flash possession, Southard broke off a 43 yard touchdown run and Holloway added 2. Southard scored again after runs of 43 and 8. Holloway ran in to make it 23-6. Southard would score again before halftime, this one from 69 yards out after a Koestler gain of 18.

The Flashes scored twice in the 3rd with a Koestler 19 yard run and Holloway 12-yarder. The last was set up by a Cockrell punt block of McGee at the Chief 39. With reserves on the field, the Chiefs dotted the board for the final points with :30 left when McGee hit Duane Lock from the 43. *"We got after them pretty good"* said Bumgarner while heaping praise on Southard, James Smith and the offensive line.

GAME 8:   SAINT AL (5-0-2) vs JACKSON SAINT JOSEPH (5-2)
                          FINAL: ST AL 30 JACKSON SAINT JOE 7
                          October 24, 1975

CAC games were over and, with their 5-0-2 record, they would have to hope that Raymond and Madison-Ridgeland would tie to gain the title. For now, JSJ had 9 seniors on the squad and were *"probably the most physical team we'll face. It's a big game."*

For the second straight week, the opponent got on the board first. Saint Joe drove 78 yards in 10 plays behind a 49 yard run by Al Nuzzo. Maxey made the initial touchdown-saving tackle, but Mike Henderson dove in from the 1 and then converted the PAT. Two plays later Saint Al answered with a 60 yard Southard touchdown set up by a slashing kickoff return by James Smith. Southard converted on a pass from Smith to make it 8-7.

The Flashes scored again on their next possession in 10 plays covering 68 yards. Smith found Hollway from the 13 and then hit Southard for the two-pointer. Cockrell picked off a Rebel pass two plays afterwards and then John Smith finished the 31 yard drive from the 6. Beasley was good to make it 22-7 at half. Nuzzo would be done for the game with an injured leg after 74 yards on 8 carries. Saint Al put one more touchdown up in the 4th after Holloway fell on a Rebel fumble at their 38. The drive was iced with :50 left to go when Southard ran in from the 3 and Smith hit Cockrell for the 2.

"It was a tremendous team effort. We did a good job of controlling the line of scrimmage." Bumgarner also praised a number of Flashes on their efforts and commented on the loss of Robert

Koestler with a separated shoulder. *"It'll be a big loss on the team. Other folks are going to have to step in and take up the slack".*

GAME 9:   SAINT AL (6-0-2) @ NATCHEZ CATHEDRAL (5-3)
FINAL: ST AL 41 NATCHEZ CATHEDRAL 19
October 31, 1975

Coming off of a big win, the coach said *"It was such a big win for us; I hope we don't have a letdown. (They) are a power team. Not a lot of finesse; they just line up and run at you."*

Saint Al struck quick on the road. On the first play, John Smith gained 42 and 5 plays later Holloway dove in from the 2. Beasley made it 7-0. Cathedral took advantage of a Flash fumble at the 6 with a 2 yard score by D'Antoni. McKinney's PAT tied it. The Flashes added a score in the 2nd on a 53 yard drive finished by a Holloway 13 yard touchdown. He also picked off a Greenie pass at the Flash 13 and finished that drive with a 3 yard score. Smith's two-point conversion made it 21-7 going into the locker room.

Holloway wasn't done. He scored again in the 3rd from the 3 and Smith converted for the 2. On the next Cathedral possession, the Greenies fumbled at the 34 and Mike Patton recovered. Smith hit Cockrell from the 28 for the touchdown. The last tally came from the same duo when Smith hit Cockrell from the 10. Cathedral was able to add two more touchdowns before the end of the game in front of Saint Al reserves with runs by D'Antoni (1) and David (1). Both PATs were unsuccessful.

GAME 10:   SAINT AL (7-0-2) @ GREENVILLE SAINT JOSEPH (2-7)
FINAL: ST AL 35 GREENVILLE SAINT JOE 0
November 7, 1975

The Mississippi Bowl and the Sturgis Lions Bowl had both shown interest in post-season contests, *"but we won't know anything before Saturday".* Kyle Lawler was finally back after a hand injury and the coach said of the Irish, *"They've had a lot of hard luck, but they have a scrappy ball club. We're looking for a fight out of them".* In the contest, only 8 reserves were on the Irish sideline while all Flashes were able to play.

Saint Al's first drive of 70 yards in 10 plays saw a Southard touchdown from the 3. The PAT was a Smith to Cockrell pass of 35 yards. On the ensuing drive, the Irish's Harold Permenter was picked off by Holloway but the Flashes could not cash in until the 2nd. There Holloway scored from the 1 later followed by a Smith to Cockrell 13 yard touchdown pass. Two Beasley PATs and a Smith interception of Permenter would make the halftime score 21-0.

The Flashes started their first drive of the 3rd with a fumble that was recovered by Peter Sherman. Shortly afterwards, Smith was picked off by the Irish at their 20. The defense rose both times to hold GSJ to effectively no gain. Southard increased the lead and his scoring totals by putting two more into the endzone. The first was 4 yard run and the second was from the 1. Smith converted the two-pointer after the first Southard score.

The Flashes announced after the game that they had unanimously voted to accept an invitation to The Mississippi Bowl in Clinton. The opponent was not announced.

GAME 11:   SAINT AL (8-0-2) vs MADISON RIDGELAND (9-0-1)
FINAL: ST AL 7 MADISON RIDGELAND 6
November 22, 1975

On Monday, the Mississippi Bowl announced that Saint Al would be enjoying a rematch with CAC champion Madison Ridgeland. An official delegation came to the school for signatures and a photo opportunity. MR was bringing a 24 game winning streak against Saint Al's 16 games. It would not be for CAC title, but it would be for pride. *"… we wouldn't be playing them again if we didn't want to prove we've got a better ball club. We're just not satisfied with the tie. Madison is a powerful, experienced team. If they have a weakness, we're still looking for it. I think maybe they want a replay because they didn't play a good game. They didn't give us any credit for playing a good game."*

Madison gave Saint Al a gift in the 1st on a fumble caused by Steve Jefferson that was recovered by Matt Patton at the Braves 13. Southard converted from the 1 and Beasley made it 7-0. The Flashes came close to scoring on their very first possession but got no further than the Braves 7. A Smith fumble at the Madison 9 in the 2nd was another close call. In the 3rd, Maxey picked off a Bubba

Martin pass and returned it 63 yards to the 9. The response from the Braves didn't come until the 4th after Edward Bracy ran in from the 13 to cap an 80 yard drive. Bubba Martin's PAT was no good and the Flashes had all they would need. The Flashes almost added to the lead but a Southard FG of 42 yards was wide left.

Southard won "Outstanding Offensive Back" while Jefferson won "Outstanding Defensive Lineman". And Bumgarner, after the All-CAC selection debacle, had to be happy his prediction that *"Our kids will be out to prove that they are more deserving of recognition"* was realized.

Southard ended up winning the Virgadamo Trophy and the CAC scoring title with 92 points. John Smith also took home the honor of league leader in touchdown passes with 10. Three other Flashes accounted for 116 points on the season.

All CAC awards were announced on November 21st. Southard, named "Most Outstanding Back", shared first team honors with Matt Patton and Steve Jeffferson. Honorable Mentions went to David Holloway, Ricky Cockrell, James Smith, John Smith, Kyle Flowers, Steve Holloway, Murray Pinkston, Mark Koestler, Robert Koestler and Denis Hogan. Bumgarner was not pleased. *"We felt like we deserved more than three players on the team. Pelahatchie, a team we beat 41-12, also had three picks and their record ... was 1-5-1. Puckett had two players and they were 1-6 in conference play"*.

He went further by saying, *"I feel like some of the coaches got together, and I won't say that they voted against us, but they voted for each other's' players. I felt like we had four other players (Cockrell, Holloway, the Smith brothers) that were really done an injustice. We had only two touchdowns scored on our defense in the CAC and we had only one player to make the defensive team."*

1976 (7-3-1)

There was rebuilding to be done, but Bumgarner did have two players (Gerald Maxey and Tommy Alonzo) up to the task for QB. Maxey would eventually go to the RB spot. *"I believe with good leadership and barring a rash of injuries, we should be in the thick of the race for the conference title"*. Though hurt by lack of depth, he noted *"We don't have a lot of kids out, but those we have have shown a lot of dedication. We haven't been able to scrimmage enough due to the lack of depth, but we've looked good in the three scrimmages we've had"*. The Flashes would hit the road for the first three contests in a string Bumgarner noted as *"...the three toughest conference opponents we'll play and all of them back-to-back on the road. It makes the challenge that much greater. If we come back 3-0, they had better watch out for us"*.

GAME 1:   SAINT AL (0-0) @ RAYMOND (0-0)
                   FINAL: ST AL 2 RAYMOND 0
                   September 3, 1976

The last two years were played to a 0-0 tie. Thanks to turnovers, this year would be the same until the 4th. The Flashes fumbled in the 1st, had three-straight miscues in the 2nd, two more in the 3rd and a couple in the 4th. Added to that, the Flashes were picked off by Odis Harvey in the 1st at the Ranger 21. *"I have never seen anything like it"*, said Bumgarner.

Saint Al was attempting to close the game late in the 4th but fumbled on the Raymond 4 on an Alonzo pitchout to Maxey. However, with 2:29 left, the Flash defense led by Tim Beasley and Mark Koestler was able to sack Drew Walker (or Jeff Allen) for a safety and the win. *"We need to work on our goal line offense. We made several crucial mistakes inside the 10. We've got a long way to go to be as good as we were last year. We looked good. We averaged 4.8 yards per carry on the ground. I was especially pleased with the way our young line blocked. They did a good job opening holes. We just couldn't hold onto the football."*

GAME 2:   SAINT AL (1-0) vs PUCKETT (1-0)
                   FINAL: ST AL 46 PUCKETT 6
                   September 10, 1976

Bumgarner scouted Puckett on the 2nd during their 21-0 rip of Pisgah and pronounced that *"We're going to have our hands full if we bog down our offense"*. Ricky Cockrell had the flu game week but would play at RB by game time. The coach was also switching numerous players around to give rest and experience. Instead of nine players going both ways, he planned on only six.

The Flashes put up 376 yards while holding the Wolves to 87 (64 on one play). Scoring was early and often. In the 1st Cockrell took it in from the 1. In the 2nd, a 57 yard Maxey reverse (with a leap over a defender for good measure) put them up 12-0. Cockrell converted the 2 pointer. Maxey hauled in a 32 yard pass at the Wolves 10 in the same quarter and was rewarded with an 8 yard touchdown carry. Tim Beasley's kick was good. Before halftime, Mike Koestler picked off a Puckett pass and brought it back 35 yards to the Wolves 20. Alonzo found Marty Randall from the 16 to make it 27-0.

The Flashes added to the lead in the 3rd on a 63 yard drive with Battalio plunging in from the 4 and Beasley adding the PAT. Puckett's only score came toward the end of the quarter on a surprise 64 yard pass from James Anderson to Clifton Mangum. In the 4th, Maxey took the helm and hit Jay Barnett from the 16 score. Koestler added the last Flash touchdown.

GAME 3:   SAINT AL (2-0) @ UTICA (1-1)
FINAL: ST AL 0 UTICA 0
September 17, 1976

The previous two games against Utica had been 7-0 and 6-0 wins. This CAC game was predicted to "be a dandy". Said Bumgarner, "This one could be for all the marbles. They … are tough to beat down there. We've got to win this one because we could stumble somewhere down the road". Denis Hogan had a badly bruised elbow, sat out of practice on doctor's orders and "… definitely won't start and may not play at all, depending on how the game is going".

The only serious threat in the game from Utica came in the initial quarter. They had driven 57 yards to the Flash 1, but a Don Taylor fumble was recovered by Murray Pinkston. Saint Al got to the Wave 13 but missed a 42 yard FG attempt. Chris Cox contributed by recovering 2 Utica fumbles. Hogan didn't play and was joined by an injured Matt Patton with a right ankle sprain in the 1st.

"I feel like we had a real good effort most of the time. Injuries to key personnel, fumbles, penalties, and poor execution at times on offense definitely hurt us. It seemed like every time we got something going, one of those things happened to kill it. We've got to work on putting together a sustained drive. It was one of the hardest hitting games I've seen in a long time. Utica was sky-high for us. I was proud of our defense for the way it stopped them on the goal line."

GAME 4:   SAINT AL (2-0-1) vs TERRY (2-1)
FINAL: ST AL 27 TERRY 6
September 24, 1976

A win against Terry would be crucial to another CAC title. "Terry is coming in here … and if we don't rededicate ourselves this week, we could be in trouble". Practices went well during the week, so much so that Bumgarner said "We've had the best practices this week that we've had all year. Our seniors have gotten together and held a couple of team meetings. We're beginning to get the kind of leadership we've got to have. Attitudes and team spirit are better than at any time this fall. I guess sometimes it takes adversity to get a group pulling together".

The Flashes scored on their first two possessions. In the 1st, it was an Alonzo pass from the 16 to Randall to cap a 67 yard drive. In the 2nd, it was a 99 yard push capped by an Alonzo 15 yard touchdown pass to Cockrell. Carlos Lee, making his Saint Al debut, converted both PATs. They actually added one more on a Maxey 85 yard touchdown run, but it was called back for illegal motion.

The only 3rd quarter score came from Terry on a 53 yard drive highlighted by a 20 yard touchdown pass from Burleson to Brown. Saint Al iced the game in the 4th with two more scores. The first was set up by a Koestler sack of Burleson causing a fumble he also recovered on the Jacket 14. Three plays later Randall caught one from the 6. Greg Evans helped on the last score with an interception at the Terry 43 that was returned to the 4. Cockrell converted it from the 3. Bumgarner called it "one of our better efforts. Our backs did a better job of running with the ball this week, too."

GAME 5:   SAINT AL (3-0-1) vs LELAND (3-1)
FINAL: ST AL 19 LELAND 22
October 1, 1976

Leland was "the perennial kingpins of the Delta Valley Conference" and finished 1975 at 10-0. They also had a 20 game win streak that dated back to October of 1974. "It's the first time in several years that St. Al has taken on a team the caliber of Leland. It gives us a chance to compare ourselves with a team from a larger conference and an opportunity to see just what we're made of. They have a fine team. Their strength lies in their defense. They are quick and pursue extremely well. It's hard to break the long one on them".

Saint Al started well in the 1st on a 34 yard Battalio touchdown run. Leland came right back with a Frank Broussard score from the 2 to make it 7-6 in favor of Saint Al. The Flashes punched back with a 1 yard touchdown by Cockrell and a Lee PAT in the 2nd. But Leland was good for a response when a bad punt snap went over Cockrell's head and gave the ball to the Cubs at the Flash 9. Broussard plunged in on the next play and added the two-pointer. Halftime was a Leland lead of 14-13.

The Flashes regained the lead on their second possession of the 3rd. A drive of 82 yards in 20 plays resulted in a Battalio touchdown from one foot away. They attempted the two-pointer but it failed. As time wound down, Alonzo picked off a Cubs pass for 19 yards to the Leland 40. They got as far as the 9 but a 26 yard FG was missed. It was here that Leland completed a 19 yard pass from Jackie Blaylock to A.J. Jones and added a 15 yard run by Anthony Gray to the Flash 49. On 4th and 14, Blaylock found a gap and took the ball the distance for the game winner and added the PAT. The Flashes could get only to the Cub 42 before turning the ball back over on downs.

Said Bumgarner, "It's a shame to put forth as good an effort as we did and make two or three errors and lose the game. We really took it to them. Our kids did everything we asked of them. We were pleased with the way we controlled the ball. We held our mistakes to a minimum, but those we made were costly." Leland coach Butch Inman reportedly told Bumgarner that they "hadn't had anybody drive the ball on them like (St Al) did in five years".

GAME 6:   SAINT AL (3-1-1) vs BYRAM (3-2)
                 FINAL: ST AL 64 BYRAM 0
                 October 8, 1976

According to Bumgarner, "Byram has a good team. We'll try to pick up where we left off last week." The only injury for the week was Tim Beasley who had suffered bruised ribs against Leland.

The first three possessions were touchdowns, each from runs coming behind no-huddle offenses. Cockrell capped a 70 yard drive from the 4 and added the 2 points. A Byram fumble on the next possession allowed Cockrell to slam in from the 4. In the same quarter, starting at their 30 and after a Cockrell gain of 31, Maxey raced in from the 24. Battalio added the 2 points.

Byram fumbled again in the 2nd and on the 6th play, Koestler scored from the 3. Alonzo got the call for the 2. A Mike Ray interception was later matched by a Donnie Head pickoff, and Saint Al went 55 yards in 9 plays before Cockrell ran his third touchdown. Lee made it 37-0 at halftime. It appeared that Byram would avoid the shutout in the 3rd at the Flash 1, but their third fumble set up the next Flash touchdown. Alonzo took it over from the 1 and Lee made it 44-0. They made it 51-0 in the quarter when a 60 yard drive was highlighted by a 22 yard Maxey touchdown and a Lee PAT.

The Flashes added two more scores in the 4th. Set up by a Cockrell run of 56, Battalio went in from the 4 and Lee converted. Head ended the game on a two yard dive. Tim DeRossette finalized things with another interception. Cockrell had "well over 100 yards in rushing" and Maxey and Battalio "turned in 100-yard performances".

GAME 7:   SAINT AL (4-1-1) vs PELAHATCHIE (3-1)
                 FINAL: ST AL 0 PELAHATCHIE 8
                 October 15, 1976

The biggest game of the year was now in Vicksburg. A win over Pelahatchie would give them the inside track for the CAC title. A loss would take everything out of their hands.

The first three quarters were scoreless, but Saint Al was ahead in first downs (10-3) and offense (173-69). The bad news was that Tim Beasley appeared to have broken his collar bone. Pelahatchie threatened in the 3rd by getting to the Flash 2 but the defense stood tall and denied them. In the 4th, however, the Chiefs were able to complete two passes (10 and 20 yards) taking them deep into Flash territory. Scottie Irwin pushed in from the 2 at the end of the game and Moses Beeman converted the 2.

Saint Al attempted to make good on their final opportunity. Alonzo hit receivers for 14, 15, 14 and 13 yards in successive passes. But his last was tipped and picked off by Duana Lock to finish things. Said Bumgarner, "It seemed like something happened every time we got into scoring position. I felt like we controlled the game in the first half, but they made up their minds they could play with us *and came back after us in the second half. They showed a lot of respect for us. We didn't show enough for them."*

GAME 8:   SAINT AL (4-2-1) @ JACKSON SAINT JOSEPH (UNREPORTED)
                             FINAL: ST AL 8 JACKSON SAINT JOE 0
                             October 22, 1976

Saint Al's destiny for the title was out of their hands. *"We had it (CAC title) in our hands and let it slip away".* Of his upcoming opponent, the coach said, *"Nobody wants to beat us any worse than they do. The kids are accepting of the fact that we got beat and we are getting ready for St. Joe. They are getting that fire in their eyes. I can't think of a better team to come back with than (them). It is our biggest game of the year and last week's loss makes it even bigger..."* Beasley was out for the season with his injury.

The Flashes scored the only points of the contest in the 2nd. Starting at the Flash 8, Alonzo found Koestler for 28 and then *"it was run,run,run".* On 4th and 1 from the 6, Battalio took it in and Maxey converted the two points. Alonzo had fumbled on an earlier drive to Bobby Franciscato at the Bruin 25 and threw a pick to Bobby Hogg in the 3rd. *"We would drive for seven or eight minutes and then come up with nothing",* said Bumgarner. Cockrell stopped a 4th quarter drive with a hit on QB Mike lupe that caused a fumble recovered by Murray Pinkston. Bumgarner praised downfield blocking by saying *"That's one reason why Cockrell has such a good night".*

The game was marred in the final seconds by a fight that even included some fans. *"Instructed to take two steps in the remaining seven seconds of the game, Flashes QB Tommy Alonzo ran out the time playing tag with Bruin defenders."* Bruin head man Bill Raphael said *"I regret the incident at the end of the game because it's no indicative of either school. It's a big rivalry and with high school kids concerned, it's hard to control."* Bumgarner echoed that. *"Both teams were aggressive and fired up and the tension was a little high".*

GAME 9:   SAINT AL (5-2-1) vs NATCHEZ CATHEDRAL (2-6)
                             FINAL: ST AL 34 NATCHEZ CATHEDRAL 6
                             October 29, 1976: HOMECOMING/POSTPONED

The coach warned about Homecoming activities shading the job at hand. *"...there are a lot of activities going on and we've got to guard against getting sidetracked to the point where we forget about the main event. Natchez Cathedral has been up and down this year and we expect them to be up for us. Natchez always gives St. Al a good game."* The coach would not have to worry about Homecoming festivities. *"A bone-chilling rainstorm"* in 40 degree weather postponed festivities until the following week and resulted in *"fewer than 200 spectators"* on hand. Koestler would miss with a pinched nerve in his shoulder.

The first Flash score came on their second possession; a drive of 80 yards in 15 plays highlighted by 51 yards of Cockrell runs before Maxey scored from the 17. Cathedral appeared ready to match the Flashes and opened the 2nd with a 54 yard touchdown pass from Charles Westmoreland to Joe McCoy to even it at 6. Cathedral also missed a 35 yard FG in the quarter. With seconds remaining until half, and sitting at his 10, Cockrell burst through the middle and followed blockers 90 yards for the go-ahead touchdown. Maxey's run made it 14-6.

On the first possession of the 3rd, Cockrell did it again with an 84 yard touchdown run. Alonzo converted the 2 points. The Greenies were in a giving mood, fumbling to Gerry Galloway on the Flash 45 and then to Head at the Cathedral 40 in the 4th. Cockrell added his third touchdown from the 5 ten plays later. Pete Tarnabine helped the cause with a pick-six from the Cathedral 20 to end the game. Ricky Cockrell had amassed a whopping 262 yards of rushing on the cold and rainy night.

GAME 10:   SAINT AL (6-2-1) vs GREENVILLE SAINT JOSEPH (UNREPORTED)
                             FINAL: ST AL 29 GREENVILLE ST JOE 0
                             November 5, 1976: HOMECOMING

According to Bumgarner, the Irish had *"five kids on the bench that started last year".* Also in the balance was the "Catholic Championship", with Saint Al already beating Saint Joe and Natchez Cathedral. The possibility of a bowl bid was also at stake, and as a stretch, the Flashes could still win the CAC if Terry upset Pelahatchie, but the coach conceded that chances were *"slim".*

For the make-up Homecoming game in weather "*near-freezing*" conditions, the Irish were "*punchless*". Just four minutes into the game. Cockrell ran 54 yards for a touchdown. Maxey converted the 2 points. On the first play of the 2nd, Battalio went in from the 4 after a 12 play drive. Alonzo carried for the PAT to make it 16-0. Battalio put it in again before halftime from the 3 to make it 22-0.

The Irish avoided disaster when two touchdowns were called back to start the 3rd. The Flashes picked off an Irish pass at the Flash 42 afterwards, but an Alonzo pass returned the favor to GSJ four plays later at their 15. The Irish then threw another interception, this one by Jimmy Shamoun to Denis Hogan. The big guy rumbled 73 yards for the last score and Lee added the final points. The 4th was marked by two Alonzo fumbles and another interception by Saint Al.

GAME 11:   SAINT AL (7-2-1) vs BRANDON (8-2)
              FINAL: ST AL 0 BRANDON 26
              November 18, 1976: RED CARPET BOWL

Pelahatchie ended CAC hopes with an 8-0 win, but the Flashes were hosting the 14th Annual Red Carpet Bowl. The Bowl Committee, headed by Herb Wilkinson and Oren Bailess, funded two Vicksburg students with scholarships as a result of the contest. The Flashes would have two-weeks rest but be underdogs against a Little Dixie Conference team. Both coaches were complimentary of one-another. Henry Rath noted that "*They do a lot of things well. They have done a good job. I look for a tough game*", while Bumgarner called Brandon "*a fundamentally sound team and well-coached. We saw them play Pearl and they made few, if any, mistakes. They execute extremely well*".

Brandon hit early in the 1st on a 69 yard march capped by King from the 4. They added a 35 yard pass from Dan Davis to Charles Fletcher in the 2nd, and Fletcher put up his 2nd score after intercepting Alonzo for a 33 yard pickoff return. Randy Robbins kicked the two PATs. Rath said that "*We got a little sloppy just before the half, but that interception picked us up*".

The Bulldogs had gotten deep into Flash territory more than once in the interim and had missed a 32 yard FG. Greg Evans had picked off one threat at the Flash 10. In the 3rd, King added another score from 57 out. Fletcher had already picked off another Flash pass but even with more deep drives by Brandon, they fumbled to Koestler at the Flash 33.

After the game, Toney's Sidewalk Café hosted an event for all participants. David King and Charles Fletcher won awards and Rath was presented with the winner's trophy. Said Bumgarner, "*They were just teeing off on us and smothering everything we tried. We never really got a chance to get our offense going. It was a case of going into a game knowing you've got to play flawless ball and you invariably make mistakes you don't' ordinarily make. We've … met a team just as strong but a lot faster. I'm proud of our kids for not giving up. After that interception it took a lot of courage to come back and give it all they had*".

All CAC awards were announced on November 25th. Murray Pinkston, Matt Patton and Dennis Hogan topped the list. Honorable Mention nods went to Mark Koestler, Joe Battalio, Gerald Maxey, Tim Beasley, Tommy Alonzo and Ricky Cockrell. With his ACT of 30 and numerous community activities, Murray Pinkston won the Vicksburg Warren County Thom McAn Award, an honor to the area's outstanding scholar athlete. He also won the Virgadamo Trophy.

1977 (11-1)

The Capital Athletic Conference underwent a change in 1976; moving to a North and South split with 5 teams in each division. Saint Al was chosen by coaches to be the front-runner for the title. "*We've got a good group of experienced running backs returning. I feel that we will be better this year, but so will Utica, Raymond and Pelahatchie. We should be able to compete for the title.*"

Bumgarner had 5 senior captains in Denis Hogan, Tommy Alonzo, Gerald Maxey, Chris Cox and Donnie Head. "*It's been the difference in our club so far. The leadership we're getting out of our seniors is immeasurable. Team attitudes and hustle have been excellent so far, and I credit much of it to our senior captains.*" He also gained a new player from Maine in a 5-10 170-pounder named John Laboda.

Commenting on one scrimmage, he noted that they "*moved the ball well and should be ready for Utica … with a little polishing up. Our players are aware that this game with Utica is an important one and I think that they are setting their sights now instead of waiting until Friday. I think that we will be ready for Utica Friday night.*"

Utica head man Terry Clark commented "*It's always an honor to play St. Al. They have possibly the finest winning tradition of any small school in the state. Whoever makes the mistakes will come out on the losing end.*" Bumgarner returned the compliment by saying "*Utica is a well-coached team. They are hard to score on, which is evidenced by only 13 points we've been able to score on them in three years. Anytime you've got 10 or 11 people back, you've got to have something. We've done about all we can do to get ready. However, we've got several untested kids in there and if they come around, we'll have a pretty good ball team.*"

GAME 1:   SAINT AL (0-0) vs UTICA (0-0)
             FINAL: ST AL 28 UTICA 6
             September 2, 1977

The Flashes first possession was an "*electrifying*" Tommy Alonzo touchdown pass to Gerald Maxey for 60 yards. In the 2nd, the Wave's Grover Hunter fumbled and gave the ball to Dennis Hogan. Thirty-five yards later, Joe Battalio made them pay with a score from the 1. It was 14-0. Before halftime, Hunter fumbled again and it was Billy Coomes recovering at the Wave 14. On 3rd down, Alonzo found Carl Smith open on a roll-out. By intermission, it was 21-0

In the 3rd, Utica used up 9:30 of the clock driving to the Flash 17 but they couldn't get further. The Flashes responded when Alonzo hit Maxey for a 49 yard touchdown. Carlos Lee made his 4th PAT of the night. Utica scored in the 4th on a 70-yard drive that resulted in a 5-yard pass from James Schuller to McGriggs. The defense stopped the Wave inside the Flash 15 twice with one being an Alonzo interception in the endzone. Utica gained 299 rushing yards (Taylor had 234), prompting Baumgarner to attempt to "*find a couple of stoppers to plug up the holes...*" Utica also ate most of the clock; a whopping 19:53 versus the Saint Al 4:07, but it couldn't compete with Alonzo's 169 yards in passing. Most of those (131 yards) were to Maxey.

Said Bumgarner afterwards, "*You've got to give them a lot of credit. If they hadn't fumbled in the first two times they had the ball, it could have been a different story. Taylor is probably the finest running back we'll see this year.*" Maxey won "Player of the Week" honors.

GAME 2:   SAINT AL (1-0) @ BYRAM (1-0)
             FINAL: ST AL 33 BYRAM 8
             September 9, 1977

The Bulldogs were 1-0 after beating Jackson Saint Andrews 13-8. Bumgarner was concentrating on the previous game, saying "*We missed some blocks and made a few mistakes that we've got to work on. We've got some defensive adjustments to make. We're going back to an 'even' front*". Going into the game, the only injury of note was to Donnie Head. He had gotten a right-eye cut that required six stitches.

On the first possession, Saint Al drove 56 yards in 9 plays. Battalio went in from the 4 to make it 6-0. Holding the Bulldogs on their next drive at the Flash 21, the Flashes went the other way in 10 plays. Alonzo found Carl Smith from the 11 and Carlos Lee made it 14-0 at halftime. In the 3rd, Bulldog QB Mike Statham threw a pick to Tim DeRossette. He raced the 40 yards for the touchdown to make it 20-0. Byram came back when Statham hit Mike Norwood for a 60-yard score followed by a Claude Jackson two-pointer to make it 20-8. The Flashes took the ensuing kick and marched 46 yards in 5 plays. Nelson pushed it over from the 3.

Byram took the next kick, but two plays later they threw yet another interception. After a 54 yard drive in 10 plays, Alonzo ran in from the 10. Lee converted the PAT. "*I still felt like we committed too many turnovers and made too many mistakes*", said Bumgarner. "*We showed a definite improvement in our execution and blocking on offense. We are trying to go for the bomb too much.*"

GAME 3:   SAINT AL (2-0) vs RAYMOND (2-0)
             FINAL: ST AL 21 RAYMOND 0
             September 16, 1977

Nagging injuries hampered scrimmaging this week. Maxey and Smith had muscle and groin issues, while Tony Patton had a bruised calf. While he didn't rule them out for the upcoming game, he said "*I know it's dangerous to be scrimmaging this time of year, but we needed it and we had a good one. We've got to be full speed for Raymond.*" He had watched the Raymond-Pelahatchie game and was impressed. The Rangers outweighed the Flashes by an average of 28 pounds, returned 12 starters from a 7-2-1 team, and had just defeated the defending CAC champions.

The Rangers took the opening possession 53 yards to the Flash 19, but Denis Hogan ended their drive with a sack of Bart Ballard. He also blocked a Mitch Thomas FG attempt afterwards. The Flashes took possession, ran 11 straight times, and capped the drive with a Mike Ray touchdown from the 2. Carlos Lee's PAT was good. The defense stood tall on Raymond's next possession. Standing at the Flash 36, Nelson sacked Ballard for a 5 yard loss and forced a punt. Saint Al took advantage and drove 92 yards with a 40 yard pass from Alonzo to Carl Smith for the touchdown.

Three plays later, Nelson forced a Ballard fumble recovered by Battalio. Saint Al's final touchdown came in the 4th. Battalio (already having 2 fumble recoveries, an interception, and 11 tackles) came up with yet another pick and returned it to the Raymond 40. Alonzo eventually found Carl Smith again, this time for the 10 yard score.

"I am extremely pleased with both our offensive and defensive lines. I felt like we controlled the line of scrimmage. I was real happy with our defense. We're beginning to jell. I was particularly happy with the shutout. I felt Hogan's block of that field goal was a big play. Battalio and Nelson played well, but so did others. It was a good team effort. We were ready." Mike Ray quietly added 147 yards of rushing in the contest. *"I don't think I've ever seen a kid who wants to run the ball as badly as Mike does. He's improving every day."*

GAME 4:   SAINT AL (3-0) @ SAINT ANDREWS (0-3)
              FINAL: ST AL 35 ST ANDREWS 8
              September 23, 1977

Baumgarner knew nothing about Saint Andrews except that he couldn't overlook them. *"St Andrews is having their problems but we still can't take them too lightly. We really don't know what to expect... They keep changing because they've had a lot of injuries and we haven't known how to prepare for them. So we're trying to cover all bases."* The Saints were very small in numbers with only 23 players reported on their roster.

On the first play from scrimmage, Ray went 63 yards for the touchdown to make it 6-0. The next Flash score came on a Saint fumble recovered by Carl Smith at the 45. After 10 plays to the 11, Ray did the honors again. Lee made the PAT and it was 13-0. In the 2nd, Doug Varney hit Kirk Strong at the 34, but fumbled to Saint Al. Though forcing a punt, the Saints fumbled it again at the 26. Five plays later, Battalio went in from 4. Lee's PAT made it 20-0. Saint Andrews scored with 3:52 remaining when a bad snap evaded Battalio and rolled out of the endzone for a safety.

The second half fumbles continued for Saint Andrews. Their opening drive was fumbled into the hands of Matt Halford. Nelson pushed them to the 20 where Alonzo found Smith for the score. Maxey converted to make it 28-2. The Saints got their lone touchdown in the 3rd when sub QB Mike Yarbrough fumbled and Chris Scott took it back 72 yards. The last touchdown was by Ray; a 23-yarder.

"We just wanted to win the ball game without getting any injuries. We were aware of that Saint Andrews had their problems with injuries ... I think they did a good job." When asked about the 110.5 yards of flags against the Flashes, Bumgarner said *"I don't think that I have ever seen that many penalties called in one ballgame. We started substituting in the 2nd quarter and it looks like we might have started a little too early. We had a real good team effort, and we had the chance to get a look at a lot of our second and their teamers."*

Mike Ray won "Player of the Week" for his 129 yards on the grounds and 3 touchdowns.

GAME 5:   SAINT AL (4-0) @ GREENVILLE SAINT JOSEPH (0-4)
              FINAL: ST AL 49 GREENVILLE ST JOE 6
              September 30, 1977

The Irish had a number of injured players before the game. Coach Raymond Faulkner said of the Flashes, *"They are as good as anyone on our schedule, and are probably our biggest rivals. We are sure not going into this ball game with the idea that we can't win. We don't have anything to lose, while they (are primed) for a letdown and might be getting overconfident.*

The fourth play from scrimmage had already featured runs by Ray and Battalio runs for 20, and Nelson finished it from the 35. They forced a safety on the Irish next possession after a punt snap went out of the endzone. The ensuing drive saw Alonzo hit Carl Smith for a 40 yard touchdown, and the next included a Ray run for 55 yards and the score. More was to come when, starting at the Irish 44, the Flashes drove to the 1 behind work from Battalio, Ray and Maxey. Battalio pushed in from there. Greenville got their only points when they ran a reverse to Hugh Outzen for the 90-yard score. Alonzo found Donnie Head on 4th down from the 39 to make it 35-6. The Flashes had one more chance before half, and made the most of it. Battalio went 30 yards on the first touch to make it 42-6.

The reserves took the field for the 2nd half and held the Irish scoreless. Coomes, Fordice, Koestler and others continued the pressure. DeRossette rushed 7 times for 38 yards, intercepted one, and threw the final touchdown to Dan Fordice from the 18. Carlos Lee made 5 of 7 PATs, the Flashes rushed for 266 yards, and the Irish had only one first down; coming with only :27 left in the game. *"We were probably in the best frame of mind we've been in all year. The coaches and administrators from both schools made an all-out effort to keep it a good clean game. I was real pleased with the sportsmanship and good conduct shown on the part of players and fans. It was the best that we've had with them in quite a whi*le." Bumgarner also commented about the downfield blocking of his line by saying *"That's why we were able to break three long ones."*

GAME 6:   SAINT AL (5-0) vs PUCKETT (2-3)
               FINAL: ST AL 49 PUCKETT 0
               October 7, 1977: HOMECOMING

With a 5-0 start, the Mississippi Prep Poll put the Flashes at #14 and tied with Mendenhall at 4 votes each. Coomes was back but Hogan had now torn wrist ligaments after a practice. *"He fell on it the wrong way during a blocking session. There is an outside chance that he may play some, but it will definitely be limited. I don't want to take the chance on losing him for the year. That would be a real blow"*.

About the week, Bumgarner said *"The thing that we have got to do is remember the most important part of homecoming for us: the game and Puckett. Our long range team goal is to make it into the Top 10 teams in the state and if we are going to do that, we can't afford to have a letdown against anyone."* Puckett had an All-Conference LB but were a *"little weak in depth"*. Meanwhile, Saint Al was starting the Scoring Leader of Warren County in Carl Smith. With 36 points, he was 6 ahead of teammates Ray and Battalio (30) in 2nd. Lee was 5th (18) and Maxey was 6th (14).

On the fourth play of the game, Alonzo hit Smith from the 50 and Lee made it 7-0. After four-and-out by the Wolves, on the Puckett 26, Alonzo hit Maxey for the score to make it 14-0. Following yet another Puckett punt, Ray broke one for 58 yards and another touchdown. In the 2nd from the Puckett 19. Ray and Battalio ran to the 3 before Alonzo hit Smith in the endzone. Lee made it 28-0. Donnie Head fell on a Johnny Cameron fumble at the Puckett 44 and Alonzo later hit Nelson for a 22 yard score. Battalio made it 35-0. The Flashes took over again at their 44 led by QB Tim DeRossette. He drove into Puckett territory before Bob Benton picked him off to send it to halftime.

After a Puckett punt on their first possession, the Ray/Nelson/Battalio combination rushed into Wolves territory. Alonzo would find Nelson for 10 and then the touchdown. On the following possession, Puckett fumbled and John Kellum gathered it in. Saint Al gave it right back on a Head fumble to Michael Ward. At the Flash 43, DeRossette ran for a couple before finding Fordice for 27 yards. DeRossette hit Fordice again for a 22 yard score. Lee made it 49-0. The final quarter saw two Puckett fumbles recovered by Pat Koestler and Doug Whitaker, and one Wolves interception by Laurence Newsome. But the scoring was done.

GAME 7:   SAINT AL (6-0) @ PISGAH (1-5)
               FINAL: ST AL 54 PISGAH 6
               October 14, 1977

Hogan would return after clearance. Only a few small injuries remained and the Flashes would be healthy for the 1-5 home team. Pisgah fumbled four plays into the game to give Saint Al the ball at the 49. On the 2nd play, Alonzo hit Carl Smith for a 43 yard touchdown. Pisgah gave the ball back afterwards on downs, Ray went from the Flash 42 to the Dragon 10 on the first play, and two plays later Battalio pushed it in.

On the first play of the 2nd Alonzo hit Maxey from the 48 for the touchdown. Their first play afterwards, Alonzo found Maxey for a 58 yard score. Pisgah fumbled on their ensuing drive and Hogan recovered at the Dragon 21. One play later, Ray scored to make it 33-0. Fordice picked off a Carl King pass afterwards and brought it to the Dragon 14. Coomes ran it in from the 10 three plays later and Lee made it 40-0 at the half.

The reserves manned the 2nd half, with DeRossette driving the team 56 yards in 14 plays. He then found Fordice for the touchdown to make it 47-0 after Lee's PAT. Pisgah managed a score on a 76 yard drive of 11 plays when King plunged in from the 1. Saint Al quickly answered when they went 52 yards in 7 plays. Head capped it from the 8 and Lee finished the scoring at 54-6.

The coach was blunt afterwards. *"They gave us all they had, but there is really no comparison between our two programs. I really don't think a game like this is fair to our players when they practice all week, and then have to sit our half the ballgame because we are leading by 40 points. We don't need wins like this. We are trying to build up a first rate football program and you don't do it by blasting a weaker team out like we did tonight."*

GAME 8:   SAINT AL (7-0) vs JACKSON SAINT JOSEPH (4-3)
                 FINAL: ST AL 53 JACKSON ST JOE 6
                 October 21, 1977

Though the Flashes had beaten them 4 straight years, Bumgarner said *"We will be up against our toughest rival since Raymond ... They are always our biggest game of the year .... This is St. Joe's season ... and it's their biggest game of the year. They point to us like we point to them. All the teams that have beaten them are real good clubs. But you can throw the record book out the window when these two teams play. "*

In the 1st, Alonzo found Maxey for a 52 yard score and quickly put it in again on their next possession with a Ray 26-yard touchdown. The defense helped next when Maxey picked off a Saints pass and allowed Alonzo to find Carl Smith from the 11. It capped a 76 yard drive of 11 plays. With 4:00 left in the 2nd, Ray went 43 yards for the touchdown. Before half, Battalio got in from the 9 and it was 33-0.

Ray started the 3rd on a 66 yard run for yet another score. The Saints got on the board when quarterback Mike Iupe pushed in from the 1, but the Flashes quickly responded. A 47-yard touchdown from Alonzo to Maxey was called back for interference, but eventually Nelson scrambled in from the 3. In the 4th, Maxey sealed it with another pick and a 100 yard touchdown return. Ray had 214 yards of rushing and Lee had 6 PATs to help the effort in the game. Ray won "Player of the Week" honors.

"They were simply awesome. I had no idea we could beat St. Joe like we did. Here I am worrying myself sick all week. Boy, they really surprised me.

GAME 9:   SAINT AL (8-0) @ PELAHATCHIE (4-4)
                 FINAL: ST AL 56 PELAHATCHIE 13
                 October 28, 1977

There were *"five bowl inquiries to start the week"* and the coach was concerned. *"We've had a lot of distractions, with the win over St. Joe and all the talk of bowls, and we're just not as hungry for Pelahatchie right now as we've got to be Friday night. I recall several years ago St. Aloysius was 8-0 and went over (there) and got beat 30-14."* Nelson had a bruised shoulder, and DeRossette and Tuccio were doubtful after being out all week with the flu.

"Our first objective of the night will be to establish our running game and then we'll see what else we can do against them. ...Their QB will probably be the best veer QB that we have faced. They beat us last year and went on to win the CAC title. ...It's going to be a big one for us." But Saint Al did have the county's rushing leader in Ray with 970 yards. And he was tied with Carl Smith in scoring; both with 10 touchdowns.

On their first possession, Alonzo found Smith for 24 yards to the 1. Ray took it in and Lee made it 7-0. The Chiefs answered from their 25 on 5 plays, capped by a Scottie Irvin touchdown run from the 9. Michael Wilson made it 7-7. It was all Flashes afterwards. Starting at the 30 after a penalty, Alonzo immediately found Maxey for a 70-yard score. On their next drive, it took 4 plays for 76 yards. Alonzo hit Nelson for 38 and Ray found the endzone from the 21. Maxey converted the 2 to make it 21-7. In the 2nd, Nelson went in from the 5 and Lee made it 28-7.

Still in the first half, Maxey returned a Chief punt to the Pelahatchie 48. Four plays later, Alonzo hit Maxey from 22 and Lee made it 35-7. Smith later picked off Irvin for a 66 yard touchdown to make it 42-7. The 2nd half saw numerous reserves playing but Saint Al still added more points. Alonzo was picked off by Duane Lock, but Battalio returned the favor on the next play. After 3 plays, Alonzo found Maxey to the 26 and then handed off to him to cover the rest to make it 56-7. With :12 left, Irvin hit Michael Wilson from the 32 for their final score. The defense was helped in the half by a Coomes interception and another fumble recovery by Nelson.

GAME 10:   SAINT AL (9-0) vs TERRY (5-4)
                      FINAL: ST AL 31 TERRY 0
                      November 4, 1977

Bumgarner was looking at his second undefeated team since 1975 (9-0-2). "*I think that they are beginning to realize what we can accomplish this season.*" Though praising Terry players, he added "*We consider it a tune up for Utica and we're not going to hold anything back.*"

A pouring rain had caused Bumgarner to ask Terry head man Ricky Clopton to postpone the game. But since rain can be an equalizer, that request was denied. Chris Cox blocked a Calvin Baggett punt on the first 2nd quarter play resulting in a Lee FG from 33 away. The Flashes then went for the onside kick and Doug Whitaker recovered it. Six plays and 45 yards later, Battalio went in from the 1. Lee made it 10-0. Said Bumgarner, "*I think that's what got us going. Carlos' field goal and then recovering that on-side kick.*"

The last score of the half was on a Ray burst from the 17 to make it 17-0. In the 3rd, Cox blocked another Baggett punt at the 1 that was recovered by Pete Tarnabine. Nelson took it in and it was 23-0. In the 4th, a Baggett punt hit the center in the back and was recovered by Battalio at the Terry 8. On the next play, Ray went in and Maxey converted the 2-pointer.

The Flash defense never let the Jackets inside of the 40 and held Reggie Funchess to -3 yards to give the Flashes their first perfect regular season since 1958. "*I was really pleased with our defense. I believe Battalio, Hogan and Cox (who won "Player of the Week") probably played their best defensive games. It feels good to be 10-0. We really shut them down. But we don't have time to enjoy it. We've got to start thinking about Utica.*"

GAME 11:   SAINT AL (10-0) vs UTICA (NOT REPORTED)
                      FINAL: ST AL 29 UTICA 8
                      November 10, 1977: CAC CHAMPIONSHIP; BYRAM, MS

The Flashes had turned down Natchez, Crystal Springs and Kosciusko bowl bids in order to play in either the Mississippi Bowl or the Red Carpet Bowl. "*We can't have any distractions for this game. We have got to get ready to meet our toughest challenge of the season. That's why we are going to wait until after Thursday night to decide anything. But we will go wherever the boys vote to go.*"

The Flashes had played Utica on opening day and won 28-6. "*We didn't really stop their running attack when we played them before. I felt like we bent, but never broke. We are going to have to keep them from controlling the ball and grinding it out. They had a tough running game with Donald Taylor, and now their other back, Grover Hunter, has added a new dimension to their attack. If we can play our game and execute well, then I think that we stand a good chance of winning. The key for us is to control the line of scrimmage, both offensively and defensively.*"

The Flashes jumped out with two touchdowns in the 1st. The first was a Flash drive from their 37 in 4 plays. Alonzo hit Smith for 42 yards at the 7. A penalty moved it to the 4 and Ray went in for the score. The second was courtesy of a Wave fumble by Taylor on the Flash 9 recovered by Head. Four plays later, Ray went 68 yards for a touchdown. Lee made the PAT and made it 14-0. Utica came right back and went 62 yards in 8 plays, capped by a Taylor score. James Schuller added the 2 to make it 14-8. The Flashes had the only other score before half. On a 15 yard Ray run, a 15-yard personal foul was added. In all, the drive covered 45 yards in 4 plays and was finished with a 1 yard dive by Battalio. The Flashes faked the kick and Maxey hit Head in the endzone to make it 22-8.

In the 4th, Arthur Burse blocked a Flash punt and David Newman recovered at the Flash 22. They got to the 14, but on 4th down, Pete Tarnabine stopped Taylor for a 2-yard loss. Bumgarner called it a "*super play. It broke their back. The play Pete made was the culmination of our defense efforts. We had a lot of outstanding plays leading up to that, but it was the big one.*" Said Tarnabine, "*I knew they were coming my way... I saw Taylor try to cut to the outside and I was ready for him.*" Afterwards, the Flashes went 84 yards in 6 plays. Nelson started it with a 36 yard run that set up a Mike Ray touchdown run of 29. Lee made the final score 29-8.

"*We had to fight for everything we got. Both teams played a super game. Utica is a much improved ball club from the first of the season and they gave us all that we could ask for. Ray had a* great night for us. I think he would have gained more, but we let the other backs run more in the second half." Said Utica's coach, "I felt that we hurt ourselves with turnovers. We had the momentum a couple of times and we just couldn't capitalize on it. I felt that we were still in it until late in the fourth quarter. They beat us twice, so obviously they have the better ball club. Saint Al has a well-balanced ball club and if they have a weakness, I don't know where it is."

GAME 12: SAINT AL (11-0) vs KOSCIUSKO (11-0)
FINAL: ST AL 3 KOSCIUSKO 21
December 2, 1977: MISSISSIPPI BOWL; JACKSON, MS

The CAC champions were now ranked number 11 in the AP Prep Poll and Ray was firmly entrenched in the Warren County leader board with 107 points. The All-CAC Team winners were announced during the week with Bumgarner elected "Coach of the Year" and Denis Hogan as "Best Lineman". Other first teamers included Head, Cox, Ray, Alonzo, Maxey and Smith. Honorable Mentions included Battalio, Tony Patton, Nelson, Randy Johnson and Tarnabine.

Saint Al learned that they would play undefeated Kosciusko in the Mississippi Bowl on ABC after a three week layoff. Thanksgiving and the weather had pushed both teams into practice adjustments. The Mid-Mississippi Conference foes outweighed the Flashes, had a lot of depth and were favorited. Said Bumgarner, "They pursue real well; they gang tackle. We don't know what we can do. We've never been there. But we've got the kind of kids who can rise to the occasion. I believe we're ready. We're going to give it our best shot. We've got a lot of respect for Kosciusko but we're not afraid of them."

Three thousand spectators were in Newell Field to see the matchup. Kosciusko didn't disappoint, taking the opening kickoff and driving 11 plays for 83 yards. Tommy Hodge snuck in from the 1 and Charlie Hodge made the PAT for a 7-0 lead. The Flashes scored in the quarter when Alonzo hit ray for 40 yards on a 58 yard drive. On 4th down, Lee nailed a 29 yard FG to cut it to 7-3. In the 2nd, the Whippets added points with a Lamar Moore touchdown run of 23 and a Hodge PAT. Down 14-3 just before half, penalties helped to push the Flashes to the Whippet 26, but a pass by Ray to Maxey was picked off to end the half.

The Flashes had the ball all but 3 plays in the scoreless 3rd. Their first drive marched all the way to the Kosciusko 33 and, on 4th and 4, Ray took the ball 7 yards for an apparent first down. But a flag for too many men in the backfield killed the drive and forced a punt. The second drive took them 46 yards to the Whippet 20, but an incomplete pass from Alonzo to Maxey on 4th and 6 gave it back to Kosciusko.

With 3:19 left in the game, Tommy Williams hit Robert Williams for 47 yards. Andrew Carter took it in from the 2. "That broke our backs," said Bumgarner. "Coming up empty-handed twice and them converting that big third down play. Alonzo was defending on the play, but got turned around." In the end, the 1977 Flashes put together a team that people would remember for years. They finished a respectable 10th in the AP Poll, The Virgadamo Trophy went to Donnie Head and the much-loved Coach Bumgarner found a new home in Brookhaven.

1978 (9-2)

After the departure of Les Bumgarner to Brookhaven, Saint Al put their program in the hands of a bulky and boisterous 6'4" redheaded 1971 MSU grad who had excelled as a three-year starter offensive tackle for the Bulldogs. With four years assistant coaching experience and two years as head man at Pearl High School, Edwards took over a football "machine" in Vicksburg. He was missing 12 leading players from the past year's 10-1 CAC Bowl runner-up, but his 1,400 yard rusher in Mike Ray was back. As were many other talented Flashes on the 33-man team.

"I have been very impressed with this group. I don't think that they would quit under any circumstances because that's something that they don't know how to do. We will be young in some spots, but if several key positions develop rapidly, we expect to have an excellent season."

After scrimmages, he was pleased with his running backs (Ray, Bart Bell, Tim DeRossette and Joe Battalio) and the QB-receiver part of the team (Lanny Barfield, Mike Yarbrough, Donnie Gordon, Mike McCain, Bell and Cicero LaHatte). "If we can give our backs a few cracks to get through, we'll be able to move the football." They were trying hard to rebuild an offensive line losing 5 starters to graduation and were "..making progress. Most of our linemen are young and don't have a lot of experience, but they are really giving it a good effort." He was particularly proud of the progress of

John Laboda, Dave Tuccio and Phil Hogan. Ironically, Hogan would not see the season. Before the first snap against Utica, he had broken his ankle.

As game day approached, he was "...*trying to prepare ... for what we think (Utica) will do. Their offense is pretty simple, but they do a good job of running it. With the success they had last week (a 10-0 victory versus Franklin County), I don't see them making a whole lot of changes.*" The day before kickoff, he added "*We are going to go down there and try not to beat ourselves. If we can play good football, I think we can stay with them.*"

GAME 1:   SAINT AL (0-0) @ UTICA (1-0)
                                 FINAL: ST AL 29 UTICA 0
                                 September 1, 1978

On their first possession, set up by a 13 yard pass from Yarbrough to Donnie Gordon, Ray scored his first touchdown of the night on a 9-yard sweep. Ray also put the PAT through to make it 7-0. Said Edwards, "*I was proud of the way Yarbrough kept his cool in the clutch. He had a lot of pressure on him and he took some hard licks.*" Ray also found the endzone late in the 2nd on an 11-yard run to make halftime 13-0.

Saint Al continued the pressue to begin the 2nd half. On their first possession, they drove 78 yards in 11 plays with Battalio finishing on a 1-yard dive. DeRossette added the two-points to make it 21-0. The final score came in the same quarter as Tuccio picked up a fumble late. Yarbrough hit Battalio for an 11-yard touchdown and Ray added the two-points. Saint Al had put up 292 yards compared to Utica's 45, had 17 first downs versus the Gold Waves' lone chain movement, and Ray had 168 yards with most (130) in the first half.

"*I thought the kids did an excellent job. Our running backs were exceptional. Ray, Joe Battalio, Timmy DeRossette, George McConnell and Bart Bell put together an outstanding ground game. Our defense did well. Any time you shut down a team, you know you have a good defense. And having a defensive secondary that allows no pass completions is also great.*"

He was also complimentary of the one aspect of his team that had his focus early. "*Coach Bob Hitchins did a marvelous job on the offensive line and Coach Jimmy Salmon tuned up the running backs into perfect condition. But to beat Byram and Raymond, we will have to continue to improve. It's going to be tough. We aren't anywhere near reaching our potential. We made technical mistakes ... that we are going to have to overcome.*"

GAME 2:   SAINT AL (1-0) v BYRAM (1-1)
                                 FINAL: ST AL 14 BYRAM 19
                                 September 8, 1978

Mounting injuries sum up the agony that faced the head man during the week. Hogan had already been lost for the year and now lineman Tim Smith had fallen from a vehicle that Sunday and separated his shoulder. He could also add John Laboda to the list with an ankle injury from the Utica contest along with Ray and McCain. Both were suspended by the school for reportedly missing an assembly. "*I hate to see it happen, but I fully support Father Camp (Saint Al's principal) in this. They broke the rules and it was the only decision he could make. We have had some bad luck but we are going to have to keep fighting to overcome it. We are going to be depending on some of our younger kids to come around and do the job for us.*"

Byram was already a tough opponent. "*We have a lot to do to get our people ready for (them). We had them scouted last week in their game (loss 14-0) with St. Andrews and they were in it until the fourth quarter. They just line their backs up behind that big line and run straight at you. We aren't nearly as big as they are, but we think our kids will do a good job against them.*"

Byram scored two touchdowns in the first half; one in the 1st when Jimmy Booth found Sylvester Joiner from the 18 yard line. In the 2nd, it was a 61 yard run by Steve Coleman that made it 13-0. Saint Al cut the lead when McConnell scored from the 3. The two-pointer was no good and the halftime score was 13-6. The Flashes went ahead when Billy Coomes took the ball to the 1 on a 4th down pass from Yarbrough. George McConnell dove in from there and then converted the two-points on a dive. But with under 2:00 left, Booth hit Coleman on a pass and the senior took it 55 yards for a touchdown and the win.

"*We had far, far too many penalties (100 yards on 10 flags) to win. We spent way too much time on the other end of the field without scoring. That, and the penalties, really lost the ball game for* us." McConnell had 83 yards in his replacement role and garnered praise. *"I think George played one of the finest ball games I have ever seen a running back play. He gave us ... the supreme effort. I think his whole performance cold be exemplified by the two-point conversation. He made that on his own."* Afterwards, that effort gave McConnell the "Player of the Week" nod.

The Vicksburg Evening Post's Michael Logue asked about the effects of missing four players. *"I know our kids thought they could win this ball game. They showed that by the way they came back in the end. Of course you miss people ... but I certainly don't want to take away from the job by McConnell, Joe Battalio, Timmy DeRossette and Bart Bell. I think they all played a superb ball game."*

GAME 3: SAINT AL (1-1) @ RAYMOND (3-0)
FINAL: ST AL 12 RAYMOND 14
September 15, 1978

The Flashes worked Monday and Tuesday in the gym due to weather. Wednesday was back on the fields where they made a few switches on defense and worked full contact sessions. DeRossette moved from linebacker to tackle, Tuccio moved to guard and Barfield was now in at linebacker. *"I believe Timmy will help us more at defensive tackle, not that Dave wasn't doing a good job. But we'll be able to utilize Timmy's height more at tackle and use Dave inside at guard."* David Ray, a freshman lineman, saw some valuable practice time and gained praise from Edwards. *"He has the potential to help us."* Edwards said of the kids, *"They aren't down; they're ready to bounce back."*

On Raymond's very first play, they coughed up the ball and it was recovered by Donnie Gordon. The Flashes moved to the Ranger 18 before Ray gave the ball back on the next play. The defense held and set up the first Flash score in the 2nd. A 54-yard drive was capped by a 20-yard touchdown run by Ray to put the Flashes up 6-0 at halftime. Raymond evened the score at 6-6 in the 3rd. The Flashes fumbled on their own 48 and a few plays later, James Cooper went in from 34 yards out. Saint Al regained the lead in the 4th on a Ray touchdown from the 7 to make it 12-6. But the game was sealed when Battalio launched a 53 yard punt to the Ranger 19 only to see sophomore James Cooper return it to tie the game. With 4:12 left, Thomas Bunton caught the two-point pass to make the final 14-12.

"We made some mistakes, but played well in the open field. We've just got to keep working and trying harder. We had to practice in the gym a couple of times ... and didn't get in the running we needed. But we will work hard on that this week." As for player efforts, he praised Battalio, DeRossette and Perry Cox. *"Perry is really coming around. He's developing into the kind of player we knew he could be. There's still room for a lot of improvement but he has made a lot of progress."* Ray rushed for 234 yards in the loss.

GAME 4: SAINT AL (1-2) v SAINT ANDREWS (4-0)
FINAL: ST AL 20 SAINT ANDREWS 0
September 22, 1978

Guard Will Raiford would now be out with a knee injury. The line was already depleted and another injury was not welcome news. *"Will had been doing a real good job for us. He didn't play ball last year, but was showing good senior leadership and an excellent attitude. We will miss him the rest of the season."* Junior Tony Franco would fill his spot. Edwards didn't put the team through much contact work due to the thin ranks. But conditioning was strenuous and the kicking game was getting some work.

The Flashes had only scouting reports on Saint Andrews. They had had beaten Byram, Terry, Jackson Christian and Cathedral by a total of 77-6. *"Evidently they are a real fine football team. We're expecting a tough ball game. It's a real big game for both teams. Coach (Terry) Clark has always stressed defense so we're expecting them to be strong there."* When game time arrived, Saint Al had two quarterbacks. Barfield was to handle most of the duties while still sticking with a two-man system in Yarbrough. This was not a surprise since Edwards had commented earlier in the week that *"Lanny has really come along and we want to see what he can do under fire."*

Saint Andrews was held and forced to punt. Ray returned the kick to the Saint 21 and four plays later, he got in from the 1 to make it 6-0. In in the 2nd when, after an 18-play drive of 70 yards, Battalio went in from the 1. Ray added the two points and Saint Al was now up 14-0. In the 3rd, the Flashes would put on the finishing touches. Starting at their 22, they used nine plays to get Ray into the endzone from the 5. *"We had to have it and the kids gave it to us. It's our first conference win and we are proud to get it. St. Andrews has a good team and they were well prepared."*

Saint Al amassed a staggering 155 yards in 13 penalties. One of those erased a 95-yard Ray kick return for a touchdown. The other eliminated a 52-yard burst. But Ray still had 105 yards in rushing and the only pass completion of the night (a 43-yarder to DeRossette). *"Ray had an outstanding game. I also thought that our offensive linemen (Cox, Tuccio, Gordon, Franco and Bob McConnell) all did an exceptional job. We couldn't have asked for any more."* On defense, Battalio had 11 tackles and 3 assists. Running the ball, he gained 22 yards and a score. *"Joe hasn't gained that many yards this season, but everything he picks up is hard earned. He blocks well for us and he is the leader of our defense."* For his work, Ray was named "Player of the Week".

GAME 5:   SAINT AL (2-2) v GREENVILLE SAINT JOSEPH (2-2)
                              FINAL: ST AL 42 GREENVILLE ST JOE 0
                              September 29, 1978

The Flashes were back on track but Edwards was only looking forward. *"It was great to win, but we remember the previous two weeks too well. We know that if we aren't ready for every game, we could get beat again."* Fortunately there were no new injuries to report. Coomes had broken two of his front teeth in a pre-practice warmup and Ray, Warren County's scoring leader, had a slightly pulled upper hamstring. Both were still expected to play. *"He says it doesn't hurt when he's running, only when he slows down. I told him not to slow down."*

Edwards through his rival more of a passing-oriented team. *"We hope to offset that with speed and quickness. If we can stop their passing attack, we can win the ball game. Their quarterback, Greg Mernardi, is a good passer and they have one the finest individual athletes we'll see at wide receiver (Reggie McCray). They try to get the ball to him most of the time."* Tuesday was devoted to this pass defense. *"We worked on all the coverages we plan to use."*

Saint Al led only 13-0 at halftime. In the 1st, Battalio ran in from the 3 and Ray kicked the point after. In the 2nd, Ray tacked on a 69-yard touchdown run. In the 3rd, the "massacre" began. Barfield went in from the 1 and Ray added the 2. Ray scored from the 6 but missed the kick. Finally, the Saint Al defense smothered Reggie McCray in the endzone for the safety to make it 29-0. After that, the paper notes that *"Everyone got a piece of the action as Edwards cleared out his bench in the fourth stanza."* Freshman Barry Breithaupt took in a two-yard run, sophomore Sam Brown took one in from the 8, and freshman David Ray kicked the final point to finish it.

The stats were gaudy. Ray rushed for 199 of the Flashes 315 yards on the ground. By comparison, the Irish had 22. Though lots of Flashes saw action, Edwards noted that *"We got some good individual efforts, but as a team we've got room for improvement. We didn't play real well, but maybe that had something to do with who we played. We made some mistakes that could have made a difference a good club. Sure, I'm happy for the win, but our opponent wasn't very strong. And I'm pleased that everybody got to play."*

GAME 6:   SAINT AL (3-2) @ PUCKETT (2-3)
                              FINAL: ST AL 6 PUCKETT 0
                              October 6, 1978

Ray was now Warren County's leading scorer (71 points) and rusher (734 yards) by a large margin. And, Tim Smith was now back with the team after being out a month with the shoulder injury. *"We'll bring him along slowly until he gets back in shape."*

Edwards was complimentary of Puckett. *"I feel they are the best team we have seen all year, although they have lost three games. It's a big game for us, our biggest so far. I expect it to be a close ball game. Puckett is not very big; in fact, they are about our size. But they are exceptionally quick. We're going to have to run straight at them. The best way to play a team that is as quick and pursues as well as they do is run straight at them. With their quickness, we don't expect to be able to get outside. Also, we plan to use a lot of play-action passes."*

The first half had only one close shave with the endzone. The Flashes made it all the way to the 12 before fumbling back to the Wolves. The second half saw Puckett return the gift. On the kickoff, Puckett fumbled and Sam Brown scooped it up. Ten plays later, Ray went in from the 3. That would be the only scoring of the night. Bart Bell ensured the win late by picking up a Puckett fumble. *"It was a hard-hitting game but we won when we had to. Our offensive linemen … did an outstanding job. Our* first half left much to be desired, but this group really came out in the second half. I was also proud of our defensive unit. This is their third straight shutout and fourth on the year." He finished with praise for Coaches Hitchens and Salmon for their work on the lines. With his 206 rushing yards, Ray was again named "Player of the Week" by The Vicksburg Evening Post.

GAME 7:   SAINT AL (4-2) v PISGAH (1-5)
                              FINAL: ST AL 34 PISGAH 0
                              October 13, 1978

Bob McConnell had taken a *"hard lick"* to the head the previous Friday but Edwards said that *"He's okay, and the doctor has given him the go-ahead."* Cox Smith and DeRossette were banged up but all were expected to play against Pisgah. Saint Al was closed on Monday along with all Catholic schools, so Edwards took the opportunity to review the Puckett game film with the team. He took the time to praise a number of people on both sides of the ball. But of Bob McConnell he said that he was *"the best nose guard I've ever coached."*

Game night was messy with a constant drizzle that sent many fans home by the 3rd. The game was such a one-sided affair that there was nothing left for them to really see anyway. The opening kickoff went only a yard and the Flashes had the ball to start on the Dragon 41. Ray and Battalio runs set up a Ray 13 yard score to make it 7-0. The next possession had Ray going 68 yards for the score. Ray went in from 34 anf DeRosette added the two to make it 22-0. The half would end with yet another Ray touchdown. This one was from the 40 to put it 29-0. Pisgah's only score came in the 3rd with many younger Flashes on the field. Windale McCrary finished a 57-yard 14-play drive when he found the endzone from the 7.

"It was clearly a mismatch. We could have scored 70-80 if we had tried. A lot of people may wonder why we didn't beat them worse. But there wasn't any need to. That sort of thing comes back to haunt you. Besides, all of our kids got to play and I was glad of that. You have to give Pisgah credit for not quitting. They came back in the second half and put together a good drive." Yet again, in what was becoming an expected honor, Ray was named "Player of the Week".

GAME 8:   SAINT AL (5-2) @ NATCHEZ CATHEDRAL (3-4)
                              FINAL: ST AL 34 CATHEDRAL 11
                              October 20, 1978: HOMECOMING

Homecoming week against a non-conference opponent saw a few more slight injuries. Yarbrough had wrenched his back and was questionable, Smith and Cox still had hurt ankles and DeRossette had a virus. By game time, all would be back and suited up. As for Cathedral, they had suffered a far worse injury. The Green Waves' starting quarterback had suffered a broken neck early in the year and remained paralyzed. As for their attack, Edwards commented that *"This is the first time that I've ever had to prepare for something like this* (Cathedral's Notre Dame Box Offense). *We have to get our defense ready to react to their offense so that we can stop it."* As for the other side of the ball, he said *"They run a multiple defense. They give you a lot of different looks and we've been trying to piece together what we've got to do to be ready for them. I think it will be a close ball game. They've been wanting to get us down there for a couple of years. They are a lot bigger than we are. They have a couple of big kids on the line and our kids are going to have to dig in and play hard to win. "*

In the 1st, Saint Al put it in twice. Between the running of Ray and Battalio, they rushed to the 40 in six plays. Ray then went in from the 43 for a score. After forcing a punt that put the Flashes at the 19, they engineered a 7-play drive that resulted in a Barfield to Ray 38-yard touchdown. Barfield then hit DeRosette for the two and the quarter ended at 14-0. Cathedral came back in the 2nd with a Greg Whitman FG of 37 yards to make it 14-3. At halftime, the homecoming team was in early control.

Natchez tried an onside-kick to start the 2nd half, but Saint Al recovered. Ray had 3 rushes to the 24 and then Battalio converted for the score. The Greenies managed to score in the 4th when a snap on a Flash punt deep in their territory went out of the endzone to give them a safety. Later, Bart Bell recovered a fumble by at the 50. Ray eventually went in from the 19. Scoring was finalized by both teams afterwards. Mike Fortunato drove the Green Wave 59 yards and ran it in from the 9. Ray, however, sealed it with a 59 yard touchdown run and again garnered "Player of the Week".

"It was by far the best game we have played. Both the offensive and defensive teams played an excellent game." For Ray, it was an understatement. He rushed for 304 yards in the game; his 4th 200+ game of the year. *"It was Mike's best performance of the year. He was fantastic."* As for the

team effort, and aside from numerous individual praises, he said *"We had poor kickoff coverage and poor punt protection ... things that can get you beat in a hurry."*

GAME 9: SAINT AL (6-2) v PELAHATCHIE (2-6)
FINAL: ST AL 21 PELAHATCHIE 0
October 27, 1978

Injuries still dogged the Flashes, but that was usual for 1978. As for the game, Edwards said *"We've got to have this one to win our (CAC) division. Pelahatchie has had most of its success running outside. They beat Saint Andrews (14-12) outside and we expect them to do the same against us. (They) run a tight wing, with the wingback cracking down on the defensive ends, so we're going to have to rely more on our corners to stop them."* In practices, defense was emphasized. *"We don't use a lot of different defenses; we just try to perfect what we do. Week-to-week we make adjustments in our two basic defenses. Simplicity and the kids' assurance that they know what they are supposed to do are essential."*

In the 2nd it was a trick play that put points up first. After a Barfield interception and John Kellum fumble recovery, Saint Al sat at the Pelahatchie 6. Penalties eventually put them back to the 34. With Barfield going out on a fake "bruised back", Yarbrough then pulled a flea-flicker by handing off to Battalio, who handed off to Coombs, who flipped it to back to Yarbrough. He subsequently hit Ray from the 34 for a touchdown. Ray took it in from the 2 to make halftime 8-0. *"I can't believe it worked"* screamed Edwards.

In the 3rd, Ray fumbled at the Pelahatchie 14 but redeemed himself in the 4th. After six carries for 45 yards, he scored from the 4 and then threw a 15-yard pass to Coomes for another touchdown. He also ran for the two-pointer and kicked an extra point. With that, Ray ran his Warren County Leader total to 136 points of scoring and 1,640 yards of rushing.

Things could have been worse for Pelahatchie. The Flashes had interceptions and fumbles that cost them at least two more scores. Battalio fumbled on the opening series that saw Saint Al move from their 48 to the 24; and an ineligible receiver call brought back a Ray-to-DeRossette 76-yard touchdown. In all, the Flashes had 105 yards in penalties. *"It wasn't pretty. We did some things a good football team does, but we also did some things a good football team doesn't do. We did it with a good kicking game."* Battalio earned "Player of the Week". Ray and DeRossette shared Honorable Mention.

GAME 10: SAINT AL (7-2) @ TERRY (3-6)
FINAL: ST AL 21 TERRY 6
November 3, 1978

With the Division CAC already won, Edwards conceded that there was no way they could get psyched up to play Terry. Barfield would not be playing and was doubtful even for Raymond. Battalio had infected tonsils and was out of school most of the week. The Flashes scored late in the 1st. when Ray finished a 14-play drive of 61 yards with a 1 yard run to make it 6-0. Late in the 2nd, Ray hit Coomes for 51 yards. It was a big play, but Coomes would sit out the remainder of the game with an injured leg. DeRossette finished the drive with a score from the 1 to make it 12-0.

The only score for Terry came in the 4th when a punt snap went over Battalio's head and Vernon Green recovered for a touchdown. The extra point failed and it was 12-6. Immediately afterwards, Saint Al went 71 yards in 11 plays. DeRossette finished it with a touchdown from the 3. Yarbrough hit Gordon for the two-pointer and it was over.

The headline said *"St. Al Rips Terry"*. But it could easily have noted that Ray had another stellar performance with 196 yards on the ground. He now sat at 1,836 for the season and needed only 167 to break the astonishing 2,000 yard mark. Edwards was somewhat happy. *"I was pleased with the way that our offensive line and our entire defense played. The defense didn't give up a touchdown and the offensive line gave our backs plenty of protection. Terry was keying on Ray and I was proud of the way that he kept his composure. He took several shots and he came right back at them."*

"We were expecting a tough game with Terry. Terry has a much better team than its record indicates, but we didn't play well. If we play this way against Raymond next Thursday, they will beat us by three touchdowns. I don't expect us to play like that. Terry was a lame duck for us and we lost our composure at times. We weren't fired up and it hurt us." But after thinking about it the following week, he did go on to say that *"considering the situation, it wasn't all that bad a game."*

GAME 11:   SAINT AL (8-2) v RAYMOND (10-0)
                 FINAL: ST AL 21 RAYMOND 0
                 November 9, 1978

Both coaches had coached at Pearl together and were mutually respectful. Ken Granberry, an Edwards assistant at Pearl, called the game *"a little wholesome friendly competition"* and added *"We're looking forward to tomorrow night. Saint Aloysius has a lot of incentive because we've beaten them already, but I feel that the team that is mentally ready will win it."* Edwards said of Granberry *"I knew Ken would make a good head coach. He has done a real good job. Raymond is the best club we've played. They are well coached."*

But he was still high on this Flashes team. *"They don't fear Raymond a bit. They respect them, but they are not awed by them."* The Rangers beat the Flashes 14-12 in week 3 but now Saint Al had reeled off 7 straight victories and was fairly healthy. Both running backs were ready. Ray sat at 1,838 yards on the season, but James Cooper has 1,306 for the Rangers. The heralded duel between these two teams was highly anticipated.

The Flashes scored on their first two possessions. The first was a 57 yard drive that saw Battlio with runs of 11, 8 and 7. Ray then went in from the 1, made the extra point, and it was 7-0. The second was set up by a DeRossette pick of Raymond QB Bart Ballard. His 15-yard return to the Ranger 25 led to his touchdown on a pass from Yarbrough. The Flashes almost scored again when DeRossette picked up a Ranger fumble near the 50. The drive ended at the Raymond 13, but halftime was 13-0.

The Flashes kept the ball 10:26 of the 3rd quarter and almost cashed in a score. But Yarbrough's fumble on the 3 was recovered by Robert Earl Jones to keep them out. However on Ballard's pass attempt afterwards, Bob McConnell got the safety (driving him 3 yards past the goal post) to make it 15-0. The final points were on a Battalio dive from the 2 that finished a 68 yard drive. Raymond finally got past the 50 when they drove from their 14 to the Flash 45, but Bart Bell sacked Ballard on the next play for a loss of 12 to seal the game.

Said Granberry afterwards, *"Their line dominated us. We couldn't get the ball. They whipped our butts. Our line whipped 10 lines this year. Tonight they whipped us. ... tonight they were a better ball club."* The defense was astounding. Only once did the Rangers get past the 50, and that was late in the contest. The offense helped by keeping the ball for 32:17 of the 48 minutes of the game. *"We think shutout every game. That's the goal of our defense. You look at any outstanding football team and they've got a good defense. We're real proud of our defense. We didn't do anything unique tonight. It was what we've run all year."*

Battalio, defensive captain and the individual credited with the "Gold Crush" nickname, added *"Everybody wanted to win and everybody did his job. It was a team effort. We played together as a team. We stuck together and worked hard. And we've had good leadership from our seniors."* Despite the landmark rushing record by Ray, it was DeRossette who earned "Player of the Game". But a CAC Championship was of much more importance. And the Flashes were holding it.

Ray rushed for 202 yards in the game and put him at 2,040 for the season even though he missed one game due to suspension. The previous year, he had rushed for 1,557. Afterwards, he gave all of the credit to the line and his teammates. But the blow to come was announced at halftime of the Raymond game. To put it in the words of <u>The Vicksburg Evening Post</u>: **"CAC Coaches Deny Ray Of Rightful Honor".** Curt Nix, Sports Editor, was emphatic in his criticism.

"It's difficult for me to conceive that there are grown men, coaches by title, who would deny a 17-year old youngster an honor that is rightfully his simply because they don't like his style of play. I'm referring to five head football coaches in the Capital Athletic Conference who conspired to keep Saint Aloysius' Mike Ray from wearing the crown of "Most Valuable Back" for 1978."

Cooper and Ray were split winners in a 5-5 vote. But Ray had 148 points and 2,040 yards in 10 games. Cooper had 118 points and 1,364 yards in 11 games. While Nix was complimentary of the achievements and character of Cooper, he continued. *"That, friend, I can't comprehend. It's a miscarriage of justice. It makes a mockery of the system the CAC employs to select its all-conference athletes and denotes time for a chance in the format. For what reason, I ask, could five coaches, allegedly possessing the ability to judge football talent, pick Cooper over Ray unless there was another motive? ... Ray is not only the best back in the CAC, he's the greatest back the league has ever produced."*

The article was lengthy, scathing, insightful, statistical and more. Even Utica head man George Walker was noted as saying *"Ray's the best back. It's beyond me."* Edwards agreed. *"I couldn't compare Ray and Cooper. .. Ray is a senior; Cooper is a sophomore. I think Cooper has a lot of potential, but he's not a Mike Ray."* Lost in this were the numerous accolades to other Flashes. Laboda made All-CAC as center. Battalio was named at linebacker and Tim DeRossette at defensive tackle. Honorable Mentions went to DE Kellum, guard Bob McConnell, tackle Perry Cox, QB Barfield, split end Billy Coomes, DE George McConnell and TE Gordon. Battalio won the Virgadamo Trophy.

The Flashes were invited to play in the Wendall Ladner Bowl on the Mississippi Gulf Coast. But, the team turned down the offer with Edwards commenting *"We felt we would have to have near 100 percent vote of our kids to go. But there were too many who didn't want to go."* After the CAC issue, it's not hard to wonder why.

1979 (7-4)

"Edwards Tries To Put Together Another Title" was the headline of the first article about the 1979 campaign. Joe Edwards was confident that another CAC championship was possible. *"Given the right set of factors, we have the team that can repeat as champions. We certainly have a lot of room for improvement. Our kids are going to have to get themselves ready to play this fall, both mentally and physically. There are other things to look at, too. We don't have that much depth and, should we come up with a lot of injuries, we are going to be in trouble. Also, we are a senior ball club. (We) are going to have to have some untied people come on and perform like we thing they can. We have the team that can repeat as champions, but we must guard against complacency. We cannot let down."*

The Flashes concentrated on their offense in the first few days. *"We think that we may be a little quicker in the backfield. We may not have the strength that we had, but I think we have a good group of players to work with.*" In-between, they worked on special teams. *"Right now, this has me worried more than any other phase of our game. We are going to have to do a lot of work on this before the season starts."*

They were trying Perry Cox as punter and Mike Yarbrough as kicker. There were, however, two more players in Tony Franco and Phillip Hogan vying for the kicking job. *"The fastest way in the world to lose a ball game is to have a breakdown in your kicking game. Perry is certainly capable of handling the kicking, but he is going to have to get faster."* By full practices, he said *"We did a little hitting today. We worked with a half line scrimmage and went at it. We are still getting into shape and we will get better. These kids know what they have to do and they have too much character not to get ready. Our line has the potential to be as good as anyone's."*

On game week, Phillip Hogan (bruised knee) and Mike Yarbrough (pulled muscle) were injured and a virus was going around the school. Tired of hitting one-another, he said *"What we need now is a ball game against someone. We have been out long enough and our kids are getting into shape. They are tired of hitting each other and are ready to (go) after someone else."* The slate was formidable. *"We have a tough schedule. Our division of the CAC conference may not be as strong overall, as is the otherwise. But we are playing some good teams and if we stay healthy and get the good, sound senior leadership we are expecting, we will do alright."*

GAME 1:   SAINT AL (0-0) vs TERRY (0-0)
                    FINAL: ST AL 21 TERRY 0
                    August 31, 1979

Terry's 1978 finish at 3-7 had Edwards say *"We really don't know what to expect from them defensively"*, though he was expecting a run-oriented offensive attack. The report from the paper was sparse, but Saint Al scored twice in the 1st to take the early lead. George McConnell scored from the 11 and Mike McCain made it 7-0. Later in the quarter, Sam Brown took a pitch from Lanny Barfield from the 12. Though the kick wasn't good, the 13-0 score would hold until the 4th. With 5:00 left, McConnell scored again with an 11-yard run and added the two-point conversion to ice it 21-0. And the run-oriented attack Edwards was expecting put up only 41 yards. The Yellow Jackets had a total of 69 yards in passing for the game.

"I don't think we looked too pretty, but we won and that's what counts. Our offensive line did a really good job of blocking tonight, but we've got to work on conditioning. I was really disappointed with the number of cramps we got tonight. Compared to last year's team, we are probably fundamentally more sound but not as explosive. We won't find out how we really are until we play teams like Utica, Bryan and Raymond."

McConnell and teammate Phillip Hogan won Honorable Mentions that week. No Saint Al player would reach *"Player of the Week"* status.

GAME 2:   SAINT AL (1-0) vs UTICA (0-0)
                 FINAL: ST AL 0 UTICA 8
                 September 7, 1979

After Monday film, Edwards said *"I thought the offensive line came off the ball well and our backs did a good job blocking. We made mistakes, but they were technique mistakes, like not coming off on the right foot. There was no loafing, and with more work, I think we'll be able to correct our errors and become a good football team. We only had one fumble, but I noticed in the films that there could have been more. We weren't holding the ball the way that we should, and we will correct this during the week."*

The Gold Wave had first played Saint Al in the 1977 CAC Bowl and was optimistic about their prospects. Said head coach George Walker, *"We have had one of the best springs that we have ever had, and I think we are ready for our opener. This year's team seems to be a more disciplined ball club. How we play against St. Al will really tell us what kind of a year we are in for."* Edwards echoed his statement. *"We are looking for a good game with Utica. They are saying that they have on the best teams... they ever had and we will be tested. Any resemblance between Terry and Utica will be totally accidental. We are in for a tough game this week and we will have to play a lot better than we did last week to win".*

The only score of the 1st half would be a special-teams mistake. On a punt attempt, the ball would sail over Cox's head and roll out of the endzone for a safety. Mistakes on both teams built, but the score was still only 2-0. The Gold Wave put up the final points in the 4th. On their own 20, the Flashes fumbled and gave the ball to linebacker Joseph Caston. The next play was a 17-yard gain by Robert Pollard and, three plays later, he drove in for the score from the 2. The Flashes had one final chance to tie. A Utica fumble at the 13 late in the contest was recovered by Mike McCain. McConnell ran for 6 yards but got no further. Barfield was sacked for a loss of 5 and then, on 4th down, he was picked off by Larry Carson. Coach George Walker told Steve Swogetinsky afterwards, *"We were going to win. I could feel it. It was by far my biggest win as a coach. Our kids worked hard for it and they deserve all the credit."*

Said Edwards, *"I saw it coming all week during practice. Our players didn't seem to be taking the game as serious as they should during practice, and it showed up in the game. You have to give Coach Walker a lot of credit. He had the guts to say all week long that he was going to win and he went out and did it. I could see from the first minute that we were in for a heck of a ball game. They stuck it to us. They deserved to win."*

"The loss was the responsibility of the whole team. We win together and lose together. I think we are going to see real quick what we are made of. We are going to have to find out who wants to play and take it from there. It all depends on how the kids respond after this loss. We can have a 5-6 team or we could go on and have an 11-1 record." The only week award was for George McConnell as Player of the Week Honorable Mention.

GAME 3:   SAINT AL (1-1) @ BYRAM (UNREPORTED)
                 FINAL: ST AL 20 BYRAM 10
                 September 14, 1979

On practice week, Edwards said *"We have a hard week's practice ahead. We have had some heart-to-heart talks with some of our players and we may be making some changes this week. Our offensive line didn't block anyone. Utica had a good football team and they whipped us. But I would like to get another shot at them. They are on the same side of the conference with Raymond and it will be tough for them to make it to the CAC Bowl. But if Raymond isn't ready to hit the night they play Utica, they are in for an upset."*

"I looked at a film... and saw what I expected to see. For us to beat them, we will have to stop their passing game. They have a good passing quarterback and an excellent receiver. Their running game is a supplement to their passing attack and our defensive backs will be tested." There were no injuries unless you count *"Just some hurt feelings."* It was time for redemption.

Of the first 34 plays, 27 of them were by the Flash offense. The first possession was an 85-yard drive in 15 plays to the Bulldog 8 only to lose control on a fumble. The Flashes soon had the ball again, and this time it was Sam Brown carrying 4 times for 51 yards. He capped the work with a 5-yard touchdown to make it 6-0. Just before halftime, Byram scored when Jimmy Booth hit Steve Coleman from the 12. The two-pointer was good for the lead of 8-6. The pass must have awakened the defense as Booth eventually ended up with just 3 completions on 17 attempts to go with 4 interceptions.

On the next drive, powered mostly by Brown and McConnell rushes, Brown went in from the 4 to polish off a 7-play 44-yard drive. They almost scored again when LaHatte picked off Booth at the Byram 41 and brought it back to the 25. But the next three passes fell harmlessly and it was halftime. In the 3rd, McConnell threw a pick to the Bulldogs at the Flash 15. Byram returned the favor on a fumble recovered by Barfield near the goal. Instead of risking the turnover or easy touchdown, the Flashes gave up the intentional safety on 4th down. Cox took the punt and stepped out of the back of the endzone to make it 12-10.

Byram took the kick and moved downfield before a DeRossette interception at the 44. The Flashes didn't score as they fumbled at the 1 after a 12-play drive of 84-yards. The Bulldogs were trying to get points before the final gun but lost on downs on 4th-and-4 at the 7. DeRossette then went in from the 3 and McConnell ran in the 2-pointer. With a combined 5 interceptions, 6 fumbles, and 20 penalties, it was a sloppy game from any perspective. Assistant coach Jimmy Salmon stated later, "*What worries us most is the motion penalties. We were called on some clipping penalties, but that was judgement on the part of the officials. We have got to eliminate our mistakes against Raymond.*" Edwards didn't mention either of those things afterwards. "*We played a good defensive ball game. I thought our defensive backs played real well.*"

DeRossette told Austin Bishop, "*We were firing off the ball real well. We have been working real hard and we have decided that we don't want to lose anymore*". He, Brown and John Laboda won Honorable Mentions in the paper for their efforts on the night.

GAME 4:   SAINT AL (2-1) vs RAYMOND (3-0)
               FINAL: ST AL 8 RAYMOND 21
               September 21, 1979

The flu bug was back and the number of starters that would miss the game was unknown. "*I would have to say our backs are against the wall. We are going to be hurting depth wise. When we lose someone, we can't just run someone else in. We have to adjust our personnel and because of this we have people going both ways.*" Coupled with bad weather, it meant a tough week to get ready for an undefeated CAC opponent ranked Number 1 in The Clarion Ledger's BB-B Poll. Fortunately, Raymond was in the conference, but not in the division. They had outscored their opponents 136-0 thus far, with 64 coming against Saint Andrews. Salmon said "*If they get a chance, they are going to score big against us. But don't think it's going to be an easy game. I don't think Raymond has been tested yet but they will be this Friday night.*"

Edwards said, "*If we win, good; and if we lose, well, Saint Aloysius will still be here. It's a big game for us, but it won't make or break our season. We were 2-2 last year and went on to win the championship. We are more worried about how we are going to stand at the end of the year that we are about one game. (But) we fully intend to win this game. Raymond is a good solid team but they aren't awesome. They can be beaten just like anyone else. It is going to take a monumental effort for us to beat them. But I think we are about due one.*" The Flashes had beaten Raymond in the 1978 CAC Bowl 21-0. The Flashes were the conference champion. Raymond was not.

Saint Al moved all the way to the Ranger 36 before fumbling on 4th down. Afterwards, the quarter belonged to the Rangers. On 4th-and-25 from the Flash 25, the snap to punter Cox went over his head and resulted in Allen Williams tackling Cox for a safety. This had happened two games previously against Utica for the same result. After 38 yards in 5 plays, Lenal Freeman scored a 28 yard touchdown to make it 8-0.

In the 3rd, Bunton picked off a Barfield pass and took it back 71 yards for a 15-0 lead. But the Flashes were to get the same gift in the 4th. Bart Ballard threw an errant ball and DeRossette came up with it for a 45 yard touchdown. DeRossette converted the 2-pointer and it was now 15-8. The Rangers put the finishing touches at the close of the game. Behind Cooper's running, the Ranger drive was a total of 105 yards when penalties are counted. Ballard went in on a 1-yard sneak, Bob Bell blocked the extra point attempt, but the game was over. Said Cooper afterwards, "*The line just bore down and started blocking. The line just did the job when it was needed.*"

In spite of the loss, Edwards was fairly upbeat. "*I thought our defense did a good job. Besides the one long drive late in the game, they only got about 100 yards (statistically 80). So actually, the defense played them real well. For the first time this season we looked like St. Al is supposed to. We play to play Raymond in the CAC Bowl. Either them or Utica."* For his interception, 10 tackles and 7 assists, DeRossette was named "Player of the Week". Perry Cox garnered Honorable Mention.

GAME 5:   SAINT AL (2-2) @ SAINT ANDREWS (0-4)
               FINAL: ST AL 27 SAINT ANDREWS 0
               September 28, 1979

Edwards remained positive. *"We aren't hanging our heads. You can tell them that the Flashes are going to be alright. We are 2-2 right now, and in the two games we have lost, I felt like we beat ourselves. We are striving to improve in every game. If we continue to improve and win every week, then by the end of the season, no one is going to think much about those two losses. We are still in good shape, but we are going to have to make some changes. We have to get the right combination. We are looking for the right combination of players. I think these moves are going to strengthen our team and put a few of our players where they will be in a position to help us more."*
       LaHatte would step in to help at the QB spot. *"Lanny Barfield will start, but we want to play Cicero more. Lanny plays a big leadership role for us as linebacker and we have been asking a lot of him. He does a lot of hitting on defense and then turns around and plays quarterback. Toward the end of the game, he starts getting worn down and Cicero will be able to give him a breather."* Among other changes, freshman Pat Evans would now be playing after earning his spot at nose guard. For this week, Bob McConnell was doubtful with a sore ankle.
       The only first half score was in the 1st by Brown from the 9. Hogan's PAT made it 7-0. The purple and gold were driving again in the 2nd but penalties and fumbles extinguished any hope to pad the lead. Brown added two more touchdowns in the 3rd on runs of 5 and 6. Brown added a two-pointer to make it 21-0. Scoring was finished when LaHatte found Breithaupt from the 25.
       Brown's 224 yards were stellar. *"By far it was my biggest night as a player. My line was blocking well and gave me the protection I needed. It's a start, and I hope I am able to continue to do as well. I loved every yard of it."* Edwards agreed. *"Sam had a good night. He performed well..."* As for the team, he added *"As a whole, I thought under the circumstances that our kids came out in the second half and did a good job. We are still making a lot of mistakes that we are going to have to correct, if we are going to win against some of the teams we still have to play."* Brown was the obvious selection for "Player of the Week".

GAME 6:   SAINT AL (3-2) vs MISSISSIPPI SCHOOL FOR THE DEAF (0-5)
               FINAL: ST AL 34 MSD 0
               October 5, 1979

Edwards was concerned about looking ahead to Puckett. *"We aren't overlooking MSD because it will be a division game. ... We cannot afford to be upset. We have to play heads-up ball against anyone we play to win. But the next week we have Puckett, and that will probably be the biggest game of the year. If we are going to do anything in this division, we are going to have to win that game."*
       The Flashes were still dealing with injuries that include Bob McConnell (ankle), Perry Cox (knee) and Tony Franco (knee). *"We have some people hurt right now. But we are hoping that they are all going to come around. It seems to be more of nagging types of injuries more than anything real serious."* To be cautious, both Cox and Bob McConnell sat out to ready themselves for Puckett. Practices focused to *"eliminate penalties (that) have hurt us all year. We have a good team and we are going to get better. But it is going to take work to do it."*
       On the first possession of the game, Mike McCain took it back 90 yards for a 6-0 lead. After a 4-and-out by MSD, the Flashes were back in business. It took Brown only two plays to convert. The first was a run of 25 and the second was the 15 yard score and a 12-0 lead. After starting at their 32, MSD gave up a fumble that was recovered by Paul Koestler. Barfield immediately hit a wide-open DeRossette from the 20, followed by a McConnell dive for the 2-pointer to make it 20-0.
       The Saint Al defense held MSD yet again, and this time Brown found the endzone from the 8 after 6 plays. Barfield hit DeRossette for the 2 and it was quickly 28-0. Younger players took the field and showed that they, too, had talent. Freshman Craig Stamm dropped a 19-yard pass into freshman Johnny Gussio's hands for a quick 19-yard touchdown. The 34-0 scoring would be finalize the game.
       There were a couple of other Bulldog turnovers for the Flashes benefit. Both Gussio and Keith Ehrhardt picked off passes, and fumbles were pounced on by Koestler and Mike Mahoney. The

younger brother of Sam Brown outrushed him in the game. John Brown has 21 carries for 131 yards while his older brother had just 86 yards on 5 carries. As for MSD, they amassed only 88 yards of total offense. As expected, Edwards wasn't overly excited about the win. *"We didn't get a lot accomplished... Our first team really didn't break a sweat. I was glad that the younger players got in some experience."* John Brown won Honorable Mention in voting for "Player of the Week".

GAME 7:   SAINT AL (4-2) vs PUCKETT (4-2)
                     FINAL: ST AL 0 PUCKETT 14
                     October 12, 1979: HOMECOMING

The CAC game Edwards frequently mentioned would probably determine who would play for title on November 15th in Byram. Both teams had lost to Utica and Raymond, and the winner was sure to face one of them again. *"I don't think there will be a lot of points scored by either team. It should be a defensive struggle all the way. They have a quick, hard-hitting defense. We are going to try a few things that we haven't done so far to put some points on the scoreboard. We had better play the best game of the year if we hope to win."* Sickness had taken its toll this week with LaHatte, Bob and Bart Bell, and Phillip Hogan all missing school and practices. This would combine to hurt the home team in a pivotal game to determine their future.

The scoring began in the 2nd when, with the ball at the Saint Al 34, the Wolves drove 9 plays resulting in a Johnny Cameron plunge from the 2. His PAT made it 7-0. Later in the half, George McConnell grabbed a fumbled Puckett punt at the 39. Saint Al got to the 19 before LaHatte was picked off by Lawrence Newsome on a 3rd-and-14 pass. *"It hurt us when we didn't score in the first half. If we could have put some points on the boards when we got inside their 20, we would have had a good chance of winning."* The Wolves last touchdown came in the 3rd. The 61-yard drive in 8 plays was keyed by an Archie Fletcher run of 40 yards all the way down to the 5. Cameron took it in from the 1

"We got whipped by a good team. We had some people hurt and we couldn't do a lot of the things that we had planned to do." The injury comment was directed toward Sam Brown who suffered a hip-pointer in the 1st quarter and wouldn't return. *"When we lost Brown, we lost our speed to the outside. We had to either run up the middle or pass. George McConnell did a good job just getting out there tonight. He was still feeling the effects of being sick, but we had to have him and he showed what he was made of by giving everything he had."* For that effort, McConnell was Honorable Mention for "Player of the Week".

What Edwards didn't mention was the fact that the Flashes had topped the 100-yard mark in penalties for the 4th time in 7 games with one other game netting 95 yards in flags.

GAME 8:   SAINT AL (4-3) @ PISHAH (5-1)
                     FINAL: ST AL 27 PISGAH 0
                     October 19, 1979

Said Edwards, *"I'm looking forward to going over there and playing Pisgah. I used to coach over that way and I know some of their people well."* But this wasn't a friendly visit. *"They are 5-1 and they will be tough. They are very big on defense and we have our work cut out. Pisgah is a much improved team. You don't stumble around all season and come up with five wins."* Brown still had the hip-pointer but DeRossette would be back. Edwards also planned on playing a host of younger Flashes including Evans, Gussio, and Keith Ehrhardt.

The first offensive play for the Flashes was a Mike McCain fumble that gave Pisgah the ball at the Flash 43. But a few plays later, the favor was returned when a handoff from Brandon Bright to Robert Williams ended up in the hands of Bob McConnell. After holding Saint Al, another fumble by Williams was recovered by McCain and resulted in a 52-yard dash to the endzone for a 6-0 lead.

On the ensuing drive, the Dragons pushed the ball to the Flash 32 in 12 plays before Bart Bell intercepted Bright at the goal and took it back to the Pisgah 17. McConnell then hit the endzone behind blocking from Evans and Laboda make it 12-0. Late in the 2nd, Pisgah punted to LaHatte, who received it at the 35. While returning it, it was knocked away. But DeRossette was there, grabbed the ball on the run and took it to paydirt. LaHatte found Breithaupt for the two points to make it 20-0. The final score of the game came in the 4th when Breithaupt returned a punt to the Dragon 43. McConnell did the rest, carrying 4 times for 30 yards. The last seven was a blast into the endzone to make the final 26-0.

There could have been a score by Pisgah before the clock expired. With: 38 left, Bright pitched to Williams who, in turn, tossed a touchdown to Clyde Grant. But a flag was on the field. The

Dragons tried it again to Pete Halbrook and got to the 5, but the ensuing fumble was recovered by Steve Butler and the game was over. Said Edwards post-game, *"This was a big game. I was real satisfied. Things have been kind of tough lately. They're not the best team we have played but this game was important. They are much improved from last year. They surprised us the way they moved the ball in the early going. I was a little scared* (during that early drive), *but things turned out alright. We have three tough games left, but I think we should win those."*

Though Saint Al blanked their opponent, statistically Pisgah had done very well. They doubled Flash first downs (12-6), had more rushing yards (151-126), more passing yards (56-0) and completions, and fewer penalty yards. But their turnovers were deadly. McConnell's 132 rushing yards helped his team. *"The line was blocking real good. Mike McCain did a good job on the ends also."* For the game, McConnell and DeRossette shared "Player of the Week" nods.

GAME 9:   SAINT AL (5-3) vs FRANKLIN COUNTY (5-2)
             FINAL: ST AL 14 FCHS 10
             October 26, 1979

Saint Al would face a big Class AA team this week. *"They are as big physically as Warren Central. By no means are they as talented as the Vikings, but we have to worry about their size and depth."* Edwards worked two days on defense and tweaked the formation to an eight-man front. *"We are going to have to take our chances. We are going to have to stop their running game and contain their passing. So far, they haven't looked outstanding with their passing and we are centering more on their running game. They have two good back that we will have to watch."* Brown would play while still bothered by the hip, but otherwise the team was fairly injury-free. *"I think we are heading up. Physically, we are in the best shape that we have been in all year."*

Saint Al gave up their first possession on a mishandled snap between Barfield and Laboda that was recovered by Dewayne Whittington at the Flash 36. Ten plays later, Henry Jones made a 25-yard FG to make it 3-0. The Bulldogs drove again in the 2nd, but this time Jones missed the 53-yard attempt. The Flashes got on track shortly thereafter when Sam Brown took a pitchout and raced 79 yards for the score. Barfield hit DeRossette for the two-points to make it 8-3. Franklin County responded with a six-minute drive where Alonzo Harris picked up 17 yards to the Saint Al 5. From there, Steve Kennedy found Gary Rodgers for the go-ahead score. Jones' PAT made it 10-8. Franklin County almost scored again before half when a blocked punt by Larry Hickinbottom put the Bulldogs at the Flash 18. But an interception by Mike McCain stopped the scoring opportunity to end the half.

The second half really came down to three drives. First, the Flashes were inside Bulldog territory following the kickoff, but a Breithaupt fumble gave the ball back to FCHS. Second, and also in the 3rd, the Bulldogs missed a 46-yard FG. The final drive of note was early in the 4th when starting at his own 28, McConnell gained 13 on a run. A flag gave the Flashes an additional 15 yards for roughness. The drive was capped by Brown who took in from the 8. The final score was secured at 14-10.

Said head man Michael Goff, *"We weren't ready to play ball. We just came here to go through the motions. Every time we got the ball in good field position, a flag would hit the ground. This was our worst game of the year."* In contrast, Edwards was upbeat. *"It was the best that we have played all year. They were a good team and our defense faced the best offensive line it has faced all season. They didn't have that much speed, but we had to work to stop them. We have had a better attitude in the last two weeks. I think our players realize they're playing for St. Al and they have a lot of pride."*

For his 13 tackles at linebacker while also quarterbacking the club, Barfield was "Player of the Week". Sam Brown's 155 yard game and Bob Bell's efforts made them Honorable Mention.

GAME 10:   SAINT AL (6-3) @ PELAHATCHIE (3-6)
              FINAL: ST AL 6 PELAHATCHIE 0
              November 2, 1979

Flashes now faced a 3-6 Pelahatchie team but nobody was willing to overlook anyone this year and *"intense"* workouts were underway. *"They are better defensively than they are offensively. We are going to put some time into our offense today to see what we can do against them. They have been coming on lately and I feel like they are an improving team."* But the kicking game was always on the agenda. *"You can never have a letdown on your kicking game; because that's the best way I know* to get beat. We spent some time on this and used the remainder of the practice working on fundamentals and conditioning."

On their second possession, McCain gained 24 and Barfield got them to the 6. But then a mishandled snap gave the ball to the Chiefs. In the 2nd, Barfield hit Breithaupt in the endzone but the referee ruled him out of bounds. That drive fizzled three plays later at the Pelahatchie 31. In the 2nd half, James McAllister had a 26 yard run that would have scored were it not for a McCain tackle from behind. Next was a 20 yard run by Sammy Johnson to the 10. But LaHatte deflected a Shannon King pass on 4th down to give the Flashes the ball. DeRossette would fumble to end the scoring chance.

The next Flash drive was repeated when McCain fumbled the ball to the Chiefs. The defense held, but on their next possession, it was George McConnell who fumbled at the Flash 15. Once again, the defense held and regulation ended scoreless. The Flashes received to start overtime but could not drive. On the ensuing Chief possession, the Flashes avoided disaster when Perry Cox blocked a King 28-yard FG attempt. On the next possession, Barfield ran the sneak to the one-inch line and DeRossette went in for the score. The game was over when LaHatte intercepted a King pass. Saint Al had gone through double-overtime and survived a turnover-infested contest.

"We will take it any way we can get it. We had many breaks fall against us, but we won it when we had to. We were down for this game. The Franklin County game emotionally took a lot out of us. We looked real flat." For defensive line efforts that resulted in 10 tackles, Bob McConnell won "Player of the Week", with DeRossette and Bart Bell tabbed for Honorable Mention.

GAME 11:   SAINT AL (7-3) @ JACKSON SAINT JOSEPH (5-5)
            FINAL: ST AL 8 JACKSON ST JOE 9
            November 9, 1979

Saint Al was healthy and, in Edwards' words, "getting ready and on Friday night we are going to get after them." He had seen his Class A opponent. "They run a varied offense. They have a fine passer in Joe Rooks and we expect them to throw the ball a lot. They are going to be a lot bigger than we are and we will be depending on our quickness. They are by far the best defensive team that we have had to face all season. Their line outweighs up by 20 pounds per man, and we are starting two freshmen and a sophomore while they are starting three seniors."

Edwards inserted a few stunts in the defense to defend the pass. "We really don't want to use these stunts, but we may need to put pressure on their passing game if they start slicing us up. ..What we were mainly concerned with is eliminating mistakes. We didn't play them last year, and I think some of the intensity of the game has worn off. This is the first game with St. Joe that I have been involved with since I came here, but I have coached against them and they do a good job. They are well coached and I'm expecting a tough game."

The Flashes came close to scoring first in the opening stanza. They moved from their 34 to the 4 with catches by Breithaupt of 29 and 14 yards and a McConnell run of 15. But penalties and a Mike Barranco sack forced them to end up punting from the Bruin 46 and halftime remained scoreless. Saint Al looked to get going on the Bruins' first possession of the 2nd half when Bob Bell picked off a Rooks pass and brought it back to the St Joe 17. But on fourth down, a mishandled snap gave the ball back to the home team. The defense held and DeRossette took advantage of a bad snap on their punt. Saint Al had the ball at the 3. Four plays later, DeRossette went in from inches out followed by George McConnell's two-point sweep to make it 8-0.

On a third-down play, Edwards called on Cox to punt, and he boomed it 51 yards to the Bruin 19. But Saint Joe was to go 81 yards in 14 plays, with Kevin Campbell going in from the 4. Laboda and Cox stuffed the two-pointer but the Flashes were in control 8-6. As the rain continued to fall, there were three straight turnovers before the gun sounded. First, Bob McConnell's fumble on third down was recovered by Paul Byers. But he avenged himself when, on the next play, Rooks did the same only to have McConnell recover. Finally, a bad exchange between Barfield and McConnell gave the ball to the Bruins' Paul Harkins. Saint Joe was now at the Flash 25 with 1:06 left.

A distraught Edwards said of the last play, "Do not blame George or Lanny on the fumble. I made a poor call. The call I made would have worked, but it shouldn't have been called. We had them beat. We played good the whole ball game. You can't blame anyone but me. I made a stupid call late in the game under pressure. We just got greedy.""

The Bruins immediately moved to the 15 on a slant pass from Rooks to John Tiller, and then with just :07 left in the game, Rooks hit a 24-yard FG on a Mark Trebotich hold for the win. Bruin Head

Coach Bill Raphael told Miles Marcus of <u>The Vicksburg Evening Post</u>, *"We were very fortunate. We didn't play an inspired football game. However, they never gave up and came back under pressure."*

The All Warren County Football Team was announced in December. Barfield, McCain, McConnell were tabbed. Honorable mentions went to DeRossette, Bart Bell, Laboda and Franco. Lanny Barfield was the recipient of the Virgadamo Trophy.

"Going into the season, anything short of a repeat CAC Championship would be a letdown. We had a strong group of returning seniors. Unfortunately, we fell short with losses that still sting today. That's part of what makes Saint Al great; a winning tradition and deep pride that hurts with any loss.

That being said, the good memories far outweigh the bad. Dedicated coaches, Edwards barking "weight room" and eight-eighty", and Salmon riding the two-man sled. We had a lot of brothers on that team. Bells, Browns, DeRossettes, McCains, McConnells, and even a "Brother Franco". Looking back, we were all brothers. The friendships made were lasting, the roots of which took hold during two-a-days in the August heat on the Saint Al football field."

Lanny Barfield; August 1, 2016

1980-1986

SAINT ALOYSIUS 1982 TEAM (10-1)

1980 (7-5)

Starting where they left off. That's the term Edwards used about opening practices. *"We worked on our kicking game in the morning practice, and on offense in the afternoon practice. We are starting where we left off last spring and try to improve each day."* They lost 13 seniors and younger players would have to be ready mentally and physically. *"We are going to have to stay away from any big injuries. We are kind of young this year. I won't say that we don't have any depth; just no experience. I think that it is safe to say that we are untested. We are going to be a steadily improving team. They just don't have any playing experience. We are going to have to play (the younger guys) some. We plan to work on basic alignments and fundamentals this week. We have to concentrate on this because we are so young. We will be putting a lot of time into conditioning. We have a ways to go there before we play Utica."*

The first week had Edwards say that George McConnell, Cicero LaHatte, Barry Breithaupt, Sam Brown and junior transfer from Warren Central Greg Hull *"have looked real well"*. The pads came out the following Monday. *"The fun part is over. Now we are going to get down to the tough stuff."* It went well, noting that they were *"looking better every day"*. A stickler for perfection, he added *"We still have a lot of room for improvement, but I can see that we are headed in the right direction. We scrimmaged some today and looked real good. We have some people who can play in spots, but our second unit is not coming around as well as we had hoped. I'm really displeased with this group because I know that they can play better than this."*

As for predictions, Edwards said *"The first ball game will be important. If we can go down there and win, we could have a great season. If we lose, we still could have a good year. I would hope that we would be in a position to challenge for the overall championship. There will be no let-ups for us this year. We have some tough opponents at their place. It's going to be tough right out of the box. Our first three ball games are going to be tough. You really never know whether you are ready or not. You have to play and find out."*

GAME 1:   SAINT AL (0-0) @ UTICA (0-0)
            FINAL: ST AL 7 UTICA 6
            SEPTEMBER 5, 1980

Speaking of Utica's first win against the Flashes the previous season, Edwards said *"Most of the kids on this team didn't play in that game last year. Each game is a new situation. You can't go back and bring up the past while getting ready to play."* But George McConnell hadn't forgotten. *"I remember at the game last year, they came up to us saying 'we finally beat St. Al'. I felt they were laughing at us. I'm sure they are going to be tough again, and it is a big game for both teams. I would like to see us win it and kind of even the score from last year."*

Utica coach Coach George Walker wasn't hanging everything on that 1979 game. *"St. Al may be young, but I know that they have some fine players. We respect these people and we are going to be ready to play a tough football game. Last year, it seemed to our kids that the season hung in the balance with the St. Al game. It's a good rivalry and we are expecting a good game. But we aren't pushing it like we did in 1979."* Edwards added *"We are probably playing one of the top two teams in the CAC. Our young defense is going to have its work cut out for it. Utica has an explosive offense and we have to stop their big play. If we are going to stay with them, we are going to have to contain them."*

In the 2nd, Utica started at their 26 and marched 11 plays finalized by a 34-yard pass from Tom Cole to Clifton Callahan. The 2-pointer was picked off to keep it 6-0. The second half started with a rush for 62 by tailback Sam Brown. LaHatte went in from the 6 to finish the drive and Ehrhardt's kick made it 7-6. The only threat afterwards was a Utica march from their 23 to the Flash 15. In spite of 20 yards in Saint Al penalties to give the home team the ball so close, the defense held and secured the first win of the season.

The Vicksburg Evening Post had the headline **"Young St. Al Stuns Utica"**. Said Edwards *"One thing that I was a little disappointed in was our passing attack. We didn't try very many passes and this is something that we are going to have to work into our offense. We made some technique mistakes. But one thing our kids did was hustle. I thought Greg Hull did a good job blocking while he was at fullback, and Barry Breithaupt, Brian DeRossette and David Gamble id a good job on the defense. Overall I was pleased with our defense. We bent a little and gave up some yardage. But we didn't break. Offensively, we made a few mistakes that hurt us. I thought Cicero LaHatte ran the ball club* well, and Sam Brown and George McConnell did a good job running. We were able to run better than I anticipated. I feel that in Sam and George, we have two of the best backs in the CAC."

For their work, McConnell and Brown won Honorable Mentions for "Player of the Game".

GAME 2:   SAINT AL (1-0) v BYRAM (1-0)
       FINAL: ST AL 27 BYRAM 0
       SEPTEMBER 12, 1980

Edwards' practices for Byram were intense. *"It was kind of sloppy. But it was because of the heat. We went right out and worked on some fundamentals and we just wore them out. It must have been about 100 degrees when we went out there."* He'd seen film from the previous week in which they trounced Saint Andrews 44-12. *"They have some big backs. They are running behind a senior offensive line. They are much better than years past. I hope I can get that across to our boys. (They are) a much improved ball club. They are more disciplined and they are starting six across the line. Their quarterback is young, but he seemed to do everything that they asked of him well."*

When asked about the passing game, he said *"If we can put together a passing game, it would be a big help to our runners. It's hard to really tell what is wrong... We had several receivers open during the game, but failed to hit them for some reason or another. It is hard to build a passing game. ..They don't have much time to spend on it."* The team had only one slight injury on deep-snapper John McCain (wrist) and Edwards was confident. *"I expect to win the game. I think our kids are going to be ready to give a good effort. We are going to do what we can to beat them. We are definitely ready."*

By kickoff, injuries had demolished the Bulldogs. Three starters were lost including the quarterback. The helmsman (Ken Churchill) would be a 9th grader, as were many others. Said Coach Gary Post, *"Whenever I turn to our bench, all I see is ninth-graders."* The Flashes scored two plays after the kickoff when LaHatte pitched to Gussio who hit Breithaupt from the 17 for a touchdown. Ehrhardt made it 7-0 early. In the 2nd, Brown and LaHatte moved from their own 11 to the Bulldog 14 in 9 plays. Brown reached the endzone and, with Ehrhardt's kick, it was 14-0.

Brown and McConnell's rushing around the ends put the ball at the 2 to start the 2nd half. McConnell capped it to make it 20-0. Later with 2nd-and-16 from the Flash 14, LaHatte found Breithaupt for 25 and he went the rest of the way for the final touchdown. For offensive and defensive efforts, McConnell was "Player of the Game". Edwards gave praise to 10 others by name. *"We played well in spots. I thought our entire offensive unit played a pretty good game, but I was a little disappointed in our defense."*

GAME 3:   SAINT AL (2-0) @ RAYMOND (1-1)
       FINAL: ST AL 0 RAYMOND 36
       SEPTEMBER 19, 1980: HINDS JUNIOR COLLEGE

Defending CAC champion Raymond was coming off of a 35-15 victory versus North Pike. *"Raymond has a lot of talent. They have big players that will probably outweigh us by as much as 20 pounds per man. In this game, we cannot be making the mistakes that we made in our first two and hope to win. Our defense is going to have to be on its toes the whole game. But Raymond is not a one-man team. We are going to have to play a near perfect game to win. I scouted their first game against Cathedral which they lost, and I think they were a little over-confident. I don't think they will let that happen again. I seriously think we can win this football game. ..with our group this year, I know we will have a supreme effort from all of our players. If we lose the game, it will be because they beat us. We won't beat ourselves."*

The Flashes started from their 20 and drove to the Ranger 19 in 15 plays. But on a second 4th-down attempt, LaHatte came up six inches short and gave the ball to Raymond. Afterwards, Edwards noted that *"If we had picked up that six inches on the first drive, I think it might have been different. We could have stopped their momentum if we could have gotten it in, and it would have been tough on them."* Raymond then took the ball to the Flash 19 but missed a 29-yard FG. The drive also saw George Thomas go down with a shoulder injury and would be expected to miss at least a couple of weeks. In the 2nd, the Rangers held the Flashes on 4 plays and began a drive at their 47. Eight plays later, James Cooper punched it in from the 11 for a 7-0 halftime lead.

The 2nd half started with a Cooper score from the 4 after 7 plays. Thomas Bunton added the PAT to give them a 14-0 cushion. After that, the wheels came off of what had been a turnover–free game for Saint Al. The first was an Allen Williams fumble recovery at the Flash 3 that resulted in a Tim Vance touchdown from the 1. Bunton was the recipient of the next turnover: a mishandled snap from center at the 42. The Rangers took that opportunity and drove 11 plays. Elijah Paige scored from the 2 with seconds remaining in the 3rd to make it 27-0. Said Edwards afterwards, *"Things went the wrong way for us in the 3rd quarter. We got some people hurt and they just had the numbers on us."*

Two plays later, another fumble put Utica at the Flash 3. Cooper ran it in and it was now an overwhelming 34-0. Scoring was completed when the Rangers sacked LaHatte in the endzone for a safety. *"Our kids didn't quit. For as many bad things that happened to us, we didn't quit. You have to credit Raymond with those fumbles. They were bigger, stronger and they probably played their best game of the year. This is the worst St. Al has lost by in a while. But Raymond is the best team that we have played in a while, too."* Cooper, with 200 yards of rushing, lived up to the expectations of the Saint Al coach. Said Raymond Coach Ken Granberry, *"St. Al has a good club, but our bunch was fired up. We lost our opener and they didn't want it to happen again."*

"I thought Cicero kept his composure real well. He showed me a lot of leadership and he really took some shots". For that effort, LaHatte was the "Player of the Game". Sam Brown and George McConnell garnered Honorable Mentions.

GAME 4: SAINT AL (2-1) v SAINT ANDREWS (1-2)
FINAL: ST AL 32 ST. ANDREWS 12
SEPTEMBER 26, 1980

Thomas was out for at least 4 weeks, Gamble's back was still an issue, Hull bruised a bone in his hand and Gussio had fluid on the knee. *"We are pretty well beat up, but we are going to have to get ready to go again. We need to do some work out there, but I can't afford to get anyone else hurt. We are so thin as it is anyway. We are hurting right now."*

He had reviewed film of the Raymond game and said *"I was kind of pleased with the defense. We gave them the ball inside our ten three times. That was 18 points right there. Besides that, we held them pretty good. I haven't quit and I don't think the players have either. I think it brought our players back to earth."* Edwards was a mixed bag for another CAC opponent. *"I'm not trying to say that St. Andrews is as good as Raymond. But I do know that they have a fine defensive team and they will hit you. Offensively they are strong in running the ball. I think they will try to run at us. We are going to have to play well to win. They have beaten Terry and they are coming to beat us."*

It would be a "coming out" party for senior tailback Sam Brown. With 296 yards of rushing, he set a record that wouldn't be threatened for years. In the 1st, and after 4 plays and 2 penalties, they were only at the 30 when LaHatte hit Breithaupt for the first score to make it 6-0. In the 2nd, Gussio picked off a Chris Nichols pass and brought it back to the Saint 26. Four plays later, LaHatte closed it out with a 7 yard touchdown run. The Flashes were now up 12-0. The 1st half closed when Brown pushed it in from 18 yards on a 6-play drive of 36 yards.

In the 2nd half, the Flashes poured it on. On the initial play, Brown went 48 for another touchdown. The kick made it 25-0. Saint Andrews' answering drive started at their 27 and went 73 yards in 10 plays, capped by a Scott Vanlandingham pass to Chris Nichols. The 2-point conversion was not good and the lead was now 25-6. After the ensuing kickoff and on the 2nd play from scrimmage, Brown went 65 yards up the middle for the final Flash score. The Saints had one last chance against the second team and threw four "bombs"; the last one connecting with Charles Fowler at the 38 with :10 left to make it 32-12. *"I was glad we were able to play the second string team. When you only have four of five seniors on your whole team in the first place, (they) play a big part. Of course we're glad to win. But I'm really not as proud of the way they played this week as I was last week. We did too many things poorly that we usually do better."*

The "Player of the Game" was obviously Brown, while LaHatte and Breithaupt shared the Honorable Mentions.

GAME 5: SAINT AL (3-1) @ MISSISSIPPI SCHOOL FOR THE DEAF (0-4)
FINAL: ST AL 48 MSD 7
October 3, 1980

"On paper, this is not supposed to be one of the better teams on our schedule. But you never know. If we don't prepare for them, they could sneak up on us. They have a lot of speed. But they are really young and aren't that strong. We made a lot of mistakes last Friday night (on offense) and we

need to correct them. This is the type of game that really worries me because we should win it. But if we go in there and make a lot of mistakes, it could get tough."

Edwards ran the team through an hour-and-a-half Tuesday practice. "We cannot keep making the mistakes that we made last week and I feel like we made some progress today. We had a good workout and I feel that our kids responded well. MSD has good, quick receivers and a good quarterback, and we have to be ready to stop them." The injury situation was better with North Division CAC foe Puckett upcoming. "We aren't planning to run up the score real bad, and we hope to play our reserves a lot. But the main thing I want to do is go over and win the game and get our without any injuries."

Not much is written about the game. We know that it was Brown who paced the Flashes early, scoring two touchdowns of 30 and 31 yards. At the end of the 1st, it was 14-0. In the 2nd, LaHatte hit Breithaupt for 2 touchdowns covering 24 and 30 yards. Ehrhardt made his 4th extra point to make it 28-0. Edwards then called on freshman quarterback Kevin Mahoney to steer the squad. And he was successful, driving down to the 2 and then carrying it in himself. The extra point attempt was no-good and it was 34-0.

The only MSD score came courtesy of a 3rd quarter Flash fumble when Terry Jenkins picked it up and went 68 yards. Bobby David was good on the try and it was 34-7. On the ensuing kickoff, Brown took the ball 89 yards for the touchdown to make it 41-7. Scoring was finished in the 4th when Bill Hoxie bullied in from the 10.

Edwards was happy with the players. "I thought several of our younger players (Hoxie, Chris Gardner, Mike & Kevin Mahoney, and Marty Agostinelli) had a good game. They were able to get some experience, which will be good for our team in the long run. We really didn't need to play this game the week before the Puckett game. We really didn't accomplish that much. I was glad that our younger players got to see some action. But our starters needed to play a tough game to get tuned up for Puckett. MSD has improved a lot over last year. They got out there and played hard. But I had really rather have played this game the first week of the season or the last week."

No Flash won "Player of the Game", but Hoxie and Brown did get Honorable Mentions.

GAME 6:   SAINT AL (4-1) @ PUCKETT (3-2)
                FINAL: ST AL 13 PUCKETT 21
                October 10, 1980

The game would probably determine the CAC North Division champion. The Wolves had beaten the Flashes 14-0 the previous year to end what Steve Swogetinsky called "the Flashes two-year dominance of the CAC Bowl". Said Edwards, "I've seen Puckett play once, and watched them on film twice. If we play at our best, we can beat them. But we can't have any letdowns. … They have one of the best running backs in the conference in Johnny Cameron."

As for injuries, Pat Evans hit his hand during practice and Edwards didn't know if it was "either jammed or broken. (But) it really hurts us because we are thin on our line, as far as experienced people go." He added later that week, "We'll do alright if we are well. Basically, we are going to have to stop their outside running. They have a couple of fine backs, and their quarterback has shown that he can be effective in short passing situations. We … feel that we are prepared for it. But this can change. Puckett can be unpredictable and we have to be ready to stop whatever they throw at us. They know how much this game means and they will be getting up for this game."

Edwards eerily noted before the Tuesday practice that the Flashes had emphasized the kicking game that Monday. "I have a funny feeling that the team with the best kicking game will win. It will play an important factor."

The Flashes scored first on a 10-play 70-yard drive that culminated with a LaHatte-to-Breithaupt touchdown from the 25. Ehrhardt made it 7-0. Puckett responded immediately when Bubba Newsome went 72 yards on the ensuing kickoff to tie it up. Edwards was right about the kicking game and its importance. "We had a lot of young kids on the kickoff team, and it hurt us tonight. You always try to find a place for your younger players to come in and get some experience, but we can't do that anymore. Next week, we will have the best eleven players on our team on the kickoff team."

LaHatte had the lead-changing touchdown from the 1 later in the 2nd to give Saint Al a 13-7 advantage. Prior to the touchdown, the Wolves' Johnny Cameron went down with what appeared to be a broken leg. After the play, Puckett running back Bubba Newsome went up the middle for a 90-yard touchdown to give them the lead 14-13 with 3:51 left in the half. "That one play cost us the game. We had a chance to go into the half with a two touchdown lead and, instead, we were down by one."

Before the last whistle, Saint Al had committed a host of penalties, fumbles and shanked punts. Puckett had one more score in them when a Flash fumble gave Jackie Parker a clear shot for 69 yards and the touchdown. He also added the extra point.

"We gave the game away. I think we have a better team, but we gave it away. We will just have to put this behind us. We are going to be working harder this week than we ever had before. We can still have a good season and we can still make the conference playoffs. Anything can happen between now and then." Only Sam Brown gained status in the "Player of Game" as Honorable Mention.

GAME 7:   SAINT AL (4-2) v PISGAH (4-2)
                            FINAL: ST AL 21 PISGAH 0
                            October 17, 1980: HOMECOMING

The Flashes heavily practiced the kicking game on Monday. *"I thought we showed a lot of improvement in this area today. We are going to use our best 11 players on these teams from now on, because we can't afford to have another breakdown like we did against Puckett. They have two fine backs with a lot of speed. I don't think they have that good of a passing attack, but they run the ball well. They have some big linemen ... run a misdirection offense and what they basically try to do is to get you going one way, find a crease and then run a back through it and go."*

Sam Brown had suffered a hip pointer and would be watching from the sidelines. He was leading the county in rushing with 878 yards; 478 yards more than Warren Central's Carl Otis in second place. McConnell would step in and take over his place. Edwards knew the importance of this contest. *"If we have any chance at all to be in the conference race, we have to win Friday night. I expect them to run a lot. They have some real hard running backs to bring down. We have been doing some extra work on tackling, getting ready for them."* He had his starting OL back; the first time since the 1st quarter of the Raymond game.

Scoring was limited in the rain to only the 2nd and 4th quarters. In the 2nd, LaHatte hit Breithaupt for a 44-yard score and Ehrhardt made it 7-0. The Flashes struck again in the 4th when McConnell got away from the Green Dragon defense and scampered 65 yards for another touchdown to make it 13-0. Scoring finalized when McConnell put it in from the 4 with :40 left in the game. The Flashes went for 2 and made it when LaHatte hit Gussio. The Flashes survived the rain and another CAC opponent standing in the way of a conference crown.

"The conditions definitely had an effect on the game. I thought it would hurt us more than Pisgah. But our defense came on and played a heck of a game. Our entire line, David Gamble, George Thomas, Brian DeRossette and Pat Evans played a great game, as did our linebackers and defensive backs. George McConnell is the toughest athlete I've ever coached. If some major college doesn't sign him this winter, they are going to be missing one heck of an athlete." That athlete won "Player of the Game", with Briethaupt and LaHatte as Honorable Mentions.

There was more reason to be happy. Puckett lost to Pelahatchie 6-2, putting the Flashes right back into contention. *"I don't know what this will do to us, as far as standings in the CAC go. But this puts us back in it. Puckett still has to play Pisgah and we will have to play Pelahatchie."*

GAME 8:   SAINT AL (5-2) @ FRANKLIN COUNTY (6-0)
                            FINAL: ST AL 0 FRANKLIN COUNTY 37
                            October 24, 1980

The Flashes were facing undefeated Class A Franklin County in Meadville. *"It's just another ball game for us. I know that they are an improved club and we are going to have to get ready for a tough game."* They had a "spirited" Tuesday practice; one that Edwards had to shorten for fear of injury. *"They really got after each other. I really feel that we need to hit, but I'm afraid we are going to get somebody hurt, and at this time we can't afford any injuries. We know that we are playing an excellent team. The main way for us to stop their power offense is for our offense to move the ball and keep our defense off the field as much as possible. We are going down there with the idea that we are going to win the game. Our kids are working hard, and we are looking for a good game. Our defense is showing lots of aggressiveness, which is what we are going to need."*

There aren't recorded box scores in either team's local papers. But we know that Franklin County scored their first touchdown in the 1st with a Nolan Booker run of 13-yards to make it 6-0. Their next points came in the 2nd. Joseph Smith scored from 42, Booker scored from the 9, and then

Smith blocked a punt and took it back 15 yards. It was 24-0 at the half. Breithaupt was not to return, as he had hyper-extended his knee.

In the 3rd, Steve Kennedy hit Booker from the 25 for the score and, in the 4th, Booker took it in from the 3. Regardless of what the stats may have looked like, it was all Franklin County. Two runners went over 100 yards (Booker with 144 and Alonzo Harris with 109) and the Bulldogs put up 345 yards of offense versus the Flashes' 63. *"Since I've been coaching, I've seen a few better teams than Franklin County, but not many. They are probably one of the Top 10 teams in the state. I was very proud of our kids. They never quit. Franklin County just outmanned us and our players kept fighting back. I really want to compliment Sam Brown and George McConnell. They were getting popped real good and they stayed in there. They didn't quit."*

There were not-surprisingly any mentions regarding "Player of the Week". The Flashes had played a non-conference opponent and the result didn't matter; unless pride was a factor.

GAME 9:　　　　SAINT AL (5-3) v PELAHATCHIE (4-0 CONFERENCE)
　　　　　　　　FINAL: ST AL 28 PELAHATCHIE 0
　　　　　　　　October 31, 1980

The CAC championship was on the line for the North Division against undefeated Pelahatchie. The math was complicated as to what would happen should Saint Al win but the only thing that mattered was that they won. *"We are the only thing between Pelahatchie and the division championship. I feel like our kids will be ready to play their best game of the year this Friday night. The only thing we have to worry about is beating Pelahatchie. That's the only control we have over the division. This is a big game for us. And we are going to try to do to someone like we were done last Friday night."*

Practices that started in the August heat were now done in the rain and cold. Edwards cut it short this week saying *"I think we got some things done. It started raining and I didn't want to get anyone sick."* Edwards told Steve Swogetinsky, *"They have a better team than I thought they did. Their quarterback (Shannon King) is a big kid who can drop back and throw the ball. They have pretty good team speed. And what they run on defense is a mystery to me. Pelahatchie always plays good defense and their offense is much better this year than it has been in the past."*

As for his approach, he said *""We have to get our running game going, and then pass at the right time. That's what we believe in and that's what we will be doing. I'm sure that they will be fired up for us. They can win the conference if they beat us. This game is going to be up to the players. The team that wants this game the most will be the team that wins".*

In the 2nd, the Chiefs went three-and-out, punted and LaHatte gathered the ball in at the 12 and went 99 yards for the first Saint Al score. Ehrhardt made it 7-0. On the next possession, Pelahatchie mishandled a punt snap and the Flashes took over at the 6. Two plays later, Brown went in from the 4. McConnell gained the two-pointer to finish scoring in the half.

In the 3rd and starting at the 20, Saint Al moved to their 42 on the ground before LaHatte hit Breithaupt for a 53 yard gain to the Pelahatchie 5. Brown went in to make it 21-0. Finally, after a punt to the Flashes put them at their own 42, McConnell ripped a 21 yard run to set up another Brown score. This time it was from the 37 with: 25 left. Ehrhardt closed it out to make it 28-0. With 99 yards, Brown eclipsed the 1,000 yard mark in this game and sat at 1,028. But no "Player of the Week" honors were apparently handed out that week.

GAME 10:　　　SAINT AL (6-3) @ JACKSON SAINT JOSEPH (5-4)
　　　　　　　　FINAL: ST AL 0 JACKSON ST JOE 7
　　　　　　　　November 7, 1980

The second Class A game in three weeks would now be on a Saturday night in order to avoid competition with the Warren Central-Clinton game. *"We are hoping that their fans will come out and see us play on Saturday night. They run a very diversified offense. They will throw the ball, run a sweep or run the option and we have to be ready for all of these things. I've seen five films on (them) and they have a good team. I'm not ready to put them in the same category with Franklin County, but I know we are going to have to play well to win."*

He added, *"If we maintain good field position and don't make the big mistakes, we will be alright. We have to play a good defensive game. You can plug along on offense, and play strong* defense and win your share of games. But if you can't play defense, you can't beat anybody. We will be trying to establish our running game. And we will be passing sparingly but wisely."

This was the seniors' last time to play at Balzli Field. "It's their last home game and they want to go out winners. .. and Sam and George will be closing out outstanding careers." Said McConnell, "It's hard to believe that this is my last home game. This year has gone by quicker than I thought it would. I feel that is our biggest game of the year. They kicked a field goal to beat us last year (9-8) and we want to even that up Saturday night." According to Edwards, "Everyone is ready to play."

The game came down to one play, and with under 1:00 to go. Brown had a close call for a long touchdown called back in the 2nd when his foot was ruled to have touched the stripe at the 49. Edwards agreed with the call saying "I think it was a good call. A couple of people on the sideline who had a good view said his foot just touched the line." And in the 3rd quarter, Saint Joe was going for a 27-yarder that was blocked by Gussio.

Rushing was about even in the end (148 to 176); penalty yards were close (35 to 50); neither team had punted, and Saint Joe had 13 yards of passing versus Saint Al's 0. But the last play was all that counted. With a minute left, Cedric Love went 35 yards on a run only to be pushed out by Brown at the Flash 3. The Flashes had rushed 8 after the QB in hopes of a fumble or sack, but Love got away. On the next play, he plunged in for the dagger. Mark Trebotich kicked the PAT and scoring was done. "I felt we needed the big play to stop them. We sent in an eight-man blitz. Someone missed a tackle, and they made the big run."

As for Brown and his 122 yard effort, Edwards said (despite a 296 yard performance weeks before), "I thought it was the best game that Sam had played all year. He hung in there and fought for some tough yardage." The Flashes were still tied with Puckett and Pelahatchie for the North Division championship. All three had a 4-1 record. We aren't going to be worrying about Puckett and Pelahatchie. We are going to do our best to beat Terry and let the rest take care of itself."

GAME 11:　　　　SAINT AL (6-4) @ TERRY (UNREPORTED)
　　　　　　　　FINAL: ST AL 13 TERRY 6
　　　　　　　　November 14, 1980

The Flashes had to beat Terry and hope that Byram beat Pelahatchie in order to have a chance in the CAC Championship against Natchez Cathedral in Raymond, MS. "The Terry game is crucial for us. It is one that we can't overlook because they have nothing to lose. They have a fine quarterback in T.C. Holley. And they have a lot of team speed. Terry throws the ball real well and they have a lot of speed. If we start letting them have any success against us, we could find ourselves fighting for our lives. We are going to have to be ready for whatever they throw at us."

In the rainy 2nd, Terry's Charles Arthur got around the left for a 5-yard touchdown. It capped a Yellow Jacket drive that started after a Flash fumble at their 30. A failed 2-point conversion kept it 6-0. With 1:54 remaining, LaHatte finished a 9-play drive of 60 yards by diving in from the 2. Ehrhardt gave Saint Al the 7-6 lead going into halftime. Scoring would finish late in the 3rd when LaHatte took his team from the Flash 17 to the Terry 17. Sam Brown then went the rest of the way for the final points.

"It wasn't a pretty win, but it's a win in the record books. Terry has been playing some people close this year. They have some good athletes and they always play us close. I never had any doubt that we weren't going to win, even though they scored first. I think after they scored, our kids realized that we weren't down here on a picnic and stated playing."

In the end, there was more than one reason for celebration. Byram had not only beaten Pelahatchie, but shut them out 27-0. Saint Al was now North Division champions and playing in the CAC Bowl against a 9-1 Cathedral team. When asked about whether Saint Al was going 'through the back door' to win the berth, Edwards said "You could look at it that way. But if you think about it, whoever went to the CAC Bowl for the north was going through the back door. I think the best team in the north is going. It remains to be seen whether or not we can beat Cathedral. I feel like we can."

GAME 12:　　　　SAINT AL (7-4) v NATCHEZ CATHEDRAL (9-1)
　　　　　　　　FINAL: ST AL 7 NATCHEZ CATHEDRAL 14
　　　　　　　　November 20, 1980; BYRAM, MS

The team that was "kind of young this year" and "untested" found themselves 48 minutes from claiming the CAC championship. There was only 2 days to get ready for the big game and because of the cold and wet conditions, Brown and Alonzo were sick. "This has really put us at a disadvantage.

Cathedral has had two weeks to get ready for us and we have two days. They present us with several problems. They run out of the box some, but they also use several other formations. They don't have that break-away speed as someone like Raymond does. But they have several top notch players and they are going to be tough to beat."

Both teams were pre-season surprises. Cathedral lost 13 seniors and was expecting a rebuild. Said Edwards of Saint Al, "You always hope that you can win a championship. But with our inexperienced players at the beginning of the season, I'm a little surprised that we are in the final game. I felt like we lost a couple of games this year that we should have won. But now we have everything to gain and nothing to lose."

For head man Ken Beesley, who would be playing the championship on his birthday, he said "We are looking forward to playing St. Al. They have a good, aggressive football team", while also predicting that this game would come down to the Greenie's offense versus the Flashes defense. Edwards was more on the mental side of the coin. "I think emotions will have a lot to do in this game. We haven't really played at the right emotional peak since our second or third game. If our kids get mentally right, we are going to be tough to beat."

The Flashes were first on the scoreboard in the 2nd quarter. With the Greenies keying on Brown, it was McConnell who went right for 65 yards. Ehrhardt made it 7-0. In the same period, Greenie QB Michael Garcia hit Juan Thompson on a 4th down touchdown play from the 18. After Thompson converted the 2-points, it was 8-7 with 1:56 left in the half.

The 3rd was scoreless. The Flashes had a chance at the Cathedral 18, but McConnell fumbled. "I fumbled it. What else can you say? Someone had my leg and as I was twisting to get away, I was hit from behind. As I hit the ground, the ball got loose." Midway through the 4th, Garcia again struck through the air. This time it was Bobby Irby for 25 yards and the touchdown. The 2-pointer missed but the game was in the books. The Flashes didn't go down without a fight, but two interceptions by the Greenies' Walter Brown killed both opportunities. Beesley said, "We tried to get outside of St. Al but they cut us off. So, we got in our T formation and came straight at them. When we got in range, we went for the score with the pass."

Edwards summarized the season for Steve Swogetinsky that night. "We had a good season. We came close to having a great season, but we fell short. From what we had to work with when we started fall practice, I would have to say this team has come further than any team that we ever had. When we started, we didn't have that much experience on the offensive line and we only had four kids who had played any defense. We are going to have to put this game behind us and look forward to next season. We are only losing four seniors, and we have around 30 players returning. We are going to have a to hit the weight program this fall and build ourselves up so that we will be pushing some people around instead of having them dominate us, as was the case in a couple of games this season".

The honors that year included Breithaupt, Brown, DeRossette, Evans and McConnell as All CAC. Honorable Mentions went to Alonzo, Gamble, Gussio, Hull and LaHatte. All Warren County members included Breithaupt, Brown, Evans and McConnell with Mentions to DeRossette, Gamble, Gussio and Lahatte. The Virgadamo Trophy went to George McConnell.

1981 (11-2)

The first week of practices saw about 35 players in shorts as they "put in (the) base offense". Said Edwards, "Overall, I'm pleased with the shape that the team is coming back in. Of course there are some that aren't in too good a shape but we hope to get them into shape as quickly as possible." The first week saw a stomach virus spread to at least ten players. Injuries were numerous in Newell Simrall (broken toe), Barry Breithaupt (knee), Greg Hull (groin), Lawrence Koestler (wrist) and Bill Hoxie (ankle). All were expected to play except senior George Thomas.

On one of the last plays of a game-week scrimmage, he tore two knee ligaments and would be lost for the season. "After I found out about George, I almost called the scrimmage off. But we need the work." The next scrimmage wasn't very long for the starters because "we don't need to get anyone else hurt". As for the Madison Ridgeland game, he said, "I think (conditioning) will be the deciding point in the game. I feel that the two teams will have about the same amount of ability, but the one that is in the best shape will have the edge in the final quarter."

Edwards had Breithaupt and Johnny Gussio as solid running backs and a returning QB in Cicero LaHatte, but needed bench strength. "We have to find some depth there. But offensively, I think *we are going to be okay."* Craig Stamm would eventually settle in at number two, and Pat Evans would join the backfield as a fullback.

Beau Cathey had found his spot receiving, earning Edwards' praise. *"I have also been very impressed with the way (he) has been catching the ball. He has been like a vacuum cleaner pulling in everything."* On the season's prospects, one sportswriter agreed with those that voted Saint Al as preseason District 6B favorite. *"The Flashes could be on their way to a place in the Class B state championship playoff game. In regular season, they will finish 9-1."* The pre-season All County Team included Evans and DeRossette for offense and Ehrhardt , Gussio, and Breithaupt for defense. The fans were high on the potential, too. They sported bumper stickers that read **"Number 1 In '81"**.

GAME 1:   SAINT AL (0-0) vs MADISON RIDGELAND (0-0)
      FINAL: ST AL 15 MADISON RIDGELAND 9
      SEPTEMBER 4, 1981

Edwards said of Madison's Class A team, *"I'm expecting a tough game out of them. They are supposed to be one of the better Class A teams in the district, and they will have one of their better teams in a few years this season. I hear that they are supposed to have as good a team as the one that (USM star) Sammy Winder was on. I feel like we can win, but we are going to have to play one of our better games to do so. It's going to be nip and tuck in these first two games."*

The Flashes scored first when LaHatte snuck in from the 2. Ehrhardt made it 7-0. The Braves answered in the 2nd when Tray Earnhart lobbed a pass to Bart Williams from 37 away. The missed PAT had Saint Al clinging to a 7-6 lead. In the quarter, starting RB/LB Breithaupt sprained his ankle and had to be helped off of the field. Greg Hull filled his defensive spot. *"I was proud of the way that Hull came in and held the team together. Barry is one of our leaders and we missed him. But Hull got the job done and that's what we need. I feel like we have three starting linebackers and that's a blessing."*

In the 4th, the Braves found themselves at the Flash 4 but the Gold Crush held Earnhart to a game-leading field goal of 21 yards. A subsequent Braves punt was received by LaHatte at the Flash 40 and he took it back for the touchdown and capped it with a pass to Robert McDaniel for the two-points.

LaHatte noted, *"Coach Edwards says that if we work hard on the specialty teams, they can win a game for us. It did."* Edwards added *"Both teams were worn out. And unless you really stress it, the one area in a game when a player may tend to loaf a little is the specialty teams. That punt was our opportunity to win the game. And our kids took full advantage of it. Our kids didn't quit. They did what they had to do to win and I'm as proud of them as I have ever been of a team in my life."*

The Gold Crush defense were definately the stars. *"There's no doubt that our defense played a heck of a game"*, Edwards said, mentioning each of their names as praise. For his special teams play, LaHatte earned "Player of the Week". Gussio, Simrall and David Gamble earned Honorable Mention.

GAME 2:   SAINT AL (1-0) @ BYRAM (0-1)
      FINAL: ST AL 17 BYRAM 0
      SEPTEMBER 11, 1981

Asked about Byram, Edwards said, *"Byram is supposed to be one of the better BB teams around this year. (They) are probably the biggest B-BB team that we have faced since I've been here. They are huge on the line, but they aren't as quick as we are. They will outweigh us by 30 to 40 pounds. We are going to have to load up our defense to stop them. If we can do that, we will be successful."*

Of his team, he said *"I think some of our kids found out that they need to be in a little better shape. We will do a good bit of running today to try and fix that."* Breithaupt's injury was going to keep him from playing and Gussio had been sick all week with a virus. Edwards was confident in his reserves. *"These kids can get the job done. But they don't have that much experience and it will be hard on them."*

Saint Al struck first on a 7 play 25 yard drive with a LaHatte pass to Chris Alonzo from the 8. Ehrhardt made it 7-0. A Bulldog fumble was recovered by Robert McDaniel and over the next six plays, LaHatte had completions of 26 and 25 yards. Gussio would score and Ehrhardt converted to make it 14-0. The only scoring after would be a 36-yard FG by Ehrhardt in the 3rd to make it 17-0. *"That field goal was very important. That meant even if Byram scored two touchdowns and got both two-point conversions, they would still be behind. We had an outstanding defensive effort tonight. I was not pleased with our overall effort. I thought we played very sloppily and showed no enthusiasm whatsoever. But, we did play well defensively."* Gussio rushed for 100 yards while Hoxie pitched in with

40. "Johnny ran the ball real well tonight. He gave it his all every time he carried the ball. I also thought Hoxie did a good job running the ball when he was in there."

The defense limited Byram to 21 rushing yards and 25 passing. The visiting crowd, according to sportswriter Austin Bishop, chanted "Gold Crush, Gold Crush, Gold Crush" at Bulldog Stadium afterwards. Ehrhardt won "Player of the Week" while Gussio and Gamble were the Honorable Mentions.

GAME 3:   SAINT AL (2-0) vs EAST FLORA (2-0)
                              FINAL: ST AL 42 EAST FLORA 8
                              SEPTEMBER 18, 1981

"The fun is over. We are starting our district schedule with East Flora this week and every game from here on out is going to count. We don't know that much about East Flora. We know that they are big. It seems that everyone we play is bigger than we are, but in a way, I would rather play the bigger teams than the ones with exceptional speed. They seem to thrive on the big play. And we are going to have to guard against it. If they jump out with a long run or a pass, we could really be in for a battle."

Practice week rain forced the Flashes inside, as it had the week before opener and the injury report was not much better. Breithaupt was out, Hoxie had injured a rib and DeRossette had a pulled muscle. "Right now we are a little bumped up. We are going to get some folks well and ready to play. But we don't play anyone too early and chance them getting hurt where they will be lost for the season."

Midway through the 1st, the Flashes got on track. On 3rd and 5 from the Flash 39, LaHatte hit Cathey for a 61 yard touchdown. Ehrhardt made it 7-0. On their next possession, LaHatte hit Robert Hite for 50 yards to the Hawk 24. Five straight Gussio runs put them at the 3 and LaHatte found Cathey for another touchdown. In the same frame, the Hawks put up their only points after a jarring LaHatte fumble was returned by Keith Ranson 46 yards. L.V. Ball then hit James McField for the 2-pointer to make it 14-8.

LaHatte extracted revenge later in the half when he picked off a Ball pass and ran it back to the Flash 4. Two plays later Gussio scored and Ehrhardt's kick made halftime 21-8. "Cicero's interception was a big play. I thought our secondary as a whole did a fine job. We were expecting their passing game to be strong, but we pretty well shut them down." The 3rd saw two more Flash touchdowns. Gussio scored from the 14 and LaHatte found Alonzo from the 15. In the 4th, it was McDaniel's turn on a 6-yard score. Ehrhardt made the EP to end the scoring 42-8.

LaHatte "threw the ball as well as any quarterback that I have ever had". That included 167 yards of passing and 3 touchdowns. Cathey grabbed two touchdowns and Gussio rushed for 140. The defense limited East Flora to 78 total rushing yards, 11 passing yards and only 3 first downs. Said Edwards, "I was also pleased with our receivers (Hite, McDaniel and Alonzo). They held on to the ball well tonight." For his 4 catches and 2 touchdowns, Beau Cathey was "Player of the Week". LaHatte and Gussio were the Honorable Mentions.

GAME 4:   SAINT AL (3-0) @ SAINT ANDREWS (0-2)
                              FINAL: ST AL 47 SAINT ANDREWS 0
                              SEPTEMBER 25, 1981

The Vicksburg Evening Post expected "an air raid". "I really expect them to put the ball in the air. From what I can tell they like to throw the ball and use a lot of motion and a lot of different formations. We have been working with our defensive backfield to get prepared for them." Edwards knew that the ground game was Saint Al's strength. "...our basic philosophy is still built around the running game. We are still pretty much a running team." Gussio was averaging 4.9 per carry with 336 yards and Breithaupt was expected to see action again. "Barry isn't 100%, but he has gotten the okay from the doctor and it's time he plays again. We plan to use him in spots. I won't say how much.... He is coming along real well but he will have to work himself back into shape."

Edwards was not overlooking Saint Andrews. "When you start looking ahead, you are asking for trouble. St. Andrews doesn't have that impressive of a record, but I have seen a film of them and I know that they have a good football team. They are a young team, but they are much improved from their first game and nothing more would make their season than to beat St. Aloysius. You wouldn't believe the improvement they made from the first game to the second. They learned from their mistakes in the first and put it into practice. We have all the respect in the world for them." Despite 42 points from the week before, Edwards said "Our offensive line is going to have to play better. We just had too many break downs in this area and we are going to have to improve."

In the 1st, Gussio went in from 3 on a 76 yard drive to make it 7-0. Two possessions later, he went 56 yards to the 1 setting up a Pat Evans touchdown dive to make it 14-0. Starting their next drive at the Saints 26, LaHatte gained 17 and then Gussio did the honors. Ehrhardt's PAT made it 21-0 going into halftime. In the 3rd, Gussio broke a long 60 yard run to the 1. This time he earned the score. Backup QB Craig Stamm drove the Flashes 45 yards in 6 plays later, with McDaniel going in from 24 for a 34-0 lead.

The only bright spot for the Saints was an interception. But the Gold Crush was too strong, holding on 4 downs and giving the ball back to the offense for the night's longest drive. This one tallied 73 yards and resulted in a Cathey 20-yard score from Stamm. The final touchdown came with only: 55 left when Breithaupt got in to cap a 44-yard drive. Gussio had 176 yards and 3 touchdowns; 7 other players contributed for scores; the Flashes never punted; and Saint Andrews had only 3 first downs and -7 yards of rushing.

"I was pleased with the maturity of our older players. They put us ahead early and allowed us to play some of our less experienced boys. I was proud of our younger players, too. Robert McDaniel and Craig Stamm played well, and also our young defensive backs. Greg Hull had 14 tackles at linebacker to earn "Player of the Week". LaHatte and Gussio again gained Honorable Mention status.

GAME 5:   SAINT AL (4-0) vs MISS SCHOOL FOR THE DEAF (UNREPORTED)
                 FINAL: ST AL 30 MSD 0
                 October 2, 1981: HOMECOMING

Starting the week, Gussio , LaHatte, Koestler, Alonzo and Cathey were hobbled. "We are probably in the worst shape that we have been all year. We are hoping to get these folks ready for this Friday night." Those cleared up a bit during the week and had him feeling better. "We should be in pretty good shape for the game. What we have to do is get our minds right for MSD. There have been a lot of distractions this week with homecoming and everything. But Friday night, we are going to have our minds on our business. MSD has a good deal of speed, and they can break one on us if we aren't careful. We are going to have to contain them. I think this is the best club that they have had in a while. Last year, they were weak, but it was Coach (Terry) Clark's first year there and he is doing a fine job with them. They have some pretty good size kids in the offensive line. They are supposed to be better offensively than they are defensively."

Saint Al started by driving to the MSD 16 and 18 but lost the ball via fumbles on both. With 2:30 left in the 1st and after a 55-yard drive, Gussio took the ball 29 yards for the touchdown. It was now 7-0. The 2nd was a scoreless affair and gave the head coach cause for concern. "We played a flat first half" We played with no motivation and no enthusiasm. .. I was proud of the way we came back in the second half. I think we learned some things tonight."

Saint Al received the opening kick at their 45, and seven plays later, Gussio scored from the 10. Ehrhardt made it 14-0. On the ensuing kickoff, MSD fumbled at their 23. It took only 5 plays for Breithaupt to score from the 1. With :24 left, Robert McDaniel had his turn to score from the 3 on a Flash 49-yard drive. The 4th was memorable only for a MSD fumble on their own 18, 25 yards in penalties against the home team and a 30 yard Ehrhardt FG.

Gussio had 154 yards rushing while Breithaupt had 90, and they had held the visitor to 84 yards. Despite that, Edwards said "I'm very disappointed with the game as a whole. But it didn't surprise me. We really didn't have our minds on the game during the week because of Homecoming, and I knew that MSD was going to be vastly improved." Gussio received "Player of the Week" while Ehrhardt and Gamble garnered Honorable Mentions.

GAME 6:   SAINT AL (5-0) vs PUCKETT (5-0)
                 FINAL: ST AL 7 PUCKETT 0
                 October 9, 1981

Like Saint Al, Puckett was undefeated and held the key to the 6B championship. And, the Wolves had beaten the Flashes 2 years straight. Said Edwards, "Puckett isn't bigger than we are, but they have played tougher than we have. This game is for all the marbles in District 6B, and if we don't beat them on our home field, we don't deserve to win district. It's just a matter of our kids being ready mentally for the game. (They) will be one of the best teams we face this season. We have to prove that we are the best."

"They do so many things well. They have a good option quarterback. He can run the ball and he throws well. They do a lot of things on offense... They run a multiple offense where they can either throw or run. You never know which, and it is going to put our defense to the test. They have real good team speed on defense. They stunt a lot with their linebackers, and, with their speed they can make a mistake and make up for it." Koestler and Carl Brown were the only injured players reported that week. It was time to show that Saint Al's 151 points this year versus their opponent's 17 wasn't a fluke.

Late in the 1st, LaHatte hit Alonzo for 20 yards and the lone touchdown. Ehrhardt made it 7-0. We know that the Wolves had an unsuccessful 4th quarter drive and, if the box scores are accurate, that there were a total of 9 fumbles; 3 interceptions; and lots of defensive stands by both teams. Said Edwards, "I thought we had the game under control. But one break and they could have scored and won the football game. We had several opportunities to put more points on the scoreboard. But we kept making mistakes that would cost us points. The first three and a half quarters were played on their side of the field. They put together a drive in the final minutes that could have won it. We played well in every phase. Our linebackers, line and secondary all did an outstanding job."

The headline afterwards read "ST. AL DRUMS PUCKETT". Though Saint Al controlled the stats, a 7-0 victory could hardly be called a "drumming". Two Saint Al players had been named "Player of the Week": LaHatte for punting and Evans for defense. Hull and Alonzo made Honorable Mentions.

GAME 7:   SAINT AL (6-0) @ PISGAH (3-3)
                 FINAL: ST AL 26 PISGAH 6
                 October 16, 1981

Edwards had good words for Pisgah. "We are expecting a pretty tight game. ... They can beat us if we don't have our minds on the game. They have some fine athletes on their team, and we certainly can't overlook them. (Don) Ragsdale was out last week with a shoulder injury. If he is back.., we could be in for a hard time. I consider (quarterback Roy) Williams one of the best athletes in the district. He just does everything well." Injuries were limited. "We are probably as healthy as we have been all year long. George Thomas is the only player that is out with an injury, and the doctors have told him that it will be another week until he will be back."

Saint Al started at the 24. Eleven plays later, Breithaupt went in from the 2 and Ehrhardt made it 7-0. On Saint Al's next drive starting at the Flash 16, LaHatte was picked off by Melvin Grant who took it into the endzone. The kick was missed and it was 7-6. The 2nd was all Saint Al. An errant Dragon pass was picked off by Cathey at their 30 and taken back to the 17. Gussio plunged in two plays later to make it 13-6. On the ensuing kickoff, Roy Williams mishandled the ball and Stamm fell on it at the 35. It took 3 plays before LaHatte hit Alonzo from the 23 for the score to make it 19-6. "I was pleased with the way we responded... We came back and held them right there (after Grant's interception for a touchdown)."

The scoring and the half came to a close with a Gussio touchdown from the 28 that finished a 51-yard drive in 2 plays. Referring to 9 penalties that caused Saint Al to lose 130 yards, a 22 yard Gussio touchdown and an Ehrhardt 44 yard FG, Edwards said "We didn't play very well at all. We did real well for the first 12 minutes. After that, we got tired and began to lose our edge. We did too many things wrong. We were just not very excited." With 126 rushing yards rushing, his 4th 100-plus game of the year, Gussio was "Player of the Week". Honorable Mentions went to Evans and LaHatte.

GAME 8:   SAINT AL (7-0) v SEBASTAPOL (3-3)
                 FINAL: ST AL 35 SEBASTAPOL 6
                 October 23, 1981

The Flashes had never played Sebastapol and Edwards hadn't seen them on film. In fact, The Vicksburg Evening Post used the heading "ST. AL FACES UNKNOWN". Within a day or two, he got a tape of the Bobcat team. "They are a passing team. I would say they go to the air about 40 percent of the time. They will try to trick us with some misdirection plays and putting their backs in motion. But I think our defense will be up for the challenge. Sebastapol has about the same size that we do. And they seem to be a well-coached team. We will have our work cut out for us. We will have to make whatever adjustments we have to as we go along."

DeRossette had apparently torn thumb ligaments against Pisgah and looked to be out. *"We will surely miss (him) on the line."* McDaniel (leg muscle) would be watching, too, but even that wasn't enough to stop a surging Flashes team. On the first drive, they went from their 44 to the Sebastapol 4. But the next play was a mishandled pitch to the Bobcats at their 6. Forcing a punt after holding for only 4 yards, Saint Al took over at the Bobcat 42. Three plays later LaHatte found Cathey for a 28-yard touchdown and Ehrhardt made it 7-0. The next score for the Flashes ate 89 yards in 5 plays with LaHatte taking it in from 2 yards out to make it 14-0 at halftime.

Early in the 3rd from the Flash 40, Gussio drove it to the Sebastapol 16 and then hit the endzone on the next play. Ehrhardt made it 21-0. In the same quarter, Breithaupt came up big with an interception of Barry Hudson, and 47 yards later, LaHatte found Hite for a 25-yard touchdown. Hoxie later went 60-yards that finished the scoring for the purple and gold. Ehrhardt was true again and made it a 35-0 affair.

Earlier in the game, the defense held a Sebastapol drive that started at the 25 and marched all the way to the Flash one-inch line. Against younger Flashes, Hudson hit receiver Bruce Patrick for the touchdown. *"Our defense has played well all year. They were able to score on the younger kids, but we played it real well. Defensively you really can't single anyone out. All of our kids did an excellent job. Our offense still made a few mistakes, like some fumbles, but there was a lot of improvement. Cicero ... had another excellent outing at quarterback."*

LaHatte was "Player of the Week", with Gussio and Evans gaining Honorable Mentions.

GAME 9:   SAINT AL (8-0) @ PELAHATCHIE (7-1)
            FINAL: ST AL 20 PELAHATCHIE 0
            October 30, 1981

Pelahatchie had lost only their opener against Puckett and this game would decide the District 6B championship. *".. I feel we have the team that can win the district. It will be a hotly contested, physical ball game. But one way or another, it is going to settle the issue and that will be it. Our kids know what is riding on this game. They will be ready."*

"I saw a film on them from the Puckett game and I saw one on them from last week. And if you didn't know it was the same team playing, you would never believe it. They have some big kids on the line and we are going to have to isolate them in some areas. They are a completely different team from the Pelahatchie teams that we are used to playing. They are the biggest and fastest team that we have played all year. And when you add this with how well coached they are, you know that you are going to have to battle to win.

The Flashes opened by moving 71 yards on 9 plays with Ehrhardt making a 22-yard FG. In the 2nd and from his own 40, LaHatte kept the ball for a 48-yard pickup to the Chief 12. After 5 plays, Earhardt hit another 3-pointer to make it 6-0. The 2nd half started well when Breithaupt picked off a Chief pass at their 35 and ran it to the 31. But five plays later, Pelahatchie picked off an errant Flash pass in the endzone. Late in the 3rd, the Flashes capped a 59-yard drive when LaHatte found a wide-open Cathey for a 36-yard touchdown. *"I looked up and saw him wide open on the play,"* said LaHatte. *"So I just laid the ball up there. I threw it easy. I didn't want to overthrow it, so I just tried to ease it in there."*

The 3rd also had one more highlight. Gussio would pass the magical 1,000 yard mark for rushing in a season. *"I really wasn't thinking about the 1,000 yards during the game. I was just thinking about winning the game. All I had to do was follow the blocking I have been getting all year. They have opened some holes in the line you wouldn't believe. All I have had to do was run through them."* In the 4th, Pelahatchie was unsuccessful on a fake punt. The Flashes drove 42 yards in 5 plays, capped by a Gussio 36-yard touchdown. Ehrhardt's kick finalized scoring.

Edwards said *"I thought we would win the game. But to be honest with you I thought it would be a lot closer. You know, sometimes I have a bad habit of underestimating my own team. They wanted this game very bad. They really wanted to be district champions. Overall, it was the best that we have played all year. This group has continued to work very hard and have become an outstanding football team."*

LaHatte added, *"I am very excited. There are 12 seniors on this team and we all wanted this win very much."* Said Ehrhardt said about the Gold Crush, *"Our defense played a good game tonight. We hung in there with them all night long and didn't let them get anywhere."* And as a big part of that defense, he earned the "Player of the Week". LaHatte and Gussio were co-Honorable Mentions.

GAME 10:   SAINT AL (9-0) @ GREENVILLE SAINT JOSEPH (6-2)
                  FINAL: ST AL 3 GREENVILLE ST JOE 34
                  November 6, 1981

Saint Aloysius was going for its first undefeated season, not counting bowls, since 1977 when they had lost to Kosciusko in the Mississippi Bowl. Greenville Saint Joe had won their District 3B title this year to go along with the Flashes' district title. Immediately after going to 9-0, Edwards said *"Even though we have clinched the district now and are assured of making the state playoffs, I don't fear a letdown next week against St Joe. All of the players really want to go undefeated, so they want to beat (them) badly. I don't think there is any danger of them being down. Besides that, St. Joe has let it be known all year that they were up there waiting for us at the end of the season to knock us off. So we want to go up there and show them what we can do. They have a big team and they seem to do things well. We are looking for a tough ball game. They have lost two games by a total of four points. I'm sure they have a fine football team."*

But before the East Flora game, when speaking to The Vicksburg Evening Post, he said *"The thing about this district is that everyone is about even. You can't overlook anyone. I wouldn't be a bit surprised to see the winner of the district with a loss. We don't go to lose a football game. But if it should happen, we won't be out of the running."*

The paper's Austin Bishop said, *"The way the Flashes moved the ball on their first possession, it looked like it would be another solid victory for the Vicksburg crew."* The Flashes received the kickoff and, after 80 yards in 13 plays, got to the Irish 17. Ehrhardt's FG was good to make it 3-0. They didn't score again. The Irish answered quickly, and for an extended drive. They took the ball 75 yards on 17 plays with Jimmy Lang taking the ball in from the 1 and hitting the extra point to make it 7-3. Their defense held the Flashes to 3 plays and took over the punt at the Irish 44. Four plays later, Wade Love muscled in from the 22 to make it a 14-3 lead at halftime.

The Irish opened the 3rd with a missed 36 yard FG by Lang. Saint Al had only two possessions in the 3rd, neither resulting in a first down. With :07 remaining, Wade Love hit Jerry Katawar for a 20-yard crossing pattern touchdown. Lang made it 21-3. After a 3-and-out, LaHatte was forced to punt. It was blocked, landed in the endzone, and was recovered by Gene Snipes. The kick was no good but the lead was 27-3. The final score was by the home team on their next possession when Love raced in from the 17 to cap a 40 yard drive. Saint Al finished the contest by throwing an interception in the endzone.

Greenville turned the tide with two fake punts, a reverse and a double-reverse. In fact, those plays that set up the touchdowns were the one thing on Edwards' mind. *"If I had to select a turning point in the game, it would be the first fake punt. It was a total mental breakdown on our part. We had somebody watching for that, but he turned and ran down the field."*

He continued by saying *"The turning point of the game was the first practice of the week. We just weren't ready to play. You have to be prepared mentally to play every ball game. I kept telling our players that they were tough. But I guess (they) just thought I was crying wolf. There have been several teams that I told them were tough, then we went out and whipped their socks off. I guess they thought the same thing would happen again this week. Saint Joe was just ready for the game and we weren't. They whipped us all over the field, in just about every way."* In all, Saint Joe not only won on the scoreboard. They also won in 1st downs, rushing yards, and penalties.

GAME 11:   SAINT AL (9-1) v MOUNT OLIVE (8-2)
                  FINAL: ST AL 24 MOUNT OLIVE 10
                  November 20, 1981
                  PLAYOFF ROUND 1: FARRELL FIELD

Warren County statistical leaders featured a number of Flashes. Gussio led in scoring (72 points) and rushing (1,137 yards on 181 carries). Warren Central's Jim Warren was 2nd with 898 yards on 29 more carries. Lahatte sat in 7th for scoring (432) but led in passing with 559 yards. As for 6B champion Mount Olive, they had lost to Topeka-Tilton 19-13 during the year that snapped a 20-game losing streak. Additionally, the Pirates had won two games in overtime.

Edwards felt good about the chances. *"I think we are capable of winning the football game. But we are going to keep them on the inside. They have explosive speed that we are going to have to contain. I believe that if we can keep them from breaking the big play on us we will be okay. We have been working extra hard on our defense in order to stop their two (perhaps three in Lewis Mitchell, Harold Carter and James Mickell) good running backs. We haven't even worked on offense yet. I believe* there will be some points on the board Friday night. I think three touchdowns will be necessary to win the football game. We are also working hard on our coverage of kickoffs and punts. We can't afford to let those speedsters burn us with a long one. We will not be making any real changes in our offensive game plan. We took a close look at the St. Joe film and it wasn't anything we did wrong that beat us. They just whipped us."

Carter led his team with 604 yards, while Mickell was close behind with 600. Ramon Johnston, head coach for Mount Olive, talked about his squad, too. "We are a big play offense. We need to get our backs loose on the corners if we expect to break one. They have more of a grind-it-out type offense. It was that kind of offense that beat us in our second loss (New Hebron 34-19). We couldn't get the ball against New Hebron. We scored every time we had the ball; we just didn't have it enough. We need to stop them from keeping the ball for a long time."

Ehrhardt had been working on kickoffs with the ball on its side to keep the two big returners from big returns. It worked as neither had the chance to really get going on that part of the game. On Mount Olives' second play from scrimmage, Hull caused Mickell to fumble and Ehrhardt was there to scoop it up at the Pirate 27. Evans ran twice for 7 and 4, and then Gussio took in from 16 to make it 7-0. The Flashes kicked and Mount Olive went 56 yards all the way to the Flash 11. The defense held and forced a Todd Mangum 23-yard FG to make it 7-3. The second Pirate mistake came when LaHatte waived for a fair catch at the 49 but an opposing player ran over him and put the ball at the Pirate 36. It took 5 plays before LaHatte would score from the 9 to make it 14-3 with 1:43 in the half.

Mount Olive quickly moved downfield and with :07 left, Mangum hit Carter for a 5-yard touchdown to make it 14-10. In the 3rd, Saint Al proved it wasn't folding. On their second possession, in 2 plays, Gussio ran it in from 8 to make it 21-10. The only other score followed a Pirate fake punt in the 4th, which resulted in a 34-yarder from Ehrhardt to finish it.

"It was the best game we have played all year. We came out here tonight and played as hard as we could. We took advantage of some mistakes and played tough, hard-nosed defense. I couldn't believe we held them to just 10 points. And they shouldn't have gotten those. We could have shut them out. Our defense just played outstanding tonight. The whole team was outstanding. I am very proud of these players. They came out ready to play and did what they had to do to win!"

As the team waited for the gymnasium locker door to be opened, you could hear the chants of the players. "Dexter, Dexter, Dexter."

GAME 12:   SAINT AL (10-1) v DEXTER (10-0)
                       FINAL: ST AL 21 DEXTER 12
                       November 27, 1981: PLAYOFF ROUND 2: FARRELL FIELD

At the MHSAA meeting in Jackson on Sunday, the Flashes found that their semi-final game would be at Farrell Field. "I couldn't believe it.", said Edwards. "Now if we can just beat this bunch!" Dexter Coach Jimmy Lowery was also taken aback. "We came and were told where we were going to play. I had thought we would be at a neutral site, but I guess we didn't have anything to say about it."

But there was more good news. All District Honors for 6B, voted on by district coaches, were issued and the Flashes were well-represented. Joe Edwards was named District 6B Coach of the Year. "It's an honor to be named coach of the year. But I can't take all the credit. It really isn't that tough standing over on the sidelines when you have a group of kids playing like we have had this year. And our assistant coaches have done an outstanding job." LaHatte was All-District QB/Most Valuable Back. Other offensive awards went to Simrall, McCaffrey and Gussio. "I'm sure Cicero feels this way. These honors are team honors, not just individual. It takes the team to put you in a position where you can receive this type of recognition." On defense, Evans, Alonzo and Ehrhardt were tabbed. Honorable Mentions included Hull, Breithaupt, Stamm, DeRossette, Gamble, Hite and Koestler.

Their opponent would not only be holding the District 7B crown, but also riding a 28-game win streak. They had just gotten their 10th win, shut out 6 teams and had given up only 28 points (none from rushing). Their head coach, a 1974 USM grad, was 58-7 at Dexter and his team, according to him, was fully healthy. "Unless we have something come up this week, we will have everyone ready to go. We are happy to be in the playoffs. It is a boost for our football program and helps us get publicity from all over the state. And, it gives some of our kids recognition that they wouldn't get before."

Said Edwards, "They have a good football team. They look bigger on film than their roster says they are. And they are quick. They are a scrappy bunch which will really come after you. We had better be ready to play one of our better games of the season." As for his team, he said "I'm glad it's at our place. Our kids always seem to play better at home. We have had a couple of good practices. We *are going to work Wednesday, take Thursday off for Thanksgiving and then meet briefly Friday morning."*

The Flashes set the tone for the game on just their second play. LaHatte ran an option play to the right; Breithaupt took out the defensive end and left the quarterback with only the cornerback between him and paydirt. Evans delivered what the paper called *"a devastating block"* on the defender and cleared the way for a 67-yard scamper. Ehrhardt made it 7-0. Said a smiling LaHatte after the game, *"It really surprised me that I outran them. I just ran as hard as I could and they never caught me. That shocked me."* Edwards, however, talked about the Breithaupt block. *"That block Barry made allowed us to make that play. We had the containment inside and all we had to do was beat one man. Pat took care of him and Cicero just took off down the field with Gussio following him just in case of a pitch out on down the field."*

After the kickoff, the Bulldogs responded with a drive to the 1 and a Matt Cooley touchdown to make it 7-6. The Flashes answered on the next possession when Breithaupt hauled in a 46-yard pass for a touchdown. Ehrhardt made it 14-6. Said LaHatte, *"He was wide open all the way. All I had to do was hit him with the pass. I knew he would catch it."* And Breithaupt was happy, too. *"Scoring that touchdown really made me feel good. I really felt like I was making a contribution to the team again. It felt good to be able to pitch in and help."* Of Breithaupt, Edwards said, *"Really, we have been playing Barry out of position this year. We started him off at fullback and he got hurt in the first game with a badly twisted ankle. But Pat has done well at running back and we were able to put Barry back at end."*

Late in the 3rd at their 12, Saint Al committed one of their 4 fumbles on the night. Dexter recovered and, in a two-play drive, it was Cooley again from the 1. Again the Bulldogs were unable to convert the 2-point play and the Flashes were clinging to a 14-12 lead. In the 4th, Dexter punted to Saint Al and LaHatte put the Flashes at their 41 after a return of 34 yards. Two plays later, he did the work himself and kept it for a 38-yard touchdown. Ehrhardt finished with the PAT to make it 21-12.

"The play is an audible all the way. Actually, I don't even call an audible. I just slap Newell (Simrall) on the rear end and away we go. I call it if there is a wide gap between their linebackers and I see that I can make it through the hold. Newell just makes a block on the play and I follow him down the field." The offensive line had once again powered the rushing attack by creating opportunities for long gains. Edwards was quick to point out that *"Our line (Simrall, DeRossette, Koestler, Gambell and McCaffrey) gave our backs the protection they needed as they have all season long."*

Edwards praised the entire unit on their effort. *"It (the single-wing offense) gave us problems but we didn't throw up our hands and go crazy because we were playing a Notre Dame box-type offense. We made a lot of things happen on defense."* Said Gussio, *"Our defense has really dug in and played tough when it had to. We had our backs to the wall a couple of times against Dexter, but didn't let them score and that turned the game around."* Though entering the game with a twisted knee, Ehrhardt was perfect on kicks. *"It like to scared us all to death. We have gotten where we expect to make the extra point or a field goal every time we try. Keith doesn't miss many. And I would have hated to have had to go into the game without him."*

Said an excited LaHatte, *"The whole team played very well tonight. We were ready to play and we gave it our all. I really thought we could beat them if we played our best. The blocking was tremendous. Everyone blocked well on the line of scrimmage and Pat Evans made some key blocks also. Now that we have gotten this far, we want to win the State Championship."*

GAME 13: SAINT AL (11-1) v STURGIS (13-0)
FINAL: ST AL 13 STURGIS 26
DECEMBER 4, 1981
PLAYOFF ROUND 3: NEWTON, MS

On Sunday at Provine High, Dr. Woodrow Marsh let Saint Al know that they would be playing in Newton. *"Of course we would have liked to play at home. But since we can't, I think Newton is a good place to play. It's not but about 30 miles east of Pelahatchie on I-20. I know that's a pretty good piece, but it is about even between the two schools. We need to have good fan support. I hope we have quite a few people get out and come to the game to back us. In a game like this it helps to have a lot of fans yelling for you."*

In the final contest, he was facing another solid squad. There may have been only 269 people in Sturgis, but they played like a much larger school. Like Dexter the week before, they were undefeated. Coach Jimmy Fulce was in his 16th season at Sturgis and had never had a losing record. Gussio said, *"I just want to win the state championship. I don't care who scores or runs with the ball as* long as we win. That is what matters." Said Breithaupt, "I really believe we can win the game. And I honestly mean that."

Said Edwards, "They are supposed to be the class of the B schools in the state. They have a quarterback (Kirby Jackson) that is flat our fast. If he gets past you he is gone. Their two running backs (Joe Lampkin and Paul Thompson) are good runners, too. They all have good speed and are exceptionally quick. They also have a good receiver in Rodney Gray. He can flat fly. He is a very dangerous receiver. I believe we are going to hit them as hard as they have been hit all year. From looking at the films it looks as if they haven't played anybody that hits like we do. We are going to square off and lay it on them. We are in for a tough battle, but no matter how the final game turns out, we have had an outstanding season and I'm very proud of each of the players on this football team."

At the Flash 44, LaHatte hit Cathey on a pass to the Lion 20. A combination of Gussio, Evans and LaHatte runs moved it up to the 1. From there, LaHatte dropped one step and then followed Simrall into the endzone. Ehrhardt put the squad up 7-0. Sturgis received the ensuing kickoff and drove to the Flash 27 courtesy of two big third-down conversions. That resulted in a second down run around the right by QB Jackson for the touchdown. The Curt Jordan PAT tied it. On Sturgis' next possession, facing third-and-long, Jackson appeared to be stopped. But instead, he launched a 30-yard touchdown to Jordan. With only :05 left in the half, Gussio tried a halfback pass that was picked off. Sturgis, however, was flagged for a penalty that gave the Flashes one more chance. Ehrhardt attempted a 32-yard field goal that was just wide. The Flashes were down 14-7 at half.

The only scoring of the 3rd came via a Jackson sneak in from the 1. Simrall blocked the PAT to keep the score 20-7. On the initial play of the 4th, Gussio broke a run of 32 to put the Flashes at the 12. Again, Gussio and Evans pushed the pile to the 1 and allowed LaHatte to plunge in to make it 20-13. Disaster struck, when after a Gussio fumble at the Flash 7, Joseph Lampkin took it in from the 1. The PAT was missed, but scoring was over. And so was the successful season for the boys from Vicksburg.

Said Edwards, "We aren't making any excuses about losing the game. Sturgis came out and did what they had to do to win... It was real crucial on the third down play and the touchdown pass. But it is like that in every ball game. You can look back in two or three plays that really made the difference. We came over believing that we could win the ballgame. And had a few things happened differently, I think we could have won. I'm proud of our players. I'm as proud of them as I was last week when we won the South State championship. We lost the ball game but we had a good year."

Said LaHatte, "We would like to have won it all. But we didn't. We had a good year. We won the South State Championship. It was my best year ever." Added Simrall, "I thought we should have won. But we didn't and we have to live with it. No one can say we were losers because we are champions. Tonight we weren't the best, but we didn't quit. We fought to the end."

The Honors continued outside of the All District. Pat Evans was First Team All-State Defensive Line, Gussio was Second Team All-State Offense (RB) and Cicero LaHatte was Second Team Offense (QB). In addition, LaHatte shared the coveted Virgadamo Trophy with Breithaupt.

"The 1981 Flashes were led by 12 seniors (Rabalais, Koestler, Hull, Butler, Simrall, Thomas, Alonzo, Gamble, Hite, Brown, Breithaupt and LaHatte) were the first Saint Al team to play in the State Playoff system in effect today. We won the South State Class B Championship by beating Dexter 21-12 and broke their 28 game winning streak; the longest active winning streak in the state. We then went on to play for the Class B State Championship against 14-0 Sturgis and lost 26-13. They were led by Kirby Jackson who went on to play for Mississippi State and the Buffalo Bills, as well as playing in four Super Bowls. Our team ended with an 11-2 record to continue the winning tradition of Flashes football."

Cicero LaHatte; August 8, 2016

1982 (10-1)

Only one small step from Class B State Champions the year before had expectations high. The Flashes were projected as winners in the sub-district. "Sure, we would like to go back and win the state championship this year. But you really couldn't call that our goal. We are not going to determine how good our team is this year by whether or not we win the state title. We could be a better team and not even win our district. Last year we got some big breaks and some balls bounced our way at critical times. This year they may bounce the other way and we could lose some tight games."

A second-week scrimmage went well four good running options. Johnny Gussio had 1,496 rushing yards and 14 touchdowns the previous season and fullback Pat Evans saw lots of playing time during the State Playoff run. Rounding it out were John Brown and Bill Hoxie. *"With these four backs, we have the potential for a faster and more explosive team than in the past. All four played well. Johnny had a fine season last year and we believe that he has the ability to have another banner year."*

At QB, there were two capable alternatives in Craig Stamm and Kevin Mahoney. But as kickoff neared, Stamm had a sprained ankle and Mahoney had a possible torn hamstring. Sophomore Corey Pinkston, the third option, was nursing a knee injury. The line was in good shape, with Edwards saying *"we have a couple of guys returning that did a good job for us last year and a couple we feel like will become good linemen as the season goes along."*

Defensively, the "Gold Crush" defense was solid, especially at linebacker where Evans and Keith Ehrhardt were in charge. The Vicksburg Evening Post called them *"devastating hitters"*. Edwards agreed. *"Those two are a pair of tough ones. They will tear somebody's head off. They both love to hit and they know how to do it."* The week before the Red Carpet Bowl, he said *"I don't know of two better high school linebackers anywhere. I know I haven't run across them, anyway. These two love to play the game and don't mind laying somebody out. They would rather hit than eat."*

GAME 1: SAINT AL (0-0) @ MADISON RIDGELAND (0-0)
FINAL: ST AL 10 MADISON RIDGELAND 7
SEPTEMBER 2, 1982

Edwards was concerned about his first opponent. *"We have to contain their running backs. They have several big backs that can fly. Their QB has a pretty good arm and some good receivers to work with. They have a fine football team and we are going to have our hands full."* Stamm, in his first QB start, had healed and the team was fairly healthy.

A punt on the Braves' first series was errant and the Flashes grabbed the ball at the Braves' 29. Ehrhardt's FG was good from 35 yards and the score was 3-0. *"Keith gave us what we needed. It was a straight shot through the middle of the goal posts."* In the 2nd, the Braves took the lead when Eddie Courtney took it in from 11 and kicked the PAT. But Saint Al came right back. On a halfback option, Gussio threw a 29-yard strike to Brown and Ehrhardt made it 10-7. The Flash defense stood tall with Beau Cathey breaking up a big pass attempt and both De Ferguson and Stamm recovering fumbles.

"It was a defensive struggle, especially in the 2nd half. It seemed like we stayed on our side of the field during most of the half. Our defense bent some, but it never broke." The Braves had 92 yards in rushing and 39 in passing while giving up 65 yards on 7 penalties and losing two loose balls to the Flashes. *"The offensive line did a good job blocking. Joe Evans, Brian DeRossette, Marty Agostinelli, David Wilson, Tim McCaffrey all did us a good job. (But) everyone played well. You really can't single anyone out in a game like this. It was a team win."* Ehrhardt was the recipient of "Player of the Game" for his defensive efforts and kicking. Wilson and DeRossette shared Honorable Mentions.

GAME 2: SAINT AL (1-0) VS BYRAM (0-1)
FINAL: ST AL 28 BYRAM 6
SEPTEMBER 10, 1982

Edwards noted that *"It's always good to win the first one. And it was a nail-biter."* The AP Small Schools Poll honored the Flashes with a #4 ranking. *"It's nice to be ranked in the polls. But it's still very early in the season. Where we are at the end of the season is more important. We still have a lot of football to play."*

As for his opponent, Edwards said, *"Byram is big, but they always seem to have good size. They like to get the ball outside to their tight end and this is something we are going to have to stop."* As for team health, *"Actually, we are in better shape this week than we were going into the Madison Ridgeland game last week. We have some bumps and bruises, but nothing real serious. We are so thin in numbers, we can't afford to get anyone hurt in practice."*

The non-district game was described by sportswriter Danny Garnett as being *"an impressive show for the hometown fans here at Farrell Stadium."* After 14 plays and 73 yards on the opening drive, Gussio scored from the 1 and Ehrhardt converted. In the 2nd, Brown scored from the 9 to cap a 78 yard drive. The Flashes struck again with a Stamm-to-Cathey touchdown covering 67 yards. Ehrhardt was good for a 21-0 halftime lead.

In the 3rd, aided by two penalties, the Bulldogs drove from their 26 to the Flash 7. But the Gold Crush defense held the visitors for no points. *"I was very proud of our goal line stand"*, said Edwards. *Our kids showed a lot of determination and hustle."* Saint Al's final points came in the 4th after a 90 yard and 11 play drive. This time it was Stamm with a 25-yard TD run to make it 28-0 after Ehrhardt's kick. The only Bulldogs points came with :58 on the clock; a Jason Dozier to Harvey Ford TD.

The Vicksburg Evening Post reported that Flash penalties actually cost them 2 touchdowns. Gussio had 199 yards of rushing, and for that he was awarded "Player of the Game". Brown and Stamm were Honorable Mentions. Gussio also earned the head coaches respect, saying *"Johnny Gussio ran the ball as hard as we have ever had a back run."*

"I was very pleased with our play in the first half, but we didn't look too good after. We had some crucial penalties in the third quarter and we lost our composure a couple of times. We executed very well on offense. Craig did a good job of running the offense and Johnny ran the ball harder than he's ever run it before. We will do some more things this week. I think we will throw more to open our running game up more."

GAME 3:   SAINT AL (2-0) @ EAST FLORA (2-0)
                 FINAL: ST AL 6 EAST FLORA 12
                 SEPTEMBER 17, 1982

A key sub-district game was at hand. *"This is one game we have to have. If we don't win this one, we could be in for a very short season. East Flora always has good size and speed. And they have scored 94 points in their first 2 games. What we have to do is take the early momentum and not let them get started. We could lose to East Flora and still win the district, but someone else would have to beat East Flora. We can control our destiny with a win. And I feel like we can win if we play the way we are capable of playing. East Flora has a good football team. But so do we."*

Early in the 2nd, East Flora fumbled the ball at their 12 to Mike Mahoney. Gussio scored the lone Saint Al touchdown from the 6 after a 4 play drive. It wasn't until the 4th that the Hawks were to get on the board, courtesy of a Flash fumble at the 19. Two plays later, running back David Crosby hit paydirt from 25 yards out. The two-pointer was no good and Saint Al was clinging to a 7-6 lead.

With 2:25 left, a Gussio punt pinned the Hawks back on their 6. With just over a minute left to go, the Hawks sealed their destiny. In spite of 5 defensive backs waiting, L.V. Ball hit Carl Wilkerson for the 84-yard touchdown. *"We prepared for that one thing and didn't do what we were supposed to do. We just made too many mistakes tonight and they beat us. I'll take the blame for it. Now we have to suck it up. We have 7 more games to play this year."*

Edwards said of the play the next week, *"We aren't making any excuses. We made mistakes and now we have to correct them. You can't blame the loss on one big play. And it wasn't a lack of hustle on our team either. You don't quit at Saint Aloysius."* Mike Mahoney and Gussio were named The Vicksburg Evening Post Honorable Mentions for the week.

GAME 4:   SAINT AL (2-1) vs SAINT ANDREWS (NOT REPORTED)
                 FINAL: ST AL 47 SAINT ANDREWS 0
                 SEPTEMBER 24, 1982

Monday was mainly watching film and light conditioning. Edwards was upbeat about the week and the rest of the year. *"We have had some good practices and I feel a lot better about this team. We are going to see a lot better football before this season is over. I don't think we will lose another game. Whether we make the playoffs or not is another matter. That's out of our hands."* He planned to open the pass and option up to prepare for later in the year. As for Saint Andrews, he noted that *"They do basic things. They throw the ball well and they will try a little option play. We have to be ready for a tough football game."*

The back-and-forth 1st included a fumble by the Saints' Jack Duggan recovered by Mike Mahoney at the 33. A 10-yard sack on Stamm ended the opportunity. On the Flashes next possession, Gussio returned a Paul Catherwood punt to the Saint 27. Stamm and Gussio runs were aided by a Saints penalty. Now at the 3, Stamm converted and Ehrhardt was good on one of his 5 extra points. In the 2nd and starting at their 5, Gussio and Brown got to the 49 before Brown broke away for 51 yards and the score. Halftime would see the Flashes up 14-0 but at least one other score was brought back in the quarter. Gussio found the endzone from the 24 but there was a flag for clipping

The 2nd half was a Flash scoring barrage courtesy of the defense. From his own 15, the Saints' Catherwood threw a pick-6 to Cathey. Four plays later, Kevin Mahoney hit Ronnie McDaniel in the endzone from the 18. Before the crowd could keep up, Ehrhardt picked off yet another

Catherwood pass at their 42. Mahoney ran for 26 and 20, and then gave to Gussio from the 12 for a touchdown. It was suddenly 34-0.

Stamm returned as the 3rd ended. From their 45, he ran twice for 33 yards and then hit Brown at the 5. Edwards put in the younger players for experience. Corey Pinkston handed off to De Ferguson for a touchdown to make it 40-0. Ferguson got the last score with a 33 yard carry. Saint Al had 462 yards of total offense (394 rushing) versus the Saints' 51. DeRossette was "Player of the Game". Gussio and Brown were Honorable Mentions.

GAME 5:   SAINT AL (3-1) vs WEST UNION (0-4)
           FINAL: ST AL 41 WEST UNION 13
           OCTOBER 1, 1982

Practice week began with four injuries in Brown (swollen knee), DeRossette (bruised shoulder), Tim McCaffrey and Jim Fordice. *"We won't be at full strength. We have four starters who will be out or at least slowed because of injuries. I'm hoping they can play this week."* As for his opponent, he said *"For all indications, West Union has a good football team. They are small in numbers, but they seem to be solid with what they have."*

In the 1st, Gussio took a 10 yard rush to paydirt for a 6-0 lead. After West Union gathered penalties of 15 and 10 yards, Stamm picked off a Terry Torroll pass for a 23-yard touchdown return. The extra point made it 13-0. Two plays later, Ehrhardt picked off Torroll at the 29 for a touchdown and Gussio added the two points. In the 2nd, Mahoney had a run from the 1 for the next touchdown. On the Flashes next drive, they started at their own 30 after a penalty. But, 6 plays and 70 yards later, Pat Evans got his turn to score from the 6 to make it 35-0.

The Bulldogs got on the board on a 7-play 62-yard drive when Edward Sandifer scored on a reverse. On the next possession, Mahoney hit Cathey for 60 yards and a first down at the 13 followed two plays later by a return pass to Cathey for the score. Halftime sat at 47-0. The only notable action of the 2nd half was a West Union touchdown. Perry Davis hit Sandifer on a 41-yard pass to the Flash 38 and a return pass to Sandifer on the next play was good for a touchdown with :38 left.

"I was real pleased with the way we played tonight. I was especially happy with the play of both of our quarterbacks. With West Union not really being a tough opponent, I was afraid the kids were having a hard time getting up for the game. But we were ready to play." Gussio had 101 yards on 6 carries and was The Vicksburg Evening Post Honorable Mention along with Beau Cathey. Pat Evans won "Player of the Game".

GAME 6:   SAINT AL (4-1) @ PUCKETT (3-2)
           FINAL: ST AL 24 PUCKETT 0
           OCTOBER 8, 1982

The playoff season was official. East Flora's victory over Bentonia gave them a 5-0 record and the crown. *"There is nothing we can do about that now. We are aiming for a 9-1 record and then maybe a bowl game. Records don't mean anything in this game. No matter how they do before or after our game, Puckett always gets tough for St Al. We are going to have to contain (Ronnie) Newsome. He will be one of the quickest players we have gone against this year. Newsome adds another dimension to Puckett with his quickness and speed. Puckett basically tries to run the ball down your throat, but Newsome can break something open if you don't watch him."*

To prepare, Edwards spent more time on the option and outside blocking schemes. *"Puckett has a big team. They are very physical up the middle and our offensive line is going to be tested. We haven't done real well with our outside blocking and we have put a lot of time in there. I think we will be able to run inside and outside on Puckett. Pat Evans is a quick, hard-hitting fullback and he can stick it up in there for us. We have good outside speed with Johnny Gussio at tailback and John Brown or Beau Cathey at the flanker, so we do alright there. I don't know if we can sit there and pound it out with Puckett. We have to make them do some things that they don't like to do."*

On the kickoff, Cathey took the ball 75 yards for a touchdown and Ehrhardt made it 7-0 and before the home team crowd could get settled. And it was déjà vu for the Puckett crowd as the same thing had happened the week before against Richland. *"The kickoff return got us started on the right foot and set the stage for the rest of the game"*, said Edwards afterwards. The Flashes scored again when Mahoney capped a 66-yard drive in 9 plays by diving in from the 1. Mike Mahoney recovered a

Puckett fumble later, but the only remaining scoring of the 1st half came when an unsuccessful fake punt by Puckett at their 30 allowed Ehrhardt to hit a long 47-yard FG.

In the 3rd, the visitors drove 47 yards in 8 plays with Gussio diving in from the 1. At 7:36, the scoring was over and the Flashes were up 24-0. John Brown did add an interception in the half, and the defense stopped the only promising Wolves drive at the 10. *"Overall, we played our best game of the year tonight. Both our offense and defense executed well. Johnny ran better than he has all year."* The Gold Crush had limited Puckett to only 109 offensive yards. John Brown won "Player of the Game". McCaffery and Cathey were Honorable Mentions.

GAME 7:   SAINT AL (5-1) vs BENTONIA (3-2)
                  FINAL: ST AL 53 BENTONIA 6
                  OCTOBER 15, 1982

The Flashes worked in the high school gym on Tuesday due to weather. *"We got some things done, though we were somewhat limited in what we could do. We need to get out. We need to spend some time on the kicking game, especially kickoffs. We can't let them have a big play in this area. We are facing a very solid offensive team in Bentonia. They have two fine running backs who are going to be tough to catch if we let them get outside on us. They have excellent speed and we will have to contain them."*

The 1st quarter alone accounted for 27 Flash points. Gussio was first on a 28-yard run. Evans had an interception two plays later and Gussio did it again; this time from 36 yards out. On the next possession, Mahoney hit Robert McDaniel for a 21-yard score to make it 20-0. Finally, Gussio had a 6-yard run to make it 27-0. First half scoring for the Flashes was finished when Mahoney took off for a 62-yard score. Joe Evans hit the PAT to make it 34-0. But the Wolves didn't give up. Andrea Yancey caught a Ronnie Hubbard pass for 4 yards and the score. The two-pointer was no good and the score sat 34-6.

After receiving to start the 2nd half, Mahoney led a 48 yard drive of 7 plays and capped it off with a 5-yard touchdown. Three plays later, Cathey picked off the Wolves and set the purple and gold up again. This time, it was John Brown from the 4. Ronnie McDaniel plunged in from the 1 for the last touchdown. The extra point failed and the final was secured at 53-6.

"We just had them outmanned. They had some kids hurt and only dressed out 14 players. We had more manpower (and) had a good effort from everyone who played. We were able to give some of our younger players some playing time and this will help in the long run." Those included Brent Barfield, De Ferguson, Ronnie McDaniel, Chris Gardner, Rory Beard, Lee Speyerer and John Moss. Saint Al had 363 yards in total offense compared to the Wolves' 70. David Wilson grabbed the "Player of the Game" honor, and Mahoney joined McCaffery with Honorable Mention nods.

GAME 8:   SAINT AL (6-1) vs TERRY (2-5)
                  FINAL: ST AL 50 TERRY 0
                  OCTOBER 23, 1982

By unanimous vote, the Flashes accepted an invitation to The Red Carpet Bowl. *"It gives us something to play for again. I really didn't know if our kids would go for it and I certainly didn't want to go if they didn't. But they are really fired up about it. The Red Carpet Bowl is one the top bowls in the state and it's an honor for us to get a chance to play in it."* The Flashes had competed in the 10th, 13th and 14th RCBs. *"It's always a pleasure to have St. Aloysius participate in the Red Carpet Bowl,"* Chairman Dr. Briggs Hopson said. *"The Flashes have played in the game several times and always bring a good crowd. We hope to match them with another top notch team."*

The Flashes were ready physically with exception of Pat Evans' bruised shoulder. *"We have had it x-rayed and it is not fractured. It's a deep bruise."* As for Terry, Edwards said *"I don't care who we are playing. If we don't play well, I'm never happy with a game. We have to guard against overlooking Terry because, admittedly, they aren't the best team we will face this year. We should be able to beat Terry, but we have to be ready to play. We have to guard against overlooking (them). They have a fine running back in Bobby Jackson. Terry has pretty good size on defense. And they are so quick. We will need another good effort out of our offensive line."*

Gussio scored on the 2nd play of the game. He ran twice; 21 on the first and a 32-yard touchdown on the second. Ehrhardt made it 7-0 with only 1:02 off of the clock. Mahoney later hit Robert McDaniel for a diving 17-yard touchdown to make it 14-0. The next possession saw Stamm intercept a Terry pass at the 21. Evans would get in from the 1 for the touchdown. After holding, Beau Cathey returned a punt for a touchdown behind Saint Al blockers to make it 28-0 going into halftime.

The Flashes maintained the fire with Robert McDaniel intercepting a Terry pass to set up an eventual Gussio touchdown. And when Terry had the ball at their 5 on the next possession, Ronnie McDaniel stepped up to pick off an Alfonso Willie pass. Moss grabbed a pass at the 20 followed by three John Brown runs; the last a 5-yard touchdown to make it 42-0. In the 4th, Pinkston hit Moss for a 5-yard strike for the final offensive score. The game was finished with a sack of Willie for a safety. *"As far as the game is concerned, I'm proud that we won"*, said Edwards. They had held Terry to 28 yards. But the turnovers were the engine that made it happen. *"I felt like we were ready to play, but it was difficult for the players to get psyched up for the game. I was afraid we might have a letdown, which could hurt in our game next week against Pelahatchie."*

Evans won "Player of the Game" while Gussio and Moss made Honorable Mentions.

GAME 9:   SAINT AL (7-1) VS PELAHATCHIE (8-0)
                      FINAL: ST AL 13 PELAHATCHIE 10
                      OCTOBER 29, 1982

Though the Flashes had the Warren County rushing leader in Gussio with 858 yards, nobody could say this was a guaranteed victory. *"We have a tough one coming up this week for sure. They are undefeated and have most of their players* (21 starters) *returning of last years' team. We beat them 20-0 last year at their place. It was a tough game all the way. I expect a very tough game from them. They want to come in here and win very badly. This is a B-I-G, big game for us. We might could prove a little something by beating them."*

Had Saint Al not dropped that early game, this would be even bigger. Pelahatchie won their sub-district and the two schools would have eventually faced each other for the District 6B title. Mahoney was now lost for the season with torn ligaments in his ankle from the last game. But Stamm was a proven QB and had Edwards' confidence. *"Craig is going to get the job done for us. We have been putting a lot of time in on the option. I have all of the faith in the world in Craig. He has looked good in practice and he has really been throwing the ball well."*

"Pelahatchie is one of the best teams we have played in the four years that I have been at St. Al. They are going to be hard to score on, and they have a good offense themselves. They have some kids who can catch the ball. Pelahatchie is so big and strong and it is going to be tough for us to muscle it up the middle on them. We are going to have to get outside and utilize our speed against them."

On their first possession, the Chiefs went 62 yards on 12 plays resulting in a Dwight McNair FG of 36 yards. Two plays later, Stamm hit Cathey for a 68-yard score to make it 7-3. The next possession for the Flashes started well, driving to the Pelahatchie 31, but ended on a fumble. The Chiefs capitalized with a 69 yard drive in 14 plays resulting in a Pete Stokes plunge from the 2. With 3:57 until half, the Chiefs made it 13-10 with McNair's extra point.

The Chiefs started the 2nd half by moving the ball to the Saint Al 4 thanks to a 65-yard Dwight Brown run. Once again, the defense held and forced the Chiefs into lost yardage of 1, 12 and 6 yards. The 38 yard FG try by McNair was subsequently wide right. The last score of the game belonged to the Flashes. In the 4th, Gussio hauled in a Pelahatchie punt at the Flash 45 and took it all the way to the endzone. The PAT was blocked, but the 13-10 lead would hold for the Red Carpet bound home team.

"This was a very big win for us. Pelahatchie is a good football team, but we just made the plays when we had to. We had some breaks at key times that really helped us out." John Brown nabbed "Player of the Week", with Stamm and Gussio named Honorable Mentions.

GAME 10:   SAINT AL (8-1) vs GREENVILLE SAINT JOSEPH (0-8)
                      FINAL: ST AL 49 GREENVILLE ST JOE 0
                      NOVEMBER 4, 1982

The Flashes rejoined the rankings, moving back into the Small Five poll at number 5. The Vicksburg Evening Post published a nice article on the seniors that week: **ST. AL SENIORS HOPE TO GO OUT WITH WIN.** *"These kids (seniors) have been the backbone of our program for the last three years. They have contributed a lot to make out program successful and I want them to have a good game to go out on."* The visiting Irish were 0-8, but Edwards still remembered the beating at the hands of the opponent last year. *"Records don't mean a thing when St. Al and Greenville St. Joe hook up. Greenville is hungry for a win and I can't think of a team they had rather beat than St. Al. You really can't tell* anything about the Greenville team from their record because they have been playing some pretty tough teams. Overall, they probably play a tougher schedule than we do."

He was also adamant that they not look to play this game based on revenge. "One thing we have stressed in getting ready for this game is we have to go out and play our regular type of game. I have seen teams go out looking to get even and not play well. We have to have our minds on the game."

The Irish started by moving down the field to the Flash 15. There, the defense came alive and dropped the visitors for losses of 1, 1 and 3 before sacking the QB for a 10 yard loss and possession of the ball. Then it was all Flashes. The first drive went 69 yards on 11 plays, with Gussio going in from the 3 on 4th down. Ehrhardt's kick (one of 7 on the night) made it 7-0. Greenville would have an opportunity after a fumbled punt in the 2nd at their 47. But again, even after another red-zone drive to the 10, the defense came through when they dropped the QB for a 14-yard loss and stalled the drive. Two plays later, Gussio went 52 yards for the touchdown to make it 14-0.

The half came to a close when, with :32 left, Gussio dove in from the 7 to cap a 79 yard drive on 9 plays. It was 21-0 and Gussio already had 151 yards. He continued the assault in the 2nd half. Taking the opening kickoff, he ran it back 90 yards to make it 27-0. The kickoff wasn't as kind to the Irish, as they fumbled the ball and gave possession to the Flashes. Five plays later, and after he tacked on a 19 yard run, Evans bulldozed in to the endzone from the 2 to make it 35-0.

The Flashes continued the pressure. Their very next possession was a 58-yard drive in 8 plays with Gussio going in from the 4. The scoring ended with a 3-yard run by Ferguson midway through the 4th. He had helped his cause with 8 carries and 39 yards on the drive. The final play of significance was from Jim Fordice who hauled in a Greenville fumble.

With 170 yards and 5 touchdowns, Gussio was an obvious "Player of the Game". He was also the Warren County leader with 1,084 rushing yards on 151 carries with 16 touchdowns. Stamm and Ehrhardt were Honorable Mentions. "I was pleased with the way we played tonight. I really expected a lot tougher game out of them. They got after us early pretty good. But after we got rolling, it was over with. Maybe this will be a pretty good springboard for us going into the Red Carpet Bowl next Thursday. We know Wesson has a good team and we are looking forward to playing them. We are proud to host the Red Carpet Bowl and consider it quite an honor."

GAME 11:   SAINT AL (9-1) vs WESSON (9-1)
                       FINAL: ST AL 28 WESSON 0
                       NOVEMBER 10, 1982: RED CARPET BOWL; CITY PARK

Saint Al wasn't playing for a ring this year, but was excited about their 4th RCB appearance. Said Edwards, "I'm not saying that this takes all of the sting out of missing the playoffs. But it sure soothes the pain. A lot of our kids have been attending the Red Carpet Bowl since they were young kids and getting a chance to play in it is like a dream come true."

Both teams sported 9-1 records. "I think their team is very comparable to ours. They play very good defense and they don't make many mistakes. You have to beat Wesson. They don't beat themselves." Head Coach Ricky Clopton was also complimentary of the Flashes. "We have been the type of team that plays strong defense and waits for the other team to make a mistake. The thing that worries me about St. Al is that they everything so well. It's hard to stop a team that executes as well as St. Al does."

Wesson had a capable two-man rushing tandem. Wade Alexander had tallied 917 yards and teammate Michael Coleman had 578. Both teams featured strong defenses. Wesson gave up only 49 points, while the Flashes surrendered 56. And both teams had losses to the eventual sub-district winners. The most accurate measuring stick for comparison would be Puckett. Saint Al defeated the Wolves 24-0 and Wesson 22-6. The previous year, the Flashes had won the South State Class B Championship over Dexter. Wesson, likewise, won the River City Bowl over Natchez Cathedral. On paper, it was a very evenly-matched game.

A reported 2,500 fans watched as Saint Al struck first; the only score in the first half for either team. Stamm capped the 9-play 79 yard drive from the 10 by hitting Cathey. Ehrhardt was good and the Flashes were up 7-0. The next possession was a heartbreaker. Stamm got loose for an apparent 35-yard touchdown, but illegal motion forced the Flashes to punt to the Wesson 33. Another opportunity was lost after a Stamm interception of Mike Lewis at the Cobra 45. A penalty pushed them back and Ehrhardt's 51-yard FG attempt hit the crossbar.

The Cobras had the ball 4 times for 14 total plays in the 1st half. The Gold Crush defense was doing well. Said Clopton, *"Those suckers kept the football the whole first half. We couldn't get the ball away from them. I don't think our team has ever been dominated like that offensively. We were just hanging in there during the first half. Which is really what we have done all year. We have looked for the break and capitalized on it. We were overpowered. That sums it up best."*

The Flashes stopped the opening 3rd quarter drive to take over on the Wesson 40. Stamm orchestrated an 8-play drive with an 8-yard touchdown and Ehrhardt was good again to make it 14-0. The next possession saw Lewis throwing yet another pick; this one to Cathey who returned it to the Wesson 16. Evans did the honors afterwards, taking it in for the 21-0 touchdown. Scoring was finalized when Stamm hit Cathey from the 20 to cap a 51-yard drive on 14 plays. The Cobras got to the 1 in the final minutes, but penalties kept them out.

"We played well in the 2nd half. I was very pleased with the way our defense played. We just never let them get started." But the sting of the East Flora loss was still present. *"We would have liked to have been playing Pelahatchie for the District 6B championship. As far as I'm concerned, we are the best team in the district. But this was a good experience for our team. The Red Carpet Bowl Committee did a great job putting this on and we were happy to be a part of it."*

Offensive MVP Awards were shared between Gussio and Stamm. Gussio had amassed 182 yards of rushing to put him at an unofficial 1,264 yard on the season. Stamm rushed for 110 and threw for 41. David Wilson won the Defensive MVP Award. The sharing of the trophy meant that there was just one piece of hardware, and 35 years later, there is still argument about who gets to hold the momento.

The All-County Football Team list was released a few weeks after the last game and 8 Flashes were named. Among them were the county's leading rusher in Gussio along with Cathey, DeRossette, Ehrhardt, Evans, McCaffrey, Stamm and Wilson. Honorable Mentions went to Mike Mahoney, Robert McDaniel, Fordice, John Brown, and Joe Evans. Pat Evans won the school's Virgadamo Trophy.

"Coach Edwards demanded hard work, sacrifice and discipline on the field, in the weight room, and in the classroom. He ensured that we were prepared and better-conditioned than anyone we faced. We played a very simple, physical style of football and enjoyed success that few teams can rival.

Our record on the field was strong, and the bond of friendship and trust among us even stronger. The seniors on this team began to form a unique chemistry as early as the third grade at Saint Francis. We were trained early to attack at the snap of the ball and play until the whistle blew. We were mentally, physically and spiritually prepared, and we expected to win every time we stepped on the field. We remain very close friends to this day.

As boys we would go to the Flashes games on Friday nights and dream of playing as many of our families had in days past. We understood that wearing the purple and gold jersey was a great honor. We knew how blessed we were to play football, the ultimate team game, and knew that the Saint Aloysius family was counting on us. We fought with all of our might to make them proud and left everything we had on the field."

On Behalf of the 1982 Flashes. Pat Evans, Johnny Gussio and Michael Mahoney; July 27, 2016

1983 (6-4)

"If they put on the purple and gold on September 1st, and go out on the field against Madison-Ridgeland, they WILL be in shape." That was Edwards' opening quote for 1983. It was based on a prior experience he had about conditioning and was *"all the education he needed. I took a team that wasn't in shape the second season I was here and was embarrassed. I said it would never happen again. You may think you're in shape, but you never can tell until after you put on the pads and carry them around during practice for a week or so. We have had a week in shorts and I think most of the kids are used to the heat. Now we are really fixing to go to work."*

As two-a-days continued, he said, *"The offensive line has looked real good in the first couple of practices, especially Joe Baladi, Joe Evans and Brent Barfield. The entire line has been working exceptionally hard."* Media questions centered on opening day. *"Madison Ridgeland has a good football team. They are well coached and have several good players. But we can beat them and conditioning will be the key of the ball game. We have a long way to go but we can get there with hard work and a tough mental attitude."*

He also told The Vicksburg Evening Post "Right now we have around 15 boys ready to play Varsity football. I think we get several others ready to go with practice and a few junior varsity games. However, we are going to have some kids who will have to suck it up and go both ways and we can't afford to get any hurt."

GAME 1:   SAINT AL (0-0) @ MADISON RIDGELAND (0-0)
                          FINAL: ST AL 7 MADISON RIDGELAND 27
                          SEPTEMBER 1, 1983

Said Edwards before kickoff, "We have a lot of untested people. But we have done just about everything we can do to prepare. Now we need to play. Ready or not, we are fixing to kick it off." Madison was returning their starting running backs from a 6-4 season, while Saint Al had only Beau Cathey playing the same position on defense.

Saint Al drew first blood on a fumble recovered by Cathey at the MR 48. Kevin Mahoney capped an 11-play drive with a 1-yard TD keeper. Joe Evans' PAT made it 7-0. Two plays later, the Braves' Wesley Jackson broke away for a 65-yard touchdown. Bubba Simpson's PAT notched it 7-7. Afterwards, it was Cathey who coughed up the ball on the kickoff, setting up a Carl Powell 1-yard sneak. The Flashes responded when they showed FG formation on the 21 but Cathey instead took the snap and hit Pinkston at the half-yard line. Unfortunately, the Flashes had too many men downfield and the drive was nullified.

Two plays later, sophomore Mark Simrall gave Saint Al apparent life by recovering a fumble at the MR 14. But Jessie Winder intercepted a Mahoney pass on the drive and ran it back 98 yards for the score to make it 20-7. The final score came on a David Winder 39 yard touchdown run and, combined with the PAT, finished the contest at 27-7. Saint Al had more rushing yards (155-151), more first downs (11-8); fewer penalty yards (65-45) and much more possession time (30:44 – 17:16). Nobody completed any passes, but two Flash turnovers led to touchdowns.

Mahoney landed The Vicksburg Evening Post "Player of the Game". Afterwards, Edwards praised him, Ferguson, Speyerer and Rory Beard for "outstanding play". "We played a good football game. We have a lot of inexperienced players and they didn't do a bad job. We aren't going to play anyone faster. That's not to say we won't play teams that aren't as good as Madison-Ridgeland. But they hurt us with their speed."

GAME 2:   SAINT AL (0-1) @ NATCHEZ CATHEDRAL (1-0)
                          FINAL: ST AL 14 NATCHEZ CATHEDRAL 11
                          SEPTEMBER 9, 1983

Edwards was adamant that they needed more work on offensive line blocking. "I feel like the kids tried hard. But we didn't get the blocking we need on the line or with the downfield receivers and we are going to spend a lot of time in this area starting Monday. We have inexperienced players in this area and they will improve as the year goes a lot. But we need a lot of work."

During practice week, it was learned that Cathey had an ankle and knee injury from the previous game and wouldn't play. De Ferguson moved in at tailback to take his spot. As for the Greenies, Edwards noted that they were a power-type offensive team with good size. "They are a senior ball club. They are big and strong, but I don't think they will be as quick as Madison-Ridgeland. We must counter this with our quickness and hope our conditioning will help us in the final quarter. If we can go down there and play well, we can win. It is a matter of us doing it. We are thin in numbers right now but I think we have the people to get the job done. "

He also added some strong words for the team in Natchez. "This is an intense rivalry. We feel that they have been dodging us for the last three years and we are glad to finally be playing them." If Edwards was looking to fire up his team and reverse course, he got his wish.

Freshman Jeff Jones got the purple and gold going by taking the opening kickoff 68 yards to the Cathedral 21. Ferguson burst around the end for 20 to the 1, followed by a Mahoney QB keeper touchdown. Evans' PAT made it 7-0. Said Edwards afterwards, "We were extremely unhappy with our special teams play last week against Madison. We put in a lot of extra time on it and Jeff Jones made the big play for us." The 2nd started with Mahoney attempting a keeper to the right but fumbled to give it to Cathedral. The Wave took advantage and Tommy Kimbrell booted a 37-yard FG to make it 7-3.

The Greenies gave the ball back to the Flashes later in the quarter on a fake punt, but then Saint Al fumbled back to Natchez. Halftime sat with a Flash lead of 7-3. Edwards was unhappy, saying

"We made mistakes in the first half that kept us from putting the game away. That's one thing that really bothers me. We would have a good play and then lose it on a penalty."

In the 3rd, Lee Speyerer fell on an opening drive Cathedral fumble at the 22. Six plays later, and four Mahoney carries, Ferguson took it in from the 5. Evans made it 14-3. In the same frame, the Flashes again turned it over. Combined with a number of penalties, it resulted in a Reagan White two-yard touchdown. The 2 point conversion lowered the lead to 14-11.

In the 4th, on Cathedral's last effort, Speyerer knocked down a Wave pass, Brian Breithaupt had a big tackle on a reverse, and a Speyerer interception sealed the game. *"This is the most important win we've had since I have been here. We still have a lot of work to do, but I'm extremely pleased with the victory and the effort our kids put out."* Beard was named "Player of the Week", with Honorable Mentions going to Mahoney and Ferguson. Mahoney was now the second leading rusher in Warren County with 154 yards on 43 carries and 2 touchdowns.

GAME 3:   SAINT AL (1-1) vs EAST FLORA (0-2)
                 FINAL: ST AL 0 EAST FLORA 15
                 SEPTEMBER 17, 1983

When speaking of the Hawks, Edwards said *"Our kids have their work cut out. East Flora has a fine football team. They have a large team and they will come straight at us. They do that, but they also run the sweep and the reverse. So we have to be ready to play defense. I think their Keith Ranson will probably be the best football player we face all year."* The game wasn't a district contest, but was somewhat of a grudge match. The previous year, East Flora eliminated the defending District Class B champs Flashes from a return State Playoff visit by beating them 7-6. *"I've talked to coaches whose teams have played East Flora. And they don't see how East Flora is 0-2. They have a good group of athletes with size and speed."*

In the 1st, David Cosby scored on a 5-yard run and Leavelle Hollins' extra point made it 7-0. In the 2nd, the Hawks were held at the one-half yard line to give the Flashes a chance to stay in the game. That same defense held strong until late in the 4th until East Flora managed a 49-yard touchdown pass from Kenneth Horton to Willie Robinson. This time Horton got the 2-point conversion to make the final score 15-0.

"They were bigger and stronger than we were. And they outmuscled us. I was proud of our kids. They fought tooth-and-nail. But East Flora was just too much for us to handle. Our kids played well and don't have a thing to be ashamed of. I'm glad that they don't like to lose, but they need to look ahead." Saint Al, who had already lost Beau Cathy at the starting tailback spot, now saw starting Rory Beard with a broken arm requiring surgery, Pat Gordon with a knee injury requiring surgery, and De Ferguson with a bad muscle tear. Beard and Gordon were gone for the season. *"We can't afford these injuries, but now that we have them, our kids have to fill in the holes."*

GAME 4:   SAINT AL (1-2) vs SAINT ANDREWS (2-1)
                 FINAL: ST AL 39 SAINT ANDREWS 16
                 SEPTEMBER 23, 1983

Edwards ended the last game positively, in spite of the damage. *"We will match up better with the next three teams we play and have a good chance of winning."* Cathey was a possibility after practicing during the week for the first time since injury, but he still noted that *"If we get anyone else hurt in the backfield, I really don't know what we will do. We were thin in numbers to begin with. And with these injuries, (we) don't have many left."*

Of Saint Andrews, he said *"They have an improved team. Saint Andrews has a straight passing attack and they run the option well. They don't make mistakes. They are going to be more our size, but make no mistake. We will have to play well to win. They are going to be getting after us, so our kids had better be ready to get after them."* In the end, the home-standing Saints had 5 fumbles (losing 3), threw 2 interceptions, and had more penalty yards (40 vs 6).

Saint Al took the opening kickoff, using now-playing Cathey, to score from 5 yards out. Three plays into the Saints' first drive, David Biggar fell on a loose ball at the 43. The Flashes got into the endzone on that drive to start the 2nd; a 1-yard keeper by Mahoney. The 2-point conversion failed, but Saint Al led 12-0. Later, Mahoney hit Pinkston for 13 followed by Cathey runs of 15 and 3 for another touchdown to make it 18-0. A Saints fumble on the next possession was recovered by Evans.

Mahoney hit Pinkston for 19 but a fumble afterwards turned the ball back over. After regaining possession, Pinkston hit Mahoney on a fake punt for 43 yards to the 2 as the half expired.

In the 2nd half, it was more of an air game. Mahoney to Pinkston for gains of 12 and 9 set up their 21 yard connection for a touchdown. Evans was good to make it 25-0. The Saints fumbled at their own 8 after and Saint Al immediately responded. Three plays were capped by a 1-yard Speyerer TD to make it 32-0. The final score was a 1-yard plunge from Pinkston now playing quarterback. The drive was set up by Jeff Jones, who carried 27 of the 28 yards. Reserves came on for the Flashes.

Bev Bishop hit Jerome Franklin twice for a total of 45 yards and then carried the load himself for a 23-yard touchdown. A pass to Paul Catherwood made it 39-8. Immediately afterwards, Bishop threw another 57 yards and rushed 19; the last 4 of which for his 2nd TD. Catherwood hauled in the 2-pointer to finish the scoring. *"We got to play everybody tonight. I just wanted to avoid any injuries whatsoever."* Everybody included Jones, a freshman who picked Bishop off twice in the game.

The Flashes led every category but passing (145-122). Speyerer won The Vicksburg Evening Post's "Player of the Game" with Moss as Honorable Mention.

GAME 5:   SAINT AL (2-2) @ WEST UNION (1-3)
                 FINAL: ST AL 7 WEST UNION 8
                 SEPTEMBER 30, 1983

The Flashes were starting without Mahoney at signal caller and John Moss as receiver, but had a capable backup QB in Pinkston. Even so, had someone told Joe Edwards that his team would be inside the South Union 20 six times, keep West Union on their side of the field all but once and still lose; he probably would have scratched his thinning reddish hair and given you his distinctive stare. But that is exactly what happened to open District 6B South competition in Pinola.

On the first possession of the game, the Flashes drove 80 yards in 7 plays, with Ferguson gaining a 2-yard touchdown. Joe Evans made it 7-0. It was a back-and-forth affair until Pinkston intercepted a Bulldog pass with 1:38 left in the half. The Flashes drove to the 2 yard line, but time expired. In the 3rd quarter, Brent Barfield picked off a West Union pass and returned it 25 yards to the Bulldog 30. But, the Flashes would stall at the 18. In the same quarter, West Union's Terry Terrell hit his own safety blocker in the helmet with the punt and the Flashes recovered at the 20. The drive would get no further than the 8 before turning over on downs.

In the 4th, it was Perry Davis scoring on a 7 yard run to make it 7-6. West Union opted for a 2 point conversion. On a freak play, the underthrown pass from Davis was tipped, but Mike Johnson was able to grab it to make the final score 8-7. The Flashes still had chances. The first was a drive from their 42 to the Bulldog 20 that ended on downs. The next was a drive from the Bulldog 40 to the 17 that ended in a Johnson interception of Pinkston to seal the win.

The Flashes had won in first downs, passing yards, total offense, turnovers, return yards and fewer penalties. Nevertheless, the scoreboard was in favor of West Union. Bulldog Coach Dwayne Yates was thrilled. *"I really don't know what to say. Saint Al has a fine football tradition, and beating them takes a fine effort by any football team. This has to be the biggest football victory in West Union High School history."* A somber Edwards said *"We got many chances to put the ballgame away, but we couldn't capitalize on our breaks. But give credit to West Union. They played a real fine game and did what they had to do to win."* Pinkston won "Player of the Game.

GAME 6:   SAINT AL (2-3) vs BENTONIA (0-5)
                 FINAL: ST AL 47 BENTONIA 0
                 October 7, 1983

The Flashes now had Mahoney back and hopefully a solid backfield as well. *"We haven't had the same backfield for any two games in a row. The talent at our backfield position varies so much that these changes make a difference in timing as well as other things. Maybe this week we will have them all together."* There were injuries, though, in Evans (fluid on the knee) and Biggar (sprained neck). Still in playoff contention, it would take defeating both Bentonia and Utica. *"We're not only struggling trying to get back into the sub-district race. We are struggling trying to get back to winning some football games. After the game we played against West Union last week, we have plenty of room for improvement. West Union proved to me that you can never count a win before you earn it. We are going to have to be the best team Friday night to win the game. That is the only way you can win games."*

In his return, Mahoney rushed for 115 yards, scored 3 touchdowns, and passed for 2 more to Pinkston. *"We're a different ball club with Kevin out there. He helps us out when he is on the field."* On the first drive that started at the Wolves 45, Mahoney found Pinkston for an 11-yard touchdown. Evans' PAT made it 7-0. On their next drive, starting at the Wolves 39 and it was Mahoney again; this time on an 18-yard run. Evans made it 14-0. Before the halftime, Mahoney scored yet again on a 48-yard run. Bentonia had threatened only once when they made it to the Flash 9. But the defense was up to the challenge and stopped any opportunities.

In the second half, the Flashes took over at the Wolves 37. Speyerer carried the ball 19 yards to set up a Ferguson 25-yard score to make it 28-0. Mahoney later picked off a Wilford Griffin pass and took it to paydirt. Mahoney would later find a diving Pinkston for a 35-yard TD followed by a Joe Baladi fumble recovery that gave Ferguson a 10-yard rushing touchdown. The PAT made it 47-0. With time eroding, Mark Simrall picked off a Griffin pass to seal the win.

"We played a real good game overall, especially in the second half. We made some mistakes in the first half. We weren't concentrating on what we were doing. We scored 21 points in the first half when we should have had 35." Pinkston had just shy of 100 yards in receptions on 4 catches; the Flashes had 372 yards of total offense and kept Bentonia to 42 rushing yards. Noted the head coach succinctly, *"We have Utica next week for Homecoming. They have a real fine ball club. We have got to beat them to have a chance at the playoffs."*

Mahoney was "Player of the Game". Ferguson and Pinkston made Honorable Mentions.

GAME 7: SAINT AL (3-3) vs UTICA (3-3)
FINAL: ST AL 9 UTICA 0
October 14, 1983

The Flashes were putting up respectable numbers in Warren County. Pinkston was the leading receiver with 12 catches for 186 yards and Mahoney was 3rd in rushing with 366 yards on 88 carries. Before the game, Edwards noted that *"We would like to win the game and get back ... but the world will not come to an end if we don't."*

The game was one that would be on the ground throughout the contest. In the 2nd, the Flashes received a gift when an errant punt snap sailed over Casey Fisher's head recovered at the 15. The Flashes couldn't score on three plays and elected to go with an Evans FG. But a Wave procedure penalty gave Saint Al a 1st down at the 5. Ferguson wasted no time and immediately stormed into paydirt for the 7-0 lead.

In the 3rd, Speyerer blocked a punt and then joined a horde of Flashes to tackle Fisher in the endzone for a safety. Saint Al could have scored again in the 4th when a TD pass inside the 20 from Mahoney to Pinkston was called back for holding. In between, it was the Flash defense that saved the day. Joe Evans not only had a fumble recovery, but Pinkston also picked off another pass. And in his punting, Pinkston averaged 40 yards on 4 punts, even with a 55-yarder called back due to a penalty.

Post-game, Utica head man Joe Walker said, *"We let them have that touchdown right there before halftime, and that really hurt us. Coming into the game, I told our players that if we could hold St. Al scoreless for three quarters, then we had a good chance to win. But give St Al all the credit. I think they wanted it a tad more than we did."* Edwards told Danny Garnette, *"We had to win tonight, and I am proud of our players for going out there and doing just that. The defense played fairly well, but the offense had several chances to score and couldn't put it in."*

As for playoffs, West Union had already beaten the Flashes 8-7 and sat 2-0 in division play. If they beat Utica, they would be 3-0 and the crown was theirs. A Utica win by 18 or more would give the Golden Wave the championship. Only a Utica win under 18 would wrap purple and gold on the trophy.

For *"steady defense"* and fumble recovery, Joe Evans was named "Player of the Week", with Pinkston and Mahoney Honorable Mentions.

GAME 8: SAINT AL (4-3) @ GREENVILLE SAINT JOSEPH (1-5)
FINAL: ST AL 27 GREENVILLE ST JOE 0
OCTOBER 21, 1983

The win against Utica the week took a lot out of many players. Mahoney was slowed with an ankle injury but would be play. Nothing was decided on the playoff situation by game time. Utica and West Union were to battle much later and all the Flashes could do was get ready for GSJ and stay sharp.

"The Greenville St Joe game is in our hands... We need to play well and try to win these next three games and not worry about anything else."

Speaking of the loss that ruined the perfect 1981 season, Edwards said "We return to the scene of the massacre. They really beat us up bad. It was just as bad as the score indicated. This is also a big game for us because Saint Joe is one of our Catholic school rivalries. We will always be able to get up for them. It's hard to tell just what kind of team they have. They play a lot of teams in Arkansas and then some in the Delta that we are not that familiar with. Because of that, we have nothing to compare them with and can't fairly say what kind of team they have. The record of a team can be very deceiving."

On their first drive, Ferguson took them to the 7 yard line where Mahoney capped the drive by finding Pinkston over the middle. In the 2nd half, Mahoney fumbled a wet ball to give the Irish life, but Speyerer picked off a Cedric McCray pass at the Flash 49. Ferguson would cap it from the 30 around for another Saint Al touchdown. Mahoney hit John Moss for the 2-pointer. Speyerer hauled in another pick before it was over. Intercepting at the Flash 25, he ran it back to the Irish 9. Three plays later it was Ferguson for his 2nd of two TDs; this one from the 2. Evans made it 21-0. Scoring was ended when Moss picked off the 3rd McCray pass of the evening and returned it to the Irish 22. The 6-play drive was capped when Pinkston scored from two yards out.

Edwards told Calvin Stevens, "We played a very poor game in the first half. We weren't as sharp as we should have been. After we got ahead we slowed things up some. St. Joe isn't that strong and we didn't want to run all over them. We played a conservative ball game after we finally scored. We had some mistakes, but we got lucky. We had three fumbles that could have hurt us and this is where the luck came in."

For his 157 yards and 2 touchdowns, Ferguson was "Player of the Game". Edwards said of him, "De played a real good game. He has the speed that it takes to be a good tailback, but he still needs to learn when to make his cuts." Pinkston and Simrall were Honorable Mentions.

GAME 9:   SAINT AL (5-3) @ PELAHATCHIE (7-1)
            FINAL: ST AL 6 PELAHATCHIE 17
            OCTOBER 28, 1983

In hindsight, this game versus Pelahatchie would be important. The Chiefs had already secured the East Division Championship the week before by beating Puckett 14-7. They would be the next opponent should everything come together for the Flashes. "I don't look at this game as a championship preview because we don't have any control over it. We had our chance to control it, but we didn't take advantage of it. If we are able to play for the district title, good. But if we don't, it is our own fault." The West Union loss was the difference in the year. And the way they lost made the bitter taste worse. "I feel like we have the best team on this side of the district. But whether we make it to the playoff is another matter." As for Pelahatchie, he said "Our scout was tremendously impressed with (them). They are a huge, power-I team that lines up and comes straight at you."

The Chiefs scored late in the 1st after Vance Jones intercepted a Mahoney pass at the Saint Al 25 yard line. It took 6 plays for Dwight Brown to score from the 6 with only: 01 on the clock. Mitch Marin added the PAT to give the home team a 7-0 lead. Saint Al punted after 3-and-out, but the Pelahatchie team had 12 men on the field and gave new downs to the Flashes at the Chief 42. They orchestrated a 7-play march topped by a 20-yard Mahoney to Moss touchdown to make it 7-6.

Two Flash fumbles afterwards, at the 35 and 34 yard lines, resulted in 10 Pelahatchie points. Martin had a 21-yard effort in the 3rd that was good, followed by a 1-yard Eric Holman touchdown with 5:35 left to ice the game. Edwards told Danny Garnett afterwards. "You can't turn the ball over four times deep in your own territory and hope to win against a good team." And the fact was that no Pelahatchie drive was longer than 40 yards the entire game was more insult than injury. "I just hope we get a chance to play Pelahatchie again in the championship game. Pelahatchie is good, but they are definitely not the strongest team we have played this year. If we meet them again, we will be better prepared and do something differently. If we meet them again, we will whip them. You can print that."

For his 20-yard TD reception, Moss was "Player of the Game". Honorable Mention went only to Mahoney.

SAINT AL (5-4) vs MISSISSIPPI SCHOOL FOR THE DEAF (6-3)
            FINAL: ST AL 27 MSD 0
            NOVEMBER 3, 1983

Edwards was cautious about MSD. *"We are probably facing one of the best...teams in their history. They have excellent speed and do a lot of things well. We can't let them get outside on us or they will break it open."* Referring to Steve McNeese, he said *"He's one of the best backs around."* The last time a Flash team wasn't above .500 was 1969. And a lot was riding on containing that speed for the win.

The recap for this game in print is not very long. The Flashes scored two 1st-quarter touchdowns; one on a 2-yard Mahoney run and the other on a Ferguson 9-yarder. With both PATs missed, it was 12-0. In the 2nd, it was Ferguson from the 15 followed Mahoney to Moss for the 2 point conversation to make it 20-0. Ferguson scored again in the 4th to seal the victory on an 8-yard run. In all, the Flashes rushed for 249 and passed for 37. McNeese, for the record, put up 127 of his own.

But the bad news was to follow the good. West Union has stomped Utica 56-6, ending the hopes of the Flashes for another game. *"On behalf of Saint Aloysius, I want to congratulate West Union. They did what they had to do and we wish them all the luck in the world."*

The awards came in for some 1983 Flashes after the season. All-County nods were given to Evans, Mahoney, Pinkston and Speyerer. All-District went to Agostinelli, Baladi, Barfield, Evans, Mahoney, Pinkston and Speyerer. Joe Evans won the coveted Virgadamo Trophy.

"The Vicksburg Evening Post sports headline would read "It's All Over", but that night after the last regular season game, hope remained in the Saint Aloysius parking lot. After fans and players had gone, at least two vehicles remained: a blue VW Beetle (Coach Edwards) and an old 4-wheel drive Chevy (mine). We hung around the gym awaiting the results of the Utica-West Union game. Coach Edwards was inside his office listening to results on the radio. When the news came, he stepped outside the gym and said that Utica crushed West Union. He didn't have to say anything else. That was the end of the 1983 season. No playoffs.

Our senior class followed possibly the greatest Saint Aloysius team ever. The 1982 loss to East Flora denied them a state championship. The 1983 season was our chance to do something that even they didn't: go to the playoffs. So, when it ended, there was regret and disappointment at what 'should have been'. Plain and simple, we should have beaten West Union. I should have been on the field that night with my team. I placed my teammates and coaches in a tough situation. For that I'm eternally sorry.

Having said that, our team had notable accomplishments. We beat both Catholic schools on our schedule (if you're reading this, you know that isn't an easy task). Cathedral would go the rest of the year into South State Championship with ours being their only loss. I'll never forget Coach Edwards, with a minute or so to go, coming into our huddle. His fist was clenched in front of his face and, with a determined expression, said 'Fellas, hold on to the ball and we got this game won!' That 6'4" and 270 pounds of grown red-headed man would strut back to the sidelines ... happy. We beat a very good Utica team that won our district and went to the playoffs in what should have been our spot. We ended with a 6-4 record (7-3 officially due to the Madison Ridgeland forfeit) but could have easily been 8-2.

Football teaches young men a lot about life and provides many great memories. Many I recall like they happened yesterday. If you played for Coach Edwards, you have good stories and probably an impersonation of him (sincerest form of flattery). Sharing memories with other past players is one of the things that bonds our school football history together."

Kevin Mahoney; July 30, 2016

1984 (5-5)

This year will be remembered not for what happened on the field, but rather for what happened off. David Atkins, a member of the senior class, was killed in a car wreck. The players wore a "41" sticker on their helmet to honor him. And when you see a dedication that includes him, you will know why.

As for football, the Flashes began the season with what Edwards termed, *"a lot of question marks"* due to departures and graduation. Edwards had 13 returning seniors; many seeing valuable playing time the previous year playing both ways. But it was obvious that underclassmen would be called upon to contribute. *"I just don't want to throw our younger players into a game situation before they're ready unless I absolutely have to."*

The outlook was still positive for the Flashes. They received 12 points, including 3 first place votes, in the District Six 1-A preseason coaches poll. Edwards noted that *"We are going to be a team that steadily improves as the season progresses. Right now, we have made some position changes and some people are having to get used to doing something new. But they will get better as we play."* One reporter noted: *"In my opinion, St. Aloysius is the surprise of the season. There were a lot of questions about that group when the fall practice session opened and Head Coach Joe Edwards seems to have found the answers. What impresses me is their versatility. The Flashes can run or throw on offense. And while their defense bends at times, it doesn't have many breakdowns. It is going to be hard to keep this group out of the State Playoffs."*

Months of weight-lifting and weeks of two-a-day practices had been invested. Edwards still boomed out his *"Sunshine and blue skies"* cries as he blew the whistle on the Monday 880s. The Flashes were increasingly tired of hitting each other and it was time to see what the team with so much promise had to offer.

GAME 1:   SAINT AL (0-0) @ MADISON RIDGELAND (0-0)
                               FINAL: ST AL 32 M.R. 8
                               SEPTEMBER 7, 1984

The Braves had beaten Saint Al the previous season 27-7 (despite forfeit) and were returning with many starters. *"We're going up there untested. It will be tough, no mistake about it. They beat us pretty good last year, but we are hoping we can turn that around."*

The Flashes scored first on a five-play drive of 85 yards: Four carries by De Ferguson and a 63-yard pass from Corey Pinkston to Herman Biedenharn made it 6-0. With 1:43 to go in the 2nd, Ferguson ran eight yards for a touchdown, capping a 4-play drive of 32 yards. Pinkston converted the 2-pointer with a pass to Speyerer to make it 14-0. On the next play, a Braves fumble on their 22 and was recovered by Brent Barfield. Pinkston then hit Speyerer again with :56 left to make halftime 20-0.

In the 3rd Pinkston hit Biedenharn again for an 11-yard touchdown to make it 26-0. The St Al defense, spurred by Barfield and Joe Baladi, helped its cause again when Pinkston picked off a pass on the very next play from scrimmage. Unfortunately during the 3rd, senior Brave back Ronnie Travis suffered a broken leg and was carted from the field after a 20-minute delay.

The Flashes would add to their lead. A 4th down catch by Delvan Irwin put them in scoring position, and then Pinkston hit Speyerer once again for a 13-yard touchdown. The final score of the game came at 7:16 on a 60-yard TD by Madison Ridgeland's Ras Greer. *"Suddenly I looked up at the scoreboard and we were winning 32-0"*, said Edwards. Pinkston added *"Everything seemed to fit, didn't it? Those straight drop-back passes worked like a charm. It's funny, we had worked hard during the summer on this passing game and all week our receivers couldn't exactly find the handle. But it all fell into place tonight."*

Pinkston went 13-16 for 230 yards; Biedenharn had two passes, both for touchdowns, for 74 yards; and Speyerer caught 8 passes for 122 yards with a TD and an extra point. Edwards praised the linemen afterwards. *"David Biggar played well at center, especially with the pass protection. Brent Barfield, Joe Baladi, James Peck and DeRossette did well on defense. They have a lot of work to do but at least we have some size."*

Pinkston was recognized as Player of the Week by the Jackson Touchdown Club and QB Player of the Week by the paper. Honorable Mentions went to Biedenharn and Speyerer. Afterwards, the Flashes made the Small School Top 5 AP Poll as the state's number 2 team. Edwards said *"I'm tickled to death we're number 2 but I would be a lot more tickled if we were to win that one (Natchez Cathedral) Friday night."*

GAME 2:   SAINT AL (1-0) vs. NATCHEZ CATHEDRAL (1-0)
                               FINAL: ST AL 24 NATCHEZ CATHEDRAL 12
                               SEPTEMBER 14, 1984

Edwards was candid about the next game. *"We're going to have to work better and harder to win Friday's game with Natchez. They're kind of our rivals; there's no love lost between the two teams. We expect a tough game. I'm sure they are looking at this as a grudge match."* Cathedral opened their season with a 21-20 win over Salem. The senior-laden squad had a revenge factor in mind as Saint Al was the only team to beat them (14-11) the previous year.

Cathedral opened the game with Jim Willard's 23 yard touchdown run to make it 6-0. With running by Ferguson and two pass completions by Pinkston that moved them to the 4, Pinkston hit Speyerer for the game-tying score. In the 2nd and after working their way to the 4, FB Ronnie McDaniel got the call and carried a host of Greenies in to make it 12-6 with 4:09 remaining.

It was Ferguson who scored on the opening drive of the 2nd but the game was sealed in the 4th when Speyerer returned a punt 44 yards to set up a Pinkston keeper for a TD. As time expired, and with many reserves in the game, Natchez scored again when QB Michael Richardson hit Willard for a 38-yard TD. Ferguson was named Player of the Week, while Speyerer and Barfield were named Honorable Mentions. Afterwards, Edwards said *"I knew it was going to be a tough game. Our kids showed a lot of character on a hot night as they came back to score the next 24 points. I'll tell you who what won this game and it was the offensive line".* Cathedral Head Coach Ken Beasley noted that *"Their line dominated ours. They were just too big for us and that was the difference in the game."*

GAME 3:　　　　　SAINT AL (2-0) @ RICHLAND (0-2)
　　　　　　　　　FINAL: ST AL 14 RICHLAND 3
　　　　　　　　　SEPTEMBER 21, 1984

It would have been easy to be overconfident as the Rangers were 0-2, starting five sophomores on offense, and Saint Al had just beaten their arch-rivals to stay undefeated. *"There is some green paint still on my helmet",* noted lineman Baladi to a reporter this week. And even though he finished that statement with *"I expect them to give us a good game",* a possible case of overconfidence was in the air.

The first half was penalty-laden; keeping either team from putting together worthwhile drives. And at half, it was Richland who held a 3-0 lead courtesy of a Greg Honeycutt interception of Pinkston. With time waning, he helped his cause with a 45-yard FG. The Flashes almost pulled off a potential lead before the whistle. Pinkston completed passes of 18, 16, 13 and 11 to march his squad to the Richland 17 before fumbling a snap from center.

Halftime brought the Flashes out of hibernation. On a short Richland punt in the 3rd, St Al set up shop at the Ranger 42. With a quick option to the 14, they then faked a handoff that resulted in a Pinkston QB keeper touchdown. Bill Landes' PAT made it 7-3. In the 4th, the Flashes stayed with the option and run game. Speyerer runs of 10 and 12 yards set up a Pinkston dive from 2 yards out to cap a 52-yard drive. Landes was good again, and the scoring was done.

Edwards summed saying *"I was fearful coming here tonight. We had our eyes on their 0-2 record and everyone – coaches, players, even the bus driver – was overconfident. Only our defense played well the first half. Brent Barfield, Lee Speyerer and the rest did a good job keeping us out of the hole."* Lineman Matthew DeRossette was named "Player of the Game", with Pinkston and Ferguson tabbed for Honorable Mention. Ferguson rushed for 139 yards on 23 carries and the Flashes kept their number 2 spot in the Little Five AP poll.

GAME 4:　　　　　SAINT AL (3-0) vs. JACKSON SAINT ANDREWS (2-1)
　　　　　　　　　FINAL: ST AL 14 ST ANDREWS 29
　　　　　　　　　SEPTEMBER 28, 1984

With a 3-0 record, the purple and gold had high expectations of an undefeated record before going into district play. They sat 18th in the AP Top 20 Poll, 3rd in the Clarion-Ledger Class B Poll, and 3rd in the Little 5 Poll. But Edwards knew the potential was there for a letdown. Prior to kickoff, he said *"We can't play sluggish, uninspired football like we did in the first half of the Richland game and expect to win. Saint Andrews is improved and I expect they will take it to us. We expect a tough game."* There were injuries coming into the contest. Pinkston had jammed his wrist against Ridgeland and Ferguson had bruised knees.

In the 1st, the Flashes sat at their 2 after a Saints punt. On the first play, Ferguson, limited by injury from the previous game, fumbled at the goal line. On the ensuing play, Saint Andrews immediately scored on a Craig Bluntson run to make it 7-0. On the next drive, Ferguson ran 8 times on a 10-play, 68-yard drive. Pinkston kept from the 1 and the Flashes were down 7-6. The bad news was that Ferguson injured his shoulder on the march and would be gone for the remainder of the game.

The quarter ended on a Saints touchdown catch by Collier Simpson and a Paul Catherwood 2-point conversation to put them up 15-6. Before halftime, the Flashes would have four more fumbles, two penalties and 2 incompletions to keep them from scoring as deep as the 15. The timing was off on the option and the offense was out-of-sync.

In the 3rd, it was Speyerer who fumbled on the Saint 47. This set up a 46-yard Lee Winfield touchdown run to go along with a Catherwood 2-point conversion to make it 23-6. Then, with 11:00 to go in the 4th, Bev Bishop ran a 7-yard keeper to finish their scoring for the night. Immediately afterward, Speyerer returned the kickoff 43 yards and caught 2 passes for another 45 to get the purple and gold to the Saint 2. From there, Ronnie McDaniel pushed it in for the touchdown. That was followed by a 2-point conversion from Pinkston to Biedenharn to make it 29-14. The game ended with a Payton Monroe interception of Pinkston to run out the clock.

"We have not played physically well in the last two weeks, to say the least. I guess we just can stand prosperity. We appreciate the ranking and we appreciate the confidence everybody's expressed in us and we just hope we can come back and earn it again." A few days later, said *"It was the first time since I've been here that we didn't hit and play good defense. We can't expect teams to bow down to us because we wear purple and I think that is what our kids thought was going to happen. Coach Freddie Lee did a good job getting Saint Andrews ready to play. But we didn't do well at all."*

Pinkston was more direct. *"In the past, we would go out and run a few series against St. Andrews and have the game won. But that wasn't the Saint Andrews we've played in the past. They played a good game but we weren't ready. It was the most disappointing loss for me since we lost the State Championship in 1981."*

GAME 5: SAINT AL (3-1) @ WEST UNION (2-2)
FINAL: SAINT AL 13 WEST UNION 14
OCTOBER 5, 1984

Saint Al had suffered their first loss but district play was starting with no injuries. While they lost to West Union the previous year only 8-7, Edwards was wary about this contest. *"Right now, I would have to say West Union is the favorite to win our district. They are the best team we have played so far. They play extremely tough defense and hit well. We will have our work cut out for us."* Before the season, Corey Pinkston told Steve Swogetinsky he wanted to make it one to remember. *"I don't know if we can win the State Championship or not. But I want to see us in the State Playoffs. If we make it that far, anything can happen."* For that goal to have a chance, this district game mattered.

Meanwhile at Farrell Field, torrential rain had left the field a muddy mess. In the 1st, West Union was set to punt but a penalty pushed the Bulldogs back to the 32 to try again. This time, the snap got away from punter Trey Griffin, and he was downed at the 15 in an attempt to recover. Though it took 6 plays, along with a penalty, the Flashes got into the endzone on a Pinkston keeper from the 1. Junior Greg Gussio hit the PAT to put Saint Al up 7-0.

In the 2nd, WU got to the goal line before Bulldogs QB Perry Davis was stuffed for a loss of a yard on 4th down. The Flashes then mastered a 99 yard drive ending in a Pinkston touchdown pass to Biedenharn from the 19. The kick was no good, but the halftime score was 13-0. Ferguson returned the opening 3rd quarter kickoff 20 yards and carried 4 more times before finally fumbling at the 25. Thirteen plays later, Davis cut the lead to 13-6. Before the whistle ended the 3rd, the Flashes had fumbled twice more and both teams traded punts.

In the 4th, Steve Hubbard intercepted a Pinkston pass at the 11. Three plays later, Davis scored from the 6 and found the endzone for the 2-pointer. Saint Al managed to get to the WU 32 afterwards before an interception by Bulldog Wade Dampeer put a dagger in any comeback attempt. Edwards said *"This was the most gut-wrenching loss I've had in all of my years of coaching. We're a better team than they are now. Anybody who saw that game knows we are a better ball team than West Union. But we turned the ball over at critical times and let them come back. We came out and turned it over four times and it's really nobody's fault. The kids played hard, they did the best they could, but I guess fate just wasn't on our side tonight. We can still turn this into a good season and maybe have a shot at the playoffs. But it's up to the seniors."*

For the record, he was right statistically. Saint Al had more first downs, rushing yards and passing yards. Even though the Flashes had lost control of their destiny after the loss, it would take beating Utica in 2 weeks and hoping that Utica beat West Union on November 8th. Barfield was named "Player of the Week" while Speyerer and Pinkston grabbed Honorable Mentions.

GAME 6:   SAINT AL (3-2) vs BENTONIA (1-3)
                    FINAL: SAINT AL 29 BENTONIA 0
                    October 12, 1984 - HOMECOMING

Bentonia was coming off of a 0-7 season and was just the thing Saint Al needed to get headed in the right direction in front of a capacity homecoming crowd. *"They have as good a chance as anyone. Our kids want to come out of this. We can still have a good season and maybe even have a shot at district. But we have to take care of business."*

The opening kickoff was fielded by Pinkston, who promptly went 75 yards for the 6-0 lead. In the 2nd, they orchestrated a 65-yard drive capped off by Speyerer getting the last 10 yards for the touchdown. Landes made the extra point and the purple and gold headed to the locker room up 13-0. Their next score was a gift in the form of a Bentonia fumble at their own 34, scooped up by Gussio who returned it to the 10. The next play was a Pinkston keeper for the touchdown, followed by Pinkston finding Biedenharn for the 2-points.

In the same quarter, McDaniel took the ball away from Edward Williams and returned it 32 yards for the score. John Kavanaugh ran for the PAT. Kavanaugh, stepping in for the injured Ferguson, led the rushers with 90 yards on 13 carries. Speyerer won "Player of the Week" honors while Pinkston and Kavanaugh were Honorable Mentions.

GAME 7:   SAINT AL (4-2) @ UTICA (2-3)
                    FINAL: SAINT AL 0 UTICA 19
                    October 19, 1984

The hopes for a trip to the Class A Playoffs ended this night in a place dubbed by the locals as "The Pit". The nemesis of the purple and gold's 1984 season, namely fumbles, was ever present. A win would have the Flashes watching the outcome of the Utica-West Union game to determine the district champion. A loss ended any hopes.

Ferguson, sidelined by shoulder injury after 544 yards on 90 carries, was out. Even though this was touted this as being a potential *"barnburner"*, Edwards was less confident. *"They play the best defense of anybody I've seen this year. They have two super backs that are going to give us some problems. That (James) Handy kids scored three touchdowns in the first period last week against Anguilla. What it boils down to is that we will have to play exceptionally well to win this game."*

In the scoreless 1st, Saint Al had only 2 first downs, had fumbled at their own 26 and 35 yard lines and were punting to start the 2nd quarter. But Pinkston was drowned at the 25, with Robert Scott blocking the punt and James Handy returning it 20 yards for the touchdown. Three plays into the 2nd half, Pinkston was picked off by Richard Caston who returned the interception 55 yards to make it 13-0. Unfortunately, the Flashes would fumble again, this time at the Saint Al 24. Eric Snow hit Caston for 12 yards and a 19-0 score that never changed.

In all, the Flashes fumbled 5 times and lost 4. And with negative rushing yardage (-21), it would have taken a miracle to pull out a victory. With 8 tackles in the game, Junior Mark Simrall was named Player of the Week. Tim Holder and Joe Baladi were Honorable Mentions. After addressing his team, Edwards said *"We have our backs to the wall. We are fighting for our lives the remainder of this season. We are going to have to fight to break even. We can suck it up and have a good record or we can let tonight's game haunt us and lose our next three. What we do is in our hands."*

GAME 8:   SAINT AL (4-3) vs. GREENVILLE SAINT JOSEPH (5-1)
                    FINAL: SAINT AL 14 GREENVILLE ST JOE 27
                    October 26, 1984

In 1983, the Irish finished with a 1-8 record. Only 5 starters returned on offense, and 5 on defense. But their record of 5-1 showed their improvement for the 1984 season.

The Irish scored on the first play of the 2nd via a Duke Palasini run to make it 6-0. The Flashes moved the ball to the Irish 24 but lost the ball on downs. Eight plays later, a 24-yard pass from John Canale to Britt Virden (along with a 2-point conversion by Canale) made the score 14-0. The 2nd half started more successfully for the Flashes. A 65 yard drive resulted in a 22 yard pass from Pinkston to Delvan Irwin for the first TD to make it 14-6. The remainder of quarter was back-and-forth, and ended with a Pinkston interception on the 23 after a long Irish drive. The turnover drive to start the 4th failed, and the punt to the Flash 49 eventually resulted in a 9-play touchdown when Canale scored from 13.

The Flashes blocked the extra point. Greenville led 20-6, but added to it on a Palasini 23-yard run. Saint Al came back 17 seconds later when Speyerer returned the kickoff to the 17, and then Pinkston hit Biedenharn for the final touchdown of the night. The 2-point conversation from Pinkston to Junior TE David Baker was good for the final score of the night.

On paper, the game wasn't close. GSJ had 359 yards of total offense versus 141. They had no fumbles, fewer penalty yards, more first downs and dominated the rushing game (292-62). A somber Edwards, who had seen his squad start strong and highly ranked, said afterwards: *"We just weren't physically strong enough to stay with them. Physically, we couldn't match up. They ran straight at us and we couldn't stop them. We got some of our younger kids some playing time. They are our future."*

GAME 9:   SAINT AL (4-4) vs. PELAHATCHIE (6-2)
                        FINAL: SAINT AL 20 PELAHATCHIE 28
                        November 2, 1984

Pelahatchie was coming off of a 10-2 season and the Flashes had lost 3 of 4. Corey Pinkston had said a few weeks before *"This is my senior season and I want to go out a winner. The other seniors feel that way. We know what it is going to take for us to win."* Edwards added *"They have a huge line. Across the front, they're 225, 200, 260, 190, and 190. And they've got tall boys; several 6'4" and 6'5" players. They're probably the best team we've played this year."* Hopes were high that the battered team would finish strong.

An early 1st quarter scoring opportunity by the Flashes was turned over on downs after an initial McDaniel fumble recovery on the Pelahatchie 14. Seven plays later, Eric Perry scored from their 29 and it was 7-0. The Chiefs scored twice in the 2nd. Mike Johnson scored on a 13-yard run and then from the 1 with: 16 left. After an extra point and a two-point conversion, it was 22-0.

Later in the 2nd, Speyerer capped a 72-yard, 14 play touchdown from the 2. Pinkston hit Kette Dornbusch for the two points to make it 14-8 at half. In the 3rd, Pinkston picked off a pass for a 46-yard Flash touchdown to make it 21-14. The Chiefs came right back on the kickoff and went 60 yards in 12 plays with Perry scoring from the 15.

The Flashes did punch back. Pinkston hit Speyerer on a 3-yard touchdown pass with 6:25 remaining but could not get the ball back to attempt the tie. Though Ferguson amassed 151 yards on 18 carries, his 4th game of the season over the 100 yard mark, the game marked 5 losses in 6 games for the Flashes. *"We got a good effort from our kids. But we made the mistakes that got us beat."*

GAME 10:   SAINT AL (4-5) @ MISSISSIPPI SCHOOL FOR THE DEAF (3-6)
                        FINAL: SAINT AL 35 MSD 12
                        November 9, 1984

The season had not gone as envisioned during pre-season two-a-day practices and hard work in the Mississippi heat. What had started as a 3-0 ranked team was now facing a best-case scenario of a 5-5. Edwards was thinking about that group just before the game. *"We're going with the same people who've been starting all year because these seniors don't want to go under .500. I know it's been a disappointing season for the kids and the Saint Al people. We'll just have to do the best we can tomorrow and then start regrouping for next year."* As for MSD, Edwards was impressed with their junior tailback Steve McNeese. *"He's got national rushing records for players in deaf schools with (over 4,000) yards in 3 years. He's the best running back we'll play all year..."* Unfortunately, McNeese was unable to go due to a knee injury. But notably, his replacement (Dan Ford) did manage to get 129 yards and a touchdown on 17 carries.

Ferguson opened scoring by taking the kickoff back 85 yards. Sophomore John Agostinelli booted the PAT to make it 7-0. Ferguson also scored the next two touchdowns on runs of 4 and 60 yards. Agostinelli and Landes added extra-points. With 3:55 left in the 2nd, MSD got on the board with a 9-play, 62 yard drive capped by a 12 yard TD run by Ricky Burns to make it 21-6. Saint Al scored next with a Mark Simrall 2-yard run at the 1:10 mark. Landes made the extra point to pad the lead to 28-6. The Bulldogs punched right back with a 2 play drive ending in a 67 yard touchdown by Ford. A high-scoring halftime was in favor of the Flashes 28-12.

The third was uneventful, but strangely, included Pinkston picking off Burns at the 2, followed by Burns picking off Pinkston in the endzone. In the 4th, Ron Cocilova recovered a MSD fumble at the 34 and, three plays later, Ferguson put in his last touchdown as a Flash: a 15 yarder. Agostinelli converted the PAT. The final play was an interception by Pinkston at the 25.

Said Edwards, "This was a good win for the seniors. It's been a disappointing season because we had so many high expectations for this team. We let the junior varsity play a good bit, but they weren't that fired up because they didn't know they were going to play as much as they did." Ferguson led rushers with 145. A .500 mark was disappointing in contrast to expectations, but the new perspective of it being the last game for a group of seniors that worked so hard together was a tough pill for 13 young men as they walked off of the gridiron; most for the final time.

An overall record of 5-5 was, at best, unexpected. Before the season began, Joe Edwards had been quoted in a preseason article as saying "If (we) work hard, avoid injuries and have a little luck, they could be in the State Football Playoffs. If things go the other way, it's going to be a long season. We'll have to see how it works out. This could be one of our better years. It just depends on how bad the kids want it."

As Brent Barfield noted in his write-up in The Vicksburg Evening Post the week of the MSD game, "I can remember on the Thursday afternoosn before practice, coach (Edwards) would say 'To win them all, you've got to win this week'. Now, it's so much different because we've got a whole different attitude. We're not looking at an unbeaten season by far and we're not looking at any type of playoff or any type of bowl game whatsoever."

The All County and All District awards went to Baladi, Barfield, Pinkston and Speyerer. Barfield also received the inaugural David Atkins Memorial Scholarship. Pinkston, meanwhile, got, Most Valuable Back in District VI A, Mississippi High School All Star Game, and the Virgadamo Trophy.

"The 1984 season, oddly enough, is captured well by Charles Dickens' famous quote "It was the best of times, it was the worst of times, it was the season of light, it was the season of darkness. It was the spring of hope, it was the winter of despair, we had everything before us, we had nothing before us ..." Everyone thought Saint Al had a lot of question marks going into the season, except for us. We believed this would be one of Saint Al's best seasons since the 1981 team that made it to the state championship. The only real concern was experienced depth because injuries at key positions could seriously put our season in jeopardy.

It was the best of times. We opened with a 32-8 thrashing of 3A Madison-Ridgeland, followed by a big win over our rival Natchez Cathedral. In the third week of the season, we overcame a trap game between two rivals, Cathedral and Saint Andrews, when we beat Richland to maintain our number 2 ranking in the "Little Five" AP Poll and garnered a number 18 spot in the AP statewide Top 20 Poll.

It was the worst of times. Our primary fear happened against Saint Andrews when our best, fastest and most experienced runner (De Ferguson) went down with a shoulder injury that lingered for the remainder of the season. We lost for the first time in anyone's memory to Saint Andrews, but we did not get beat. We had more total offense and the number of first downs was equal, but we had seven turnovers due to the timing differences and lack of experience at running back taking over for the injured Ferguson.

It was difficult for all of us to recover after that game, and not having our tailback for a large portion of the remainder of the season weighed heavily on us all. We lost some games we should have won, but what I remember through it all is the significant support we received from everyone even though we did not know how to get out of the tailspin at times.

The theme I remember most coming down the stretch was the pride. No one could remember the last time Saint Al had a losing season, and it was not going to start on our watch. Our focus turned to fighting for our Alma Mater, for Aloysius purple and gold. We were the men who never say die. We wanted to give those who were here a reason to stand up and cheer for Aloysius High.

I loved my time at Saint Al, I love the guys I played football with, and despite the promising season having gone unfulfilled, I would not trade that time for anything.

Joe Baladi; July 22, 2016

1985 (6-6)

Practices under Edwards started with both intensity and rain. "I'm pleased with the condition that our kids returned in. And they worked hard this week. They did everything we asked them to do". Eleven seniors had been lost, including starting QB Corey Pinkston. Junior Jeff Jones took his spot. "Jeff threw the ball well. So far, he has done ... even better than I thought he would". Of many others, he noted *"They are all young and inexperienced. But they are working hard. They may fool some people this year"*.

"We are going to make mistakes and we'll lose some games. But we'll have to keep our heads high, suck it up and do the best we can. We are going to play to the best of our ability."

GAME 1:   SAINT AL (0-0) vs MADISON RIDGELAND (0-0)
                        FINAL: ST AL 0 MADISON RIDGELAND 7
                        SEPTEMBER 5, 1985

Madison Ridgeland fielded a team of 46 players with 30 sophomores and freshmen. Edwards knew the feeling with his squad. Though his opponent finished 1984 at 1-8, Edwards said *"They are bigger than we are and Coach Walker does a good job with them. It will be a good game"*.

On the third play of the game, Mike Marshall recovered a Braves fumble but the Flashes couldn't get far. After a trade of turnovers (a John Kavanaugh fumble and a Mike Nassour interception), the only scoring threat for the half was a Bryan Pryon 46 yard FG attempt that missed. First year punter John Agostinelli pinned Madison Ridgeland deep in the 4th. But from the Braves 21, Ras Greer broke away for the game's only touchdown. Pryon's PAT finished it at 6-0.

Said Edwards, *"We had our chances. We have a lot of things to work on, but we did some good things. This isn't a time to hang our heads. It's a time to learn and improve"*. Two-way player Mark Simrall won Player of the Week honors with Honorable Mentions to Kavanaugh and Agostinelli.

GAME 2:   SAINT AL (0-1) @ NATCHEZ CATHEDRAL (1-0)
                        FINAL: ST AL 3 NATCHEZ CATHEDRAL 24
                        SEPTEMBER 13, 1985

Edwards took time to scout Cathedral against Salem. *"We had better be ready to play well. We are facing the best Natchez Cathedral team that I've seen. Cathedral may be the best team we play all year"*. Still optomisic, he said *"… we are going to Natchez feeling we have a good chance to win the game"*. Greenie coach Ken Beesley had played Saint Al in a Jamboree and said *"We have a lot of respect for Saint Al. They beat us last year in a very physical game"*.

The Flashes fumbled on the game's second play at the Flash 44. Michael Richardson would take it in 8 plays later from the 16 to make it 6-0. In the 2nd, Cathedral put up to scores with a Kevin Jenkins 6 yard score and a Ken Beesley, Jr push from the 1. Halftime stood 18-0. The final Cathedral tally came in the 3rd when Jenkins ran in from the 9. The Flashes' only points came later when Agostinelli made a 25 yard FG.

Kavanaugh led the rushers with 108 yard on 21 carries but Jones would the Player of the Week. Kavanaugh and Agostinelli shared Honorable Mentions for the second straight week.

GAME 3:   SAINT AL (0-2) vs RICHLAND (0-2)
                        FINAL: ST AL 16 RICHLAND 6
                        SEPTEMBER 20, 1985

"The attitudes are good. We have made a lot of progress in the first two games and we are going for our first win Friday night". Those were Edwards' word going into an unknown Richland squad. *"Our scout thinks we can play with them, but our defense has to be ready to stop a balanced attack"*.

Richland opened scoring in the 2nd when John Sullivan capped a 10 play drive of 68 yards by going in from the 2. After the ensuing kickoff, Kavanaugh finished a 13 play drive of 66 yards from the 10 with just :52 left in the half. Agostinelli made it 7-6. In the 3rd, Jones picked off a Richland pass and took it to the endzone, but it was called back for clipping. In the 4th the Flashes got in twice. Kavanaugh went in from the 3 and Agostinelli drilled a 31-yarder with 2:44 remaining.

"Player of the Week" Kavanaugh had 133 rushing yards on 25 carries in a game later called *"John Kavanaugh Night"*. Agostinelli and Jones were Honorable Mentions. *"It was nice to get our first victory. I was proud of the way our kids have hung in there and practiced hard"*.

GAME 4:   SAINT AL (1-2) @ SAINT ANDREWS (2-1)
       FINAL: ST AL 14 SAINT ANDREWS 0
       SEPTEMBER 27, 1985

Said Edwards, "*Saint Andrews did a good job of hurting our feelings last year and we would like to even that score. They may not have all of their kids back from last year, but (they are) a well-coached team and we know we'll have our hands full*".

A Saint Andrews snap over the punter's head in the 1st set up a two yard sneak by Jones 11 plays later. A Kette Dornbusch punt return in the 2nd got to the Saints 38. He then gained 23 and, three plays later, Kavanaugh drove in from the 9. Jones found Greg Gussio for the two points and a 14-0 halftime lead. The Saints got only as far as the Flash 15 in the 2nd half, but Mark Simrall recovered a fumble to stop the drive. Jones would also pick off a Saint Andrews pass in the 4th.

Gussio's three receptions and a PAT conversion gave him Player of the Week. Jones and Kavanaugh were Mentions. "*This was a very big game for us. This is a young team, but we are making progress. This win has to help our confidence. I was especially proud of the defense. They bent some, but they didn't break. It was a good effort on everyone's part*".

GAME 5:   SAINT AL (2-2) @ SIMPSON CENTRAL (1-3)
       FINAL: SAINT AL 6 SIMPSON CENTRAL 0
       OCTOBER 4, 1985

This District 6-1A West Division game would likely determine the champions. Defending champs Utica (formerly known as West Union) were disqualified and on probation by MHSAA for playing an ineligible player. Edwards said "*Our kids realize what this game is for and I'm sure their kids do, too*". SC coach Dwayne Yates said "*I really don't see either team having an edge. The only advantage we have is playing at home … and I don't know how important that is*".

The game's only score was in the 2nd. After taking a punt at their 40, the Flashes marched to the endzone in 12 plays capped by Kavanaugh from the 9. Simpson Central drove to the Flash 22 late in the 4th, but Simrall stopped the run to give Saint Al the ball. Though two FGs were missed, the Flashes had taken a step toward the conference title.

"*This win was fantastic. It was a big accomplishment to come down here and beat Simpson Central. We didn't play that well, but we are going to improve*". Kavanaugh had 122 rushing yards via 24 carries to lead the Flashes. Simrall, with 19 tackles that included the 4th quarter stop, won Player of the Week. "*Mark made several key stops for us on defense and he also blocked well on the offensive line*". Honorable mentions went to David Baker, Kavanaugh and Dornbusch.

GAME 6:   SAINT AL (3-2) @ BENTONIA (0-4)
       FINAL: SAINT AL 21 BENTONIA 0
       October 11, 1985

A win sealed the District 6-1A subdistrict title. But it didn't come easily against a team with only 15 players. Edwards said afterwards, "*I'll tell you what happened. We came up here expecting the old Bentonia. We weren't sharp in practice Wednesday or Thursday and we started the game with fumbles and penalties*". A couple of fumbles, two interceptions and a missed FG resulted in a scoreless first half. Saint Al put up their first points in the 3rd on a Kavanaugh plunge from the 5 to seal an 8 play 59 yard drive. Agostinelli made it 7-0.

An ensuing fumble by Chris Counts was recovered by Michael Nassour at the Wolves 26. Four plays later, Dornbusch moved in from the 3 and Agostinelli padded the lead to 14-0. The last tally came from a Jones' sneak from the 1 in the 4th followed by an Agostinelli PAT. David Baker and Paul Pierce added interceptions afterwards but there would be no more scoring. Kavanaugh had 165 yards on the ground but Baker would get the nod for Player of the Week.

GAME 7:   SAINT AL (4-2) vs UTICA (3-2-1)
       FINAL: SAINT AL 13 UTICA 26
       October 18, 1985

Though probation would keep Utica from post-season, they were playing for pride. Edwards called it "*… the most important game right now for us. We take each game one-by-one. Utica has one* *of the best defensive teams I've seen since I've been here at Saint Al. They have a bunch of aggressive kids. I expect a tough game".*

As the 1st ended, Dicky Caston found the endzone from the 15 to cap an 11 play drive. The 6-0 score held until the 3rd before both teams found the board. Jones hit Gussio from the 12 and Agostinelli put the Flashes up 7-6. Caston responded with a 58 yard tear and Lee Robinson connected on the point-after. After a bad snap to a punting Dornbusch, Robinson got in from the 1 to make it 20-7. In the 4th, Caston again scrambled for a touchdown; this time from the 20. The Flashes tightened the loss with a 28 yard touchdown pass from Jones to Gussio. The two-pointer failed.

"We stunk overall. I take the blame for this loss. We didn't have a good week of practice and that's my fault". Dornbusch, with two fumble recoveries and a 31.4 punting average, won Player of the Week. Gussio, Baker and Brent Biedenharn were Mentions.

GAME 8: SAINT AL (4-3) @ GREENVILLE SAINT JOSEPH (2-5)
     FINAL: SAINT AL 12 GREENVILLE SAINT JOE 32
     October 25, 1985

Edwards called GSJ the *"best 2-5 team in the state. Actually, they're better than Utica offensively. And you better believe they'll be after us and we'll be after them".* The Flashes started strong with an opening drive touchdown from Jones to Brad Warnock from the 14. But the Irish began adding points. Jason Cole scored from the 1 in the 1st and Pratt Lewis added two touchdowns in the 2nd along with 2 PATs.

In the 3rd, Gussio recovered an Irish fumble that allowed a Kavanaugh dart from the 7 to make it 20-12. But Saint Joe added two more scores before the game was over. One was a Danny Hillhouse pass to Rob Ward for a 5 yard score and the last was a Ward run for another. *"We got a good ole tail kicking. We tried everything offensively and defensively, but nothing seemed to work. We just weren't ready to play and they took it to us. This was an embarrassing loss for us. But we are going to have to put it behind us and start working for next week's game with Jackson Saint Joseph."*

GAME 9: SAINT AL (4-4) vs JACKSON SAINT JOSEPH (4-4)
     FINAL: SAINT AL 7 JACKSON SAINT JOSEPH 17
     November 1, 1985: HOMECOMING

Bad weather forced the Flashes into the gym where they worked on defensive changes. *"This is going to be one of the biggest teams we've faced and we have made some adjustments to try and counter their size".* Edwards predicted as many as 9 sophomores on the field at any given time during the game.

The Flashes once again started the game strongly, moving 62 yards for a touchdown. Jones capped it from the 2 and Agostinelli's PAT made it 7-0. In the 2nd, a high snap to punter Agostinelli put the Bruins at the Saint Joe 49. The 14 play drive was capped with a 15 yard pass from Jeff Artigues to Herbert Loving. Artigues' kick ended scoring until the 4th. A 22 yard Artigues FG put the Bruins up 10-7 and a Tutu Green touchdown run of 26 was followed by an Artigues PAT to ice the contest.

Said Edwards, *"I'm disappointed we lost. But the truth of the matter is that St. Joseph was a little bigger, older and more experienced than we are. Our day will come, but it is going to take a lot of work in the off-season to get there".* Larry Rocconi won Player of the Week for his defense. Jones and Baker were Honorable Mentions.

GAME 10: SAINT AL (4-5) @ PISGAH (1-8)
     FINAL: SAINT AL 43 PISGAH 0
     November 7, 1985

Edwards wanted desperately to win this game to provide momentum for the playoffs. The good news was that, though not overlooking them, his opponent had 16 players and was *"mainly a 10th grade football team. I said at the beginning of the year we can't take anybody for granted and we certainly can't Thursday night".*

Saint Al again took the opening drive for a touchdown when Jones hit Baker from the 23. Agostinelli made it 7-0. In the same frame, Gussio returned an interception 57 yards for a score to make it 13-0. Gussio added two more in the 2nd with the first from the 14. A pass to Baker made it 21-0. His second came from the 2 after blocking a Dragon punt at their 14. Biedenharn's fumble recovery in the 3rd allowed Kavanaugh to score from the 25.

The ensuing kickoff resulted in a safety when the receiver stepped out of the endzone. With the second string playing, Jerry Hosemann put up the last points on a 6 yard scamper. *"It was a good game for us. Everybody got to go in and play. It was a good way to finish the regular season and we needed that going into the Puckett game"*. Gussio was the obvious Player of the Week choice while Jones and Kavanaugh received Mentions.

GAME 11:   SAINT AL (5-5) vs PUCKETT (9-0)
                       FINAL: SAINT AL 14 PUCKETT 10
                       November 15, 1985: FLORENCE, MS

An optimistic Edwards said of his undefeated foe, *"… we're not in awe of them. We've played some teams as good as Puckett this year, but I don't think their schedule's been as tough as ours. I'm not saying they don't have a good team. In fact, they probably have to be favored. But I think we have a good chance of winning the football game"*. A win gave them the District 6-A Championship.

The first half belonged to Puckett. Greg Stevens connected on a 32 yard FG in the 1st to make it 3-0. In the 2nd, Stevens scored from the 1 and added the PAT to make halftime 10-0. *"They won the first half…"* said Edwards. *"They just got a couple of breaks. If we hung in there, I figured we would get some of those breaks, too"*.

Saint Al came roaring back in the 3rd with their only points to seal the win. Jones' scoring run from the 8 capped a 10 play drive of 67 yards. Agostinelli tightened the game 10-7. On the ensuing possession, Saint Al went 67 yards in 12 plays. Gussio got in from the 1 and Agostinell's PAT finished scoring for both clubs. The Wolves did try a 30 yard FG early in the 4th but missed. Said Coach Lennis Stevens, *"The turning point was when we missed the field goal. We normally don't have any problems from that distance, but we did this time"*. Rocconi later recovered a Puckett fumble and Warnock picked off a pass.

"I'm glad we won it for the school and the Saint Al fans. Maybe that puts some salve on some of the wounds. This team has realized a lot of disappointments this year and this win might make up for some of them".

GAME 12:   SAINT AL (6-5) vs McLAIN (5-4)
                       FINAL: SAINT AL 14 McLAIN 31
                       November 24, 1985: MIZE, MS

This would be McLain's fourth trip to the playoffs. Their team was more junior-laden while Saint Al was dependent on sophomores. Kavanaugh and Gussio each had 891 yards of rushing while McLain's Lamar Cherry had 997. Coach Barry Sharpe said *"I look for a good close ball game. But we know Saint Al will get after you on offense and defense"*. Responded Edwards, *"We may go down there Friday night and get beat, but we're just pleased to be at this point already. And whatever we do, we've got something over in the school (the district trophy) that nobody can take away from us"*.

As usual, Saint Al got going early. After a dropped McLain punt was recovered at the Ram 8, Jones crashed from the 3 and Agostinelli made it 7-0. The Rams responded with a 70 yard drive when Cherry went in from the 2 to make it 7-6. Cherry would end the evening with 205 yards on the ground. Saint Al bounced right back to start the 2nd with a 2 yard Gussio run and an Agostinelli PAT. McLain cut the lead to 14-12 when Cherry broke away for 66 yards in the frame. The final 1st half score was via a Nathaniel Bolton pass to John Street for 74 yards and an 18-14 lead that would not be given back.

The Rams added another score in the 3rd when Cherry got in from the 1 to cap a 73 yard drive. Late in the 4th, after a blocked Flash FG by the McLain, Cherry added the last on a 35 yard bolt. Commented Edwards afterwards, *"We won some big games this year and we've had a good season. I have no complaints about our season."*

Among other honors, Jones would make the All-County team at safety while Mark Simrall would garner the Vigadamo Trophy honor.

"What a memorable season! This team started 0-2 but fought through the season to win the division and a playoff game against then-undefeated Puckett! In our playoff game, we were losing 10-0 in the first half (no thanks for me throwing an interception in the endzone at the end of the first half). But just like during the regular season, Coach Edwards made adjustments to the game plan and the team stepped up to achieve our goal of advancing through the playoffs. Flashes win 14-10!"

Jeff Jones; November 17, 2016

1986 (6-4)

Though Joe Edwards had more depth for the season, there were still minor injuries hampering conditioning at the start of practices. *"You can't do any full conditioning until you get the full pads on. Most of them are in fair shape. We're a little bit bigger this year so you have to condition that much more"* The club had only 5 seniors but returned 8 starters. *"We're not going to use the excuse that we're young. Most of them have a year under their belt. As far as experience wise, it's time to buckle down"*.

Jeff Jones returned at QB alongside a backfield of John Kavanaugh and Kette Dornbusch. This gave hope to a high-powered offensive attack. *"If we can keep our running backs healthy, we could have the best team I've had here"*. Edwards was also focused on the defense and depth, saying *"It's all up going to be up to their attitudes. They have to learn how to punish ball players. Last year, we weren't very good defensively. They weren't very aggressive. This year, someone's really got to step forward to show leadership"*.

GAME 1:   SAINT AL (0-0) @ MADISON RIDGELAND (0-0)
                    FINAL: ST AL 7 MADISON RIDGELAND 3
                    SEPTEMBER 5, 1986

The day before kickoff, Edwards said *"We need to play a game. The last three days we pretty much have spun our wheels. It's a matter if they want to get after some people. Physically, we won't play a team as good as we are. This group has got to prove to me that they have the heart to play up to their potential. Whether they are tough enough to do what it takes to win is the only question that needs to be answered"*.

It would be the Braves who got on the board first after the opening kick. A drive to the Flash 10 allowed Brian Curley a 27-yard FG to make it 3-0. In the 2nd, Dornbusch picked off a Billy Lanthrip pass and brought it to the Braves 17 but the eventual 47 yard FG attempt by Saint Al was short. But the Flashes got their lone points afterwards on a Jones scamper for 29 and then a run from the 3. John Agostinelli's PAT finished scoring for the game.

The remainder of the contest was filled with turnovers. Fred Russell picked off a Jones pass while Woodie Mitchell gave it back on a fumble to Jones. Jones picked off a late pass after the defense held a deep Madison drive and Nassour added another interception later. *"I was proud of the defense. Time and time again they held them. Tryon Rosser played a super game and Kette Dornbusch was outstanding at linebacker. It wasn't pretty, but it's a win. We were fortunate to win it. I'd say that's the understatement of the year"*. Rosser won Player of the Week.

GAME 2:   SAINT AL (1-0) vs NATCHEZ CATHEDRAL (1-0)
                    FINAL: ST AL 0 NATCHEZ CATHEDRAL 25
                    SEPTEMBER 12, 1986

The storied Catholic rivalry was at hand and Edwards was ready. *"Both teams feel like they have to get after each other and believe me, they do. This is a Catholic school rivalry. They have a good team and we hope to give them a good ball game"*. Despite an impressive 47-13 Greenie win over Salem, Cathedral coach Ken Beesley wary. *"Saint Al always seems to play us their best game of the year. In this game, you might as well throw out the records"*.

The Greenies marched down the field on their first drive for a score. Ken Beesley capped a 12 play drive of 65 yards from the 1 to make it 6-0. Then with :01 left before halftime, Ricki Fulton caught a Beesley pass for 26 yards to the Flash 26. Beesley then used that one second to find Fulton for the 12-0 intermission lead. Said Cathedral's coach, *"I think the touchdown right at the half was key to the game. They were still in the game, but we got the momentum on our side going into the locker room"*. Cathedral opened the lead in the 3rd with a Michael Richardson touchdown run from the 15 and added to it in the 4th with a Frank Sanguinetti pickoff of Jones for a 50 yard return and score.

Edwards commented that *"The most disappointing thing to me was our composure and the mistakes we made. I'll bet we had 100 yards in penalties (7-65) and you can't do that and beat a good football team"*.

GAME 3: SAINT AL (1-1) @ MISS SCHOOL FOR THE DEAF (UNREPORTED)
     FINAL: ST AL 39 MSD 14
     SEPTEMBER 19, 1986

Edwards was emphatic that the Flashes would be prepared this week. *"You better believe we are getting to work hard this week to get ready for MSD. We're going back to training camp; square one. We're going to find out who wants to play and who doesn't. I took the positive approach with this team, telling them that they had a lot of talent and could beat anyone. That might have been a mistake. We will not have a repeat of last Friday"*. Meanwhile, MSD coach Terry Clark had only 3 seniors and started a 7th grader and two 8th graders.

John Kavanaugh took the opening kick back 86 yards for the opening touchdown. Jones hit Paul Pierce from the 19 just before the end of the 1st to make it 14-0. An interception by Hunter Galofaro, aided by two Kavanaugh runs, resulted in a 19 yard Kavanaugh touchdown run. Agostinelli converted his third PAT to make it 21-0. Pierce immediately picked off a MSD pass for a 22 yard touchdown less than a minute later to make it 33-0 at half.

With Flash reserves on the field, the second half opened the door for MSD. Roy Latham dashed in from 28 and Lovell Jones ran in from the 27 later in the 4th. Esaw Smith found Lemeaul Moor for the two-pointer. Brian Boykin finished Flash scoring midway through the 4th from the 1. *"You can't tell if you've accomplished anything in a game like this. It's nice to win, but I don't think we gained very much from this. We didn't accomplish much with this. Our reserves played well in sport. You've got to realize we won't have another game like this the rest of the year."*

For his 63 yards of rushing on 4 carries, Boykin won Player of the Week honors. *"He's our future. It's tough for a freshman to go out there and play ..."*

GAME 4: SAINT AL (2-1) vs SAINT ANDREWS (2-1)
     FINAL: ST AL 29 SAINT ANDREWS 0
     SEPTEMBER 26, 1986

Though Edwards said *"We don't like Saint Andrews very much and they don't like us"*, both head coaches worried about the other's running backs. But it would be Kavanaugh with 200 yards on 24 carries and two touchdowns that told the tale. His first came from the 3 in a rainy opening quarter. Jones got in from the same distance :35 before halftime with Agostinelli adding both PATs to make it 14-0. In the 3rd, a Kavanaugh fumble at the Saint 13 stalled the next drive and a Jones interception killed the next. But in the 4th, Kavanaugh broke away for a 76 yard score and made it 21-0 with Agostinelli's PAT.

A Leroy Winfield fumble on the following kickoff set up a Michael Abraham touchdown pass to Paul Montalvo from the 27 one play later. Michael Nassour's two-pointer followed to finish scoring. *"Kavanaugh finally broke out and Jeff Jones held our offense together. We played pretty well, but the real test will be next Friday against Southeast Lauderdale. They have a power football team but we fell we have more speed"*. For his performance, Kavanaugh gained Player of the Week.

GAME 5: SAINT AL (3-1) vs SOUTHEAST LAUDERDALE (3-1)
     FINAL: SAINT AL 13 SOUTHEAST LAUDERDALE 14
     October 3, 1986

Southeast had not allowed a touchdown in their three wins. Said Edwards *"We'll have to play our best Friday night to win. We are on a roll, but so are they. ... we'll have to wait and see"*. A few new injuries hampered the team, but none that took away a chance for a Flash win.

Saint Al hit the board first on a Jones pass to Larry Rocconi from the 5. Agostinelli made it 7-0. But the killer play came with 5:12 left in the 2nd when Mike Fuller blocked an Agostinelli punt and returned it 39 yards for the score. Deshon Davis' PAT made it 7-7. *"I have never won a game that I've had a blocked punt go for a touchdown. We were playing well defensively, but you can't win and let something like that happen"*.

In the 3rd, the Tigers padded the lead when Davis hit Greg Bailey from the 21 and added the PAT. Down 7 with 2:23 remaining, Abraham found Nassour from the 6 to cut the lead to 1. A two-point pass attempt for the win fell incomplete. Saint Al was held back by 94 yards of penalties on 13 calls while SE held Kavanaugh to just 43 yards of rushing. Said Southeast coach Dwane Taylor, *"I have to give a lot of credit to Saint Al. They are a well-conditioned football team. I'm glad we don't have to play them again next week".* Rocconi's defensive play earned Player of the Week accolades.

GAME 6:　　　　　　SAINT AL (3-2) vs BENTONIA (1-3)
　　　　　　　　　　FINAL: SAINT AL 62 BENTONIA 12
　　　　　　　　　　October 10, 1986: HOMECOMING

Bentonia had only 15 players on the season (7 true freshmen) and their lone victory had been against Mississippi School for the Deaf. But they had a running back (Edward Williams) that had tallied 690 yards on the season. Said Edwards, *"Numbers-wise, they don't have it. But their front-line people probably are as talented as we are. When you come right down to it, we haven't beaten a good football team yet. We just haven't hit on all cylinders yet. It's mystifying. About the time we get something corrected, something else breaks down."*

The Flashes would entertain a Homecoming crowd with plenty of scoring. Kavanaugh ran the first in from the 14, Dornbusch was second from the 11 and Jones found Rocconi from the 9 to make it 21-0 after Agostinelli PATs. Bentonia managed to dot the board in the 2nd with a Williams dash from 85 yards away. Afterwards, Dornbusch went in from the 34, Kavanaugh picked off Lee Davis to set up his 3-yard run and Abraham found Pierce to make it 41-6. Bentonia's final score came with :11 left in the half when Williams raced 19 yards and closed it at 41-12.

Pierce dove in from the goal line in the 4th and Brad Warnock added the PAT. Omar Logue picked off a Davis pass for a 16 yard return touchdown and then picked off another just afterwards that set up a 1 yard run by Abraham. *"We came ready to play. It was homecoming and it did have a little extra special meaning to the boys".*

GAME 7:　　　　　　SAINT AL (4-2) @ UTICA (4-2)
　　　　　　　　　　FINAL: SAINT AL 16 UTICA 27
　　　　　　　　　　October 17, 1986

The conference matchup had huge implications. Should the Flashes win, they were guaranteed a spot in the 1A playoffs while a loss kept them home. Utica had two rushers over 300 yards and would be hard to stop. *"We haven't beaten a good football team yet. It hasn't been the type of year I hoped for, but all that could change with a win this week. I think we can beat them. We're a better football team, but I know we'll have to prove that on the football field".*

Saint Al started well when an early Dickie Caston fumble was recovered by Brent Biedenharn at the Utica 32. It led to an Agostinelli FG from 35 yards and a 3-0 lead. On their next possession, it was Lee Robinson fumbling to Kavanaugh followed by a Nassour punt block at the Wave 8. Kavanaugh crossed the goal on the next play and Agostinelli made it 10-0. Three more Utica fumbles followed before Jones found Warnock for 34 and then kept it for a one-yard score.

It would be all Utica afterwards. Their first came on a Caston pass to Robinson from the 5 along with a two-pointer to Kevin Cassell. Before halftime, a snap to punter Agostinelli sailed over his head and was recovered in the endzone by Cassell. Halftime saw Saint Al clinging to a 16-14 advantage. In the 3rd, Robinson put Utica ahead with a run from the 6 and finished scoring on a run in the 4th. Edwards said of Caston after the game *"He's done it the last two years. I think I'm going to send him a graduation present".*

GAME 8:　　　　　　SAINT AL (4-3) vs GREENVILLE SAINT JOSEPH (2-5)
　　　　　　　　　　FINAL: SAINT AL 27 GREENVILLE SAINT JOE 2
　　　　　　　　　　October 24, 1986

The Flashes were pointing toward ensuring another winning season while also beating a Catholic rival. *"It's going to be very important to us that we win this week. If we lose, we're going to have to buckle up for the last two games".* They would do it with numerous players injured or out. Morris Peck and Tim Vollor were out for the season with knee injuries while three others were doubtful.

Another special teams error put the Irish up early in the 2nd when a snap went over punter Agostinelli's head for a safety. Fortunately, the Irish also had turnovers, with a Mitch Womack fumble recovered by Scott Hosemann at the Irish 47. Kavanaugh ripped off 34 yards for the score four plays later and Agostinelli made it 7-2. Saint Al added to the halftime lead when Jones found Pierce from the

4. Agostinelli made it 14-2. After returning for the 2nd half, another Womack fumble was recovered by Rocconi at the Irish 17. Jones would convert from the 2 and Agostinelli made it 21-2. The last score came in the 4th when Jones snuck in from the 3.

Said Edwards, *"Our defense did just an outstanding job. They got the lead and kept hitting hard"*. But Kavanaugh had 165 yards of rushing in the contest to power the offense. For his efforts, he received the Player of the Week. Now at 773 on the season, Edwards noted *"John's a kid who really works hard in practice and in the offseason. He's a joy to work with"*.

GAME 9:   SAINT AL (5-3) @ JACKSON SAINT JOSEPH (6-2)
               FINAL: SAINT AL 18 JACKSON SAINT JOE 34
               October 31, 1986

Another Catholic rival awaited, and the Bruins were much better than the previous parochial opponent. *"We're looking forward to going over there and playing them. They've got the best ball club they've had since I've been here"*. It was always a bitter contest and the paper wrote that *"No one is quite sure how it started, but somehow (it) has turned into a war"*. Saint Al was hoping for two more victories that could lead to a potential bowl invitation.

At the end of the 1st, Saint Al got on the board with a 25 yard Agostinelli FG. Saint Joe answered immediately with a 72 yard drive capped by a Gary Pearson touchdown from the 3. Jeff Artigues' PAT made it 7-3. The Flashes responded with a Pierce touchdown run from the 4 and an Agostinelli PAT. But on the drive, Kavanaugh bruised a hip and would sit the remainder of the game. Problems worsened on the next drive when Dornbusch twisted an ankle and joined Kavanaugh on the bench.

Down 14-3 to start the 3rd, the Bruins' offense came to life. Artigues found Pearson for a 40 yard strike, Artigues hit Herbert Loving from the 35, and Artigues again hit Loving for another score. Artigues added all three PATs. The Flashes' last points came in the 4th when Jones hit Rocconi from the 16 and then for the two-pointer. Saint Joe finished the contest with an Artigues touchdown scamper of 40 yards. *"We had lost our leading rusher ... our second leading rusher, and left all the weight on (Jones). I think he did an outstanding job of just holding the team together. They had a good team. Our young kids got a lot of experience tonight. I just hope that we can regroup for next week."*

GAME 10:   SAINT AL (5-4) @ JACKSON ALTERNATIVE SCHOOL (1-7-1)
               FINAL: SAINT AL 32 JACKSON ALTERNATIVE 12
               November 7, 1986

The Knights were in the first year of football and had a less-than-stellar record. But, Saint Al's injuries continued to mount. Two more players were lost as a result of the Bruins game and Edwards would have to play younger personnel. *"I've never had this many injuries before at Saint Al"*. A winning season was hanging in the balance and Kavanaugh needed 181 yards to break the 1,000 mark.

Saint Al's first score came as a result of a shanked Thomas Sawyer punt that rolled back into the endzone and was recovered by Paul Montalvo. Nassour added the two points for an 8-0 lead. A Dornbusch interception on the next drive put the ball at the Knights 13. Kavanaugh went in from the 8 and Agostinelli made it 15-0. With :08 left in the half, the Flashes made it 18-0 on an Agostinelli boot from the 31. Near the close of the 3rd, Dornbusch dove in from the 1 to finish a drive of 73 yards. The final points came in the 4th when Jones got in from the 13 on a keeper.

The Knights would finish the game with two scores. Sawyer took the first in from the 11 and Victor Winston darted 30 yards for the second. More importantly, Kavanaugh finished the night with 182 yards on the ground. This put him at 1,001 for the season and resulted in Player of the Week. John Agostinelli and Jeff Jones would share the Virgadamo Trophy for 1986.

"After coming off of a playoff run in 1985, we expected to repeat that success in 1986. Even though those goals weren't met, this team was led by only five seniors who (despite not being the biggest or the fastest playes) played with effort, grit, and pride for the Purple and Gold. Leadership was shown not in wins and losses, but in heart and spirit. RIP Ron Cocilova."

John Agostinelli; November 17, 2016

Joseph T. Balzli
July 31, 1914 – December 17, 1981
"The Father of Saint Aloysius Football"

No book on the history of Saint Aloysius football could exist without some deep reflection on the importance one man played in its success. That man was Joe Balzli. Initially, the idea was to have this chapter a recollection of the "man" by former players, known proudly as "*Balzli's Boys*"; former youngsters now much older but who still remember him fondly. There would be no lack of people ready to shower compliments on his memory. Casual conversations with some of his oldest players can bring tears to their eyes.

As this project grew, I knew early-on that nothing I could write would encapsulate him properly. The stories are endless and it would take much more ink than I believe Joe Balzli would be comfortable in me producing. Charles Faulk wrote of him in the following (paraphrased) words:

The young mentor grew up on the docks of Mobile, Alabama. His father was captain of an ocean liner; his mother died when he was young. Instead of falling in with others that would make bad decisions as to their future, the young Balzli turned to the Brothers of the Sacred Heart. "*They did for him what the Brothers used to do for us. They gave him something to do to keep him in the yard*", recalled Frank Logue. After being appointed as principal, Brother Ignatius brought him to Saint Al in 1936. When he took his first step into coaching, he was barely older than his players. "*His eyes would twinkle and he had a sly, foxy expression that seemed always ready to break into a grin. The job paid poorly. He kept books for an ice house to make ends meet*".

"*I never heard him curse his men. He never laid a hand on one. After a football game, he'd be driving the bus, a cigar between his fingers on the steering wheel. He'd call out the name of the captain and tell him, 'All right, now. Say your prayers.' We'd ride back reciting rosaries*", recalled Logue.

After over twenty years of producing staggering results while influencing so many young men and deflecting any opportunity at credit, Joe retired and handed the reigns over to Andy Bourgeois. He would go on to start a new career at Karl's, the men's store in downtown Vicksburg.

While researching this book, I came across a great piece written by <u>The Vicksburg Evening Post</u> on July 1, 1963. The reflections on him were so much better than anything I could have written. So with much respect to the unknown author, and sincere appreciation to <u>The Vicksburg Post</u>, I humbly submit the (condensed) recap of "*The Father of Saint Aloysius Football*".

In the mid-thirties there came a tough gridiron general to the beloved "Brothers School" on the dusty plateau atop Grove Street hill. Joseph T. Balzli, fired with all the zeal of youth, threw his energy into helping Brother Ignatius in the important work of training young men. For one quarter of this century after the surrender of Vicksburg Joe Waged his own campaign of conditioning young men for action and life: a work that demanded a trinity of effort of the spiritual, mental and physical.

As in every battle, all aspects and times are tough in their own way, and so Joe admits today that it was a battle from the start. Balzli generaled his meager band much in the same manner with much the same limitations of men and materials as did the Confederate commander of these bluffs, for up until the last five years, the school had less than 70 students in the high school.

It was a one-man coaching staff. In his quarter century at Saint Aloysius, Joe amassed a win average of 70%, five undefeated seasons, three years with only one defeat, Middle Mississippi Class A Championships three years, and winner of all three bowl games played. A total of twenty-one straight wins was registered with the club he brought up as an assistant in 1936 as freshmen and sophomores. These players became top-flight juniors and seniors in 1938 and 1939. During that period of 21 straight wins, Balzli's 16 man brigade scored 471 points while holding the opponents to a stingy 38. The troops that assailed the double stripe of Aloysius during these 21 games flew the battle colors of such teams as Hazlehurst, Yazoo City, Magee, Shreveport, Belzoni, Brandon, Newellton, Tallulah, Clinton and Menard of Alexandria, LA.

With the coming of the attack on Pearl Harbor, Joe entered the service in February 1942. He spent four years in the U.S. Marine Corps, 34 months of his hitch was spent in the combat areas of the South and Central Pacific from Guadalcanal to Palau. On return to the States he was utilized in the Corps training program.

When Joe returned to civilian life, Monsignor D.J. O'Beirne appointed him Athletic Directors and coach of all sports in the two Catholic schools. The job was a demanding and responsible one coaching the football and basketball teams for Saint Aloysius and Saint Francis, and drill master for the band. During the summer months, Joe supervised camp trips for students of the two schools to the Mississippi Gulf Coast.

His personal concern was so great for the young people that he felt more comfortable driving the school bus himself. He would shrug this duty off with the quip, *"They could get someone else to replace me, only they couldn't find as good a bus driver as I am."* Again, the real spirit of the man: a big of quick humor, a joke on himself to cover up the responsibilities.

In October 1947, Joe married former Margaret Chatham. They were blessed with two children, Tom and Ann, and have been a close part of the parish school program for years. Margaret (taught) first grade at Saint Francis, Ann (was) in seventh grade, and Tom, as a freshman at Saint Al, (was) making a good try for the varsity sports roster.

A good general always leads his men, and Joe Balzli led his. He always called them men, never boys. He was with them in the church, in the classroom, in the locker room, on the athletic field, always working with and in close accord with the teachers. He was one of the first to dispel the specter of the *'meathead'* athlete. His rule was strict: in body discipline, spiritual *"gentlemaness"*, and efficient use of intelligence. From his first five years, teams (gave) 100% participation in the Second World War.

Back home from the service, Joe found some good material reporting to practice and though the senior group really lent itself for to a power system, Joe put a few more embellishments on his post-war "T" formation and had a bruising "T" for one year in 1946. However, the next two years saw the "T" flexed into every shape of the alphabet, with split lines, men-in-motion, flankers, floaters, etc.; things people consider fundamental today but which were new at that time.

Again, Joe had picked up more schooling in his clinics. He went to clinics regularly from his first year even if he had to go distant states. This "T" formation group of 1946-1947 scored a total of 380 points while winning 15 out of 17 games. They were just as rock-ribbed on defense as they were lancer-like on offense, holding 11 of these games scoreless. (They won) two bowl games defeating Menard of Alexandria, LA for the CYO title and upended Tylertown in the 1947 Lions Bowl Game.

When his player material began arriving in bolts of "Single Wing" design, back Balzli went to the *"thumper system"*. Never one to dally with an idea, Joe said one game was a turning point and he switched from the "Split T" to the "Single Wing" in mid-season to win the last five games on the schedule.

Brother Cecil began to coach the younger players and for his time in such association he provided Balzli with you, well-schooled players as they entered high school. The only such junior team assistance Joe ever had. From this era came the strong unit of the late fifties. From the four-year span from freshmen to seniors, this club lost only two games. They blitzed the opposing elevens for a crushing 961 points...

Joe completed his coaching activities with this system: his "Single Wing", a system that he had helped evolve from the plodding wedge-attack from the late fifties to the intricate and mechanically beautiful units of the present. He devised what all coaches seek today: the best rule blocking for an unbalanced line. He was always eager to help others and pass on anything that would improve the game: the game he believed sired no weaklings.

During the campaigns of his strong clubs in the fifties, Joe was nominated and selected as coach of the annual Mississippi High School All-Star football game, but due to other commitments of that year, we was unable to accept.

He was a devoted exponent of the best equipment and playing conditions that were possible. As early as the thirties he had SEC officials working his games. Their worth to the evolution of the game in this area is above price. Balzli's was the first team in the state to require every man on the squad wears a face mask. All ankles were taped even in the days when the norm was to tape only a player that had an injured foot. Three spring and summer seasons, he devoted to the building of a stadium and track and turf. The gridiron was sodded with the best grass that could be put in any stadium, college or otherwise.

Looking back over the years, Joe admits to having enjoyed every minute but when the time arrived, he knew it and was ready to get out. He was then coaching the sons of the men of his first ball clubs. The ex-coach states that a 25-year term is really too long for any coach to stay at one school.

Had Joe hung up his whistle and cap at the close of the very successful 1958 season, he would have been considered by most as a greater coach record-wise. However, he says that he isn't sorry for staying to start a new cycle. Thinking back over his years of coaching, Joe says that what stands out most in his mind is the performances of his men both on and off the field. He feels that it is all but impossible to pick out or compare teams of the 30s, 40s, 50s and 60s.

Even the scholarships awarded to his players, three to LSU, two to Ole Miss, one to Mississippi Southern, two to Millsaps, two to Loyola and one to Princeton cannot be used as a gauge since Joe feels that all his players were top caliber if they gave all that they were capable.

Balzli called it a career end after the 1960 season to accept a job in one of Vicksburg's leading men's stores. However, regarding football, Joe says he's just transferred his enthusiasm and love of the game from the sidelines to the stands and likes to think of himself as the school's Number One Fan. His praise for the Bourgeois-Conlin duo is unlimited. He especially praises the conditioning, fire and hustle of the teams of the past two seasons. From his background, he can be happier than anyone else to see his school now fully and completely manned with a complete athletic staff.

The Balzli era closed out a phase in high school coaching in this area and he went out not only the last in the line of the one-man-coaches, but as one of the best of the lone campaigners of grid warfare.

To keep his memory alive, and in recognition for all that he had done for the school, Saint Aloysius' field was renamed Balzli Field on November 3rd, 1995.

Anthony Paul (Tony) Virgadamo
July 30, 1929 – December 2, 1950

The extremely popular Virgadamo was not only a great athlete, but also a fine student and leader. The young and talented kid with boyish good looks and charm is still well-thought of by those who knew him. A member of the Flashes from 1944 to 1947, he had not only captained the squad his senior year, but also played in the band. Shortly after graduation, he enlisted in the United States Marine Corp and was assigned to the Headquarters and Service Company; 5th Marines; 1st Marine Division. Corporal Virgadamo was killed in action with the United Nations forces in Korea on December 2nd, 1950. His remains were never recovered.

The military assigned Tony an honorary burial at The Courts of the Missing in Honolulu, Hawaii. Vicksburg remembered him, along with so many other hometown sons, on a downtown memorial. For his service, he was awarded The Combat Action Ribbon, Korean Service Medal, United Nations Service Medal, Republic of Korea Presidential Unit Citation, Republic of Korea War Service Medal, The Purple Heart and The National Defense Service Medal.

From 1941 to 1949, Saint Aloysius had been awarding the Cunningham Trophy to the most outstanding person in the classroom and on the gridiron. It had been named in honor of Mr. Walter W. Cunningham, Superintendent of the Illinois Central Railroad. Winners for those years included:

1941:	Dan Mahoney	1946:	Gordon Bailey
1942:	John Kolb	1947:	Tommy Thomas
1943:	Joe Derivaux	1948:	Jack Stamm
1944:	James Bres	1949:	Al Ford
1945:	Donnie Derivaux		

Beginning in 1950, and at the request of the players, the award became known as The Virgadamo Trophy and given on the same merits. It continues to this day. Winners of this trophy for the years noted in this publication are:

1950	Robert Baylot	1969:	Carl Franco
1951	Clint Schlottman	1970:	Bobby Baylot
1952	William Carrigan	1971:	Paul Rocconi
1953	Joseph Durst	1972:	David Hosemann
1954	John Banchetti	1973:	Bill Loyacano
1955	William Gargaro	1974:	Murray Whitaker
1956	Karl Nicholas	1975:	Dennis Southard
1957	Tom Morrissey/Paul Hosemann	1976:	Murray Pinkston
1958	Eddie Habert/George Evans	1977:	Donnie Head
1959	Bobby Gordon/Jim "Monk" Monsour	1978:	Joe Battalio
1960	John Downey	1979:	Lanny Barfield
1961	David Nohra	1980:	George McConnell
1962	Greg Doiron	1980:	Cicero LaHatte/Barry Breithaupt
1963	Roy Woody	1982:	Pat Evans
1964	Joe Maggio	1983:	Joe Evans
1965	Tom Balzli	1984:	Corey Pinkston
1966	Billy McCain	1985:	Mark Simrall
1967	Bernie Callaway	1986:	John Agostinelli/Jeff Jones
1968	Frank Koe		

In the first 75 years of Saint Al's football program, at least 871 young men donned pads for the team at some point. In that time frame, the small Catholic school gridiron players produced 6 undefeated/untied regular seasons, 8 undefeated seasons, and 8 more one-loss seasons.

When bowls were available, the Flashes went to 11 of them. They laid claim to 15 championships and at least three runner-up spots, all while scheduling some of the toughest teams available for decades.

The best effort at the all-time Flash roster follows. For those who may be missing, or for those with whom I have missed a playing year, my deepest and most sincere apologies.

Abraham	UNK	1929	Basche	Kenneth	1968
Abraham	Michael	1985-1986	Battalio	Joe	1975-1978
Agostinelli	John	1983-1986	Battalio	Vincent	1937-1940
Agostinelli	Marty	1980-1983	Baugh	Billy	1944-1945
Alonzo	Chris	1979-1981	Bauni	Henry	1950-1951
Alonzo	Johnny	1969-1970	Baylot	Bobby	1947-1950
Alonzo	Terry	1973	Baylot	Bobby	1967-1969
Alonzo	Tommy	1976-1977	Baylot	Charles	1945
Alvarado	Bob	1952-1953	Baylot	David	1971-1974
Amborn	Charles	1958-1960	Baylot	J.	1943
Amborn	William	1933	Baylot	Jimmy	1969-1971
Amborn	William	1938	Baylot	Mark	1986
Ammon	Preston	1943	Baylot	Robert	1970
Anderson	Glen	1945-1946	Beard	Glen	1980
Anderson	Larry	1970-1971	Beard	Patrick	1971-1974
Andress	Peter	1970-1972	Beard	Rory	1982-1983
Andrews	Dean	1985	Beasley	Tim	1973-1976
Andrews	James	1932-1934	Beasley	Tommy	1969-1971
Angelo	Freddy	1960-1962	Bell	Bart	1978-1979
Angelo	Larry	1958-1096	Bell	Bob	1979
Anklam	Fred	1970-1971	Bell	Charles	1937
Antoine	Charles	1962-1964	Bellan	John	1912-1913
Antoine	Ricky	1968-1970	Bellan	Paul	1912-1913
Arenz	Billie	1935	Bellan	Paul	1941-1942
Arenz	Joe	1927-1929	Bellan	William	1944
Atkins	David	1983	Bendinelli	Ralph	1933-1936
Bagby	Claude	1966	Biedenharn	Brent	1984-1986
Bagby	Craig	1966	Biedenharn	Herman	1982-1984
Bagby	Greg	1969	Biggar	Craig	1984
Bailey	Beau	1984	Biggar	David	1982-1984
Bailey	Gordon	1945-1946	Black	W.L.	1924
Bailey	Joe	1974-1976	Blackwell	John	1925-1927
Baker	David	1961	Bliss	Francis	1929-1930
Baker	David	1984-1985	Bobb	William	1934-1935
Baker	Jackie	1956	Bolton	Dick	1943-1944
Baker	Rip/Russell	1946-1948	Bonelli	Joseph	1931-1933
Baladi	Joe	1982-1984	Bonelli	Robert	1936
Balzli	Tom	1962-1965	Boolos	Frederick	1933
Banchetti	John	1952-1954	Boolos	Joseph	1931-1933
Banchetti	Paul	1966-1968	Booth	Andy	1966-1969
Bankston	Harry	1912-1913	Booth	Bubba	1967-1970
Bankston	Ray	1944-1946	Booth	George	1965
Bankston	Willie	1924-1935	Booth	George	1927-1930
Barber	John	1943	Booth	Joe	1935-1939
Barfield	Brent	1981-1984	Booth	John	1970-1971
Barfield	Lanny	1978-1979	Booth	Mike	1965-1966
Barnes	Ronnie	1966-1967	Booth	Paul	1957-1958
Barnett	Jay	1975-1978	Booth	William	1929-1931

Boykin	Brian	1986	Canizaro	Jack	1948-1950
Brabston	Bryan	1947	Canizaro	Joe	1936-1939
Bradera	Eddie	1954	Canizaro	Pete	1928
Bradway	John	1986	Canizaro	Vincent	1925-1927
Bragg	Albert	1934-1935	Canizaro	Vito	1932-1933
Bragg	Floyd	1937	Cantin	Carl	1976
Branan	Otto	1964-1967	Cappaert	Dan	1963-1966
Branciere	Andy	1966-1967	Cappaert	Steve	1969-1972
Branciere	John	1936	Carrigan	Bill	1950-1952
Breithaupt	Barry	1978-1981	Cassino	Frank	1961-1964
Breithaupt	Brian	1981-1984	Cassino	Nick	1932
Breithaupt	Ernest	1937	Cassino	Vincent	1941-1942
Breithaupt	Freddy	1947-1948	Cathey	Beau	1980-1983
Bres	James	1943-1944	Caughlin	Charles	1912
Bridgers	Dave	1963-1965	Chatham	Griffin	1944-1947
Brooks	Jim	1966	Chatham	Paul	1954-1956
Brooks	John	1963-1965	Chatham	Richard	1956-1957
Broussard	K.P.	1931	Coccoro	Bart	1957-1959
Brown	Al	1962-1965	Coccoro	Clement	1933-1935
Brown	Carl	1980-1981	Coccoro	John	1978
Brown	E.W.	1925	Cocilova	Ron	1983-1986
Brown	Henry	1924-1925	Cockrell	Ricky	1974-1976
Brown	John	1979-1980, 1982	Conerly	Marion	1966-1968
Brown	Paul	1959-1962	Conner	Samuel	1971
Brown	Ricky	1967-1968	Cooke	William	1953-1955
Brown	Sam	1977-1980	Coomes	Billy	1975-1978
Brunini	Joseph	1924-1926	Coomes	Bobby	1971-1973
Bucci	Philip	1969-1970, 1972	Coomes	Ken	1970-1972
Buell	Billy	1959-1961	Coomes	Mike	1969-1970
Buell	Jimmy	1959-1961	Coomes	Robert	1970
Buell	Tommy	1960-1964	Corts	Angelo	1946
Bufkin	Billy	1948-1950	Cotten	Irvin	1940-1942
Butler	Pat	1981	Cox	Chris	1975-1977
Butler	Steve	1977-1979	Cox	Paul	1927
Byrd	Thomas	1955	Cox	Perry	1976-1979
Cabanero	Fernando	1975	Cox	Steve	1966, 1969
Caesar	Charles	1968	Cox	UNK	1925
Caesar	John	1937	Crandall	UNK	1913
Caldwell	James	1968	Crevitt	Joe	1953-1955
Callaway	Bernie	1965-1967	Cronin	A.J.	1934-1938
Callaway	Fisher	1963-1966	Cronin	Earl	1925
Callen	Freddie	1958	Cronin	Jerry	1954-1955
Campbell	Jerry	1961	Cronin	John	1958-1961
Campbell	Jerry	1933-1934	Cronin	Pat	1959-1960
Campbell	John	1950, 1952-1953	Cunningham	Ivan	1956-1958
Campbell	Mark	1979	Cunningham	Lee	1984-1986
Campbell	William	1927	Davidson	Bobby	1957
Canizaro	Eddie	1962-1964	Davidson	Jack	1949-1951

Davidson	Jim	1944	Evans	Joe	1944-1945
Davidson	Robert	1955	Evans	Joe	1980-1983
Davis	Danny	1964-1966	Evans	John	1937
Davis	William	1926-1928	Evans	John	1953
Day	Billy	1978	Evans	Keith	1986
DeLewis	Andy	1967-1968	Evans	Mark	1964-1967
Derivaux	Charles	1943	Evans	Miller	1937-1939
Derivaux	Donald	1943-1945	Evans	Pat	1979-1982
Derivaux	Jerry	1944-1947	Evans	Robert	1947-1950
Derivaux	Joseph	1942-1943	Evans	Wade	1967-1969
DeRossette	Brian	1979-1982	Ewing	Sam	1935
DeRossette	Frank	1971	Fabenstock	Jack	1935
DeRossette	Matthew	1983-1984	Falgout	Larry	1959-1962
DeRossette	Tim	1976-1979	Farish	Bob	1950-1951
DeRossette	Wally	1968-1970	Ferguson	Claude	1939-1941
Dicks	Guy	1969-1970	Ferguson	De	1982-1984
DiRago	Joe	1927-1928	Files	Clay	1945
DiRago	Marion	1929=1930	Finane	Charles	1937-1938
DiRago	Vincent	1960-1961	Finane	J.B.	1930
Ditto	Frank	1944-1947	Fitzgerald	James	1926
Doiron	Greg	1959-1962	Fletcher	John C.	1913
Doiron	Phillip	1956-1958	Flowers	Kyle	1973, 1975
Doiron	Warren	1952-1953	Flowers	Shelby	1940-1941
Donovan	P.	1928	Flowers	Teddy	1942
Donovan	Robert	1930-1933	Foley	Bill	1939
Donovan	W.	1948	Foley	Charles	1943-1946
Dornbusch	Kette	1984-1986	Foley	Mike	1969-1972
Downey	John	1958-1960	Foley	Robert	1942-1946
Dugan	Joe	1936	Foley	Robert	1964-1967
Dunlap	Cas	1983	Fontenot	Mike	1963
Durst	Joe	1951-1953	Ford	Al	1947-1949
Durst	John	1949-1951	Ford	Bill	1964
Edwards	Charles	1927-1928	Ford	Charles	1943-1944
Edwards	Franklin	1928	Ford	Wilmer	1932
Ehrhardt	Bert	1965	Fordice	Dan	1977
Ehrhardt	Keith	1979-1982	Fordice	Jim	1979-1982
Ellis	George	1947-1951	Foster	Steve	1959-1960, 1962
Ellis	Ira	1930	Franck	Chuck	1967
Ellis	John	1951	Franck	John	1925
Emfinger	Milton	1947-1949	Franck	Larry	1945-1948
Ettinger	George	1954-1957	Franco	A.	1925
Evans	Bob	1947-1949	Franco	Angelino	1957-1959
Evans	Earl	1941-1942	Franco	B.	1933
Evans	Edwin	1940	Franco	Bob	1966-1969
Evans	George	1954-1958	Franco	Carl	1967, 1969
Evans	Greg	1974-1976	Franco	Gary	1973
Evans	Harry	1941-1943	Franco	Guy	1970-1973
Evans	Jett	1964-1965	Franco	John	1953

Franco	Mike	1959-1962	Guider	Warren	1962-1963
Franco	Raphael	1930-1932	Guillott	Bryan	1960
Franco	Robert	1970	Guimbellot	Herman	1961
Franco	Tony	1929	Guiney	Charles	1933-1934
Franco	Tony	1950-1952	Gullette	Benny	1959-1960
Franco	Tony	1977-1979	Gussio	Greg	1984-1985
Franco	UNK	1925	Gussio	Johnny	1979-1982
Frohn	Martin	1933-1936	Habeeb	Albert	1931
Gabe	Robert	1931	Habert	Eddie	1955-1958
Galloway	Jerry	1974-1976	Hagan	Charles	1964-1966
Galofaro	Hunter	1984-1986	Hale	Perry	1954-1955
Gamble	David	1979-1981	Hall	Linus	1985-1986
Ganzerla	Mike	1964-1965, 1967	Halford	Matt	1974-1977
Gardner	Chris	1980-1983	Hamilton	J.C.	1931
Gargaro	John	1950-1951	Hanes	Francia	1957-1958
Gargaro	William	1952-1955	Hanisee	Harold	1934
Garmon	Bill	1982-1983	Hardin	Eddie	1959-1962
Garraton	Charles	1929-1931	Hardin	Harry	1952-1953
Garvey	Andrew	1912	Hardin	John	1964-1965
Garvey	Kelly	1934-1936	Hardy	Ben	1977, 1980
Geary	Jack	1944-1947	Hardy	Paul	1978
Geary	Mike	1961	Harris	Dreher	1964-1965
Geary	Robert	1955	Harris	Preston	1966-1969
Geary	Robert	1927-1930	Harrison	Bill	1945-1947
Geary	Wade	1958	Harrison	UNK	1931
George	Mike	1924	Hartley	John	1952-1955
George	Richard	1966	Harwood	Laurence	1942-1943
Gerache	Joe	1966-1968	Harwood	Roy	1936
Gerache	John	1972-1973	Hatchettee	Bill	1936-1939
Geter	Marvin	1979, 1981-1982	Hawkins	Richard	1939-1941
Goff	Percy	1947-1948	Hazard	John	1926
Gordon	Bobby	1957-1959	Hazel	Hilton	1912-1913
Gordon	Chris	1983-1984	Head	Donnie	1974-1977
Gordon	David	1971-1972	Head	Greg	1971-1974
Gordon	Donnie	1977-1979	Head	Joey	1985-1986
Gordon	Patrick	1982-1984	Head	Reggie	1969-1972
Gordon	Tommy	1955-1957	Hearn	Angus	1924
Grant	Anthony	1971-1972	Hebeler	Mort	1959
Grant	Harvey	1927	Hebeler	Patrick	1934
Grant	John	1929	Hebeler	R.	1931
Gray	Clarence	1927-1928	Hebler	Mart	1961
Green	Andy	1948-1950	Helgason	Ted	1952-1953
Grey	Cliff	1982	Henegan	Gene	1946
Groome	Fred	1950-1953	Henegan	William	1942
Groome	Red	1929-1930	Hennessey	John	1957-1958
Gugert	Frank	1959	Hennessey	Larry	1952
Guider	Clarence	1937	Henry	Richard	1940
Guider	George	1925	Herbert	James	1938

Heron	Norbert	1912-1913	Hummel	Jack	1927-1928
Hess	Freddie	1958	Hunter	John	1935-1936
Hickman	James	1932-1933	Irwin	Delvan	1983-1984
Hickson	Kevin	1964-1967	Israel	Gil	1966-1968
Hite	Jack	1972-1973, 1975	Israel	Joe	1968, 1970-1971
Hite	Robert	1978-1981	Israel	Ricky	1975
Hogan	Ben	1941-1943	Jabour	Jamie	1972
Hogan	Charles	1967	Jabour	Paul	1973
Hogan	Dan	1944, 1946-1947	Jabour	Will	1946-1949
Hogan	Denis	1975-1977	Jacquith	William	1928-1930
Hogan	Mike	1969	James	Caston	1927-1929
Hogan	Pat	1963, 1965-1966	James	O.E.	1926-1929
Hogan	Philip	1976-1979	James	Wyatt	1926
Hogan	Tom	1936-1940	Jamison	O.B.	1928
Hogan	W.	1933-1935	Jamison	T.A.	1926-1929
Holder	Tim	1983-1985	Janes	Phillip	1933-1934
Holland	Skipper	1967	Jaquith	William	1931
Holloway	David	1972-1975	Jefferson	James	1974-1976
Holloway	Steve	1973-1975	Jefferson	Lynn	1971-1974
Holly	UNK	1925	Jefferson	Steve	1972-1975
Hopkins	Bert	1957	Jennings	Bill	1956-1957
Hosemann	Anthony	1933-1934	Johnson	David	1979
Hosemann	Bob	1961	Johnson	Jerome	1957-1959
Hosemann	David	1970-1972	Johnson	Norbert	1952-1955
Hosemann	Delbert	1940-1941	Johnson	Randy	1976-1977
Hosemann	Delbert	1961-1964	Johnson	Rex	1970
Hosemann	Jerry	1966-1969	Johnson	Richard	1970
Hosemann	Jerry	1985-1986	Johnson	Ricky	1969
Hosemann	John	1957-1959	Johnson	Steve	1968
Hosemann	Marcel	1924	Jones	Freddy	1960-1962
Hosemann	Mike	1956-1957	Jones	Jeff	1983-1986
Hosemann	Paul	1930-1931	Jones	Jesse	1953-1956
Hosemann	Paul	1956-1957	Jones	Mike	1972-1973
Hosemann	Robert	1934-1937	Joseph	Fred	1934
Hosemann	Scott	1985-1986	Katzenmeyer	Bill	1959
Hossley	Bill	1932	Katzenmeyer	Brent	1935-1936
Hossley	Dan	1957-1959	Katzenmeyer	George	1937-1939
Hossley	James	1952-1954	Katzenmeyer	Leonard	1937-1938
Hossley	Joe	1955-1956	Kavanaugh	John	1984-1986
Hossley	Louis	1927-1928	Kellum	John	1977-1978
Hossley	Mike	1972	Kelly	Frank	1929-1930
Hossley	Tom	1925-1927	Kelly	Mike	1962-1964
Howell	Billy	1956-1957	Kelly	Patrick	1912-1913
Hoxie	Bill	1980-1982	Kelly	Wilsey	1960-1962
Hoxie	Rip	1978	Kennedy	Joe	1935-1936
Hude	Harry	1937-1940	Kent	UNK	1927
Hude	Jack	1933-1934	Kette	Charles	1942
Hull	Greg	1980-1981	King	Martin	1932

King	Robert	1939-1941	Little	Walter	1956-1957
Kirchmayer	Steve	1957	Loboda	Steve	1986
Kittrell	Howard	1975	Logue	Chris	1984
Kline	John	1912	Logue	Hicks	1945-1946, 1948
Koe	Frank	1966-1968	Logue	John	1942-1947
Koe	Lester	1966-1967	Logue	Louis	1955-1958
Koestler	Bobby	1946-1948	Logue	Omar	1985-1986
Koestler	Charles	1944-1945	Long	Horace	1947-1950
Koestler	Lawrence	1981	Louis	Tom	1947-1949
Koestler	Leo	1954-1957	Loyacano	Bill	1971-1973
Koestler	Mark	1975-1976	Loyacano	P.	1930-1931
Koestler	Mickey	1950-1951	Loyacano	Paul	1955-1956
Koestler	Mike	1971-1974, 1976	Lucchesi	Bobby	1962-1965
Koestler	Pat	1976-1977	Lucchesi	Eddie	1953-1956
Koestler	Paul	1979	Lucchesi	Larry	1950-1951
Koestler	Robert	1980	Luckett	Robert	1912
Koestler	Robert	1973-1975	Lusco	Sam	1983-1984
Kolb	Rudolph	1941-1943	Lyons	Michael	1986
Kolb	Tony	1967-1970	Mackey	Clarence	1924-1926
Kowaluk	Nick	1959	Mackey	Jackie	1955-1958
Laboda	John	1977-1979	Mackey	Joe	1957
LaHatte	Cicero	1978-1981	Mackey	John	1959
Lamb	Keith	1967	Madison	Howard	1951-1953
Lambert	John	1938-1942	Madison	William	1960
Lambert	O.B	1936-1937	Maggio	Joe	1961-1964
Lambert	Richard	1959	Mahoney	Ashley	1963-1966
Landers	Harvey	1970-1973	Mahoney	Daniel	1938-1941
Landes	Bill	1982-1984	Mahoney	Kevin	1980-1983
Laster	Irving	1938-1941	Mahoney	Michael	1979-1982
Lauderdale	Bill	1936	Mahoney	Mickey	1958-1961
Lauderdale	Bill	1961-1964	Mahoney	Mike	1979-1980
Lauderdale	Charles	1930	Marlett	Bob	1949-1951
Lavecchia	Joseph	1912	Marshall	Charles	1913
Lavecchia	Nick	1926-1927	Marshall	Charles	1961
Lawler	Ed	1971-1974	Marshall	Mike	1984-1986
Lawler	Kyle	1972-1973, 1975	Marshall	Robert	1912
Lawrence	George	1975	Marshall	Teddy	1953-1955
Lee	Billy	1944-1945	Marsicano	Joe	1942-1943
Lee	Carlos	1976-1977	Marsicano	John	1952-1953
Lee	Lester	1938	Marsicano	Paul	1953
Lee	Tommy	1960-1964	Matherne	Dick	1956
Lefoldt	Richard	1930	Matherne	Earl	1944-1945
Leist	Jack	1971	Mattingly	John	1934-1935
Leist	Joe	1971-1972	Mattingly	Steve	1939
LeMay	Mark	1966	Mattingly	Wally	1966
Leo	Jerry	1964-1966	Maxey	Gerald	1974-1977
Lindigrin	Joe	1957-1958	McCaffrey	Tim	1979-1982
Little	Phillip	1959	McCain	Billy	1963-1966

McCain	Joe	1972, 1974	Morgan	Hollis	1925
McCain	John	1979-1980	Morrissey	Mike	1955-1957
McCain	Mike	1976-1979	Morrissey	Tommy	1944
McConnell	Bob	1978-1979	Moss	John	1980-1983
McConnell	George	1977-1980	Muffaletto	Ronnie	1966-1969
McCormack	Charles	1955-1956	Muirhead	Frank	1944, 1948
McCormack	John	1945	Mulligan	Lloyd	1934
McCormack	Pat	1945-1948	Murphy	Newell	1952
McCoy	Brad	1969	Nassour	John	1960-1961
McDaniel	M. Thomas	1933	Nassour	Michael	1983-1986
McDaniel	Robert	1963	Neal	Bart	1975
McDaniel	Robert	1979-1982	Neal	Eric	1966
McDaniel	Ronnie	1982-1984	Neil	David	1959-1960
McGuffie	John	1960	Nelson	Bobby	1974, 1977
McHann	Tom	1948	Nelson	Gordon	1935-1937
McIntosh	David	1964-1965	Nelson	Joseph	1928-1930
McKay	Billy	1986	Nelson	P.	1932
McKinney	Eli	1938-1941	Nelson	Tommy	1971
McKnight	Theodore	1933-1934	Nicholas	Karl	1953-1956
McMillan	Clifton	1953, 1955	Nichols	Larry	1970-1973
McNamara	Albert	1970	Nichols	Robert	1975
McNamara	F.X.	1928-1929	Nohra	David	1958-1961
McNamara	Mike	1963, 1965-1966	Nohra	George	1948
McNamara	Patrick	1970, 1972	Nosser	Mike	1985-1986
McNamara	Roy	1961-1962	O'Brien	Red	1924-1927
McNamara	Tom	1931-1932	O'Connor	Robert	1915
McNamara	Tom	1960-1961	Odom	Bruce	1973
McNamara	William	1927-1928	Odom	Danny	1973
McTaggart	Thomas	1952-1953	Odom	UNK	1934
Meacham	T.	1927	O'Neill	Bob	1948-1951
Melsheimer	Albert	1934-1935	O'Neill	Jack	1945
Melsheimer	Bob	1955-1956	Owen	Pat	1961
Melsheimer	Edwin	1932-1933	Palermo	Dick	1947-1949
Melsheimer	Gerald	1930-1931	Palermo	Jack	1951-1952
Melsheimer	Jack	1934-1936	Palermo	James	1935
Melsheimer	Julius	1933	Palermo	Joseph	1912
Melsheimer	Marion	1925, 1927	Palermo	Vincent	1935
Melsheimer	Sam	1935-1936	Patin	Sean	1985-1986
Menger	Kenneth	1912	Patton	Matt	1973-1976
Messina	Gerry	1969	Patton	Tony	1975-1977
Messina	Jerry	1966	Peacock	James	1952-1954
Meyer	Tommy	1957-1960	Peck	James	1981-1984
Miller	W.H.	1925	Peck	Morris	1984-1986
Monsour	Jimmy	1955-1959	Piazza	Bob	1968
Montalvo	Paul	1986	Piazza	Charles	1943
Montgomery	Bob	1966-1968	Piazza	Donnie	1968-1971
Montgomery	Mac	1962	Piazza	Harry	1936-1940
Moore	UNK	1928	Piazza	Harry	1961-1964

Piazza	John	1967-1968	Rocconi	Larry	1964-1967
Piazza	Julius	1912-1913	Rocconi	Paul	1968, 1970-1971
Piazza	Julius	1931-1932	Roesch	Donald	1983, 1985-86
Piazza	Mike	1985-1986	Roesch	George	1943-1944
Piazza	Vincent	1936-1938	Rogillio	Scott	1981-1982
Piazza	Wiley	1966-1969	Romano	Andrew	1952-1954
Pickett	Drew	1984-1986	Rosser	Tryon	1985-1986
Pierce	Paul	1984-1986	Roth	Donald	1952-1953
Pinkston	Corey	1981-1984	Russell	Blaine	1935-1938
Pinkston	John	1945	Ryan	Ferguson	1930
Pinkston	LaBarre	1912	Sadler	Robert	1941
Pinkston	Murray	1974-1976	Sadler	Robert	1963-1964, 1966
Platzer	Paul	1939	Sadler	William	1964
Potts	Tom	1967	Sadol	Milton	1929
Price	Donald	1930-1932	Salmon	James	1966-1969
Price	Donnie	1966-1970	Sam	William	1934
Price	Frank	1964-1967	Sanders	Will	1947-1949
Price	John	1952	Saucier	Sidney	1952-1953
Quin	Marvin	1962-1964	Schaff	Clement	1961-1962
Quirk	Atwood	1950	Schaff	Meredith	1948-1949
Quirk	Roland	1955	Schaff	Meredith	1950-1951
Rabalais	Mark	1981	Schlottman	Clint	1947-1951
Raiford	Will	1978	Schuler	Henry	1913
Randall	Martin	1973	Schultz	Jim	1964-1966
Randall	Marty	1976	Schultz	Joe	1960
Randall	Neil	1972-1973	Scott	Sam	1952-1953
Ray	Bobby	1966-1968	Seidel	Milton	1930-1934
Ray	Eddie	1961-1965	Setaro	Dan	1958-1960
Ray	Lloyd	1938	Setaro	Joe	1952-1954
Ray	Mike	1975-1978	Seymour	Leo	1951-1952
Ray	Ricky	1973	Seymour	Sidney	1964-1967
Ray	Tommy	1964-1967	Shannon	Winfield	1912
Rebert	Nick	1983	Sheffield	Ernest	1925-1926
Reddoch	Donald	1943-1946	Sherard	Harry	1931
Reddoch	Leo	1941-1943	Sherard	James	1933
Renaud	Louis	1952-1953	Shrewsbury	Steve	1965
Reynolds	Earle	1924-1926	Signa	Carmel	1960
Reynolds	Walter	1941-1942	Signa	Conan	1985-1986
Riddle	Albert	1952-1953	Simrall	Karsten	1986
Riddle	Billy	1958-1961	Simrall	Mark	1982-1985
Riddle	Don	1955-1957	Simrall	Newell	1981
Riddle	Mike	1950-1953	Smith	Carl	1977
Ring	Charles	1964-1965, 1967	Smith	Homer	1913
Ring	John	1959, 1961	Smith	James	1972-1975
Ring	Pat	1961-1963	Smith	John	1972-1975
Roberts	Jack	1926-1927	Smith	Steve	1986
Roberts	William	1912	Smith	Tim	1975-1978
Rocconi	Larry	1983, 1985-86	Smith	Walter	1950-1951

Solomon	Ed	1966-1967	Tuccio	Sam	1952-1954
Southard	Dennis	1973-1975	Tuminello	Donnie	1944-1947
Speights	Eddie	1984	Turcotte	Roy	1956
Spell	Preston	1939	Tweedle	Chip	1986
Spengler	Albert	1912-1913	Vance	Travis	1955
Speyerer	Lee	1981-1984	VanNorman	Garnett	1968-1970
Speyerer	Mike	1966-1968	Veazey	John	1935
Stamm	Carter	1972	Veazey	Pat	1935-1936
Stamm	Craig	1979, 1981-1982	Veazey	Victor	1934-1936
Stamm	Jack	1945-1948	Vedros	Mark	1972-1973
Steinriede	Bill	1967-1968	Vedros	Philip	1969-1971
Steinriede	Bob	1977	Verhine	Scott	1986
Stevens	Chuck	1976	Virgadamo	Tony	1944-1947
Stewart	Grove	1957	Vollor	Austin	1985
Stewart	Van	1936-1939	Vollor	Bill	1949
Stewart	William	1938-1941	Vollor	Frank	1963-1965
Stokes	Vincent	1932	Vollor	John	1956-1957
Stout	Tom	1913	Vollor	Tim	1984-1986
Streeter	UNK	1931	Vollor	Tim	1953, 1955-1956
Stuart	John	1935	Walker	Willie	1939-1942
Stubblefield	John	1913	Wallace	Balfour	1952-1954
Styron	Rad	1953, 1955	Wallace	Carl	1946-1947, 1949
Sudduth	Watson	1931-1932	Warnock	Brad	1985-1986
Sullivan	Bob	1957-1959	Weil	Felix	1912
Sullivan	Mickey	1956-1958	Weimer	John	1939-1942
Summers	James	1985	Whitaker	Doug	1975-1976
Sutton	Gordon	1956-1958	Whitaker	Gid	1972
Sutton	Harry	1952-1953	Whitaker	Murray	1971-1974
Tarnabine	Joe	1871-1973	White	Martin	1966-1967
Tarnabine	Pete	1975-1977	Wilkerson	Charles	1927-1930
Terry	Jim	1959-1961	Williams	Augustine	1970
Terry	Ray	1952-1955	Williams	Bob	1945-1946
Theobald	Bill	1947	Williams	Ed	1937-1938
Theobald	Bobby	1944	Williams	Francis	1970-1973
Theobald	David	1940-1942	Williams	Gus	1971
Theobald	Louis	1945	Williams	Joseph	1970
Theobald	Louis	1975	Wilson	David	1980-1982
Theobald	Ricky	1967-1970	Wilson	Don	1913
Thomas	George	1978-1981	Wilson	Jerry	1960
Thomas	Tommy	1943-1947	Wilson	Maurice	1932
Tickell	George	1941	Wilson	Neil	1946
Tickell	Talbott	1945	Witty	Bob	1956, 1958
Tierney	John	1924	Wood	Buddy	1948-1950
Trahan	Chuck	1971-1974	Wood	Jack	1952-1955
Tuccio	Ben	1966-1968	Wood	John	1951-53
Tuccio	David	1975-1979	Woods	Jerry	1960-1962
Tuccio	Joe	1961	Woods	Lloyd	1934-1935, 1937
Tuccio	Paul	1968	Woods	Ray	1934-1935

Woody	Mike	1962, 1965	Yerger	Bill	1957, 1959
Woody	Roy	1960-1963	Yerger	John	1985-1986
Wright	Norman	1927-1930	Zorn	George	1961, 1964
Yarbrough	Mike	1977-1979			

SAINT ALOYSIUS HEAD COACHES

Alonzo	Don	1969
Alvin	Brother	1944-1945
Autrey	Tommy	1974
Balzli	Joe	1937-41; 1946-60
Bourgeois	Andy	1961-64
Broussard	Elmo	1965-1968
Bumgarner	Les	1975-77
Edwards	Joe	1978-87
Harold	Brother	1933-35
John	Brother	1942
Knox	Ike	1914
Morrissey	Mike	1925
Philip	Brother	1943-1944
Regis	Brother	1945
Remigius	Brother	1936
Rhoads	Glenn	1970-73
Roberts	Jack	1929, 1932
Roderick	Brother	1942
Rogers	Ted	1926-27
Schaffer	Gormon	1931
Setaro	Fred	1931
Shannon	Walton	1928, 1930
Sylvester	Brother	1914

SAINT ALOYSIUS ASSISTANT COACHES

Albertus	Brother	1934
Ashford	Mitch	1981
Autrey	Tommy	1970
Balzli	Joe	1936
Benet	Brother	1936
Booth	Bubba	1980
Carl	Brother	1935
Conlin	Mike	1961-62
Curtis	Joe	1970-72, 1977
Downey	Pat	1966
Evans	Miller	1946-1947
Foret	Bobby	1963
Fowler	Neal	1970
Gontz	Richard	1970, 1972-74, 1977
Graves	Joe	1982-86
Guider	George	1932-33
Hitchins	Bobby	1970, 1974-78
Iverson	Gary	1973
Johnson	Tom	1975-77
Justice	Chuck	1978, 1981-82
Ladler	William	1961
Lloyd	Borther	1938
Logue	Frank	1947, 1952
Nichols	Dutch	1962
Nichols	Larry	1981-84
Patton	John	1979
Quinn	Billy	1944
Ray	Raymond	1952
Salmon	Jimmy	1970, 1976-79, 1984-86
Shannon	Walton	1927
Smyly	Gary	1969
Worsham	Jerry	1964-66

SAINT ALOYSIUS MANAGERS

Amborn	William	1938	Koestler	Barney	1976-77
Angelo	Miles	1970-71	Koestler	Leo	1977
Baker	Jackie	1958	Kowaluk	Nick	1960
Baker	Tom	1948	Lauderdale	Bill	1937
Boyd	Jessie	1951-1952	Little	Phillip	1960-61
Brabston	William	1952-1954	Logue	Frank	1941
Bradfield	Jackie	1914	Love	Marion	1934
Cabanero	Fernando	1975-76	Lusco	Matt	1971-74
Cook	William	1952	McNamara	Pat	1971
Crowley	Mart	1952	Melsheimer	Eugene	1970
Cunningham	John	1958	Nichols	Rodney	1969-70
Emerson	Paul	1983-1986	O'Neill	Edwin	1947
Ennis	John	1977	O'Neill	Neil	1956
Epperson	Epp	1935	Palmer	Matt	1938
Ethridge	David	1956	Partridge	Scott	1978
Ethridge	Francis	1952-1953	Puckett	Johnny	1961
Floyd	Paul	1973, 1975	Reeder	Robert	1972
France	John	1954	Rogillio	Scott	1980
Franco	John	1954	Sadler	William	1961
Gargaro	Bill	1952	Schlosser	Frank	1958
Hale	Perry	1953	Smith	Carl	1974
Halpin	Willie	1979	Speights	Eddie	1984
Haydel	Rusty	1963	Strickland	O.L.	1954
Henegan	Richard	1942	Thweatt	Joe	1963
Herrod	Thomas	1955	Wallace	Carl	1948
Horton	John	1947-1948	Wilkerson	Robert	1955-1956
Irby	Thomas	1952-1953	Wilson	Neil	1947
Jabour	Jamie	1973, 1976			

CONFERENCE CHAMPIONSHIPS	
CAPITAL ATHLETIC CONFERENCE - CHAMPIONS	1971, 1972, 1973, 1977, 1978
CAPITAL ATHLETIC CONFERENCE NORTH CHAMPS	1980
CLASS A CHAMPIONS	1939, 1940
DISTRICT 6-A CHAMPIONS	1981, 1985
MID-MISSISSIPPI CLASS A CO-CHAMPIONS	1947
MISS CATHOLIC CONFERENCE - CHAMPIONS	1962, 1963
SOUTH STATE CLASS B - CHAMPIONS	1981, 1985
CHAMPIONSHIP RUNNER-UP	
CAPITAL ATHLETIC CONFERENCE - RUNNER UP	1975, 1980
STATE CHAMPIONSHIP - RUNNER-UP	1981
BOWL APPEARANCES	
CRYSTAL BOWL	1970
GOODFELLOW BOWL - CHAMPIONS	1938
JAYCEE BOWL	1967
LIONS BOWL - CHAMPIONS	1947
MISSISSIPPI BOWL	1965, 1975, 1977
RED CARPET BOWL	1971, 1974, 1976, 1982
HONARARY	
UNDEFEATED - UNTIED REGULAR SEASON	1938 1939, 1955, 1958, 1975, 1977
UNDEFEATED REGULAR SEASONS	1938, 1939, 1955, 1957, 1958, 1974, 1975, 1977
ONE-LOSS TEAMS	1927, 1946, 1947, 1952, 1972, 1973, 1977, 1981
C.Y.O. CHAMPIONSHIP	1947

Made in the USA
Columbia, SC
29 January 2024

30818876R00163